ENGLAND AND THE
CATHOLIC CHURCH UNDER
QUEEN ELIZABETH

ENGLAND AND
THE CATHOLIC CHURCH
UNDER
QUEEN ELIZABETH

Arnold Oskar Meyer

Translated by
Rev. J. R. McKee

Introduction to the 1967 edition
by John Bossy

LONDON
ROUTLEDGE AND KEGAN PAUL LTD

First published in Great Britain by
Kegan Paul, Trench, Trübner & Co., Ltd

Reissued (with new Introduction) 1967
by Routledge & Kegan Paul Ltd
Broadway House, 68-74 Carter Lane
London, E.C. 4.

Printed in Great Britain by photolithography
At the Alden Press in the City of Oxford

AUTHOR'S PREFACE TO THE ENGLISH TRANSLATION

THE volume now before the reader was planned originally as a short introduction to a work on England and the Catholic Church under the Stuarts. Although it has grown into a book, still it does not claim to give as full a treatment of the subject as I hope to give for the period between 1603 and 1689. I saw no reason to repeat what has been told so often and so well, *e.g.* the story of catholic rebellions and conspiracies against Elizabeth, the schemes of which the imprisoned Queen Mary was either actively or passively the centre, the diplomatic history of the projected invasions, and the military history of the naval war with Spain. These incidents and events, dramatic as they are, have always claimed the largest share of attention, and I doubt whether anything really new and important can be said about them. I therefore decided to sketch these chapters as briefly as possible, and to lay the stress on questions which have not yet found definite and satisfactory answers. These questions are : At what time and to what extent did catholicism lose its footing on English soil ? Was it reduced through force, or through change of opinion ? What were the strongest weapons, both spiritual and temporal, which Rome employed in her struggle to regain her lost dominion ? How did the scanty remnants of the catholic church in England persevere and develop under the pressure of the penal laws? I soon found that these questions could not be answered in a short introduction, nor from the materials already accessible in print. I had to go to the archives and to make 1558, instead of 1603, as originally intended, the real starting-point of my history. It is true, as perhaps the most competent of my critics has observed,[1] that the question, *when* did catholicism lose its ground in England? cannot fully be answered without reference to a still earlier period. English church history during the later middle-ages contains the key to the problem. To go back as far as that lay outside the scope of my book. But I preferred, rather than leave this problem aside altogether, to attempt a solution, which, though imperfect from a more general point of view, may still hope for acceptance as a contribution to our knowledge within the limited period here in question.

Whereas foreign politics and military history, as far as they touch the subject of this book, are only briefly summarised, the history of the Armada has been given a chapter to itself. This is not written, however, from the point of view of diplomatic or military history, but, looking upon the great year 1588 in its bearings upon the Anglo-Roman struggle, is occupied with the defeat of the Armada as the turning-point in the history of Elizabethan catholicism as well as of the counter-reformation of Western Europe. In this chapter, instead of describing the course of events in detail, I have consequently tried to depict the spirit in which the conflict was waged, and to show its moral significance as a trial of strength rather than its material effects.

It is my intention to bring the work to a conclusion in

---

[1] Prof. A. F. POLLARD in the *Göttingische gelehrte Anzeigen*, 1912, pp. 169 *et seq.*, and in the *English Historical Review*, 1912, pp. 159 *et seq.*

two more volumes, for which the materials have been already for the most part collected. This will carry on the history up to the Act of Toleration of 1689.

Among the Roman archives and libraries which I have consulted for the present volume, the general archives of the Vatican hold the first place. The chronological list of unpublished documents which I give at the end of the volume (p. 533) shows at once how much more I am indebted to these archives than to all the rest put together— principally, of course, for a knowledge of the papal policy, but not by any means for this alone. I am beholden, for instance, to the dispatches of the nunciatures for much light thrown upon the policy of Spain and international relations of various kinds ; while the memorials and letters of prominent English catholics lay bare the internal condition of catholicism in England, the views held by catholic exiles on the continent, and their relations with Rome and Spain. The Vatican Library, of which the importance for my work will be more apparent in the following volumes, contains sources of information similar to those among the archives. I found it, moreover, useful for pamphlets and broadsides (in the Barberini collection). From both the archives and the library I was able to draw important and original matter for the history of the English seminaries (Appendix XVI. and XIX.). For the history of the seminaries and the mission, the archives of the English College in Rome afford matter supplementary to what exists at the Vatican, which was most welcome. Among the remaining Roman collections, I need only name the Minucciana belonging to the Prussian Historical Institute, and the Caetani archives, in connection with this volume. To the latter, I owe a single document, but one of value (Appendix XXI.).

Outside Rome, only a few Italian archives were of

b

service, chiefly—thanks to England's ancient commercial friendship with Tuscany and Venice—the state archives of Florence and Venice and the National Library of Florence. To the archives of the Holy House of Loreto I am indebted for a few documents which throw light on the doings of English pirates in the Mediterranean (Appendix XXIII.). Papers in the Vatican suggested the idea of making researches in this little used collection.

Among English archives, the most important are those belonging to the catholic cathedral of Westminster. No others can compare with them in value for the inner history of English catholicism. As their contents, however, are of importance only from the end of the sixteenth century, the letters, reports, and memorials of English catholics and Roman officials which they contain, are only of service for the last chapter of this volume. The rich treasures of the Public Record Office have been already largely made public in the Calendars of State Papers. However, for some series (especially *Italian States*), I have been able to draw upon fresh sources of information. As regards the results yielded by the Recusant Rolls, I must refer to Ch. I., § 4. The British Museum and the Bodleian Library were invaluable to me on account of their original editions of royal proclamations, and, above all, for their rich store of pamphlets and broadsides. For although it was only in the seventeenth century that the classical period of political pamphleteering dawned for England, still as early as the time of Elizabeth, broadsides and pamphlets had become such a power in public life that no student of history can pass over these sources of information with impunity. This is perhaps more true for the history of English catholicism than for any other department (*cf.* the entries in the index under Pamphlets).

Through the kindness of Father J. H. Pollen, S.J.,

I have obtained copies of the instructions furnished to the English Jesuit missionaries, the originals of which are preserved in the archives of the Society of Jesus.

Out of the mass of documents contained in the above-named collections I could print only a small portion in the Appendix, for my chief aim was to write history, not to publish documents. My choice of material was also conditioned by regard for the labours of others. Hence I give none of the letters of the leading Jesuit, Robert Persons, of which I have made repeated use, being, as they are, one of the chief sources of information for the history of catholicism in England, because I did not wish to encroach upon the complete edition of these letters projected by Father Pollen.

Among the acknowledgments due from me in this place, those which I owe to the Prussian Historical Institute in Rome must come first. I was a member of it from 1903 to 1908, and had it not been for the opportunity thus offered me of spending years of study in Rome, I could never have entertained the idea of attempting this work. Professor Paul Kehr, the Director of the Institute, kindly allowed and encouraged me to follow out my own scientific inclinations side by side with the official work connected with my post. For this I shall always remain deeply indebted to him.

Any one who has had the good fortune to work in the Vatican cannot fail to remember with especial gratitude the kindness and unfailing attention which he experienced from the superintendents and officials in the archives and the library. It is my pleasant duty to thank, before others, the deeply respected Prefect of the Vatican Library, Father Franz Ehrle, S.J., for the personal interest which he took in my work from the first, and for the assistance he gave me by his unerring knowledge of existing materials.

Every facility for prosecuting my researches in the Westminster archives was most freely given me by His Eminence Cardinal Bourne, archbishop of that see, and for this I offer him my respectful thanks.

Among my English fellow-workers Father J. H. Pollen, S.J., who is hardly surpassed as a specialist in Elizabethan catholic history, has given me the most valuable help through a frequent interchange of opinion both by letter and in personal intercourse. Although we disagree in our general view of Elizabethan England, it is, nevertheless, a satisfaction to me that the English Jesuit and the German Protestant are able to agree, as a whole, on a question of such decisive importance as the estimate of the religious character of the catholic missions. I express to Father Pollen my best thanks for assistance in various instances, to which attention is drawn in the footnotes.

The German edition of this book [1] received a good many reviews which, as I am grateful to say, not only kindly acknowledged what I have tried to give in my book, but also helped me on in my studies by suggestive and instructive criticisms. I wish to mention one of my reviewers, at least, Professor A. F. Pollard, in whose copious remarks [2] I found a rich mine of the fullest and most detailed information on many points. I have to thank him and other critics, if the English edition is in some points improved upon the German. Of course, I also benefited by the literature published since the issuing of the original edition.

It is with very great pleasure that I finally thank my translator, Father J. R. McKee, of the Oratory. He undertook the task at his own initiative, and has carried

---

[1] Published as Vol. VI. of the *Bibliothek des Kgl. Preussischen Historischen Instituts in Rom.* Rome, 1911 (Loescher & Co.).

[2] In his two reviews indicated in Note 1, p. vi.

it through with a sympathetic interest and untiring assiduity. It has been his ambition to render the sense faithfully, but to avoid the harshness of a literal translation. He has also taken the trouble to give the quotations from English sources and literature in their original wording. Moreover, he placed me under an obligation by making some valuable suggestions and references, and by bringing to my notice several works bearing on the subject which have appeared since the publication of the German edition. He also submitted his translation to me and patiently examined my revision of it. For all this I wish heartily to thank him.

A. O. MEYER.

ROSTOCK,
June 21, 1914.

PUBLISHERS' NOTE

THE Author's preface above, with its generous acknowledgments to Italian and British scholarship, was written and dated before the outbreak of the European War. The Publishers, after consultation and careful consideration, see no cause to withhold from scholars and students the English translation of this historical work.

K. P. T. T. & Co., LTD.

LONDON

TRANSLATOR'S PREFACE

I HAVE translated this book because it seems to me a remarkable confirmation of the view of the Reformation which English catholic historians, from Dodd to the present day, have expressed in their writings—a confirmation all the more impressive because given by one not himself a catholic.   That Dr. Meyer's work should contain views which a catholic historian would reject, and should pass over considerations which he would emphasize, goes without saying, but no one who reads it can fail to be struck with the author's endeavour to be always fair and impartial.   The translation, which does little justice to the picturesque vividness of the original, owes much to the careful revision given to it by Dr. Meyer in days when communication between England and Germany was easier than now.   In several instances he altered or modified statements in the first German edition, and added references to works published since its appearance.   To these, I am sure, he would have added references to the series of articles on the "Appellant Controversy" contributed by the REV. J. H. POLLEN, S.J., to *The Month* during the present year.   *Parish Life under Queen Elizabeth*, by W. P. M. KENNEDY (London, Herder, 1914), supplies some further details to those given by the author of this work.

I am indebted for help in the translation and correction

of proofs to the Reverend A. H. Paine and Mr. G. F. Engelbach, and to Brother Vincent Hayles of the London Oratory, for assistance in verifying references.

J. R. McKEE,

Chaplain H.M. Forces.

Dunfermline.

TABLE OF CONTENTS

CHAPTER III

CHAPTER IV

APPENDIX

ABBREVIATIONS

The references to the various series of *Calendars of State Papers* are given as follows :—

DOM. CAL. = Calendar of State Papers, Domestic Series, of the Reign of Elizabeth.

FOR. CAL. = Calendar of State Papers, Foreign Series, of the Reign of Elizabeth.

SPAN. CAL. = Calendar of Letters, Dispatches and State Papers, relating to the negotiations between England and Spain, preserved principally in the Archives of Simancas.

VEN. CAL. = Calendar of State Papers and Manuscripts relating to English Affairs, preserved in the Archives of Venice and Northern Italy.

INTRODUCTION
TO THE 1967 EDITION

John Bossy

A HISTORIAN may count himself lucky if he writes a book which is still read more than fifty years after its publication. To write one which, as the decades go by, maintains its reputation as "a great work ... still, after forty years, the 'last word' on its highly important subject", as "still indispensable", as "easily the best thing on the subject"[1], is a notable achievement. This has been the fortune of Arnold Oskar Meyer and his *England and the Catholic Church under Queen Elizabeth*. Entering, as a young man of thirty-four and a pure outsider, a territory scarred by three and a half centuries of real and verbal conflict, he succeeded in equipping it with a plan which has since imposed itself as fruitful, even inevitable, on experts of very divergent views. How do we account for this success? Meyer has been widely complimented for the diligence of his research, the impartiality of his attitude, and the vigour of his writing; on the last point credit should also be given to his translator who by dimming, in

---

[1] PHILIP HUGHES, *The Reformation in England*, iii (London, 1954), 357; GARRETT MATTINGLY, *The Defeat of the Spanish Armada* (Penguin edn., 1962), 429; G. R. ELTON, *England under the Tudors* (London, 1955), 485. To which one may add J. B. BLACK, *The Reign of Elizabeth* (2nd edn., Oxford, 1959), 501—"scholarly, dispassionate, reasonable" (should this be "readable"?); and CONYERS READ, *Bibliography of Tudor History* (2nd edn., Oxford, 1959), 198—"of first importance"; 194—"the best general account [of Elizabethan Catholicism]".

a way for which he apologizes in his preface, the boldly dramatic lighting of his original, may have enabled the book to keep better than it might otherwise have done. But his greatest virtue is surely, by his choice of problems and steady illumination of what he saw as the major issue, to have lifted the subject to a level of historical seriousness much above what it had hitherto reached. Refusing to attempt unanswerable questions, prising his readers away from an obsession with conspiracy on the one hand and martyrology on the other, asserting in the face of venerable tradition that "to speak of *guilt* in connection with these questions is quite to misunderstand them" (162), he marched directly to the heart of his book, a presentation of the encounters and dilemmas of the priests of the Elizabethan mission worthy of the tragic status which he claimed for their predicament.[1] He made a number of suggestions about the general history of English Catholicism—that, for example, its decline in the post-reformation period had little to do with persecution[2]—the value of which later investigation has tended to enhance. His attempt at a statistical description of it (59–65), crude as it is, offers a more convincing outline than anything else in the field, and in so far as it relates to the seventeenth century has hardly received the attention it deserves. There is more than enough in the book to justify golden opinions.

It would be surprising if after fifty years there were nothing to be said on the other side. The impression which Meyer has given in England of being above the *mêlée* depends partly on his having rather a German than an English axe to grind. A

[1] Meyer's tragic view has been influential; see especially BLACK, *op. cit.*, 185f: "Both parties to the conflict were victims of a tragic dilemma . . ." His account of the trials of priests (150–63) should be read in conjunction with the criticisms in HUGHES, *op. cit.*, 357–62.

[2] 72f. The lack of effect of the Elizabethan recusancy legislation has now been amply demonstrated by F. X. WALKER, "The Implementation of the Elizabethan Statutes against Recusants, 1581–1603" (London Univ. Ph.D. thesis, 1961). See also H. AVELING, in C[*atholic*] R[*ecord*] S[*ociety*], liii (1961), 291f.

nationalist with a Prussian and Lutheran background, born in 1877 of a university family, his views were those which predominated in the German academic world during the ripest years of the second *Reich*.[1] His early work on English history was part of a large body of writing, most of it much more directly intended to fulfil what he felt to be the duties of a history professor in the newly unified state: to clarify the national identity, to promote the cause of national unity and greatness. He grew up with a view of England as the type of Protestant nationhood; the *Kulturkampf* led him, as it led other German scholars, to the Counter-reformation. Having begun by studying these two topics separately,[2] he conceived a large-scale work which would unite them. In his strong but not very subtle mind, the dichotomies national/universal, modern/mediæval, Protestant/Catholic, stood out plain; he saw them embodied in the conflict between the England of Elizabeth and the Spain of Philip II, and resolved to the advantage of the former by the events of 1588. He came to the history of religion armed with the further dichotomy spiritual/political, related to the previous ones by the belief that a properly spiritual religion was the true complement of a properly political state; and he turned to Elizabethan Catholicism as to a retort in which the essence of these conceptions could be found reacting together at the highest possible temperature. He saw them at work in an underlying conflict of English and continental influences, and in the visible opposition of secular and Jesuit, descriptions which also, in his hands, acquired something of an ideal character; the outcome of the greater conflict had, as he felt, resolved them also before the death of the Queen in favour of the progressive view. This framework of ideas stands out the more nakedly in that the book was originally intended as an introduction to a larger study of

---

[1] Cf. Schüssler's obituary, below, p. 11, n. 3.
[2] In *Die englische Diplomatie in Deutschland zur Zeit Eduards VI und Mariens* (Breslau, 1900), and his work in Rome on the series of *Nuntiaturberichte aus Deutschland*.

the topic during the seventeenth century, and retained the rigidity as well as the clarity proper to an interpretative essay rather than to a substantive work. Readers of a later generation will notice that Meyer's range of problems excluded the full consideration of levels of his subject which might lie between the universal principle and the private dilemma; that it excluded, among other things, those matters of a roughly sociological order which, since he wrote, have attracted much attention from English historians of the period. This attention he would probably have deplored as arising from a materialist conception of history.[1]

One may, without reflecting on the general usefulness of Meyer's categories, feel that there are points in his book at which they have run away with him. His obsession with an English national character, revealed as far as one can see chiefly in a Germanic respect for women and a "love of travel", may pass as harmlessly odd, though one will note the degree of racial determinism which these remarks imply.[2] It is rather more crucial, and not of course unrelated, that his English/ Spanish contrast is far too sharply drawn, whether in respect of the spirit and achievements of the parties, the fatal nature of their conflict, or the decisiveness of its outcome.[3] In particular he much exaggerated at least the short-term consequences of the failure of the 1588 Armada. One of his grounds for arguing

[1] Cf. his *Deutsche und Engländer* (below, p. 11, n. 2), where (263) he quotes Schiller: "Es ist der Geist, der sich den Körper baut."

[2] 84, 205, etc. On the first point the German version is somewhat stronger (70): ". . . eines Volkes, das nach germanischer Art die Frauen stets geehrt hat . . ." See also his essay, "Charles I and Rome", *American Historical Review*, xix (1913), 13f; and *Deutsche und Engländer*, 264— "Nicht die Geographie ist das Schicksal, sondern der Character, die Rasse."

[3] Examples of more modern treatment of these points will be found in the works of ELTON and MATTINGLY cited above, p. 1, n. 1, and in R. B. WERNHAM, "English Policy and the Revolt of the Netherlands", in J. S. BROMLEY and E. H. KOSSMANN (eds.), *Britain and the Netherlands* (London, 1960), 29f.

that 1588 brought in a new era in the relations of England and the Catholic Church is certainly untenable, since England and France had been allies since 1572; similar objections might be raised to the others.[1] His surprising judgment that "England's victory over Spain brought the career of the Counter-reformation in western Europe to a standstill" (462) implies both a narrow view of what the term "Counter-reformation" might cover, and too ready an identification of its political aspects with the conduct of Philip II.[2]

On all these more general points, readers will find excellent guidance elsewhere; but this is less easily come by in the tangled thickets of the inner history of English Catholicism, and here some more detailed comments seem called for. Those which follow concern Meyer's general categories, his discussion of the *émigré* leaders William Allen and Robert Parsons, and his treatment of the Archpriest Controversy.

His use of the dichotomy secular/Jesuit is not altogether reliable. Taking a long view of the internal quarrels of the English Catholic clergy, we should find it difficult to accept his equation of secular with national and Jesuit with non- or anti-national. Put crudely, there is a sixteenth-century problem, which is about allegiance to the state but not between secular and Jesuit, and a seventeenth-century problem, which is between secular and Jesuit but not about allegiance to the state. We can hardly, that is, read "national" for "secular" without getting ourselves into the position that most sixteenth-century seculars are Jesuits and most seventeenth-century Jesuits seculars.[3] It is important to notice that Meyer extended the term Jesuit to include all secular priests trained in seminaries which were

[1] 369f. On Anglo-papal economic relations (358–63), cf. J. DE-LUMEAU, *L'alun de Rome, xve–xixe siècle* (Paris, 1962), 45f, 207f.

[2] J. LYNCH, "Philip II and the Papacy", *Transactions of the Royal Historical Society*, 5th series, ii (1961), 23f.

[3] Cf. T. CLANCY, *Papist Pamphleteers: The Allen-Persons Party and the Political Thought of the Counter-reformation in England* (Chicago, 1964), 94–106.

under Jesuit supervision.[1] He was thus led to speak of a secular mission begun from Douai in 1574, and a "Jesuit mission" launched from Rome in 1580, of "two bodies of missionaries" obliged to "co-operate" when they got to England (131f, 190f). This is misleading: the achievements of the seminaries, as well as many of their problems, depended on their being, in their foundation and early history, closely integrated organs of a single enterprise. There was, eventually, a split between Douai and Rome, but Meyer pre-dated it. His view that the Jesuits strove "to get the management of the whole English mission into their hands" (111) is unrealistic as well as rather tendentious: the Society had, after all, quite enough on its plate without that, and the complaint, at this time, was rather that it was taking perfectly good Englishmen and sending them off to Poland or India or Brazil.

His treatment of Allen and Parsons is on the whole remarkably fair and accurate; but he was unable altogether to escape the tradition of putting down to Parsons anything which might seem unfortunate in their joint conduct.[2] Thus there is no reason to ascribe the Invasion Memorandum of 1582 specially to Parsons;[3] unspecified "evidence of style" is a flimsy ground for supposing that he helped Allen to write his *Admonition* of 1588 (326); and though Meyer noted at one point that the *Conference about the next Succession* of 1594 was a collective production, he persisted throughout the rest of the book in treating it as an individual effort of Parsons.[4] In any case half the book was, as was pointed out at the time, cribbed *quasi ad*

---

[1] Thus p. 190, where this explains what would otherwise be Meyer's howler of having Jesuits schooled in seminaries. Neither Alexander Briant (146, n. 3) nor Anthony Tyrrell (268) was a Jesuit.

[2] Cf. GARRETT MATTINGLY, "William Allen and Catholic propaganda in England", in G. BERTHOUD, etc., *Aspects de la propagande religieuse* (Geneva, 1957), 325f.

[3] 278, 293–8. L. HICKS, in *C.R.S.*, xxxix (1942), 148, n. 1.

[4] 200, 347f, 383f. HICKS, "Fr. Robert Persons and the Book of Succession", *Recusant History*, iv (1957), 104f.

verbum from the *De justa reipublicae christianae . . . authoritate* of the Reims professor William Reynolds, published six years before.[1] One may add that, had the scope of the *Conference* been simply "to pave the way for the Spanish succession to the English throne" (200), the authors' Protestant fellow-countrymen would hardly have gone to the bother of reprinting it three times during the following century. It is not easy to see how Meyer reconciled the text of the book with the idea that dislike of it expressed "constitutional feeling . . . against a purely dynastic conception of the succession" (385); but his view that Parsons was a proponent of absolute monarchy depends on what anyone who looks at his footnote (385, n. 4) will see is a mistranslation of a remark about Parsons's personal behaviour.[2] Meyer's preconceptions have here led him to get the position more or less back to front. His statement, finally, that at the end of his life Allen "separated himself from the extremists" and fell out with Parsons and the Jesuits (359, 388f), is at the least far too dogmatic. All the evidence produced since Meyer wrote[3] tends to prove the contrary. And although this is quite the obscurest period in the history of Elizabethan Catholicism, it would now seem fairly safe to say that Allen retained his attachment to the Spanish connection, to the Society of Jesus in general, and to Parsons in particular, until the end of his life; but that, the sense of his responsibilities as Cardinal reinforcing what his government of the seminary had shown to be a natural bent, he tried to kill dissent with kindness and so laid himself open to misinterpretation from people of simpler loyalties.

[1] CLANCY, *Papist Pamphleteers*, 62.

[2] I would take the correct translation to be: "Parsons is determined to get absolute control of England (or, 'of English affairs') into his hands . . ."

[3] By HICKS, "Cardinal Allen and the Society [of Jesus]", *The Month*, clx, (1932), 342f, 434f, 528f, especially the last part; and by P. RENOLD, in the forthcoming *C.R.S.* lviii, Introduction, section i, and Appendix C. I am very grateful to Miss Renold for letting me see these before publication; the view expressed in the next sentence of the text is my own.

In the peculiarly difficult matter of the Archpriest Controversy Meyer did well enough, though one must allow for his point of view and for the fact that, when he wrote, more material was available from one side of the argument than from the other. Later investigation would suggest some revision of fact: for example, the reforming spirit shown by Father Weston in the goings-on at Wisbech took rather a passive than an active form;[1] and there is nothing to show that Parsons had anything to do with the appointment of an archpriest.[2] John Bishop's *Courteous conference* (420f) was written about 1580. But the chief flaw is once again over-simplification. Meyer's determination to concentrate on the question of nationality is here particularly restricting; he seems to have been aware that many other problems were involved,[3] but he pays them little attention. He treated this question also too much as a conflict of secular and Jesuit, too little as a conflict within the secular clergy itself, of which the Appellant priests formed at this period a distinct though growing minority. And he equated it too crudely with an over-simplified view of the attitude and behaviour of Catholics in the matter of the succession to Queen Elizabeth (444). The position up to 1603 would seem roughly to be that a large section of the Catholic gentry was in favour of James, irrespective of his position in religion; that Parsons was usually in favour of James on condition that he became a Catholic, and not otherwise;

[1] J. H. POLLEN, *The Institution of the Archpriest Blackwell* (London, 1916), 7.20; P. RENOLD, in *C.R.S.*, li (1953), p. xiii, etc. Fr. Pollen's book provides the best general treatment of the controversy, and Meyer's account should be checked against it.

[2] POLLEN, *op. cit.*, 25f; HICKS, in *C.R.S.*, xli (1948), 127.

[3] Some of them are explored in my own articles, "The Character of Elizabethan Catholicism", *Past and Present*, no. 21 (1962), and T. ASTON (ed.), *Crisis in Europe*, 1560–1660 (London, 1965), 223f; "Rome and the Elizabethan Catholics: A Question of Geography", *Historical Journal*, vii (1964), 135ff, especially 140; "Henri IV, the Appellants and the Jesuits", *Recusant History*, viii (1965), 80–122. I would refer to these for more constructive suggestions about the history of Elizabethan Catholicism than will be found here.

and that the Appellant priests held a variety of views, but seem predominantly to have been in favour of James on condition that he granted toleration, and not otherwise.[1] Those who will be inclined to agree with Meyer that to envisage a "Spanish" succession to Elizabeth was, after 1588, "blindness and fanaticism" (375, 383) should be aware that a suggestion has been put forward which would place Sir Robert Cecil among the blind and the fanatic.[2] And although Professor Hurstfield has found the evidence unconvincing and proposed an alternative explanation,[3] it would seem a little premature to regard the question as entirely closed. Here again we are brought up before what Dr. Rowse has called "the undescried heart of Robert Parsons";[4] one can do little but sympathize with the feeling that fifty years of devoted research have left us little nearer than Meyer was to a total grasp of this very remarkable man, and offer the suggestion that if there is a key to the enigma it may lie in that *Memorial for the Reformation of England* to which he seems nowhere to refer.[5]

In his preface to the English translation of his book, dated June 21, 1914, Meyer still expressed the intention of following this introductory work with two substantive volumes for which

[1] The most exact description of the Appellant point of view that I know of will be found on p. 387 of Professor HURSTFIELD's article cited below, n. 3.

[2] L. HICKS, "Sir Robert Cecil, Fr. Persons and the Succession", *Archivum historicum Societatis Jesu*, xxiv (1955), 95–139.

[3] J. HURSTFIELD, "The Succession Struggle in Late Elizabethan England", in S. T. BINDOFF, J. HURSTFIELD, C. H. WILLIAMS (eds.), *Elizabethan Government and Society: Essays presented to Sir John Neale* (London, 1961), 369–91. Fr. Hicks's argument had previously been accepted by Professor BLACK in the second (1959) edition of his *Reign of Elizabeth*, 430–51.

[4] A. L. ROWSE, *The England of Elizabeth* (London, 1950), 462.

[5] See T. CLANCY, "Notes on Persons's *Memorial*", *Recusant History*, v (1959), 17f. It will be difficult to blame anyone for failing to understand Parsons as long as the publication of his letters and papers, suspended now for over twenty years (1st volume, to 1588, ed. L. HICKS, *C.R.S.*, xxxix, 1942), remains incomplete.

the bulk of the research had been done and part of which seems already to have been written.[1] One may ask why he never did so. The decisive reason seems to have been the outbreak of war between Germany and England; two pamphlets written under its impact, in which Meyer propounded the plutocratic theory of the British Constitution with a passion bordering on hysteria, and argued that an invasion was the only way to instil into the English a sense of moral responsibility, point to some emotional crisis.[2] If he had already, as one may suspect, got into interpretative difficulties in pursuing his work, this change of perspective must have multiplied them; and since he could no longer regard England as a model, to a man of his belief in the national responsibilities of the historian there can have seemed little point in devoting one's career to its history. In any event, he now abandoned virtually his whole historical work, and turned for the rest of his life to the history of nineteenth-century, and specifically of Bismarckian, Germany. He held a succession of chairs in Kiel, Göttingen and Munich, gave his full allegiance to the third *Reich*, and was amply rewarded by it. In 1935 he took over the directorship of the *Handbuch der deutschen Geschichte*, published under the auspices of the *Deutsche Akademie* with the object, among others, of "providing the German people with an essential piece of equipment in the struggle for its inward reconstruction".[3] Shortly after, when the community of

---

[1] Preface, vi–vii. In an introduction to Meyer's essay, "Zur Geschichte des Wortes Staat", published posthumously in *Die Welt als Geschichte*, x (1950), 227f, G. FRANZ mentioned the existence of two chapters of the second volume of *England and the Catholic Church*, and indicated that they were shortly to be published. So far as I know this never happened.

[2] *Deutsche Freiheit und englischer Parlamentarismus* (Munich, 1915); *Worin liegt Englands Schuld?* (Stuttgart/Berlin, 1914), especially p. 31. There is a copy of the first in the British Museum, and of the second in the Seeley Historical Library, Cambridge.

[3] *Vorwort* by O. BRANDT to the first fascicule of the *Handbuch* (Potsdam, 1935). Brandt, the original director, having died before this was published, Meyer added another brief foreword.

German historians was reconstructed, he was appointed as consultant, with eight other professors, to the new *Reichsinstitut für Geschichte des neuen Deutschlands*,[1] and moved finally to a chair in Berlin. A volume of essays issued in 1937 as a *Festschrift* on his sixtieth birthday, in which he returned briefly to English problems, implies that the march of history had once again altered perspectives. "England [in the sixteenth century] ... ordained for herself a strong leadership, as Germany does today ... As age towards youth, so stood Spain towards England."[2] But he was now embarked on what he felt to be the crown of his life's work, and eventually as his contribution to the national effort in another time of war, a large biography of Bismarck finished shortly before his death in a riding accident in East Prussia on June 3, 1944.[3]

A knowledge of Meyer's later career is certainly more relevant to a judgment of *England and the Catholic Church* than it might be to that of a less ideologically founded work. It may confirm the suspicion that he allowed too much weight to considerations of nationality, and provoke one to question his judgment of the proper delimitation of the spiritual and the political; it indicates the pitfalls of writing history with the issues of the present too patently in mind. But we are after all concerned with a book and not with a man; and in this respect one must conclude that his options were more fruitful than otherwise. Anyone who has

---

[1] See *Historische Zeitschrift*, cliii (1935–6), 220f.

[2] *Deutsche und Engländer. Wesen und Werden in grosser Geschichte* (Munich, 1937), 265–6.

[3] *Bismarck, der Mensch und der Staatsmann* (Leipzig, 1944); *Vorwort*, 5—"In schwerer Zeit entstanden, bildet das Buch meinen Beitrag zur nationalen Arbeit während des Krieges." This edition was never in fact published, though there is a copy in the British Museum; in the 2nd edition (Stuttgart, 1949) an obituary by W. Schüssler (ed. 1, 790–1) was suppressed, and an introduction by H. Rothfels added, where a number of points are made similar to those made here. Cf. A. J. P. Taylor, *Bismarck* (London, 1955), 271–2. There is another obituary of Meyer in W. Goetz, *Historiker in meiner Zeit* (Cologne/Graz, 1957), 379f.

tried to make sense of the history of English Catholicism in the seventeenth century will testify to Meyer's achievement in imposing a comprehensible pattern on the Elizabethan period, and deeply regret that he did not pursue his work. One can ask little more of a history book than that it should inspire rational disagreement until something better comes along; and though one may boggle at Father Hughes's "great", and feel Dr. Elton's "easily" a little unfair to Father Hughes, one cannot but agree, with no more than a mild "Alas!", that Meyer's is the best book on the subject. It seems likely to remain so for a good while to come.

ENGLAND AND THE CATHOLIC CHURCH IN THE AGE OF ELIZABETH

INTRODUCTION

FEW epochs of English history have been so often and so brilliantly portrayed as the period of the Tudors and the Stuarts. It has not been, however, the fortunes of catholics, then forming only a small minority of the English people, which have drawn historians of the first rank to undertake repeated investigations into those times. They have devoted their labours rather to the disputes over doctrine and questions of church government which broke out within the protestant religion, or to the great conflict between crown and parliament. The Hosts of the Lord who fought against Anti-Christ under Cromwell stand well in the foreground. The priests of the Roman church and the Knights of the Standard of Jesus, who entered the forbidden land disguised, and laboured there in secret, pass unnoticed in the background, or are eyed with suspicion. And yet the history of English catholicism, in the time of its sorest sufferings under Elizabeth and the Stuarts, in no way falls behind those other questions in importance and interest. For it was only during this period that England finally decided to be a protestant country, a decision equally important for both the old world and the new. And the spectacle which the catholic church, so accustomed to rule and have pre-eminence, here presents—dispossessed and outlawed in the midst of a great nation—is so strange and even unique that it would call for treatment on psychological grounds alone, were its historical significance less than it actually is. The material which well repays study has been often and successfully handled from the point of view of edification ;[1] but, so far, no historical work exists which gives an unprejudiced account of the fortunes of English catholics during this lengthy period.[2]   In contrast to the pious belief which regards every one as a saint and martyr, we still come across the ancient prejudice which looks upon every emissary from Rome as a conspirator or assassin—a prejudice by no means confined to the popular mind.   One of the most distinguished of English historians brands the English catholics who resided abroad in Elizabeth's time, and more especially the seminarists, as "desperate intriguers," and speaks of "the deterioration of the English character under

[1] There are two large and, in parts, historically valuable collections : (1) *Memoirs of Missionary Priests and other Catholics of both Sexes that have suffered death in England on religious accounts from* 1577 *to* 1684, by Bishop CHALLONER.   2 vols. (1st ed. 1741–2, and frequently reprinted afterwards).   (2) JOSEPH SPILLMANN, *Gesch. der Katholiken Verfolgung in England,* 1535–1681.   In 4 parts (Freiburg i. B. 1900–5).   Ends with 1654 ; uncritical.

[2] The Elizabethan period has been chiefly dealt with ; for the history of the catholic mission we have the rich collection of materials by JOHN MORRIS, S.J., *The Troubles of our Catholic Forefathers, related by themselves,* 3 vols. (London, 1872–7) ; for the political history of the catholics in Elizabeth's time we have the excellent series of articles by J. H. POLLEN, S.J., in The Month, published during the last fourteen years, of which the most important is, *The Politics of English Catholics during the Reign of Queen Elizabeth* (1902).   The sources of the history of the Jesuit mission in England are collected by HENRY FOLEY, S.J., *Records of the English Province of the Society of Jesus.*   7 vols. (London, 1877–83).

foreign influences."[1] It is not necessary to waste time on theories so devoid of foundation. Whoever accepts as historical the statement that Englishmen "living beyond the seas" were "rebellious and traiterous subjects," speaks from the standpoint of the Elizabethan government,[2] not from the standpoint of history. Those were days when a heroic spirit, an eager quest of unworldly gains, fired the whole English people, and it would indeed be strange if this spirit of high enterprise led to a deterioration of the English character exclusively in catholics. Rather it is precisely in them we see manifested the very power which Englishmen justly reckon their best characteristic and which they can well lay claim to after Waterloo—the power of holding their ground in the face of heavy odds.

It is the hopelessness of the conflict between religion and country in which catholics were involved from the outset that gives to the history of English catholicism under Elizabeth and the Stuarts its particular character. A similar conflict raged in other countries of mixed religions too, but not with the same severity and hostility. Again, in no other country was hatred against the catholic church so impassioned and so lasting as in the England of Elizabeth and the Stuarts. The explanation of both these facts is to be found in the peculiar line which the reformation took in England. The distinction between the reformation and the institution of a state church must be

---

[1] MANDELL CREIGHTON, *The English Church in the Reign of Elizabeth*, in *Historical Lectures and Addresses* (London, 1903), p. 162.

[2] *E.g.* "Her rebellious and trayterous subjects living in the partes beyond the seas," *Proclamation of July* 1, 1588, etc., etc. I have always used the proclamations as originally published and preserved in the British Museum, Public Record Office, Bodleian Library, etc. I may, however, omit references to the places where these documents are to be found, since all bibliographical information is contained in R. STEELE's *Tudor and Stuart Proclamations* (Oxford, 1910).

more sharply drawn in English than in German history.   In England, the two things are quite separate in point of time, origin, and sphere of action.   The establishment of a national church was the offspring of the late middle ages and was political in its origin, while its sphere of action was confined to Great Britain.   The English reformation, on the other hand, only started after the national church had become an accomplished fact, *i.e.* about the middle of the sixteenth century, and it ran its course well into the second half of the seventeenth.   It was religious in its origin and had a world-wide importance.

The English state church [1] had its commencement in English law, with the founders and patrons of churches— the king and the nobles—as the supreme owners of church property.   The supreme head of the universal church—the pope—had, therefore, no right to dispose of the property and revenues of the English church.   This view, derived in some measure from the *Eigenkirche* [2] of Teutonic countries, took shape in the legislative acts of the fourteenth century directed against the exactions of the popes.   The statute of 1351 [3] declared invalid all appointments to English benefices by way of papal provision, and, two years later, appeals from the king's courts to any foreign court (*i.e.* the papal curia) were forbidden by the statute of " Præmunire." [4] Both statutes were subsequently renewed and confirmed. Although at first the actual results of these enactments fell short of the letter of the law, these statutes nevertheless

---

[1] *Cf.* for what follows, J. HALLER, *Papsttum und Kirchenreform*, I. (Berlin, 1903), pp. 375–465.

[2] *Cf.* ULRICH STUTZ, *Die Eigenkirche als Element des mittelalterlich germanischen Kirchenrects*, Berlin, 1895. *Cf.* POLLOCK & MAITLAND, *The History of English Law*, I. (1898), p. 497.

[3] *Statutum de Provisoribus*, 25 Edw. III. 4.

[4] *Statutum contra Adnullatores Judiciorum Curæ Regis*, 27 Edw. III., i. c. i.

remained in force in spite of all papal encroachments as well as of all infringements by the king. They were also so successful in checking the stream of papal provisions to benefices for two generations as to reduce them to insignificance. The freedom of the church in England from foreigners was already an accomplished fact long before the storm against foreign benefice-hunters broke out in Germany. The English national church existed in fact long before the formal separation from Rome. The act of Henry VIII. in disowning the pope was not so much the beginning of a fresh development as the end of an old: it is rather the keystone of anglicanism than the foundation stone of the reformation.

The opponents of the reformation in England, both ecclesiastics and laymen, whether English or not, are never tired of insisting upon its "impure origin"[1]—the unholy

[1] As one example among many, NICHOLAS SANDERS' words may be quoted: "Anglicani protestantes . . . incestuosas Henrici et Annæ Bolenæ nuptias adorabant velut fontem evangelii sui, matrem ecclesiæ suæ, originem suæ fidei." *De Origine ac Progressu Schismatis Anglicani libri tres* (Romæ, 1586), p. 97. In much the same style Cardinal F. Barbarini wrote to George Panzani the papal agent in London on May 9, 1635. His letter (Bibl. Vat., Cod. Barb. 8634, fol. 20), along with the most important pieces of the correspondence, will be printed in a subsequent volume. It is rare to find any disposition on the catholic side to take a deeper view of Henry's action. Fr. Joseph Creswell wrote to Clement VIII. on April 26, 1596: "Certo è che, benchè la passione de Henrico 8° per maritarsi con Anna Bolena fu la immediata causa et la ultima occasione per rompere coll' papa, con tutto ciò non haverebbe il re havuto ardire de intentarlo, nè li suoi de consigliargli nè consentire a tal cosa, se non vi fussero preceduti molti altri disgusti, con che già havevano perso l'amore et il rispetto alla Sede Apostolica che furono come tante dispositioni per discomporre il re et il regno et disporgli a poco a poco a così grande ruina cagionata non solo da quel ultimo eccesso, con che se discuoprì il male, se non ancora dalli altri già preceduti, senza li quali quel ultimo o non haverebbe mai accaduto o non sarebbe stato bastante per fare così grande rottura." Arch. Vat. Borgh. III., 124 g. 2, fol. 93.

passion of a king who desired his marriage annulled. The day when Henry first gazed into Anne Boleyn's black eyes is still popularly regarded as the birthday of the English church and reformation. Now if reformation means something more than merely changing the form of church government and suppressing monasteries, then no name has less right to figure in the history of the English reformation than the name of that king, whose religion was mere formalism, who spared no woman in his lust and no man in his wrath. Charles I. was right in saying: "No man who truly understands the English reformation will derive it from Henry VIII." [1] If reformation means something that concerns the revival of the religious life of a nation and leaves its stamp for centuries upon the national character, then the reformers of England are the puritan Ironsides with their sword and bible. The religious movement associated with their name has made a deeper impression on the souls of the people than the reformation succeeded in making in any other country, not even excepting the land of Luther. The inheritance of the puritans is, even to this day, among those characteristics which differentiate the English from other nations. It is shown in the religious zeal which inspires even laymen to assume the office of teacher and prophet and speak to the people on the mysteries of the Godhead as the spirit moves them ; in the moral earnestness that never wearies of listening to preachers of repentance in the streets and public parks ; in the tendency to introduce moral considerations into political and artistic questions ; in the ecclesiastical tone of mind which makes attendance at divine worship both a christian and a social duty as well as the satisfaction of a real inward need ; in the sanctification

---

[1] *The Papers which passed at New-Castle betwixt His Sacred Majistie and Mr. Al. Henderson, A.D.* 1646 (London, 1649), p. 16.

of Sunday which forbids or restricts not only business but pleasure too; in the disciplinary restrictions and respectability of university life. It is shown too, in its darker side, in the tendency to prudery and pharisaism, and in the dread of scandal. Neither a religious statesman like Gladstone nor a popular religious movement like the Salvation Army—perhaps the greatest of its kind since the foundation of the great religious orders—would be conceivable without the puritan reformation. If Germans raised protestantism to be a power in Europe, puritan England made it a power throughout the world; wherever the English have taken possession of fresh territory, there, all the world over, we soon perceive some fruits of the puritanical spirit.

This mighty religious movement, which has not even yet spent its force, utterly anti-catholic as it was, laid hold on the English people at a time when the Roman church, with renewed vigour and newly fashioned arms, was joining battle with Lutherans and Calvinists all along the line, and was seeking also to retrieve its losses in England by pen, pulpit, and sword. In other words, reformation and counter-reformation synchronized in England. Movements which followed each other on the continent, and consequently did not collide with the full shock of their first encounter, appeared simultaneously on the scene in England, and the result was a life and death struggle. In this conflict the puritans were, so to speak, the rocks against which the waves of counter-reformation beat in vain.

There was yet another combination of ideas, equally pregnant with results for catholicism, which gave the English reformation its power—the union of religion and patriotism. The first beginnings of English protestantism under Henry VIII., and the earliest essay at a protestant state church under Edward VI., show little sign of this combination.   But under Mary, the wife of Philip II., and more completely under Elizabeth, the identification of protestantism with national aspirations was effected.   The English reformation became national in the country's fight for independence when threatened by Spain, the pope's right arm.   It remained national when continental customs and culture from Italy and France became fashionable at the court and among the nobles to the detriment of English manners and ways.   The country's enemy, whether he appeared in the guise of an armed force or in the guise of outlandish fashions, was always catholic, and so the country's fortunes came to be bound up with those of the reformation ; patriot and protestant became synonymous.

CHAPTER I

THE BREACH BETWEEN ENGLAND AND ROME

I. *English Catholics and the Re-establishment of the State Church*

WHEN Elizabeth ascended the throne it was difficult to tell with which religion the future of the country lay. The question has often been asked whether catholics or protestants were in the majority at Mary's death. There was no one then living in England capable of answering the question and proving his answer, and even to-day we are no more able than they were to find a satisfactory reply. In reckoning catholics as two-thirds of the population,[1] Count Feria, the Spanish ambassador, based his estimate on subjective considerations and not on any data as to the actual numbers. It is possible he may not have been far wrong, still, taking into consideration the strength of his prejudices and the vehemence displayed in his judgments upon English affairs, it is more than probable his wishes influenced his estimate. We have at the present time fuller data to go upon than the ambassador of Philip II.

---

[1] KERVYN DE LETTENHOVE, *Relations Politiques des Pays—Bas et de l'Angleterre sous Philippe II.*, t. I. (Brussels, 1882), p. 477. Summarized in SPANISH CALENDARS, 1558–67, p. 39 : *cf.* pp. 67, 77. So too N. SANDERS, *De Origine ac Progressu Schismatis Anglicani libri tres* (Romæ, 1586), p. 364. Upon what J. R. GREEN, *Hist. of the Engl. People*, II. (1878), p. 403, bases his idea that catholics were in a majority of three-fourths, I cannot say.

and his contemporaries, and yet we cannot be certain whether the English clergy were more inclined to the old or to the new state of things. The remarkably small number of them deprived for refusing to take the oath of supremacy—only five hundred clergy in six years, to strike an average among various estimates [1]—would tell in favour of a strong anglican and protestant majority, were it not that the extreme delicacy shown in the treatment of at least the lower clergy seems on the contrary to betray dread of a strong catholic party. Since we cannot be certain of the numerical strength of the two parties even among the clergy, and must rest satisfied with a vaguely approximate result, any attempt to claim the majority of the nation as a whole for adherents or enemies of Rome must be regarded as merely conjectural and devoid of solid proof.

The question of religious majorities in England is premature for the period under consideration. A nation which allowed itself to be transferred from one church to another, three times in twelve years (1547, 1553, 1559) without serious opposition cannot have been very strongly attached to any party, and it matters little which party numbered most adherents at a given moment. Things were still in the making, and the masses were as yet in a state of flux and could be led in any direction.

For generations the religious life of England had been in a state of unrest. Long before the reformation, foreigners had noticed that although divine service was attended with great devotion, there were, nevertheless, many persons who held various opinions of their own, concerning religion.[2] At a later date also, critics on the

---

[1] For particulars, see p. 29.

[2] *A Relation of the Island of England*, translated from the Italian by C. A. SNEYD, Camd. Soc. (1847), p. 23.

catholic side declared the English to be "naturally religious and careful for the salvation of their souls."[1]   But, unlike Germany, when the great movement began, a leader was lacking to urge on the people and give them his name for a war-cry.   The government, accordingly, assumed the office of a leader of the people in matters religious also, and it did so with all the greater ease since the monarchy was then at the height of its power in England.   Circumstances too of a purely personal nature helped to make every change of government a change in the religious system.   The despotism of Henry VIII., who burnt protestants for heresy and hung Roman catholics for high treason, created a state of legal confusion and religious uncertainty which could only produce alarm and perplexity.   The protestant government of Edward VI. and the catholic government of Mary were both the beginnings of a development in definite directions, but they were too short to produce a permanent result in either direction. People in England did not therefore fully realize how incompatible the two religious systems were with one another. Even on the continent, where the separation between catholicism and protestantism was effected earlier, men were not yet reconciled to the idea that Christendom was now for ever broken up into hostile camps.   The Jesuits, those champions of the counter-reformation, had scarcely begun their labours, and had not yet entered England when Elizabeth ascended the throne.   It was on the one hand, only the work of the catholic mission which, in the spirit of the council of Trent, repudiated all compromise, and, on the other hand, the increasing strength of puritanism, which synchronized with it, that

[1] From an anonymous memorial on England addressed to the Cardinal Protector of England between 1581 and 1585. Bibl. Vat., Cod. Ottoboni, 2419, pars. I., fol. 21ᵛ.

brought home to the majority of Englishmen the essential
and irreconcilable difference between catholicism and
protestantism.

So long as there was any possibility of reconciliation
between the contending parties, the government which won
the people's confidence by its political measures, had also
the best chance of influencing them in matters of religion.
Instead, then, of asking which religion numbered most
adherents at Mary Tudor's death, it is more to the point
to inquire which government—the protestant or the catholic
—enjoyed the confidence of the people.   The protestant
government under Edward had by no means won the
people's affection, but, on the other hand, Mary's catholic
government was hated.   Protestantism could not have
wished for any more effective propaganda than the stake
and the faggot : in the martyrs, Mary gave the new creed
its most eloquent apostles.   Towards the end of her reign
irritation had reached such a height that probably only
the hope of the sick queen's speedy death prevented a
protestant rising.   And as the day of release at length
drew nigh, the people did not await its actual arrival, but,
as the Spanish ambassador sadly remarks, "as soon as
they knew the queen's last hour was approaching, began
to insult images and religious." [1]   The "lively representations of love, joy, and hope," with which the Londoners
went "many miles out of the city to see" Elizabeth,[2]
was something more than the noisy welcome usually
given to a new ruler ; it was due to something more than
curiosity and the love of a spectacle.   For Elizabeth
was no "dark horse" : people knew that Anne Boleyn's

[1] KERVYN DE LETTENHOVE, *Relations Politiques*, I., p. 295.
SPAN. CALENDAR, 1558–67, p. 1.

[2] *Cf.* the fine description in SIR JOHN HAYWARD'S *Annals of the
first four years of . . . Elizabeth*, ed. Bruce, Camd. Soc. (1840),
pp. 6, 7.

daughter was no daughter of the Roman church, no creature of the king of Spain.

The second consideration weighed with them quite as much as the first. As the daughter of a Spanish mother and the wife of a Spanish king, Mary was out of touch with English sentiment and had no sympathy for national and political ideals. When she threw herself into the arms of her idolized Philip, Mary sacrificed England's welfare to the world-wide schemes of Spanish politics. An unfortunate war, the loss of Calais, and a severe blow inflicted on the nation's prestige were the results of Mary's reign. It is due to her that in England the catholic religion and Spanish politics were to be associated with one another in the popular estimation for generations to come ; by the marriage with Philip of Spain, the cause of the reformation became for the first time identified with the cause of the nation.

A ruler in close touch with the aspirations of the nation could not have a moment's doubt as to the political attitude he ought to assume. In nothing did Elizabeth appear greater and more self-confident than in her knowledge of Englishmen. Philip's ambassador had unwillingly to confess that the new queen "thinks as they [her people] do." [1] One of her earliest decisions clearly showed that the Spanish diplomatists were no longer the advisers of the English crown ; the queen would be a free princess and listen to what her new ministers said.[2] However obvious this resolution might appear, it showed great boldness under existing circumstances, and Elizabeth bravely kept her word.

In the eyes of the pope and catholic Europe,

---

[1] SPAN. CAL., 1558–67, p. 4.

[2] JOHN STRYPE, *Ecclesiastical Memorials*, Vol. III., pt. ii. (Oxford, 1822), p. 147. *Cf.* CAMDEN, *Annals rer. Anglic . . . regn. Elizab.* (Lugd. Batav. 1625), p. 16.

Elizabeth was the illegitimate daughter of an excommunicated king, and it was entirely a question of politics whether or not these authorities would consent to set aside canon law in her favour. Her rival, Mary Stuart, emblazoned the arms of England on her shield immediately after the death of Mary Tudor.[1] As queen of Scotland and dauphiness of France, she could summon both countries to arms and attack England from north and south, provided only the pope would say the word —the word for which all France was waiting[2]—Elizabeth is illegitimate, Mary is the lawful queen. In this predicament Spain, until now the ally of England and rival of France, seemed to be Elizabeth's sole support. But Spain's support could only be continued on condition that the government of England remained in catholic hands as it had done under Mary Tudor. From the point of view of foreign politics the accomplishment of the reformation in England seemed a hopeless task.

And it was a woman of five-and-twenty who girded herself up for the task. The familiar picture of Elizabeth gives undue prominence to the weaknesses which showed themselves chiefly as she grew older, and more especially in her unqueenly conduct during the trial of Mary Stuart. In the critical days at the beginning of her reign, and in all moments of peril, the queen never failed to exhibit a masculine and statesmanlike greatness which made up a hundred-fold for all that was petty in her character. Masculine courage, royal self-consciousness, and pride of

---

[1] The Heralds' College condemned her arms as unauthorized and bad heraldry. STRYPE, *Annals of the Reformation, etc.*, I., i. (Oxford, 1824), pp. 12 *et seq*. FOREIGN CALENDAR, 1558-59, No. 845. CAMDEN, pp. 29 *et seq*.

[2] The French government pressed for a declaration of Elizabeth's illegitimacy in Rome. KERVYN DE LETTENHOVE, *Relations Politiques*, I., pp. 333, 455.

country yielding to none, unfathomable cunning, too, when necessary, and skill in dissimulation that flouted all the rules of diplomacy—these were the characteristics of Elizabeth in the years when she was engaged in delivering the country from Spanish tutelage and in building up the reformation.

Among the great statesmen who joined battle with the church of Rome in the sixteenth and seventeenth centuries there are only two who can compare with Elizabeth in the world-wide importance of their actions, Gustavus Adolphus and Oliver Cromwell. It may be disputed to which of them protestantism is most indebted. In one point, however, the woman is sharply distinguished from the two men—her soul was scarcely ever touched by anything of the nature of religious enthusiasm. As far as we know, Elizabeth's birth, of a marriage condemned by Rome, was the main reason why she threw herself into the arms of the national church. It was not so much religious, or, if you will, personal, motives as national considerations, however, which in the last analysis made her the champion of the English reformation, and, as a result, the foundress of the first great protestant power.

The first steps were taken with remarkable foresight. The difficulties of the situation prevented the queen from at once putting out a religious programme. The proclamation announcing her accession abstained on this account from all allusion to matters of belief.[1] A phrase towards the end was capable of receiving a conservative interpretation against reforming opinions; the queen forbade all attempts to change the actual state of the country.[2] The

[1] Of Nov. 17, 1558.
[2] ". . . not to attempt uppon anny pretence the breache, alteration, or chaunge of any ordre or usage presently establyshed within this our Realme."

view that Elizabeth was herself undecided at the time and wished to keep both roads open [1] is contrary to all probability. It would imply that Elizabeth, who for years, had been looking forward to ascending the throne, now saw clearly for the first time, thanks to Cecil's eloquence, that belief in her legitimacy would be possible only in a protestant England. The truth is rather that Elizabeth appears from the beginning as a strongly marked personality, clear as to her aims, though still cautious in the choice of means.

The selection of new advisers showed how the land lay. Without immediately dismissing the catholic councillors of her predecessor, the queen added protestants to their number and so formed a privy council composed equally of both parties.[2] In all practical affairs, Sir William Cecil, afterwards Lord Burleigh, was the man in whom she trusted from the start; he was the coming man. Her choice of him is as clear an indication of her statesmanship as the orders she gave her waiting women are of her practical sense. She forbade these ladies, once and for all, ever to speak to her on affairs of state.[3] From the first day of her reign, then, she showed herself a born ruler. It was no mere way of speaking which made a contemporary writer say, "None knew better the hardest art of all others, that is, of commanding men." [4]

At the beginning of her reign, Elizabeth received a loyal welcome from catholics and protestants alike. The Archbishop of York, Nicholas Heath, proclaimed her

---

[1] Cf. DODD, *Church History of England*, ed. by TIERNEY, II. (London, 1839), p. 120, note 2—quoted hereafter as "Dodd-Tierney."
[2] The list of members is given by CAMDEN, *Annal rer. Anglic. regn. Eliz.* (Lugd. Batav. 1625), pp. 2 *et seq.*
[3] KERVYN DE LETTENHOVE, I., p. 368. SPAN. CAL., 1558–67, p. 21.
[4] HAYWARD, *Annals*, Camd. Soc. (1840), p. 8.

accession in the House of Lords, but when he saw the turn things were taking, he knelt down before her Majesty and with great freedom of speech bade her remember her sex and youth which were so ill-suited to bear such weighty responsibilities. Elizabeth replied she would undertake nothing without the consent of her councillors and parliament.[1] She did in fact keep her religious intentions in the background for a remarkably long time. Every attempt to draw some avowal from her failed on the spot. A few days after her accession when an amnesty had been granted to prisoners, a witty courtier presented a petition to the new sovereign on her way to chapel, and cried out, " There are four or five more innocent men in prison, the four evangelists and the apostle Paul, who have long been shut up in the prison of an unknown tongue." The queen's answer was ready, " The prisoners have to be asked first if they want to get out." [2] When the Spanish ambassador seized the opportunity of his first audience to beg Elizabeth "to be very careful about religious affairs," all the answer he got was "that it would indeed be bad for her to forget God, Who had been so good to her."[3]

For nearly six weeks this state of uncertainty lasted without any one being the wiser ; on the one hand there was a gradual spread of protestantism at court and among the officials of the crown,[4] and, on the other, a strict adherence to the forms of Roman Catholic worship. The requiems for the deceased queen and for Charles V., both

[1] Sanders to Card. Morone. Report of 1561. Catholic Record Soc., *Miscellanea*, I. (London, 1905), pp. 2 *et seq.*
[2] LORD FRANCIS BACON, *In felicem memoriam Elizabethæ*. Works, ed. SPEDDING, etc., VI. (London, 1858), pp. 301 *et seq.*
[3] " La respuesta me parecio algo equivoca," remarks Feria. KERVYN DE LETTENHOVE, I., p. 341. SPAN. CAL., 1558–67, p. 10.
[4] KERVYN DE LETTENHOVE, I., pp. 338, 339. SPAN. CAL., pp. 7, 8.

C

celebrated in December,[1] were carried out in full accord with the rites of the ancient church. The explanation of these apparent contradictions is not hard to find ; by necessary changes among the courtiers and officials, Elizabeth wished to make sure of her footing before passing over to the protestant camp.

The people remained perfectly quiet during this period of transition. A few protestants here and there showed their zeal for religion by insulting images in the churches ; among catholic priests there were more frequently found some who felt bound to declare " My Lady is a bastard." [2]

Towards the end of the year, the atmosphere of the court was cleared of everything catholic. Count Feria, the Spanish ambassador, found himself in a position of painful isolation ; " they run away from me as if I were the devil." [3] At Christmas the queen at length threw aside her reserve, and went out from mass before the elevation of the host.[4] To the same date belongs the first authoritative pronouncement concerning divine service —the gospel, epistle, the ten commandments, etc., were to be recited in English, but at the same time it was strictly forbidden—" until consultation may be had by parliament by her Majesty and her three estates of this realm "—to add anything whatsoever to the Word of God,[5] or "gyve audience to any manner of doctrine or preaching " contrary

---

[1] HAYWARD'S *Annals*, pp. 12, 13.

[2] JOHN STRYPE, *Annals of the Reformation*, I., i. (Oxford, 1824), pp. 63 *et seq.* ; p. 69.

[3] Letter dated Dec. 14, 1558. KERVYN DE LETTENHOVE, I., p. 339. SPAN. CAL., p. 8.

[4] KERVYN DE LETTENHOVE, I., p. 365. " El domingo de Pasqua," in a letter written on Dec. 29, is of course a mistake for " Natal." SPAN. CAL., p. 17, has correctly, " Christmas." *Cf.* VENETIAN CAL., VII., p. 2. For further evidence, see C. G. BAYNE, *The Coronation of Qu. Eliz.*, in the Engl. Hist. Review, XXII., p. 662, note 47.

[5] Proclamation of Dec. 27, 1558.

to it. The services in the chapel royal were reformed in accordance with these injunctions, and married chaplains were allowed to officiate.[1] In a country grown accustomed to almost absolute monarchy, and where the mere form of parliamentary government was kept up, it was of great importance that the sovereign had already taken up a definite position with regard to religious questions before parliament was consulted. In spite of much that was inconsistent in her conduct, Elizabeth now left no one in doubt as to her religious opinions. Although at her coronation (January 15) a few things still remained ambiguous, all important points were already settled, or as good as settled. The queen, it is true, took the ancient oath containing the promise to maintain the privileges of the church,[2] but the spirit that was to rule the church was plainly shown by her conduct during the ceremony. As at the mass on Christmas day, Elizabeth withdrew before the elevation of the host took place in order to avoid being present at the outward sign of transubstantiation, which was then regarded in England almost as the symbol of the Roman church, she also refrained from receiving the Holy Communion, which was given according to the ancient rite under one kind.[3] Shortly afterwards (January 25), on her way to Westminster to open parliament, the queen refused to be received in procession by the monks of Westminster Abbey according to their custom ; "away with those torches for we see very well ! "[4]

---

[1] KERVYN DE LETTENHOVE, I., p. 366. SPAN. CAL., p. 18.

[2] See the actual words in MASKELL, *Monumenta ritualia Ecclesiæ Anglicanæ*, II. (Oxford, 1882), pp. 9–11.

[3] The proof of both facts, almost amounting to certainty, is given by C. G. BAYNE, *l.c.*, pp. 650–73. *Cf.* H. A. WILSON, *The English Coronation Orders*, Journal of Theol. Studies, II. (1901), p. 497.

[4] VENETIAN CAL., VII., p. 23. KERVYN DE LETTENHOVE, I., p. 413. SPAN. CAL., p. 25.

was her mocking comment on their festal array. When
the religious question was described in the speech from the
throne [1] as the chief task with which parliament had to
cope, this alone, without any further indication, was tanta-
mount to a condemnation of the existing order. Only
a few days later, a step forward was taken in the same
direction, when diplomatic relations were broken off with
the pope, "in consideration there was no further cause"
for them.[2]

The parliament which now assembled to decide the
religious future of England has been stigmatized by
catholics as "the Packed Parliament." Nicholas Sanders,
the historian of catholicism under Elizabeth and a
prominent man among catholics, was the first to reproach
the government with having brought undue influence to
bear upon the elections.[3] Later on, in the time of Charles I.,
it was also stated that the government had in each case
put forward three or five candidates from amongst whom
the electors must choose their representative.[4] A careful
investigation, however, has not substantiated these charges.
Elizabeth's first parliament was neither more nor less
representative of the people's will than Mary's last. Both,
like all other parliaments in Tudor times, contained a
number of government officials, privy councillors, and
courtiers, upon whose votes the government could count.
The large majority in Elizabeth's first House of Commons
(about eighty per cent.) was made up of independent

[1] STRYPE, *Annals*, I., 21 (1824), pp. 78, 80.
[2] Letter recalling Sir Edward Carne, the English ambassador in
Rome, dated Feb. 1, 1559. STRYPE, *Annals*, I., i., p. 51. FOREIGN
CAL., No. 299. *Cf.* MAITLAND, *Queen Elizabeth and Paul IV.*,
Eng. Hist. Rev., XV., pp. 326 *et seq.*
[3] See more fully, H. N. BIRT, *The Elizabethan Religious Settlement* (London, 1907), pp. 44–52.
[4] CLARENDON, *State Papers*, I. (Oxford, 1767), pp. 91 *et seq.*

members whose election had been quite regular. The contrary charges were entirely due to the wish to impugn the ecclesiastical legislation of this parliament, not only from the standpoint of canon law,[1] to which it undoubtedly ran counter, but also from the standpoint of English civil law. This accusation is unsupported by facts. The laws of 1559 which severed England finally from the Roman church were framed in a constitutional manner. One thing alone has to be remembered—the parliament was much more subservient to the crown in those days than fifty years later.

It did undoubtedly weigh with the parliament that even before it assembled, Elizabeth's government had indicated the line it intended to take in ecclesiastical affairs. But this, of course, did not in the least impair the constitutional character of the statutes enacted, and did not differ in any respect from what had been done by Elizabeth's predecessors.

The work of this first parliament of Queen Elizabeth was briefly this : the repeal of Mary's catholic legislation, *i.e.* the mediæval statutes against heresy which she had revived, and the re-enactment of the anti-Roman legislation of Henry VIII., not, however, in all its fulness, but in all essential points. In the first place, appeals to Rome and the payment of annates were once more forbidden, and the supreme jurisdiction in spiritual and temporal matters was given back to the crown.[2] The re-introduction of the

---

[1] *I.e.* "Against God's church." In Card. Allen's estimation, for example, the laws against the catholics are "no laws" solely on this ground. *Apologia Gul. Alani pro Sacerdotibus Soc. Jesu et Seminariorum Alumnis* (1583), cap. iv. F. DE MARSYS seeks to prove that the laws against the catholics are opposed to the laws of nature, of God, and of man, and to English and Roman law. *Histoire de la Persécution présente des Catholiques en Angleterre* (1646), livre II.

[2] See the contents of the Act of Supremacy, 1 Eliz. c. 1 : "An Act restoring to the crown the ancient jurisdiction over the state

Book of Common Prayer as the directory for public worship was a return to the work of the reformation under Edward VI. Clergy who refused to use this book suffered for the first offence the loss of a year's income and six months' imprisonment, for the second offence, deprivation and a year's imprisonment, and for the third, imprisonment for life. The same punishments were inflicted upon all clergy who should " preach, declare, or speak anything in the derogation and despraising of the same book "; attendance at divine service was made an obligation binding in law, and all who absented themselves without due cause forfeited " for every such offence twelve pence . . . to the use of the poor of the parish." [1]

In one point easily overlooked, and which, I think, is usually misunderstood, the Elizabethan legislation stood upon a different basis from that of Henry VIII., *i.e.* its conception of the royal supremacy. By proclaiming himself " supreme head of the church of England after God," Henry VIII. assumed to himself the position of pope—his supremacy was an imperial papacy, a " Cäsaro-papismus." His son Edward followed suit. There was nothing to prevent the holder of a supremacy so conceived from defining the doctrine of the church or performing spiritual functions in person. The question never became a practical one, for Henry VIII. remained catholic in all other points of doctrine, and Edward VI. died while still a child. Still, in the confession of faith of Edward's reformed church, the forty-two articles of 1552, no restrictions were placed upon the royal supremacy.[2] It was this absence of all

ecclesiastical and spiritual and abolishing all foreign power repugnant to the same."

[1] 1 Eliz. c. 2 : " An Act for the uniformity of Common Prayer and Divine Service."

[2] The thirty-sixth article ran : " The King of England is Supreme Head in Earth, next under Christ, of the Church of England and

limitation which made it impossible for catholics to accept the supremacy and even caused offence to many protestants.

When it was now proposed to give the same title to Queen Elizabeth, Archbishop Heath delivered a great speech against the royal supremacy in the House of Lords, his chief point, to which he always returned, being that a woman cannot be the pastor of Christ's flock ; cannot teach, preach, or administer the sacraments, and, therefore, a woman cannot be " supreme head of the church." [1] Heath never tired of putting this idea, this "therefore," in new forms. His speech plainly shows that the title, "supreme head," pure and simple, as borne by Henry VIII. and Edward VI., was understood in a "cæsareo-papal" sense. Nicholas Sanders [2] fully agreed with the archbishop and directed his attack against the royal supremacy on the same lines.

But Elizabeth, calmer and more calculating than her father, and always desirous of avoiding extremes, would not take the title. In no other point of her ecclesiastical legislation do we find the personal wishes of the queen so clearly expressed, and, although she offended many by her point-blank refusal, she nevertheless held to her point.[3] The title she chose and bequeathed to her successors to

Ireland. The Bishop of Rome hath no jurisdiction in this realm of England. The civil magistrate is, etc." A. SPARROW, *A Collection of Articles, Injunctions . . . of the Church of Engl.*, 4th impr. (London, 1684).

[1] DODD-TIERNEY, Vol. II., pp. ccxlviii. *et seq.*

[2] *De Origine ac Progressu Schismatis Anglicani* (Romæ, 1586), 361 : " Henricus non quidem fuit, sed per sexum atque ætatem poterat fuisse divini verbi . . . administer. Edouardus nec fuit nec adhuc per aetatem poterat esse minister verbi, quanquam per sexum potuisset. Elizabetha vero ne per sexum quidem poterat verbum dei . . . administrare."

[3] *Cf.* Feria's dispatches in KERVYN DE LETTENHOVE, I., 476, 482, 502. SPAN. CAL., 1558–67, pp. 37, 43, 55.

the present day sounds at first a mere modification of form without any change of meaning—"the only supreme governor of this realm, as well in all spiritual or ecclesiastical things or causes as temporal." But the explanation of the title given by Elizabeth herself, and then accepted in the anglican confession of faith, avoided from the first all "cæsareo-papal" interpretations. In the thirty-nine articles, the supremacy is limited by the following words:[1] "We give not to our princes the ministering either of God's word or of the sacraments, the which thing the injunctions[2] also lately set forth by Elizabeth our queen do most plainly testify, but that only prerogative which we see to have been given always to all godly princes in holy scriptures by God Himself; that is, that they should rule all estates and degrees committed to their charge by God, whether they be ecclesiastical or temporal, and restrain with the civil sword the stubborn and evil doers."[3] By these words, the Elizabethan supremacy is undoubtedly taken to mean the subordination of the spiritual to the temporal order, but nothing more. And so, when Elizabeth on several occasions assured the Spanish ambassador in set terms that she would not be head of the church or discharge spiritual functions,[4] her words must be taken as an indication that she wished to allay the fears of Archbishop Heath and others by explaining that, while the earlier title was the expression of a cæsareo-papal power, or could at least be so interpreted, the new one did not express this and could not be

[1] Article thirty-seven, corresponding to the thirty-sixth of the forty-two articles.

[2] Of 1559, *Injunctions given by the Queen's Majesty as well to the clergy as to the laity of the realm:* printed in SPARROW, pp. 65 *et seq.*

[3] What follows corresponds to the words in the forty-two articles: "The Bishop of Rome . . . etc."

[4] *Cf.* the passages referred to p. 23, note 3.

understood in that sense. The general opinion that there is no difference between the supremacy of Henry VIII. and Elizabeth's overlooks the point that the former was unlimited (in theory at least) and the latter limited.[1] No less a legal authority than Selden can be quoted in support of the interpretation given here. In his *Table Talk* (*s.v.* King), this great lawyer says : " There's a great deal of difference between head of the church and supreme governor, as our canons call the king. Conceive it thus : There is in the kingdom of England a college of physicians ; the king is supreme governor of those, but not the head of them, nor president of the college, nor the best physician."

This modification in the title of the royal supremacy explains, at least to a considerable extent, the remarkable fact that Elizabeth's ecclesiastical reform met with so little opposition. The bishops alone opposed it as a body, for Mary had taken care the regained bishoprics should not be filled with half-hearted catholics. The convocation which met at the same time as parliament opposed the change of religion in the strongest way, and professed its belief in the fundamental doctrines of the catholic church, especially in the papal supremacy.[2] Not satisfied with this, the more ardent of the bishops considered it their right and duty, as appointed guardians of the true faith, to proceed against the heretical queen with spiritual censures, a view of the situation in full accord with the prescriptions

---

[1] RANKE, *History of England* (English translation, Oxford, 1875), Vol. I., p. 230 : " It made, however, no essential difference." FROUDE, *Hist. of Engl.*, VI., p. 189 : " A variation of phrase was all that was necessary." The best explanation of the supremacy as restored under Elizabeth is given by G. W. PROTHERO, *Select Statutes and other Constitutional Documents . . . of Elizabeth and James I.*, 4th ed. (Oxford, 1913), Introd., pp. xxxiii. *et seq.*

[2] WILKINS, *Concilia Magnæ Britanniæ et Hiberniæ*, IV. (1737), pp. 179 *et seq.*

of canon law.[1]   The most influential of them, however, Archbishop Heath of York, was not in favour of this step, and the majority sided with him.   We know none of the details of this abortive attempt,[2] but it seems to be a fact that the idea of excommunicating Elizabeth was first entertained, not in Rome or in any other foreign country, but in her own land and among her English subjects.

It has been a moot point whether the treatment of the deprived bishops was mild or severe.[3]   The quantity of documents relating to the subject and the great variety in the treatment meted out to individuals allow room for indulging in sentiment both over the prisoner's hard lot and over the queen's tender heart.   Those who are on the look-out for sufferers will find what they seek, and those who seek for signs of grace and indulgence will find them too. In reality neither Elizabeth nor Cecil were animated by sentiment in the matter, but acted from motives of policy. Each case was decided on its own merits.   Was it more to the government's credit to treat a bishop well or ill ?   The highly respected archbishop of York, Nicholas Heath, who had proclaimed Elizabeth's accession in the House of

[1] " Si vero dominus temporalis, requisitus et monitus ab ecclesia, suam terram purgare neglexerit ab hæretica fœditate, per metropolitanum et cæteros comprovinciales episcopos excommunicationis vinculo innodetur, etc.," cap. 13, § 3, X.   De hæreticis, V., 7.   FRIEDBERG'S ed. of the Decretals, col. 788.

[2] ROBERT PERSONS, *Domestical Difficulties*, ed. J. H. Pollen, Catholic Record Soc., II. (1906), p. 59.   CAMDEN, *Annales*, p. 13. *Cf.* C. G. BAYNE, *Anglo-Roman Relations* 1558-65 (Oxford, 1913), p. 53, note 41.

[3] The chief works on the subject are T. E. BRIDGETT and T. F. KNOX, *The True Story of the Cath. Hierarchy deposed by Qu. Elizabeth* (London, 1889) ; HENRY GEE, *The Elizabethan Clergy and the Settlement of Religion* 1558-64 (Oxford, 1898); G. E. PHILLIPS, *The Extinction of Ancient Hierarchy* (London, 1905).   The first and third books are written from the catholic point of view ; the second from the anglican.

Lords, who had quashed the attempt to excommunicate her, whose speech against the royal supremacy, in spite of all its vigour, had avoided giving offence, this man, whose past was free from stain of cruelty and who had gained the esteem of his opponents by his dignified conduct and courage, was not treated like a political offender, but rather like a deserving state official forced into retirement by untoward circumstances. After a short and easy confinement to save appearances, he was allowed to retire to his estates in Kent and to pursue his studious life in peace. The visits by which the queen openly honoured the deprived prelate were a sign of her political tact and of her gratitude. The bishop of London, on the contrary, Edmund Bonner, the best hated of the judges of heresy under Mary, could not hope for clemency. When the bishops paid their respects to the queen on her way into London, she snatched away her hand from Bonner and would not allow it to be touched by lips that had pronounced sentence of death upon so many protestants. Here again it was Elizabeth herself who struck the note, and, whether she acted from calculation or impulse, she hit upon what was politically expedient. It was no nominal confinement to which Bonner was subjected; death alone set him free after long years of imprisonment. Yet care was taken, even in his case, not to give the catholics a martyr. The new law declaring any one who repeatedly refused to take the oath of supremacy guilty of high treason was a convenient weapon by which to condemn this inflexible prisoner, nevertheless, the authorities were careful to see that he died without the crown of martyrdom and was buried in the silence of the night. Other bishops were imprisoned for a time, heavily fined and then released when it was no longer feared they would prove troublesome; others were kept in a state of semi-imprisonment, but it was always possible to prove that the full rigour of the law had not been put in force against them. This was due neither to clemency nor pusillanimity, but to political shrewdness. In a country that only a few years before had seen protestant bishops burnt to death, and catholics, before that again, beheaded for refusing the oath, the new system must have seemed a change for the better; fines and imprisonment replaced the scaffold and the stake.

The large mass of the clergy was treated still more leniently than the bishops. One of the ritual innovations which must have been most repugnant to catholic priests was communion in both kinds. It showed great political tact that on a point like this, which did not interfere with the authority of the state, consciences were at first left undisturbed. If a priest, the queen declared shortly before Easter, 1559,[1] refused to give communion in both kinds, the parishioners were not further to molest him, in order not to wound in any way christian charity, but to go to some other priest from whom they might receive the sacrament under both kinds. She was aiming at a peaceful transition, trusting to time and a mild application of the law. The fact that in this the authorities were not mistaken is a clear proof that strong religious convictions were to be met with only among the leading spirits and a few others, and not yet among the mass of the people and clergy. "The difference between catholics and Lutherans was not of much importance in substance," declared the queen to the Spanish ambassador.[2]

Among strict catholics the royal supremacy, even in its new and modified form, naturally caused the greatest scandal. Nevertheless the oath of supremacy was not

[1] Proclamation of March 22, 1558–9.   Easter fell on March 26.
[2] SPAN. CAL., 1558–67, p. 170.   Dispatch of July 25, 1560.   *Cf.* similar remarks made in 1565, p. 425.

condemned in Elizabeth's first years with anything like the same vehemence as it was later on [1] when the pope's excommunication and the activity of catholic missionaries had awakened the conscience of the adherents of the ancient faith. Even allowing for the fact that the oath was not at first exacted everywhere with equal insistence, the percentage of those who were deprived for refusing to take it was remarkably small. Out of about eight thousand clergy,[2] only from two to three hundred, according to the usual reckoning,[3] were deprived in the first six years of Elizabeth's reign. A more recent calculation,[4] however, raises the number to seven hundred. Various explanations have been sought to account for this pliability in the clergy. There is much to be said for the argument that the recent change of religion was looked upon as no more likely to be permanent than the two which

[1] *Cf.* Card. Allen's words : "This intolerable othe, repugnant to God, the church, Her Majestie's honour, and al men's consciences." *An Apology . . . of the two English Colleges* (1581), p. 12. Nicholas Sanders considered that by this oath of supremacy Elizabeth surpassed all the "Athalias, Machas, Jezebelas, Herodiadas, Selenes, Constantias, Eudoxias" ; *De Origine ac Progressu Schismatis Anglicani* (Romæ, 1586), p. 364.

[2] For this number, instead of 9400, usually given, *cf.* H. N. BIRT, *The Elizabethan Religious Settlement* (London, 1907), pp. 124, 161 *et seq.*

[3] CAMDEN, *Annales*, p. 23. DODD-TIERNEY, II., Ap. No. XLIV. See especially H. GEE, *The Elizabethan Clergy, etc.* (Oxford, 1898), pp. 145 *et seq.*, ch. xii., xiii.

[4] BIRT, p. 197 : "I have the names of over 700 holders of benefices who underwent deprivation before the end of 1565." I am unable to control this number ; the conjectures upon which Dom Norbert Birt relies (pp. 200–3), in order still further to increase the percentage of those who were deprived, are in many cases open to criticism and have not brought conviction to me. A. F. POLLARD, *Hist. of Engl.*, 1547–1603 (London, 1910), in HUNT-POOLE'S *Political Hist. of Engl.*, VI., p. 217, and J. P. WHITNEY, *The Elizabethan Reformation*, in the Quarterly Review, No. 430, also decline to accept Dom Birt's calculations.

had preceded it.[1] Who could tell in the year 1559 that
Elizabeth was specially destined to mould things into their
permanent shape ?   Many persons might provisionally
comply with the law while waiting for a change in the
immediate future, and, when no such change came about,
what began by being provisional would end by becoming
permanent. The supposition cannot be entertained that
the see of Rome had given English catholics a secret
dispensation to take the oath of supremacy and attend
anglican services.[2] A dispensation of this kind would be
irreconcilable with the principles of the catholic church.
Whoever does not admit this, but continues to regard the
dispensation as a fact, is bound to explain, amongst other
things,[3] why at the outset the oath was refused at all and,
later on, rejected by so many. Every martyrdom for Rome
would have been meaningless if Rome permitted the oath.
As I have already pointed out, a more probable explanation
seems to me to be found in the often overlooked fact that
Elizabeth's supremacy was different from Henry's. Now
that the title " head of the church" had been dropped, many
persons would quiet their conscience with the assurance
that the new title, " governor," had no spiritual significance,
but only claimed their obedience on civil grounds.[4]

[1] PETER HEYLYN, *Ecclesia Restaurata, etc.*, ed. Robertson, II.
(Cambr., 1849), p. 295. J. H. POLLEN, *Politics of Engl. Catholics*,
in The Month, Jan., 1902, p. 50. H. N. BIRT, *Elizabethan Relig.
Settlement*, pp. 167, 298, 375.

[2] GEE, p. 198. FROUDE, *History of England*, VII., p. 177, treats
the dispensation as an established fact. The *sole* evidence for it is
a forgery of the seventeenth century, the absurd inventions contained
in a report supposed to have been written in Italy by an English spy,
E. Dennum. STRYPE, *Annals of the Reformation*, I. ii., p. 56.

[3] Especially the express orders of the Inquisition in 1562 pro-
hibiting attendance at anglican services. BAYNE, *Anglo-Roman
Relations*, Ap. 48.

[4] " In hac iurisiurandi formula, cum . . . . Supremi Capitis appella-
tionem indoctiores omissam viderent, pro simplicitate sua lætabantur

The caution with which the clergy were taken in hand at first was also shown in the treatment dealt out to the laity. A degree of consideration was shown them little in accord either with the prevailing views of the period or with the practice followed later on. Many catholics whose conscience forbade them to accept the new order of things were allowed to leave the country and retain their property, provided only they did not settle in Rome.[1] It must be noted, however, that passports were not granted indiscriminately to catholics, and a good many of those who wished to emigrate complained of the difficulty they experienced in obtaining permission to go abroad.[2] This can hardly surprise us, for only noblemen and merchants were allowed to go abroad by the laws of that day as a matter of course.[3] Still, on the whole, the government was content at first merely to get rid of catholics. Clergy and religious, too, were free to leave England, and many availed themselves of this unusual permission.[4] As the departure of catholics was welcomed, so, too, was the influx of protestants. Not only did English protestants who had fled abroad under Mary return home again,[5] but oppressed protestants from Holland came too. "They are

non eousque progressum esse, ut id sexui fœmineo tribueretur, quod antea viris Henrico et Edouardo honestius concedi posse videbatur, ex eoque plurimi non modo Calvinistæ, sed aliquot etiam utcunque catholici putabant magis excusabile, si hoc iuramentum præstarent." SANDERS, 369 *et seq.*

[1] See the reference to Sir Francis Englefield in Appendix I. : " Gli è stato concesso di poter goder le sue entrate, purchè non venghi habitare a Roma," and, towards the end, the reference to Sir Edward Carne. The permission to live abroad without forfeiting his property in England was withdrawn between 1565 and 1570. For Englefield, *cf.* SPAN. CAL., 1558–67, p. 615, n., 1568–79, pp. 46, n., 62, 82.

[2] R. LECHAT, *Les réfugiés anglais dans les Pays-Bas espagnols durant le règne d'Elisabeth* (Louvain, 1914), p. 22.

[3] CAMDEN, *Annales*, p. 47.

[4] SPAN. CAL., 1558–67, p. 77.

[5] FOREIGN CAL., 1558–59, n. 290. VENETIAN CAL., VII., n. 7.

all welcome. I at least will never fail them," replied Elizabeth to some who complained of the Dutch immigration.[1]

In London itself, afterwards the headquarters of puritanism, the abolition of catholic worship was carried out by the people with a good will. The removal of the crucifixes, statues, and altars from the churches not only met with no opposition,[2] but was the occasion of popular rejoicings. The zeal for destruction bordered on licence and vandalism. Stained glass windows were broken, walls scraped bare of frescoes, the figure of St. Thomas cast down and beheaded, missals, vestments, and altar-hangings burnt by the mob with noisy applause, "as if it had beene the sacking of some hostile city."[3] In some parts of the country there was opposition to the change of worship, as in the neighbourhood of Winchester and in the northern counties[4] which were afterwards the chief stronghold of catholicism.   However much in certain circles men might murmur against these innovations, even an unsympathetic observer was forced to admit that the most striking phenomenon of these months was the revival of protestantism after its five years' oppression. "In six months," wrote the Spanish ambassador in July, 1559, "[Elizabeth] has revived heresy and encourages it everywhere to such an extent that it is recovering rapidly all the credit it had lost for years past."[5]

[1] SPAN. CAL., pp. 118, 119.

[2] KERVYN DE LETTENHOVE, I., 539.   SPAN. CAL., 76, 89.

[3] HAYWARD'S *Annals*, Camd. Soc. (1840), p. 28.   These words contradict Camden's attempt to give a more favourable description : "imagines sine tumultu amoventur," *Annales*, p. 22 ; *cf*. VENETIAN CAL., VII., p. 11.

[4] K. DE LETTENHOVE, I., pp. 554, 548.   SPAN. CAL. 1558–67, pp. 79, 82.

[5] K. DE LETTENHOVE, I., p. 559.   SPAN. CAL., p. 85. Not *furiously !* The Spanish *a furia* means "with the greatest haste," not *furiously*, as Hume renders it in the SPAN. CAL.

II. *England and the Catholic Church in their International Relations* (1558–63)

The chief danger which menaced the reformation came not from within the country, but from without. Between the two supporters of Mary Stuart's claims, France and Scotland, England lay almost defenceless.[1] For the moment, indeed, little was to be feared, thanks to Mary Tudor's alliance with Spain, which so far remained unbroken, although the ecclesiastical changes must in time lead to a breach with that country and to political isolation. France was soon fully occupied with the wars of religion and so for a long time ceased to be numbered among England's most dangerous enemies ; but Spain could not calmly stand aside and permit a protestant power to grow into greatness in the immediate neighbourhood of her possessions in the Low Countries. It therefore became a necessary aim of Spanish politics to bind England to Spain either as an ally or a vassal. When Elizabeth ascended the throne, the question, whether Spanish influence could be better secured in England by marriage or war, naturally presented itself to Count Feria, the ambassador of Philip II. He inclined towards the latter alternative, for victory seemed assured,[2] but his master decided to "serve the Lord"[3] by marrying Elizabeth. She did not for a moment think of accepting the proposal made to her almost in the spirit of self-sacrifice, though she refrained from giving a definite

[1] A good description of the dangerous and defenceless state of England is given by the ambassador Wotten in a letter to Cecil of Jan. 9, 1559. K. DE LETTENHOVE, I., p. 393. The English forces numbered 8000 infantry, 2000 cavalry, and 4000 marines. SPAN. CAL., 1558–67, pp. 137, 146.

[2] SPAN. CAL., 1558–67, p. 3.

[3] "Me he resuelto determinadamente de hacer este servicio a Dios Nuestro Señor, etc." K. DE LETTENHOVE, I., p. 400. SPAN. CAL., p. 22.

D

answer until parliament had passed the Act of Supremacy. Then only did she bluntly tell Count Feria she could not marry the king of Spain because she was a protestant.[1] Neither this answer nor Philip's own marriage with Elizabeth of France put an end to the hope that the queen of England might yet be drawn by marriage—this time with one of the archdukes—to play a part in the world-wide political schemes of the Hapsburgs.[2] It does not fall within the scope of this work to follow in detail the moves in this political game.[3]   Our only concern is to show how it affected the fortunes of English catholics and Elizabeth's attitude to Rome.

It was quite natural that at the first indications of religious change, English catholics who wished for a return to the old state of things both in religion and politics, should turn their eyes in the direction of Spain.[4]   "The catholics in this country, who are many, place all their hope in your majesty," wrote Feria to the king.[5]   Philip II. could not help at first utterly disappointing these hopes. Just because he was seeking to win Elizabeth by gentle means, he was unable to enter into an understanding with that section of her subjects who were opposed to her.   He had to put up with many unfavourable criticisms for never having once essayed to intervene diplomatically in favour of his English co-religionists.   His ambassador warned him not to throw away altogether the good will of the

---

[1] K. DE LETTENHOVE, I., p. 473.   SPAN. CAL., p. 37.   The word "heretic" which Feria places in Elizabeth's mouth can hardly have been used by her of herself.

[2] FOREIGN CAL., 1558–59, *passim.*   K. DE LETTENHOVE, I., pp. 498 *et seq.*   SPAN. CAL., 1558–67, p. 53.

[3] For a detailed narrative, see C. G. BAYNE, *Anglo-Roman Relations* 1558–65, Oxford Historical and Literary Studies, Vol. II. (1913), pp. 31–39.

[4] K. DE LETTENHOVE, I., p. 364.   SPAN. CAL., 1558–67, p. 16.

[5] K. DE LETTENHOVE, I., p. 414.   SPAN. CAL., 1558–67, p. 26.

catholics, while some among them were heard to declare that if Spain would not help them, "they would appeal to the French, or even to the Turks rather than put up with these heretics." [1]   There is no sign that English catholics were treasonably mixed up with Spanish politics in the first years of Elizabeth. It does not alter this fact that even then several Englishmen had entered the service of Philip II.   One of the first, if not the first, to do so was Sir Richard Shelley,[2] Knight of St. John, and he is a proof that it was then quite possible to enter the service of Spain without any ill will towards Elizabeth's government.[3]

The less the advantage English catholics gained from the policy of Spain, the greater was that gained by Elizabeth. Fertile though the period was in strange contradictions between religion and worldly policy, one of the strangest is the circumstance that the catholic king, who was afterwards to be the executor of the bull of excommunication, began, without intending it, by being the ally of the English reformers.   Having once assumed the character of protector of the little island kingdom, Philip II. was not in a position to estimate so correctly the altered state of things. The idea that England, poor and defenceless as she was, could ever be anything else than a pawn on his political chess-board, which might be either useful or troublesome to him, never once entered into the mind of the king or his diplomatists.   Philip's attitude towards Elizabeth was based

---

[1] SPAN. CAL., pp. 124, 132, 171.

[2] Philip II. commended him to Card. Morone on April 24, 1561, with the words: "Por perseverar en nuestra verdadera fee y religion . . . no solamente se ha querido desterrar dù su naturaleza y perder los bienes que en ella tenia y grado que pudiera tener, pero aun va agora a servir con su persona a Dios y a su religion." Arch. Vat., Arm. LXIV., t. 28, fol. 78.

[3] *Cf.* the life of Shelley by A. F. POLLARD in the *Dict. of Nat. Biogr.*, LII., p. 40.

on the supposition that England could never cause him alarm while it might be made useful. He therefore allowed himself to be brow-beaten by the queen and her government to an extent that a state more powerful than England would never have ventured upon. Elizabeth's self-importance was increased by the consciousness, only too well fostered by Spain, that she was the most eligible match in Christendom. When parliament had re-established the supremacy of the crown over the church, she haughtily [1] inquired of the Spanish ambassador if the king had aught to say against it, and, when Count Feria replied she would be ruined in this way, she merely asked, " By whom ? By your master or the king of France ? " Elizabeth's astonishing audacity and rudeness can best be explained by the fact that in the Spanish representative she had to do with a man whose behaviour exhibited, and even exaggerated, all that the world of those days meant by Spanish pride. Don Gomez Suarez de Figueroa, Count of Feria, carried himself in England as if it were a vassal state, and treated Elizabeth as if she were queen by the grace of Philip. The way she received his threats and warnings was incomprehensible to him ; " she is convinced of the soundness of her unstable power, and will only see her error when she is irretrievably lost." [2]

The passages of arms between the ambassador and this young woman of twenty-five are among the most entertaining episodes in diplomacy. Partly owing to her masculine common sense and happy knack of repartee, partly, also, owing to her thorough acquaintance with various languages, Elizabeth possessed from the beginning of her political career a readiness of tongue which reduced many a professional diplomatist to despair. In the way she played

---

[1] " Con sobervia." K. DE LETTENHOVE, I., p. 482.
[2] *Ib*. I., p. 574. SPAN. CAL., p. 89.

with this Spanish grandee and ambassador—sometimes domineering and sometimes cajoling, sometimes sarcastic and sometimes amiable—she showed herself at once a woman and a real queen. But the thorough success she achieved by this quick play of manner and by what looked like mere banter could not have been surpassed by the wiliest diplomatist. While one enigma followed another she gained time and continued to be wooed. " I could not tell your majesty," wrote Feria to Philip II., "what this woman means to do with herself, and those who know her best know no more than I do." [1] His final summing-up was that Elizabeth "is a daughter of the devil," [2] and his successor, Bishop Quadra, came to the same conclusion when he wrote, " This woman must have a hundred devils in her body, notwithstanding that she is for ever telling me that she yearns to be a nun and to pass her time in a cell praying." [3]

The chief result of Elizabeth's policy and procrastination was her immunity from the papal excommunication. That the anglican reformation enjoyed ten years of undisturbed progress, and that the excommunication when published was only " a paper thunderbolt " [4] was due more to the two Hapsburgs, the king of Spain and the emperor of Germany, than to any one else.[5] The hope of winning Elizabeth by marriage and of thereby gaining over England to side with the Hapsburgs in politics would be instantly

[1] K. DE LETTENHOVE, I., p. 504. SPAN. CAL., 1558–67, p. 57.

[2] " Hija del diablo." K. DE LETTENHOVE, I., p. 519. SPAN. CAL., p. 67.

[3] K. DE LETTENHOVE, II., pp. 157 et seq. SPAN. CAL., 1558–67, p. 119.

[4] JOHN JEWEL, A Viewe of a seditious Bul sent into Englande from Pius Quintus, Bishop of Rome (London, 1582), p. 81.

[5] SPAN. CAL., 1558–67, pp. 60, 61, 62, 88. NICHOLAS SANDERS, De Origine ac Progressu Schism. Angl. (1586), p. 416. J. H. POLLEN, The Politics of English Catholics, The Month, Jan., 1902, p. 53.

dashed to the ground as soon as the pope cast out Elizabeth from the communion of the faithful. From the
catholic point of view, the future justified those who
appealed to the pope to release all Elizabeth's subjects
from their oath of allegiance and to recognize the claims
of Mary Stuart,[1] as a direct answer to the revival
of the anglican state church. "Good fruit cannot be
expected from so bad a tree [Henry VIII.], whatever is left
undone in compassing her destruction will never be made
good";[2] such was the justification of this policy towards
Elizabeth. There can be no question that the papal
excommunication would have been incomparably more
dangerous for the queen and her designs in 1560 than in
1570. No one pretends that Elizabeth was universally
beloved in the early years of her reign,[3] many catholics
openly cast doubts upon her legitimacy,[4] the English
universities looked askance at her for many a year to
come,[5] and every one was asking who was the heir to the
throne.[6] The unforeseen result of the policy adopted by
Spain and the empire during these critical years was to
shelter Elizabeth from Rome and France, and to leave the
English reformation to take its course free from foreign

---

[1] *Vid. ante*, p. 14, note 2.

[2] "Fructus bonus ab arbore tam mala non potest expectari, totum
amittitur, quicquid in illa deiicienda omittitur." An anonymous and
undated letter apparently belonging to the year 1561. Arch. Vat.,
Arm. LXIV., t. 28, fol. 174. Now printed by BAYNE, *op. cit.*,
Appendix 35.

[3] SPAN. CAL., *passim*.

[4] "Los catolicos muy descontentos y tan mal con esta reyna, que
publicamente dicen non la tienen por reyna ni por legitima." The
Spanish ambassador Quadra to Philip II., June 6, 1559. K. DE
LETTENHOVE, I., p. 534.

[5] *Ib.*, II., p. 643. SPAN. CAL., p. 218. Letter of the Spanish
ambassador of Nov. 15, 1561. *Cf.* H. N. BIRT, *Elizabethan relig.
Settlement* (1907), ch. vii.

[6] SPAN. CAL., *passim*.

interference. So long as Elizabeth continued to be courted by Philip and Ferdinand little was to be feared from France's threat of a papal excommunication.[1]

Philip II., as Elizabeth's protector in spite of himself, rendered his first important service in the summer of 1560 when pope Pius IV. was seeking means for reopening diplomatic relations with England after a year's breach. Abbot Vincenzo Perpaglia was to have gone to England as nuncio with a papal letter calling upon Elizabeth to return into the bosom of the catholic church.[2] If the queen refused to listen to friendly admonition, Perpaglia was ordered to have recourse to threats.[3] An invitation to the council of Trent would have been a sure and natural test of the queen's good will, and it would have been difficult for Elizabeth to have adhered, on such a point, to her habitual policy of procrastination. The report, therefore, that the nuncio had started on his journey gave her a disagreeable shock,[4] while it raised the hopes of English catholics both at home and abroad. In Italy, where hardly any doubt was entertained of the mission's success, people realized that "in England all men did not yet pull together,"[5] but in the Low Countries, where the real state of affairs was better understood, people mocked at the man "who was travelling to England to persuade the queen in religious matters."[6] In England, catholics

---

[1] SPAN. CAL., 1558–67, p. 136.
[2] Brief of May 5, 1560, printed in CAMDEN, *Annales* (Lugd. Bat., 1625), pp. 47 *et seq.* BARONIUS ET RAYNALDUS, *Annal. Eccles.*, ad annum 1560, § 42. In English in DODD-TIERNEY, II., Appendix No. XLVII. For the correct title of the abbot (*S. Solutore*, near Turin, not *Salvatore*, as it is nearly always given), *cf.* MAITLAND, Engl. Hist. Rev., XV., pp. 759 *et seq.*
[3] BAYNE, *Anglo-Roman Relations*, p. 48.
[4] K. DE LETTENHOVE, II., p. 440. SPAN. CAL., 1558–67, p. 159.
[5] FOREIGN CAL., 1560–61, n. 74.
[6] *Ib.*, No. 224, 5.

who were suspected of being implicated in the undertaking were arrested.[1]

All these hopes and fears were brought to nought in a way men least expected. Perpaglia was considered to be a pronounced partisan of France.[2] The policy of France was to have Elizabeth excommunicated. This was sufficient to make it the policy of Spain to prevent the fulfilment of his mission. Pius IV. had commended his nuncio to the protection of the two Hapsburgs,[3] but the Emperor Ferdinand, who scarcely knew Perpaglia, alone furnished him with the desired letter of introduction to Queen Elizabeth.[4] The courts of Spain and Brussels, on the contrary, were scarcely better pleased with Perpaglia's journey than the English court itself, and begged the pope to nominate another nuncio.[5] Orders from Rome reached Perpaglia in Brussels instructing him not to proceed to England until he should receive further instructions.[6] Painful as it was for the Spanish ambassador in London to undertake the task of once more dashing the hopes of English catholics to the ground and of keeping the unbidden guest at a distance from the queen, there was nothing for him to do except write to the nuncio strongly dissuading him from continuing his journey to England.[7] The sole result of Perpaglia's mission, from which so much

[1] SPAN. CAL., pp. 170 et seq. For fuller particulars as to this episode, see BAYNE, Anglo-Roman Relations, pp. 46–61.

[2] " Es Frances por la vida," writes Quadra, the Spanish ambassador in London. K. DE LETTENHOVE, II., p. 441.

[3] Briefs of May 5, 1560, to Philip II. and Ferdinand I. BARONIUS ET RAYNALDUS, Annal. Eccles., ad ann. 1560, §§ 43, 45.

[4] Vienna, June 20. Copy in Arch. Vat., Arm. LXIV., t. 28, fol. 64.

[5] VENETIAN CAL., VII., p. 229 ; the Venetian ambassador with King Philip to the Doge and Senate.

[6] FOREIGN CAL., 1560–61, No. 507.

[7] SPAN. CAL., pp. 170 et seq.

had been expected, was the distribution of five hundred
ducats of papal alms among the English catholic exiles in
Brussels.[1]

Immediately afterwards, the question of the council was
brought to a conclusion in Rome. On November 29,
1560, the bull announcing the reopening of the council
of Trent was published.[2] Nuncios were nominated to
carry the news to catholic princes, including England.
Elizabeth and her government had so cleverly made a
pretence of being ready to take part in the council, and
acted so astutely, that even in Spain, where people were
best informed, they were thought to be in earnest. At the
court of Philip II. men were wondering whom the queen
would send as her representative.[3]

Taught by his experience of the previous year, the pope
this time came to an understanding with Spain over the
mission of the new nuncio. In order to avoid giving
offence to either party, Pius enjoined upon Abbot Girolamo Martinengo, whom he chose for this undertaking, to
show his commission to the ambassadors both of Spain and
France and to listen to the advice of each of them.[4]
Before matters should reach this point, however, the
nuncio was to write to the queen from Brussels asking
for a letter of safe conduct. It was by no means certain
that he would receive one, but Martinengo himself, who had
undertaken the mission much against his will,[5] was more
afraid of being badly treated in England than of being
refused admission. In the list of questions he drew up

---

[1] FOREIGN CAL., 1560-61, No. 815, 7. It was commonly said in
England at a later period that Perpaglia's mission had been thwarted
by Elizabeth. CAMDEN, *Annales* (ed. 1625), p. 48.

[2] BULLARIUM ROMANUM, VII. (1882), pp. 90-92.

[3] FOREIGN CAL., 1560-61, No. 762, 3.

[4] Instructions of March 9, 1561, Appendix III.

[5] FOREIGN CAL., 1560-61, No. 816, 1.

before his departure,[1] the following difficulty is pro-pounded : "What am I to do if the queen does not receive me as the nuncio of the Supreme Head of the church, but only as the envoy of a (secular) prince ? " Cardinal Morone, who superintended the proceedings, wrote on the margin : " This is out of the question, and, if it should still happen, he must do the best he can." To the further inquiry, " How am I to behave if the queen speaks dis-respectfully of the pope's person ? " the cardinal replies, " Answer courteously and calmly."

This time, Spain had no objection to the person of the nuncio, and was in full sympathy with the object of his mission, but she dreaded the consequences of failure. Should Elizabeth refuse to admit Martinengo or decline the papal invitation, her excommunication, and possibly even war also, might be the result. Such a turn of events would put an end to the catholic king continuing his policy of friendly protection towards England. Philip, therefore, recommended the pope to defer the mission to England until it would be ascertained that the other potentates were going to take part in the council.[2] Pius rejected this advice, Martinengo was sent in March 1561, and Spain had no choice left but to do her best to assist the nuncio at Elizabeth's court. The affair did not look hope-less at the outset, for Elizabeth declared at one time she was ready to send representatives to the council, provided it was free, *i.e.* met on this side the Alps, and, at another, that she was just on the point of choosing them.[3] In fine, she was trying to keep up her policy of procrastination to the very last minute. Cecil, unlike his mistress, appeared during these weeks to fight with his visor up. When,

[1] Appendix II.
[2] BAYNE, *Anglo-Roman Relations*, pp. 73-78 ; *cf.* his Appendix XXV.
[3] SPAN. CAL., 1558-67, pp. 179, 187, 197.

however, he suggested that some theologians should be sent into England on the pope's behalf to discuss controverted points, or when he made the equally impracticable proposal that the pope must give the queen all her titles— even including " Defender of the Faith "—else she would not receive his letters—it was plain to any one who had eyes to see that Cecil was not acting straightforwardly.[1] It is significant that the secretary of state is described by the Spanish ambassador in the following words : " Cecil is a very great heretic, but he is neither foolish nor false." [2]

It was he more than any one else who drew from Elizabeth the clear uncompromising " No " she so much dreaded. Up to this time England had been in a position to regard its own reformation as its private concern, but now the time was come to defend this department of its domestic policy openly before the world. The queen's manner had roused hopes in the Spanish ambassador that she would never venture to shut the door in the face of the pope's messenger. In order to protect the nuncio from hostile demonstrations in the London streets, Greenwich was chosen as the meeting-place. The ambassador hired a lodging for himself there in order the better to help Martinengo, and looked forward with longing to the day of his arrival.[3] So sure did he feel of that arrival and of the issue of the nuncio's mission that he expressed the hope that the imprisoned catholic bishops—England's natural representatives at the council—would now soon be set at liberty. These incautious words, carried about and interpreted in various ways, afforded the first pretext for pretending that the Spanish embassy was the headquarters of a catholic conspiracy.[4] " The papists' humours," thought Cecil, " grow too rank by the queen's lenity." [5]

[1] SPAN. CAL., 1558–67, pp. 189–191.   [2] Ib., p. 191.
[3] Ib., pp. 193–195.   [4] Ib., pp. 195–199.
[5] FOREIGN CAL., 1561–62, No. 187, 2.

At last, on May 1, 1561, the final decision on the nuncio's reception was taken. The Privy Council met at Greenwich and declared it was dangerous to the state to give an audience to the representative of a power which regarded the laws of England as contrary to its laws and constitutions as well as to the law of God.[1] According to the official report of the sitting and the information given to the Spanish ambassador, the resolution was unanimous without one dissentient voice. But it was nothing of the sort. It appears rather that the majority was in favour of allowing the nuncio to land, but Cecil and the lord chancellor, Sir Nicholas Bacon,[2] took the opposite view and carried their point.[3] When the Spanish ambassador went to see the queen after receiving this astonishing piece of news, he found her "confused and upset."[4] It is possible Elizabeth may have been dissembling in order not to seem a party to this mortifying decision, but more probably she dreaded a step which might have the immediate effect of bringing about her excommunication. A year before, during Perpaglia's mission, the pope had threatened that if his exhortations proved fruitless he would either employ against the queen the authority God had committed to him or enjoin upon the council the duty of punishing her obstinacy.[5]

[1] FOREIGN CAL., 1561–62, No. 162.

[2] In an anonymous account of this meeting of the Privy Council, it is said of Bacon: " Custos sigilli publici, qui cum Cecilio moderatur et regit omnia, ita rem posuit, ut diceret, se non videre quemquam posse absque manifesto crimine laesæ majestatis huic nuntio admittendo suffragium prebere." Arch. Vat., Arm. LXIV., t. 28, fol. 335.

[3] For the arguments employed in the discussion, cf. HEYLYN, Ecclesia Restaurata, ed. Eccles. Hist. Soc., II. (Cambridge, 1849), pp. 354 et seq. See also FOREIGN CAL., No. 248, 2. BAYNE, op. cit., p. 110.

[4] SPAN. CAL., p. 202.

[5] J. H. POLLEN, Papal Negotiations with Mary, Queen of Scots, 1561–67, Scottish Hist. Soc. (Edin., 1901), p. 46. BAYNE, op. cit., p. 48.

The danger of excommunication now threatening was dreaded not only by Elizabeth, but quite as much, if not more, by her protector, Philip II. Immediately on hearing at Madrid of Martinengo's rejection—a defeat also for Spanish politics—the king endeavoured to dissuade Rome from fulfilling her threat. Philip II. represented to the pope [1] that however justifiable such a measure directed against the queen of England might be, the present moment did not seem to him to be the proper time for it. If the pope pronounced Elizabeth schismatic and deposed without putting his sentence into execution, he would only damage his own prestige and exasperate the queen to no purpose.[2] Philip, however, upon whom as the church's most devoted son the execution of the sentence would devolve, was just at that moment quite unequal to the task. A Spanish attack upon England, which would mean the break-up of the peace of Europe, would also bring with it the break-up of the council, the sole means for remedying all religious abuses. Therefore the king begged the pope to postpone his sentence against Elizabeth to a more convenient season, declaring he would himself be ready to carry out the sentence with all his power, when the proper time came.

Philip's anxiety about the excommunication was now groundless. Rome had no wish to regard Martinengo's rejection as final. It was thought that the responsibility of the action rested, not on the queen, but on her advisers.[3] At this moment Cardinal Ippolito d'Este was on his way to France as papal legate, and the pope in an autograph

[1] Philip II. to his ambassador Vargas, July 16, 1561. MIGNET, *Histoire de Marie Stuart*, I. (Paris, 1885), pp. 405–407.
[2] ". . . si la declara [cismatica] y procede a privacion y non se ejecuta, es perder reputacion y irritarla y ponerla mas dura y en mayor desesperacion sin nigun fructo . . ."
[3] FOREIGN CAL., 1561-62, No. 247, 1.

letter commissioned him to treat with the queen of England and to accede to her wishes, " provided only that she and her kingdom return to the true religion and to our catholic faith." [1]   We can only explain this action as being due to hopes of yet winning over Elizabeth.   Even before Cardinal d'Este entered upon his legation, the nuncio at Paris, Bishop Gualtieri, tried his hand at the ill-fated task.   He paid an unexpected visit one day to the English ambassador and authoritatively told him what the world had known for some months past, *i.e.* that in sending Abbot Martinengo the pope had no other end in view than to invite England to take part in the council of Trent, like the other Christian nations.   What harm, then, he asked, can come to the queen of England if she receives the nuncio ?   His action brought him into contact with a man of Cecil's views.   The ambassador, Throckmorton, answered curtly and to the point that his instructions were to have nothing to do with him or with anything that came from his master, moreover the nuncio had no doubt heard that the affair had already been settled in London.[2] After such an answer it is difficult to understand why Cardinal d'Este made further attempts and endeavoured to ascertain the feeling in London regarding the council. He naturally fared no better than his predecessors ; still Pius IV. could now console himself with the consciousness that he had left no stone unturned.[3]

The English government, however, had in the mean time made every attempt to impair still further the œcumenical character of the council, which it accepted no more

[1] Josef Šusta, *Die röm. Kurie u. d. Konzil von Trient*, I., p. 196. The document is dated June 29, 1561.

[2] Throckmorton to Elizabeth, July 13, 1561.   Foreign Cal., No. 304.

[3] Šusta, p. 335.   *Cf.* H. de la Ferrière, *Lettres de Catherine de Médicis*, I. (Paris, 1880), p. 259.   For detailed account of Card. d'Este's mission, see Bayne, *op. cit.*, ch. vii.

than any other protestant state, by preventing France also from sending representatives to Trent. These attempts, indeed, failed utterly ; it produced no effect either on Catherine de' Medici or Antony of Navarre to draw their attention to Germany's disinclination to send representatives to the council.[1] Still the attempt is significant ; for it is the first instance of English protestantism carrying the war against Rome into the enemy's country. Here, for the first time, England started on the road which just fifty years later led her to become the ally of Venice against the pope, and after another fifty years, made Cromwell the dreaded champion of Italian protestants. The common view, which would have us believe that England's attitude to Rome was solely one of self-defence and compulsory self-justification, cannot be maintained. The English reformation defended itself by adopting a policy of aggression, and therein, for the most part, lay its success and its greatness.

Even while the council was sitting England aimed a fresh blow at catholicism. The massacre of Vassy in Champagne (1562) showed the world what great dangers menaced protestantism in France. The north of England, too, was disturbed by the proceedings of Mary Stuart, Elizabeth's catholic rival. England could not regard with equanimity a revival of catholicism in the sister kingdom. The equipment of Elizabeth's fleet led to a sharp diplomatic encounter with Spain who would not suffer any interference on behalf of the protestant movement in France and the Low Countries. This gave rise to a heated dispute between the Spanish ambassador and Cecil who defended England's right to come to the aid of her co-religionists.[2] The

[1] FOREIGN CAL., 1560–61, No. 1030, §§ 7, 11–15, 17, 18, 21, 25. Full details are given by BAYNE, *op. cit.*, pp. 80–84.

[2] See Quadra's instructions and dispatches for July, Aug., Oct., and Nov., 1562. SPAN. CAL., pp. 251 *et seq.*, 255, 258, 264, 268. The two first documents are also in K. DE LETTENHOVE, III., pp. 81, 91.

gravest menace, however, to the new church of England
was the queen's dangerous illness in October, 1562, which
suddenly brought the question of the succession into
prominence.[1] The two last reigns showed how the state
religion must stand or fall along with the views of the
individual ruler. Elizabeth recovered, but every one who
desired to see England protestant now realized to the full
how precious her life was. Owing to anxiety about the
queen, upon whose life everything depended, Cecil was
unwearied, and even feverish, in detecting conspiracies
which had no existence. In the first year of Elizabeth
he was already on the look-out for Spanish assassins whom
Philip II. never sent over.[2] But while the Spanish
ambassador was now closely watching the tactics of the
aspirants to the English throne, Cecil interfered in a way
that in any other case would have brought about a suspen-
sion of diplomatic relations, but not, however, in the present
instance, since Philip could not relinquish the hope of one
day bringing England to side with him in politics. The
chance occurrence that a murderer sought refuge in the
Spanish embassy, and was given shelter for a few minutes,
provided Cecil with the opportunity of charging the
ambassador with encouraging conspiracies against the
English government and weaving seditious plots around
the queen. Not satisfied with casting these mortifying
reproaches on the ambassador, the secretary of state
threatened him with the rigour of the English law. In
order to make the insult complete, the government gave
notice to the ambassador to leave his residence, which he
had occupied up to that time, on the ground that he had
allowed it—crown property—to fall into a dilapidated
state.[3] And as if to show that Elizabeth was afraid of no

---

[1] Span. Cal., pp. 262, 263. K. de Lettenhove, III., pp. 165–168.
[2] Dispatch of Quadra, Nov. 27, 1561. Span. Cal., p. 220.
[3] Span. Cal., pp. 276–290 (Jan., 1563).

one, Cecil made a still bolder move shortly afterwards. The English government had certainly the right of forbidding its own subjects to attend mass in the chapel of the Spanish embassy, but the right of foreigners to practise their religion freely within the limits of their own embassy, was then regarded by theorists as an open question, while in practice it was really a question of political strength. Elizabeth's government, therefore, showed great confidence in its own power when, in February, 1563, it began to imprison Spanish subjects for going to mass at their own embassy and only gave them their freedom when they found bail. What the king of Spain did not allow to protestant Englishmen in his kingdom, the queen of England likewise denied to catholic Spaniards in hers! Cecil had given orders that if need be opposition was to be overcome by force without respect even to the embassy itself.[1] England placed herself over against Spain as one power with another and made the equal treatment of the two religions a question of international law. The monarch whose empire extended over half the world found no other answer than to exhort his ambassador to be gentle and conciliatory![2]

At home, as well as abroad, England pursued an aggressive policy against the catholic religion. Stirred by what had happened in France and Scotland, the Commons in January, 1563, petitioned the government to take measures for the safety of religion and the church of England.[3] The result of this petition was the bill for the assurance of the royal supremacy which came into force on April 1.[4] By this new law the obligation of

[1] SPAN. CAL., pp. 301, 305.
[2] See letter of Philip II. of March 31, 1563. SPAN. CAL., pp. 315 et seq.
[3] HENRY GEE, The Elizabethan Clergy, etc. (Oxford, 1898), p. 187.
[4] 5 Eliz. c. 1. "An Act for the assurance of the Queen's

E

taking the oath of supremacy was laid upon private individuals such as schoolmasters, as well as public officials, and refusal to take it was visited with heavier penalties than ever.   The punishment of " præmunire," *i.e.* total confiscation of property, was now incurred by the first, instead of the second, refusal, and the punishment for high treason (death) by the second, instead of the third, as formerly.   Between the first and second presentation of the oath, an interval of only three months was granted. It has been justly observed, however, that the draconian severity of this law was even from the first intended more *in terrorem* than in earnest.[1]   Still this does not alter the fact that a law of this nature must have pressed heavily on consciences.   The government wanted no reconciliation with Rome, but rather to oppress, or, if possible, destroy catholicism.   It was dominated by the conviction (doubtless correct in those days) that political power could only be guaranteed by religious unity ; a truth to which the state of affairs in Germany, France, and the Low Countries bore eloquent testimony.

III. *The Proposed Excommunication of Elizabeth at the Council of Trent*

Such was the state of affairs in England when at Trent the council was confronted by the question whether or not it should excommunicate Elizabeth.   According to canon law, the queen had long ago deserved to be expelled from the church.[2]   As we have already seen, it was consideration for the political aims of the house of Hapsburg, more than anything else, that had hitherto restrained Pius from

Majesty's royal power over all estates and subjects within her Majesty's dominions."

[1] GEE, p. 195.

[2] For the passage in the decretals, see p. 26, note 1.

acting in accordance with the requirements of the church's law. Reasons in favour of the excommunication had grown stronger since then, and now the question was to come before another court. The pope himself asked the council to consider what both parties, the council and the pope, had to do in the affair,[1] and the catholics of England also made their voice heard. The English refugees had obtained from the theologians of Louvain university a memorial dealing with the promulgation of the excommunication and forwarded it to Trent at the beginning of June, 1563.[2] This document gave prominence to the consideration that the prolonged indulgence shown to the queen must have the effect of misleading English catholics. If the council merely appeared to be influenced by political motives, then worldly considerations would be the deciding factor with catholics too. If the assembled fathers of the council put the fear of man before the fear of God, how can a private individual be expected to do otherwise? The church, therefore, ought not any longer to leave her children in the lurch.

The history of English catholicism in the next ten or fifteen years amply justifies those who considered that this great question of Elizabeth's excommunication should be approached from a purely spiritual point of view. The council took the opposite line and yielded to the fear of men, and the result among English catholics was the

---

[1] Card. Borromeo to the papal legates at the council, Rome, June 2, 1563. Appendix IV. J. H. POLLEN gives a chronological summary of the most important documents dealing with the question of Elizabeth's excommunication at the council; *Papal Negotiations with Mary* (Edin., 1901), pp. 173 *et seq.* To this I add the letters of Card. Morone (see Appendices), and the correspondence of the nuncio Delfino.

[2] PALLAVICINO, lib. xxi., c. vii., § 4. F. B. V. BUCHOLTZ, *Gesch. der Regier. Ferdinands I.,* Vol. IX. (Vienna, 1838), pp. 699–701.

adoption of half-measures with regard to the anglican church. A number of prelates, amongst whom were Cardinal Morone, Cardinal Charles de Guise, and the clerical representatives of the emperor, were formed into a commission in the middle of June and came to the decision to seek advice from the emperor and the pope.[1]

The Emperor Ferdinand, as soon as he heard of this from his ambassadors in Trent, expressed his strong disapproval of this "new and unlooked-for proceeding," and brought forward reasons that would easily commend themselves even to the judgment of ecclesiastics.[2] If the queen of England is to be excommunicated and deposed for contempt of the church's authority, then must the same treatment be meted out to all princes who, since the rise of these divisions in the church, have actually, if not formally, set at naught the same authority. It may be doubted whether it was real alarm or only the wish to intimidate the council which made the emperor warn them that Elizabeth's excommunication would mean the destruction of the catholic church and her bishops not only in England, but also in Germany, for the German protestants, fearing lest they should meet the same fate as Elizabeth, would unite together, and, by their superior power, drive the catholics out of the country. The emperor's weightiest reason against the excommunication was couched in the form of a question—where in all Christendom is the prince

[1] Card. Morone to Card. Borromeo, Trent, June 21, 1563. Appendix V.

[2] (1) Ferdinand I. to his envoys at the council, Innsbruck, June 19, 1563. TH. SICKEL, *Zur Gesch. des Concils von Trient* 1559–63 (Vienna, 1872), pp. 551 *et seq.*   (2) The nuncio Delfino to the legates at the council, Innsbruck, June 17. STEINHERZ, *Nuntiaturberichte aus Deutschl.* 1560–72, III. (Vienna, 1903), p. 351. (3) Card. Morone to Card. Borromeo, Trent, June 28. Appendix VI. *Cf.* also RAYNALDUS, *Ann. Eccl.*, ad ann. 1563, § 115.

who will undertake to carry the excommunication into effect? "How absurd and unworthy of a general council it would be to frame a decree that could not be executed, needs no proof."[1]

Following closely upon this, a second opinion—unsolicited—reached Trent. The most prominent statesman who then served the Hapsburg dynasty, Cardinal de Granvelle, now entered the lists.[2]   He ridiculed those who favoured the excommunication and yet would leave its execution to providence. He reminded them of the hostages in Elizabeth's power—the imprisoned catholic bishops—who would probably have to pay for the excommunication with their life, and, as a primary consideration he harked back to the cherished idea of Spanish policy —King Philip was constantly striving to bring England "to a better way of thinking," and the queen's excommunication would spoil all his plans. Therefore he earnestly warned the fathers of the council not to allow themselves to be persuaded by the French, or any one else, to decree the excommunication unless they had first obtained the consent of the king of Spain.

Here again we have the old state of things—the emperor and Spain protecting Elizabeth from excommunication, while France desired it! These two weighty opinions practically decided the question even before the council had ascertained the opinion of the pope. Cardinal Morone communicated the emperor's ideas to Rome and forwarded

---

[1] SICKEL, pp. 551 *et seq.*   Philip had already expressed himself in the same sense in June, 1561, *vid. ante,* p. 45, note 2.

[2] EDM. POULLET, *Correspondance du Card. de Granvelle,* I. (Brussels, 1877), p. 553. Summarized in RAYNALDUS, ad ann. 1563, § 115.   In a letter of the same date (June 27) to the Spanish secretary of state, Don Gonzalo Perez, the statesman's view of the question is expressed still more strongly.   CHARLES WEISS, *Papiers d'état du Card. de Gr.,* VII. (1849), pp. 111–113.

Granvelle's letter with the comment: "If, as we believe, the pope will not order otherwise, we shall leave the matter until it please God to show what is to be done and when and how."[1]   In the mean time, however, Pius IV. had "ordered otherwise," having been convinced by the arguments of the Louvain theologians.   He found "this consolation," *i.e.* Elizabeth's excommunication, must be given to the English catholics,[2] but a week later, the emperor's arguments in support of the contrary opinion struck him as prudent and well-founded, and without more ado he revoked his former decision.[3]   "Rome," says the official historian of the council, "decided not to cut off the diseased limb since its amputation would not be for the healing but for the injury of the whole body."[4]

The refusal of pope and council to employ spiritual weapons was a symptom of profound significance.   The catholic church no longer ventured to employ against the queen of a small country weapons which once she had not shrunk from using against the Roman emperor.   Deference to the policy of the Hapsburgs regarding treaties and marriages cannot *alone* explain this refusal, and even if it did, would itself be a confession of weakness.   Both advisers, especially the emperor, touched on a more fundamental reason—the inability of the church to carry her own verdict into effect.   The earlier excommunication of Henry VIII. had been the paper protest of the middle ages against the advent of the new era.   Before repeating this exhibition of impotent wrath, it was thought more prudent to make every attempt to avoid a breach and gain the object in view by friendly means.   So little was Rome the aggressor in

---

[1] Card. Morone to Card. Borromeo, July 7, 1563, Appendix IX.

[2] Card. Borromeo to the legates in Trent, June 30, Appendix VII.

[3] *Ib.*, July 6, Appendix VIII.   Borromeo to the nuncio Delfino, July 10.   STEINHERZ, p. 363.

[4] PALLAVICINO, lib. xxi., c. vii., § 6.

the conflict with England that she did not even attempt to defend her own rights. The pope was more afraid of his own bull than Elizabeth was.

Since Rome's declaration of war against England was postponed chiefly owing to the emperor's advice, the duty of promoting the friendly representation of the church's claims upon England devolved upon him. Ferdinand I. therefore complied with the pope's request and pleaded with Elizabeth on behalf of her catholic subjects that she would grant them at least *one* church in each town.[1] In a highly flattering letter the emperor recommended to her the pope's petition;[2] Elizabeth's answer was a decided refusal couched in equally courteous terms. In this, the strong hand of Cecil is clearly to be seen;[3] to grant the use of churches to members of another faith would be against the law, in the first place, and, in the second, would be incompatible with the domestic peace and security of the realm.

In proportion as England waxed bolder Rome grew feebler, and Pius IV. now caught at every straw. Towards the end of the year (1563) young Thomas Sackville came to Rome, not on any political errand whatsoever, but merely as a humanist making the tour of Italy. Through his father, Sir Richard Sackville, under-secretary of state, he was in touch with the English government, and, therefore, the pope and Cardinal Morone seized upon him as a means for making a fourth attempt,[4] almost incredible as it seems, at reopening diplomatic relations with

---

[1] The legates to the emperor, Trent, Aug. 23, 1563. BUCHOLTZ p. 702.

[2] Ferdinand I. to Elizabeth, Sept. 24. STRYPE, *Annals of the Reformation*, I., ii. (Oxford, 1824), pp. 572 *et seq.*

[3] On Nov. 3. STRYPE, I., ii., pp. 573 *et seq.*

[4] Or even fifth ! *i.e.* 1560, Perpaglia; 1561, Martinengo, the nuncio Gualtieri, and the cardinal legate d'Este. *Vid. ante*, pp. 39 *et seq.*

England. Young Sackville was to find out if, despite all rebuffs already received, a nuncio might even yet be dispatched to London! The under-secretary replied to his son that it must not even be hinted that he was mixed up with an affair of this kind, and, forthwith, advised the juvenile diplomatist not to show himself in England for some time to come, for his relations with the curia, did they leak out, might be fraught with serious consequence for both father and son. Cardinal Morone had once more to relinquish the attempt, although, as he hoped, only for a time ; still he begged Thomas Sackville to let him know later on if ever there should be any likelihood of a nuncio being received in England, for in that case the pope would at once send one.[1] To the end of his life Pius IV. never abandoned this hope. When news reached Rome in the summer of 1565 that Elizabeth was treating her catholic subjects more leniently, the pope declared in consistory that they must not yet entirely give up all hope that Elizabeth might still return to the right way through marriage with a catholic consort and so bring back with her the whole English people.[2]

This catholic consort was also the cherished hope of Spanish politics during all these years. Philip's claims lost ground year by year, yet before he could make up his mind to recover by arms his lost influence in England, he left no peaceable means untried. Although he had at first thought of marrying the queen himself, he later on put

---

[1] J. H. POLLEN, *Four Papers relative to the Visit of Thomas Sackville . . . to Rome in* 1563–64, Cath. Record Soc., II. (1906), pp. 1–11. *Cf.* MAITLAND, *Thomas Sackville's Message from Rome*, Eng. Hist. Rev., XV., pp. 757 *et seq.* For additional material, see the dispatch in SPAN. CAL., 1558–67, pp. 390 *et seq.* *Cf.* BAYNE, *Anglo-Roman Relations*, pp. 206 *et seq.*

[2] Consistory held on June 8, 1565. The acts in BRADY, *The Episcopal Succession in England, etc.*, II. (Rome, 1876), p. 327.

forward one of his German cousins as a suitor, and, after
1561, the Spanish ambassadors played the part of match-
makers between Elizabeth and her favourite, Lord Robert
Dudley, afterwards Earl of Leicester. The idea was
to carry the match through somehow under Spanish
auspices, in return for which the wedded pair were to
pledge themselves to restore the catholic church in
England. The most effective way of checking Cecil, the
secretary of state, Spain's most dreaded enemy, and the
church's greatest foe, seemed to be a marriage with some
prince favourable to catholicism and Spain.[1] Elizabeth
now surpassed herself in the arts of deception and procrastination. Protestants saw with alarm that the Spanish
ambassador, Bishop Quadra, had gained the ear of Elizabeth and her lover.[2] Nevertheless, all the ambassador's
attentions and flatteries in dealing with this affair of the
heart did not succeed in consolidating the influence of
Spain.[3]

However, the comedy ran its course and even entered
on a new phase with the arrival of a new ambassador. All
the diplomatic rebuffs received between 1561 and 1563
over the matter of the nuncio and the council did not
prevent Philip II., a year later, from renewing his
endeavours to find a prince-consort for Elizabeth. What
every one, who was not a diplomatist, saw clearly in those
days, *i.e.* that the policy of the queen of England was all in
favour of protestantism, was made to appear by the queen
herself as if it were a question still under discussion.
During the first ten years of her reign, Rome and Spain
were led to believe that a difference of opinion on this
point existed between the queen and her ministers. In

---

[1] SPAN. CAL., 1558–67, pp. 192, 195, *et passim*.
[2] *Ib.*, pp. 208, 209, 224–226.
[3] *Ib.*, pp. 232, 234.

reality it was only a difference of temperament, though, thanks to Elizabeth's skill in dissimulation (a skill surpassing what was usual even in that age), it bore the appearance of a fundamental difference in their attitude towards religion.   Elizabeth was an adept in assuming airs of injured innocence and in the use of ambiguous phraseology.   She had to conceal, so she declared, her real sentiments, but God knew her heart, how faithful it was in His service, etc., etc.[1]   Accordingly, a third Spanish ambassador, Guzman de Silva, was encouraged to set to work with renewed hope at the task of bringing about the match with Leicester as a prelude to the longed-for change in ministry and policy.[2]   The idea of a marriage between Elizabeth and the Archduke Charles also played its part in the comedy,[3] and the day was now not far distant when the last of the Spanish ambassadors to Elizabeth's court, Mendoza, was to start the witticism : the queen of England plights her troth yearly, but never marries.[4]

And so Spain continued to be the ally of the English, and therefore also of the Scotch, reformation.   Without Spain's friendly neutrality, England could not have played an effective part in the defeat of the French catholic party in Scotland, which entailed the triumph of protestantism throughout Great Britain.[5]   English catholics were left forsaken by pope, emperor, and " catholic king."

---

[1] Dispatch of the Spanish envoy of Oct. 9, 1564.   *Coleccion de documentos inéditos para la hist. de España*, t. 80, p. 47.   *Cf.* the similar statements of March 24, 1565, p. 86.   In English in SPAN. CAL., pp. 387, 410.

[2] SPAN. CAL., pp. 366 *et seq.*, 369, 371 *et seq.*, 388 *et seq.*

[3] *Ib.*, pp. 380, 395 *et seq.*, 407, 436, etc.

[4] Recorded by RAYNALDUS, *Annal. Eccles.*, ad ann. 1561, § 52.   The saying dates from the time of Mendoza's embassy in London, 1578-84

[5] This has been already noted by RANKE, *Hist. of the Popes* (Eng. trans.), Bk. III., § 5.   *Cf.* J. H. POLLEN, *The Politics of Engl. Catholics*, The Month, Jan., 1902, p. 58.

IV. *The Decline of English Catholicism*

In the history of English catholicism, it is still a moot point when and how the great bulk of the nation abandoned the church of Rome. An answer to these questions will be attempted in what follows.[1] A completely satisfactory result, however, can be obtained only by minute researches among local and provincial records,[2] nevertheless, in my opinion, the sources already available are sufficient to enable us to follow the main lines of the movement.

The purely arbitrary calculations in favour of the existence of a catholic majority in England in the days before the Armada, absurdly exaggerated as they are,[3] are worthless for serious statistical purposes. The sole object of the amateur politicians, for such they were for

[1] I have searched in vain the *Recusant Rolls* in the Public Record Office in London for reliable statistics. They are arranged by counties and years, yet (1) only the well-to-do were enumerated in them ; (2) there is no reason to suppose that the officials, who had a free hand, dealt uniformly with the different counties ; (3) the supervision exercised upon the catholics varied in strictness at different times ; (4) the recusants who owed fines for previous years, as well as the possessors of goods of deceased recusants, are included in the roll for a given year, and so an accurate estimate can only be arrived at by means of an index of names.

[2] An attempt to solve the question on these lines has been made by H. N. BIRT, O.S.B., in his painstaking but yet unsatisfactory book, *The Elizabethan Religious Settlement* (London, 1907), chs. viii.–x.

[3] In one of the numerous memorials on the proposed invasion of England we read : " Si appareret auxilium externum, suis viribus, id est nummis, armis, et copiis Anglorum Catholicorum, qui (ut *minimum* dicam) *sextuplo* superant numero ibi hæreticos, subjugari posset illa, quæ ecclesiam Dei contempnit et catholicos opprimit ac sacra omnia prophanat." Arch. Vat., Arm. LXIV., t. 28, fol. 354ᵛ ; there is a second copy of the document, fol. 371 *et seq.* In this case the exaggeration is explained by the fact that the writer came from Wales when the catholics were in the majority. The memorial was written shortly before or after 1580.

the most part, who framed countless memorials on the proposed invasion, was to stir up the courage of the pope and the king of Spain to undertake the enterprise against England in real earnest. A memorial of 1583, which shows greater knowledge of details and, from a political point of view, deserves more serious consideration than most of the others, makes choice of the guarded expression that " catholics and discontented persons " together formed a majority in the country.[1] This, however, throws no more light on the actual number of catholics than did William Allen when he congratulated Pope Sixtus V. on his accession in 1585 *majoris et sanioris nostræ gentis nomine.*[2]

An approximately correct answer to the question seems to be obtainable from the history of the catholic mission under Elizabeth taken in connection with the statistics of English catholics under the Stuarts. In the first year of the Jesuit mission (1580–81), the number of converts, according to one reading, was 10,000, according to another, 20,000.[3] Up till 1585, *i.e.* after five years of Jesuit missions and ten years of catholic missionary labours in general,[4] the total number of converts is said to have reached the figure of quite 100,000 who openly declared themselves, while about 40,000 kept their conversion secret.[5] Will any one seriously believe that in five, or even ten, years[6]

---

[1] T. F. KNOX, *The Letters and Memorials of William Cardinal Allen* (London, 1882), Introd., liv.

[2] J. H. POLLEN, The Month, April, 1902, p. 406.

[3] KNOX, *op. cit.*, p. 98. DOMESTIC CAL., 1581–90, p. 21. The statement is taken from a letter of Allen dated June 23, 1581.

[4] The Douay mission began in 1574.

[5] The report of the visitation of the English college in Rome, 1585. Appendix XIX. [§ 16].

[6] According as we take 1574 (the beginning of the mission from Douay college), or 1580 (the beginning of the mission from Rome) as the starting-point.

some two hundred and fifty priests,[1] travelling through
the country disguised and in the greatest secrecy, constantly
oppressed and persecuted by the laws,[2] converted 150,000
protestants to catholicism ? This means, on an average,
six hundred converts for each priest whose brief period
of activity in most cases extended over a year or perhaps
a little longer. I think the statement has only to be made
in order to be rejected. But are these figures nothing
more than empty words and exaggerations ? We are not
bound to think so, and, in my opinion, they have hitherto
been wrongly interpreted. As we shall see more clearly
later on, it was the custom of English catholics before the
beginning of the " mission " to join " externally " in anglican
worship. It was the chief work of the mission to contend
against this faint-hearted compliance with the law. Nothing
is more natural than that each person who withdrew from
attendance at the state church should be counted as a
" convert." The distinction mentioned above between
(100,000) public and (40,000) secret converts does not
militate against this interpretation, for there would always
be degrees of boldness in confessing the faith. If we accept
this interpretation, the numbers would still bear witness
to the astonishing success of the mission, without continuing to be incredible. If once even a small number
of catholics ceased attendance at church, others would
follow their lead without much urging from the mission
priest. The force of example to produce this effect
would be practically *nil* if the conversions spoken of
were actual conversions from the anglican to the catholic
church.

[1] Of whom only forty-two were from the English college, Appendix
XIX. [§ 12], while about two hundred were from Douay. T. F. KNOX,
The First and Second Diaries of the Engl. College, Douay (London,
1872). See " Diarium secundum," *passim.*
[2] See the description in ch. ii., sects. iii. and iv.

Whoever rejects this interpretation and accepts the tradition literally, *i.e.* whoever believes that converts in the strict sense are meant, and, consequently, that the actual number of catholics increased, comes at once face to face with an insurmountable difficulty.   He would find that after thirty years of presumably successful propaganda, catholics were a small and insignificant minority of the population of England.   Friend and foe agree in this, that the labours of the catholic mission between 1580 and 1585 produced remarkable results, and that even later its success was well sustained.   Again, all the calculations as to the number of catholics in England made by well-informed persons in the seventeenth century agree with each other, and these, which we shall shortly quote, not only preclude us from accepting an increase in the number of catholics during Elizabeth's reign, but also throw a new light upon the census, or rather the estimate, of 1585.   The figure 100,000 or 140,000 (perhaps, to be within the mark, 120,000) so-called *converts*, which we find given in 1585, is nearly the same—allowing for the slow increase of population—as that given in the seventeenth century for *catholics*.   That the *converts* of the Jesuit mission are to be understood in the sense we have explained above is thus shown to be highly probable.   In this way alone can all that will be said about the success of the mission be reconciled with the actual statistics of the later period.   The mission " converted" careless catholics into strict ones ; it did not attempt a widespread propaganda (which would indeed have been impossible), but created a strong base of operations for the catholic church.   This work was achieved in a few years, but had to be continually defended.   In the fact that this was carried through in the face of persecution lies the real "success" of the mission.

In the figures for 1585 (120,000 *circ.*) we have in all

probability the earliest indication of the number of English catholics. While the accepted view leads to a contradiction, strangely overlooked by almost every one,[1] viz. that the number of catholics both increased and decreased between 1580 and 1600, we have now, for the whole period from 1585 to 1685, a steady increase of catholics in relation to the increase of the whole population.[2] If we grant that catholics were still largely in the majority at Elizabeth's accession, then we must conclude that they were reduced to a minority between 1558 and 1580.

In the first place, let us take the estimates of the seventeenth century already mentioned. One of the men on the papal side best acquainted with England was Guido Bentivoglio, nuncio at Brussels, who for years had been gathering information from English catholic exiles, and was also in touch with the mission. He stated in 1613 that about six hundred priests were working in England and that the mission reckoned fully thirty families to each priest.[3] A family, including servants, in seventeenth-century England would number some six or seven persons.[4] This would give a total of at least a hundred and twenty or a hundred and thirty thousand catholics.[5]

[1] As far as I see only A. F. POLLARD is aware of the contradiction, and tries to give a solution. *Cf.* his *Hist. of Engl.* 1547–1603, Vol. VI. of the *Political Hist. of Engl.* (1900), p. 371.

[2] See A. F. POLLARD'S criticisms on the first German ed. of this book in the *Göttingische gelehrte Anzeigen*, 1912, No. 3, p. 170.

[3] "Dello stato della religione in Inghilterra." *Relationi fatte dall Illmo. Card. Bentivoglio in tempo delle sue Nuntiature di Fiandra e di Francia, date in luce da* ERYCIO PUTEANO (Anversa., 1629), pp. 178 *et seq.* MS. in Arch. Vat., Borgh. I., 269–272, fol. 72–84, and Borgh. II., 17, fol. 41^{v}–50.

[4] *Cf.* p. 64, note 3.

[5] The figures 6·5 and 600 can safely be regarded as approximate. The estimate of thirty families to a priest is in Bentivoglio's opinion somewhat too low, and there would also be a number of unmarried persons belonging to no family who must also be taken into account.

The papal agent at the court of Charles I. (1634–36), Gregorio Panzani, being on the spot could consult the best sources of information, and he estimated the number of English catholics, inclusive of those who did not openly declare themselves, at 150,000.[1]

In 1670, *i.e.* nearly two generations after Bentivoglio, the Venetian ambassador in London, Piero Mocenigo, stated there were over thirty thousand catholic families living in England.[2]   Edward Holt, agent of the English secular clergy in Rome at the same date, gives the number of priests in England as eight hundred, and of catholics as two hundred thousand.[3]

The total population of England about 1600, according to the most scientific method of calculating known at that time, was three millions.[4]   A calculation based on the number of anglican communicants and catholic recusants gives about three millions and a half.[5]   The most probable estimate, based on the number of births, marriages, and deaths, reaches a still higher figure.   According to these, the total population of England in 1570 would have reached three millions and three-quarters ; in 1600, almost

[1] " Relatione dello stato della religione catholica in Inghilterra." Contemporary MSS. in the archives of the Propaganda, Anglia Miscell., t. I. ; in the Bibl. Vat., Cod. Barb. lat. 5222 ; transcript in Brit. Mus. Add. MSS., 15389 ; and a free English rendering in J. BERINGTON'S *Memoirs of Gregorio Panzani* (Birmingham, 1793). A new translation is to be given by the Cath. Record Soc.

[2] Dispatch of 1669–70, Jan. 10.   State archives, Venice, Senato Dispacci Inghilterra, 54.

[3] BRADY, *Episcopal Succession in England, etc.,* III. (Rome, 1877), p. 167.   Since thirty thousand families amount to "about 200,000" persons, the accuracy of the figure 6·5 given above (p. 63) becomes highly probable.

[4] *Mundus alter et idem, sive terra Australis antehac semper incognita . . . authore* MERCURIO BRITANNICO [William Knight] (Hannoviæ, 1607), pp. 113 *et seq.*

[5] JULIUS BELOCH, *Die Bevölkerung Europas zur Zeit der Renaissance.*   Zeitschrift f. Sozialwissenschaft, III. (1900), p. 774.

four millions and a half; in 1630, five millions and a
quarter; and in 1670, five millions four hundred thousand.[1]
With this agrees the total of five millions and a half given
by a contemporary for 1690.[2]

Hence it follows that in the hundred years during
which the persecution of catholics lasted (1580 to 1680, in
round numbers), the entire population of England, and
with it the number of catholics, increased at the rate of
40 per cent.[3] Catholics numbered from 2·3 to 3 per cent.
of the whole population.

So far the result can be tested by the sources of information already accessible. But in all probability the
period of the decrease in the number of catholics, who,
according to their own reckoning, formed at least half the
population in 1558, is to be restricted to even narrower
limits than the years from 1558 to 1580—the outside limits
of the whole period of the change. In the years between
the close of the council of Trent and Elizabeth's excommunication (1563–70), the catholic church had plainly lost the
greater number of her adherents.[4] Several things justify

---

[1] According to the calculation of the Register Office, *Population of
England and Wales* (1841), p. 36. I have to thank Professor Beloch
for this reference. I give the calculation in round numbers.

[2] On this and other calculations, see MACAULAY, *Hist. of Engl.*,
ch. iii.

[3] With this agrees the fact that the number of catholic priests rose
from six hundred in 1613 to eight hundred in 1670 (see above), *i.e.*
increased about 33⅓ per cent. in about sixty years.

[4] The repeated assurances of the Spanish ambassador that the
catholics were "daily increasing" (SPAN. CAL., 1558–67, pp. 390, 418,
638, 687; 1568–79, p. 87) prove nothing. "Daily increase" is the
accepted phrase which meets us all through the course of the history
of English catholicism from 1558 to 1688. Every party not resigned
to its own extinction believes it is increasing. So, too, the statements
of the ambassadors from time to time that there was a catholic
majority between 1565 and 1570 (SPAN. CAL., 1558–67, pp. 389, 393,
672; 1568–79, p. 87) prove nothing either, for it was the interest of
English catholics to appear to the Spaniards as a strong party with

F

this conclusion.   First, the catholic rising under the Earls of Westmorland and Northumberland (1567) looked for its support exclusively to the northern parts of the country. This shows that already the rest of England had for the most part abandoned the catholic church.   There is other evidence to show that this geographical partition of the two religions was already an accomplished fact.[1]   Second, the complete failure of the pope's excommunication in the following year shows, too, that the strong catholic feeling on which Rome relied no longer existed.   In addition to these external indications, which are not conclusive in themselves, another very weighty reason belonging to the internal condition of catholicism must be added.

From the establishment of the anglican state church to the excommunication of Elizabeth there was very little spiritual supervision over English catholics, and what existed was entirely without organization. The deprivation of the bishops destroyed the hierarchy, while the insistence on the oath of supremacy led to the removal of most of the catholic parish priests.   Many, indeed, especially in Wales and in the northern counties, still exercised their ministry in secret,[2] and many a beneficed clergyman of the state church was a priest in disguise, yet for the large majority of catholics there existed nothing of the nature of regular

whom it might be profitable to make an alliance. After 1570 the Spaniards themselves realized that now only the majority " of respectable people " were catholics (SPAN. CAL., 1568–79, p. 309).

[1] Dispatch of the Spanish ambassador of 1569 : "Todo norte y Valia son por la mayor parte catolicos." *Coleccion de documentos inéd.*, t. 90, p. 231.   SPAN. CAL., 1568–79, p. 147.   *Cf.* p. 422, "the people in the north being all catholics " (1572).

[2] *Records of the English Catholics under the Penal Laws*, Vol. I. *The First and Second Diaries of the English Coll. Douay*, T. F. KNOX (London, 1878), Introd., p. lxi.   MARY BATESON, *A Collection of Orig. Letters from the Bishops to the Privy Council*, 1564, Camd. Soc. Miscellany IX. (1895), pp. 3, 19, 34, 67.   *Cf.* H. N. BIRT, *The Elizab. Relig. Settlement* (1907), chs. viii.–x., *passim.*

spiritual ministrations or guidance for their conscience. It was only in 1576 that catholic missions emanating from the English seminary, founded in Douay in 1568, were started, and only in 1580, two years after the foundation of the English college in Rome, did the missions attain to their full activity under the guidance of the Jesuits. In the previous period there is no sign of the least attempt at the organization of any spiritual oversight deserving the name. Catholics in the capital at all events had the opportunity of hearing mass in the ambassadors' chapels, but even this could easily be prevented, and was, in fact, prevented often enough.[1] The vast majority of catholics were entirely left to themselves without any bond of union with their church. No doubt the long history of the sufferings of English catholics comprised periods of much greater oppression than the first twelve years of Elizabeth, but at no other period did catholics see themselves so utterly forsaken by the church, or so entirely cut off from all communication with Rome, as at this period—especially in the seven years between the close of the council of Trent and the queen's excommunication.[2] Neither pope nor council, neither emperor or Spanish king, had done anything whatsoever for them ; not one priest had been sent to them. "Who would ever have believed that until now (1570) the Roman court would have done so little to win back this island which has always been so faithful ?"[3]

[1] For instances of the imprisonment of those who had attended mass at the French, Spanish, and Portuguese embassies, see SPAN. CAL., 1558–67, pp. 126, 686 ; 1568–79, p. 80, *et passim*. Cf. NICHOLS, *Diary of Machyn.*, Camd. Soc. (1848), p. 225.

[2] Numerous statements in support of this view are to be found in the reports of the Spanish ambassador. *Coleccion de doc. inéd.*, t. 89, 90, and the SPAN. CALS.

[3] "Chi havrebbe mai creduto che si fosse tenuto fin qui così conto nella corte di Roma della reduttione di questa isola, la quale è stata

Even if our sources of information said nothing more than this, we might venture to conclude that the decline of English catholicism must have taken place chiefly between 1560 and 1570. But enough has come down to us to place this conclusion beyond a doubt, and, at the same time, to supply the answer to the further question, how was it that the large mass of catholics conformed to protestantism?

In 1562 English catholics asked the Spanish ambassador to obtain for them an authoritative decision on the question whether or not they might attend the services of the reformed church. The ambassador, Quadra, a bishop of the catholic church, wrote accordingly to Rome, and himself pleaded that an answer might be given in the affirmative.[1] The English prayer-book, he maintained, merely omitted catholic doctrines but contained no positive heresies. However, the inquisition bethought itself of the words, " he that shall be ashamed of Me and of My words, of him the Son of Man shall be ashamed," and forbade attendance at protestant services.[2] The council of Trent, when approached through the Portuguese ambassadors at London and Trent, gave English catholics the same answer, and strictly prohibited them from attending the services of the anglican church.[3] The mission priests

sempre tanto devota?" Anonymous *Discorso venuto d'Inghilterra del* 1570 *in Venetia*, Arch. Vat., Miscell. Arm. II., t. 84, fol. 32.

[1] SPAN. CAL., p. 258. More fully in FROUDE, *Hist. of Engl. from the fall of Wolsey to the defeat of the Spanish Armada*, Vol. VII., pp. 22 *et seq.*

[2] Decision of Sept., 1562, printed by BAYNE, *op. cit.*, Appendix XLVIII. *Cf.* FROUDE, p. 24. *Coleccion de doc. inéd.*, t. 87, p. 426. SPAN. CAL., p. 267. For the quotation from the Gospel, *cf.* St. Mark viii. 38 and St. Luke ix. 26.

[3] The opinion of the committee at Trent, which alone is known for certain, is printed by BAYNE, *op. cit.*, Appendix XLVI. *Cf.* pp. 163-173.

succeeded at a later date in making this prohibition effective, but in the days when they were bereft of pastors, the faithful of the flock discovered strange expedients for obeying the catholic church and the law of the protestant state at one and the same time. They drew a subtle distinction between taking part in divine service and merely being present at service without joining in it. Rome forbade the former ; there could be no harm in the latter. Many, therefore, entered the church some time before service began and left before it was over, persuading themselves that there was no real connection between their time spent in the church and the performance of the heretical service. Others fancied they satisfied their conscience by going to service but abstaining from communion ; others, again, considered even the protestant communion harmless so long as it was received without inward participation—they ate " Calvin's profaned bread " with the heretics that they might secretly receive " the Lord's Body " when opportunity offered.[1] There were even

[1] This is the description of the conduct of English catholics in the period before the mission given by the *Relatione del presente stato d'Inghilterra . . . Roma, appresso F. Zannetti*, 1590. A copy of this rare pamphlet is in the Vatican Lib. (Stamp. Barb. H. II., 12, No. 2). See pp. 7, 8. Printed in part by KNOX, *Letters and Memorials of Card. Allen*, p. 57, note. For further details, see *Popish Questions and Answers*, 1580, printed in STRYPE, *Annals of the Reform*, II., ii. (Oxford, 1824), pp. 348–351, also *Quaertio 17a* of the paper *Ad consolationem et instructionem catholicorum*(1570–79), printed by CREIGHTON, *Engl. Hist. Rev.*, VII., p. 85, and, for a later period, Topcliffe's letter in STRYPE, IV., No. XXXI. The picture presented by these documents is further borne out by the *Historia ecclesiastica del scisma del regno de Inglaterra* by PEDRO DE RIBADENEYRA, S.J. (Madrid, 1588), p. 257 : " . . . por una parte [los catolicos] tomavan los sacramentos como catolicos, y por otra en publico como hereges. Y yvan a los templos de los calvinistas, y oyan sus sermones y se con aminavan con sus impias ceremonias participando del caliz del Señor y de los demonios, y juntando a Christo y Belial, como se hizo en tiempo del rey Eduardo. Con esta flaqueza y pussilanimidad de los catolicos tomaron animo los hereges."

some catholic priests—so the most trustworthy evidence assures us [1]—who adopted the doctrine which distinguished between inward belief and outward obedience, and brought themselves to say mass in secret and go publicly to the protestant communion service on the same day.

The great apostasy from the catholic church did not therefore take place suddenly and of set purpose, but was the result of silent compromises with conscience. What began as outward compliance with the law would only gradually result in actual membership in the national church. Priestly supervision, with confession and absolution as a means of discipline, would probably have checked this movement towards protestantism, as in fact it did later on, but the church did not provide in time a body of clergy able to exercise the necessary discipline in accordance with her mind. Catholic priests themselves bore witness that absolution was given, not on condition of staying away from anglican services, but on the easier condition of abstaining merely from receiving the anglican communion.[2] It was only in 1567 that the attempt was made to bring about a change in obedience to an order of St. Pius V. Since avoidance of all kinds of religious intercourse with protestants was now required as a condition for receiving absolution, a clear dividing line was traced for souls. Only a section of the catholics submitted at once, while the rest required further proof that the new system was really ordered by the pope.[3]

And when the Spanish ambassador—who in spite of all was still the last refuge and hope of English catholics—preached to them to be temperate in all things not contrary to their conscience, and reminded them of the text, " Let

[1] In a letter of Card. Allen. KNOX, *Letters of Card. Allen*, p. 56.
[2] See the letter of the priests Harding and Sanders of 1567. Appendix XII.   [3] *Ib.*

every soul be subject to higher powers," [1] and when English catholics saw the imperial ambassador going to church with queen Elizabeth,[2] could they regard it as unlawful to do likewise ?

They were all the less likely to do so, since the protestant service offered them something denied them (wrongly, as they thought) by the catholic service, *i.e.* the use of their native tongue. It would be incorrect to account for the general desertion from the catholic church entirely, or even chiefly, by the pressure which the law of England put upon consciences. It was not merely that something negative drove people into the anglican church, there was something positive that attracted them as well. As in Germany, so in England, the reformation had aroused a vehement desire to have the Holy Scriptures in the vernacular. On this point there was no difference between those of the ancient faith and the reformed. The great literary achievement of the English seminaries on the continent— the catholic translation of the Bible made at Rheims and Douay [3]—owes its origin to this desire which had to be satisfied. " Experience has taught that even under catholic jurisdiction the people were so unwilling to give up their bibles [4] that they rather clung to them all the more strongly the more the law forbade it." [5]

Along with the desire for an English Bible went the

---

[1] SPAN. CAL., 1558–67, p. 389.

[2] *Ib.*, p. 436.

[3] The New Testament was finished at Rheims in 1582 and the whole Bible at Douay in 1609. In a revised form, it remains the Bible of English catholics up to the present day.

[4] The allusion is to the authorized translations of the Bible in the time of Henry VIII., which were again forbidden under Mary the Catholic. *Cf.* KARL STÄHLIN, *Sir Francis Walsingham u. seine Zeit*, I. (Heidelberg, 1908), pp. 39, 43.

[5] See the letter of Harding and Sanders already mentioned. Appendix XII., towards the end.

demand for divine service in English.   In vain catholics
sought to obtain from the authorities of their church permission to use the vernacular, if not for the whole, at least
for parts, of the service [1]—what the Roman church denied
the anglican granted.

To all these yet one more motive for joining the
anglican church is to be added.   Under Elizabeth,
England once more enjoyed a blessing she had not known
for half a century—ten years of settled government free
from foreign wars and civil bloodshed.   We may believe
the queen that at her accession she had asked God for the
grace to rule in gentleness without shedding blood.   The
first ten years of her reign laid the foundation of her subsequent popularity.   Elizabeth took pride in all manifestations of her people's love, but most of all she rejoiced to
hear a "vivat regina!" from the lips of a catholic priest.[2]
That she was able to enjoy even this triumph was due,
not, of course, to the penal laws, but to the feeling which
had for the first time revived under her rule that the
country was being governed with a firm hand, and, after
years of weakness and vacillation, England once again
stood on her own feet.   A government that possesses the
confidence of the people has great power of recuperation.

Not force, primarily or by itself, one may confidently
affirm, could ever have made the catholic church in England
shrink so quickly to a small remnant of what it once had
been.   No doubt Elizabeth's legislation hastened the
growth of protestantism in the country, but the final
decision was not caused by fear of the state but by the
religious and national sentiments of Englishmen.   Had
it been otherwise, how are we to explain the fact that
catholicism declined when there was comparatively little

[1] STRYPE, *Annals of the Reform*, II., ii. (Oxford, 1824), p. 348.
[2] SPAN. CAL., 1568–79, p. 51.

persecution, while, later on, in the period of bloodthirsty legislation,[1] the boundaries of the two religions remained stationary ? We should under-rate the catholic church if we thought she could be abolished by laws ; and we should also under-rate Englishmen if we thought they would allow the state to dictate their religion to them.[2]

V. *The Excommunication*

Pius IV was succeeded in January, 1566, by the saintly Pius V. The monasticism of the middle ages once more ascended the throne of the apostolic see. No one could cast the least reflection on the pope's moral character, for Pius remained a mendicant friar even on the throne. Sobriety with him meant asceticism—food, he was wont to say, must be taken like medicine. His midday meal was also his supper. He refused a gift of fine woollen cloth and remained faithful to his friar's habit. He often worked late into the night and rose next morning long before day. When friends and physicians urged him to take care of his health, he answered that God had placed him where he was to take thought for others, not for himself.[3]

A pope of this kind regarded politics merely as the handmaid of religion. His nickname, " Fra Scarpone," (" Brother Woodenshoe ")[4] indicated the monastic limitations of his outlook. Together with monastic ideals, the

---

[1] Ushered in by the 23 Eliz. c. 1, in 1581.

[2] The view I have here put forward, and, as I hope, proved, is directly opposed to that taken by J. H. POLLEN, S.J., in his series of articles in The Month for 1902, *The Politics of English Catholics during the Reign of Queen Elizabeth*, which in other respects are among the most valuable that have been written upon catholicism in England under Elizabeth. Fr. Pollen maintains that the destruction of English catholicism was brought about by brute force.

[3] J. A. GABUTIUS, *De vita et rebus gestis Pii V.* (Romæ, 1605), pp. 229 *et seq.*

[4] *Attioni e costumi di Pio V.*, Arch. Vat., Borgh. I., 268, fol. 116.

mediæval conception of the papacy was to him a reality. The order to which he belonged was that of St. Dominic ; his post as cardinal had been that of Inquisitor-General. It was not to be expected that such a man would be restrained, like his predecessor and the fathers of the council, by fear of men and political considerations, from excommunicating the great heretical queen.

But even a Pius V. must wait for the right moment to ensure the success of such an act. The conflict between the two rivals, Elizabeth and Mary Stuart, was alone able to afford him the desired opportunity.   The year in which Pius ascended the throne was the turning point in the tragedy of the Queen of Scots ; it was the year of her breach with her unworthy husband, Lord Darnley, the murderer of her secretary, Riccio.   From a breach with her husband, the queen descended in her turn to the shedding of blood, and from the shedding of blood to marriage with Darnley's murderer, and then, in order to keep in with her people, to the abandonment of the catholic cause in Scotland.   "Catholic Europe was in despair at the depths to which their favourite had fallen."[1]

The pope, at first, was fully resolved to support Mary by all the means in his power,[2] but he now had doubts which of the two queens was the better—or worse.[3]   Still, when Mary forsook her throne and fled to England and became the prisoner of her rival, and figured as a martyr

---

[1] T. G. LAW, *Mary Stuart*, Camb. Mod. Hist., III. (1904), p. 275. *Cf.* FROUDE, *op. cit.*, VII., p. 523.

[2] BRADY, *Episcopal Succession in Engl.*, II., p. 329.

[3] Card. Michele Bonelli [Alessandrino] to Giov. Castagno, nuncio in Spain [afterwards Pope Urban VII.], Aug. 17, 1568 : " Io per hora non ho da darle commission alcuna in nome di Il. S^te, non essendo ben rissoluta S. Sta. nell' animo suo, qual delle due regine sia la migliore." MARTIN PHILIPPSON, *Hist. du règne de Marie Stuart*, III. (1892), p. 496.

for the catholic faith, the conviction was borne in upon her contemporaries—a conviction endorsed by posterity—that Mary Stuart's misfortune surpassed her guilt.   The hopes of English catholics were centred in her, the Duke of Norfolk offered himself as a suitor for her hand, and her release was the object of the catholic rising of 1569. After Elizabeth, Mary was nearest to the throne—"they wanted to raise Absalom against David"[1]—the struggle was for the crown of England.

The imprisoned queen sent word to the king of Spain that, if he would help her, she would be queen of England in three months and mass would be said all over the country.[2] The man to whom she turned for assistance was one who spent months in deliberation while the decisive moment slipped by, and was just then taking everything calmly in order to strike when it suited himself.[3] It was at this juncture that Spanish ships laden with gold for the troops in the Low Countries were being seized by England, while the Spanish ambassador was threatened in London, kept in custody, and had his letters opened. "It is disgusting," wrote the bewildered man to his master, "to hear Cecil talk about the queen being a monarch, and that no other Christian prince is a monarch but she."[4] It had long been realized in England that no provocation was great enough to rouse Philip II. Just now, moreover, when Spain was wrestling with the rebellion in the Low

[1] *Coleccion de doc. inédit.*, t. 90, p. 266. SPAN. CAL., 1568–79, p. 180.

[2] Letter of the Spanish ambassador in London, Jan. 8, 1569. *Coleccion, etc.*, t. 90, p. 171. SPAN. CAL., p. 97.

[3] For Philip's attitude towards the "Northern Rebellion," see his own remarks to the nuncio Castagno. Appendix XIV.

[4] *Coleccion, etc.*, t. 90, p. 213. SPAN. CAL., 1568–79, p. 135. On the ill-treatment of Spain and of the Spanish ambassador in connection with English politics, see K. STÄHLIN, *Sir Francis Walsingham*, I., pp. 214 *et seq.*, 217.

Countries, it would have required an unwonted degree of determination to undertake a campaign against England as well.

And now, when things seemed coming to a head and it appeared to the Spanish ambassador "that God is now opening a wide door which will lead to the great good of Christendom," [1] Philip II. merely indulged in edifying reflections, and made a few suggestions, calmly admitting he was endangering his reputation "by deferring so long to provide a remedy for the great grievances done by this woman to his subjects, friends, and allies." [2]

The hour now struck for God's champion in Rome. As soon as Pius V. learnt through his English informant [3] that the moment was propitious, he, "with exceeding joy," ordered the process against Elizabeth to be opened. Although the matter under consideration was notorious, the production of evidence in connection with the case was required in strict adherence to prescribed form.[4] There was a sufficient number of Englishmen in Rome able and willing to bear witness to the queen's conduct, among whom were men of mark, such as the sole surviving bishop of catholic times, Thomas Goldwell, bishop of St. Asaph, and Sir Richard Shelley, the last English grand prior of the Knights of Malta.[5] The examination of these and others—twelve in all—was judged sufficient to prove the guilt of the accused. The chief points in the accusation were the assumption of authority as *head of the*

---

[1] Letter of Sept. 17, 1569. *Coleccion, etc.,* t. 90, p. 285. SPAN. CAL., p. 192.

[2] Letter of Dec. 16. SPAN. CAL., pp. 217 *et seq.*

[3] Dr. Nicholas Morton, *Annal. Eccles., cont.* LADERCHIUS, ad ann. 1569, § 270 *et seq.,* 1570, § 321. *Cf.* J. H. POLLEN, The Month, Feb., 1902, p. 140. DODD-TIERNEY, III., p. 12, note.

[4] The acts of the process in *Annal. Eccles.,* ad. ann. 1570, §§ 322–345.   [5] *Vid. ante,* p. 35.

English church, the deprivation and imprisonment of bishops, the assumption of visitorial rights, the introduction of an oath injurious to papal authority, the passing of laws against the pope, the encouragement of heresy, etc.

On February 5, 1570, the cause was opened before the judicial authorities of the Apostolic Chamber, on the 12th the hearing of evidence was concluded, on the 25th judgment was pronounced "against Elizabeth, pretended queen of England, and her heretical followers." [1] So little did Pius V. trouble. himself over the views of temporal sovereigns on spiritual matters, that he not only entirely ignored the king of Spain during the process, but when the trial was at an end, he did not even send him word of what had been done. It was hardly forgetfulness, but must have been deliberate purpose, which kept the nuncio in Madrid, who was in constant correspondence with Rome, in total ignorance of the excommunication.[2] Nor was it fear of the catholic king's displeasure which kept Pius V. from sending him an account of what had been done. Philip II., who had put obstacles in the way of the excommunication for political reasons, was now to realize that his will was not to be the determining factor in a spiritual matter of this kind, but the will of the chief pastor of the church alone. France, who had always desired the excommunication, seems to have been informed of its accomplishment through diplomatic channels.[3] Philip was deeply offended

---

[1] The bull has often been printed ; in *Bullarium Roman., Annal. Eccles.*, in Camden, Sanders, Dodd-Tierney, etc. Two copies of the original—a sheet of 12 × 18 inches—are in the Arch. Vat., Miscell. Arm. II., t. 67, fol. 244 ; t. 84, fol. 27.

[2] See the letter of the nuncio Castagno of July 17, 1570. Appendix XIII.

[3] " Dicono che detto breve [*sic*] è stato mandato al re di Francia da S. Santità." From Castagno's letter already mentioned. Appendix XIII.

that at such an important crisis no one had consulted him, the greatest authority on English affairs as he claimed to be, and expressed his astonishment at "this sudden and unexpected step"[1]—the very words used against the excommunication by the Emperor Ferdinand at the council of Trent seven years before![2]   So clearly did the king realize that all his plans were upset by the publication of the excommunication—of which he was later to be the champion—that he sent word to the excommunicated party that nothing the pope had ever done so displeased him as the late declaration.[3]

The Emperor Maxmilian II. was of the same opinion as his cousin of Spain, and also sent a sharply worded message to England showing his strong disapproval,[4] and, at Elizabeth's request, asked the pope either to recall his bull or prevent its diffusion by the press.[5]   Pius V. returned the only answer possible—a flat refusal.   There could be no idea of recalling the bull so long as Elizabeth held aloof from the communion of the church.   The pope is unable to understand why the queen can feel so distressed by the bull ; if she acknowledges its validity, why does she not return to the bosom of the church ?   But if not, why does she feel ill-used ?   The circulation of the bull cannot be stopped and is no longer under his control.[6]

Notwithstanding the history of the preceding ten years, the bull *Regnans in excelsis* was at last the work of a moment, called forth by the necessity for prompt action.

[1] SPAN. CAL., p. 254.   [2] *Vid. ante*, p. 52.
[3] FOREIGN CAL., 1569–71, No. 1083.
[4] *Ib.*, No. 1267.
[5] W. E. SCHWARZ, *Briefwechsel Maximilians II. mit Pius V.* (Paderborn, 1889), No. 123, The emperor to the pope, Sept. 28, 1570. *Cf. Ann. Eccles.*, ad ann. 1570, § 381.
[6] *Ann. Eccles., cont.* LADERCHIUS, ad ann. 1570, § 381 : Pius V. to Maximilian II., Jan. 5, 1571.

The careful observance of form in the eight days devoted to the hearing of evidence cannot disguise the fact that the verdict—excommunication and deposition—violated the forms of law.[1] No doubt, from the standpoint of the catholic church, Elizabeth had richly deserved both excommunication and deposition, but the way in which both these sentences were formulated against her was uncanonical. English protestants as well as catholics have with justice pointed out that a prince ought not to be excommunicated without previous warning, and, after excommunication, ought not to be deposed unless within a year he has not obtained nor even sought release from excommunication.[2] But Elizabeth, as was represented to the pope, had been excommunicated and deposed "even at the very first choppe." [3]

To judge a political act from the standpoint of law may at the first glance appear misleading and beside the mark, but in this case the point of law very soon assumed political importance. Since it was not the queen but the luckless catholics who had to bear the brunt of the papal anathema, the legal flaw in the pope's sentence gave a handle to harassed and feeble consciences on the look-out for any proof of invalidity in the bull. The division of English catholics into two hostile camps of reconcilables and irreconcilables really turned upon the different positions they took

---

[1] This fact is passed over by modern historians.

[2] Cap. 13, X., *De hæreticis*, V., 7. In FRIEDBERG'S ed. of the *Corpus Juris Canonici*, I. (Leipzig, 1881), col. 788.

[3] JOHN BISHOP, *A Courteous Conference with the English Catholickes Romane* . . . (London, 1598). *Cf.* CAMDEN, *Annales*, p. 182, "Illam non prius admonitam nec citatam, etc.," and p. 186. The ineffectual "prayers and exhortations of catholic princes," mentioned in the bull, formed no part of the canonical process, not having been framed with reference to the threatened punishment. An example of an admonition in due form, allowing time for a change of mind, is given by the bull against Henry VIII.

up regarding the question, does the bull of excommunication bind us or not ?

In answer to the first objection, *i.e.* that the excommunication had been pronounced without warning, the legal acumen of the curia[1] had provided that a warning need precede an *excommunicatio ferendæ sententiæ* only, while Elizabeth, as a heretic and fautor of heretics, having, *ipso facto*, incurred excommunication, it was a case of *excommunicatio latæ sententiæ*, where the preliminary warning was not required. The passages, however, quoted in support of this view[2] have reference to all heretics in common. But special modes of procedure over-ruled the ordinary methods in the case of the excommunication of heretical *princes*,[3] who were first to receive warning before being excommunicated.[4] So too the reference to the other point of law, *i.e.* that in notorious cases of guilt no warning is required, proved nothing ; for the law had in view very different offences from those with which Elizabeth was charged.[5] Moreover the hearing of the evidence showed that those who conducted the case were not satisfied on the point of notoriety.

Furthermore, to couple deposition with excommunication was also against the law. The requirement of a year's

---

[1] I have followed the detailed account given by LADERCHIUS, *Ann. Eccles.*, ad ann. 1570, §§ 366–369.

[2] Cap. 8, X., *De hæret.*, V., 7 (FRIEDBERG, col. 779) ; cap. 9, *ib.* (780) ; cap. 49, X., *De sententia excomm.*, V. 39 (910) ; cap. 2, in VI., *De hæret.*, V., 2 (1069).

[3] See p. 79, note 2.

[4] Cap. 5 in VI., *De pœnis*, V., 9 (FRIEDB., col., 1902), to which Laderchius refers, contains a decree according to which even princes incurred excommunication *ipso facto quapropter si princeps*, etc. Still the offences therein specified (failure to take proceedings against murderers of a cardinal, etc.) have no bearing on Elizabeth's case.

[5] I.e. *crimen adulterii et incestus*, and concerns, moreover, clerics, and not laymen ! Cap. 15, X., *De purgat. canonica.*, V., 34 (FRIEDB., col. 875 *et seq.*).

delay between the two sentences is so clearly stated in canon law [1] that even the champion of the curia [2] can produce no passage from the church's law in favour of pronouncing both together. The legal method of procedure, such as is laid down by the fourth Lateran council, obviously gave to the framers of the bull no grounds for passing sentence of deposition. In the first part of the bull, before any mention of excommunication or deposition had been made, Elizabeth is styled *prætensa Angliæ regina*, and in the actual words of deposition the pope deprives her, not of her right to rule over the kingdom, but of her *pretended* right.[3] The defenders of the bull scored a logical advantage [4] inasmuch as the verdict against Elizabeth does not recognize her as rightful queen, but as the wrongful occupant of the English throne ; owing to her illegitimate birth, Elizabeth was incapable of succeeding to the throne—Pius V. did not actually depose her, but only pronounced sentence on the non-existence of her right.

This view corresponds with the actual wording of the bull, removes at once the difficulty about the absence of warning, and is the only possible way of bringing the sentence of deposition into agreement with canon law. It was, however, far from agreeing with the papal policy of the last ten years! Had not Pius IV. again and again tried to enter into diplomatic relations with this " pretended" queen ? His brief of 1560 gave her the royal title,[5] and all through the years that followed Rome never

---

[1] Cap. 13, § 3, X., *De hæret.*, V., 7.

[2] LADERCHIUS, *loc. cit.*, §§ 370–374.

[3] " Declaramus . . . ipsam *prætenso* regni prædicti jure . . . privatam."

[4] Laderchius here follows the learned Dominican Alexander Natalis.

[5] *Vid. ante*, p. 39, note 2.

questioned the queen's legitimacy. So belated an objection
could have no force. From a legal point of view it was
out of the question to tack on a charge of illegitimacy to
the excommunication, *i.e.* to mix up a question of civil
status and a penal sentence, two things which have nothing
whatever to do with each other. For since Elizabeth was
ostensibly being punished for her misdeeds by being
deposed on grounds of illegitimacy, the criminal sentence
of deposition is founded on the constitutional idea that she
was incapable of reigning. It is plain that here the politician
speaks, and not the jurist !

And so, the bull against Elizabeth is indefensible from
a strictly legal point of view.[1] It was enough for a man
like Pius V. to feel justified in his own conscience that he
had fulfilled the spirit, if not the letter, of the law. He
could not foresee that it would be just those English
catholics whom he desired to help who would fasten on
the letter in order to oppose the spirit of the sentence.
The political situation in the winter of 1569-70 required
action, not threats. Only a man like Philip II. would have
been capable of going through the whole long legal process
step by step—first warning, then excommunicating, and,
finally, deposing—to end by becoming the laughing-stock
of the world. Pius V. struck while the iron was hot.

The breach of canonical form being thus explained, the
ground is cleared for the explanation of another error which
must have astonished the catholics of England less than
the anglicans. That people in Rome were ignorant of the
ecclesiastical title borne by the queen of England, throws
light on the insufficiency of the knowledge of English

[1] The tone of Laderchius, who defends the bull, is characteristic.
Having no legal grounds of defence to fall back upon, he indulges in
rhetoric and finally appeals to a number of precedents from the Bible
and history which have as little bearing on the case as quotations
from the decretals.

affairs in the Eternal City.   So vividly did they remember
Henry VIII. that they took for granted his daughter also
styled herself *supremum caput*.   Elizabeth was excommunicated on account of a title she had emphatically rejected![1]
Nothing could have presented a more welcome target for
the adversary's wit.   " Where is she ever called Supreme
Head ?   Peruse the acts of parliament, the records, the
rolls, the writs of chancery or exchequer, where is she ever
called Supreme Head of the church?   No, no, brethren,
she refuseth it, she would not have it, nor be so called." [2]

Eagerness to detect as many flaws and errors as possible
in the bull produced a fine show of learning on paper, but
far more did it call forth expressions of attachment to, and
confidence in, the queen.   Every one joined issue with the
bull on his own ground ; the historian showed the evils
that had resulted from the unlimited authority of the popes
over the nations, the ecclesiastic turned his attention to
the theological errors, the popular pamphleteer, with his
usual vulgarity, made gibes serve for learning.   But no
one of those who plied his pen on the protestant side
allowed himself to be out-done in venting his indignation
against the subversive, godless doctrine which gave a mere
human being the right to release subjects from their oaths
of fealty and allegiance.   The ages of Gregory VII. and
Innocent III. had spoken by the mouth of Pius V. ; the
age of Luther answered, " O vain man! As though the

---

[1] *Vid. ante*, pp. 22–26.   The words of the bull are, " supremi
ecclesiæ capitis locum in omni Anglia . . . monstrose sibi usurpans."
A lenient interpretation might well appeal to the use of the word
" locum " instead of "titulum," but leniency of this kind could not be
taken for granted by the framers of the bull.   Elizabeth's correct legal
title, moreover, does not occur in the acts of the trial.

[2] JOHN JEWEL, bp. of Salisbury, *A View of a Seditious Bull, etc.*
(London, 1582), p. 48.   Reprinted in *The Works of Bp. Jewel*,
Parker Soc. (1850), " fourth portion," p. 1144.

coasts and ends of the world were in his hands, or as if no prince in the world might rule without his sufferance ! " [1]

Equally unanimous was the resistance to the attack on Elizabeth's legitimacy. The thought that the love of the people constituted the ruler's true legitimacy found expression in words which were sometimes touching and sometimes bombastic. In times of intense national excitement the enthusiasm for king and country takes a religious turn. The nation identifies its own and its sovereign's cause with the cause of God. In Elizabeth's England, however, where in the minds of most men the religious movement and national sentiments were closely interwoven, the Roman thunderbolt kindled a blaze of loyalty towards the throne and its occupant such as had not been known in the country for centuries and has perhaps never been experienced since. The innumerable political pamphlets of the day are fond of breaking out into prayer for the protection of the queen and the destruction of her (*i.e.* God's) enemies, while the sermons were wont to conclude with outbursts of impassioned patriotism. That the crown was worn by a woman was in itself an appeal to the chivalrous sentiment of a people who have always shown a Teutonic respect for the weaker sex.

Popular writers never wearied of making merry over the similarity of *bull* in English and *bulla* in Latin. The broad taste of the period found delight in drawing extraordinary comparisons between bellowing bulls and excommunicating bulls ; [2] the more fastidious taste of literary euphuists composed Latin verses about bursting bubbles

---

[1] JEWEL, *ib.*, p. 83.   Parker Soc. ed., " fourth portion," p. 1153.

[2] E.g., cf. *A disclosing of the great Bull and certain calves that he hath gotten and specially the Monster Bull that roared at my Lord Bishop's gate.* [Allusion to the nailing of the bull to the door of the bishop of London's palace by John Felton]. *Imprinted at London by John Daye.* Brit. Mus., C. 37, d. 36 (2).

(*bullæ*).[1] Nor was there any lack of ribaldry. No figure of speech was too coarse to serve as an insult, no mud too dirty to throw at the catholic church. Obscenity and quotations from Scripture were mingled in a loathsome compound.

No event in English history, not even the Gunpowder Plot, produced so deep and enduring an effect on England's attitude to the catholic church as the bull of Pius V. Englishmen never forgot their queen's excommunication. Whenever in later ages men's minds were stirred up against the Roman church, the remembrance of 1570 was enough to justify their implacable hatred. When more than a century after the days of the excommunication, the excitement roused by the Popish Plot spread throughout the country and fanned men's passions into a blaze, it seemed as though the times of Elizabeth had returned to warn men against all charity and conciliation. The story of the excommunication, and of the pope who freed men from their oaths, and subjects from their allegiance, was a weapon that kept its edge for centuries and effectively put a stop to every thought of toleration for the papists.[2]

Elizabeth's excommunication has been called "the supreme effort of the counter-reformation."[3] One might

[1] *Cf.* HENRY BULLINGER, *A Confutation of the Pope's Bull* (London, 1572).

[2] The countless pamphlets, etc., published between 1678 and 1681 contain many allusions to the bull of 1570. The bull itself was the object of several new publications—quite in the style of the previous century. Cf. *A bull sent by the Pope Pius to encourage the traytors in England, pronounced against Queen Elizabeth of ever glorious memory, showing the wicked designs of Popery* (London, 1678). This pamphlet turns the bull into verse. The learned discussion of the question was also revived. Cf. THOMAS BARLOW, bishop of Lincoln, *Brutum Fulmen or the Bull of Pope Pius* V., an edition and translation of the bull with a learned historical commentary on the excommunication of princes which went through two editions in one year (1681), notwithstanding its ponderous scholarship.

[3] T. G. LAW in the *Cambr. Mod. Hist.*, III., p. 282.

add that in the whole history of the Christian church no other papal excommunication called forth such mighty efforts to carry it into effect as the one launched against Elizabeth.   It was the church's last and most striking attempt to withstand the reformation in the spirit of the middle ages and restore her broken unity by the aid of spiritual and temporal weapons combined.   This last attempt, however, recoiled on its authors with a force which no aggressive action against the church on England's part could have equalled.   This fact alone would be sufficient to make English history in the Elizabethan age a matter of world-wide importance.

The excommunication completely failed in its object in England because the pope, far from the scene of action and deriving his information from partisans, had been entirely mistaken as to the number and influence of English catholics.   When John Felton, with frenzied heroism, nailed the bull to the door of the bishop of London's palace, the only visible result of the catholic rising in the north was the gibbets of the condemned. The small disturbances which took place here and there in the years that followed were unable to cause the government any alarm.

Abroad, too, the bull failed in its effects because the separation of Europe into rival parties of catholics and protestants, and, in addition to that, of Hapsburgers and French, rendered the combined action of the powers against England as impossible now as in the days of the excommunication of Henry VIII.   The church forbade all social and commercial dealings of any kind whatsoever with excommunicate persons, *i.e.* with those who had been cut off from Christian fellowship.   The ultimate consequence of the excommunication of Elizabeth and her followers —nearly all England—ought to have been, according to the church's intention, the breaking off of all diplomatic relations with the island-kingdom, and, furthermore, the proclamation cf a continental blockade. The former— cessation of political relations—almost came to pass else- where on a later occasion, for when Paul V., in 1606, laid the republic of Venice under an interdict, all the catholic courts ceased from at least *direct* dealings with the Venetian ambassadors. The bull against Elizabeth did not produce even this result, to say nothing of the *com- plete* rupture of all diplomatic relations. The latter —cessation of commercial dealings—or, in the case of England, the declaration of a continental boycott, sounds like an anachronism in the sixteenth century. Neverthe- less it was not only suggested by English catholics but definitely aimed at by the papal diplomacy.

Giovanni Castagno, afterwards Pope Urban VII., then nuncio in Madrid, had an interview with Philip II. a few months after Elizabeth's excommunication, and requested him to give practical effect to the bull in the form of a continental blockade. The undertaking, for which even the resources of a Napoleon were insufficient, appeared unpractical to the king ; if Spain by herself proclaimed the boycott, Philip thought she would only injure herself, for France had made peace with England, and no co-operation was to be expected from Germany.[1] It is worthy of notice that soon afterwards the idea of blockading England was realized in the very country from which Philip anticipated the chief opposition, Germany. Shortly after the excom- munication, when the Hanse towns were compelled to fight for their ancient privileges in England, the first (1579) suggestion was to exclude English trade from the Rhine or

[1] See Castagno's letter of Sept. 7, 1570. Appendix XV. For further evidence for the plan of a continental blockade, see STÄHLIN, *Sir Francis Walsingham*, I. (1908), p. 215, note 2.

at least from the Prussian ports ; then to break off entirely all commercial relations with England ; finally (1597) an imperial edict was published forbidding under pain of outlawry all trading with the Merchant Adventurers.[1] Far removed as all this was from any connection with the bull, yet the accidental community of interests between the Lutheran Hanseatic towns and the catholic church could inspire a passing hope that the bull might find its accomplishment in the prohibition of all trade with England, which, in the words of a contemporary, would "clip the wings of that wicked woman."[2] Thanks to Elizabeth's

[1] R. EHRENBERG, *Hamburg u. England im Zeitalter der Königin Elizabeth* (Jena, 1896), pp. 151, 158 *et seq.*, 195.

[2] *Informatione della lega di Hansa et del commercio che ha con Inghilterra*, a paper by MINUCCIO MINUCCI (1589), Bibl. Vat., cod. Urb. lat. 814, pt. ii., fol. 344, 345. There is another copy in the archives of the Prussian Historical Institute in Rome. Minucciana, t. 22 : *De fœdere Hanseatico*, No. I. *Cf.* HERMANN KEUSSEN, *Der päpstliche Diplomat Minucci u. die Hanse* (Hansische Gesch.-Blätter, 1895, p. 111). Minucci earnestly advocated that the statute of the Diet of Augsburg of 1582, which expelled the Merchant Adventurers from Germany, should at length receive the requisite consent of the emperor : " Se la Santità di N. S^{re.} et insieme la M^{tà}. del re cattolico, considerando la medolla di questo negotio, faranno finalmente risolvere l'imperatore al sudetto bando et proscrittione, ogn'uno s'accorgerà che questo sarà un cavare a quella mala femina le penne maestre . . . Quelli che conoscono questo negotio della radice, credono che'l demonio, al quale serve la regina per instromento della perditione di tante migliaia d'anime, acciechi gl'occhi degl' huomini a fine che non si accorghino che questa saria la strada di vincere al sicuro quasi senza adoperar armi, levando a quel regno tutte le commodità non solo del danaro, ma anco del grano che sogliono ricevere in permutatione dagl' Ostrelenghi." The idea of boycotting England had already come to the fore after the excommunication of Henry VIII. in 1539. *Letters and Papers of Henry VIII.*, Vol. XIV., pt. i., No. 603 ; *cf.* the preface, p. vii. G. DE LEVA, *Storia documentata di Carlo V.*, Vol. III. (Venice, 1867), p. 250. In a somewhat different form, the idea appears even in the early middle ages. HEINSCH, *Die Reiche der Angelsachsen z. Zeit Karls d. Gr.* (Breslau, 1875), pp. 54 *et seq. Cf.* BÖHMER-MÜHLBACHER, *Regesta Imperii*, I², No. 309a. Again,

lucky star, the breach with Rome and the breach with
the Hanseatic towns were too far separated in time for
the idea of a continental boycott to be realized.

And as the excommunication produced no effect on the
international relations of England, so its failure in the sphere
of politics could not have been more complete. In the
country itself, the only effect of the bull was that catholics
were watched more closely than ever, and the number of
them imprisoned since the Northern Rising increased.[1]
When Elizabeth, at the beginning of the next year (1571),
raised her minister, Sir William Cecil, to the peerage as
Lord Burleigh, it was at once a proof of her gratitude for
the destruction of her enemies and an indication of her
future policy. Full of confidence in her good fortune
and in Burleigh's iron hand, Elizabeth bent herself hence-
forward to his will. "The queen's opinion is of little
importance," wrote the Spanish ambassador about this
time,[2] "and that of Leicester still less, so that Cecil un-
restrainedly and arrogantly governs all." Elizabeth herself
had no hatred of the catholic church and religion. Here,
as in everything else, Burleigh was aiming at political
power, and for this, unity between church and state was
necessary ; there was no room for the catholic church in
Lord Burleigh's England.

The bull gave him an opportunity for further anti-
catholic legislation. On July 1, 1571, the act against the
introduction of papal bulls came into force.[3] In this
the law is laid down that whoever procures or brings into

---

later : C. DE LA RONCIÉRE, *Le blocus continental de l'Angleterre sous
Philippe le Bel.*, Revue des Questions historiques, Vol. LX. (1896),
pp. 401–441.

[1] SPAN. CAL., 1568–79, pp. 261, 269.

[2] In Aug., 1570. *Coleccion*, t. 90, p. 386. SPAN. CAL., p. 265.

[3] 13 Eliz. c. 2. An act against the bringing in and putting into
execution of bulls and other instruments of the see of Rome.

England, or makes known a bull of the " bishop of Rome "
or any other written or printed proclamation, whatever may
be its contents, is guilty of high treason, and forfeits his
life and goods.   Whoever brings into England or receives
Agnus Dei " or suche lyke vayne and superstitious thynges "
forfeits life and property.   A year before this, the system
which encouraged espionage and delation had been introduced, to the demoralizing effect of which, the most revolting features of the persecution of the catholics are due.
A royal proclamation [1] promised that those who gave
information as to seditious books and bulls " should
be so largely rewarded, that during his or their lives
they should have just cause to think themselves well
used."   With regard to accomplices who turned informer,
it is said, " the discoverers should be preserved from
the note of blame of accusing, as far forth as might
be any ways devised."   The battle with poisoned weapons
began.

There was not much to choose between the contending
parties.   Nothing shows up the temper of the time better
than the way the pious biographers of the pope describe
the part he played in Ridolfi's conspiracy.   " Since neither
the apostolic nuncio nor any other representative of the
Roman see was allowed in England, the pope laboured
with all zeal to excite the English to rise and destroy
Elizabeth through Roberto Ridolfi, a Florentine gentleman
residing in England in the guise of a merchant. . . . To
aid and strengthen the conspiracy, Pius resolved to employ
the utmost means in his power (the excommunication)." [2]
But " God, according to His secret counsel, permitted that

[1] Of July 1, 1570.   Proclamation against seditious and traitorous
books and bulls.

[2] J. A. GABUTIUS, *De vita et rebus gestis Pii V.* (Romæ, 1605),
pp. 102 *et seq.   Cf.* GIROLAMO CATENA, *Vita del gloriosissimo
Papa Pio V.* (Romæ, 1647), pp. 113–118.

Elizabeth should be informed of it beforehand." [1] The plan of seizing Elizabeth living or dead,[2] either by insurrection, revolution, or assassination, was considered in those days quite as pious a work as the naval league which Pius V. formed about the same time, and which in the great battle of Lepanto gained for the cross one of its greatest victories over the crescent. When the pope encouraging the catholic earls in "the pious and religious beginnings" of their rising, wrote in his biblical style, "God is mighty who overthrew Pharaoh and his hosts in the sea"; [3] when he exhorted Elizabeth's prisoner, Mary Stuart, to place her trust in God, "who rescued David from the hand of Saul and the apostle Paul from the jaws of the lions," [4] his words explain the contradiction which only a later age would draw between the saint and the abettor of conspiracy. It would be an anachronism in morals to reproach the zealous pope with his share in the conspiracy [5] or to refuse to believe he had any.[6] It is nowadays a universally recognized rule that every man must be judged by the moral standard of his own day.[7]

[1] CATENA, op. cit., pp. 117 et seq.

[2] The word "or" has long been overlooked. Ridolfi's conspiracy contemplated Elizabeth's assassination only as an alternative. J. H. POLLEN, The Month, Feb., 1902, pp. 145, 146.

[3] F. GOUBAU, Apostolicarum Pii V. epistolarum libri quinque (Antwerpiæ, 1640), pp. 292 et seq. Brief of Feb. 20, 1570, five days before the publication of the bull of excommunication.

[4] Brief to Mary Stuart of Jan. 9, 1570. GOUBAU, op. cit., pp. 263-265.

[5] DÖLLINGER AND REUSCH, Die Selbstbiographie des Cardinals Bellarmin (Bonn, 1887), pp. 307-311.

[6] LINGARD, History of England, VI., p. 260, endeavours to represent Ridolfi's success with Pius V. as "very indifferent."

[7] Of the extensive literature on Ridolfi's conspiracy, I mention only Fr. Pollen's researches in The Month (Feb., 1902, pp. 143-147), which, in a brief space, contain all that is essential in the sources of information. His conclusions are moderate and just. See his articles for the most important literature on the subject.

Measured by this standard, Lord Burleigh's actions also lose the revolting character which has been attributed to them by catholics until the present day. The weapons with which the English legislature sought to overthrow the catholic church were the same as those with which the catholic church sought to destroy Elizabeth's government. It was not a fight in open day, but in the twilight and the dark. The true heroes of the warfare were those who entered the forbidden land in spite of all dangers, and risked their lives for no other object than the spread of the catholic faith. The foundation of the missionary colleges on the continent opens a new period, the heroic age, in the history of the catholic church in England.

VI. *The Founding of the Seminaries on the Continent*

From the account given of the progress of events up to this point, it would seem as if the complete destruction of English catholicism was merely a matter of time. That such was Burleigh's object cannot seriously be denied—the character of his legislation is too unmistakable—and he would have been no child of his age had he, as a statesman, favoured religious toleration. He treated English catholics more or less in the same way as protestants were treated in catholic countries, and, notwithstanding all the inquisitorial severity of his rule, we must not overlook the fact that English history is free from such blots as the massacre of St. Bartholomew and the murders of protestants in Ireland.

That neither Burleigh nor any of his successors succeeded in uprooting catholicism in England is due chiefly to the revival of the religious spirit stirred up by the seminary priests from abroad. The decline of catholicism ceases with the establishment of the "mission." Although the lost ground could not be regained, yet catholicism in England henceforth stood firm amid all storms of persecution.[1]

It was not Rome, the centre of the catholic church, which took the first step in this work of rescue, but the victims of persecution themselves, the English catholic exiles. Without the assistance given them by Rome they could not have carried out the work on so large a scale as they actually did, but it will always be a glorious proof of the self-sacrifice and vitality of English catholicism that it created for itself and kept going a second centre, a little Rome of its own, far from the capital of catholic Christianity. Cardinal Allen said not a word too much when, shortly before his death, he commended to all his "godlye friends" the dearly loved work of his life, "the Semynarie of Dowaye, which is as deere to me as my owne life, and which hath next to God beene the beginninge and ground of all the good and salvation which is wrought in England." [2]

William Allen was a student of theology at Oxford when, at the age of twenty-six, the Elizabethan reformation brought forceably home to him the alternative either to accept the new order of things or leave the country. He decided in favour of the latter course, and, like many others, betook himself to the Low Countries. The circumstance that his own fate was involved in that of his country matured in him an idea which had been much in men's minds since the council of Trent, the foundation of a seminary for the education of priests. Various aims, not all clearly developed, presented themselves to the mind of the founder.[3] He wished to create a spiritual centre for

---

[1] *Cf.* the statistics given in sect. iv.

[2] Letter of Allen of March 16, 1594.   T. F. KNOX, *Letters and Memorials of Card. Allen* (London, 1882), p. 358.

[3] *Cf.* his later letter, of 1578 or 1580, in KNOX, p. 54.

catholic exiles from England ; he wished to give English catholicism a substitute for the lost universities ; he wished to found for his countrymen an establishment for the instruction of catholic youth. The idea of the mission in England itself was at first far from his thoughts, for he regarded such an undertaking as impossible under the existing regime. His intention was rather to train up a spiritual army which at the right moment, *i.e.* after Elizabeth's death and the accession of a catholic sovereign, would be ready at once to invade England and win back for the church her lost territory.

Trusting to providence, without other support than voluntary contributions and his own private resources, Allen proceeded in 1568 to the foundation of his seminary. He chose Douay in Flanders, the seat of a newly founded university, where he had himself just then finished his theological studies. In the event, Allen's venture surpassed his highest expectations. What he had at first scarcely dared to contemplate—a catholic mission in protestant England—became the chief aim of the seminary, and for fully two centuries, Douay was the religious centre of English catholicism. In the course of the next fifty years, besides the seminary for secular priests, there came into existence colleges of English Benedictines and Franciscans, along with Scottish Jesuits and Franciscans, and an Irish seminary for secular priests as well.[1] The various forms

[1] DANCOISNE, *Mémoires sur les établissements religieux du clergé séculier et du clergé regulier, qui ont existé à Douai avant la révolution.* Mémoires de la société (impériale) d'agriculture, de science et d'arts, séant à Douai, 2nd series, Vols. IX., X., XII., XIV. (1868–79). *Cf.* especially Vol. IX., pp. 496, 497, and Vol. XIV., Etablissements britanniques. By the same author, *Histoire des établissements religieux britanniques fondés à Douai avant la révol. franç.* (Douai, 1880), and *Le collège anglais de Douai pendant la révol. franç.* (Douai, 1881). This latter work is a translation from the English of F. HODGSON. *Cf.* also, *Histoire du collège de Douai*

and ideals of the religious life—contemplative and active,
cloistral and secular, educational and studious—all found a
home in Douay.   English catholicism is not bound by so
many memories even to Rome itself as to this town in
Flanders.

Near at hand to England, and at the same time under
Spanish dominion, the Low Countries became a second
home for English catholics.   Monasticism, destroyed in
England first by Henry and then by Elizabeth, sprang
up anew on the soil of the Netherlands.   Of about forty
English religious houses founded on the continent under
Elizabeth and the Stuarts, the majority were crowded
together in the confined territory of the Low Countries,
while the rest were scattered over France, Spain, and
Germany.[1]   But Douay ever remained the centre of this
ecclesiastical colony, and Douay owed its character to
Cardinal Allen's foundation.

Naturally the rise of this catholic England beyond the

à laquelle on a joint la politique des Jésuites anglois, trans. from
English (London, 1762), written from an anti-Jesuit point of view.
Further works quoted in Hodgson-Dancoisne, Introd., pp. xxxviii.
et seq. Also J. B. MACKINLAY, O.S.B., The City of our Martyrs,
Dublin Rev., 3rd series, Vol. XI., 1884.

[1] MANN, A Short Chronological Account of the Religious Establishments made by English Catholics on the Continent, Archælogia or
Miscellaneous Tracts relating to Antiquity published by the Society
of Antiquaries of London, XIII. (1800), pp. 251–273.   J. J. E. PROOST,
Les réfugiés anglais et irlandais en Belgique à la suite de la réforme
religieuse établie sous Elisabeth et Jacques I., Messager des Sciences
Historiques . . . de Belgique (Gand, 1865).   ED. PETRE, Notices of
the English Colleges and Convents established on the Continent after
the Dissolution of Religious Houses in England, ed. by HUSENBETH
(Norwich, 1849).   To a great extent these earlier investigations are
now superseded by the excellent essay of ROBERT LECHAT, Les
réfugiés anglais dans les Pays-Bas espagnols durant le règne
d'Elisabeth (Louvain, 1914), and by P. GUILDAY, The English
Catholic Refugees on the Continent 1558–1795, Vol. I., The English
Colleges and Convents in the Catholic Low Countries, 1558–1795
(London, 1914).

seas did not escape notice at home in protestant England. Had not the colony of English exiles at Louvain, who had exerted themselves to get Elizabeth excommunicated at Trent,[1] already made themselves obnoxious by their publications and the secret distribution in England of catholic writings![2]   The foundation of a seminary for priests abroad could not possibly escape the watchful eye of the English government for long.   The act "against fugitives over the sea" (1571)[3] was the response given by parliament to the seminary and other foundations abroad.   This statute severed once and for all the bond between the fatherland and its catholic children abroad.[4] Loss of hearth and home and whatever property they possessed was the punishment inflicted on all who from the date of Elizabeth's accession had left the country without permission or remained abroad beyond a specified time, provided they did not return home by a certain date. Whoever incurred loss of property by this law might regain it within a year if he returned home in a contrite spirit and submitted himself in all respects to the state religion.   The law was aimed indeed at all nonconformists, but had special reference to catholics settled abroad.   To facilitate the working of the act, lists of catholic exiles were drawn up.[5] The religious character of the penal legislation became

---

[1] *Vid. ante*, p. 51.

[2] M. BATESON, *Original Letters from the Bishops to the Privy Council*, 1564, Camd. Soc. Miscell., IX. (1895), p. 67.

[3] 13 Eliz. c. 3.   An act against fugitives over the sea.   The act is further explained by 14 Eliz. c. 6.

[4] The "fugitives over the sea" were henceforth excluded from enjoying the benefit of amnesties.   See 13 Eliz. c. 28, § 8; 23 Eliz. c. 16, § 8; 27 Eliz. c. 30, § 10; 29 Eliz. c. 9, § 8; 31 Eliz. c. 16, § 8; 35 Eliz. c. 14, § 8; 39 Eliz. c. 28, § 8; 43 Eliz. c. 19, § 8; 3 Jac. I. c. 27, § 9; 7 Jac. I. c. 24, § 8, etc.

[5] STRYPE, *Annals of the Reformation*, II., ii. (1824), pp. 596 *et seq.*   The same list with some variations in COLLIER, *The Egerton Papers*, Camd. Soc. (1840), pp. 63-65.

much more clearly defined after the excommunication. We cannot tell how the act worked or how many re-entered on the enjoyment of their property through the door of the state church. One thing alone is certain, scarcely one individual returned home in a contrite spirit from Douay.

Even in the first years after its foundation, the education at Douay seminary was distinctly directed towards the training of missionaries. More importance was attached to the practical side of the ecclesiastical calling than to purely scientific equipment. The seminarists were exercised in preaching and dialectic, and were made familiar with the chief doctrines of protestantism. Pastoral theology formed a prominent feature in the course of instruction, while devotional exercises aimed at deepening the religious feelings. Instruction in church history, especially English church history, supplemented the theological course.[1] The spirit of the council of Trent and of the Society of Jesus strongly influenced the tone of the seminary in its early years, though it was soon to come into sharp conflict with the latter. Among the benefactors who gave financial aid to the new foundation, the Jesuits probably

---

[1] *Cf.* also for this point, Allen's letter mentioned above, KNOX, *Letters of Allen*, pp. 62–67. The chief sources for the history of Douay college are contained in KNOX, *The First and Second Diaries of the Engl. Coll., Douay* (London, 1878). The third, fourth, and fifth Diaries are published by the Catholic Record Society (London, 1911). For a description of life in the college, *cf.* Introd., pp. xxxvi. *et seq.* Among earlier works, see N. FITZHERBERTI, *De antiquitate et continuatione Catholicæ religionis in Anglia et de Alani Card. vita libellus* (Romæ, 1608), pp. 52, 66 *et seq.* BELLESHEIM'S *Wilhelm Cardinal Allen und die englischen Seminare auf dem Festland* (Mainz, 1885) is valuable as a collection of materials, but in conception and style ranks rather as hagiology than history. The most recent Life of Card. Allen is by MARTIN HAILE, *An Elizabethan Cardinal, William Allen* (London, 1914). For life in the Engl. coll. at Douay, see ch. ii.

headed the list with their monthly contribution of fifty crowns.[1] The catechism of Peter Canisius was a text-book at Douay,[2] and the relation of the college to the disciples of Loyola was not that of rivals but of brothers in arms.[3]

In 1575, Gregory XIII. granted the Douay seminary an annual pension of twelve hundred gold scudi.[4] Although three years later the anti-Spanish and anti-catholic movement in the Low Countries forced the college to remove to the university town of Rheims, it was never able to put a stop to the rapid growth of the institution.[5] During the fifteen years spent in its new home (1578–93), in spite of occasional financial difficulties,[6] the seminary gave signs of steady progress, and successfully fulfilled its function as a house for training missionaries and promoting scientific studies. In 1582 appeared the Rheims New Testament, the first instalment of the English catholic translation of the Vulgate,[7] a work which was originally forced upon the catholic church by the reform movement,[8] and then in turn exerted considerable influence on the anglican bible. This interchange of good offices between

---

[1] R. PERSONS, S.J., *The First Entrance of the Fathers of the Society into England*, ed. J. H. POLLEN, S.J., Cath. Record Soc. *Miscellanea*, II. (1906), p. 190.

[2] KNOX, *Letters of Allen*, p. 65.

[3] KNOX, *Douay Diaries*, p. 310 ; Letter of Gregory Martin to Edm. Campion, S.J., 1575. *Cf.* KNOX, *Letters of Allen*, p. 33.

[4] DODD-TIERNEY, II., Appendix, No. LII. KNOX, *Allen*, p. 24.

[5] KNOX, *Douay Diaries*, Introd., xlix.–liii.

[6] See the exhortation to support the seminary addressed to catholic Christendom by Gregory XIII. on Jan. 21, 1582. COCQUE-LINES, *Bullar. Roman. Pontif.*, t. IV., pt. iv., p. 8.

[7] See entry in the diary of the seminary for March, 1582 : " Hoc ipso mense extrema manus Novo Testamento anglice edito imposita est." KNOX, *Diaries*, p. 186 ; cf. *Letters of Allen*, p. 112.

[8] *Vid. ante*, p. 71.

the hostile churches is a gratifying feature, however slight
it may be.[1]

In the same year that Douay college received recognition from the pope in the form of a grant, its founder and
rector was summoned to Rome to take part in the proposed erection of an English college there.   In the middle
ages, England, like most other Christian countries, owned
a house for pilgrims in Rome.[2]   The idea of converting
this hospice into a seminary for priests was mooted immediately after the separation of England from Rome.   In
1559 or 1560 a memorial was laid before Pius IV. asking
him to appoint a number of exiled prelates and priests,
who had lost their position and income, to be teachers in
the English hospice for the purpose of giving catholic
education to the sons of exiles and training up a supply of
English priests.[3]   The proposal was disregarded until
fifteen years later, when the example of Douay kindled
renewed zeal.   The adoption of the plan had become a
pressing necessity in the interval, and the only question
was how best to carry it into effect.   Allen could no longer
find room in Douay for his young fellow-countrymen who
felt called to the ecclesiastical state.   In 1576, he sent the
first batch of students for whom he had no accommodation

[1] The relation between the catholic and protestant English
bibles has been sufficiently investigated from the point of view of
philology by J. G. CARLETON, *The Part of Rheims in the making of
the English Bible* (Oxford, 1902). *Cf.* the essay by T. G. LAW,
Collected Essays and Reviews, ed. H. BROWN (Edin., 1904), and the
earlier work by H. COTTON, *Rhemes and Doway. An attempt to
show what has been done by Roman Catholics for the Diffusion of the
Holy Scriptures in English* (Oxford, 1855). *Cf.* also W. F. MOULTON,
The History of the English Bible (London, 1878), pp. 181-189.

[2] W. J. D. CROKE, *The National English Institutions in Rome
during the Fourteenth Century*, Dublin Review, Vol. 134 (1904),
pp. 274-292. Cf. *Atti del congresso internazionale di scienze storiche*,
III. (Roma, 1906), 555-572.

[3] See Appendix I.

to Rome, where they were lodged in the English hospice ; the next year, he sent a second batch, and by that time the income of the hospice could support no more, and the foundation of a college became a necessity.[1] Gregory XIII. carried this into effect in 1579 and gave substantial endowments for the support of the college.[2] In addition to a yearly rent of 3600 gold scudi, three times the amount given to Douay, he gave the college the abbey of San Sabino, near Piacenza, which brought in a yearly income of 3000 ducats. The number of students was at first fixed at forty, but since Allen, who was the chief mover here also, continually kept adding to their number, it very soon (1585) was increased to seventy.

The great importance and representative character of the *Venerabile Collegium Anglorum de Urbe* justifies a short account of the inner life of the community. For a full and accurate understanding of the nature of the catholic mission in England, as well as of English catholicism as a whole, it is necessary to go back to the source whence the vitality of the entire movement

[1] The history of the foundation is given by Philip Sega in his report of the first visitation of the English college. See Appendix XIX. Another contemporary account is by Robert Persons, S.J., who was rector at a later date, printed by J. H. POLLEN, S.J., in Cath. Record Soc. *Miscellanea*, II. (1906), pp. 83–160. Some of the *acta* added by Persons to his account are now preserved along with a large number of other (still unprinted) papers in Arch. Vat., Miscell. Arm. XI., t. 94 (De collegiis urbis). See also *Brevis narratio de origine ac progressu collegii Angl. . . . ab* 1578 *usque* 1582, in Cod. Vat. lat. 3494. The report of the second visitation (1596), the college diary, annual reports, and other sources of information, translated into English, are given by H. FOLEY, S.J., *Records of the Engl. Province of the Soc. of Jesus*, Vol. VI. (London, 1880). Among more recent accounts may be mentioned MORONI, *Dizionario di erudizione storico-eccles.*, Vol. XIV., pp. 170 *et seq.;* and KNOX, *Douay Diaries*, pp. lvii.–lix.

[2] Bull of foundation of April 23, 1579. COCQUELINES, *Bullar. Roman. Pontif.*, t. IV., pt. iii. (Romæ, 1746), pp. 359–63. DODD-TIERNEY, Vol. II., Appendix, No. LVII.

proceeded—the missionary establishments on the continent. For no other English seminary have we such abundant and varied sources of information as for the college in Rome ; *acta*, statutes, and visitation reports sketch clearly the objective outlines of the picture, while personal judgments from friend and foe fill in the subjective colouring.

The statutes direct that the students must not be under fourteen years of age [1] or over twenty-five, physically sound, of blameless conduct, and of good parts. It was part of the blamelessness of the aspirant's conduct that he should not have already lightly cast aside the ecclesiastical habit. The new-comer took an oath to be true to the pope and the catholic church, and spent the first eight or ten days separated from the others in order to prepare himself with due recollection for entering on his new life. This began with a general confession. Not until a few months later was the college oath tendered to the student, of which the most important passage ran—" I swear to Almighty God that I am ready and shall always be ready to receive holy orders in His own good time, and I shall return to England for the salvation of souls whenever it shall seem good to the superior of this college to order me to do so." [2] From this moment the alumnus became a full member of the college.

The short notes of the lives of the new-comers are the confession of a voluntary renunciation in which pride and humility are strangely mingled. There is scarcely one

[1] See the statutes of 1579, Appendix XVI. *Cf.* the *Constitutiones Coll. Angl.* in Sega's report of 1585, Appendix XIX. [§ 57]. In these eighteen is suggested as the earliest age at which students should be received.

[2] Printed in DODD-TIERNEY, Vol. II., p. cccxliii. Also in the *Liber ruber*, fol. 3ʳ, Arch. of the Eng. College. Persons slightly altered the wording afterwards. *Cf.* HEURICUS MORUS, S.J., *Historia missionis Anglicanæ soc. Jesu ab a.* 1580 *ad a.* 1635 (Andomari, 1660), pp. 57 *et seq.*

among them who had not once and for all forsaken family or friends, property or career (some even forsook their brides), because the Spirit had seized him and called him to a higher service.[1]   Many were converts and many were sons of noble houses—a distinction of which the anglican clergy of that date could but seldom boast.[2]

The rule of life[3] which the new-comer undertook to follow was based on the system of education elaborated by the Jesuits, and was essentially the same as that which still forms the foundation of the training given in catholic seminaries.   The whole life was devoted to one end.   Each day began with half an hour's meditation, prayer, and examination of conscience.   Mass was heard daily, and a sermon in addition on festivals.   All the important acts of the day were accompanied by prayer, such as rising and going to bed, going out and coming home, the beginning and ending of meals.   At dinner and supper spiritual books were read.

The forenoon was devoted to study, *i.e.* attendance at

[1] Public Record Office, STEVENSON'S *Roman Transcripts*, 9, *Students' Interrogatories*.   FOLEY, *Records*, Vol. I., pp. 142 *et seq.*

[2] "... non ex fœce hominum, ut vestri verbi ministri, sed nobilibus plerumque orti familiis et copiosis nati parentibus huc adveniant, et ausim sane dicere maiorem esse longe nobilitatis florem in his tribus tantum seminariis Anglicanis, Rhemensi, Romano et Vallesoletano, quam in universo vestro clero domestico reperiatur." ANDREAS PHILOPATER [*i.e.* ROB. PERSONS, S.J.], *Elizabethæ Angliæ reginæ hæresim Calvinianam propugnantis sævissimum in catholicos edictum . . . promulgatum Londini*, Nov. 29, 1591 (Romæ, 1593), p. 262, *cf.* p. 236.

[3] In addition to the sources mentioned on p. 101, note 1, *cf.* PHILOPATER, *op. cit.*, pp. 272–284.   The course of studies and rule of life observed in the English college followed the usual rules adopted in the colleges of the Jesuits, and were only distinguished from them by their greater strictness and by a few particulars.   *Cf.* EB. GOTHEIN, *Ignatius von Loyola u. d. Gegenreformation* (Halle, 1885), pp. 415 *et seq.*, 447 *et seq.*   B. DUHR, *Gesch. der Jesuiten i. d. Ländern deutscher Zunge*, Vol. I. (Freiburg, 1907), pp. 568 *et seq.*

lectures in the *Collegium Romanum*.[1] The scheme of studies followed fixed rules which left no room for personal choice. The length of the course of studies depended on the ability and previous education of each, but never extended beyond seven years—three for philosophy and four for theology. The lectures were followed by instruction in singing. Waiting at table was performed by the students in turn. The food was good and plentiful, with a sweet for dessert, "for they know Englishmen love sweet things." [2]

In the afternoon, there was first an hour's recreation in the garden or cortile. Every third or fourth day the members of the college issued forth under the direction of the superiors, either for a holiday at their own *vigna* [3] or for a pilgrimage to the Seven Churches.[4]   In this also we see a feature of the Jesuit system of education which provided recreation as a counterpoise to the severe mental strain.   After the usual recreation came an hour's preparation and the resumption of studies.   The students were exercised in debate ; the young priest must learn to restrain his impetuosity, sarcasm, and irritability, and to keep his temper in argument.   When the afternoon studies were over, the bedrooms were to be put in order, for each student had to make his own bed and was liable

---

[1] " Gymnasium societatis Jesu," as it is called in the institutions. Appendix XVI. : *De eo quod pertinet ad studia.*

[2] ANTHONY MUNDAY, *The English Romayne Life. Discovering the Lives of the Englishmen at Rome, the Orders of the English Seminarie* (London, 1582), pp. 26, 27.   *Cf.* GOTHEIN, *op. cit.*, p. 417.

[3] If the " Vigna del Collegio Inglese " was the same then as now, it was situated on the Tiber below Rome opposite the hunting-castle of Magliana.   Even at the present day the students of the English college often go there for an excursion.   The *Collegium Romanum* had also its *vigna* at this period.   COCQUELINES, *Bull. Roman. Pontif.* t. IV., pt. iii. (1746), p. 325.

[4] MUNDAY, *op. cit.*, p. 29.   The Seven Churches are S. Giovanni, S. Pietro, S. Paolo, S. Lorenzo, Sta. Maria Maggiore, Sta. Croce in Gerusalemme, and S. Sebastiano.

to be punished for untidiness.   After supper, all went into
the church for the litany.   The day ended as it had begun,
with an examination of conscience.   The time allowed for
sleep was seven hours and a half.

The books to be read out of study hours were as strictly
prescribed as the studies themselves.   They were confined
to devotional books and lives of the saints.   No student
was allowed to buy or keep any book he had chosen for
himself.   The language spoken throughout the day was
Latin, the language of the church.   Italian was limited to
the hours of recreation.   Personal intercourse was subject
to strict supervision.   No one could go out alone or choose
his companion.   He must state beforehand why he wished
to go out, and, without the rector's permission, could not
pay a visit or take anything to eat.   Intercourse with
laymen was reduced to the narrowest possible limits.   Only
with special permission could visits be paid to friends, and
no layman was admitted into the college.   Intercourse
with the servants of the house was forbidden.   Even in
the intercourse of the alumni with one another no freedom
of choice was allowed ; the order in which they walked out
together was regulated in every case.   Correspondence as
well as personal intercourse was supervised ; without the
rector's leave no one could write or receive a letter.
After what we have said, the reader will not be surprised
to learn that, without leave, the students had no command
over their money and could not, without permission, carry
any about with them.

To judge fairly of this system of education, we must
view it exclusively in relation to the future calling of the
students.   Bearing this in mind, we are bound to admit that
the result aimed at—the complete transformation of the
worldling into the ecclesiastic—could only be attained by
this entire renunciation of self-will.   All that belongs to

the man's own individuality must be suppressed in order
that all that is sacerdotal may arise in unmixed purity.

The system, however, was over-done. In the attempt to
gain complete mastery over the inner life of the students,
means were employed which, justified as they may have
been in the hands of a Burleigh on the look-out for conspiracies, cannot be excused in teachers of youth. A
student who had spent over four months in the English
college in Rome, and during that period had conceived
the germs of his subsequent hostility to the Jesuits,
describes in detail how the rector spied on the alumni
of the college by means of their own companions.[1] "At
recreation time," these so-called *Angeli costodes*, "speake
liberally against their superiors, of their goverment and
usage towards them, of their apparell, meate and drinck,
and against the straight keaping of them in, and against
whatsoever they thinke is not wel done in the colleadge.
And all this to sounde their compaignons," and then "carry
the whole discourse straight to the Rector. . . . Nothing
so contrary to an englishmans nature, as to be betrayed by
him whom he trusteth. If such spies were in Oxford . . .
they would be plucked in peeces."[2]

And so, in spite of all the care taken, there arose such
a degree of irritation in the English college that a number
of the alumni rose in arms against the Jesuit management

---

[1] HUMPHREY ELY, *Certaine briefe notes upon a briefe apologie set
out under the name of the priestes united to the archpriest. Drawn by
an impassionate secular prieste, friend to bothe partyeş, but more friend
to the truth. Imprinted at Paris by Peter Sevestre* [1603]. It would
be arguing in a vicious circle to refuse credit to Ely's experiences
because of his opposition to the Jesuits, for it was these experiences
which contributed to make him their opponent. Moreover his
evidence is supported by that of others. *Cf.* the references in note
above. GOTHEIN, p. 439, gives further proof of the system of
espionage and eavesdropping carried on in the college.

[2] ELY, *op. cit.*, pp. 81, 82.

and the principle of *Divide et Impera*. If there is any
truth in these indignant accusations [1]—and, however highly
coloured, they can hardly be altogether without foundation
—then it is clear that the Jesuits had by favouritism won
over a certain number of the students who acted as their
trusted agents and to whom the rest were handed over
without defence. It is hard to believe the statement that
the Jesuits not only appointed these " elect " to posts of
responsibility, and gave them better treatment than the
others, but even overlooked their flagrant infringements of
the college rules. The bitterness of the complainants may
have led them to misrepresent the facts or generalize
unduly. However, the fact remains that the institution
of "guardian angels" was in itself a serious mistake.

The complaints against the management of the English
college in Rome were not the only ones. When a Jesuit
was appointed confessor to the college of secular priests at
Douay, the experiences of the alumni of the college in
Rome were repeated there. While it is certain that complaints of the secular clergy against the Jesuits must be
received with caution, being the accusations of unsuccessful
rivals, still, where the charges agree as they do in these
two cases, the evidence even of opponents has its value ;
and what Matthew Kellison, rector of Douay,[2] has to

---

[1] Mentioned in Card. Sega's report of the second visitation of the
English college, March 4, 1596. Bibl. Vat. Ottob., 2473, fol. 187–226,
especially the sect. *De Superioribus collegii Anglicani*, fol. 200. In
English in FOLEY, *Records of the Engl. Prov. of the Soc. of Jesus*,
Vol. VI., pp. 20 *et seq.* The same complaint had been already made
ten years previously at the first visitation, though not with the same
insistence. Appendix XIX. [§ 31].

[2] In a letter to Card. Borghese of June 6, unfortunately without
the year, Arch. Vat., Borgh. I., 691, fol. 91. Kellison (who signs his
name *Matthæus Chelisonus*) was rector of the English college at
Douay, 1613–41. His letter contains a request for the removal of
the Jesuit confessor. " Nam ex quo collegium hoc confessarium
habuit Jesuitam (cuius præsentia et domi gravis et foris toti clero et

say of the Jesuit confessor in his house as the cause of disturbances there, agrees only too well with the complaints of the Roman students. "He was wont to gain information about everything from secret informers and secretly to mix himself up with all our affairs, which caused him to be hated, and also deprived the confessions of all freedom and openness."

The protestant controversy of the time naturally seized on such an educational blunder as a useful weapon in its campaign against the hated Jesuits and seminary priests.[1] For the life at the English universities at the same period —about which we are sufficiently well informed—knew no more of such a system of supervision then than it does now.[2]

Many of the methods of humbling self-esteem were quite as exaggerated as this system of espionage, which searched even into their very thoughts. The custom observed in other Jesuit colleges, that the students should wash the feet of the guests,[3] was certainly quite justified and full of significance in the English college in Rome, which had formerly been a hospice.[4] But the degrading punishments meted out for small breaches of rule did not seem

quamplurimis catholicis Anglis ingrata est) perpetuis quidam dissensionum fomes extitit . . . ipse semper solitus est per delatores secretos de omnibus se informare et omnibus nostris negotiis sese clanculum insinuare, quæ res, cum illum reddat odiosum, tum confessiones reddit non adeo gratas, liberas et apertas."

[1] *Cf.* THOS. JAMES, *The Jesuites Downefall, threatned against them by the secular priests for their wicked lives, accursed manners, hereticall doctrine, and more then Matchiavillian policie* (Oxford, 1612), pp. 46 *et seq.*

[2] E.g. *College Life in the Time of James I., as Illustrated by an unpublished Diary of Sir Symonds D'Ewes* (London, 1851).

[3] DUHR, *op. cit.*, p. 581.

[4] In the *Annuæ litteræ Coll. Angl.* for 1585 it is said, "Hospitio excepti sunt ex veteri consuetudine hujus hospitalis multi peregrini, quibus alumni pedes lavabant et prompte ministrabant," Arch. of the Engl. coll., *Liber ruber.* Translated in FOLEY, VI., p. 115.

calculated to promote good discipline. The student who did not make his bed properly, or kneel down to say his prayers at the prescribed hour, or missed mass, was punished by having his rations curtailed, or by being made ridiculous at meal-time, when his plate was set on the floor and he had to eat from it standing, which necessitated his kneeling down for each mouthful—and other such-like things.[1] Heavier penances still were enjoined in the confessional. The penitent had to appear in a long linen garment like a sack, with openings for the eyes alone, which left part of his back bare. In this costume he had to walk up and down before a number of his comrades scourging himself till the blood flowed.[2] "When a man doth it at the first, he is so farre ordinarily from amendment that in his hart he doth grutch and repine at his superiors for the geving of it. But when he is used 3 or 4 times to doe it, then he maketh a very scoff and mocking or may game of it : so farre is it from a true penance as it engendreth (as I said) both hatred and mockery." [3]

It would be unfair to judge of the whole system from these extravagances. The exaggerations of the system did not prevent it from producing magnificent results.

The whole scheme of education in the seminary culminated in the "Spiritual Exercises" drawn up by the founder of the Society of Jesus for his disciples. But the end which these exercises held up to those who were going to be priests in England was something far higher than that which most men aimed at by this means. For them these Spiritual Exercises were not merely an occasion for

---

[1] A. MUNDAY, *op. cit.*, p. 23. In other Jesuit colleges this punishment seems to have taken the form of eating separately at a low table. GOTHEIN, p. 449.

[2] A. MUNDAY, *l.c.*

[3] HUMPHREY ELY, *op. cit.*, p. 80.

deepening the spiritual life, they were a conscious preparation for martyrdom. *Seminarium Martyrum* was the
glorious epithet bestowed upon the English college,[1]
paintings of the torture-chamber and the scaffold covered
the walls of the building,[2] and it was with the salutation,
Salvete flores martyrum! that St. Philip Neri used to
greet these future martyrs when he met them in the
street.[3] To prepare men for this fate was the loftiest
and most exacting labour of the English college, and in
none was its success more glorious.

Once a year, in autumn, a body of students met to go
through the Spiritual Exercises.[4] Separated from the
rest for a few days, they devoted themselves to meditation
in common on the life of Jesus, to acts of self-humiliation,
and lived uninterruptedly in the contemplation of the
sufferings and death of the martyrs which lay before them,
whose fate they might be called upon to share, and that
perhaps at no distant date. If in other respects their whole
education aimed at destroying self-esteem and implanting
humility in these young souls, whatever pride or longing after
distinction might yet remain in them was now centred upon

[1] *Annuæ litteræ collegii Angl.*, 1585.
[2] KNOX, *Letters of Allen*, p. 186, note 6. *Cf.* EPHRAIM PAGITT,
Christianography, 3rd ed. (London, 1640), p. 264 ; Engl. Hist. Rev.
Vol. XXI., p. 377. The original frescoes by Circignani (usually
called Pomarancio) have perished, but the series of engravings, taken
from them by Cavalieri and published by Grassi in Rome in 1584,
indicate the subjects represented. See J. MORRIS, S.J., *The
Pictures of the English College at Rome, etc.* (Stonyhurst college,
1887), where Grassi's engravings are reproduced. Some idea of the
character of the original paintings can be gained from the terrible
series of martyrdoms by the same artist on the walls of S. Stefano
Rotondo in Rome.
[3] MORONI, *Dizion. di erud. stor.-eccl.*, Vol. XIV., p. 173.
[4] Described in the *Annuæ litteræ coll. Angl.* for 1582. Arch. of
the Engl. coll., *Liber ruber*. FOLEY, *Records*, VI., pp. 81 *et seq.*

these representations of torture and blood and transformed into a consciousness that they were called to the loftiest of all vocations. For Divine mercy had snatched them alone as a small remnant out of the ruin of their country [1] to set it free from the curse of heresy and damnation by their teaching and example. It is to youths at their most impressionable age that these thoughts speak. Love for their country and their religion, longing for high achievements, every noble enthusiasm—all were fused together into one burning desire, to die for England's conversion. Not only death itself lost its terrors—that was as nothing —but the lingering and painful tortures which went before were lit up by a halo of glory. There was only one thing on earth worth anything—the martyr's sacrifice.

And so were trained up in Rome those incomprehensible men who kissed the instruments of torture, blessed their hangmen, and embraced the ladders as they mounted to the gallows. Seldom has education won a grander triumph over human nature. Among all the achievements of the counter-reformation which filled the whole of Christendom with new centres for the diffusion of spiritual life, nothing grander is to be found than these seminaries of English priests. When a German or a Frenchman, an Italian or a Spaniard donned the ecclesiastical habit, he might be influenced quite as much by the thought of a mitre or red hat as by a true inward vocation. No such career with its worldly honours lay before the Englishman. When a man subscribed the college oath in most cases he signed his own death-warrant. We are here interested in the history of the English college in particular only so far as it reflects in miniature events repeated on a large scale in the history of English catholicism as a whole. The first rector of the college, Maurice Clenock, who had previously been warden

[1] ". . . velut raptas e patriæ funere reliquias."

of the hospice, soon showed himself unsuited for the post by the unfairness with which he, as a Welshman, favoured his own countrymen in preference to the English.[1]   At the earnest request of the English students, who threatened to leave, the management of the college was taken over by the Jesuits in 1579.   This action was quite in keeping with the spirit of their institutions.   " We ask not for freedom, but for discipline," declared the students in their petition to the Cardinal Protector Morone.[2]   The high expectations with which the college welcomed the Jesuits were partly realized and partly not.   We have already pointed out the strength and weakness of their system, and, after what we have said, it will be easily understood how the strain induced by their methods of training endangered the domestic peace of the establishment.   A second factor contributed to produce the same result.

The Jesuits, as was only natural, tried to influence the students to enter the Society of Jesus.   In full consciousness that they were the staunchest champions of the counter-reformation, they strove to get the management of the whole English mission into their hands.   It was a fixed idea of their order that the church could best be served by the extension of their own power—be it even at the cost of the other orders and the secular clergy.   But here again the bow was too tightly strung for endurance. The Jesuits, so ran the complaint of the English college students, made use of the confessional to attract novices. Those whom they won over were unduly favoured—

---

[1] The disputes between English and Welsh are spoken of by H. MORUS, *Hist. missionis Angl. soc. Jesu* (1660), pp. 55 *et seq.* FRANC SACCHINUS, *Hist. soc. Jesu*, pt. iv. (Romæ 1652), lib. vii., § 22, *et seq.*   PERSONS' *Memoirs, l.c.* and *passim.*   The original acts are in the Arch. Vat., Miscell. Arm. XI., t. 94, fol. 101 *et seq.   Cf.* the documents in DODD-TIERNEY, Vol. II., Appendix, No. LIX. *et seq.*

[2] Printed in DODD-TIERNEY, Vol. II., p. cccxlviii.

"beardless youths," not in orders, who had joined the Society were placed in the refectory above other alumni who were priests but not Jesuits.[1] The formation of a Sodality of the Blessed Virgin [2] in the college acted as a sort of preliminary stage to entering the Jesuit order. The sodality seems to have stood to the rest of the alumni as an exclusive students' club does to students who do not belong to it. Before the formation of the sodality, said the malcontents,[3] peace had reigned in the college, only with it did discord find an entrance ; followers of the rector and the Society of Jesus alone were admitted as members, and these enjoyed more consideration than the others, were placed as prefects over the rooms, presumed to defend publicly philosophical and theological questions, and were more quickly promoted to orders. All this moved the less favoured ones to band themselves together with the object of obtaining the dissolution of the sodality, the removal of the Jesuits from the management of the college, and the prohibition of joining a religious order.[4]

This abuse of authority, and the espionage described above, threatened more than once the peace, and even the very existence, of the college.[5] Twice the supreme authority had to interfere, by means of a visitation (1585 and 1596), to decide between the Jesuit party and its

[1] These grievances are given in the report of the visitation of 1596. Bibl. Vat., Ottob. 2473, fol. 201ᵛ, 202. FOLEY, *Records*, VI., p. 23.

[2] *Cf.* the statutes of the *Sodalitas Bᵐᵃ Virginis in Collegio Anglicano.* Appendix XIX. [§§ 87–139].

[3] Appendix XIX. [§ 21].

[4] Report of visitation of 1596. Cod. Ottob. 2473, fol. 204ᵛ. FOLEY, VI., pp. 50 *et seq.*

[5] Humphrey Ely's description in *Certaine Briefe Notes, etc.* (*vid. ante*, p. 105), and the grievances of the anti-Jesuit students enumerated in the reports of the visitations agree so well together, both as to the general tone of things in the college and many particular points, that no room is left for doubt as to the causes of these internal disturbances.

opponents.   Both sides had a hearing, but the papal visitors, with Cardinal Sega at their head, felt it was important before all things that ecclesiastical authority should be upheld.   All complaints and attempts at stirring up opposition were sternly suppressed.   The first visitation ended in the alumni being forbidden even to criticize the management of the college among themselves; all complaints were to be laid before the rector; to hold *conventiculæ* without leave was threatened with punishment; [1] and the obnoxious sodality was to be treated with due respect, all murmurings against its members or statutes being forbidden.   However, the visitors enjoined the formation of a second sodality within a month, and that those who wished to join it should be examined by the visitors in the presence of the rector, showing by this that they wished to set up a counterpoise to the privileged position of the first sodality. [2]   Moreover a concession was made to the discontented party by allowing any student to depart from the English college, "honourably and in peace," within eight days and transfer himself to the college in Rheims, and so change his Jesuit superiors for secular. [3]   But no fault was found with the management of the college, and the Society of Jesus had every reason to be satisfied with the result of the visitation. [4]

The second visitation [5] only confirmed the ruling of the first.   Sega was convinced that under no circumstances were the fathers to be removed from the management of

[1] See the "decreta" of the visitation of 1585. Appendix XIX. [§§ 43, 44].

[2] *Ib.* [§§ 45, 46].

[3] *Ib.* [§ 52].

[4] "Approbarunt omnia," says Persons, referring to the visitors. *Initia et progressus Collegii Anglicani de Urbe*, ed. by POLLEN in Cath. Record Soc. Miscellanea, II. (1906), p. 95.

[5] This will be treated from a more general point of view in ch. iv., sect. i.

I

the college, and that everything must be done to prevent fresh disturbances.   He even went so far as to direct that separate cubicles should be made in order to remove all possibility of secret conferences among the alumni.[1]   Next year (1597), a man hastened from Spain to be placed at the head of the college who was to quench forthwith all spirit of insubordination, a man possessed of a gift of governance second to none among his fellows—the greatest of the English Jesuits, Fr. Robert Persons.

" When I came to Rome," he says, " I found the colledge as a field with two hostile campes." [2]   Although this man's iron will succeeded in suppressing all opposition to the domination of himself and the Jesuits, nevertheless two hostile camps were to be found not only in the English college in Rome, but nearly everywhere wherever there were English catholics both in England and on the continent. The feud was kept up from generation to generation, and not even the common enemy was able to force the wranglers to keep the peace among themselves.   The hatred of members of the same religion for one another was at times more intense than their hatred for their oppressors, and it was both the disgrace and the tragedy of English catholicism that its forces were not united, and it had to present a broken front to the enemy.   The trouble in the English college revealed only one of many roots of bitterness, though the deepest and strongest of all—the quarrel between the Jesuits and the secular clergy.

In Scotland as in England, there were catholics with enough zeal and enterprise to make an independent effort for the defence of their own church.   What William Allen did for catholicism in England, William Creighton the

---

[1] Cod. Ottob. 2473, fol. 216-226.   FOLEY, VI., pp. 50-63.
[2] Letter of July 13, 1598 [WILLIAM WATSON], *A Decacordon of ten quodlibeticall questions concerning religion and state* (1602), p. 127.

Jesuit seemed destined to do for it in Scotland.   Similar
beginnings promised a similar result, but the development
of the Scotch seminary falls far short of the success
attained by the English college.   Although Rome did its
part and contributed the necessary funds and erected the
Scots' college alongside the English *Collegium de Urbe*,
the result was insignificant, not to say a failure.   For
the most indispensable thing of all was lacking—youths
eager to embrace the ecclesiastical state.   There were
officers, but no men.   Creighton was labouring under a
misapprehension when he wrote to Cardinal Caetani, the
Protector of England and Scotland,[1] that if only the means
were forthcoming a large body of students from the three
Scotch universities would at once flock to the new seminary,
and even if they were heretics to start with they would
easily be converted.   His aim was to win souls by charity
and patience, and he hoped in two or three years to see a
new catholic priesthood in his native land.

The first Scottish seminary, a private venture like the
English, was founded in 1576 at Tournay.   For many
years it vegetated in different places ; during the first
thirty-six years of its existence we find it in no less than
six different localities—Tournay, Pont-à-Mousson, Douay,
Louvain, Antwerp, and finally Douay again.[2]   The expectation that the pope or the king of Spain would support
the undertaking encouraged those at its head to purchase
" a fine property " in Louvain.[3]   There were only sufficient
funds for the support of seven or eight students.[4]   Yet

---

[1] On Sept. 7, 1595, from Louvain.   Appendix XXI.

[2] A. BELLESHEIM, *Hist. of the Cath. Ch. in Scotland* (Engl. trans.
by Dom O. HUNTER-BLAIR, O.S.B., London, 1889), Vol. III., ch. vii.

[3] William Creighton to Card. Caetani, Louvain, Sept. 7, 1595.
Appendix XXI.

[4] Report of Mgr. Malvasia of 1596, Brussels.   BELLESHEIM, *op. cit.*,
Vol. III., p. 355.

even this was a success compared with the work done by
the seminary at Braunsberg, which in the course of over
sixty years (1579–1642) sent only seven or eight missionaries back to Scotland.[1] A few foundations, dating like
the English hospice in Rome from earlier times and now
adapted for the training of missionaries, were scarcely
more important. The Scottish monasteries in Germany
(Würzburg and Regensburg) did not take up missionary
work nor did the Scots' college in Paris flourish like the
English sister house. Originally founded in the middle
ages in connection with the university,[2] towards the end
of the sixteenth century a legacy entitled it to fulfil
its new task. It had now sufficient for the support of
twenty-four students, but up to the beginning of
the seventeenth century there were actually only five
or six.[3]

The history of the Scots' college in Rome also plainly
shows that failure was due to no want of means or lack
of good will, but to the absence of suitable men. The
Collegium Scotorum de Urbe was founded by Clement VIII.[4]
in 1600 on the model of the English college.[5] Although
well able to support twenty alumni out of its annual
income of 1400 Roman scudi, it contained at first only a
third or a half of that number,[6] and even later it never

---

[1] See the list in BELLESHEIM, Vol. III., Appendix VI.

[2] For details, see BELLESHEIM, Vol. II., p. 24, *et passim.*

[3] Petitions from the Scots' college in Paris (without date but
soon after 1600) ; Bibl. Vat., Barb. 8614, fol. 85, 87.

[4] Bull of foundation of Dec. 5, 1600. COCQUELINES, *Bull. Roman.
Pontif.*, t. V., pt. ii. (Romæ, 1753), pp. 319–323.

[5] The statutes (undated copy of the seventeenth century) in the
Bibl. Vat., Barb. 8629, fol. 9–22. They agree in all essential features
with the statutes of the English college.

[6] *Narratio brevis de collegii Scotorum gubernatione*, Bibl. Vat.,
Barb. 8629, fol. 7, 8. Belonging to the first years of the seventeenth
century.

increased beyond it.[1] Lamentations over the small results gained from this and the other Scottish seminaries constantly made themselves heard, while the not infrequent outbursts of insubordination among the alumni, and their unwillingness to pledge themselves by oath to receive Holy Orders and devote themselves to missionary work in Scotland [2] clearly proves that in the land of John Knox it was far rarer to find enthusiasm for the catholic church among the rising generation than in England, whence numbers of young men came to fill the continental seminaries to overflowing.

Soon the need of increased accommodation for English priests could no longer be supplied by Rheims and Rome alone. "We are a hundred and sixteen," wrote the rector of Rheims in July, 1590, to the rector of the college in Rome,[3] "and for some time have received no assistance from England; new students are constantly arriving. Your reverence must take at least sixteen or seventeen of them at once. Reverend Father! this is not the time to ponder how we are to make ends meet. Between Easter and now, twenty have arrived, others are announced and are already on the way. We dare not refuse them; God sends them to us. I have reduced the quantity of food in the refectory to the smallest possible amount; their clothing is worn out, but never were the brigade happier or more content. Better youths, more full of promise in virtue and talents than these, we have never seen."

[1] *Quaedam proponenda cardinali Barberino, protectori Scotiæ*, Barb. 8628, fol. 22 ; *cf.* fol. 43, 44.

[2] See the petitions of the students of the Scots' college in Rome in Barb. 8629, fol. 39, 40. Additional material in the same codex and in Barb. 8628 and 8614.

[3] Letter of July 17, 1590, printed in the *Relatione del presente stato d'Inghilterra* (Roma, 1590), pp. 14, 15.

The necessity for additional foundations was evident. After Rome and the English catholics themselves, no one showed more interest in the spread of seminaries than the king of Spain. To number England among the states subject to Hapsburg influence was a fixed idea in Spanish politics. A first step to the attainment of this end was the return of England to catholicism. Philip II. was furthering his political as well as his ecclesiastical interests when he gave an annual donation of two thousand ducats to the insufficiently endowed college at Douay.[1] Still this arrangement could not be regarded as final. Two seminaries alone could not hold all who aspired to the priesthood in order to devote their life to working in the vineyard. And so, in conjunction with Rome and the catholics of England, the king of Spain figures as a third founder of seminaries and schools. Robert Persons, who had intimate relations with the Spanish court, took an active part in their organization. He took care at the same time that the new missionary centres should be placed under Jesuit management. Nothing shows more plainly the dauntless courage of these two men, the English Jesuit and the Spanish king, than the fact that the two most important foundations, the English colleges at Valladolid (1589)[2] and Seville (1592),[3] followed almost immediately upon the defeat of the Spanish armada. But their astonishingly rapid growth—in spite of the open war between England and Spain—shows, too, how much stronger the sense of religious unity was amongst many of the oppressed catholics in England than the

[1] THEINER, *Annal. eccles.*, III., p. 477.

[2] The papal confirmation of the foundation was given only on Nov. 3, 1592. Arch. dei Brevi., Diversorum Clem. VIII., lib. i., 1591–97, fol. 120–123.

[3] Papal confirmation on Feb. 9, 1594, *l.c.*, fol. 124.

feeling of hostility to their national foe.   Three years after its foundation, the seminary at Valladolid numbered seventy-five alumni, and "since God sends us nearly every month fresh reinforcements for the holy work from England, the foundation of a new colony has become a necessity." [1]   This new foundation, the seminary at Seville, in spite of straitened means at its start, flourished quite as rapidly as the mother house at Valladolid.[2]   It is an unusual example of an ecclesiastical institution receiving practical support not only from church and state, but from the civic authorities as well; for the city of Seville bestowed on the English seminary, shortly after its foundation, a yearly rent of six hundred ducats for ten years.[3]

The history of these and other foundations which sprang up in Madrid, Lisbon, and the Spanish Netherlands, partly through means given by the state and partly through private liberality—seminaries for priests, boys' schools, noviciates, etc.[4]—enters still less into the scope

[1] Fr. J. Creswell, S.J., to Clement VIII. Seville, Dec. 1, 1592. Arch. Vat., Borgh. III., 124g, 2, fol. 51.   The number of students in the seminary at Valladolid was somewhat smaller afterwards, *e.g.* in 1604, forty-three. *Annuæ litteræ soc. Jesu anni* 1604 (Duaci, 1618), pp. 165–69 ; Seminarium Angl. Vallisoletanum.

[2] Creswell to Clement VIII., April 19, 1593. Borgh., 124g, 2, fol. 52.

[3] *Copia de una relacion hecha en el cabildo de la cuidad de Sevilla . . . sobre un caso, si la cuidad . . . podia continuar la* [limosina] *que hazia al seminario de los Ingleses.   Impresso en Sevilla por Clemente Hidalgo a 6 Julio de* 1604. Arch. Vat., Miscell. Arm. I., t. 15, fol. 1–14.

[4] In addition to the still unpublished letters of the Jesuits, Creswell and Persons (Arch. Vat., Borgh. III., 124g, 2), the works already mentioned above on pp. 94–5 may be consulted, also the valuable references to the seminaries in Panzani's *Relazione* (*cf.* p. 64, note 1). What TH. FULLER says in his *Church History*, Vol. IV. (1845), pp. 350–358, is incomplete and in several particulars untrustworthy. For the houses founded by the religious orders who took part in

of this narrative than does the history of the two principal institutions of Douay and Rome. One point only must be mentioned which has an important bearing both on the character of these institutions dependent upon Spain and on the judgment passed by protestant England on catholic missionary houses in general. Whoever entered one of these seminaries supported by Spain left it, not only as a catholic priest, but as a partisan of the catholic king.[1] The conflict between loyalty to the state and loyalty to the church was hard enough already for English catholics, but when dependence on Rome entailed dependence on Spain, their country's foe, then the conflict became indeed war to the knife. Since the days of Mary Tudor, the wife of a Spanish sovereign, the English protestant was accustomed to regard Spanish and catholic as the same thing. The development now taken on the continent by English catholicism could only intensify this prejudice. Catholic, Jesuit, Spanish, were for the large majority only different names for the same thing. But even if a man looked closer and succeeded in distinguishing the two hostile currents in English catholicism, this only enabled him to borrow weapons from one party in order to deal harder blows at the other. It was no English protestant but a secular priest who wrote the words—"And sure, he or she hereafter that shall send their children, or go themselues, to become students at

the English mission, *cf.* P. LEANDER, *Apost. missionis status in Anglia* (1634), in the Clarendon State Papers, I. (Oxford, 1767), pp. 199 *et seq.* For the college for secular clergy in Lisbon, *cf.* W. CROFT, *Historical Account of Lisbon College* (London, 1902). For Valladolid, *cf.* the articles by DOM BEDE CAMM and Fr. J. H. POLLEN in The Month, Oct., 1898; Sept., Oct., 1899.

[1] *Cf.* the description of the seminaries at Douay and St. Omer given by Card. d'Ossat in a letter to Henry IV., Nov. 26, 1601. As a Frenchman and an enemy of Spain, the cardinal exaggerates, still his chief points are correct. *Lettres du Card. d'Ossat*, p. 757.

Rome or elsewhere under their [the Jesuits'] governement, do either by consequent cast themselues into a voluntary slavery, as bad as if under the great Turke: or else must they change the true nature of an English heart, and become traytors or fautors of conspiracies against their Prince, countrey, and dearest friends." [1]

How utterly unjust this accusation of disloyalty to their country was, the history of the catholic mission will show.

[1] W. WATSON, *Decacordon* (1602), p. 141.

CHAPTER II

THE PERSECUTION, AND THE CATHOLIC MISSION IN ENGLAND

THE history of the persecution of catholics and of the catholic mission in the England of Queen Elizabeth is wont to be represented to the reader in a series of narratives of the life and sufferings of individual mission priests. This way of dealing with the subject, although it may easily become monotonous, appeals, beyond doubt, most forcibly to our human sympathies and needs little art to render it intensely pathetic. It was on these lines that in 1582, Cardinal Allen, while the impression created by the news from England was still fresh in his mind, wrote the earliest history of the catholic mission, of which he was the organizer, a work which is at the same time a history of the persecution endured by English catholics.[1] The artless and touching simplicity of these histories of the earliest martyrdoms has influenced most of the later historians.[2] But since the writers have aimed at

---

[1] *A Briefe Historie of the Glorious Martyrdom of XII. reverend Priests, etc.* Reprinted by J. H. POLLEN, S.J. (London, 1908), along with additional evidence from the early period of the mission, from the only known copy of the original book in the British Museum. For the changes and variations from the original made by translators and editors, see Father Pollen's introduction to his reprint.

[2] In addition to the works already mentioned (p. 2, notes 1 and 2), *cf.* T. G. LAW, *A Calendar of the English Martyrs of the Sixteenth and Seventeenth Centuries* (London, 1876); J. H. POLLEN, *Acts of the Engl. Martyrs hitherto unpublished*, with a preface by J. MORRIS

producing works of edification rather than history, the persecution and mission have never yet been treated from a strictly critical and historical point of view. The scope of the work now before the reader excludes altogether the treatment of the subject in the usual hagiographical style. The consequence of dealing with it in this way has been that the historical problems, upon the solution of which depends the formation of an equitable judgment on the persecution and mission, do not stand out with the distinctness one could wish. Instead of compiling a new *Acta Martyrum*, the attempt will here be made to find an answer to the most important questions relating to the subject as a whole, and everything purely biographical will be reduced within the narrowest limits.

Since the persecution of catholics and the catholic mission in the time of Queen Elizabeth appear inseparably bound up together, the first question is, was there a causal connection between them ? If so, which of the two is cause and which effect ? This naturally leads up to a preliminary question, when did the persecution begin and when the mission ? Or, more exactly, when were they both reduced to a system ?

Granting there is a relation of cause and effect between the persecution and the mission, then a further question— the most important of all—presents itself ; one might almost say it is *the* question of the whole history of the persecution of catholics and the catholic mission in Elizabeth's reign — was the persecution political or

(London, 1891); DOM BEDE CAMM, O.S.B., *Lives of the Engl. Martyrs declared Blessed by Leo XIII.*, Vol. II. ; *Martyrs under Elizabeth*, Introd. by J. H. POLLEN (London, 1905) ; J. H. POLLEN, *Unpublished Documents relating to the Engl. Martyrs*, Vol. I., 1584–1603. Cath. Record Soc., V. (1908). *Lives of the English Martyrs*, 2nd series, Vol. I., 1583–88, ed. J. H. POLLEN, S.J., and E. H. BUXTON, D.D. (London, 1914).

religious, and did the mission aim at religious or political ends ? Although a plain answer to this important question may not be forthcoming, still it is worth while to see how near we can approach to a satisfactory solution.

I. *The Beginnings of the Persecution and Mission* (*before* 1580)

According to the catholic tradition, the persecution dates from the re-establishment of the anglican state church, the deprivation of the bishops, and the imprisonment of those catholic bishops and priests who refused to take the oath of supremacy. But these measures aimed only at effecting the inevitable revolution in the personnel of the church. By *persecution*, the age of the reformation and counter-reformation meant something very different. The English legislation of 1559, and even of 1563, did not entail the persecution of catholics but only their exclusion from public offices and honours (pp. 21–49). According to the adage, *cujus regio ejus religio*, the government aimed at bringing about religious unity by moderate means— moderate, that is, in the sense of the period.

There were, indeed, a few signs which seemed to imply the contrary. The secret celebration of, and attendance at, mass was usually passed over in silence, yet from time to time, as in June, 1561, a number of catholics, chiefly persons of position, were suddenly thrown into prison on no other charge than that of having been present at mass.[1] The explanation of this is to be found in the political situation, for it happened just in the weeks immediately following the refusal to allow the papal nuncio to land in England (p. 44). The long-cherished hopes of English catholics had suddenly been dashed to

---

[1] Dispatches of the Spanish ambassador Quadra, *Coleccion de documentos inéditos*, t. 87, pp. 358-359. SPAN. CAL., 1558-67, pp. 206, 208.

the ground and the glove had been thrown down to the
pope and council. The authorities dreaded what might
ensue at home and in Rome or Trent. Hence the government's nervousness and restlesness, hence the preventative
measures against real or imaginary dangers. A government conscious of its own strength and safety does not
persecute. It was always the feeling of insecurity either
at home or abroad, and the consciousness of England's
isolation in European politics,[1] that stirred up the government in the first ten years of Elizabeth's reign to make sure
more than once of its catholic subjects. But a deliberately
planned persecution, or, still more, a persecution solely on
religious grounds, is not to be thought of at this period.

But only towards 1570, when Scottish affairs reached a
critical stage, when Mary Stuart, Elizabeth's heiress and
rival, took refuge on English soil, and when the feudal
rising in the north threatened alike Elizabeth's throne
and England's state church, then evil times for catholics
began in earnest. What had been up to that time merely
a precautionary measure, due to the need for ensuring
the safety of the nation, now gradually assumed the
character of a systematic policy. This change took place
about the end of 1567. Domiciliary visits now became
more inquisitorial than ever in all the houses in London,
and returns were made of the religion and church attendance of their inmates. Catholics who heard mass at the
Spanish embassy were summoned and asked to take the
oath of supremacy.[2] The priests Harding and Sanders,

---

[1] This was expressly admitted in Feb., 1563, as a reason for fresh
measures against catholics. Cf. Cecil's speech in Parliament reported
by Quadra, Col. de doc. inéd., t. 87, p. 481. SPAN. CAL., 1558–67,
p. 303.
[2] The ambassador Guzman de Silva to Philip II., Dec., 1567,
Col. de doc. inéd., t. 89, p. 564 ; t. 90, p. 3. SPAN. CAL., 1558–67,
pp. 686, 687.

who had been provided with episcopal faculties for reconciling converts, were accused, as "trumpettes of treason," [1] of undermining the allegiance due to the queen, and of making their proselytes the creatures of a foreign power, the pope, the queen's deadly enemy, because they laboured to bring back their country to the Roman church. So even then, three years before Elizabeth's excommunication, the logical conclusion drawn from the idea of a national church was that conversion to a foreign church meant treason. Next year (1568) imprisonment for attendance at mass increased in frequency [2] and was carried to such lengths that it encroached even on the privileges of the ambassadors of foreign powers. [3] The rising of 1569 rendered the situation still more acute. The prisons were filled with catholics, [4] and when, the year following, the bull of excommunication arrived from Rome, the feeling of insecurity, which always accompanies a fight against a hidden foe, reached its climax. In the first weeks or months after the excommunication had become known, all the English ports were so narrowly watched that English catholics in the Low Countries were cut off for a considerable time from all communication with their home. [5] A

---

[1] See the broadside, *A bull graunted by the Pope to Doctor Harding and others, by reconcilement and assoyling of English Papistes to undermyne faith and allegeance to the Quene* (1567). Arch. Vat., Miscell. Arm. II., t. 67, fol. 258.

[2] Dispatches of the Spanish ambassador for March and October, 1568. *Doc. inéd.*, t. 90, pp. 32 *et seq.*, 39, 148. SPAN. CAL., 1568–79, pp. 12, 16, 80.

[3] DOMESTIC CAL., 1547–80, p. 321. *Doc. inéd.*, t. 90, p. 148. SPAN. CAL., 1568–79, p. 80.

[4] "[Cecil] casi tiene todas las carceles llenas," the ambassador Don Guerau de Spes to Alva, Feb. 29, 1569. *Doc. inéd.*, t. 90, p. 191. "Las carceles están llenas dellos [catolicos]," May 9, *l.c.*, 232. "A las catolicos perseguen agora más fieramente que nunca," May 23, *l.c.*, 239. *Cf.* SPAN. CAL., 1568–79, pp. 111, 148, 154.

[5] ". . . Nec aliquid ex Anglia propter aditus interclusos recipere

plausible excuse was now given for framing fresh and
essentially harsher laws against catholics.[1]

In these critical years originated the first measure of
self-preservation taken by English catholics—the foundation of the Douay seminary (1568, p. 94). No counter-
move was made immediately by the English government,
but when Rome issued her declaration of war—Elizabeth's
excommunication—then England too declared war, and
declared it, not only against those who accepted papal
bulls, but at the same time against all and sundry who
had fled over seas, the exiles and founders of seminaries.
The inward breach between England and her catholic sons
on the continent, which was already complete, was now
(1571) outwardly sanctioned and made lasting by law.
Even then, as in the preceding years, storm and calm
succeeded one another in the fortunes of English catholics.
The laws against them were never so uniformly enforced as
other laws of the country, but ever remained as a weapon
that the state could take up and lay down at pleasure.
The weapon, however, was always ready to hand, and, as
years passed, was brandished more and more threateningly
over the heads of catholics. For, after 1570, the English
government took a different view of its catholic subjects
than heretofore. Between 1560 and 1570 it treated them
harshly and suppressed their freedom of worship only
when the political horizon was overcast. Now, when the
Roman see had excommunicated the queen and declared
her unfit to rule, the exercise of Roman catholic worship,
even in times of peace, was considered a sufficient warrant

---

possunt." Francis Englefield to Card. Morone, Louvain, May 26,
1570. Arch. Vat., Arm. LXIV., t. 28, fol. 58.

[1] *Vid. ante*, p. 89. Lord Bacon marks the year 1571 as the date
when harsher measures were adopted against the catholics. *In
felicem memoriam Elizabethæ*, Bacon's Works, ed. SPEDDING, etc.,
Vol. VI. (London, 1858), p. 298.

for suspicion and persecution against its adherents.   Well
aware that they were about to incur the reproach of per-
secuting for the cause of religion, the government put out a
remarkable document a few months after the publication
of the bull of excommunication ; [1] "the queen would not
have any of their consciences unnecessarily sifted, to know
what affection they had to the old religion," and if she has
lately done so in the case of a few prisoners, "yet the cause
thereof hath grown merely of themselves, in that they have
first manifestly broken the laws established for religion, in
not coming at all to the church."   The first clause repels
the accusation of oppressing people for their faith, which
is just what the second clause admits.   Consciences are
free *when they are anglican !*

The state never deviated from the path on which it now
entered, but each new law marked an advance in its campaign against the church which had declared war against
it.   The English government merely drew the conclusion
which, however logical, was not always justified in fact,
that every one who accepted the bull on religious grounds
was henceforth to be eyed with suspicion because of his
religion.   Accordingly the next outbreak of persecution
fell upon English catholics as soon as Douay seminary
sent its first missionaries into the country (1574),[2] but
the worst storm that had hitherto burst on the adherents
of the Roman catholic faith broke out some years later in
consequence of the Jesuit mission (1580).

So far the chief points in the march of events are clear.
The persecution of catholics under Elizabeth preceded the
catholic mission in England.   The persecution, which was

[1] Decree of the Star Chamber of June 15, 1570.   J. STRYPE,
Annals of the Reformation, I., ii. (Oxford, 1824), p. 371.
[2] SPAN. CAL., 1568–79, p. 477.   STRYPE, *l.c.*, II., i., pp. 497
et seq.

not due to religious fanaticism but to political expediency, became systematized—still for political reasons—after 1569. From the year of Elizabeth's excommunication, the political character of the persecution became so inextricably bound up with the religious that the profession of catholicism came to be regarded as in itself dangerous to the state. And so the catholic mission, the necessity of which had been brought home to the church by the persecution, now, in its turn, added fresh fuel to the persecution.

In order to describe the further progress of events as a whole, especially the persecution, it will be useful first of all to take a general view of the development of the mission during the period with which we have just been dealing.

Catholic worship never completely died out in protestant England. From all the dioceses, and not from those in the north alone, came complaints from the anglican bishops in the early years of Elizabeth's reign about the way the mass priests, survivors from the days of Mary the Catholic, continued to perform their administrations in secret. "Popishe and peruerse priestes which, misliking religion haue forsaken the ministerie yet liue in corners, are kept in gentillemen's houses, and had in greate estimacion with the people."[1] Just as the bishop of Worcester complained of these priests who remained in hiding, so too the bishop of Salisbury desired active measures should be taken against "the stragling doctors and priestes who haue libertie to stay at their pleasures within this realme [& who] do much hurte secretlye & in corners."[2]

---

[1] M. BATESON, *Original Letters from the Bishops to the Privy Council*, 1564, Camd. Soc. Miscell., IX. (1895), p. 3. *Cf.* also the quotations above, p. 66, note 2.

[2] BATESON, *op. cit.*, p. 34. For other dioceses, *cf.* pp. 19, 67 *et passim.*

K

Even in London itself, the headquarters of the protestant propaganda, mass was still said secretly here and there.[1]

But the activity of priests, whether shut up in hiding places or wandering about the country, could not supply the want of a properly constituted ministry, and although their secret labours, like every kind of secrecy in an antagonist, may have seemed dangerous from time to time, nevertheless, as a matter of fact, English catholicism received hardly any support from these last survivors of the ancient priesthood.   It has been shown above (pp. 66–73) how, between 1560 and 1570, English catholics fell into the habit of attending protestant churches, partly through coming to a compromise with their conscience caused by a sense of their isolation, the absence of all spiritual ministrations, and the compliant attitude of some of their own priests ; partly, too, from the desire to hear their mother tongue employed in the service of the church.   A truly catholic propaganda, a " mission " as the church calls it, could only be set on foot in England after the foundation of the seminaries on the continent.   It is true that before this, the founder of the Society of Jesus, St. Ignatius Loyola himself, had formed the plan shortly before his death of including England in the sphere of his missions,[2] and the earliest forerunner of the Jesuit mission, Fr. Edmund Hay, had already appeared on English soil in the winter 1565–66, i.e. twelve years before the founding of the first seminary.   But although "in many places the catholic trumpet long since silenced was blown once more by him,"[3] this solitary effort produced no important or lasting

[1] J. G. NICHOLS, *The Diary of Henry Machyn*, Camd. Soc. (1848), pp. 291 *et seq.*
[2] F. SACCHINUS, *Historiæ Societatis Jesu*, pars. iv. (Romæ, 1652), lib. viii., § 83.
[3] *Op. cit.*, pars. iii., lib. iii., § 170.

results. The prevailing idea that the success of the mission coincided with the organized descent of the Jesuits on England (1580) is on the whole the true one, and only needs to be reduced to its actual limits. Without doubt, the commencement of the Jesuit mission was the crucial moment in the history of English catholicism under Elizabeth, but it may be questioned if its success would have been possible had not two other events prepared the ground for it.

The first of these was the publication of the bull of excommunication in 1570. Great as was its failure politically and its inability to compass Elizabeth's deposition, still it was not without effect that Rome had at last spoken after ten years of silence and inaction. After a period in which politics, and politics alone, had prevented both the church's Spiritual Head and Temporal Arm from doing anything for the abandoned outposts on the distant island, English catholics once more began to feel they were the sons of the universal church. From Lancashire came the news that owing to the bull people were withdrawing themselves from anglican worship. In York, Grindal, the new archbishop, found the ancient fasts and festivals observed.[1] The bull was the first step in recalling catholics from an attitude of half-hearted opposition, and even of friendliness, towards the protestant state church,[2] to the observance of the ancient catholic forms, and to the rejection of all compromise in matters of faith and worship.

The second event which prepared the way for the Jesuit mission was the foundation of Douay seminary (1568), which, indeed, as we have said (p. 94), was originally concerned with mission work only as a secondary consideration, but having begun in the sixth year of its existence to

---

[1] FROUDE, *Hist. of Engl.*, Vol. IX., p. 340.
[2] *Cf.* what was said above, pp. 68 *et seq.*

devote itself to missions, it soon came to regard them as its primary end and object. The work began on a small scale. In 1574, Douay sent four priests into England ; next year, seven ; in the third year, eighteen ; in the fourth year, fifteen,[1] etc. "So great is the eagerness of all to return to England that the time of their preparation seems endless to them."[2] In 1580, when the Jesuits started their mission from Rome, the Douay missionaries already numbered a hundred.[3] The reports of these priests, no less deserving of credit than the later reports of the Jesuits, speak of their labours as fruitful in results. There was so much work to do for souls that it was beyond the strength of the little band. All England, they wrote with conscious pride, resounds with praises of the Douay priests.[4]

When they assure us that the number of catholics steadily increased at this time, an assertion they never wearied of reiterating even later, this can only be understood in the sense that those who were not yet altogether lost to the Roman catholic church no longer halted between two opinions, but took a definite side, and not in the sense of extensive mission work among protestants, although a few actual conversions may occasionally have been made. Since the number of English catholics during the hundred years of persecution nearly kept pace with the increase of population, *i.e.* increased relatively, not absolutely,[5] we

[1] KNOX, *Douay Diaries*, pp. 24 *et seq.*

[2] *Alcune cose . . . parte dalle lettere annali del Seminario Inglese . . . in Fiandra per l'anno* 1578, *parte da lettere private di là,* Arch. Vat., Miscell. Arm. XI., t. 94, fol. 190. *Cf.* the Latin translation, published by Pollen in Cath. Record Soc. Misc., II., pp. 67, 69.

[3] KNOX, *Douay Diaries*, p. 27. The Jesuits at a later date questioned the truth of this, but the seculars were well able to prove it, "That theare were a hundred, I can shewe out of the register of the yeares they went in and of their names." HUMPHRY ELY, *Certain briefe notes, etc.*, Paris (1603), preface, p. 29.

[4] KNOX, *op. cit.,* pp. 98, 107.

[5] See sect. iv. above for the proof of this statement.

must not seek for the success of the mission in striking statistics of converts, but in the changed attitude of catholics towards the anglican church.

A correspondence between Mark and John Tippet,[1] father and son, in 1578, plainly shows the state of affairs among English catholics at that time, and the bitter suffering that had to be faced. John Tippet had been for a long time a student at Douay college, and so may be taken as an example of its spirit. The protestant father disowned his catholic son who had disgraced him by being whipped through the town as a criminal and branded with a red-hot iron. For the last time he asks the renegade if he is to be to him a father or a stranger. The son replied with all the faith and assurance of a martyr, that since his sufferings have strengthened him he is beyond the reach of doubt : he can obey no earthly powers, not even his father according to the flesh, but only " the call of God and Holy Church." [2]

The erection of a strong barrier between catholicism and protestantism—this was the mission's work, a work of enduring character and the most important that could be done for Rome in England at that time. As long as the sacrifice of the mass and the protestant communion did not mutually exclude one another (p. 69), as long as the dividing line between the two religions was being gradually obliterated, conversions were of little value—like acquisitions of territory without frontier defences. This achievement, the spread of a temper which rejected all compromise and concession, was not started by the Jesuits in the first instance, but by their predecessors, the priests from Douay.

---

[1] The name is written variously Tippet (Typpet, Tipett), or Tipper (Typer).

[2] PERSONS, *Domesticall Difficulties*, ed. POLLEN, Cath. Record Soc Misc., II. (1906), pp. 71-73.

The Jesuits, however, attained this result with greater zeal and success than any of the other missionary bodies at work in England. They were able to set to work with an authority quite different from that of the secular priests from Douay—*they* came from Rome, and *their* seminary was no private venture but a papal foundation. The grant of papal support to Douay and the mere resolve of the pope to found the college in Rome had already made a deep impression on English catholics.[1] A large number of youths pressed forward into the ecclesiastical state, and "catholics fulfilled their religious duties more courageously than heretofore." We hear of one who had two high masses celebrated daily, "as if he were in Rome, and not in England,"[2] and of similar examples of reckless courage in confessing the faith. A new era was dawning for English catholicism, an era of uncompromising hostility to protestantism and of unflinching steadfastness in the face of every kind of oppression and persecution.

The progress of the catholic mission, which we have just described, ran parallel to that of the persecution inflicted on catholics. The mission was later than the persecution, but they reacted on each other as aggravating forces, both were at once cause and effect.

The question then presents itself, what was the inner cause of this interaction, a question already keenly debated by contemporaries. Were the emissaries from Rome merely preachers of the word busied solely with the cure of souls and the spread of catholicism, as they themselves declared, or were they, as their opponents averred, spies and agitators, forerunners of the armada and conspirators against the life of Queen Elizabeth—in a word, executors of the bull

---

[1] This is shown in the document, *Alcune cose, etc.*, mentioned above, p. 132, note 2.

[2] *Ib.*, fol. 192 (= POLLEN, *l.c.*, pp. 68 *et seq.*).

of excommunication ?   It is only to put the same question
in other words, if we ask, was the persecution of priests and
catholic layfolk in England only a means of warding off
masked attacks on queen and country, as Burleigh and his
people assure us ?   Or was it the work of protestant
fanaticism springing from religious motives, as was the
complaint of the persecuted party ?

II. *Gregory XIII.: Interpretation of the Bull of Excommunication and the Instructions to the Jesuit Missionaries*

One of the most enlightened minds of the Elizabethan
age, Sir Philip Sidney, believed he had found the highest
political wisdom in the formula : religion and politics must
never be separated.[1]   It was the view of his time, and of
the next two generations at any rate—the period from
Philip II. to Gustavus Adolphus, or, if it is preferred, to
Oliver Cromwell.   The politics of the future took a
different turn, but in the Elizabethan age, religion and
politics were still so closely united that questions like those
dealt with above cannot be answered by a plain yes or no.

The catholic mission in England was undertaken just at
a time when the ecclesiastical and religious quarrel between
Rome and England was aggravated by political antagonism ;
to the question of conscience—might catholics be permitted
to attend anglican services ? (p. 68)—a second and more
pressing one was added after 1570—could Elizabeth be
acknowledged as rightful queen ?   By his bull, Pius V. had
placed English catholics in a desperate position between
conflicting duties.   Whoever acknowledged Elizabeth, or
even merely obeyed her laws and orders, was guilty of

---

[1] SIR FULKE GREVILLE'S *Life of Sir Philip Sidney* (1652.
Reprinted in the Tudor and Stuart Library, Oxford, 1907), p. 35.

disobedience to the pope, and, according to the letter of the bull, incurred excommunication. Obedience to the pope was high treason against the queen—the choice lay between faith and country.

It was only natural that many English catholics should not shrink from extricating themselves from such a conflict by devious paths. The legal flaws in the bull, excommunicating and deposing the queen at one and the same time, have already been noticed (pp. 78–82). Other flaws of a more technical character were soon alleged against the validity of its verdict. We have a memorial,[1] apparently from the pen of a canonist, dealing with these technical points with the object of meeting weak consciences halfway. The bull had not been published in the Campo de' Fiori in Rome as was the custom ; it had not been dispatched to England in an official way ; it was only a private individual who nailed it to the door of the bishop's palace. Other points are so sophistical as to strike us as mere quibbles—did the bull merely release men from their oaths and obedience, or did it require them in conscience to regard the queen as illegitimate ? Or take the following

---

[1] An undated and anonymous paper, apparently written between 1570 and 1580. *Ad consolationem et instructionem quorundam catholicorum in angustiis constitutorum quæstiones aliquot,* Arch. Vat., Arm. LXIV., t. 28, fol. 176–179, 171. A second copy in the Arch. Arcis S. Ang., Arm. XIV., caps. 2, No. 25. Printed by Bp. CREIGHTON from an imperfect transcript in the Publ. Record Office, in his article on *The Excommunication of Q. Eliz.* in the Engl. Hist. Review, Vol. VII., pp. 84-88. I add here the conclusion which is wanting in Creighton : " Ad 16.ᵃᵐ Non expedit pontificem dispensare in universum, sed ex causa necessitatis et vitæ, licet carnes comedere, nisi id fieret in professionem [so far Creighton] hæreseos et in detestationem catholicæ veritatis.—Ad 17.ᵃᵐ Respondetur ut paulo ante.—Ad 18.ᵃᵐ Cum nulla subest caussa, quamobrem aliquis se conferat ad cætus hæreticorum, vix excusari poterit a temeritate et merito reprehendus erit.—Ad 19.ᵃᵐ Secluso omni scandalo licet."—For a criticism on this Article, see below, p. 139.

syllogism : by the bull the pope intended to benefit English catholics, but the result has fallen out very much to their hurt ; this was not what the pope intended ;[1] therefore the bull is invalid. In all this theorizing we see the desire of English catholics to remain loyal subjects of the queen at least in civil matters. A mission which aimed at making this impossible would have had no chance of success with them.

No sooner had the bull been issued than the need of doing something to relieve English catholics in this conflict between church and state became evident at Rome. Cardinal Gesualdi, with whom the Jesuit Campion discussed the matter soon after 1570, expressed the hope that the bull might be " mitigated in such sort as the catholics should acknowledge Her Highness as their queen without danger of excommunication."[2] The difficulty of any " mitigation " of this kind lay in its formal wording. The purport of the bull was too plain to allow of its being interpreted in the interests of compromise. Pius V., therefore, ignored the question, and so at first did his successor, Gregory XIII. (1572–85). The new pope had the reputation of being especially well disposed to the English people ;[3] still he could not undo his predecessor's fateful act. To answer the question as to the lawfulness of loyalty in civil affairs simply in the affirmative would have been equivalent to withdrawing the bull. Such a confession of weakness and error would have had a most disastrous effect on the papal authority in England and elsewhere. And so the only course to take was quietly to allow English catholics to disregard the bull.

[1] " Quod non fuit ex mente legislatoris, ad quam oportet semper respicere."

[2] R. SIMPSON, *Edmund Campion, A biography* (new ed., London, 1896), pp. 75, 141, 410.

[3] Fr. SACCHINUS, *Hist. Soc. Jesu*, pars. iv., lib. vii., § 15.

But even this tacit toleration had to be communicated to the mission priests through some authoritative channel in order to enable them to relieve distressed consciences. This necessity was the cause of that momentous explanation which Persons and Campion, the two first Jesuit missionaries, asked and obtained from Gregory XIII. in April, 1580, before starting on their journey to England—"the bull always binds Elizabeth and the heretics, but, while things remain as they are, in no way binds the catholics, except when public execution of the said bull shall become possible."[1]   In other words, Elizabeth and her heretical subjects are visited with all the consequences of excommunication, while catholics, on the other hand, may remain loyal to the queen, without falling under the bann, until the sentence of deposition contained in the bull finds some one to carry it into effect.   The sentence itself was not revoked, but its execution was delayed.   The explanation was not a declaration of peace, but only a truce—for an indefinite period.[2]

It was this indefiniteness, this merely temporary recognition of Elizabeth, which brought suspicion upon the papal explanation.   A document of this nature, if ever it fell into the enemies' hands, could not fail to be a deadly weapon against its authors.   No booty came more welcome to Burleigh than this piece of paper.   From henceforth every one seized on it as evidence of Rome's double-dealing, and of treasonable intentions in the mission priests.   Ever since

[1] Contained in the faculties given to Persons and Campion. Appendix XVII. [§ 11].   *Cf.* CAMDEN, *Annales. rer. Angl.* (1625), pp. 316 *et seq.*   AUG. THEINER, *Annal. Eccles.*, III., p. 215. DOMESTIC CAL., 1547–80, p. 651.

[2] The untenableness of the Gregorian interpretation of the bull from the canonical point of view is plain, and I have not discovered that any one has tried to bring it into conformity with canon law. The only resource is to fall back upon the principle that the pope is superior to canon law.

Lord Burleigh, in 1583,[1] published these few lines in order to justify before the world his war of extermination against priests, the protestant historians of England, with few exceptions up to the present day, have re-echoed the verdict of " Guilty," which once upon a time English judges pronounced against those who promulgated Pope Gregory's explanation. " The poison of asps was under the lips of the bearers of such a message of treachery. It could not be communicated, as Burleigh fairly argued, without implied treason. No plea of conscience could alter the nature of things."[2]   Another historian, Bishop Creighton, writes in the same strain, and his verdict will suffice for the rest.[3]   "The object of the papal court was to allow the English Romanists to obtain all the advantages of seeming to be loyal to Elizabeth while at the same time they were to put her to death if possible, and to rise against her if there were a reasonable chance of success. It is small wonder that the English government waged war against those who were charged with the dissemination of such teaching ! "

These criticisms of Gregory's explanation of the bull, and others of a similar character, put an interpretation upon it which it does not bear on its face.   They assume that the bearers of this explanation, *i.e.* the mission priests, were entrusted at the same time with the task of fostering agitation against the English government, of conspiring

---

[1] In his pamphlet, *The execution of justice in England for maintenaunce of publique and Christian peace against certeine stirrers of sedition* . . . XVII., Dec., 1583.   Reprinted in Somers Tracts, 2nd ed., by W. SCOTT, Vol. I. (London, 1809), p. 197 ;   Harleian Miscellany, ed. THOS. PARK, II. (1809), p. 144.

[2] FROUDE, *Hist. of Engl.*, Vol. XI., p. 57 ; *cf.* p. 105 (the *viper* of Froude's rhetoric is transformed into a *rattle-snake !*)

[3] MANDELL CREIGHTON, *The Excommunication of Q. Eliz.*, Engl. Hist. Rev., VII., p. 82.   Similar opinions in STRYPE, *Annals of the Reformation*, III., i. (Oxford, 1824), p. 54.

against Elizabeth, or of encouraging people to attempt her life. Creighton tries to find proof for this assumption by bringing together the pope's *explanatio* and the memorial drawn up by a canonist cited above,[1] which laid stress on the distinction between internal and external obedience and contained many subtle answers for the quieting of the consciences of English catholics in all their perplexities. His conclusion is, that the pope, in an equally sophistical manner, desired to urge English catholics to external obedience and secret treachery towards Elizabeth. This conclusion might hold, supposing the document composed by the canonist was a decree of the curia. But this cannot be maintained. It begins : " It would seem expedient that it be declared by the authority of the pontif, etc."[2]   This is the language, not of a papal decree, but of suggestion. It is, therefore, impossible to maintain that this document gives us the key to Gregory's explanation.[3]   To judge from internal evidence, this important document was a private memorandum, a theological memorial prepared by some English catholics and submitted to Rome for authorization, but which, as far as the original tradition goes, never received the desired approbation. The judgment to be passed upon the defective morality of the document, until further evidence be forthcoming, only concerns the unknown theologian who wrote it.

Other interpreters of Pope Gregory's explanation[4] have pointed out that at the very time the pope was sending

---

[1] P. 136, note 1.

[2] The original (see above p. 136, note 1), runs : " Principio *videretur* [not *videtur*, as Creighton prints it], expedire declarari auctoritate pontificis . . . "

[3] CREIGHTON, " The document shows the meaning of Gregory XIII.'s rescript," *l.c.* Engl. Hist. Rev., II., p. 82.

[4] Especially FROUDE, *op. cit.*, Vol. XI., p. 55, note (against SIMPSON, *op. cit.*, p. 144).   *Cf.* J. H. POLLEN, *The Irish Expedition of* 1579, The Month, Jan., 1903, pp. 69–85.

missionaries into England he was giving practical aid to the Irish insurrection and bestowing upon it almost the sanctity of a crusade. But his action affords no proof against the mission, but only a ground of suspicion—a suspicion, indeed, which justified to some extent the English government in the measures which it took. In a period when conspiracy and assassination were common in politics, the thought could not fail to present itself that the seminary priests were simply the papal agents of the Irish rebellion in disguise, waging open war on the one hand and spreading treachery in secret on the other.[1] Yet nowhere did the papal enterprise in Ireland meet with a more unfavourable judgment than among the missionaries who foresaw only too clearly the consequences it would bring upon themselves![2] That the two undertakings coincided in time is really no ground for assuming that the mission was meant to be a political movement for stirring up opposition to the queen under the cloak of ministering to souls.

The real significance of this *explanatio* given to the Jesuits and of the spirit in which they were intended to carry it out—whether they were to act as conspirators, or as pastors of souls—can be logically drawn from one source alone. The right of expounding the bull according to this two-edged formula was part of the spiritual *faculties* granted to the Jesuits—Persons, Campion, and their successors. These spiritual powers or faculties committed to the papal emissaries were supplemented by certain directions for their exercise, *i.e.* the *Instructions*. Any one wishing to learn the real character of any nunciature or legation naturally

---

[1] " It was too much to expect that the pope should be understood to be acting in his temporal capacity in one case and in his spiritual capacity in another." M. CREIGHTON, *Queen Elizabeth* (London, 1899), p. 196.

[2] SIMPSON, *Edmund Campion* (1896), p. 146.

consults both these sources of information, and there is no reason why he should do otherwise when forming a judgment on the mission of the English Jesuits. The only difference is that the Jesuit missionaries received their faculties from the pope but their instructions from the general of their order—a purely technical distinction which in no wise affects their actual value. Now these instructions given to the Jesuits in 1580 contain the following paragraph :[1] "They must not mix themselves up with affairs of state, nor write to Rome about political matters, nor speak, nor allow others to speak in their presence, against the queen—except perhaps with those whose fidelity has been long and steadfast, and even then not without strong reasons." These are the decisive words. They contain a double prohibition, one absolute and the other conditional. The former forbade them to mix themselves up with politics as a rule. The missionaries were not to act as political agents, diplomatic go-betweens, spies, informers, etc. Obviously foreign politics and England's relation to other countries was meant in the first instance.[2] The conditional prohibition referred to attempts to stir up insurrections against the excommunicated sovereign. This prohibition is couched in terms suggestive of a very urgent recommendation to the greatest caution. No later than the next year (1581), however, in a new issue of the

---

[1] § 18 of the *Instructions*. See SIMPSON'S *Campion*, p. 140 ; POLLEN, *Politics of Engl. Catholics*, The Month, March, 1902, p. 293, gives an English translation. Fr. Pollen was kind enough to send me the Latin text of the MS. in the "Archives Gen. S.J." which he had used. This text runs : " Non se immisceant negotiis statuum neque huc scribant res novas ad status pertinentes, atque illic etiam neque ipsi sermonem injiciant aut ab aliis injectum admittant contra reginam nisi forte apud eos quos insigniter fideles et longo tempore probatos habuerint, at quidem tunc etiam none sine magna causa."

[2] I draw this conclusion from the employment of the plural— *statuum, status.*

Instructions, the recommendation was replaced by an unqualified prohibition—the words "except perhaps with those, etc.," were struck out.[1]

Although the grand object of the papal policy in those years—Elizabeth's overthrow—can be detected, as it were through a veil, in this document, still the idea of utilizing the mission as an *immediate* means of attaining this end, should opportunity offer, is merely touched upon in passing, and the whole tenor of the *Instructions* is animated by a totally different spirit.[2] The idea was soon rejected as out of harmony with the rest, and the mission was strictly confined to its own particular field of operations —the cure of souls. *Indirectly*, of course, the mission furthered the political aims of the pope. England, once reconciled to Rome, would not endure a sovereign excommunicated by Rome. Elizabeth's overthrow would have been the inevitable result of a successful catholic propaganda. In this sense, but in this sense alone, the mission was a political enterprise. It was neither meant to be a means of spying out the land preparatory to invasion, nor as an instrument of stirring up rebellion against the queen—especially after 1581.

Campion spoke the truth when he declared to his judges, "My charge is, of free cost to preach the gospel, to minister the sacraments, to instruct the simple, to reform sinners, to confute errors, and, in brief, to cry

---

[1] POLLEN, *l.c.*, p. 293, note 3. I have to thank Fr. Pollen for informing me of the exact year in which this clause was suppressed.

[2] The first paragraph of the *Instructions*, which lays down the principles to be followed, runs : " Finis huic missioni propositus est primum conservandi Christo propitio et promovendi in fide et religione nostra catholica omnes, qui in Anglia catholici inveniuntur, deinde ad eam reducendi quicunque ab ea vel inscitia vel aliorum impulsu aberrassent." The rest of the *Instructions* consists in the expansion of this programme. The bull of excommunication is not so much as mentioned.

alarm spiritual against foul vice and proud ignorance wherewith my dear countrymen are abused. I never had mind, and am straitly forbidden by our fathers that sent me, to deal in any respect with matters of state or policy of the realm, as those things which appertain not to my vocation, and from which I do gladly estrange and sequester my thoughts." [1]

And so, when immediately after Campion's execution, Pope Gregory's explanation of the bull fell into the hands of the English government, Lord Burleigh thought "the pseudo-martyr" was convicted of lying, and his office as executor of the bull was now made plain.[2] From what has been said above, it will be clear that Burleigh's conclusion, although mistaken, can be easily understood. Gregory's explanation only proved that the execution of the bull was to be desired, not that it was committed to the Jesuit missionaries. The missionaries' instructions merely confirmed and supplemented this statement. They contain no commission to execute the bull. In their original form, they permitted, under certain conditions, a prudent agitation against the excommunicate person ; in their final form, they are an absolute prohibition of any action that could be described as "an execution of the bull of excommunication."

[1] JOHN BRIDGEWATER, *Concertatio ecclesiæ catholicæ in Anglia* (Aug. Treviror, 1583), pp. 18 *et seq*. A copy of the rare first ed. of this work is in the Bibl. Vat., R. I., V., 925.

[2] "Therefore to make it plain that these two [Campion and Persons] by speciall authoritie had charge to execute the sentence of the bull, these actes in writing following shall make manifest, which are not fayned or imagined, but are the verie writings taken about one of their complyces, immediately after Campion's death, although Campion before his death woulde not be knowen of any such matter, whereby may appeare what trust is to be given to the words of such pseudo-martyrs." *Execution of Justice*, Somers Tracts I., pp. 196 *et seq*. Harleian Miscellany, II., p. 144.

III. *The Persecution at its Height*

The fact that the missionaries were not supposed to engage in politics is, however, no proof that they did not do so. The question arises, whether the missionaries kept to their instructions and confined themselves to their spiritual duties, or busied themselves in other matters besides as spies and political agents or as agitators and conspirators? The answer to this question determines the judgment we shall form of the persecution endured by these priests.

The founder of the mission, Cardinal Allen, defended his missionaries against this imputation in a fervent apology.[1] He compares the English priests from Rheims and Rome to missionaries sent out to the Indies. "For thither they go with no more danger than to England, and every way with like good will and hourly expectation of death. . . . They are sent to the heathen, to tell them 'there is no salvation without Christ'; they are sent to the English, to tell them 'there is no salvation without the catholic church.' Whether they die for the one, or for the other, all is one matter to them." [2] It was just the contrary idea that filled men's minds in England at the beginning of the Jesuit mission. "They are never done talking about the Jesuits here," a priest at that time wrote to Rome from England,[3] "and almost as many fables are told about them as about monsters formerly. But the principal thing is that like all other priests they

---

[1] [WILLIAM ALLEN] *An apologie and true declaration of the institution and endevors of the two English Colleges, the one in Rome, the other now resident in Rheimes* (Mounts in Henault, 1581).

[2] *Op. cit.*, fol. 82ᵛ.

[3] N. SANDERI, *De Origine ac Progressu Schismatis Anglicani libri tres* (1586), p. 446.

are held to have been sent by the pope as spies, traitors, and agitators."

These ideas were shared and fostered by the government. About the same time that Allen wrote his apology of the seminaries, a proclamation was issued by Queen Elizabeth.[1] The bishop of Rome has erected seminaries both in his own city and in other cities and countries, in order to draw away the queen's subjects into error. Thereby many have been estranged not only from the faith but also from their duty and fidelity to their country. Therefore the queen commands parents and guardians of children being educated on the continent to cause them to return to England within four months. At the end of this time, parents are forbidden to send any support whatsoever to their children abroad.

The proclamation had no effect. When it was renewed more than a year later, the blood of the first Jesuits had been shed in the mean time, passions were at fever heat, and the accusations against the missionaries were more violent than ever. Since the warnings of the previous proclamation had remained unheeded—as is stated in the second[2]—and even the execution of a few traitors[3] had not had a sufficiently deterrent effect, nay rather their innocence had been defended in seditious writings, the queen now declares that the Jesuits and seminary priests seek not only to overthrow religion and seduce subjects, but even to attack the throne and Her Majesty's life. All Jesuits and seminary priests are, therefore, herewith

---

[1] Jan. 10, 15⁸⁰₁. Proclamation recalling students from foreign seminaries. I give only a brief summary of the contents of this and following proclamations.

[2] April 1, 1582. Proclamation denouncing Jesuits as traitors.

[3] The Jesuits Campion and Briant and the secular priest Sherwin. *Cf.* CHALLONER, *Memoirs of Missionary Priests*, Vol. I. (ed. 1888), pp. 27, 38, 43.

pronounced traitors, and every one who shelters or helps them, accomplices of traitors. Whoever from henceforth goes overseas without leave, or does not return home from the seminaries across the water within three months, shall likewise be considered a traitor.

The legal term, treason, originally confined to a breach of fealty due to the sovereign, or an infringement of the royal prerogative, had received a manifold development in the conflict between the crown and the nobles. Since the time of Henry VIII. it was no longer unusual, in contrast to ancient and existing legal usage, to treat not merely *actions* but *opinions* as treasonable.[1] And so, when under Elizabeth it was regarded as treason to hold certain opinions, *e.g.* the unlawfulness of the royal supremacy over the church,[2] the legislature was not making a new departure but only carrying on King Henry's tradition. It was not the era of religious persecution but the absolutism of the crown which first called this new legal doctrine into existence. However, in the campaign against catholicism, it served as a most effective weapon.

Just in the first year of the Jesuit mission came into force the law which ushered in the period of severest persecution :[3] whoever withdrew the queen's subjects from their natural obedience or persuaded them to the Romish religion, for that intent, shall be adjudged guilty of high treason ; so, too, every one who shall allow himself to be "willingly absolved or withdrawn as aforesaid . . . shall suffer and forfeit as in cases of high treason." Heavy

---

[1] J. W. WILLIS-BUND, *A Selection of Cases from the State Trials*, Vol. I., Trials for Treason, 1327–1660 (Cambridge, 1879). Introduction.

[2] In so far as this opinion manifested itself by a refusal to take the oath of supremacy. *Vide ante*, p. 50.

[3] 23 Eliz. c. 1. An act to retain the Queen's Majesty's subjects in their due obedience.

fines were inflicted for saying or hearing mass [1] with a
year's imprisonment in addition. Every person above the
age of sixteen years who "shall not repair to [the anglican]
church" is to be fined £20 a month. In addition to the
unexampled severity of the law, the following points
deserve notice. A distinction was drawn between being
and becoming a catholic. The first was punishable by
fine and imprisonment, the second by death. It is true
the law refrains from plainly defining conversion to
catholicism as treason, it was rather conversion accompanied
by withdrawal of allegiance which was condemned.[2] But
since the publication of the bull of excommunication, it
followed logically, so long as Pope Gregory's explanation
was ignored, that every conversion to catholicism was held
to involve withdrawal of the allegiance due from a subject
to his sovereign, and, as a matter of fact, the history of the
trials for religion do not afford a single instance of a judge
distinguishing between conversion as a religious and as a
political act.[3] The wording of this enactment shows how
much importance the government laid upon avoiding the
charge of religious persecution, but it also shows with
pitiless clearness that any distinction between religion and
politics was no longer to be thought of after the publication
of the bull.

[1] 200 marks for celebrating mass ; 100 marks for assisting at mass.
A mark = 13s. 4d.

[2] The offence is defined as follows : "To absolve, persuade or
withdraw any of the Queen's Majesty's subjects . . . from their
natural obedience to her Majesty, or to withdraw them *for that
intent* from the religion now by her Highness's authority established
. . . to the Romish religion, or to move them . . . to promise any
obedience to any pretended authority of the see of Rome."

[3] One example may serve for many. "They asked him [James
Bell, a priest] whether he were reconciled [to the church of Rome] or
no. He answering that he was reconciled, ' *O that is hiegh treason,*'
say they." J. H. POLLEN, *Unpublished Documents rel. to the Engl.
Martyrs*, I. (1908), p. 77.

All subsequent laws against catholics and priests, laws of ever-increasing security, follow the same lines. All start with the assumption that catholics as such must be regarded as dangerous to the state. We will briefly summarize the chief points laid down in these later acts. The act of 1585 [1] orders all priests to leave the country within forty days, and condemns to death as traitors all who remain behind, as well as those who harbour them. All students at seminaries in the parts beyond the sea, who do not present themselves within six months before the justices of the peace in England in order to take the oath of supremacy, are declared traitors. All who support the seminaries or send their children "into any the parts beyond the seas . . . without the special licence of Her Majesty" are punished with heavy fines and imprisonment. Legislation against the catholic laity finally reached its height (1593) in a regulation which resembles the precautions taken against the plague-stricken. The act "against popish recusants" [2] orders that all persons over sixteen years of age shall betake themselves to "their place of usual dwelling and abode, and shall not at any time after pass or remove above five miles from thence." Special licence of the justices of the peace and the bishop was required each time a catholic had "to go and travel out of the compass of the said five miles." Disobedience to this was visited with forfeiture of goods for life. Whoever abjures his faith publicly in the church shall be free. Thus were catholics encircled by an iron wall that isolated them from intercourse with free men.

[1] 27 Eliz. c. 2. An act against Jesuits, seminary priests and such other like disobedient persons.

[2] 35 Eliz. c. 2. An act against popish recusants. The term *recusant* meant at first all those who refused to attend the protestant service, but in course of time became synonymous with Roman catholic.

While the provisions of this law show the unbounded mistrust with which the English government regarded everything Romish, the application of the law, as shown by the trials of priests and catholics, illustrates the extent to which this mistrust was justified. In these trials, no sign of guilt was likely to escape a pitiless opponent, and the ways in which the activity of the catholic missions menaced the safety of the state—whether their propaganda was political or religious—was sure to come to light.

Since, according to the prevailing legal doctrine, treason could be proved against a man either in consequence of his acts or of his opinions, the trials of catholics fall into two classes, those in which the attempt was made to prove treasonable *conduct*, and those which aimed at proving treasonable *opinions*. Naturally in many trials both the conduct and opinions of the accused were matter for inquiry, still the separate treatment of the two classes helps us in understanding the problem. It will not be necessary, then, to go into all the trials, inasmuch as a large number of them follow the same lines. The discussion of a few typical cases will suffice.

First, the trials in which the accused is charged with treasonable conduct. In the first period of the mission (1574–80), the chief danger to which priests were exposed arose from the act against the " bringing in of bulls, etc." [1] In 1577, printed copies of a papal bull of jubilee were found on Cuthbert Maine, a student of Douay seminary, and accordingly treason in the sense of the act was proved against him and he was put to death as a traitor.

The case was different when Edmund Campion, S.J., and several of his companions stood before the judge in 1581, for then they were charged with having plotted against the queen's life, the anglican church, and the English state.

[1] 13 Eliz. c. 2, *vid. ante*, p. 89.

It is remarkable that the government did not base its accusation on any of the penal laws, but on the ancient treason act passed in 1352.[1]   In this it is enacted that *treason shall be said if a man . . . be adherent to the king's enemies in his realm, giving to them aid and comfort in the realm or elsewhere.*   The government shrank from the odium of religious persecution, and Campion was to be made to appear guilty by the ancient law, which had not in the least contemplated religious controversy.   The endeavour to prove the plot failed completely, and was bound to fail, because there was no plot.[2]   The tactics were accordingly changed in the course of the trial, and the attempt was made to obtain indirect proofs of guilt by charging the accused with treasonable opinions.   This part of the trial, therefore, belongs to the second class of trials which we shall deal with later on.

In this attempt to convict Campion and his friends of conspiracy, measures were employed for the first time which only too soon became typical of the greater number of priests' trials.   Men were produced as witnesses against the priests who were renegades and had betrayed their co-religionists.   Campion protested against the witnesses as biased and of evil repute ; his protest was disregarded, and, moreover, in all cases where statement had to be weighed against statement, more credit was given to what the witnesses said than to the accused.[3]   It seemed as if

---

[1] 25 Edw. III. stat. 5, c. 2.   *Cf.* CAMDEN, *Annal. rer. Angl.* (1625), p. 347.   Prof. Pollard has drawn my attention to this fact in the *Göttingische gel. Anzeigen*, 1912, p. 174.   See also his *Hist. of Engl.*, 1547–1603, Vol. VI. of the Political Hist. of Engl. (London, 1910), pp. 376 *et seq.*

[2] I can only touch upon a few particulars, for the story of Campion's trial has been often told, and the injustice of the charge is now universally admitted.   The best detailed account is in SIMPSON'S *Campion*, ch. xv.

[3] SIMPSON, *l.c.*   WILLIS-BUND, I., pp. 236 *et seq.*

further evidence of guilt were waste of time when once the accused had confessed he was a priest and came from Rome or Rheims.   In one charge after another, Rome and Rheims were spoken of as hotbeds of conspiracy against England and Elizabeth in terms which admitted of no dispute.[1]   The fomenting of the Irish rebellion by Gregory XIII. (1579) was dearly paid for.   While the rebellion was still fresh in men's minds, many members of the juries may have felt justified in convicting even where guilt was not proved, and the majority of sentences of death were probably pronounced with an easy conscience.   Still, there are cases in which it is very hard to credit the judges with being in good faith.

While the study of most of the trials of this sort leads to the conviction that the mission priests charged with conspiracy must be acquitted, this conviction rarely rests on direct and conclusive evidence.   It is impossible to disprove a baseless assertion that a conspiracy was set on foot at a definite time and in a given place unless some fortuitous circumstance comes to light to prove the assertion false. In most cases the investigation must stop short in the impression which the trial leaves upon our mind as to the likelihood of the accusation and the amount of confidence we may feel disposed to give to the statements of the accused, or to the witnesses for the prosecution.   The favourable impression of the priests which in general is left on the mind is deepened and confirmed in several instances by the evidence of facts.   The priest James Fenn uttered these words of farewell under the gallows : " I am condemned for that I with Mr. Haddock at Rome did conspire and at which time Mr. Haddock was a

[1] J. H. POLLEN, *The Politics of Engl. Catholics*, The Month, June, 1902, pp. 614 *et seq*.   POLLEN, *Unpublished doc.*, I., *passim*.

student at Rome and I a prisoner in the Marshalsea, or at the least I am sure that I was in England, but to my remembrance I was a prisoner in the Marshalsea. Therefore, good people, judge you whether I am guilty of the fact or noe."[1] This statement was as capable of proof then as it is now.[2] In such a case, much as one desires to avoid rash judgment, it is impossible even for the most circumspect to describe the sentence as anything else than a judicial murder, due either to deliberation or unpardonable negligence.

Since such cases were not rare, and since the charges constantly brought against priests were either wholly improbable or plainly self-contradictory,[3] and since, moreover, the trade of false witness was gradually reduced to a system,[4] it becomes increasingly difficult to believe that these repeated judicial murders were due in all cases to negligence. The death sentences pronounced on these supposed conspirators constitute a heavy accusation against

[1] POLLEN, *Unpubl. doc.*, I., p. 62. For "at *Rome* did conspire," read *Rheims*. The charge was one of having conspired at Rheims, not in Rome. POLLEN, p. 55.

[2] See (1) *Diary of the Engl. College, Rome*, ed. FOLEY. *Records of the Engl. Province of the Soc. of Jesus*, VI., p. 74. (2) *Official Lists of Catholic Prisoners during the Reign of Q. Elizabeth*, ed. POLLEN, Cath. Record Soc. Misc., II., p. 231. Only this official list was known to the judges, but it was quite sufficient to prove the impossibility of the charge.

[3] As early as Campion's trial (1581), SIMPSON, p. 396. The case of the priest Thomas Ford (1582) is very similar to that of Fenn mentioned above. ALLEN, *A briefe Historie, etc.*, ed. POLLEN, pp. 57 *et seq. Cf.* the Latin adaptation by BRIDGEWATER, *Concertatio eccles. cathol. in Anglia* (1583), p. 249. The trial of Fenn is merely the most conspicuous of a group of fourteen trials of priests in Feb., 1584. POLLEN, *Unpubl. doc.*, I., pp. 51–62.

[4] See the examples in the *Concertatio* (ed. 1583), pp. 252, 256, 263–265. Further instances are given on pp. 312 *et seq.* of the *Apologia Martyrum*, a collection of stories of false witnesses, "homines profecto nullius religionis et omnis religionis, dolosi, impostores atque exploratores," p. 316. *Cf.* SIMPSON, pp. 439–441.

the administration of justice under Elizabeth. It may indeed be pleaded as an extenuating circumstance that trials of this kind, in which religion and politics were mingled, were something new and had no legal precedent in the past, while they differed from other political trials inasmuch as they appealed more strongly to the passions of all concerned and less directly to an impartial sense of justice. To this it must be added that nearly all the trials of catholics took place in London before jurymen drawn from a population deeply imbued with puritanism and strongly prejudiced against the catholic church—the ancestors of those who later on waged a war of extermination against every appearance of catholicism. Finally, we must not forget that a few priests, who did not, however, belong to the mission, actually did take part in plots against Elizabeth's life.[1] We are naturally inclined to form sweeping judgments when once our feelings are called into play, and are there not examples in political life when, even in times of peace, the action of a single individual is at once taken as typical of the whole party to which he belongs?

The few priests who brought such discredit on the mission were all men of a different stamp from the typical English mission priest. John Ballard,[2] the originator of the Babington Plot, lived a worldly life and never exercised his priestly functions. Anthony Tyrrell, who gave information of the plot, a spy in Burleigh's service, was utterly wanting

[1] I repeat what I have already said in the preface, *i.e.* a detailed description of the conspiracies against Elizabeth, which have been often told and to which an exaggerated importance has been attached, does not form part of my plan. In addition to the usual literature on the subject, I refer the reader to the fifth chapter—"Plots and Sham Plots"—of POLLEN'S *Politics of the Engl. Catholics*, The Month, June and July, 1902.

[2] For Ballard, Tyrrell, and Gifford, see also the articles in the *Dict. of Nat. Biog*.

in stability of character, the very opposite of the typical mission priest who was trained to unflinching steadfastness. He confessed and retracted and confessed again ; first catholic, then protestant, then catholic again, and yet again, once more protestant and catholic ! Such a man's story only proves that an institution like the English college in Rome had its failures as well as its successes. There was a strange nemesis in the turn of events by which men, in whose education spying had played so large a part (pp. 106–108), should now in turn be betrayed by spies in their own camp and by their former classmates.[1] The worst of these, Gilbert Gifford, who entered the employment of the English government as a spy even while a seminarist in Rome, was expelled both from the Roman college and the seminary at Rheims. A man like this, who received holy orders merely to betray his co-religionists, who plied his shameful trade, not because he was thrown off his balance, but for the sake of gain, whose life was a tissue of treachery and spying—such a man in truth brings no disgrace on the calling of a missionary, but rather on his paymasters.

Still it is easy to understand that the action of such men made the already detested priestly garb, which they wore or had worn in the past, so abhorred, that the self-sacrificing labours of hundreds could not restore it to honour. When once men had formed a mistaken idea of the character of the mission, and had grown accustomed to see plots on all sides with a priest everywhere behind them, it is unlikely they would pass impartial judgment, at a time, too, when they were being threatened with the Armada, religious fanatics were murdering princes, and political theorists were defending tyrannicide. But the amazing thing is that this false judgment, however justifiable three

[1] See below, p. 172, note 4.

hundred years ago, should have continued for so long to influence historians.[1]

The trials in which the object was to find the mission priests guilty of treasonable actions are less numerous than those which turned upon their treasonable opinions. While the modern sense of justice revolts against trials of this sort, we must remember, as we have already said (p. 147), that, according to English legal practice in the sixteenth century, *opinions* were chargeable with treason as well as *actions*. We must not be guilty of an anachronism in condemning too severely judicial proceedings of this kind, which at first sight appear to us unfair, but must remember that at that period men had the example of the Inquisition before their eyes. To probe and pass judgment on consciences was the Inquisition's task. Was it wrong, then, for the state to act in political matters as the church had acted for so long in spiritual matters? Had the English government confined itself on principle merely to propounding questions of conscience to the accused priests, and had it inquired into their political opinions alone, the catholic church could have found no fault with such a mode of procedure; she would have been met with weapons from her own armoury. The weak point in the legal proceedings against the mission priests lay in this, that Elizabeth's government adopted the Inquisition's methods without acknowledging its kinship with the Inquisition. Its motto was " Freedom of Conscience," and it acted in flagrant contradiction thereto rather than admit the opposite principle.[2]   This was a vulnerable spot in its

[1] J. R. GREEN, *Hist. of the English People*, II. (1878), p. 411 : " Fresh and more vigorous missionaries egged on the English catholics to revolt." FROUDE, XII., p. 152 : " The Jesuit mission of 1580 was the commencement of a new series of conspiracies."

[2] See the decree of the Star Chamber of 1570 mentioned above, p. 128.

armour easily detected by the enemy,[1] and this was the reason why the government vacillated between the procedure of the Inquisition and that of a criminal court, and circulated false reports of conspiracies.

The method of procedure in trials for treasonable opinions soon took systematic shape. The following questions were put to the accused :—

1. Did he acknowledge Elizabeth as his lawful queen ? Did he acknowledge her supremacy in all cases as well *spiritual* as temporal ?

2. Did he believe the pope could excommunicate and depose the queen ? This question often took the form, was Elizabeth's excommunication valid, or had Pius V. acted wrongly therein ?

After 1580, a third inquiry was often either added to these, or replaced the second—an inquiry never omitted after the Armada :—

3. In the event of a catholic invasion, which side would the accused take, the queen's or the pope's ?

Between 1570 and 1580 it was impossible for strict catholics to answer the first question in the affirmative, for, since the publication of Elizabeth's excommunication, she was lawful queen no longer. The question would either be answered in the negative—Elizabeth was illegitimate— which was proof that the accused held treasonable views, and so sentence of death would be pronounced in accordance with the law[2] ; or the accused might answer evasively[3] or decline to answer at all, which made matters

---

[1] This contradiction between the recognition of religious freedom in theory, and the force put upon conscience in practice is brought into prominence by Card. ALLEN, *Apologia pro sacerdotibus Societatis Jesu, etc.* (1583), ch. i. at the end.

[2] SPAN. CAL., 1568–79, p. 471.

[3] To the question if they recognized Elizabeth as their *lawful* queen, the answer was sometimes given that they recognized her as

worse, for then he lay open to the charge of insincerity.
A man like Walsingham, the secretary of state, did not
scruple in such cases to report that the accused flatly
refused to acknowledge the queen.[1]   After 1580, English
catholics were better able to face this question, for
Gregory XIII. had allowed them to acknowledge Elizabeth as their lawful queen (*pro tem.*), and most of them,
both priests and laymen, availed themselves of this permission.[2]   Still this did not essentially alter the situation,
for it was still impossible to give an affirmative answer
when asked if they acknowledged the queen's *spiritual*
supremacy.   Like all half measures, Pope Gregory's
explanation of the bull did more harm than good, and,
without being any real help to catholics, increased the belief
in Rome's duplicity.

The second question, concerning the pope's power to
excommunicate or the validity of Elizabeth's excommunication, was usually either answered evasively or not at
all.   Campion's explanation, when asked this question,
served as an example which others followed.   Campion
explained that it was a question of the schools which had
nothing to do with his trial.   He questioned the right of
his judges, as lay theologians, to bring such matters into
discussion.   Their business was to inquire into matters of
fact, not into opinions of the schools.   Even on the rack,
Campion did not move an inch from this position.[3]   Others
followed the example of a man whom they venerated so

queen.   *Col. de doc. inéd.*, t. 91, p. 73.   SPAN. CAL., 1568–79,
p. 488.

[1] Dispatch of the Spanish ambassador Mendoza of June, 1578.
Col. de doc. inéd., t. 91, p. 252.   SPAN. CAL., 1568–79, p. 595.

[2] ALLEN, *A briefe Historie, etc.*   *Cf.* the introd. to Pollen's ed.
(1908), p. xvii., for collected proofs ; also *Concertatio* (ed. 1583),
pp. 253, 257, etc., *passim ;* POLLEN, *Unpubl. doc.*, I., pp. 62, 86, etc.,
passim ; SIMPSON, pp. 418 *et seq.*

[3] SIMPSON'S *Campion* (ed. 1896), pp. 386, 418–420, 452.

highly as a spiritual guide.[1] Some either professed their
incompetence to deal with the point[2] or expressed a hope
that Pius V. had not erred in excommunicating the queen.[3]
Finally, some answered plainly yes, when asked if Elizabeth
had been rightly excommunicated.[4]

The two first interrogations were more legal and theological than political, and were more concerned with theory
than practice. They did not in any way prevent the condemned man from appearing before the world rather as a
martyr for religion than as an upholder of views dangerous
to the state. The case was different with the third question,
which, as "the bloody question,"[5] was more dreaded than
the others and brought the largest number of victims to
the gallows. The inquiry as to the part the accused would
take in the event of a catholic invasion followed simply
from the other questions as a conclusion from premises,
and as such it resolved itself into a religious question
affecting the conscience. But, since it was no longer a
mere theory that was in question, but its application to
practical politics, there was no denying that the third
question could be justified on political grounds. No
inquiry could be better chosen to prove to the public
mind that priests were dangerous to the state and bring
about their condemnation as conspirators. No question
put more strain upon a priest's moral courage than this
one, which, as the Jesuit Gerard said,[6] could not be

---

[1] SIMPSON, p. 426. ALLEN, *Briefe Hist.*, p. 35. POLLEN, *Unpubl.
doc.*, I., pp. 105 *et passim.*

[2] POLLEN, *l.c.*, pp. 85 *et seq.*

[3] *Ib.*, p. 290. [4] *Ib.*, p. 84.

[5] " Bloody," not in the sense of *accursed*, but in the sense of *mortal,
fatal.* Burleigh speaks of " any capital or bloody question." *Execution
of Justice*, Somers Tracts, I. (ed. 1809), p. 193.

[6] JOHN MORRIS, *The Life of Father John Gerard* (3rd ed., 1881),
p. 226. Gerard himself answered evasively that he would act as a true
catholic and true subject—just what he could *not* do !

answered without injury either to soul or body. A faithful son of the catholic church could only answer, "If the invasion was for no worldly object but solely for the restoration of the catholic religion, then I should take part with the invaders"—a reply which would certainly send him to the gallows.

That not every one had sufficient courage to give a plain answer to the question can easily be understood without assuming that he had been trained to disregard truth. It was not necessarily deceitfulness which led one man to answer somewhat as follows: "It is a future contingent and I know not what I should do," [1] and the evasive reply attributed to another, "I will pray that the catholic Romish church may prevail," [2] shows not so much duplicity as a shrinking from the painful avowal that he would be obliged to fight against his country. The refusal to give any answer at all may also have been due to the same motive, [3] for it could not spring from cowardice, since silence meant self-condemnation. It is very rare to find an answer which can really be charged with dishonesty. If one priest declared he would not take part *against* the papal army but, at the same time, refused to say whether he would take part *with* it, he showed a lack of intelligence and dignity. [4]

The cases in which the accused shrank from making a plain avowal are few in comparison to the overwhelming number where the statements are clear and precise.

These answers reveal two things. First: the traditional

[1] Answer of the priest Ingram in 1594. POLLEN, *Unpubl. doc.*, I., p. 243.

[2] Answer of the priest Edward Campion as the Armada was approaching, July, 1588. POLLEN, *op. cit.*, p. 160. Another example belonging to the same time, *l.c.*, p. 161.

[3] POLLEN, *op. cit.*, p. 162.

[4] *Ibid.*, *op. cit.*, p. 173 (July, 1589), also p. 163.

view which represents the Jesuits and other priests who
worked in England as being essentially untruthful, and
underhand, and hypocrites, is false—the truth being that
they were men who said what they thought in spite of the
gallows and the knife.   When it was a question of screen-
ing or saving a friend, it was allowed that a lie might
indeed be admissible and even justifiable, but no *reservatio
mentalis*, and no *æquivocatio* can be laid to the charge
of these men when contending for their faith and their
church—for the rights of the papacy.   Questions behind
which death lurked drew from them no lies.   One word
would have saved them, but that word never passed their
lips.   Secondly : the replies to "the bloody question"
show that the English government was driven by the
instinct of self-preservation to inquire into the opinions
which men held, and to adopt the methods of the Inquisition.   When a man frankly admits at a moment when war
is imminent that he would side with his country's foes,[1]
he cannot expect mercy.   And the greater the influence
he commands, or is supposed to command, the less chance
there is of his getting off.   Now in matters of conscience
no authority was more highly valued by English catholics
than that of their priests.   The very questions which the
judges put to the accused were also put to spiritual fathers
by their spiritual children.   "If the pope sends an army to
win back our country to the catholic church, are we to side
with the pope or the queen ?"[2]   A priest who never

---

[1] Examples in POLLEN, *op. cit.*, pp. 77, 86, 161, 171, 172, 218 *et passim*.
[2] That this question was asked is not merely probable but certain,
as appears from what the priest Wright (alias Dobson) says at the
beginning of his paper. *An licitum sit catholicis in Anglia arma
sumere et aliis modis reginam et regnum defendere contra Hispanos ?*
The author was one of the small number who in the conflict between
England and the combination of Rome and Spain was on the English
side. This paper is printed in English by STRYPE, *Annals of the
Reformation*, III., ii. (1824), pp. 583–597 (Appendix LXV.).

M

uttered a word on politics, or spoke against the heretical queen, might yet be called upon in the discharge of his priestly duties to direct consciences in regard to the chief political question of the hour—*to seduce* them, speaking from the standpoint of the English government. In the year after the defeat of the Armada, a hot-headed young priest, twenty-four years old, boldly declared before the judge, "that, if an army be sent into the realm, he will take part with that army and will persuade as many catholics as he can to do the like."[1] In the face of facts such as these it is impossible to speak of persecution from religious motives. While every priest was condemned to death who admitted he would side with his country's foes, mercy was shown to the small number who declared in favour of their country in its campaign against the church. They were not set at liberty, but their lives were spared.[2]

The trials for high treason, in which English mission priests were charged with treasonable conduct or opinions, in spite of seeming contradictions, bear a strong resemblance to each other. Whenever the judges condemned priests as conspirators and assassins, the verdicts, with a few exceptions, amounted to judicial murder. But when the labours of the priests, even of those who wished to keep clear altogether of politics, were held to be a danger to the state, the sentences were a political necessity as a measure of self-defence. Religion and politics were inseparable. The grave miscarriages of justice are due to the fact that the judicial authorities found themselves face to face with something new for which they had still to discover the formula. In the last analysis, it was not a question of law at all. To speak of *guilt* in connection

---

[1] POLLEN, *Unpubl. doc.*, I., pp. 171 *et seq.*

[2] See the list of imprisoned and examined priests in July, 1588, in POLLEN, *op. cit.*, pp. 154–156.

with these questions is quite to misunderstand them. The forces which came into conflict were so mighty—the mediæval catholic church and the modern state—that their upholders must either grind their opponents to powder or themselves be ground to powder. *Tragic* is the only word which describes a conflict such as this. All the victims, with few exceptions, showed themselves equal to the part they were condemned to play ; they faced torture without shrinking and knew how to die.

These trials for high treason are the most striking feature in the history of catholics under Elizabeth. But, in order to estimate correctly the part they played in the whole drama of the persecution, we must briefly go into the question of statistics.[1] In the first place we see that the priesthood suffered in overwhelming proportion. Of the catholic priests who came into England in Elizabeth's time, every second or third was put to death ; while of the catholic laity, only one in every two thousand suffered. The number of priests executed was more than twice as

---

[1] I rely chiefly on DODD-TIERNEY, *Church History of England*, Vol. III. (1840), pp. 161–170. His lists, though they require to be corrected and augmented in some particulars, still give, on the whole, the fairest and clearest idea of the facts. POLLEN, *Unpublished doc.*, I., pp. 1–7, compares the most important lists of martyrs. In the comparative numbers of priests and laymen given in the text, I have not included those who died in prison, since it would be impossible to estimate correctly in what proportion priests and laymen stood to each other among them. I estimate the whole number of priests who came to work in England as three or four hundred. THOS. BELL, *The Anatomie of Popish Tyrannie* (London, 1603), says in his preface, " As the Jesuits write, there are this day in England 300 priests. God eyther convert them speedily or confound them utterly ! Amen." This estimate drawn from Jesuit sources is in itself more probable than the vague estimates of between four and five hundred (KNOX, *Douay Diaries*, p. 33. DOMESTIC CAL., 1581–90, p. 161), for they do not pay sufficient regard to losses from death, etc. I estimate the total number of catholic laity under Elizabeth at 120,000, as I have said above, p. 62.

great as the number of laymen—130 to 60.   This fact has given rise to the idea that the English government attacked priests only, and left the laity in peace.[1]   It did, however, nothing of the sort.   Still, in spite of all the deeds of cruelty, it is to the credit both of the English people and Elizabeth's government that the history of the persecution affords no example of massacres such as we meet with in the Latin and Celtic nations of the period.   The characteristic which separates the religious persecution under Elizabeth from that which preceded it, or those which broke out in other countries, is the statesmanlike spirit which guided and controlled it.   During the five years Mary the Catholic reigned over England, more than three hundred protestants fell victims to religious fanaticism ; during Elizabeth's reign, which was nine times as long, scarcely two hundred and fifty, including those who died in prison, fell victims to the penal laws.[2]

It was due to this statesmanlike spirit that the various classes of opponents to the Elizabethan state church met with various kinds of treatment.   Catholics were treated differently from puritans and catholic priests from catholic laity.   The puritans,[3] who refused to conform to the state church, were banished ; they were dangerous at home but harmless abroad.   Among catholic priests we find some,

[1] In one of the most widely read English histories, it is definitely stated that " no layman was brought to the bar or to the block . . . the work of bloodshed was reserved wholly for priests." J. R. GREEN, *Hist. of the Engl. People*, II. (1878), pp. 415 *et seq.*   In the most recent edition this error is corrected.

[2] LORD BURLEIGH had already drawn attention to this contrast. *Execution of Justice*, Somers Tracts, I. (ed. 1809), p. 198.   Harleian Miscellany, ed. PARK, II. (1809), pp. 145 *et seq.*

[3] The difference in the treatment of catholics and puritans is most clearly shown in the law of 1593 (35 Eliz. c. 1 and c. 2).   On this point, see R. B. MERRIMAN, *The Treatment of the English Catholics in the Reign of Elizabeth*, American Hist. Rev., XIII. (1908), p. 482.

indeed, who were also banished.[1] Elizabeth herself would have preferred banishing them to putting them to death, but, since priests were held to be the most dangerous opponents, their trials usually ended in their execution. To avoid making too many martyrs, another measure was adopted in the second half of Elizabeth's reign with the intention of rendering priests harmless. Those who could afford to pay for their keep were isolated and put under restraint. Wisbeach Castle near the ancient Isle of Ely, the best known of these ecclesiastical prisons, has a strange history of its own. The strict watch kept over the priests at first, gradually became so much relaxed, that Wisbeach Castle finally became a sort of catholic seminary in the heart of England.[2]

The large mass of English catholics were mostly unaffected by these penal measures—death, banishment, imprisonment. Had the legal doctrine that a man could be put to death for his opinions as well as for his actions been systematically applied to the laity, as it was to the clergy, there would have been murders without end. There are, however, only a few instances of catholic laymen being executed solely for having questioned the legitimacy of the excommunicated queen [3] or having been to confession to a priest.[4] As a rule when laymen were condemned to death it was for having supported priests,[5] or kept them

---

[1] Vid. ante, p. 149, for the law of 1585, and cf. CAMDEN, Annal. rer. Anglic. (1625), p. 378.

[2] T. G. LAW, Conflicts between Jesuits and Seculars in the Reign of Q. Elizabeth (1889), Introd. xxxviii.-xliii.

[3] E.g. Thomas Sherwood in 1577. ALLEN, A briefe Hist. (ed. POLLEN, 1908), pp. 118 et seq. WILLIS-BUND, Vol. I., p. 229.

[4] E.g. Robert Sutton in 1588. POLLEN, Unpubl. doc., I., p. 291.

[5] For an especially hard case belonging to the time shortly after the Armada, see Richard Martine, a layeman executed only for being in the companye of Mr. Robert Morton, priest, and paying VId. for his supper. POLLEN, op. cit., p. 290.

in hiding,[1] or for having aided them to escape from prison.[2] The second measure of persecution, banishment, was also naturally restricted in its application. Banishment on a large scale would have been difficult to accomplish and questionable on political grounds, for Spain would have backed up the exiles, and so the danger of invasion would have been increased. Only very poor catholics whose imprisonment would be an expense to the state and who were harmless abroad were banished in 1593 in virtue of a provision of the act against recusants.[3] Imprisonment was by far the most frequent means of oppression adopted during the first period of persecution. At first catholics were confined in the same prison as thieves and other criminals.[4] This soon became impracticable. "The prisons are so full of catholics," it was said as early as 1583, "that there is no room for thieves."[5] It became obviously necessary to set aside special places for the imprisonment of catholics, both priests and laity. For a time the castle at Chester was used for this purpose, but as it was too near the sea-coast, it was judged unsuitable, and a new prison was provided in Manchester where catholics were isolated amidst good protestant surroundings.[6] Still even imprisonment could not be employed to an indefinite extent, and it became a cause of expense to the state or local community whenever prisoners could no longer pay for their own keep. An attempt indeed was made to force the local community to contribute towards the support of indigent prisoners,[7]

[1] *E.g.* Richard Langley in 1587 and Saunder Blake in 1590. POLLEN, *op. cit.*, pp. 134, 291.

[2] *E.g.* Margaret Ward and John Roche in 1588, *op. cit.*, p. 290.

[3] 35 Eliz. c. 2, § 5.   *Cf.* MERRIMAN'S remarks, *l.c.*, p. 483.

[4] Dispatch of the Spanish ambassador Mendoza of Oct. 1, 1581. SPAN. CAL., 1580–86, p. 177.

[5] *Concertatio Eccles. Cathol.* (ed. 1583), p. 104.

[6] J. STRYPE, *Annals of the Reformation*, III., i., p. 243.

[7] *Ib.*, p. 244.

but levies of this kind were not enjoined by the law,[1] and naturally yielded very little. Therefore, at last, the act of 1593 (p. 149) hit upon the cheapest and most comprehensive method of detention; catholics were restricted to a radius of five miles from their abode, and so all the catholics in England were kept in a sort of open confinement.

The economy which characterized all departments of Elizabeth's policy shows itself also in her treatment of catholics. Little disposed to waste the resources of the state in its campaign against the Roman church, the government sought rather to compel its opponents to defray all the expenses of the war. Fines were to be the chief means for oppressing catholicism. Already in the Act of Uniformity of 1559, the legislature had made the first tentative move in that direction—absence from church, without just cause, was punished by a fine of one shilling to be devoted to the poor (p. 22). After the beginning of the Jesuit mission, when the government was in search of sharper weapons, it had again recourse to the expedient of fines, and employed it to an excessive degree. The act of 1581 imposed a heavy fine for saying or hearing mass,[2] and, in addition to this, punished absence from the anglican service in a manner hitherto unheard of. It ordered[3] that any one over sixteen years of age who did not go to church should be fined £20 a month. So heavy a fine was altogether beyond the means of most men and could only be paid by a small minority without incurring financial ruin. Wherever a serious attempt was made to put the law into execution, it was shown to be impossible to exact the full penalty.[4] In the diocese of Chester "the sum total of all

[1] The communities were bound by law to pay for the relief of vagabonds and beggars only. 14 Eliz. c. 5, § 2.

[2] For particulars, see above, p. 148, note 1.

[3] 23 Eliz. c. 1, § 4.

[4] MERRIMAN, *l.c.*, pp. 486 *et seq.*

the fines imposed " in 1583 "came to £757 13s. 8d., whereof £40 13s. 0d. had been only received." [1] By orders in council, the legal penalty was reduced in a few years to a half, a third, or a quarter, according to the means of paying at the disposal of the condemned. [2]   A new act [3] soon ordained that if the payment of £20 cannot be exacted, the queen can seize upon the goods and chattels and two-thirds of the landed property instead. [4] But even in their milder form the laws were never enforced to their full extent, even when the persecution was at its height. [5] Nevertheless the amounts actually received bear speaking testimony both to the oppressive character of the laws and the readiness of catholics to make sacrifices for their faith.   In the last twenty years of Elizabeth's reign, the sum of £6000 was annually exacted from catholics for refusing to attend church, [6] i.e. a sum equal to £50,000 at least of modern currency.   Towards the close of the queen's reign, the collection of these fines was leased to an "undertaker," who naturally tried to make the best out of his enterprise, and this change in the system meant a change from bad to worse for the catholics. [7] Although, generally speaking,

---

[1] STRYPE, *Annals*, III., i. p. 246.

[2] Order of the Privy Council, Feb. 25, 1586. MERRIMAN, *l.c.*, p. 488.

[3] 29 Eliz. c. 6, § 4.

[4] For the way in which this law was put into execution, see MERRIMAN, *l.c.*, p. 490, note 27.

[5] *The Recusant Rolls* for 1593, a year of severe persecution, mention only about 1400 recusants, *i.e.* about 1 per cent. of the catholics. Pub. Record Office, *Recusant Rolls*, Exch. LTR, Pipe Series, No. 2. The working of the penal laws from a financial point of view has not been adequately investigated. *Cf.* what I say above, p. 59, note 1.

[6] F. A. GASQUET, O.S.B., *Hampshire Recusants*, a story of their troubles in the time of Elizabeth (London, 1895). Reprinted in the author's *Old English Bible and other Essays* (1897), pp. 355 *et seq.* and *cf.* MERRIMAN, *l.c.*, p. 491, note.

[7] R. G. USHER, *The Reconstruction of the English Church*, I. (New York, 1910), p. 120.

the burden was borne by the small number of wealthy catholics,[1] still the tax must have led in many cases to complete bankruptcy.[2] Catholics who were not among the first to suffer, lived in daily dread that it would soon be their turn, and felt no security in their possessions. Even in the first months after the act of 1581 had been set in motion, the Spanish ambassador had to tell of catholics whose moral courage was failing them under the strain.[3]

Even when catholics suffered neither fine nor imprisonment their lot was far from enviable. It was hard for them to be shut out from all public offices, and harder still to be banned by public opinion. Every catholic was suspected of being an enemy of his country and was treated accordingly. In every land the government had its confidential agents, officially or secretly, and sometimes mere private individuals, who kept continual watch over catholics.[4] The knowledge that they were thus perpetually watched is spoken of as being in itself most hard to bear. " If we converse openly, if we buy or sell, if we traffic in our necessary affairs, or take care of our own commodities, if we laugh, recreate ourselves, or carry any indifferent countenance, then are we either too wealthy, or else too well, to live : such prosperous fortune is not tolerable in men of our profession. . . . If we live in secret and delight ourselves to be solitary, if we cut off all access of our

---

[1] According to an example given by STRYPE, *Annals*, Vol. IV., No. CXXXII., the fines levied on only 137 recusants for six months amounted to £3323.

[2] *Cf.* STRYPE, *l.c.*, III., ii., p. 422. An anonymous letter written from London on Oct. 4, 1600, says, "Li cattolici sono persecutati nelli beni temporali più che mai, levandogli via quasi ogni cosa." Arch. Vat., Borgh. III., 124ᵉ, fol. 39ᵛ.

[3] SPAN. CAL., 1580-86, p. 177.

[4] Report of the Jesuit Richard Holtby to his superior Garnet, 1594. DODD-TIERNEY, *Church Hist.*, III., p. 78.

neighbours, or refuse to keep company with such as love us not, then do we busy our heads, in their conceit, to devise against them secret conspiracies ; and our leisure is a sufficient argument with them, that we occupy ourselves about no other matter, save only to stir and contrive seditious factions." [1] In one way or another they had all offended against the laws, either by hearing mass, or harbouring priests, or sending funds to seminaries, or sending their children to be educated on the continent. Any day they might fall into a trap set for them by avowed enemies or false friends. Indeed any one who showed little zeal for the state religion, who did not go regularly to church, and communicated infrequently ran the risk of being delated by an informer or any one who had a grudge against him.[2] The oppressiveness of this system of spying was most keenly felt in those cases where the church came into contact with family life. Marriages were celebrated in secret to avoid the protestant marriage service, and women about to become mothers hid themselves in places where no one could take their child away from them to receive the dreaded baptism of heretics.[3]

Even in the bosom of the family men did not feel safe, for they suspected that the government spies had their eyes everywhere. As early as 1564 the Spanish ambassador complained, " the evil lies in the universal distrust, for a father dares not trust his own son." [4] And this was before the government offered hard cash as the informer's reward and promised to protect him as well in the discharge of his calling.[5] Later on, both public and domestic life

[1] *Op. cit.*, p. 77.
[2] Cf. *D. Pye's Information of Popery in Sussex* (1596). STRYPE, *Annals of the Reformation*, IV. (1824), pp. 401–403.
[3] *Relatione del presente stato d'Inghilterra* (Roma, 1590), p. 8.
[4] *Col. de doc. inéd.*, t. 89, p. 50. SPAN. CAL., 1558–67, p. 389.
[5] 1571, see p. 90.

became more and more poisonously infected by the distrust
between the adherents of the legal and illegal religions.
Children and parents were set at variance, husband and
wife lost confidence in one another, one part of a family
was betrayed by the other, and the owner by his heir.[1]
The servants of catholic families were arrested and
examined about their masters.[2] No place, no man was
safe any longer from espionage, not even the prisoners in
prison. Men who enjoyed the full confidence of catholics
entered into an understanding with the government and
undertook to sound the prisoners under the guise of
friendly visits.[3]

There was no lack of the material from which spies are
made. The storm of persecution brought to the surface
a number of needy and disreputable characters. Many a
man was so tossed about by religious doubts that at
length he no longer knew where he was or which side
to take.[4] This confusion was increased by the internal
divisions within the catholic camp[5] which stirred up
enmities within the body as implacable as the hatred
between members of different religions, and produced
" wandering and lost lads, that otherwise might have
been honest and learned men, if this faction had not
been."[6] These were to be the material out of which
that past master of espionage, Walsingham, manu-
factured his best tools. This explains why so many
priests working in England were betrayed by "false

[1] From the letter of a catholic writer in 1592. DODD-TIERNEY,
III., p. 80, note.
[2] DOMESTIC CAL., 1581-90, p. 336.
[3] *Ib.*, pp. 36, 68, 336. DODD-TIERNEY, III., p. 78.
[4] *E.g.* Tyrrell, *vid. ante*, p. 154.
[5] More will be said about this in ch. iv.
[6] PERSONS, *Certayne aparent judgments of Almightye God*, ed.
POLLEN, Cath. Record Soc. Miscell., II. (1906), p. 209.

brethren."   No relationship was too sacred to escape violation—

> " I durst not trust my dearest frende,
>   Butt secretlie stole hence,
> To take ye fortune God shulde sende
>   And kepe my conseyence." [1]

Not alone in England were catholics surrounded by spies. On the continent also Walsingham kept a close watch over English catholics, saw that their letters were opened, noted their changes of abode, and even the inns they especially frequented.[2] The secretary of state merely followed the custom of his age and acted in nowise differently from the Spanish ambassador in London, who informed the Inquisitor-General of those Spaniards who fell into heresy in England, and kept a sharp look-out upon his fellow countrymen who went backwards and forwards between England and the Low Countries.[3] But it went beyond all the recognized limits of espionage when Walsingham's spies gained entrance into English seminaries, either as servants or as students, in order to collect evidence and work up material for accusations against the young recruits of the mission and their relations and friends at home.[4]

---

[1] From the ballad, *The Blessed Conscience*, written between 1580 and 1590. J. GILLOW, *The Haydock Papers* (London, 1888), p. 11. *Cf.* GILLOW's article in Cath. Record Soc. Miscell., III. (1906), p. 1.

[2] DOMESTIC CAL., 1581-90, p. 289. K. DE LETTENHOVE, VI., p. 658. LECHAT, *Réfugiés anglais, etc.* (1914), pp. 75 *et seq.*

[3] SPAN. CAL., 1558-67, pp. 353, 425.

[4] " Certe a prima huius collegii Romani origine ad hunc usque diem [1596] observatum est singulis septem annorum curriculis [*i.e.* during the seven years of their course as students in the college] aliquem sceleratum ibi latuisse, qui in Angliam rediens sodales suos, eorum parentes, propinquos, aliosque catholicos, in quorum cognitionem venire potuerat, nefarie proderet et perderet. Quo monstri genere ut perpetuo careat et collegium istud et ceteri piorum coetus, ab eo qui solus cordium scrutator est, supplicibus votis postulandum est." The names of some of these spies were : Salomon Aldred, Thos. Morgan, Gilbert Gifford, Edw. Gratley, Chas. Paget, Thos.

By this means the mission priests were well known to the English government long before they set foot in England. It greatly astonished imprisoned priests to be confronted after a mock trial with a list containing the names of all their fellow students at Rome.[1]

The work of the persecution was both negative and positive, *i.e.* it not only harassed the mission and suppressed catholic worship, but it carried on at the same time a propaganda in favour of the state church. Just as the act against fugitives over the sea (1571) had already promised an amnesty to all who returned and submitted to the national church (p. 96), so all subsequent acts opened a door of hope to those who should renounce their faith. The act of 1585 laid down certain stipulations for catholics who submitted ; they were not " at any time within the space of ten years after" to come "within ten miles of such places as Her Majesty shall be" under pain of making void their submission.[2] This restriction merely shows how much the fear of assassination had been revived in England by the murder of William of Orange (1584). It did not mean that the government intended to make submission hard. Elizabeth's last act against catholics, the act of 1593 against recusants, gives full freedom to all who publicly submitted to the national church.[3]

Throgmorton. Taken from the report of Card. Sega's visitation, March 4, 1596, Bibl. Vat., Ottob. 2473, fol. 196ᵛ-199. "De Cecilo et Walsinghamo." Given in English in FOLEY, *Records*, VI., pp. 12 *et seq.* See also PERSONS, *Memoirs*, ed. POLLEN, Cath. Record Soc. Miscell., II. (1906), p. 181. Ed. Thorney, an apostate student of the Jesuits' college at Dillingen, played a similar part as a spy. O. BRAUNSBERGER, *Petri Canisii Epistolae et Acta*, Vol. VI. (Freiburg, 1913), p. 29 *et passim* (see index to the vol.).

[1] *E.g.* the priest Haydock in 1584. POLLEN, *Unpubl. doc.*, I., p. 59. See lists of this kind in STRYPE, *Annals*, III., ii., No. LXVI.
[2] 27 Eliz. c. 2, § 13.   [3] 35 Eliz. c. 2, § 10.

The treatment of catholics in prison corresponded with the spirit of these provisions with regard to apostates. Persons imprisoned for hearing mass or similar offences were set free on promising to go to church.[1] Prisoners were forced to listen to a chapter from the anglican bible at meals. The warders made it a point of honour to proselytize.[2] There are instances of refractory papists being dragged to church by force or frightened into compliance by threats of the rack.[3] Others acknowledged their former blindness and promised to go to church in future, because they could endure no longer their intolerable existence in prison.[4] Pardon was offered to one man as he was about to be thrown off the ladder if he would promise to go to church. "Right heartily do I thank thee," he replied. "If by going to church I can save my life, surely all the world will see this, that I am executed solely for faith and religion and nothing else."[5]

The proselytizing zeal which went hand in hand with the persecution of catholics found its fullest manifestation in 1593 when the parents' rights over the education of their children were forcibly interfered with. The provision of the act against recusants, which deprived catholics of their freedom of moving from place to place (p. 149), served also as a means of keeping a sharper watch over the education of their children. When parents,

---

[1] Examples given by POLLEN, *Unpubl. doc.*, I., pp. 28 *et seq.*, 126, 128.

[2] *Op. cit.*, pp. 23–25.

[3] See the *Diarium rerum gestarum in turri Londinensi* (1580–85), printed at the end of SANDERS' *De orig. ac progr. schism. Angl.* (Romæ, 1586).

[4] STRYPE, *Annals of the Reformation*, IV. (1824), pp. 89 *et seq.* (1591). Of the condition of the prisons something will be said later on.

[5] POLLEN, *Unpubl. doc.*, I., p. 229 (1594). Similar examples among condemned priests are given in ALLEN'S *Briefe Hist.*, ed. POLLEN, pp. 20, 61, 73, 80.

notwithstanding all the penalties of the law,[1] contemplated sending their children to the seminaries on the continent for the sake of a catholic education, the state interfered and took away the children from their parents and had them educated in the houses of protestant clergymen at their parents' expense.[2] As a counter move to this action of Elizabeth's government, Robert Persons, with the aid of Spain, founded the English Jesuit school at St. Omers, south-east of Calais.[3]

The government measures just described cannot be attributed to panic caused by pressing danger. The more the danger of invasion decreased, the more pronounced became the propaganda in favour of the state church. When once the need of securing the protestant government against the possibility of a catholic reaction became less imminent, the state, conscious of its victory and security, set before itself a higher task, the attainment of religious unity.

A calculating and pitiless spirit of statecraft pervades the Elizabethan persecution of catholics. Deliberation rather than passion gave birth to the laws and watched over their working. But while religious fanaticism was

---

[1] 13 Eliz. c. 3 (vid. ante, p. 96) ; 27 Eliz. c. 2 (vid. ante, p. 149).

[2] " La regina d'Inghilterra commandò nel anno 1593 che si prendessero li figlioli piccoli dei catholici de più habilità, avanti che havessero età di uscire del regno alli seminarii, et che fussero allevati nelle case delli vescovi et ministri et altri heretici con mala dottrina a spesa delli suoi parenti." From a letter of J. Creswell, S.J. An undated autograph copy is in the Arch. Vat., Borgh. II., 448 ab fol. 226. The use of education as a means of proselytizing—" a pious and godly means "—is suggested by BURLEIGH'S Advice in Matters of Religion and State (about 1583), Somers Tracts, I. (2nd ed., 1809), p. 166.

[3] Cf. CRESWELL'S letter mentioned above, and also PERSON'S letter of 1593. KNOX'S Card. Allen, p. 453. PETRE-HUSENBETH, Engl. Colleges and Convents established on the Continent (1849), p. 46. L. WILLAERT, A Catholic College in the Seventeenth Century, Amer. Cath. Quarterly Review, Oct., 1908.

not the chief motive principle of the persecution, it still had its share therein.   Its share was sufficiently important to develop certain traits hitherto foreign to the character of the English people.   In hardly any other period of English history were men's private opinions so narrowly searched into as during the religious persecution.   The spy-system, which roused such righteous indignation when introduced into the education of youths in the English college in Rome (p. 105), was employed far more exten‑ sively at home in other departments and raised to the level of a fine art.   In the ferocity with which they treated women and children too, Englishmen acted con‑ trary to their true character, even more than by resorting to unscrupulous espionage.   The great Civil War of the seventeenth century spared women, children, and the aged, a point in which it compares favourably with the civil wars in France or the Thirty Years War.   But the perse‑ cution of catholics under Elizabeth and James I. spared neither age nor sex.   Even between 1570 and 1580 it was not uncommon for women and children to be arrested while hearing mass and cast into prison.[1]   A boy was racked and died a "traitor's death."[2]   After the beginning of the Jesuit mission, weakness of sex or age met with still less consideration.[3]   A well-known English historian believes he has discovered that the character of those

---

[1] SPAN. CAL., 1568–79, p. 477 (1574).   STRYPE, *Annals*, II., ii. (1824), pp. 660–662 ; *A List of Papists imprisoned* (1579).

[2] Thomas Sherwood (1578).   According to WILLIS-BUND, *State Trials*, I., p. 229, he was only thirteen years old, and, in ALLEN'S *Briefe Hist.*, ed. POLLEN, p. 118, he is described as "young of years." See CAMM, *Lives of the English Martyrs*, vol. ii., p. 245, for his real age. *Cf.* below, p. 184, note 1.

[3] Letter of Persons, Sept. 17, 1580.   THEINER, *Annal. Eccles.*, III., p. 216.   Reports of Trafford and Worsley, the overseers of Salford Gaol, also of Fleetwood the recorder, for 1581 and 1582.   POLLEN, *Unpubl. doc.*, I., pp. 23–25, 28 *et passim*.

Englishmen who fled overseas deteriorated under foreign influence (p. 2). The truth is just the opposite ; it was the exiles and the oppressed who were purified, it was the oppressors who were brutalized.

This is true not only of those who acted a subordinate part in the persecution, but also of men in leading positions. A man of education and intelligence like Sir Francis Walsingham, the ever-watchful secretary of state, equally skilful in discovering, inventing, watching, and organizing conspiracies, who, quite as much as Burleigh himself, was a prime mover in the Elizabethan persecution, and Rome's best-hated enemy in England— Walsingham exhibits in his conduct unmistakable marks of brutality and fanaticism. Blinded by religious passion, he honestly believed every Roman priest was deceitful and dangerous to the state, and he presided in person at their examinations for the express purpose of putting to them " the bloody question " (p. 159).[1] With all a puritan's intense hatred of papists, he flung gratuitous insults in the face of his victims, an *orator caninus*, as he is called in one account of a catholic's martyrdom.[2] In a moment of fury, he even went so far as to strike a priest, who had not fully acknowledged Elizabeth's legitimacy, so violently in the face that the man fainted.[3]

That the catholic faith was outside the protection of the law, that religion was a crime, and that a criminal might hope for more lenient treatment than a catholic—all this was driven home to people at times with great brutality. A woman once went to a man of note (in 1588) to beg him to use his influence to obtain pardon for one who

---

[1] SPAN. CAL., 1568-79, p. 595. POLLEN, *Unpubl. doc.*, I., pp. 161, 162 *et passim*. JOHN BRIDGEWATER, *Concertatio* (2nd ed., 1588), *passim*.

[2] *Concertatio* (2nd ed.), fol. 151.

[3] *Op. cit.*, fol. 140ᵛ.

had been condemned to death. She was asked if the man was a murderer. " By no means," she answered, " only a catholic." " O dear," said the gentleman, " had he been a murderer I should not have hesitated to comply with your request, but as it is a question of religion I dare not interfere." [1]

Since any means came handy in attacking those who were outside the law, the following report from the seminary at Rheims does not sound incredible. Catholic sources of information assure us that a young fanatic called Vane, having been dispatched by the English government, entered the college disguised as a student and attempted to poison the whole community, including the rector, William Allen.[2] The attempt was quite in keeping with the morals of the time, and was probably intended as a reply to the conspiracies set on foot against Elizabeth.

But it is less from isolated instances than from the whole system pursued that we realize how deeply England was saturated with fanaticism engendered by her religious struggles. This is especially clear in the administration of justice, and in the means employed for extorting information and punishing offenders— torture, imprisonment, and the gallows. It is, however, impossible clearly to distinguish how much is to be attributed to the barbarity of the time, how much to the abuse of absolute power, and how much to religious fanaticism.

---

[1] POLLEN, *Unpubl. doc.*, I., pp. 324, 328.

[2] *Relatione del presente stato d'Inghilterra* (Roma, 1590), pp. 13 *et seq.;* also Sega (1596) in his account of his visitation of the English college in Rome : " Aliquando deprehensus nefarius adolescens, nonime Vanesius, qui scholaris nomen ementitus in collegium Remense ad hoc ex Anglia missus fuerat, ut ipsum Alanum adeoque totum collegium veneno tollere tentaret." Bibl. Vat., Ottob. 2473, fol. 193ᵛ. In English in FOLEY, *Records*, VI. (1880), p. 7.

Nevertheless this last factor has left traces which cannot be mistaken.

Fairness is rightly held to be a strongly marked characteristic of the English people. How deeply this quality can be impaired by religious fanaticism is shown by the judicial murders systematically inflicted on those suspected of conspiracy (p. 152). And yet the administration of justice presents still worse features than false witnesses and unjust judges. Torture (*peine forte et dure*) was applied in England from the time of Edward I. only when the accused refused to plead. Under the Tudor monarchy torture became a royal prerogative in cases in which the safety of the state was held to be in danger. The climax of this development was reached during the reign of Elizabeth. Not only were the great majority of those who were tortured during this period—catholic priests—considered *ipso facto* dangerous to the state, but the persecution of catholics was at its height just when torture had developed into a fine art, and the treatment of prisoners was barbarous in the extreme. William Harrison, who wrote about 1570, was still able to praise English justice for its reluctance to employ torture ; [1] ten years later Lord Burleigh penned his deplorable justification of its use.[2] It is true that, while defending the right to torture those who refused to answer questions or were convicted of treason, he knew he was defending what was in accordance with the acknowledged principles

[1] W. HARRISON, *Description of England*, ed. F. J. FURNIVALL, Bk. II., pp. 221 *et seq.*, New Shakespeare Soc. (London, 1877).
[2] *A declaration of the favourable dealing of her Majestie's commissioners, appointed for the examination of certayne traytors, and of tortures unjustly reported to be done upon them for matter of religion,* 1583, by LORD BURLEIGH. Reprinted in Somers Tracts, I. (2nd ed., 1809), pp. 209–212. Harleian Miscellany, ed. PARK, III. (1809), pp. 565–568.

of English law. But he neither saw nor wished to see that torture, which had hitherto been used only as a means for extorting evidence as to matters of fact, was now being used in matters of conscience as well. It is only fair to the government to grant that this was partly at least the consequence of the intermingling of religion and politics. The question of the pope's deposing power concerned both the safety of the state and the consciences of catholics. The employment of torture could thus be justified as needful for preserving the safety of the state, while, at the same time, refusal to answer the *bloody questions* could be taken to imply refusal to submit to the law.[1] But, on the other hand, it must have been galling to the tortured catholics to feel that the government denied them the right to have a conscience at all. Burleigh himself declared in his apology that no catholic or seminary priest had been forced to answer on the rack " any question of their supposed conscience"[2]—*i.e.* questions concerning the mass, transubstantiation, and so forth—but only questions on personal matters, conspiracies against the queen and the realm, and their *conviction* and *teaching* "touching the pope's bull and pretence of authority to depose kings and princes."[3]   That is to say, it was *the* question which most of all vexed consciences at that time, and caused such a hopeless struggle between conflicting duties that had to be gone into amidst the tortures of the rack. Scarcely anywhere else do we feel the pitiless harshness of the struggle so keenly as in this

[1] So far I agree with the criticisms of Prof. A. F. Pollard in the *Göttingische gel. Anzeigen*, 1912, p. 175. I have modified the text in consequence of what he says.

[2] Somers Tracts, I., p. 211. Harl. Misc., III., p. 566.

[3] "And howe they were persuaded themselves, and did persuade other touching the pope's bull and pretence of authority to depose kings and princes, and namely for deprivation of her Majestie," *l.c.*

"Justification" of Lord Burleigh's.   If it is objected that only those persons were racked whose guilt had already been proved, and who plainly had further secrets yet to disclose,[1] we must remember that guilt in the sense of the statute included the mere fact of being a catholic priest.   We can judge of the justice of Burleigh's apology from the fact that soon afterwards one of the rack-masters himself publicly condemned the system as cruel and barbarous.[2]

It seems as if England had taken lessons from Spain in the art of inflicting torture.   At all events, the first degree of torture—hanging by the wrists until deprived of the senses [3]—was as much used in Spain [4] as in England, as was also the driving iron spikes between the finger-nails and the quick, or tearing off the nails which was called in Spain "anti-Christ's torture."[5]   As a rule the English instruments of torture differed little from those used elsewhere—for example, the horrible rack in which the victim was so stretched by means of levers as to be almost torn in pieces.[6]

---

[1] Urged by Froude, Vol. XI., pp. 71 *et seq.*, in defence of the use of torture under Elizabeth.   *Cf.* STRYPE, *Annals.*, III., i., p. 298.

[2] SIMPSON, *Edm. Campion* (ed. 1896), p. 392.   For a collection of references concerning the torturing of priests, see E. P. CHEYNEY, *A History of Engl. from the Defeat of the Armada to the Death of Elizabeth*, Vol. I. (London,1914), p. 72, note 1.

[3] The agony of being suspended for hours by the wrists is vividly described by Fr. John Gerard from his own experience.   J. MORRIS, *Life of Gerard* (3rd ed., 1881), pp. 240–247.   In one case we hear of a man being suspended by his wrists for fifteen hours.   POLLEN, *Unpubl. doc.*, I., p. 168.

[4] Account given by the Englishman Frampton who had been tortured in Seville in 1560.   STRYPE, *Annals*, I., i. (1824), pp. 363 *et seq.*

[5] SPAN. CAL., 1580–86, p. 153.   *Cf.* the threat—"they woulde racke him even till the nayls should start from his fingers."   POLLEN, *l.c.*, p. 72.

[6] Further particulars in the *Diarium rerum gestarum, etc.*, at the end of SANDERS, *De orig. schism. Angl.* (1586).   DODD-TIERNEY, *Church Hist.*, III., p. 150.   Concerning the rack, *equuleus*, see

In cases like this the torturers exceeded the point at which nature ceases to be sensible of pain. The priest Alexander Bryant, who underwent all grades of torture, declared he was no longer sensible of any pain when at the end his body was extended to the uttermost on the rack.[1] In spite of all the torturer's care to avoid putting an end to the victim's sufferings by death, death in some cases intervened and robbed the hangman of his prey.[2]

Instead of describing the gruesome details which fill the histories of the martyrs, we will confine ourselves to one observation of general application.   On the whole, the English people supported the government in its struggle with Rome ; the penal laws were the work of parliament, not of the privy council. Nevertheless religious fanaticism had not so completely destroyed the nation's sense of justice as to reconcile public opinion to the abuse of torture. Not only did catholics regard torture as practised under Elizabeth as unspeakably barbarous, and worthy of Turks or Scythians,[3] but the torture chambers in the Tower became so odious to the great majority of the people that the government had to take the matter into consideration. It did so in a manner far from commendable—" Master Topcliffe " received authority " to torment priests in his own house in such sort as he shall think good." [4]

Concertatio (1583), pp. 225 *et seq.* That priests were roasted, as Persons asserts (THEINER, *Ann. Eccles.*, p. 367), is nowhere proved.

[1] *Concertatio*, p. 232.   *Cf.* the *Diarium rerum gestarum, etc.*, under April 6, 1581.

[2] CHALLONER, *Memoirs of Missionary Priests*, Vol. I. (ed. 1878), p. 229.   DODD-TIERNEY, Vol. III., Appendix, p. cciv.   POLLEN, *Unpubl. doc.*, I., p. 362.

[3] *Concertatio* (ed. 1583), pp. 106–108.

[4] POLLEN, *l.c.*, p. 212 (1592), Richard Young seems to have had the same kind of authority : Unum istud purgatorium timemus omnes, in quo duo illi catholicorum carnifices, Topcliffus et Youngus, omnem habent cruciandi libertatem." SOUTHWELL, S.J., to Acquaviva (1590), *l.c.*, pp. 329 *et seq.*

No blot is more foul on the history of Elizabeth's latter years than the name of Richard Topcliffe. Every inhuman quality which the most heated imagination can picture is embodied in this example of unspeakable degradation. Greed and perverse delight in inflicting suffering, rather than religious fanaticism, were the motives of Topcliffe's conduct. His name became a synonym for brutality. " *Topcliffian customs* was a synonym for barbarity, *topcliffizare* became a slang term for hunting a man to ruin or death."[1] Prolonged practice had made him familiar with the amount of suffering of which man's nervous system was capable, and to invent fresh tortures became his business and his delight. The accounts handed down by eye-witnesses and by the sufferers themselves surpass all powers of description, and we gladly draw the veil over the last and most frightful scene when the condemned were handed over to Topcliffe without witnesses and inquisitors. Only a man like Topcliffe was capable of torturing afresh a man who had already been broken on the rack, who had confessed and admitted everything asked of him, and had even renounced his faith.[2] Only a man like Topcliffe was capable of continuing to insult his victim so long as he drew breath and of stifling the last words of farewell and prayer.[3] Had he not been sure of the queen's approval,[4] the wretch could not have plied his trade.

---

[1] POLLEN, *Religious Terrorism under Q. Elizabeth*, The Month, March, 1905, p. 277.

[2] As in the case of Henry Walpole, who, later on, retrieved his weakness. POLLEN, *l.c.*, pp. 258, 266.

[3] A. JESSOPP, *One Generation of a Norfolk House* (Norwich, 1878), pp. 63 *et seq.*, 231 *et seq.*, attempts to sum up Topcliffe. For what has been said above, see FOLEY, *Records*, I., pp. 361, 378 ; MORRIS, *Condition of Catholics, passim;* POLLEN, *Unpubl. doc., passim,* especially pp. 183, 186, 207 *et seq.*, 209 *et seq.*, 362 *et seq.*

[4] There is no need to believe that the queen's favour went the lengths that Topcliffe boasted, nevertheless his vaunting (POLLEN

When we hear of a recorder who could no longer control himself when presiding over the application of torture, but burst into tears,[1] or of a governor of the Tower, who was so overcome by the constancy of a man under torture that he resigned his post,[2] we are led to the conclusion that the administration of penal justice during the persecution exceeded the horrors common at the period.   We get the same impression from the treatment of prisoners during that time ; they were confined in foul and stinking dungeons, and given the worst food and water ;[3] sometimes they were tied to a manger like animals and had their scanty viands flung at them ;[4] sometimes they were yoked like beasts of burden to a sort of mill and whipped if they did not perform their tasks willingly or were unable to work from illness.[5]   Possibly we might reject these accounts as inventions or exaggerations of catholics, were they not corroborated by the large number of deaths which took place in prison.   To every four or five catholics who suffered death by execution, we must add one who died while in prison.[6]

p. 210) would have been impossible had he not felt sure of his position as a trusted servant of Her Majesty.

    [1] The torture of the youthful student Sherwood (1578) to make him betray his friends, is described in the following terms : " Il ricordatore lo fece tormentare crudelissimamente, tirando le membra sue in diverse parti con certe rote in tanto che tutte quasi le giunture del corpo si smossero del luogo suo, il quale spettacolo fu tanto horrendo che il ricordatore stesso pianse per compassione delli dolori che lo vide patir, mar con tutto ciò il giovane non volse scoprire alcuno." From letters from England, Arch. Vat., Miscell. Arm. XI., t. 94, fol. 192ᵛ.   Printed from another copy by POLLEN, Cath. Record Soc. Misc., II., 74.

    [2] J. MORRIS, *Condition of Catholics* (1871), p. ciii.

    [3] *Concertatio* (ed. 1583), p. 105.   POLLEN, *Unpubl. doc.*, I., pp. 83, 85, 168, 329.

    [4] A letter of Southwell's of 1594.   POLLEN, p. 304.

    [5] POLLEN, pp. 304, 311, 329.

    [6] The list in DODD-TIERNEY, III., pp. 161-170, gives 187 executions

The victims attributed all their sufferings solely to religious fanaticism—heresy as the catholics called it. " I blame not so much the men who have prepared such things as these (may God forgive them) as the heresy which incited men, not naturally cruel but inclined to gentleness, to such hardness of heart against their fellows that they are restrained from treating them in the most cruel fashion neither by their common nationality, nor education, nor by their youth, nor by their right to freedom, nor the immunity of the priesthood, nor prayers, nor tears." [1] The deepest indignation, however, was caused by the want of pity shown to the sick and aged, and to women.[2] In this, if in nothing else, the English character belied itself.

The mode of execution—a mere pretence at hanging, disembowelling while the condemned was still alive, and the dismembering of the corpse [3]—was nothing new, being the form of death decreed for traitors by the ancient laws of the land. But even here we see fanaticism at work. It was usual to suffer the condemned to hang until quite dead in cases where the crime was less heinous.[4] To be

of catholic priests and laity, forty-two deaths in prison. It would, of course, be of great importance to know the proportion which the deaths in prison bear to the whole number of those imprisoned. This, however, in the present state of the investigations, is impossible.

[1] *Concertatio*, p. 108. Similarly Southwell's words: " Non in opprobrium gentis, sed in hæresis pestem . . . vitium conferendum." POLLEN, *Unpubl. doc.*, I., p. 325.

[2] *Concertatio*, pp. 111, 116–118.

[3] The wording of one of these death sentences is as follows: " Suspendantur et viventes ad terram prosternantur, et interiora sua extra ventres suos capiantur ipsisque viventibus comburantur." POLLEN, *Unpubl. doc.*, I., p. 57.

[4] " Sometimes, if the trespass be not the more heinous, they are suffered to hang till they be quite dead." W. HARRISON, *Description of Engl.*, ed. FURNIVALL, Bk. II., p. 222. Hanging alone was the punishment for felony ; hanging with disembowelling, for treason.

a catholic priest, however, ranked by no means as one of the less heinous forms of high treason, and the unhappy men complained they were treated more cruelly than the basest criminals.[1]   Only too many cases are on record in which this last and most horrible form of martyrdom—tearing out the entrails—is shown not to have immediately produced death.[2]   However, it was precisely this act of excessive cruelty that turned the scale.   Torture and the sufferings of imprisonment were hidden from the public gaze, but an execution was a popular spectacle.   The numerous descriptions which have come down to us of nearly two hundred executions of catholics, plainly show how the better feelings of the people triumphed over the brutality and fanaticism then in fashion.   Of course there is a sufficient number of cases where the dying man was insulted and derided to the very end,[3] especially if, in his farewell speech, he had expressed the hope that his death might aid the catholic cause, for "there be men in the world which drink blood as easily as beasts do water."[4] Yet as time passed we find the cases become more numerous in which the spectators, and frequently even the presiding magistrates themselves, refused to allow the law to be carried out to the letter.   The cry of some one in the crowd, "Let him hang," or the order of the sheriff, often prevented the executioner from cutting the rope while

WILLIS-BUND, *State Trials*, I. (Cambridge, 1879), Introd., xxix., xxxiv., 21.

[1] *Concertatio*, p. 114.

[2] "Tam impigre nonnunquam dextreque perficerunt, ut plerumque non solum persentiant acutissime, verum etiam articulatim et distincte loquantur post eruta sibi ilia, etc." *Concertatio, l.c. Cf.* POLLEN, *Unpubl. doc.*, I., pp. 186, 207.   "He lived until that fury of hell and butchery, Knave Bull, had thrown his heart into the fire." The account of Middleton's execution, 1590.

[3] POLLEN, pp. 186, 323.   *Concertatio* (ed. 1583), pp. 114 *et seq.*

[4] A catholic's remark after Campion's execution. DOMESTIC CAL., 1581–90, p. 31.

the condemned still breathed.[1] Sometimes two sheriffs disputed as to the way the sentence was to be carried out,[2] and sometimes it was the people and the sheriff who came to words,[3] or the people among themselves. Robert Southwell, S.J., won the good will of the crowd by his simple prayer for the queen. When the sheriff gave the order to cut him down, "there was a great confused cry in the companie that he praied for the queene, 'And therefore let him hang till he be dead,' sayd they."[4]

Towards 1590, when the most bloodstained years of Elizabeth's reign were drawing to a close, the revulsion of feeling against all this cruelty seems to have gained the upper hand among the people.[5] The sense of greater security after the defeat of the Armada probably contributed to this. The usual cry of " Traitor," which had accompanied every catholic on his way to prison and the gallows, lost its force and was heard less often.[6] It took many years before this change of opinion was fully effected. There was a reaction towards the end of the century, and again after the Gunpowder Plot (1605), and, later still, on the outbreak of the civil war, fanaticism claimed fresh

---

[1] At William Hart's execution (1583), the crowd, who were held back at a distance of forty paces, pressed forward in spite of orders to the contrary in order to prevent the customary butchery. *Annuæ litteræ Coll. Angl.*, 1583. Arch. of the Engl. coll. in Rome, *Liber ruber;* given in English in FOLEY, *Records*, VI., p. 106. Similar instances in POLLEN, *Unpubl. doc.*, I., pp. 374, note 1 ; 390. The sheriff, in the last instance, ordered the still living victim to have his head cut off in order to prevent his sufferings. Many cases, where the less painful method of execution was followed, are given in ALLEN'S *Briefe Hist.*, ed. POLLEN, pp. 62, 69, 74, 83, 96.

[2] POLLEN, *Unpubl. doc.*, I., p. 62.

[3] ALLEN, p. 108. See also the references in the following note.

[4] POLLEN, *op. cit.*, I., p. 336. FOLEY, *Records*, I., p. 375.

[5] *Relatione del presente stato d'Inghilterra* (Roma, appresso Franc. Zannetti, 1590), p. 3.

[6] *Op. cit.*, p. 4. *Cf.* FOLEY, *Records*, I., p. 378.

victims.   It was only under Charles II., during the excitement caused by the Popish Plot that these sanguinary statutes were put into execution with all their ancient brutality for the last time.[1]   With the impression of those years fresh in his mind, the author of the *Letters for Toleration*, wrote in 1689 : " The horrid cruelties that in all ages, and of late in our view, have been committed under the name and upon the account of religion, give so just an offence and abhorrence to all who have any remains not only of religion, but humanity, left, that the world is ashamed to own it." [2]   These words express a sentiment that was then beginning to spread, and usher in the close of a period which had celebrated its bloodiest triumphs under the two Tudor queens.   But while the catholic queen, herself a victim to religious enthusiasm, unhesitatingly sacrificed her country's welfare to her religious ideals, the practical and patriotic protestant queen set before herself the prosperity of the nation as the chief aim of her statecraft.

Religious fanaticism has indeed cast a shadow on the brilliant picture of Elizabeth's reign without being able to obscure its glory.   Elizabeth and her ministers were never guilty of allowing religious passion to endanger the wellbeing of the nation.   England's power as a nation suffered no injury from the persecution of catholics with all its cruelties.   Neither its intellectual culture nor its commercial enterprise were impaired—things which the nation could not well have done without, rich as it was in youthful talent and genius, and in that spirit of adventurous daring and

---

[1] The Venetian representative in London, Sarotti, wrote concerning those who were condemned in the Titus Oates plot: " Sono stati appesi alla forca e senza strangolarli si sono dal carnefice aperti essendo vivi." Jan. 31/ Feb. 10, 1679.   Venice, State Archives, Senato Dispacci, Inghilterra, 66.

[2] JOHN LOCKE, *A Third Letter for Toleration*, ch. iv.

enterprise which urged it across the ocean. Every other country where religious persecution broke out suffered severely; one alone flourished and increased and out-stripped the rest—Elizabethan England.

IV. *The Heroic Period of the Mission*

More intimate knowledge of the mission priests teaches us to regard them as men of strong manly character, steadfast in their belief, and unruffled in their obedience—men whose self-control seldom failed them, and whose cheerfulness was seldom disturbed, who were transfigured by their victory over the world, and filled with love for all men without distinction—men, finally, who amidst the most terrible torments and ill-treatment remained free and unconquered, because to them martyrdom was the crown of life. "Our vocation is not to be inclosed in cells," wrote the Jesuit Southwell in his meditations,[1] "far from intercourse with men, but to combat openly, and while rebuking the irregular devices of others, we must be watchful that we are not overcome by our own. Among the loquacious observe moderation of speech, among the irascible guard the temper, among the lovers of pleasure beware of self-indulgence . . . for the least blot in a religious is a great deformity." The man who wrote these words lived up to them. The cruelties of Topcliffe makes our blood boil even at the present day, but Southwell, who had been tortured ten times, had no harder word for him than, "Thou art a bad man."[2] To accept calmly the most insulting speeches, and to answer without bitter-ness, was a point of honour with every priest,[3] especially

[1] FOLEY, *Records*, I. (London, 1877), p. 314.
[2] POLLEN, *Unpubl. doc.*, I., p. 335.
[3] "Responderunt pro tribunali omnes mansuetis ac, quantum fieri potuit, ab omni acerbitate alienissimis verbis." Southwell to Acquaviva, the General of the Jesuits, 1588. POLLEN, p. 322.

the Jesuits—their schooling at the seminary [1] stood the test when tried by this fiery ordeal.

The powers of whole classes of men, as of individuals, increase with the greatness of the task set before them. In no other European country at the time of the counter-reformation did the catholic church possess clergy who discharged their priestly duties with such a holy zeal as the little band that worked in England. "The souls of catholics are more precious than our bodies" [2] might stand as the motto for the history of the mission. The reproach of secularity usually brought against the clergy would not have had any justification in Elizabethan England. Not even the most prejudiced opponent could discover anything to find fault with in this respect. It was the heroic period of the mission. Heroism was the offspring of persecution. When the humane Charles I. put a stop to the persecution, and took the catholics, both clerical and lay, under his protection, they ceased to be heroes and saints, and once more became men subject to human frailties. The only fault that can be found with the priests of the Elizabethan age, is that their contempt for death often took the form of contempt for life, and yearning for martyrdom. No worldling ever showed greater eagerness in the pursuit of worldly honour than they did in pursuing the "crown" and the "palm." Their chief fear was that God would think them unworthy of this honour, and, in speaking of their brethren's martyrdoms, their words often ring with impatience to be following in their steps, and frequently it sounds as if they were even envious of their lot. When, at last, the hour of their passion was at hand, they gave gifts to the jailer as he put their feet in irons, or expressed their gratitude to him

---

[1] *Vid. ante*, p. 102.
[2] Words of Southwell's. POLLEN, p. 311.

in words if they had nothing else to give. To the curses heaped upon them by the people on the way to prison or to execution, they responded by blessings, and beneath the gallows they kissed the hangman's hand reddened with the blood of martyrs.[1] We may admire this or think it mistaken or fantastic, but at any rate these men were giving a practical turn to the precept, " Bless them that curse you."

The same deeply religious spirit, which reminds us of the early days of Christianity, is to be found too in the preface to the catholic translation of the bible,[2] the greatest literary achievement of the Rheims seminary. " So we repine not in tribulation, but euer loue them that hate us, pitying their case, and reioycing in our owne. For neither can we see during this life, how much good they doe us ; nor know how manie of them shal be (as we hartily desire they al may be) saued : our Lord and Sauiour hauing paid the same price by his death for them and for us. Loue al, therefore, pray for al." In this estimate of their vocation, there was no difference between Jesuit and secular. The first years of the Jesuit mission, which fell within the period when this heroic spirit was at its height, show not only an equal eagerness for self-sacrifice in all, but also the heartiest co-operation between Douay and Rome. The divisions that had already arisen in the college in Rome did not at once spread to England. " Here, forsooth, we have so many enemies in common, that there is no time for internal factions."[3] The two

---

[1] Every one of the accounts of the martyrdoms contain traits of this kind. *Vide passim*, ALLEN'S *Briefe Historie*, POLLEN'S *Unpubl. doc.*, FOLEY'S *Records*, CHALLONER'S *Missionary Priests*, and the other histories of the mission to which we have frequently referred.

[2] The Douay-Rheims version, *vid. ante*, p. 71, note 3, p. 98.

[3] Southwell to the rector of the English college, Dec. 22, 1586. POLLEN, p. 315.

bodies of missionaries held frequent meetings and consultations.

The two pioneer priests of the mission, Robert Persons,[1] and his friend, Edmund Campion [2] (a man of very different stamp), are both such strongly marked personalities, and played so important a part in the history of their time that a description of them cannot be omitted from any account which proposes to give even a brief outline of English catholicism.

Edmund Campion,[3] the first martyr of the Jesuit mission, fully realizes our ideal of what a missionary and a martyr should be. He was one of many who at the establishment of Elizabeth's state church sacrificed their convictions and swam with the stream. His position in the world, and the honourable career upon which he had already entered at the university, kept him back for a long time from declaring his catholic convictions. Yet to the man of settled catholic convictions, the period of transition through which he had attained to them seemed to him inexcusable and intolerable. After receiving anglican orders, his scruples of conscience deepened into acute distress, and in the thirtieth year of a life rich in promise for the future, Campion left Oxford, where he had achieved so much distinction and success while still a young man, to begin a new life (1569). His first step was naturally to be received into the catholic church, and

---

[1] Sometimes written *Parsons*, but it is more usual to spell the name with an *e*.

[2] Sometimes written *Campian*, from the Latin form of the name, *Campianus*.

[3] PAULUS BOMBINUS, *Vita et martyrium Edmundi Campiani martyris Angli*, *S.J.* (Mantuæ, 1620). R. SIMPSON, *Edmund Campion : A Biography* (London, 1867 ; new ed., 1896, in the Catholic Standard Library). J. H. POLLEN, *The Journey of Blessed Edm. Campion from Rome to England*, The Month, Sept., 1897.

this was soon followed by a second—admission into the Society of Jesus. When Campion, after ten years' absence, returned to England with the greatest secrecy, he was already well disciplined in the virtues of fortitude and purity, and had attained to a gentleness of disposition which nothing could embitter, and to a greatness of mind which rose above all pettiness—qualities which give a winning majesty to his personality and place him on a level with the martyrs of Christian antiquity. No other of the missionaries working in England had the power of calling forth enthusiastic admiration and commanding unselfish devotion to the same extent as this proto-martyr of the English Jesuits. No one was endowed with a greater gift of eloquence and a sweeter voice than he. Men spoke of his "honied lips."[1] No one had so unfailing a sense of humour and flow of innocent wit in the midst of all his sufferings as this man who was "merry in his misery" and joked over his limbs torn by the rack as if all were but a play.[2]

> "O constant man, O mind, O vertue strange,
>   Whom want, nor wo, nor feare, nor hope coulde change!"[3]

Campion has given the following account of his labours as a missionary.[4] "I ride about some piece of the country

---

[1] "Os tibi mellifluum, faciei grata venustas,
  Vox dulcis, lenis, plena, sonora, gravis.
  Res sacræ, eloquium sanctum, divina loquela
  Spiritus accensus totus amore Dei.
  Hæsere astantes in te vultuque manuque,
  Inque tuas voces pendula turba fuit."

Vita et martyrium Edmundi Campiani carmine scripta. [J. BRIDGEWATER], *Concertatio Eccles. Cath. in Anglia.* (Aug. Trevir, 1583), p. 206.

[2] ALLEN, *Briefe Hist.*, ed. POLLEN (1908), p. 14.

[3] *Upon the death of M. Edm. Campion, etc., op. cit.*, p. 27.

[4] This letter, written towards the end of 1580 and regarded as one of the classical documents of the English mission, has often been

O

every day. The harvest is wonderful great. On horseback I meditate my sermon ; when I come to the house, I
polish it. Then I talk with such as come to speak with
me, or hear their confessions. In the morning, after mass,
I preach ; they hear with exceeding greediness, and very
often receive the sacrament, for the ministration whereof
we are ever well assisted by priests, whom we find in every
place. The priests of our country, themselves being most
excellent for virtue and learning, yet have raised so great
an opinion of our society, that I dare scarcely touch the
exceeding reverence all catholics do unto us. . . . I cannot
long escape the hands of the heretics ; the enemies have so
many eyes, so many tongues, so many scouts and crafts.
I am in apparel to myself very ridiculous ; I often change
it, and my name also. I read letters sometimes myself that
in the first front tell news that Campion is taken, which,
noised in every place where I come, so filleth my ears with
the sound thereof, that fear itself hath taken away all fear."

For more than a year Campion was spared to fulfil his
calling. When at last he fell into the clutches of the
persecutors, whom he had so often eluded, his trial and
death only helped on the triumph of his cause. The
accusation of political scheming [1] found no evidence to
support it, and the supposed traitor died with a prayer for
the queen on his lips. "For which queen ?" some one
cried out. "Yea, for Elizabeth, your queen and mine," [2]
were Campion's last words. When questioned as to the
validity of the excommunication, and asked to declare his

---

printed ; first in the *Concertatio* (ed. 1583), pp. 23–26, afterwards by
SACCHINUS, *Hist. Soc. Jesu*, pt. iv. (Romæ, 1652), lib. viii., § 128,
and elsewhere. It is given in English in ALLEN, *op. cit.*, pp. 23–26,
SIMPSON, *op. cit.* (ed. 1896), pp. 246–250.

[1] For the trial, *cf. ante*, pp. 151, 158.

[2] ALLEN, *op. cit.*, p. 5. The question was prompted by the
suspicion that Campion was praying for Mary Stuart.

views on the conflict between church and country, he
refused to give an answer up to the very last; there was
no phrase that could come to his rescue. Nevertheless, by
his last prayer, he appeased the conflict, for nothing could
appease it save Christian love.

Campion's life and sufferings justified the name given
to the Society of Jesus by the English Jesuit poet,
Southwell—"the meek society." [1] Yet no sooner has the
word been uttered than suddenly, as if to contradict it,
another personage appears on the scene with nothing of
the saint in his demeanour and no halo of meekness
around his head, a man filled with fiery passions and
immersed in the political life of his time, the Jesuit Robert
Persons, the chief organizer of the first missionary journey.
One of his opponents among the secular clergy propounds
the question: "Whether Master Nicholas Machiavell
or Father Robert Persons excelled one the other in
policy?" [2] The portrait of this much abused and much
admired man does not stand out before us so clearly as
the straightforward personality of Campion, and it will
only be really known when his extensive political correspondence has been collected and published. [3] One point,

[1] HENRY WALPOLE, An epitaphe of Campian . . . father of the
meek society of the blessed name of Jesus (1581). Cf. the words with
which the description of the execution of some priests ends, 1584—
" and so in most mild and constant manner ended their life. Many
a one in my hearing said, ' God be with their sweet souls ! '" POLLEN,
Unpubl. doc., I., p. 62.

[2] WILLIAM WATSON, A decacordon of ten quodlibeticall questions
(1602), p. 92.

[3] " Infinita sunt quæ cum pontificibus, cum regibus, cum cardina-
libus, principibus aliisque viris, modo sermone egit modo scripto,
utroque ad persuadendum accommodatissimo." H. MORRIS, Hist.
Missonis Anglic. Soc. Jesu ab a. 1580, ad . . . a. 1635 (Andomari,
1660), p. 388. This accounts for the difficulty in collecting Persons'
correspondence. A large portion of it is in the Borghesiana in the
Arch. Vat. Many papers are unsigned, but can be identified by their
energetic handwriting.

however, is now clear ; the conception of Persons as a
political intriguer,[1] such as appears in the question of his
contemporary quoted above, and which has survived down
to quite recent times,[2] does not give a true idea either of
the depth and earnestness, or of the brilliant gifts, of this
richly endowed man.

Like Campion, Robert Persons was also a convert.[3] In
his case, too, increasing sympathy for catholicism seems to
have been the chief reason why he had to leave Oxford
and betake himself to the continent. During the jubilee
of 1575, at the age of twenty-eight, he went to Rome
attracted more, however, by the remains of antiquity than
by the splendour of the papacy or the sanctity of the holy
places. The zeal of the convert had not yet been aroused

[1] " This born conspirator." T. G. LAW, *A Historical Sketch of the
Conflicts between Jesuits and Seculars, etc.* (London, 1889), p. xiv.

[2] As in E. L. TAUNTON, *The History of the Jesuits in England
1580–1773* (London, 1901). One of Persons' contemporaries had
formed a similar opinion of him : THOS. JAMES, *The Jesuits' Downefall threatned against them by the secular priests for their wicked
lives* (Oxford, 1612), pp. 49–72. Perhaps the best appreciation
(though in some points open to criticism) of Persons is given by
A. JESSOPP, *One Generation of a Norfolk House* (Norwich, 1878), pp.
82 *et seq.* I should query his words—" absolutely deficient in those
qualities which are the main constituents of the poetic temperament."

[3] A completely satisfactory biography is still a desideratum. The
best is T. G. LAW'S in the *Dict. Nat. Biogr.* For what follows, see
especially PERSONS' *Memoirs*, ed. by POLLEN, in the Cath. Record
Soc. Miscell., II. (1906).

[4] That some dishonourable conduct was the cause of his leaving
Oxford is a charge which was brought against him at a later period,
but is without proof. A letter of George Abbot of 1601 ; H. FOULIS
Hist. of Romish Treasons (2nd ed., 1681), p. 501. *Cf.* THOS. JAMES
The Jesuits' Downefall (Oxford, 1612), pp. 52–72 : " The Life of Father
Rob. Persons an English Jesuit," the earliest biography of Persons, is
a mere caricature. So, too, is the somewhat later life by M[ATTHEW
SUTTCLIFFE, *A True Relation of England's Happinesse under the
Reigne of Q. Eliz.* (1629), pp. 219–232 : " A Legend of no Saint but of
Robert Persons his life. . . ." Concerning his leaving the university
cf. POLLEN, *l.c.*, pp. 21 *et seq.*

Persons neither went to confession nor gained an indulgence. At Padua, where he resumed his studies, he devoted himself to natural science. Here a change gradually came over him and he strove against the longing to seek for peace far from the world in some alpine monastery. He never unbosomed himself to any friend, but when he could no longer contain himself he hastened back secretly to Rome. To atone for his former indifference, he made the journey on foot in spite of the burning sun. In Rome he took the step by which he thought he could best serve the church, and entered the Society of Jesus. He followed the theological course at the Collegium Romanum, and, after barely three years, was ordained priest. The literature of religious controversy was his special study, because he judged it most important for his own particular calling— the spread of catholicism. Before offering himself for the English mission, he had some idea of giving himself to mission work in America,[1] but the proposal came to nothing. It proves, however, how little he was influenced by political motives at this stage of his life.

It was during his missionary career that the idea of politics first took hold of his mind. Not that he exceeded his instructions (p. 142) and mixed up politics with the cure of souls! Although the statement has often been made,[2] there is no evidence for thinking he in any way acted as a political agent during his brief spell of missionary work in England (June, 1580 to August, 1581).[3] The Spanish ambassador must have been better informed than

[1] Mission of the Indies. Persons to Allen, March 30, 1579. POLLEN, Cath. Record Soc. Miscell., I., p. 137.

[2] Recently by MARTIN A. S. HUME, *Treason and Plot. Struggles for Cath. Supremacy in the last years of Eliz.* (1901), p. 12, but without any attempt at proof.

[3] See POLLEN in The Month, March, 1902, p. 296 ; also T. F. KNOX, *Card. Allen* (1882), Introd., xxx.

any one else, and to him Persons was known only through his work as a mission priest after his departure from England—a departure not at first regarded as final. The ambassador regarded the presence of the Jesuit in England as desirable, not from political reasons, such as espionage or stirring up sedition, but only for the oversight of the scattered clergy and for ministering to souls.[1] It was just in the northern counties, however, that Persons chiefly laboured, and this at the very time when the catholic reaction in Scotland was carrying everything before it and Elizabeth's influence was at its lowest ebb. The idea of liberating Mary Stuart assumed a new aspect, and English catholics set their hopes anew on bringing about a change by means of force. It can easily be understood that these views would be discussed with the man who had full authority to deal with all questions of conscience that would arise in this connection.[2] Persons, accordingly, gained the impression that many catholics wished for an invasion and that the time was propitious for it.[3] He had not worked as a political agent, nevertheless, influenced by the strain of the political situation, a second change took place in him—a change from priest to politician—and he became an advocate of the policy of invasion.

It is easy to see now that Persons made a mistake and

[1] *Col. de doc. inéd.*, t. 92, pp. 145 *et seq.* SPAN. CAL., 1580-86, pp. 195 *et seq.* Letter of Mendoza, Oct. 20, 1581.

[2] Persons himself admits that he became acquainted with these ideas, *when he had treated with them of their conscience.* KNOX, *Card. Allen*, p. xxxix.

[3] *L.c.*, pp. xxxviii. *et seq.* POLLEN in The Month, March, 1902, p. 299. Concerning the conversations which Persons then had with prominent catholics about the invasion, see the words of the nuncio, at Paris, Castelli, May 8, 1582—"Padre Roperto Giesuita, che è venuto d'Inghilterra, dove è stato dui anni [a mistake, for he had only been one year] trattando questo negotio [dell' invasione]." KNOX, *Card. Allen*, p. 405. JOH. KRETZSCHMAR, *Die Invasionsprojekte der kathol. Mächte gegen Engl., z. Zt. Elisabeths* (Leipzig, 1892), p. 130.

in the end did more harm than good to his co-religionists
and the interests of the pope in England. But if he erred,
he did so in company with the best men of his age—I need
only remind the reader of Sidney's maxim quoted above
(p. 135). And if ever afterwards it was dinned into his
ears that he had once and only once[1] ventured into the
forbidden land, this reproach of apparent desertion rose out
of the natural sympathy which people felt for the martyrs,
in which a man could claim no share who seemed to count
his life so dear. But did Persons really play the deserter?
Certainly not. He was not shirking his duty, rather he was
following his true vocation. Persons the mission priest
could easily be replaced by another, but the works of
Persons the author could only be written by few,[2] and no
one could equal him in his power of organization.

The idea of treason towards his country filled Persons at
the beginning of his career with a horror equal to that with
which his opponents at a later day regarded him as a child
of hell. As he says himself, "And that which aboue all
other thinges is most grievous, injurious, and intollerable,
is the giuing out publiquelye that all catholiques are

---

[1] "Ipse ignavus miles, saluti suæ fuga quamprimum consuluit.
Desertor tamen castrorum Dei effectus, etc." [JOHN MUSH] *Decla-
atio motuum ac turbationum inter Jesuitas . . . et sacerdotes seminariorum in Anglia* (Rhotomagi, 1601), p. 24. Mush was one of
the leaders of the secular clergy in their conflict with the Jesuits.
Cf. J. BERRINGTON, *Memoirs of Greg. Panzani* (Birmingham,
1793), pp. 28 *et seq*. LAW, *Jesuits and Seculars* (1889), Introd.,
p. xxii.

[2] His works stand high above the average of the pamphlets and
controversial writings of the time. Even in the nineteenth century
they were commended as models of English prose. CH. BUTLER,
Hist. Memoirs resp. the Engl., etc., Catholics, Vol. I. (1819), p. 285.
His contemporaries said that the resurrection of a dead man could
not have brought more conviction than his forcible arguments.
LEON. COQUÆUS, *Examen præfationis monitoriæ Jacobi*, I. . . .
præmissæ Apologiæ suæ pro juramento fidelitatis (Frib. Brisg., 1610),
p. 33.

enemies and traytors to your Royall Majestye."[1] Tha
Persons nevertheless did fall into this error, not by any
sudden change of opinions, but by being led gradually
along a path of which he did not see the end, and that he
felt keenly the breach with his countrymen and the dis
grace which was attached to his name, gives a tragic great
ness to the figure of this combatant who never tasted the
joys of victory. Under the name of *Doleman*—dolefu
man—he published the book[2] which was meant to pave
the way for the Spanish succession to the English throne
and did in fact alienate its author, once and for all, not
only from his protestant fellow countrymen, but also from
the majority of English catholics. Persons has rightly
been called by Ribadeneira, "the martyr not of a moment
but of a lifetime."[3]

The political activity of this man does not belong to a
chapter the object of which is to tell the story of the mis
sion. The confidant of the king of Spain, the courtier and
diplomatist, the unwearied speaker and writer, had but
little in common with the man who had crept secretly into

---

[1] *A brief discours contayning certayne reasons why Catholique.*
refuse to go to Church. Written by a learned and vertuous man to a
friend of his in England and dedicated by J[ohn] H[owlet] to the
Queene's most excellent Majestie, Douai, 1580.   John Howlet is a
pseudonym for Rob. Persons.   The words quoted in the text are from
the dedication to Queen Elizabeth.

[2] *A conference about the next succession to the throne of England*
(1593).   The charge brought against Persons (DOM. CAL., 1601–03,
p. 170), that, by this pseudonym, he wished to father the book
on an English secular priest, Dolman, does not take into account
Persons' pride as an author.   See his defence in *A manifestation o,*
the great folly . . . of certayne in England calling themselves secular
priests (1602), fol. 51.   Persons declares he knew nothing of Dolman's
existence, and continues, "No man yet, we think, that knoweth him
and hath read the book, wil easily beleeve or accuse him of, his
talent being known to be farre inferior to such a labour."

[3] RIBADENEIRA, *Bibliotheca Script. Soc. Jesu* (Romæ, 1676)
p. 725.

London in the summer of 1580 and assembled the catholic priests under his presidency to deliberate on the affairs of the mission.

The business of the synod of London [1] of 1580 was to settle points of controversy that had arisen among catholics and to partition the country into missionary districts. The first point of disagreement to be settled was one of minor importance concerning the observance of fasts. The old priests kept to the English custom of earlier times, while the seminary priests wished to introduce the Roman customs as to fasting. It was resolved to make no change on established usage. The chief question before the synod was whether attendance at protestant services could be excused on the ground of the severity of the law, for there were still catholics who quieted their conscience with the consideration that attendance was permissible provided there was no internal assent to the new religion (p. 68). The synod decided, as the Roman See had already done, that all participation in protestant services must cease.[2] On no other point did the mission insist with greater emphasis than this. It was unwearied in bringing together every reason against going to church, and in cutting off the subterfuges that weak consciences might employ. Persons himself, in the same year that the synod met, published his pamphlet, "Why catholiques refuse to goe to church." [3] In spite of all attempts to suppress it, the little book had a wide circulation and produced considerable effect. It

[1] Called also "the synod of Southwark," from the part of the city in which it was held.

[2] Concerning the resolutions passed at the synod, see PERSONS' *Memoirs*, ed. POLLEN, Cath. Record Soc. Misc., II. (1906), pp. 176 *et seq.* *Cf.* his pamphlet mentioned above on p. 200, note 1, and also SACCHINUS, *Hist. Soc. Jesu*, pt. iv. (Romæ, 1652), lib. viii., § 114 *et seq.* SIMPSON'S *Campion* (ed. 1896), pp. 182–191.

[3] The full title is given on p. 200, note 1.

became so popular among catholics that before long it was turned into verse and was circulated in this form also.[1]

The separation of catholics from religious inter-communion with protestants was the chief point in the programme of the mission. The most important and indispensable condition for carrying through this programme was that the priests themselves should give a good example. A remarkable misunderstanding on this point gave rise among the contemporary opponents of the mission to certain ideas that have held their ground among historians even to the present day. The missionaries are supposed to have possessed secret faculties and instructions, which, had they really existed, would have meant the total destruction of the mission. It is therefore necessary once and for all to ascertain what kind of secrecy was permitted to the missionaries and what not.

The missionaries were allowed to perform their spiritual functions in secret, to administer and reserve the Holy Sacrament without ceremony, to say mass in the presence of protestants and excommunicated persons.[2] They were permitted, and even directed, to dress as laymen, and only to wear their cassock when celebrating mass and hearing confessions in cases where the chance of danger was remote;[3] they were not on any account to carry about with them objects of devotion and other articles forbidden by English law.[4] They must reveal their status as priests or Jesuits only when it was necessary, or when the knowledge of it would bring certain benefit to souls.[5]

[1] By RICHARD WHITE, a Welsh poet.   POLLEN, Unpubl. doc., I., pp. 93-95.
[2] See the faculties, Appendix XVII., A [§ 1].
[3] Instructions, § 7.   Arch. Gen. S.J., vid. ante, p. 142, note 1.
[4] Ib., § 16.
[5] Ib., § 17.

On the other hand, neither the pope nor the general of the Jesuits gave authority to priests of the English mission to pretend to be protestants in cases where they thought they might serve the catholic church by doing so. Neither priests nor laymen ever received dispensations to comply with the anglican rite and figure outwardly as ministers and officials of the anglican state church, even when this might have been of advantage to the Roman church. The tradition which maintains that they did so,[1] is shown, when examined, to be wholly devoid of solid proof. To meet a number of cases which would arise, priests received fuller powers of dispensing and absolving than were usual, *e.g.* they could absolve owners of church property from the guilt of their unlawful possessions ;[2] they could in certain cases allow forbidden books to be read ;[3] they could dispense from "irregularity,"[4] etc., grant dispensations and perform benedictions usually reserved to the higher order of the hierarchy.[5] But all these deviations from established custom are explained either by the enforced secrecy by which acts of catholic worship had to be surrounded or by the absence of a catholic bishop in England. It would have been the destruction of the catholic cause

[1] The chief source is the account supposed to be written by E. Dennum, an English spy in Italy between 1560 and 1570, but really a forgery of the seventeenth century. STRYPE, *Annals of the Reform.*, I., ii. (1824), pp. 54–57. *Cf.*, III., ii., p. 107. FROUDE, *Hist. of Engl.*, Vol. VII., p. 177, and others, including STÄHLIN, *Sir Francis Walsingham*, I. (1908), p. 172, treat the account as genuine. *Cf.* J. H. POLLEN, *The Alleged Papal Sanction of the Anglican Liturgy*, The Month, Sept., 1902, pp. 274–280.

[2] *Faculties* [§ 6]. Appendix XVII., A. The Scotch Jesuit Creighton says of the nobles of Scotland that it was the dread of having to give up church property which was the chief hindrance to their return to the church. Appendix XX.

[3] *Faculties* [§ 7].

[4] *Ib.* [§ 4].

[5] *Ib.* [§ 1]. The consecration of chalices and vestments, etc.

had the pope allowed priests and laymen to pretend to be protestants, no matter for what reason. The words, "Son, give me thy heart and it sufficeth," were falsely attributed to the pope as the motto for this masquerade.[1] But the history of the catholic mission in England tells on every page how the sons of the Roman church gave not only their heart to the pope, but their heart's blood to the hangman.

Profound secrecy necessarily surrounded the labours of the mission priests, yet the secrecy had nothing whatever to do with political intrigues. Separation from all secular affairs is the note constantly struck in all their letters. So far removed were all thoughts of politics from these men that we can scarcely detect the least trace of them in the reports which they forwarded to Rome. "About parliament I say nothing, as I desire my letter, like my soul, to have absolutely nothing to do with matters of state."[2] Had not the mission kept clear of politics in the way it did, it could never have achieved its great religious success. What was wanting in opportunities for widespread action they made up for by the concentrated intensity of their labours.

The difficulties with which the mission had to contend can scarcely be painted in too vivid colours. The narrative of Fr. Gerard, and similar accounts from other sources, give us a description of the way priests returned to their native land.[3] After making careful choice of a place for landing, they landed secretly at night, and, carefully avoiding

---

[1] "Fili, da mihi cor tuum et sufficit." STRYPE, *op cit.*, III., ii., p. 107.

[2] Rob. Southwell, S.J., to Rob. Persons, S.J., Dec. 22, 1586. POLLEN, *Unpubl. doc.*, I., p. 319. *Cf.* with this [§ 18] of the *Instructions for the Jesuit Missionaries*, quoted above, p. 142.

[3] J. MORRIS, S.J., *Life of Father Gerard* (3rd ed., London, 1881), pp. 36–44.

all human habitations and every barking dog, they spent
the first night in the woods, notwithstanding rain and cold.
In the morning they separated, and each man set out in a
different direction.   The high-road was unsafe, for watchers
stopped strangers to ask them whence they came and
whither they went.   On this account, Fr. Gerard cut across
the fields and asked the country people he met if they had
seen his escaped falcon.   His familiarity with sport helped
him to conceal his real character.   While he was talking
knowingly of falcons, dogs, and horses, no one imagined he
was a priest of the Society of Jesus.   One of the missionaries
travelled through the country dressed like a man of the
world in silks and velvets, with plumes in his hat, mounted
on horseback with a falcon on his wrist and servants at his
side.[1]   Another dressed himself up as a military captain
returning home from foreign service.[2]   A third had learnt
some trade or handiwork to serve as a blind to his true
calling.[3]   Priests, it seems, were fond of acting the part of
doctors.   Others again gave out that they had returned
home from abroad after travelling for pleasure or education
in foreign countries—the Englishman's love of travel was
then beginning to take possession of him—or hired themselves out to gentlemen as ordinary servants in order by
degrees to win the confidence of the household.[4]   But
mines only lead to counter-mines.   All householders received strict orders to make careful investigations into the

[1] FOLEY, *Records*, Vol. I. (1877), p. 332.

[2] Persons' account given in his *Entrance of the Jesuits in England*,
ed. POLLEN, Cath. Record Soc. Misc., II. (1906), p. 200.

[3] It is only in the seventeenth century that I find frequent references
to priests acting as doctors.   See the warning put out by the Assembly
in 1616 ; CALDERWOOD, *Hist. of the Kirk of Scotl.*, VII. (Edin. 1845),
p. 225 ; WILLIAM BANNATYNE'S *Mission Report of* 1660, Publ.
Record Office, Bliss's Roman Transcripts, p. 98.

[4] Proclamation on troubles of the realm at the hand of Jesuits,
Oct. 18, 1591.

parentage, standing, and civil status of the members of
their establishment, and to inquire into their means of sub-
sistence, their previous place of abode, and their attendance
at church. Whoever did not give a strict account of all
these matters had to answer for it before the justices.[1]
In the end few priests escaped detection. Many met their
fate as soon as they landed on their native shore. One
priest who thought himself safe in his sailor's dress had
scarcely left the ship when he was seized and sent up to
London.[2]

All this secrecy and disguise is easily explained by the
ever-present perils surrounding the life of a priest in
England, but their enemies did not rest content with so
simple and natural an explanation. A man who hides
his real face must be bent on mischief. "A velvet hat
and feather, a buff leather jerkin, velvet venetians—are
they weeds for dead men ?"[3] Lord Burleigh, the originator
of the penal legislation, the man who had forced priests to
adopt these secret ways, upbraided them for donning
unclerical costumes.[4] No doubt in the minds of the large
number, who never see clearly the relation between cause
and effect, suspicion of priests was increased by the dis-
guises they wore and the false names by which they went.
What was romantic in their behaviour at the time led to
lasting results. The " Jesuit in disguise " became a typical
character in popular imagination, and political aims and
schemes were attributed to him without hesitation. He
was thought to be everlastingly busied in scheming, a past

[1] Proclamation on troubles of the realm at the hand of Jesuits,
Oct. 18, 1591.

[2] POLLEN, *Unpubl. doc.*, I., p. 309. This happened in 1586.

[3] From Campion's trial. SIMPSON'S *Campion*, p. 413.

[4] BURLEIGH, *Execution of Justice*, Somers Tracts, I. (2nd ed.,
1809), p. 196 : "Campion who was found out being disguised like a
roister"; p. 205 : "All in their apparell as roisters or ruffins." Also in
the Harleian Miscellany, II. (1809), pp. 144, 152.

master in flattery, and unscrupulous in the choice of means
—a being who shrank from daylight. " I finde the polly-
ticke Jesuite to be the moste daungerous person that anye
commonwealth can nourishe or suffer." [1]

Once in England, the priests had to avoid their homes
and the dwellings of their parents and kindred, lest they
should expose both themselves and their relations to
manifest danger. All night long they tramped about the
fields and woods without getting any sleep.[2] Many of
them passed a miserable existence in hiding-places. On
the sea-coast of Carnarvon, a priest assembled his flock
in a cave "about three fathoms deep." [3] Others fared
little better in the houses of the catholic nobility in towns.
When there were only few catholics among the numerous
servants a priest was obliged to conceal himself and pass
days and nights aloft in a hiding chamber, "like a
sparrow under the roof," "snatching carefully mouthfuls of
fresh air at the window, moving with caution in order to avoid
being seen, saying mass in the presence of only a few persons,
and conversing with fewer still." [4] Whenever a disguised
priest had gained a footing in a house, without being
known to be a priest, he had to prepare the way himself,
and months might pass during which he could only put out
feelers and act tentatively and gradually in order, step by
step, to gain, by means of daily intercourse, first confidence,
then friendship, and finally the souls of the household,

---

[1] From a letter addressed to Cecil in 1600, given in summary in
DOMESTIC CAL., 1598–1601, p. 499.

[2] "A parentum et affinium tectis . . . se abstinere coguntur et
aliquando . . . insomnes per agros silvasque noctes traducunt et per
invia ad auroram usque pervagantur." *Annuæ litteræ coll. Angl.*
1582. Arch. of the Eng. coll. in Rome. *Cf.* FOLEY, *Records*, VI.,
p. 84.

[3] DOMESTIC CAL., 1581–90, p. 405.

[4] From a contemporary account, about 1595. H. MORUS, *Historia
Miss. Angl. Soc. Jesu ab a.* 1580 *ad a.* 1635 (Andomari, 1660), p. 184.

while all the time he was daily in danger of his life.[1]   The adventures of some of the missionaries are almost beyond belief.   Fr. Gerard remained for four days shut up in a cupboard concealed behind the wainscot of a room, while the persecutors searched every nook and corner, and sounded all the walls.   At the end of the time, he was released from the hiding-hole half dead.[2]   Occasionally we find it said plainly that such a life as this was made even attractive by the dangers which surrounded it.   While Fr. Southwell was once hiding from his pursuers in a place similar to that just mentioned, he declared, as if astonished at his own feelings, "Yet in the midst of perils, it is marvellous how good God is, and how bountiful of His comforts, insomuch that danger itself groweth sweet."[3]

No reader can resist the charm which exhales from the letters of Campion, Southwell, and others who took part in the first Jesuit mission.   Their religious acts were marked by a solemnity as of the catacombs.   Each service became an event.   The significance of every sacred action was felt to the full.   The common danger riveted the spiritual bond between priest and people. The heroic courage of the missionaries moved even protestants to admiration.   "God allows the same to happen here as we read of in the early church, and there are many people, even tho' they be heretics, who are so faithful to the many priests who are here in disguise that, for their sakes, they disregard wives, children, and possessions, saying that they are good people and they will not betray them."[4]   A mission priest relates

---

[1] J. MORRIS, S.J., *Life of Father Gerard* (3rd ed., 1881), pp. 96 *et seq.*
[2] *Ib.*, pp. 165–169.
[3] "Ut vel ipsa certe discrimina dulcescant." Letter of 1586. POLLEN, *Unpubl. doc.*, I., p. 313.
[4] SPAN. CAL., 1580–86, p. 140.

(1581),[1] " Sometimes when we were sitting merrily at table, conversing familiarly on matters of faith and devotion (for our talk is generally of such things), there comes a hurried knock at the door, like that of a pursuivant. All start up and listen—like deer when they hear the huntsman ; we leave our food and commend ourselves to God in a brief ejaculation ; nor is word or sound heard till the servants come to say what the matter is. If it is nothing, we laugh at our fright." The moral impression made by a mass, which might cost men their freedom or even their lives, was as much enhanced as was the reputation of the priest who was exposed by his calling to constant dangers and perils. When a priest entered a catholic house, all who knew him to be such fell on their knees to receive his blessing.[2] " The complaint heard elsewhere that mass is too long is never heard in England. A mass that does not last at least an hour appears insufficient to many. Six, eight, and more masses are celebrated in one day in the same place. There are no lawsuits between catholics, the priest's word is regarded as decisive." [3] When to this deepening of the spiritual life a moral purification is ascribed, as when we are told how every Christian duty was more strictly fulfilled " [4] and how the proverb, " A catholic pays his debts," [5] gained currency, it may be that self-complacency comes into play yet does not efface from these narratives the stamp of trustworthiness.

[1] N. SANDERUS, *De origine . . . schis. Angl.* (1586), p. 452.

[2] *Relatione del presente stato d Inghilterra* (Roma, 1590), p. 8.

[3] SANDERUS, *op. cit.*, p. 453. *Cf.* SACCHINUS, IV., lib. viii., § 129 : "Lites inter catholicos vix ullæ."

[4] " Morum tanta integritas ubique consecuta, ut jam ex ipsis Christianæ vitæ officiis catholici internoscerentur " ; P. BOMBINUS, *Vita et martyr. E. Campiani* (1620), p. 123.

[5] " Hic inter pios hæreticos, si qui sunt paulo æquiores, proverbium inolevit—catholicos esse qui argentum resolvant quod debent." From a letter of Campion's. SACCHINUS, IV., lib. viii., § 128.

P

The most important weapons for mission work were casuistry and controversy. It is true that the Jesuits were enjoined to avoid as much as possible discussing religious questions with protestants, as it was dangerous and led to no result,[1] yet the missionary might find himself any day in a position in which he had either to decide questions of conscience arising out of the conflict between religion and patriotism, or to defend the catholic faith against attacks that were making an impression upon unstable catholics. Skill in controversy was accordingly quite as necessary as a knowledge of controversial literature, and there was also urgent need for good preaching. Other departments of sacred learning were not much called for on the mission.[2] Missionaries, too, occasionally employed means which in the seventeenth century attained unfortunate notoriety—casting out devils and exorcism. The influence of exorcism in bringing about conversions was especially mentioned.[3] Remarkable examples of asceticism of a monastic type, and of endurance of bodily sufferings were related of some of the missionaries and are said to have powerfully helped on the work of the mission.[4]

[1] *Instructions*, § 12.

[2] " Certe quilibet hic sacerdos perutilis est, maxime illi, qui casus conscientiæ et controversias probe callent. Cætera enim doctrina, quamvis curiosis quandoque auribus satisfaciat, rarissimus tamen est apud nos illius usus. Concionatores hic magnopere desiderantur ideoque pernecessarium est, ut ibi [Romæ] assuefaciant se, ut et facilitatem in dicendo et rerum copiam usu acquirant." Southwell, S.J., to Agazzari, rector of the Engl. coll. in Rome, 1586. POLLEN, *Unpubl. doc.*, I., 316. *Cf.* above, p. 103.

[3] Southwell to Acquaviva, 1586. POLLEN, p. 309.

[4] " Præter enim ieiunia et flagella, præter vigilias et orationis assiduitatem quidam huius collegii sacerdos cutem sibi lento quodam igne adurere, noctu super cordas plurimis magnisque nodis in modum cratis compositas cubare et adeo in tota victus ratione austerus esse consuevit, ut vel ipsis excitet hæreticis admirationem." *Annuæ litt. coll. Angl.* 1583. Arch. of the Engl. coll., Rome, *Liber ruber.* In English in FOLEY, *Records*, VI., 103.

We can here only briefly touch upon the extensive use of printed works made by the missionaries. Both Persons and Campion wrote and were even able to get a certain number of their works secretly printed in England.[1] By special dispensation from the pope, the mission priests were allowed to publish their books anonymously, and without the name of the place where they were printed.[2] This was a dispensation from the decrees passed by the council of Trent. The seminaries continued to be centres of learned activity with a considerable literary out-put.[3] Often the fate of English catholics was sealed by the discovery of these works when their houses were searched.[4]

It did not suffice that catholic priests should labour both by word of mouth and by their writings, for so widespread was zeal for religion in these early years that young laymen too, who had been educated at Douay, worked as a secret bodyguard by the side of the priests. There were others also who in a more restricted area—sometimes as tutors in noble families—did their share in keeping alive the catholic faith in England.[5]

The mission halted before no barrier, not even the walls of the prisons. Priests confined along with criminals

---

[1] Campion's *Decem Rationes* were printed in Lady Stonor's Park at Henley. SIMPSON, p. 287. For a list of the writings of Campion and Persons, see *Dict. of Nat. Biogr.*

[2] Appendix XVII., A [§ 8].

[3] *Cf.* K. WERNER'S sketch in his *Geschichte der apologet. u. polem. Litteratur der christl. Theologie*, IV. (Schaffhausen, 1865), pp. 320–324.

[4] *The Egerton Papers*, ed. P. COLLIER, Camd. Soc. (1840), p. 164.

[5] " . . . Sed et laici iuvenes docti clam migrant Duaco in Angliam et suos parentes ac cognatos docent cum fructu fidem catholicam, ita ut inde fiat, quod aliquæ integræ familiæ Anglia relicta in Belgicam migrarint. Alii quoque se faciunt ludi magistros in familiis nobilium, ut semen catholicum spargant in Anglia." From a memorial, *De ratione et progressu seminarii cleri Anglicani in universitate Duacena.* Arch. Vat., Miscell. Arm. XI., t. 94, fol. 208ᵛ.

ministered to the souls of their fellow prisoners.[1]   Indeed imprisoned priests, as Persons once said,[2] are often more useful to the catholic cause than those at liberty, for many people resorted to them who otherwise would have been deprived of priestly ministrations.   It was often possible to have mass said in prison, though it required both daring and skilful management.   In one of the London prisons, the prisoners provided themselves with keys to their cells, and early each morning before the guards were astir heard mass together.[3]   On another occasion catholics from without came into the prison in order to hear mass there.[4]   We even hear of jailers who were so much impressed by daily intercourse with the priests that they were received into the bosom of the church by their own captives.[5]

But the death of the martyrs ever remained the catholic mission's most effective means for achieving its purpose. Somewhat in the same way as the primitive races believed that those who fell in battle passed at once into the abode of the blessed, so the persecuted catholics had an unshaken confidence that those who suffered the martyr's death had no longer any judgment to fear in the next world.

> "Your sentence wronge pronouncèd of hym here
> Exemptes hym from the iudgement for to come.
> O happie he that ys not iudged there!
> God grante me too, to have an earthlie doome!"[6]

---

[1] POLLEN, *Unpubl. doc.*, I., p. 87.

[2] Letter of Aug. 24, 1583.   THEINER, *Ann. Eccles.*, III., p. 475.

[3] J. MORRIS, *Life of Gerard* (3rd ed., 1881), p. 199.

[4] Complaint of the bishop of London, Aylmer, to Lord Burleigh, Dec. 5, 1583.   POLLEN, p. 47.

[5] *Relatione del presente stato d'Inghilterra* (Roma, 1590), p. 11. SPAN. CAL., 1580–86, p. 336.

[6] H. WALPOLE, *Epitaph of Campion*. A. JESSOPP, *One Generation of a Norfolk House* (Norwich, 1878), p. 101, and in POLLEN'S ed. of ALLEN'S *Briefe Hist.* (1908), p. 30.

One prisoner, as he lay in his cell by candle-light on the night before his execution, suddenly saw the shadow of his head on the wall surrounded by a crown.[1] To another appeared "a verie comfortable vision of a greate and cleere light in Newgate the night before he suffered."[2] Foretastes of the heavenly reward like these, joined to an excited condition of the religious feelings, which even reached the point of seeing visions, explain the almost superhuman powers of endurance with which the martyrs bore the most exquisite torture, and went forth triumphantly to meet a death scarcely less appalling. "They laugh, they care not for death!" cried the crowd in astonishment when they saw Campion and his companions dragged to the gallows.[3] Had they lived a hundred years, their friends averred, they could not have benefited the catholic cause so much as by their deaths.[4] Or, as the Jesuit poet Southwell said, the blood of the martyrs is the spring shower which waters the field of the church.[5] Great as was the care taken to prevent the people showing reverence to the relics of the martyrs, or dipping cloths in their blood, all was in vain. Relics were secured after every execution, and sometimes it was the executioner himself who sold to catholics the martyrs' bloodstained garments.[6] Well known and quite authentic is the story which tells how Henry Walpole came as a protestant to witness Campion's execution, and went away inwardly convinced of the truth of catholicism. As the limbs of the martyr were being torn asunder, a drop of

---

[1] POLLEN, *Unpubl. doc.*, I., p. 331 (1590).
[2] *Op. cit.*, p. 291.   [3] SIMPSON, p. 449.
[4] *Annuæ litt. coll. Angl. de Urbe*, 1581. Arch. of the English coll., *Liber ruber*. FOLEY, *Records*, VI., p. 78.
[5] FOLEY, I., p. 326.
[6] *Annuæ litteræ coll. Angl.*, 1583. SPAN. CAL., 1580–81, p. 153. POLLEN, *Unpubl. doc.*, I., p. 324 (1594).

blood fell on young Walpole, who thereupon was thrilled by the feeling that he must follow in the martyr's steps. He became a catholic and a Jesuit, and died a similar death to Campion.[1]   An instance like this of conversion by a sudden revulsion of feeling does not stand alone.[2] Many things concurred to enhance the impression made by the executions, such as the calm cheerfulness of the condemned men who were often quite young, their protestations of innocence at the hour of death, and the last prayer of these " traitors " for Queen Elizabeth.

Keen-sighted men soon began to utter warnings against a system which gave martyrs to the catholics, and desired that the Roman church should not be fought with any but spiritual weapons.[3]   Burleigh himself allowed it to be seen how fully he realized this, but rather from a theoretical than from a practical point of view,[4] for that violent age was not in harmony with such ideas.   In order to render the martyrs harmless, it was thought better either to forbid them to utter any last speech or prayer, or to stop their mouths by a handkerchief.[5]   Instead of the con-demned, the magistrate made a speech in order to give the people an account of the priest's treason.[6] Yet even after death, the martyrs spoke more loudly than in their life—through the lips of their poets.

---

[1] SIMPSON, *op. cit.*, pp. 454 *et seq.*

[2] *Cf.* the conversion of the family of the martyr Jennings. POLLEN, p. 207.

[3] SIMPSON, *op. cit.*, p. 463.

[4] *Advice in Matters of Religion and State*, Somers Tracts, I. (1809), pp. 166 *et seq.*

[5] POLLEN, I., p. 289 ; *cf.* pp. 186, 207, 323.

[6] " No priests are suffered to speak at their deaths, but so soon as they are dead Topclif in an oration unto the people faineth the cause to be for the assisting the intended invasion of the realm " (1592). POLLEN, p. 208.

V. *The Mission and the Persecution in Religious Poetry*

A movement so full of spiritual power and with so tempestuous a history as the catholic mission under Elizabeth could not fail to have its poets as well as its martyrs. A full and adequate treatment of catholic poetry in the Shakespearian age belongs to the history of literature, but a short sketch of the chief poets of catholicism cannot be omitted from a description of the mission, for in them we come to closer quarters with the spiritual life and sentiments of the catholics than almost anywhere else, and, moreover, poetry itself played no small part among the means employed by the catholic propaganda.

An exiled catholic, Richard Rowlands, who for a long time lived a life of great poverty in Antwerp under the assumed Dutch name of Verstegan, composed poems marked by a return to the simplest forms of religious sentiment, and a freedom of soul from all external things.[1] Unshaken confidence that the catholic cause was the cause of God sustained him in all his miseries—

> " And force of foes destroy'd may bee
> And I made safe for serving thee ! "[2]

Compared with the pressing need of the present, the past—the time before the separation of the churches—seems to him a golden age ; still not the faintest sound of political affairs interrupts the purely religious tone of his poetry—

[1] " Mr. Verstegan, whose need much requireth some help," from a letter of Henry Walpole to Creswell (1591). JESSOPP, *Letters of Henry Walpole, S.J.* (Norwich, 1873), p. 30, *cf.* p. 36.

[2] RICHARD VERSTEGAN, *Odes* (1601), p. 19.

> "The golden world long since is worne away,
> As now the golden yeare [1] hath taken end.
> The iron world doth stil remaine and stay
> And in his rust doth to his ruyn tend,
> And in the shew of vertue and of truthe
> Seeme-good, seeme-gospel turneth all to ruthe." [2]

Psalms of penitence, hymns to Our Lady, legends of the saints, lamentations over the church's lost unity, praise of the solitary life—these are the subjects of Verstegan's poems. They are at once tender and manly and full of childlike touches, pure not only in the sincerity of their religious sentiments, but pure also from all the bitterness of an exile. They are pervaded by the peace of a soul that has freed itself from all earthly things.

The grief of the persecuted and the exile finds its most successful poetic expression in a ballad that became popular called *The Blessed Conscience*.[3] The poem contains the lament of a Lancashire gentleman, Thomas Houghton, who had had to flee from the home of his ancestors—

> " For yn thys londe yo canot lyve
> And kepe yor conscyence."

He, too, went into Flanders and died there in banishment.[4]

> "At Hoghton hygh, which is a bower
> Of sports and lordly pleasure
> I wept and lefte that loftie tower
> Wich was my chiefest treasure.
> To save my soul and lose ye reste
> Yt was my trew pretence ;
> Lyke fryghted bird I lefte my neste
> To keep my conscyence."

---

[1] 1600, the year of Jubilee.

[2] From his ode—the *Complaint of Church Controversy, Odes*, p. 94.

[3] Probably, but not certainly, by Verstegan. Printed by GILLOW. *The Haydock Papers* (1888), pp. 10–15. *Cf.* Cath. Record Soc., III. (1906), p. 1.

[4] In 1580, at Liège.

The touching refrain at the end of every verse, *To kepe my conscyence*, was also his last words when dying. Forsaken by every one except a brother, he greets death as a release—

> "And nowe I shall goe wher I may
> Enjoy my conscyence."

The thought of his lost home alone makes death hard to him—

> "Fayr Englande, nowe ten tymes adieu !
> And frendes that theryn dwel.
> Fayrwel, my broder Richard trewe
> Whom I dyd love soe wel.
> Fayrwel, fayrwel ! good people all,
> And learn experience :
> Love not too much ye golden ball,
> But kepe your conscyence ! "

The best-known English catholic poet of this period is Robert Southwell, Jesuit and martyr. He is indeed the only one who has a place to-day among the poets of his country. Although his style is often marred by the euphuism in fashion at the period, his poems have a religious and poetic value for all time. Southwell was one of those born martyrs who all his life longed for the palm. He embraced the jailer who brought him word that he was condemned to death. His farewell speech at his execution shows that the invisible was more present to him than the visible. His poems were like his life and his faith. That life was to be judged not from a material but from a supernatural standpoint is taught in them in the most emphatic manner. Fr. Southwell is no longer a man living among men, he is a citizen of the other world who delights in renouncing this world, and feels nothing but compassion for those deluded people to whom all earthly things are not yet vain and empty. *Life is but loss—I die alive—At home in heaven*—are the favourite themes of his poems.

> " Plough not the seas, sow not the sands,
>   Leave off your **idle** pain !
> Seek other mistress for your minds
>   Love's service is in vain." [1]

He is strong in his treatment of missionary subjects. Things which to others are merely poetic symbols or dry figures of speech become luminous with him, and are alive with personality.   Hence the powerful fascination of his Christmas carol, *The Burning Babe.* [2]

The contrast between the sufferings of this present life and the joys of the world to come—a favourite theme with all religious poets in misfortune—enters frequently into the writings of the catholic poets of the Elizabethan age. The glories of the heavenly Jerusalem—the city built of pearls and gold, of ivory and precious stones—the ever-lasting springtime and the never-ending fruitfulness of the fields of heaven, and the triumphant martyrs " clad in scarlet red," [3] who stand in the midst of this world of wonders—all these things are depicted in the brilliant colours of a childlike faith.

> " Hierusalem, my happie home !
>   Would God I were in thee !
> Would God my woes were at an end,
>   Thy joyes that I might see." [4]

Compared with this, all earthly things seem as nought, and all men's toil and striving worthless—

> " The marchant cuts the seas for gaine ;
>   The soldier serves for his renowne ;
> The tilman plowes the ground for gaine—
>   Be this *my* ioy and lasting crowne !

---

[1] The concluding verse of SOUTHWELL'S *Love's Servile Lot.*

[2] The last edition of his *complete works* was published in 1886.

[3] " The martyrs clad in scarlet red." *A Prisoner's Song.* The Month, July–Dec., 1871, pp. 232–240.

[4] A song made by F. B. P., The Month, *l.c.,* pp. 232–235. *Cf.* FROUDE'S quotation, Vol. XI., p. 110.

> The falkener seekes to see a flight ;
>   The hunter beates to see his game—
> Long thou, my soule, to see that sight,
>   And labour to enioy the same ! "

The poetry of English catholics, however, drew its noblest inspiration from the deaths of the martyrs. Henry Walpole, the enthusiastic youth, upon whom Campion's blood fell at his execution, who came under the influence of the heavenly vision and followed the object of his admiration into the Society of Jesus, to prison and to death (p. 213)—he, too, became the poet of the martyrs. All the sentiment and passion called forth by Campion's joyous death found poetical expression in Walpole's simple verse.[1] The poem on his martyrdom spread rapidly throughout the country and perhaps did more for the catholic cause than the labours of many missionaries. The English government hunted out the stanzas on Campion's death as eagerly as it pursued priests and Jesuits,[2] for the man they had put to death in vain, lived in these verses full of triumphant joy and contempt for death—

> " You thought perhaps, when lerned Campions dyes,
>   His pen must cease, his sugred tong be still ?
> But you forgot how lowde his death it cryes,
>   How farre beyond the sound of tongue and quill !
> You did not know how rare and great a good
>   It was to write his precious giftes in blood."

The lament over his death therewith becomes a song of thanksgiving—

> " Bounden be we to give eternall prayse
>   To Jesus' name which such a man did rayse ! "

This is the language of conquerors, not of the conquered.

---

[1] *An epitaphe of the lyfe and deathe of . . . Edmund Campian, rev. father of the meeke societie of the blessed name of Jesus.* JESSOPP, *One Generation of a Norfolk House* (Norwich, 1878), pp. 97–102. A slightly different version in CARD. ALLEN'S *Briefe Hist.*, ed. POLLEN (1908), pp. 26–31.

[2] JESSOPP, p. 96.

In the considerable number of poems written about Campion's martyrdom, the same theme constantly recurs. The lament—

> "What iron hart that wold not melt in greefe?"

is changed into the shout of triumph—

> "Rejoice, be glad, triumph, sing himmes of Joye!"[1]

Among the imprisoned catholics, many were led to become poets by the solitude of their prisons, and such was Francis Tregian, who, during the long and painful hours of confinement, wrote religious poems with a nail and candle-smoke, and sent the following touching farewell to his wife :—

> "Bless, in my name, my little babes,
>   God send them all good hap!
> And bless withal that little babe
>   That lieth in your lap!"[2]

The poems of imprisoned priests bear witness to the high spirit which animated the mission. It says much both for the courage of these men, which always rose equal to the occasion, and for their education, that they occupied the long hours of confinement in writing odes to their fellow prisoners in Alcaic metre and in the style of Horace.[3]

> "Qui mecum, amici, sicut oves neci
> Hoc, destinatæ, carcere degitis,
> Durate constantes et aures
>   His adhibete animosque dictis!
>
> .   .   .
>
> Perstate fortes fortiter in fide,
> Diri Dathanis credite semita,
> Differt ; suum tandem fidelis
>   Sed reparabit ovile Christus."

---

[1] ALLEN, *op. cit.*, pp. 55 *et seq.*

[2] J. MORRIS, *The Troubles of our Catholic Forefathers*, I. (London, 1872), p. 130. The date of the poem is 1593.

[3] *Carmen sacri martyris ad concaptivos.* JOHN BRIDGEWATER, *Concertatio* (2nd ed., 1588), fol. 125ᵛ, 126. I give the first and last verses of the ode. The author is unknown.

Another imprisoned priest, John Ingram, bore the pains of imprisonment with cheerful philosophy. A cheery and even humorous strain pervades the epigrams with which he covered the walls of his cell. The man was free, in spite of chains and prison walls, who could sing of his lot in flowing Latin verse while shut up in prison and in daily expectation of death, and could give a poetic and humorous turn to all the tribulations of the hour, without allowing a drop of bitterness to fall into the chalice of his sufferings which formed the source of his poetic inspiration. In a Sapphic ode on the different prisons with which he had become acquainted, Ingram makes merry over the guest that comes unbidden to his chamber—the mouse.

> "Sanctus ut Baptista Dei Ioannes
> Matris ex alvo socios eremo
> Hinnulos, Turri [1] comites tenebam
> Sic ego mures." [2]

From this man, whom the muses followed into prison, no pains of torture could draw a single word which might betray, or even cause danger, to his friends and helpers. Under all his sufferings the poet was dumb.[3]

The same spirit, however, did not inspire all of them. Controversy, both political and religious, had its poets too, not indeed among Englishmen, but from among the more hot-blooded Celts. A son of poetic Wales, Richard White, wrote war songs in the language of his country during the heroic period of the mission, in which every note is sounded

---

[1] *I.e.* the Tower of London.

[2] POLLEN, *Unpubl. doc.*, I., p. 277. *Ib.* pp. 270–282 for other poems by Ingram along with biographical matter. His poems written in prison date from 1594.

[3] "I take God to record that I neither named house, man, wife, or child in time of, or before, my torments. . . . My bloody Saul, Top-cliffe, said I was a monster amongst all others for my strange taciturnity." From his farewell letter to his fellow prisoners. POLLEN, I., 283.

from harmless sarcasm to deepest contempt and wild ungovernable hatred.   His pæan on the murder of William of Orange is a terrible example of the lengths to which religious excitement can drive a man.   Scorn and hatred strive together with the ferocity of a wild animal.[1]

Still this is a solitary case, an ugly discord breaking in upon the pure harmony of the poetry of English catholics. But, at the same time, it is a strain which could not fail to make itself heard, if poetry is to serve as a reflection of the true state of men's feelings.

Deep religious feeling which rises victorious over the world, childlike confidence in the church, heroic courage, and implacable bloodthirsty hatred—these are the qualities exhibited in turn by English catholicism under Queen Elizabeth.

[1] I do not quote from the original because White wrote in Welsh. The original, with English literal translation, is given by POLLEN, *l.c.* pp. 90–99.

CHAPTER III

THE ARMADA

WHEN great issues are at stake, a victory or a defeat appears to simple minds as the act of God. This has always been so, but more especially is it the case in periods of religious excitement. The history of the reformation and counter-reformation affords examples of this, but none more remarkable than the impression made on contemporaries by the fate of the Spanish Armada in 1588, and the way in which that impression has sunk into the minds of subsequent generations. That a great naval engagement should die out of the popular imagination and give place to the impression left by the disaster wrought by the forces of nature; that storm and foam should take the place of the roar of cannon, and that to wind and wave should be ascribed what was due to the superior equipment of a fleet, finds no parallel in the history of modern warfare. England's first great test as a new sea-power, the triumph won by her skill in shipbuilding and gunnery, the masterly way in which she manœuvred her fleet in accordance with completely novel tactics—all this, along with the fact that the defeat of the Armada was a turning-point in the history of naval warfare, has escaped the notice of the majority of men. One fact, however, which had nothing to do with naval tactics and was of no historical importance, has made an indelible impression both on contemporaries and on after generations, *i.e.* the battered, and disabled Armada, now no longer seaworthy or capable of offering resistance, was destroyed by storms off the Scottish coast as it made its way home. The world believed it saw with greater certainty the hand of the avenging God, who once upon a time overthrew Pharaoh and his host in the Red Sea,[1] in the play of elemental forces than in feats of human prowess. The immortal inscription which Holland, in thanksgiving for its own delivery, placed on the medal struck in commemoration of the victory, *Flavit Jehovah et dissipati sunt*,[2] recalls the song of thanksgiving sung by Moses and the Children of Israel.[3] The same tone of humble thanksgiving to God, characterizes most of the inscriptions on many other medals which celebrated the destruction of the " Invincible Armada "—*Tu Deus magnus et magna facis tu solus Deus*.[4] Among the historians of the great event, many give currency to an ancient prophecy which foretold that the year 1588 was to be an *annus mirabilis* upon which depended the fate of the world.[5]

---

[1] The publisher of the fictitious *Copy of a letter sent out of England to Don Bernardin Mendoza* (Brit. Mus. 440, i. 16) adds a note dated Oct. 9, 1588—" The Printer to the Reader "—mentioning the fate of the Armada. The fight itself does not give rise to any pious reflections—in the storm alone he sees the action of " Almighty God, who always avengeth, etc."

[2] Commonly given as, "Afflavit Deus et dissipati sunt." On the tradition concerning the inscription, see GEORG BÜCHMANN, *Geflügelte Worte* (24 ed., 1910), p. 11.

[3] Exod. xv. 10, in the Vulgate : " Flavit spiritus tuus et operuit eos mare."

[4] CES. FERN. DURO, *La Armada Invencible*, I. (Madrid, 1884), pp. 217 *et seq.* The medal with the inscription quoted above is depicted in ERICH MARCKS, *Kgin. Elizabeth von Engl. u. ihre Zeit* (1897), p. 68.

[5] The prophecy that 1588 would be an "annus mirabilis, mundi climacterium " can be traced back to Regiomontan, J. Stofler, and other German astronomers. Not only protestant historians (CAMDEN, *Annal. Angliæ* [1625], p. 513 ; STRYPE, *Annals*, III., ii. [1824], p. 2 ; SPOTTISWOODE, *Hist. of the Church of Scotland*, II., [1851], p. 389),

What is the reason that, especially in this case, the thought of divine judgment is so irresistibly powerful, so powerful indeed that the historical facts connected with the event have even been overlooked or forgotten?

In 1588 the period of the religious wars reached its climax. All the massacres committed in the course of the French wars of religion, all the vicissitudes of the struggle for faith and freedom in the Netherlands sink into mere episodes compared with the great duel between Spain and England. It is as if two champions in full battle array issued forth from two hostile armies to measure their strength. Upon them are fixed the gaze of both armies and the eyes of all the world. Before joining battle, both of them invoke the God for whom they fight. All merely earthly quarrels are forgotten at this supreme moment, and the conflict becomes one for matters of faith in the purest sense, while the decision is accepted as the verdict of God.

This feeling, which speaks to us pathetically out of the documents of the period,[1] has scarcely more value for later centuries than would attach to the heightened colours given to the event by poetic fancy. The historical importance of the year of the Armada, which has now in turn thrust its religious significance into the background, far transcends the judgment passed upon it by contemporaries. Regarded after the lapse of years, the importance of the event is revealed with greater clearness. In describing the battle, modern historians use words and adjectives very seldom to be met with in historical writing, and then

but catholic historians as well (SPONDANUS, *Annal. Eccles. contin.* [1659], *ad a.* 1588, § 1), have made the prophecy their own. The catholics, however, regard it as referring, not to the Armada, but to the events of the civil war in France.

[1] The proof for this will be given later on in this chapter, especially in sect. iii., "The Decision."

Q

only when narrating the great turning-points in the world's history.   These words can only be explained by the fact that 1588 stands as a symbol of the struggle carried on during a whole period.   " The fortune of mankind hung in the balance," said Ranke.[1]   Froude is still more emphatic:[2] "The action before Gravelines of the 30th of July, 1588, decided the largest problems ever submitted in the history of mankind to the arbitrament of force."   Laughton, the historian of the Armada, regards the event as "the great battle which, more distinctly perhaps than any battle of modern times, has moulded the history of Europe."[3] These are words which surpass all that either the combatants themselves or their contemporaries were conscious of both before and after the event.   What the engagement meant for them both from a political and a religious point of view, what the destruction of the Armada actually stood for in the struggle between England and the Catholic Church, between reformation and counter-reformation— these are points which we have to investigate here.   These questions cannot be answered without first glancing at the relations between England and Spain before the Armada.   Apart from this, England's foreign policy enters as little into the scope of this narrative as would a detailed treatment of the whole naval conflict between the two nations.

---

[1] *Hist. of Engl.* (Engl. trans., Oxford, 1875), Vol. I., p. 324.

[2] *Hist. of Engl.*, XII., p. 531 (1870), Froude's date, July 30, (o. s.) is wrong.   The decisive battle took place on July 29, o. s. (= Aug. 8, n. s.).

[3] *State papers relating to the defeat of the Spanish Armada*, ed. JOHN KNOX LAUGHTON, I. (1894), Introd., p. liv.   Navy Record Society Publications, I.

I. *Spain's Increasing Weakness and England's Growing Strength*

Any one who follows out in detail the relation of England to the catholic powers during the first twenty or thirty years of Elizabeth's reign soon finds he has so many threads in his hand that he can no longer unravel any one decided line of policy from amid all the tangle. Sometimes war seems on the point of breaking out with France and sometimes with Spain, and then a treaty is made with the one and then again with the other. The scene, however, presents quite a different appearance when once it is viewed from a little distance. No matter how often England might support the Huguenots in their quarrels with the French crown, or might wish to utilize the internal dissensions in France for the purpose of regaining Calais, and no matter how much importance might be attached, on the other hand, to the long-standing commercial friendship with Spain, a comprehensive view of the whole situation leaves no doubt in the mind that throughout these years, Spain, not France, was England's real foe. Opposing interests which nothing could harmonize, an irreconcilable opposition which embraced the whole world, existed only between England and Spain, not between England and France.

This great conflict plainly cast its shadow back upon the beginning of Elizabeth's reign. In the months following the re-establishment of the anglican state church, Philip II. had expressed himself in threatening language. He declared to Elizabeth that her policy was prejudicial to Spain's interests, and warned her not to compel him to intervene.[1] At the same time he informed Paul IV. of

[1] Philip II. to his ambassador in London, July 9, 1559. *Col. de doc. inéd.*, t. 87, p. 214. SPAN. CAL., 1558–67, p. 83.

his desire to be invested with England.[1]   He dissuaded, indeed, the pope from excommunicating and deposing Elizabeth, but asked, in case the sentence should be pronounced, that the vacant kingdom should be conferred on him.   Philip thought it worth while to get the assurance given him by Paul IV. confirmed by his successor Pius IV.[2]   Public opinion in England at a later date regarded the king of Spain as co-originator of the bull,[3] with how little justification has already been shown.[4]   Still, at the root of this notion there lay the knowledge that Spain alone would unquestionably be the executor of the bull, and that Philip II. felt himself called to the task.

For the king of Spain and not the emperor was the protector of the catholic church and the temporal sword of the papacy ; the son and not the brother of Charles V. was the inheritor of his ideas.   Spain, too, more than any other power, was regarded in England as the last resource of catholicism.   " I set more hope in the help of the king of Spain than on any other," wrote Mary Stuart in the early years of her imprisonment.[5]   A generation later, towards the end of Elizabeth's reign, an English catholic [6] looking back over the past wrote, " In forty yeres space there could appeare to man's discourse no

---

[1] Philip to Card. Pacheco, Aug. 22, 1559.   MIGNET, *Histoire de Marie Stuart* (Paris, 1885), p. 404.

[2] Philip to Vargas, his ambassador in Rome, July 16, 1561. *Op. cit.*, p. 407.

[3] SPAN. CAL., 1568–79, p. 257.   DE LA MOTHE FÉNÉLON *Correspondance diplomatique*, III. (1840), p. 196.

[4] *Vid. ante*, pp. 35–58 *passim*.

[5] Memorial drawn up by Mary, Feb. 8, 1571.   AL. LABANOFF, *Lettres, instructions et mém. de Marie Stuart*, III. (1844), p. 184.

[6] *Discourse of the Providence*, Publ. Record Office, State Papers Domestic, Eliz., Vol. CCLXXXVI., No. 60.   Summary in DOM. CAL., 1601–03, pp. 281 *et seq.*

hope or means to sett upp the catholick cause in our country but only by the favour and forces of the catholick King." In spite of all deceptions this hope remained steadfast, for there was no other. Even though the king did not interfere politically on their behalf, he at least gave the poverty-stricken exiles alms,[1] and gave them more generous alms than the pope, who was glad to commend his needy petitioners to the catholic king.[2] In addition to occasional aid, Philip II. made himself responsible for the regular payment of pensions to Englishmen who had forsaken their country on account of their faith. A list that fell into Burleigh's hands in 1574 gives thirty-three names of men and women, several of whom were of noble family.[3] In Philip's mind the idea of discharging a duty incumbent upon him as catholic king and protector of the church was combined with the desire to maintain a Spanish faction among the English catholics and to keep them from leaning towards France in the hopes of receiving help from thence.[4]

The depths to which distrust of Spain had taken root in England, even between 1560 and 1570, is shown by

---

[1] " Nisi per catholici regis dignam tali principe munificentiam (a quo his duobus annis proximis duo millia aureorum accepimus) nostris consultum rebus fuisset, jamdudum ad extrema venissemus." Petition of 200 " Angli religionis erga exules " to Pius V., Louvain, March 8, 1566, Arch. Vat., Arm. LXIV., t. 28, fol. 337 ; Misc. Arm. II., t. 67, fol. 284. ,

[2] Pius V. to Philip II., Feb. 21, 1567. FRANC. GOUBAN, *Apostolicarum Pii V. epistolarum libri V.* (Antwerp, 1640), pp. 26–28.

[3] STRYPE, *Annals*, I., ii. (Oxford, 1824), pp. 53 *et seq.*; II., i., pp. 494 *et seq. Cf.* the lists in EM. GACHET, *Catholiques anglais et écossais pensionnés par le duc d'Albe aux Pays-Bas.* Comte-Rendu des séances de la commission royale d'histoire, Vol. XVI. (Brussels, 1850), pp. 19–21, and in KNOX'S *Douay Diaries* (London, 1878), pp. 298–301. LECHAT, *Les réfugiés anglais dans les Pays-Bas espagnols* (Louvain, 1914), Append. IV.-VI.

[4] LECHAT, *op. cit.*, pp. 53, 60.

the attitude taken by the English government with regard to the exiles. Thanks to bribery and treachery, the government from the first was kept informed of the secret communications which passed to and fro between its catholic subjects and the diplomatic representatives of Spain.[1] The exiled catholics to whom Philip II. gave a hospitable welcome in the Low Countries and Spain were regarded at home as deserters to the enemy's camp.[2] The government was furnished with lists of catholics who were suspected of being ready to follow any sign from the king of Spain.[3] The movements of Philip II. himself were watched from England like those of an avowed enemy. When it was said the king was thinking of visiting the Netherlands the court of Westminster felt uneasy.[4] The idea of a marriage between the heir to the Spanish throne, Don Carlos, and Mary Stuart gave rise in England to hopes or fears according to the religion men held.[5] Serious diplomatic friction, however, arose and continued for many years when England began secretly to assist the Huguenots and the revolutionary party in the Low Countries.[6]

Towards 1570 the tension between the two courts became serious and, for the first time, there was a threat

[1] See the secret information furnished to the English government for payment by Borghese Venturini, secretary of the Spanish embassy in London. K. DE LETTENHOVE, *Relations politiques des Pays-Bas et de l'Angleterre*, III. (1883), pp. 3, 4.

[2] *Op. cit.*, III., p. 414.

[3] *Op. cit.*, IV., p. 244 ; IX., p. 162.

[4] *E.g.* in spring, 1563, *op. cit.*, III., pp. 376 *et seq.*, and in autumn, 1566, *Col. de doc. inéd.*, t. 89, pp. 377 *et seq.* ; SPAN. CAL., 1558–67, p. 582.

[5] Guaras to Granvelle, Windsor, Jan. 15, 1564. K. DE LETTENHOVE, III., p. 605.

[6] The friction began in the summer of 1562, and as early as the following autumn had become acute. SPAN. CAL., pp. 251 *et seq.*, 255, 258, 264, 268. *Col. de doc. inéd.*, t. 87, pp. 419, 427.

of breaking off diplomatic relations. It is worthy of notice that the cause of this was not political but religious. It has already been said (p. 49) that England made the question of the equal footing of the two religions a point of international law, and held its own on this point even against the king of Spain. Philip II., however, refused to grant freedom of worship to the household of the English ambassador in Madrid, whereupon Queen Elizabeth took offence and threatened to recall him (1568).[1] Her ambassador, an anglican ecclesiastic, John Man, dean of Gloucester, defended his rights with more zeal than diplomatic tact. He made fun of a procession, and let fall improper remarks about the pope. The first time this happened he was warned by King Philip, and threatened with the inquisition; the second time, he was refused admittance at court. Much as Philip's lethargic nature might yield on other points, on this the king would make no allowances. He declared that he declined to see Man again, or have anything more to do with him. He had him watched by secret agents, and threatened him once more with the inquisition if he did not restrain his remarks within due limits. At the same time Philip dispatched a courtier to England to request that another ambassador, who knew better how to behave himself in a catholic country should be sent to Spain.[2]

Elizabeth took the complaints against her representative seriously and promised to investigate the affair.[3]

---

[1] *Col. de doc. inéd.*, t. 90, pp. 24 *et seq.* SPAN. CAL., 1568–79, p. 9.

[2] Giovanni Castagno, nuncio in Madrid, to Card. Alessandrino May 1, 1568. Arch Vat., Borgh., I., 606, 381ᵛ, 382. Philip II. to Guzman de Silva, his ambassador in London, April 6, 1568. *Col. de doc. inéd.*, t. 90, pp. 43 *et seq.; cf.* p. 60. SPAN. CAL., pp. 19 *et seq.; cf.* p. 28.

[3] Guzman de Silva to Philip II., May 11, 1568. *Col. de doc. inéd.* t. 90, p. 62. SPAN. CAL., p. 29.

Her minister, Cecil, on the other hand, showed great irritation at the unheard-of action of the Spanish sovereign, who had shown great disrespect to the honour of England and the queen. The king ought only to have lodged a complaint against the ambassador, but not forbidden him the court, "as no superiority could exist between equals."[1] The affair ended in the only way possible, by the recall of the unacceptable ambassador, but without the nomination of any one to replace him.[2] Philip II., who even at Man's departure kept to his point and refused to give him a farewell audience, did everything else that lay in his power to bring the disagreement to a close.[3] In London, however, the injury was not so quickly forgotten. Before long the Spanish ambassador was assaulted in the streets of London,[4] and Cecil was only waiting for an opportunity to be even with him.

The desired opportunity presented itself within the next few months. Towards the end of 1568, it seemed that the intolerable strain between the two nations must finally lead to war. In November, news came from across the Atlantic that some English ships had been treacherously seized by Spaniards, off the coast of Mexico.[5] Just at this time, a number of Spanish treasure ships laden with money for the pay of the soldiers in the Low Countries

---

[1] *Col. de doc. inéd.*, t. 90, p. 77. SPAN. CAL., p. 37.

[2] June 5, 1568. *Col. de doc. inéd.*, t. 90, pp. 81 *et seq.* SPAN. CAL., p. 40. From the beginning of May to the beginning of July, 1571, an English ambassador, Henry Cobham, did reside at the court in Madrid, but he passed *non per residente.* Dispatches of the nuncio Castagno from Madrid, May 5 and July 3, 1571, Arch. Vat., Borgh. I., 607, fol. 358ᵛ, 386ᵛ. *Cf.* FOREIGN CAL., 1569–71, No. 1683 *et seq.*

[3] *Col. de doc. inéd.*, t. 90, pp. 109 *et seq.*, 123–27. SPAN. CAL., 1568–79, pp. 59, 66–68.

[4] Sept., 1568. K. DE LETTENHOVE, V., p. 155.

[5] Engagement at San Juan de Ulna, Sep., 1568. FROUDE, *Hist. of Engl.*, VIII., pp. 478 *et seq.* JULIAN S. CORBETT, *Drake and the Tudor Navy*, I. (1898), pp. 106 *et seq.; cf.* p. 120.

took refuge in English ports from Huguenot privateers. Cecil seized them and took possession of the considerable sum of two million silver Spanish reals. Instantly the Duke of Alva placed an embargo on all English property in the Low Countries.[1] The excitement continued to increase ; England was in a ferment ; the catholic nobility were preparing to rise ; the Spanish ambassador in London had a hand in the game. However, Cecil felt strong enough to defy Spain, who now had her hands full with the rebellion in the Low Countries, and, therefore, caused the ambassador to be put under restraint in his house, his correspondence opened, and guards placed at the embassy. The humiliation which he now inflicted on Spanish pride was part payment, he announced, for the way the English ambassador had been treated in Spain.[2]

Philip II. was forced to put up with all this in his desire to keep peace with England. He had need of peace in order to become master of the Netherlands. A breach with England just then would have exposed his possessions there—already in great jeopardy from internal rebellion—to an attack from two quarters at once, for Elizabeth had friendly relations with the German protestants, especially with the Palatinate. " These people are well prepared," was the warning given by the ambassador in London, " they boast of the impossibility of your Majesty making war against them, and enlarge upon the alliances which they have in Germany." [3] England's self-confidence is to be explained less by the trust she placed in her continental alliances than by the fact that she now at length

---

[1] CORBETT, I., p. 121. STÄHLIN, *Sir Francis Walsingham*, I., p. 214.

[2] Guerau de Spes to Philip II., London, March 12, 1569. *Col. de doc. inéd.*, t. 90, p. 212. SPAN. CAL., 1568–79, p. 134.

[3] April and May, 1569. *Col. de doc. inéd.*, t. 90, pp. 217, 228. SPAN. CAL., pp. 138, 145.

fully realized the strength of her insular position.   So long
as England had a footing on the continent, she could not
be a purely island power, it was only after the loss of
Calais (1558) that the sea became the wall of her entire
empire.   It was only now, at the beginning of Elizabeth's
reign that England woke up to the fact that her power
was unassailable, and became conscious of her vocation as
a sea power, a vocation which has made so deep a mark
on her history in modern times.   It is true, that in the
first ten years of Elizabeth's reign, the government did
very little towards building a fleet,[1] private enterprise,
however, took the initiative and began the conquest of the
sea for purposes of commerce and piracy.   "All oure
neighboures nurische and   mayntayne prowesse and
chiualrie for the lande, so lette us applie our care for the
seae ; wherein   must   necessarily   consist the glorie and
availe of oure warres."[2]   Just at the moment when the
breach with Spain was imminent, England's consciousness
of her power on the sea showed itself frequently in an
enthusiastic way.   The English wished to make out that
the queen of England was "sovereign of the sea with
supreme dominion,"[3] and they thought they had nothing
to fear in their island-fortress "even though the whole
world should combine against England."[4]   The conviction was strongest in those whose zeal for religion was
greatest—the protestants of puritanical leanings.   It was
indissolubly bound up with hatred against Spain and

[1] For proof in detail, see CORBETT, I., pp. 133–144.

[2] Roger Edwards to Queen Elizabeth, March 8, 1569. STÄHLIN,
Walsingham, I., p. 164, note 1.

[3] *Col. de doc. inéd.*, t. 90, p. 223. SPAN. CAL., 1568–79, p. 142.

[4] According to a memorial of the French ambassador in London,
De la Mothe Fénélon, of July, 1570. *Correspondance diplomatique*, III.
(1840), p. 251. "Recueil de dépêches, etc., des ambass. de France en
Angl." *Cf.* the sketch of Lord Burleigh in *Col. de doc. inéd.*, t. 90,
p. 542. SPAN. CAL., 1568–79, p. 364.

contempt for her power.[1]   Like the sea-rovers of Holland,
the principal buccaneers and naval heroes of England, such
as Drake, Hawkins, and Frobisher, were at the same time
great champions of the gospel and deadly enemies of the
catholic king.   They were filled with a fanaticism like that
of the crusaders.   That to plunder catholics was a work
well pleasing to God formed an honoured article in their
piratical creed.[2]

Under these circumstances Englishmen, who had fled
for refuge to Spanish territory, could count the less on a
lenient judgment the longer they remained there.   At the
time when bands of puritans paraded the London streets
and publicly burnt pictures of our Lady and the saints
as the "Spaniards' gods,"[3] English catholics in the Low
Countries were publicly treated as allies by the Spanish
government.   When, during the crisis in 1569, to which
we have just alluded, the Duke of Alva placed an embargo
on English property in the Netherlands, he also ordered
the English residents within his jurisdiction to be everywhere put under restraint, in Bruges, in Antwerp, in
Holland, and in Zealand.   But the colony of English
catholic exiles in Louvain alone remained unmolested.[4]
Spain could give no clearer indication of what she expected
from the English catholics.   They, however, or at least
many of them, soon showed still more clearly what side
they would take in the great struggle now impending, for
at first a few only, but, later on, increasing numbers of them,
took service under the Spanish flag.[5]   Although they were

---

[1] See the memorial of R. Edwards in STÄHLIN, I., p. 219, and *cf.
op. cit.*, p. 211, note.

[2] CORBETT, *Drake and the Tudor Navy*, I., pp. 156 *et seq.*

[3] In May, 1569, *Col. de doc. inéd.*, t. 90, p. 232.   SPAN. CAL., p. 148.

[4] K. DE LETTENHOVE, V., p. 219; information of Jan., 1569.

[5] For proofs for the years 1573 to 1575, see K. DE LETTENHOVE,
VI., p. 658 ; VII., pp. 194, 448.

not all prepared to draw the logical conclusion from their own action, nevertheless some of them said openly that the attack upon heresy in the Netherlands was to be merely the prelude to a war against heretics at home. " I hope thou wilt yet see my flag floating from the walls of Yarmouth harbour," said an English catholic serving under Alva to a protestant correspondent and compatriot.[1]

But the hour for the outbreak of war had not yet struck. The external crisis of 1569 blew over because both parties had enough to do to attend to their own internal affairs. The detention of the Spanish ambassador [2] was removed with a show of politeness after it had lasted six months, but the goods seized on each side were retained. It was in consequence of this preliminary establishment of peace that the excommunication of 1570 found no one to put it into execution. In an " earnest speech," [3] King Philip declared to the nuncio in Madrid that he regarded it as a sacred duty to sacrifice everything for the service of God and the true faith ; he who had once already brought back England to the church (as the husband of Mary the Catholic), beheld the destruction of his work with deep sorrow. Still, being an enemy to mere empty demonstrations, he preferred to wait until he could strike a successful blow, and, so far, no opportunity of doing so had presented itself. It was, therefore, an act of needless caution on England's part to get her fleet ready for action, after the excommunication of Elizabeth.[4] Ever since 1570 people

---

[1] From a letter of Samuel Lyster to Christopher Hatton, Ostende, March 22, 1573. *Op. cit.*, VI., p. 689.

[2] From the middle of January to the beginning of July, 1569. SPAN. CAL., pp. 98, 105, 172.

[3] " Un grave discorso." See Appendix XIV.

[4] DE LA MOTHE FÉNÉLON, *Corresp. dipl.*, III., pp. 181, 260 *et seq.*, 303 ; letters of the French ambassador in London of June, July, and Sept., 1570.

had been prepared for anything from Spain. When, in the summer of that year, King Philip's bride, Anne of Austria, was conveyed from the Netherlands to her new home by an escort of Spanish men-of-war, signal stations were erected all along the English coast to protect the ports against a sudden attack. This precaution was repeated when the fleet returned from Spain in the autumn.[1] The writing of a learned diplomatist, Thomas Wilson, who published a translation of the speeches of Demosthenes against Philip of Macedon in the critical year 1570, shows how much the thought of a Spanish invasion weighed on men's minds at that time. The past became to him the mirror of the present, for another Philip, whose power seemed as great as the Macedonian's, was threatening the freedom of the English Athens.[2] And when the news of Lepanto reached England in the following year, this great victory of the united Mediterranean fleets of the Christian powers was at once regarded with apprehension, since Spain would now be free to direct all her naval forces against England.[3] It was merely to avoid the appearance of being allied to the infidel that

[1] *Op. cit.*, III., pp. 297, 325 ; *cf.* p. 347. Henry Cobham was sent to the Netherlands to discover what Alva intended to do with his large fleet. FOREIGN CAL., 1569-71, No. 1129.

[2] *The three orations of Demosthenes . . . in favour of the Olynthians . . . with those his four orations titled . . . against king Philip of Macedonia : most nedeful to be redde in these daungerous dayes, of all them that love their countrie's libertie and desire to take warning for their better avayle by example of others. Englished out of the Greek by Thomas Wilson, London,* 1570. The dedication to Cecil is dated June 10, 1570. The following lines are prefixed to the work :—

" Nunc quoque tempus adest, patriæ succurrere dulci,
Ne misere in præceps Anglia tota ruat."

Similar ideas occur frequently. Extracts in STRYPE'S *Annals*, I., ii. (1824) pp. 367-369. *Cf.* also Wilson's report to Walsingham of June 8, 1577. K. DE LETTENHOVE, Vol. IX., p. 329.

[3] DE LA MOTHE FÉNÉLON, *Corr. dipl.*, IV., p. 281.

the English resolved to celebrate a perfunctory service of thanksgiving for the victory.[1]

The reputation of the Duke of Alva and the Spanish reign of terror in the Low Countries only served to increase the distrust of the policy of Spain. There was, indeed, among the Spaniards no more determined opponent to a war with England than the duke himself.[2]   This cautious general formed a more correct estimate of the greatness of the undertaking than most of his fellow-countrymen, and his idea was to commit the cause of the English catholics to God alone.[3]   But none the less the terror inspired by Alva's name penetrated to England. "Without all doubt there is some great mischief meant towards us," an English protestant wrote from Antwerp [4] on Alva's entry into the Low Countries, "and I pray God that when all is done, that [sic] there be not found some false traitors within our realm, that is only all which I doubt of.'' Elizabeth's agents in the Low Countries got the impression that the duke had his eye on England.[5]   Alva's agent in London was in touch with prominent catholics there.[6] More than fifty persons in Elizabeth's entourage were reported to be in Alva's pay,[7] and, indeed, the majority of the English aristocracy were said to be on his side.[8]

---

[1] STRYPE, *l.c.*, II., i., pp. 155–157.

[2] For particulars, see J. KRETZSCHMAR, *Die Invasionsprojekte der kath. Mächte gegen England z. Zt. Elisabeths* (Leipzig, 1892), pp. 20–46.

[3] Alva to the Spanish ambassador in London, Nov., 1571. K. DE LETTENHOVE, VI., pp. 216, 218.

[4] Thos. Dutton to Thos. Gresham, Sept. 28, 1567. *Op. cit.*, V., p. 19. Cf. *Col. de doc. inéd.*, t. 89, pp. 535, 561. SPAN. CAL., 1558–67, pp. 671, 684.

[5] DE LA MOTHE FÉNÉLON, III., p. 27.

[6] K. DE LETTENHOVE, VI., p. 637.

[7] *L.c.*, p. 739.

[8] DE LA MOTHE FÉNÉLON, III., p. 27.   Memorial of the French ambassador of 1570.

While much of all this may be set down to panic, people at any rate felt quite sure that the duke would take vengeance for the assistance given to the rebels in the Low Countries, and England fortified her ports in the autumn of 1572 when fortune seemed to her to be favouring the Spanish arms.[1]

Along with the growing mistrust of Spain, suspicion of the English exiles in Spanish territory increased too. It was deemed necessary to keep the sharpest watch over them,[2] and their power of doing harm was altogether overestimated. There was a certain irony in the situation, for people in London thought the worst was to be looked for from abroad, while an English agent in the Low Countries arrived at the conclusion that the greatest danger seemed to be at home, perhaps even in Elizabeth's own court![3] In the interval, the number of those who took service under Spain increased. In 1578, there was an entire English company headed by an English captain in the army of the governor, Alessandro Farnese. No less a personage than William Allen, the founder and rector of the seminary, had given it his support. It was due to his influence that more than two hundred young men, for the most part sons of good families, forsook their country and swore the oath of military allegiance to the king of Spain.[4] Later on,

---

[1] In Oct. and Nov., 1572. K. DE LETTENHOVE, VI., pp. 545, 561 et seq., 564, 572.

[2] Numerous reports of English spies in the Netherlands, op. cit., VI., pp. 99, 171 et seq. (cf. p. 517); VII., pp. 26, 325 et seq., 427 432 et seq.

[3] Thos. Heton to Lord Burleigh, Antwerp, Jan. 3, 1574, op. cit., VII., p. 26.

[4] " Piu notabile fu la venuta di più di ducento giovani, la magior parte di loro di casa nobile per servir al re catholico contra l'heretici, li quali per mezzo de R^do dottore Alano che l'havea procurato a venir là, furono molto ben visti del principe di Parma et messi tutti insieme sotto la condotta di un molto nobile et zeloso capitano inglese,

their ranks were reinforced by the addition of Irish and Scottish catholics.[1]

While English catholics were hastening in considerable numbers to take up arms under King Philip, their protestant fellow countrymen gathered round the banner of the Prince of Orange. At the first outbreak of hostilities the inhabitants of the Netherlands turned their eyes towards England,[2] and however calculating and business-like Queen Elizabeth showed herself regarding the greatest struggle for freedom of that age, her protestant subjects were openly Orange and anti-Spanish. Year after year, from the beginning of the disturbances, the Spaniards had to complain of the assistance which England continued to give to the rebellion.[3] Although protestant Englishmen who fell into the hands of the Spaniards were treated as criminals and not as prisoners of war,[4] fresh bands were constantly crossing the sea. About 1575, at the time when the company of catholic Englishmen came to the aid of the Spaniards, quite five or six times as many English protestants were fighting for the freedom of the Netherlands.[5] Things had now come to such a pass

aspettando ogni giorno che gli cresce il numero." From the memorial *Alcune cose di consolatione*, etc., Arch. Vat., Miscell. Arm. XI., t. 94, fol. 192ᵛ; another copy in the Arch. Arcis S. Angeli, Arm. XIV., c. II., No. 37. Printed from a Latin text by POLLEN, Cath. Record Soc. Miscell., II. (1906), p. 69.

[1] LECHAT, *Réfugiés anglais*, p. 151.

[2] *Cf.* Gresham's letter to Cecil, Antwerp, Sept. 3, 1566. K. DE LETTENHOVE, IV., p. 354.

[3] K. DE LETTENHOVE, V., pp. 124–126 ; VI., pp. 460 *et seq.*, 485–489, 525 *et passim* in this and the following volumes.

[4] "In the galleis be here [Antwerp], My good Lorde, our countrimen moste crewellye and contynuallye tormented that yt wolde make an Inglisheman's harte to rende in piesses to behold ther tormentes and misserye." K. DE LETTENHOVE, VIII., p. 406 ; *cf.* pp. 336 *et seq.*

[5] An English company in the service of the Prince of Orange (1574) is mentioned in K. DE LETTENHOVE, VII., p. 132 (*cf.* p. 163) ; "quatre

that Englishmen fought against each other on the field of battle—the catholics on the one side and the protestants on the other.

It is not easy to decide whether the majority of English catholics between 1560 and 1580 really wished to see the country involved in a war with Spain or not. Since the house of Tudor would become extinct with Elizabeth, a successful invasion would at best have placed Mary Stuart on the throne, and it might perhaps have even set up a foreign dynasty over the country. There were not many catholics who declared themselves in favour of an invasion. A member of the English colony at Louvain, a man, indeed, who had brought with him from his home in Wales something of the ancient hatred of the Celt for the Anglo-Saxon, wrote to Rome in 1562,[1] "They are not to be listened to who would persuade us that the English cannot be forced under the yoke of foreign dominion. The oppression is so severe, and grows still more severe daily,

enseignes d'infanterie angloise" (1574), *l.c.*, p. 164; another company (1576) in VIII., p. 348; "nos quatre régimens" (1578), *Rel. polit. des Pays-Bas et d'Angleterre, cont. par* GILLIODTS-VAN-SEVEREN, XI., p. 53; "deux enseignes de piétons anglois" (1578), XI., p. 54. The total number of the Englishmen who fought on the Dutch side in 1578 was originally estimated at 3500, but, being "consumid with misery," was reduced to 300, *l.c.* XI., p. 114; *cf.* p. 352.

[1] Maurice Clenock to Card. Morone. It was Clenock, who as rector of the English college in Rome, fostered quarrels between the English and Welsh students by the undue preference he showed to his fellow-countrymen, and endangered the existence of the establishment (see above, p. 111). The passage quoted above runs: "Neque audiendi sunt illi, qui nescio qua ratione ducti persuadere volunt Anglos nullo modo adduci posse, ut externi et potentioris principis iugum sibi imponi patiantur. Ea enim rerum est angustia et temporum acerbitas, quæ indies magis magisque videtur, ut non nisi ab externo aliquo se liberatum iri confidant illi qui synceram fidem sequuntur. . . . Melius enim est externo duce ad salutem æternam contendere quam ab interno hoste ad ima tartara deprimi." Louvanii, Dec. 6, 1562, Arch. Vat., Arm. LXIV., t. 28, fol. 45.

R

that the confessors of the true faith hope for freedom from foreigners alone.   Better to attain eternal blessedness under a foreign lord than to be cast into the nethermost hell by an enemy at home."   Such utterances as this, however, are rare [1] and come from men who cannot be regarded as typical representatives of English catholicism.   Nevertheless the desire for a warlike intervention seems from time to time to have taken hold of the refugees in France and the Netherlands.[2]   Among the catholics at home, too, there were many to whom it appeared incomprehensible that the catholic powers could stand idly by and see England lost to the church.   "It is truly terrible to think that the Lord God should have permitted until now that not even the good will of those who have been so often besought, and are in duty bound, to take measures for the recovery of this kingdom, should come to His aid . . . It seems as if these princes had made an agreement among themselves rather to suffer gladly all evils for ten or twelve years than to take steps to retrieve the calamities and losses which their countries and states constantly suffer."[3]   When the strained diplomatic relations with Spain shortly before 1570 did *not* result in war but in the drawing up of a commercial treaty between the two nations (1573), and the idea of settling

---

[1] *Cf.* THEINER, *Annal. Eccles.*, III. (1856), p. 481, § 6.

[2] See Walsingham's warning from Paris in 1571. STÄHLIN, I., p. 351.   Also John Lee to Burleigh, Antwerp, July 14, 1572. K. DE LETTENHOVE, VI., p. 456.

[3] From an anonymous *Discorso venuto d'Inghilterra del* 1570 *in Venetia.* Arch. Vat., Miscell. Arm. II., t. 84, fol. 32 *et seq.* "Et veramente é cosa che spaventa ogni persona il considerare che il s^r dio habbia permesso fin qui che non concorra al suo rimedio pure la voluntà di coloro che per tante vie sono stati sollecitati et obligati etiando di havere per raccomandata la redutione di esso regno . . . Tutti quei principi . . . [pare che] facessero quasi una congiura tra essi di patire 10 o 12 anni continui più presto ogni male che concorrere al riparo di tante calamità et di tanti danni che patiscono tuttavia i paesi et gli stati loro."

their differences by arms was therefore once more post-poned,[1] the intransigeant catholic party in London was so angry and disappointed that it broke off negotiations with the agent of the Duke of Alva to whom the preservation of peace was due. The members of this party found no consolation in the fact that the treaty was only to last for two years and was merely a kind of truce, for even a short-lived commercial treaty would be enough to strengthen the kingdom and the government for a generation.[2]

Still it would be wrong to draw sweeping conclusions as to the attitude of English catholics from manifestations of this kind, for only a small section was in favour of bringing about a change by force. England's gradual conversion as a nation from catholicism to protestantism, and the pressure, at first moderate and cautious, put upon members of the old religion by the government, were not of a nature to call into existence a strong revolutionary party. The large majority of those who were discontented sought relief from the ever-increasing oppression by peaceful, not warlike, means; not by a Spanish invasion but by Spanish diplomacy. With every improvement in the relations between London and Madrid, the hopes of the oppressed rose,[3] only to fall again whenever things took a turn for the worse; they hoped for a *protector*, not a *conqueror*. That English catholics, notwithstanding their dire need of assistance, were unwilling to throw themselves into the arms of Spain was brought home to Philip's ambassador as early as 1569, just when the rising of the catholic lords was spreading under his eyes and with

---

[1] STÄHLIN, I., pp. 581–584.

[2] Fogaça to Alva, London, April 20, 1573. K. DE LETTENHOVE, VI., p. 716.

[3] *Cf.* Champagney, the representative of the Spanish Netherlands in London, to the council of state in Brussels, March 17, 1576. K. DE LETTENHOVE, VIII., p. 279.

his approval. The ambassador was obviously unable to understand how any one could be a good catholic without being at the same time a good Spaniard. "I have some confidence," he wrote of the leaders of the rising, Norfolk and Arundel,[1] "that they will serve your Majesty well at this juncture, although the fact that they are Englishmen, and not entirely catholic, makes one always suspicious of them." "Englishmen and not Spaniards," would have been nearer the mark! The nuncio, Niccolò Ormaneto, who soon afterwards did his best to stir up opinion in Madrid in favour of an invasion, was quite clear [2] "that the English catholics, apart from whom the enterprise is almost impossible, refuse all aid from abroad which might bring them under subjection, but desire only just sufficient for the overthrow of their self-styled queen and for replacing her by the other one from Scotland." In poetry written under the influence of the catholic mission, the idea of a restoration of catholicism by force is distinctly rejected—

> " God knowes it is not force nor might,
>   Not warre nor warlike band,
> Not shield and spear, not dint of sword,
>   That must convert the land.
> It is the blood of martirs shed,
>   It is that noble traine,
> That fight with word and not with sword
>   And Christ their capitaine." [3]

This opinion, moreover, which would have nothing to do with a compulsory conversion of England, or with a Spanish invasion, made steady headway after 1570. In

---

[1] Don Guerau de Spes to Philip II., June 14, 1569. *Col. de doc. inéd.*, t. 90, pp. 242 *et seq.* SPAN. CAL., 1568–79, p. 164.

[2] Report of Feb. 19, 1573. F. M. CARINI, *Mons Niccolò Ormaneto, nunzio alla corte di Filippo II.* (Roma, 1894), pp. 84 *et seq.*

[3] "The complaint of a catholic for the death of M. Edmund Campion," in ALLEN's *Briefe Hist.*, ed. POLLEN (1908), p. 46.

the conflict between duty to the church and duty to the country, there was one consideration that came to have more and more weight in favour of the country—the feeling of irritation at Spanish insolence. By far the larger number of those who took service under the banner of the Catholic king suffered very bitter experiences. The haughty subjects of Philip II. regarded the impecunious exiles with undisguised contempt, as if they were "Italian bandits who had been forced to quit their country on account of robbery or murder."[1] The Spaniards had no idea of placing the Englishmen who were in the pay of Alva or Farnese on an equal footing with their own countrymen. "English blood is cheap."[2] Poor pay, or none at all, and unfair treatment were not the worst experiences of these expatriated men, who had sold themselves for the lowest price in order to fight for their faith as mercenaries in a foreign legion. Worse than these was the constant violence done to their patriotic feelings and the contempt shown for their native land, which, in spite of everything, remained still dear to them. Men who had counted on being received with open arms as co-religionists were bitterly disillusioned. Even to that period could be applied the phrase which Charles I. let fall at a later date when conversing with a papal agent: "The Spaniards trouble themselves no more about the English catholics than about a dog, in so far as they have no use of them for forming a party in England."[3]

---

[1] "The Estate of English Fugitives under the King of Spaine and his ministers." *The State Papers of Sir Ralph Sadler*, ed: CLIFFORD. Vol. II. (Edin., 1809), p. 249.

[2] *Op. cit.*, p. 221.

[3] "Non si curano di loro più che di cani, se non quanto li stimano buoni a mantenere un partito qui a divotione loro." George Conn to Card. Barberini, London, May, 5/15, 1637. Bibl. Vat., Barb. lat. 8640, fol. 310ᵛ.

Many, for the sake of their faith, would perhaps have been willing to suffer all this as long as there remained any hope of Spanish arms being able to restore catholicism in England. But even this hope failed them—at least those of them who were clear-sighted—long before the English fleet put the disabled Armada to flight. It was doubtless very depressing for the deluded catholics to find that Philip II. did nothing for them between 1560 and 1570, and that he failed as well to seize the opportunity given him by the catholic rising of 1569, but yet these things did not give them a clear answer to the question, Is the king of Spain *unwilling*, or is he *unable* to help us? The years that followed answered this question, and the answer came with unmistakable plainness, in the first instance, to all those who had forsaken England and sought refuge on Spanish territory in the Netherlands.

The English government did not rest satisfied with merely keeping an eye on the exiles. It hesitated at no means to get these suspected persons back again into its power. The fate of Dr. Story is well known. Having fled from England, Story entered the service of Spain and became a naturalized Spanish subject. He was employed under the Duke of Alva as a censor of books sold in the Low Countries. One day (1570), Cecil's agents lured him on board an English ship in the port of Antwerp, that was to carry over a cargo of heretical books. The ship set sail, and soon the unfortunate man, who had unwittingly fallen into the trap, had to answer before English judges to the charge of high treason. In vain Story pleaded that, as he was a Spanish subject, the accusation was meaningless and the court could have no jurisdiction over him. Neither his legal plea nor his adopted country shielded him from being tortured, condemned, and executed with all the brutality of the period.

In reality Story's sentence was an act of retaliation for the part he had taken in the persecution of heretics under Mary the Catholic. The legal ground for accusing him of high treason was questionable; the discussion turned on the validity of the maxim, *Nemo potest exuere patriam*.[1] There was no denying that Story's abduction was an infringement of Spanish prerogatives. "It is not to be thought," reasoned the French ambassador in London,[2] "that the Duke of Alva will allow himself to be treated in this fashion." But the duke, who dreaded nothing so much as a breach with England, preferred to let the incident pass.[3] He left "good Dr. Story" to his fate, and only in the final stage of the trial made a feeble and tardy attempt to obtain his release.[4] The only thing left for Philip's government to do was to provide for Story's widow and children.[5] The lesson for the English catholics in the Netherlands was—Spain no longer protects her guests or even her own officials.

And there was yet worse to come. The abandonment of Story was not an isolated case. It was not an indication

---

[1] CAMDEN, *Annales rer. Angl.* (1625), p. 213 ; J. W. WILLIS-BUND, *A Selection of Cases from the State Trials*, I. (Cambr., 1879), pp. 214 *et seq.* Story's retort was : "Every man is free borne, and he hath the whole face of the earth before him to dwell and abide in, where he liketh best ; and if he can not lyve here, he may go elsewhere." *A Declaration of the Life and Death of John Story* (London, 1571), reprinted in Somers Tracts, I. (2nd ed., 1809), p. 486, Harleian Miscell., III. (1809), pp. 107 *et seq.*

[2] DE LA MOTHE FÉNÉLON, Letter of Aug. 26, 1570. *Correspondance Diplomatique*, III. (1840), p. 288.

[3] FROUDE, *Hist. of Engl.*, Vol. IX., p. 313; *cf.* p. 461.

[4] *Col. de doc. inéd.*, t. 90, p. 463 ; *cf.* pp. 398, 405, 425. SPAN. CAL., 1568-79, p. 312 ; *cf.* pp. 272 *et seq.*, 276, 288.

[5] *Col. de doc. inéd.*, t. 90, p. 484. SPAN. CAL., p. 327. In addition to the references already given, *cf.* for Story's case, CAMDEN, pp. 152 *et seq.* K. DE LETTENHOVE, VI., Introd. and pp. 2 *et seq.*, 279 ; DE LA MOTHE FÉNÉLON, *Corr. dipl.*, IV., pp. 136 *et seq.* LECHAT, *Réfugiés anglais*, p. 234.

of a momentary weakness but rather the prelude to
yet more disgraceful exhibitions of feebleness on the
part of Spain. In 1572 England sought to regain
authority over her refugee subjects by means of
William of Orange, who undertook to deliver over
to Elizabeth all of them who might fall into his
hands.[1] It does not appear that much came of this
attempt. Two years later, Elizabeth approached the
governor of the Spanish Netherlands, Don Requesens,
with the demand that he should hand over to her, or at
least expel from Spanish territory, the English rebels and
exiles residing within his dominions.[2] This command
could be justified by the Anglo-Spanish commercial treaty
of 1573, which laid upon each of the contracting parties
the obligation of refusing shelter to rebels against the
other. The moment was well chosen. Philip II. had
asked Elizabeth to permit that one of the Spanish fleets
on its way to the Netherlands might put into English
harbours in case of need. Under these circumstances,
Spain did not venture to withhold its consent, but yielded
so far as to entertain the idea of banishing the English
rebels,[3] while holding back from carrying this engagement into effect. But Elizabeth would not be put off with
mere words. She repeated her demands, but now drew
a distinction[4] between "rebels," who had taken part in
the rising of 1569, and "refugees," who had quitted England for conscience sake. The former were to be handed
over to her, while the latter were to make a declaration
before the Spanish authorities that they acknowledged
Elizabeth as their undoubted lawful queen. Requesens

---

[1] K. DE LETTENHOVE, VI., p. 517.
[2] Elizabeth to Requesens, May 3, 1574. *Op. cit.*, VII., p. 117.
For a full account of the following see LECHAT, *op. cit.*, pp. 98–132.
[3] K. DE LETTENHOVE, VII., p. 131.
[4] Dec., 1574. *Op. cit.*, VII., p. 368.

agreed to deliver over the rebels, provided England did likewise and refused an asylum to Dutch rebels against the Spanish crown. The second demand, that he should extort the declaration from the refugees, he emphatically declined as "unworthy,"[1] and when Elizabeth, both in writing and through her diplomatic representatives, again and again pressed for the execution of this demand, the governor on one occasion exclaimed to the English envoy, "Now, Lord! what meaneth the queen to deal thus against these wretches who can do no harm, and are rather to be pitied than punished—being all good simple catholics?"[2]

But however long Spanish pride might hold out against these proposals, and refuse to violate the laws of hospitality, Spain, that brazen colossus with feet of clay, could not in the end refuse compliance with England's emphatic and repeated demands. For the sake of her commercial interests, she was bound to remain friends with England, for only so could her merchants find protection against the insolence of English buccaneers. By her military interests also she was forced to keep the peace, for by this means alone could she hope to overcome the rebellion in the Netherlands. Not only then did Spain herself need peace with the island kingdom, it was also of vital importance for the Spanish Netherlands that they should be able to carry on their trade with England. A rupture of Anglo-Spanish commercial relations would, therefore, have meant a severe strain upon the loyalty of the Spanish provinces. To sum up—Spain had no choice but to yield to the English demands. The English diplomatists at the court of the governor, between 1570 and 1580, were fully convinced that their

[1] *L.c.*, pp. 376 *et seq.*
[2] *L.c.*, p. 411 ; *cf.* pp. 401 *et seq.*

victory was certain. "Whatsoever answer is returned, the same will be accepted, and the sharper the better, for of necessity they must yield, or they will repent!" so wrote the English envoy[1] in February, 1575, after prolonged negotiations with Don Requesens over commercial affairs and the expulsion of the English exiles. The governor, who had so long resisted this humiliating condition, had at length to yield on every point and withdraw his protection even from the English who had implored his aid.[2] These sorely tried men were deeply irritated when they found themselves treated in a manner they had never dreamt of. They received orders to quit the country within fourteen days. It was not enough that the laws of hospitality should be violated, their pensions from Spain were stopped too, because England insisted on it.[3] In letters more than polite,[4] Don Requesens informed the queen of England that he yielded to her wishes, and at the same time repeated a request already made more than once, which gave fresh evidence of the weakness of Spain. Requesens begged Elizabeth's permission to purchase or order English guns, since they were better than those to be got elsewhere.[5] It was not calculated to give England a high opinion of Spain's military efficiency to

---

[1] Dr. Thos. Wilson to Burleigh, Antwerp, Feb. 20, 1575, *l.c.*, VII., p. 453.

[2] *L.c.*, pp. 454, 465 *et seq.* Cf. J. J. E. PROOST, *Les réfugiés anglais et irlandais en Belgique, à la suite de la réforme religieuse, etc.* Messager des Sciences Historiques . . . de Belgique (Gand., 1865), pp. 282–287.

[3] K. DE LETTENHOVE, VII., pp. 460, 466. The payment of their pensions had already ceased in 1572, *l.c.* VI., p. 456. Later on it was secretly continued ; LECHAT, *op. cit.*, pp. 120, 139 *et seq.*

[4] March 5 and 14, 1575. K. DE LETTENHOVE, VII., pp. 460 *et seq.*, 472.

[5] "Laquelle artillerie j'entens se recouvrer meilleure et plus commodéement audict Angleterre que ailleurs," *l.c.*, VII., p. 461 ; *cf.* 467, postscript.

learn that Philip II. just at this juncture once more urged his request for English gunnery and gunners.[1] Queen Elizabeth knew very well why she refused to give permission for the desired exportation of cannon.[2] It was only by secret and forbidden ways that Spain was able to obtain the desired articles, for there were not wanting English merchants then, any more than in later centuries, who regarded it as lawful to sell English guns to their country's enemies.[3]

English diplomacy had won all along the line. Catholic refugees had to reckon with the strong arm of the home government even in a foreign and catholic country. It is true Elizabeth on her part now undertook to expel the Spanish rebels residing in England,[4] but this diplomatic return to Requesens was nothing more than a worthless scrap of paper. Elizabeth excepted and threw her sheltering arm over all those " who for the sake of religion and the gospel had left their home and flown to this peaceful land as to a refuge." [5] And so she held fast with one hand what she seemed to give with the other, while all the world could see that Spain was on the losing side. Naturally Spain chiefly lost the esteem of those English catholics who had trusted to her protection. "The king of Spain is as fearfull of warre as a child of fyre," wrote Nicholas Sanders in 1577, one of the political

---

[1] K. DE LETTENHOVE, VII., pp. 174, 191, 195, 448. For the estimation of English gunnery under Elizabeth, see J. S. CORBETT, *Papers relating to the Navy during the Spanish War*, 1585-87. Navy Record Soc. Publ., XI. (1898), pp. 335 *et seq.* A description of the marine gunnery from a technical point of view is given in CORBETT, *Drake and the Tudor Navy*, I. (1898), pp. 379 *et seq.*

[2] K. DE LETTENHOVE, VII., p. 483.

[3] FOREIGN CAL., Eliz., 1577-78, Nos. 19, 70.

[4] Proclamation of April 16, 1575. K. DE LETTENHOVE, VII., pp. 489 *et seq.*

[5] *Op. cit.*, VII., p. 509.

leaders of English catholicism and afterwards its historian.[1] That he wrote these bitter words from Madrid, under the impression made by what was said at court, gives them all the greater weight. The next year brought fresh proof of Spain's weakness. In the months following the triumphant entry of the Prince of Orange into Brussels (September, 1577), the religious quarrels in the disaffected provinces broke out more fiercely than ever. The English seminary in Douay had, accordingly, to give way before the rising flood of hatred against catholicism (March, 1578), owing to its failure to receive sufficient protection from the governor of the catholic king. No longer safe on Spanish territory, the seminary sought a new home across the French border in Rheims.[2] The persecuted catholics were so accustomed to regard Elizabeth as the cause of all their woes that they believed they could detect her hand even here.[3] Granting that they were mistaken in this instance, they, nevertheless, soon experienced in Rheims fresh proof of the underhand intrigues of the English government against their seminary.[4]

Little wonder then that in course of time, English catholics, both at home and abroad, relinquished those hopes which once they had fixed upon the king of Spain— Robert Persons, the most zealous among the friends of Spain and advocates of invasion, pointed out later on that Philip II. had made a great mistake in not creating and

---

[1] Sanders to Allen. KNOX's *Card. Allen* (1882), p. 38. Summary in DOM. CAL., 1577, p. 565.

[2] *Vid. ante*, p. 98 ; *cf.* Allen's letter of April 4, 1578. KNOX, p. 39. DODD-TIERNEY, *Church Hist. of Engl.*, II. (1839), pp. 161–166. Appendix, Nos. LIII. *et seq.* LECHAT, *Réfugiés anglais*, pp. 135 *et seq.*

[3] Allen : " istud ipsum hæreticorum nostrorum solicitatione evenit ut nostri omnes Duaco ejicerentur." KNOX, *op. cit.*, p. 39. Similarly Persons ; DODD-TIERNEY, II., p. 165, note 1. This agrees with the incorrect account of CAMDEN, *Annal. rer. Angl.* (1625), p. 265.

[4] KNOX, pp. 404, 109.

maintaining a party among English catholics devoted to his interests.[1] The distrust of Spain towards her English co-religionists, of which Persons complains, was not the chief cause of this neglect—Spain was not strong enough to play the gigantic rôle of champion of the catholic church against the powers of the reformation.

England's strength, moreover, increased from year to year. While wars and civil conflicts devastated the whole of Western Europe, the traders of the island kingdom flourished at other people's expense, monopolized the carrying trade of Spanish goods,[2] and penetrated into the seas of the new world which the pope had bestowed upon Spain. With that light-hearted exuberant courage of youth which characterized " merry England," and with all the love of running risks which stakes everything on one throw, these skilful seamen and discoverers, freebooters and adventurers—these *condottieri* of the English renaissance—put forth to sea in search of battles and booty wherever they might find them. Their queen, too, whom they served as a troubadour his mistress, with such a passionate loyalty and a chivalry as never was seen before or since, smiled encouragingly on the doughty deeds of her wild young subjects. Those whom they plundered, despairing of justice, realized there was nothing else to be done than to come to terms with these buccaneers, and, in a sense, become their tributaries.[3] Elizabeth finally crowned everything, and mocked Spain to its face, by knighting Francis Drake, England's greatest sea captain and most able sea-rover on board his

[1] Letter of April 4, 1591. KNOX, *l.c.*, p. 330.

[2] *Cf.* Mendoza's lamentation of the course things were taking (1580). Letter to Philip II. of Feb. 20, 1580. *Col. de doc. inéd.*, t. 91, pp. 454 *et seq.* SPAN. CAL., 1580–86, pp. 8 *et seq.*

[3] **Letter of Mendoza of 1579.** *Col. de doc. inéd.*, t. 91, 407. SPAN. CAL., p. 687.

own ship. She sportively threatened with a gilded sword to strike off his head which the king of Spain had demanded.[1]

The voyages of the sea-dogs led to other acquisitions besides booty and self-confidence ; they gave the impulse to the greatest revolution which naval warfare was to experience until the age of steam.[2] This revolution was merely the outcome of the fact that the wide ocean had now replaced the narrow seas in the seafaring of the European nations. The ship best suited for the Mediterranean, the galley, disappeared with the battle of Lepanto, the last great battle of history fought with galleys. But now in the Thames dockyards a new age was already being ushered in. Between 1570 and 1580, the leading seamen of England began to exert an influence upon the naval projects of the government. Hawkins received a post at the Admiralty. Efforts, which until now had been only tentative, began to take systematic shape. Sails replaced oars, and instead of the mediæval tactics of ramming and boarding the enemy—a land battle fought at sea—we have the battle at a distance with guns. The chief feature of the galley, its independence of the wind, was sacrificed in favour of seaworthiness. The space formerly occupied by the galley slaves was now utilized for cannon. Even the new names given to the ships, which meet us now for the first time—*Bull, Tiger, Dreadnought, Revenge, etc.*[3]—proclaim a new era, while in the

[1] On April 4, 1581. SPAN. CAL., p. 95. CORBETT, *Drake and the Tudor Navy*, I., p. 336.

[2] *Cf.* for what follows Corbett's excellent work, specially Vol. I., Introd. and pp. 132–144, and ch. vii., " The Navy of Elizabeth."

[3] The above-mentioned names are all belonging to Royal ships launched between 1570 and 1580. See the list of ships given by M. OPPENHEIM, *A History of the Administration of the Royal Navy and of Merchant Shipping, etc.*, Vol. I., 1509 to 1660 (London, 1896), p. 120. At an earlier date religious names were also usual in the English marine.

religious names of the Spanish fleet—*Santa Maria de Gracia, Nuestra Señora del Rosario, San Juan Bautista, La Concepcion,* etc.[1]—we see the survival of the mediæval spirit.

Already, towards 1580, the reform of the fleet was so far advanced that England felt herself equal to face any foe at sea. When a council of ministers at Greenwich in October, 1579, reviewed England's relations to foreign powers point by point, the question which had given the greatest cause for anxiety ten years previously, the Spanish fleet, was dismissed summarily and almost contemptuously, " His [King Philip's] own forces by sea not great, except galleys which are unmeet for our seas."[2] As regards their own defences, however, they declared with pride that under no previous sovereign had England possessed such forces either on land or sea as did now queen Elizabeth.[3]

This consciousness of their own power kept pace with the increase of the fleet, and, indeed, went ahead of it. When, in the summer of 1574, Spain sent a fleet to the Netherlands and fire-signalling stations were once more erected along the English coast with a view to calling the country to arms,[4] there awoke among the officers and seamen of the fleet the remembrance of England's ancient claim to the sovereignty of the British sea which dated back to the days of the Plantagenets. They threatened that if the Spaniards did not dip their flags in greeting as they

---

[1] *Cf.* the list of ships in C. F. DURO, *La Armada Invencible*, I.; pp. 391 *et seq.* ; II., pp. 34 *et seq.*, 138 *et seq.*, 180 *et seq.*

[2] " Poines of State considered by the Counselle at Grenwiche touching ye present state of Englande to equalle Fraunce or Spaine, the 6 of October anno 1579." *Relat. polit. des Pays-Bas et de l'Angleterre, cont. par* L. GILLIODTS-VAN-SEVEREN, XI. (1900), pp. 409 *et seq.*

[3] *L.c.,* p. 411.

[4] K. DE LETTENHOVE, VII., p. 216.

sailed by the English coast, they would fall upon them.[1] It was the same threat, which, later on in Cromwell's time, was put into execution by Admiral Blake when the Dutch under Van Tromp refused him the honour of the first salute! The warning of the distressed Netherlands, that England's freedom stood or fell with theirs, was now felt to be almost an insult. " Her Majesty's forces and means of defence," William of Orange was given to understand, in 1576, " are not, thanks be to God, so weak or feeble but she shall be able to defend herself against the said king or any other prince that shall have any meaning to attempt anything against her." [2] Not from fear, but from the sense of her own increased strength, did England at that time aid the rebels by sending them money,[3] and declared at the same time to Don John of Austria, the governor of the Netherlands, that she was quite ready to come to friendly terms with him but would tolerate no oppression in the Netherlands, and would protect her allies with all her power.[4]

It was only a question of time, when the party, who had for long been in favour of war, the zealous protestant party—Walsingham, Drake, Wilson and others of like mind—should finally gain the upper hand. The diplomatic leader of this party, Sir Francis Walsingham, had already skilfully prepared the way for a great league against Spain when he was ambassador in Paris, shortly after 1570. The preliminary steps had already been taken; in

[1] According to the dispatch of Sweveghem, the envoy of the Spanish Netherlands in London, to Requesens, June 25, 1574. K. DE LETTENHOVE, VII., p. 187 ; *cf.* p. 206.

[2] Instructions, dated June 19, 1576, for Sir William Winter, envoy to the Prince of Orange. *Op. cit.*, VIII., p. 403 ; *cf.* p. 425.

[3] In Dec., 1576. *Op. cit.*, IX., pp. 99, 105, 110 *et seq.*, 124 *et seq.*, 154 *et seq.*

[4] Instructions, dated Dec. 14, 1576, for Edward Horsey, envoy to the governor. *Op. cit.*, IX., pp. 85–90.

January, 1572, the Spanish ambassador had been compelled to leave London, on account of his share in the catholic disturbances of previous years,[1] and in April, an Anglo-French defensive treaty had been signed at Blois,[2] when, in August, the massacre of St. Bartholomew destroyed all that had been attained and snatched the power out of the hands of the war party in the English cabinet. Although the posts of Spanish ambassador in London and English ambassador in Madrid lay vacant for six years (1572-78), six years of neither peace nor war, this does not imply that all diplomatic relations were completely broken off during this interval. Diplomatic intercourse still went on between England and the Spanish Netherlands, and there were occasions when the governments in London and Madrid tried to get into immediate touch with one another. On one occasion, indeed, the irritation between the two countries broke out in a way that violated all principles of international courtesy. In 1577, an English envoy, Sir John Smith, arrived in Madrid to negotiate the release of Englishmen from the prisons of the Spanish inquisition.[3] The Archbishop of Toledo, Quiroga, a violent and fanatical enemy of England, drove Elizabeth's envoy from his house the instant he alluded to the release of the prisoners of the inquisition.[4] King Philip, to whom the envoy appealed, curtly declined to interfere in the inquisition's affairs over which he had no control.[5]

---

[1] *Col. de doc. inéd.*, t. 90, pp. 550 *et seq.* SPAN. CAL., 1567-78, pp. 370 *et seq.*

[2] STÄHLIN'S *Walsingham*, I., pp. 454 *et seq.*

[3] FOREIGN CAL., 1575-77, Nos. 1024, 1236.

[4] *Ib.*, No. 1436.

[5] *Ib.*, No. 1580. Concerning Englishmen in the prisons of the Inquisition, see J. K. LAUGHTON, *State Papers relating to the Defeat of the Span. Armada*, I. (1894), Introd., pp. xv.-xxii.

Notwithstanding all this friction, a *modus vivendi* was established in 1578. In England, the war-party had found its most determined opponents among those who regarded relations with Spain from the commercial point of view, and the queen finally ranged herself on the side of the latter. In Spain, too, the need of peace was more pressing than ever towards 1580. Philip II. was making his last gigantic effort to subjugate the Low Countries. The religious fanaticism of the royal recluse became inflamed with a passion for destruction that nothing could surpass. Philip was determined, if he could not bring back the Netherlands to the catholic faith and to obedience, "to work such havoc in the country"—these are the king's own words [1]—"that neither the inhabitants should dwell there any longer, nor any one else ever feel any desire for it."

But Philip deceived himself if he thought it possible to lay waste protestant Holland and, at the same time, live at peace with protestant England. The England to which Bernardino de Mendoza, the last Spanish ambassador before the outbreak of the great war, came in 1578, was no longer the same land that his predecessor had left six years before. It was the England that regarded conversion to the catholic faith as high treason, the land of martyrs and conspirators, of the torture-chamber and the gallows, above all, the land of ships and guns. Ever louder and more numerous swelled the voices which condemned the secret aid given to the Dutch rebellion, and

---

[1] " No queriendo los Estados guardar, como deven, los dichos dos puntos de la Religion Catholica Romana y obediencia de Su Magestad, esta resuelto de proceder tan adelante con el negocio que, quando le fuesse impossible allanarlos por otra via (que espera en Dios no lo sera, pues la causa en si es tan justa y tan endereçada a su servicio), esta determinado de destruir los Payses de manera que ni los naturales los podran habitar, ni nadie tenga cudicia dellos." Instructions given by Philip II. to Mendoza, Feb., 1578. K. DE LETTENHOVE, X., p. 298.

advocated England's open interference on behalf of the oppressed as being at once a more dignified and a wiser policy. Thomas Wilson, the English envoy at the court of the Spanish governor, the same who had turned the Philippics of Demosthenes into a controversial pamphlet of the day, was the most determined advocate of an aggressive policy in the Netherlands and of putting an end to the seeming friendship with Spain. A man wins no confidence as a suspected friend. Openness is the safest way. " Fortune favours the brave." For a long time England has not shown her power. " I pray God that I may rather see England invade than be invaded." [1] The policy which aimed at setting people at variance from a safe distance without coming to close quarters with the enemy, and the half measures and underhand dealings of Elizabeth's diplomacy were just as contrary to the spirit of puritanism as they were to any conception of the political situation that would lead to great results. " The policie is not good becawse it is not perpetual, but temporarie and for a season, and, in the ende, harme wil whollie fawle upon us that are suspected maynteyners covertlie and underhande of al these foreyne broyles and troubles. Better not deale than not to goe roundlie to worke, and oftentymes a blowe geaven without further harme dooinge costeth them deare that went no further. It is good for a man either to bee an assured frynd or els to discover hymselfe an open foe." [2]

Between 1575 and 1580, just when England's supremacy on the sea seemed assured, the prime mover in English politics, the strong yet cautious Burleigh, went over to the

[1] Wilson to Walsingham, Brussels, June 8, 1577. K. DE LETTEN-HOVE, IX., p. 329. To the same effect as early as May 8, *op. cit.*, p. 293.

[2] Wilson to the Earl of Leicester, Brussels, May 18, 1577, *op. cit.*, IX., p. 304.

party in favour of war and tried to draw over to it the queen herself. He made representations to her concerning the danger of a match between Don John of Austria and Mary Stuart; he dealt with the question on its commercial side; the Netherlands when once in the possession of Spain would be closed to English traders; he urged upon the queen the duty of succouring the oppressed. But to support the rebels openly went against the grain of Elizabeth's feelings as a monarch; she was unwilling to rouse the catholic powers unnecessarily; she refused to sacrifice English blood in defending freedom abroad.[1] Still even Elizabeth could do no more than put off what was bound to come sooner or later. She helped in once more building up a temporary bridge across the chasm.

It was a bad sign that the resumption of regular diplomatic intercourse remained a one-sided business. No English ambassador was appointed to Madrid. When Mendoza came to London, Spain's religious intolerance was no longer the sole ground why the post of English ambassador in Madrid, vacant since 1568, was not again filled.[2] Between 1570 and 1580, the papal nuncio in Spain never wearied of representing to the catholic king how dangerous and unsuitable it would be to admit an English ambassador to Madrid—it would be like having the plague in the house while wishing to avoid infection.[3] Philip could not permit a representative of the excommunicated queen any longer to reside at his court without offending the pope, who was exorting him to put the bull of excommunication into execution. This made the position of Mendoza in London all the more painful and difficult.

[1] See Burleigh's notes of Dec., 1577, and Feb., 1578, *op. cit.*, X., pp. 152 *et seq.*, 263.

[2] *Vid. ante*, p. 232.

[3] F. M. CARINI, *Mons. Niccolò Ormaneto*, II. (Roma, 1894), pp. 90 *et seq.*

The ambassador found the anti-Spanish sentiments of the English ministers so openly avowed that it was impossible for him to remain long in doubt as to the gravity of the situation.[1]   Elizabeth herself ceded nothing of her dignity for all her love of peace.   The "long arm" and "heavy hand" of the king of Spain, of which Mendoza spoke, failed to alarm her in the least.   Elizabeth exhibited a more bellicose demeanour to the ambassador than she did to her own ministers ; she declared flatly that she did not regard the Dutch as rebels, and that she would suffer neither Spanish nor French domination in the Netherlands whilst she had a man left in England.[2]

II. *The Papacy and the Plan of Invasion* (1578–84)

The open and offensive war with Spain upon which England at length entered after much hesitation in 1585 was really only a consequence of her breach with the catholic church.   The English reformation and the Elizabethan ecclesiastical settlement assumed an aggressive character from the first.[3]   Had England allowed her antagonist the advantage of striking the first blow at the decisive moment, she would have been untrue to herself. And yet, for a time it seemed as if England would in the end be the party attacked.   Not Spain, indeed, the sword-bearer of the catholic church, but Rome armed herself to strike the first blow.

Ever since Elizabeth's excommunication, there had been much talk in England of a league of all the catholic powers

[1] *Col. de doc. inéd.*, t. 91, pp. 212 *et seq.*   SPAN. CAL., 1568–79, p. 572.
[2] Letter of Mendoza of April 12, 1578.   *Col. de doc. inéd.*, t. 91, p. 215.   SPAÑ. CAL., p. 574.
[3] *Vid. ante*, pp. 48 *et seq.*

of the continent against the heretical island kingdom.[1]
The pope was naturally believed to be the head of the
league.   There never was, indeed, any league of the kind,
nor could there have been.   The idea of a united undertaking by Spain and France against "the Jezabel of the
North" was no more than a dream, such as could find
an existence only in the heated imagination of catholic
enthusiasts.[2]   The rumour, however, was the outcome of
a true estimate of the line papal policy was taking.
Gregory XIII. was unwearied in representing to his
most faithful son, the catholic king, that the invasion of
England was a duty that lay upon his conscience.   But
as Philip's answer never varied year after year—agreeing
on the essential point but postponing the hour for
action—the aged and impatient pontiff at last took action
on his own account.   The instrument employed by the
papacy was an ambitious adventurer, utterly indifferent to
religious matters, who had already been under the church's
ban in the time of Pius V., a fortune-hunter who stuck
at nothing, and withal a man who must have had great
personal powers of attraction.

> " If I should tell his story,
>   Pride was all his glory,
> And lusty Stukely he was call'd in court."[3]

The name of this strange confidential agent of Gregory
XIII. was Sir Thomas Stukeley.[4]   The English government, which had long regarded him with suspicion, once

---

[1] STRYPE'S *Annals*, II., i. (1824), pp. 375-377.

[2] *Cf.* J. KRETZSCHMAR, *Invasionsprojekte*, pp. 57 *et seq.*

[3] *The Life and Death of the Famous Thos. Stukely*.   Undated
broadside.   Brit. Mus., C. 40, m. 10 (38).

[4] *Cf.* his biography by RICH. SIMPSON, *The School of Shakespeare*
(London, 1878), and J. H. POLLEN, *The Irish Expedition of* 1579,
The Month, Jan. 1903, pp. 69-85.   See also the documents in BELLES-
HEIM, *Geschichte der Kath. Kirche in Irland*, II. (1890), Appendixes
X.–XXVIII.

more fixed its attention on him in the year 1577, when he
made his appearance among the catholic exiles in Louvain.
The English envoy in Brussels, Thomas Wilson, made
inquiries respecting him from the nuncio, Filippo Sega—one
of the rare instances of personal intercourse between English and papal diplomatists in the days of the excommunicated Elizabeth! The nuncio, "a man full of cunning and
mildness as commonly Italians are," denied everything,
both the existence of a catholic league against England
and Stukeley's connection with the pope. But Wilson
considered he had good grounds for not believing him.[1]
Before a year was out, at the beginning of 1578, Stukeley
sailed from Civita Vecchia to stir up Ireland to rebellion
against Elizabeth. In England the guards in the sea-
ports were reinforced and the fleet put in readiness for
action.[2]

Wilson's saying about the danger of striking with only
half one's force was fully justified by this fatal enterprise.
Regarded from a military point of view, the beginning
was half comic, half tragic ; the volatile Stukeley abandoned
the Irish project while on the way thither, and went off to
Africa in the service of Portugal. There he met his death,
to figure afterwards as a hero in dramas and ballads.[3] A
mere remnant of the papal soldiers reached Ireland in
the summer of 1579. Nicholas Sanders, a papal agent,
encouraged the rebellion and bestowed upon it a religious
consecration. England put down the rising without much
difficulty.[4] The political consequences of this papal enterprise were out of all proportion to the force employed.

[1] Wilson's letters to Walsingham and Leicester, of May 11 and 18,
1577. K. DE LETTENHOVE, IX., pp. 297, 302 et seq.
[2] Col. de doc. inéd., t. 91, pp. 196, 217, 258 et seq. SPAN. CAL.,
568-79, pp. 561 et seq., 575, 599.
[3] SIMPSON, School of Shakespeare, passim.
[4] POLLEN, l.c., pp. 81 et seq.

English catholics had to do heavy penance for the indis-
cretions of their spiritual head. The papal fleet had no
sooner reached the coast of Portugal than the persecution
of catholics broke out with fresh fury in England.[1] The
catholic mission, which was just then entering upon its
labours in full force, was from the outset viewed with
suspicion by the popular mind, inasmuch as at one and
the same time the pope was landing political agents in
Ireland and priests and Jesuits in England.[2] The meagre
diplomatic relations recently established between Madrid
and London were also affected. Elizabeth complained to
Mendoza of the pope's Irish enterprise, and argued from
it in defence of her own encouragement of the rebellion in
the Low Countries.[3] Although the ambassador repelled
the imputation that Spain was answerable for the pope's
action, he was unable to destroy the belief that what had
happened in Ireland was due to the concerted action of
the pope and the catholic king.[4] Since Elizabeth's excommunication, Rome had taken no more fatal step in
English affairs than this expedition to Ireland.

Gregory's Irish enterprise was an example of petty
politics. Its explanation lay in the pope's political power-
lessness where England was concerned. In the report
drawn up by the meeting of ministers at Greenwich, of
which we have spoken already, when England's relations to
foreign powers were discussed just at the time of the Irish
expedition,[5] the Roman danger was dismissed with the
brief remark, "The pope malitious, but nowe a pore

[1] In April, 1578. *Col. de doc. inéd.*, t. 91, pp. 220 *et seq.* SPAN
CAL., 1568-79, p. 577.

[2] *Vid. ante*, pp. 140 *et seq.*, 151 *et seq.*

[3] Mendoza to Philip II., March 23, 1580. *Col. de doc. inéd.*, t. 91
p. 472. SPAN. CAL., 1580-86, p. 21. *Cf.* Mendoza's letter of July 10
in *Col. de doc. inéd.*, p. 498. SPAN. CAL., p. 41.

[4] Mendoza, on June 24, 1580. SPAN. CAL., 134-136.

[5] Oct. 6, 1579. *Vid. ante*, p. 255.

chapline, etc. Countries gone from him, etc." [1] Already in the time of Gregory XIII. Francis Bacon regarded the papacy as no longer an agressive power but as a power that was forced to defend itself. "He [the pope] is not so much carried with the desire to suppress our religion, as drawn with fear of the downfall of his own, if in time it be not upheld and restored." [2] Not only did this view completely ignore the spiritual force of the counter-reformation, but, from a political standpoint also, it was contradicted by the progress of catholicism on the continent. From an insular point of view, however, it was easily explained and justified, for as long as Spain resisted the pressure put upon her by Rome, the pope was indeed nothing more than "a poor chaplain" as far as England was concerned.

In political matters, the pope could scarcely touch the island-kingdom in any other way than by seeking to disturb by some stroke of good fortune the diplomatic relations between England and the catholic powers. We have already spoken of his efforts to bring to nought the renewed diplomatic intercourse between London and Madrid. In 1578, when England's old commercial ally, the Venetian republic, was thinking of sending an ambassador to London, the nuncio in Venice received instructions to intervene and to prevent "the authority of such a fierce enemy of catholicism as the so-called queen from being strengthened by the appointment of an official embassy." [3] Attempts of this kind on the pope's part to give practical effect to the excommunication were not

---

[1] Gilliodts-van-Severen, XI., p. 411.

[2] *Notes on the Present State of Christendom* (1582). *Works of* FRANCIS BACON, ed. SPEDDING, etc., VIII. (1862), p. 18.

[3] "Di auttorizzare con un ambasceria publica una nemica tanto acerrima de catholicismo, com' è quella pretensa regina." Arch. Vat., Nunz. Venezia, 20, p. 73 ; July 5, 1578 ; *cf.* p. 127. The instructions were repeated on the following Nov. 8.

dangerous to England and—at least in Venice—were
undertaken by the pope himself with a certain degree of
hesitation.   The nuncio, who was instructed to put a stop
to relations between the republic of St. Mark and England,
was bidden to set to work "without making a noise," [1]
and, if he could not hinder the sending of an ambassador,
he was told at least to bring his influence to bear on the
choice of a person " in whom wisdom and experience were
united with real piety, zeal in God's service, and purity of
conduct . . . in order that one may look for benefit rather
than damage to the holy catholic religion from such a
mission." [2]

In reading words like these, we gain the impression that
the pope still trusted to moral tactics as the ultimate
means.   The same impression is left upon us by the
pontificate of Gregory XIII. as a whole, with its numerous
foundations of schools and seminaries throughout the
world.   In spite of all the blood shed in the wars of
religion, the papacy of the counter-reformation, taken as a
whole, chiefly regarded a moral and spiritual reformation
as at once its last means and its final object.   Nevertheless
this age of unparalleled religious fanaticism impressed
upon the papacy also its stamp of blood and murder, and
upon none of the popes so much as upon this very
Gregory, the founder of seminaries.

The employment of assassination as a political means
and the justification of murder are common to the whole

---

[1] " Ma però senza strepito."   Instructions of March 26, 1580, for
preventing a Venetian embassy to London.   *L.c.*, fol. 286.

[2] " Ricorderà che al meno si faccia elettione di tal persona, nela
quale sia congiunta la prudenza et esperienza con vera pietà et zelo
del servizio di Dio et con bontà di vita et costumi, et che la famiglia
che condurrà seco, sia simile a lui, acciò d'una tal missione si possa
più presto sperar beneficio che danno a la santa religion catholica."
L.c., fol. 286.

age of the renaissance up to the period of the counter-reformation.[1] During the renaissance, reasons of state formed the motive and justification of political murder. But since the reformation, religious hatred and considerations of ecclesiastical state-craft also entered in, and made the two principal combatants, the catholics and the Calvinists, uphold the doctrine of murder and make use of it for political ends. The years between 1570 and 1590—the most warlike of the entire period—were also the years in which murders were most frequent. Only a few men who were in advance of their age still kept their hands clean, and among them, the greatest of them all, William of Orange. No one, on the other hand, made more use of assassination as a political weapon than king Philip II., whose fanaticism amounted to moral insanity. Among the popes, Pius V. sailed very near the wind by encouraging conspiracies and rebellions, still there is no evidence that he advocated murder or regarded it as a meritorious work. It was left to his successor to do this. Gregory XIII. adopted without hesitation all the political methods of his time. He alone among the popes of the counter-reformation regarded assassination, when employed in the church's service, as a work well-pleasing to God. It was, however, his hatred for the great heretical queen, the Jezabel of the North, which more than anything else made him in this respect a child of his age. " His Holiness's soul," wrote a Venetian ambassador from Rome, " is full of contempt for this queen." [2]

According to the evidence until quite recently at our

---

[1] WALTER PLATZHOFF, *Die Theorie von der Mordbefugnis der Obrigkeit im XVI. Jahrh.* In EBERING'S *Histor. Studien* (Berlin, 1906).

[2] Giov. Corraro (1581), ALBÈRI, *Le relazioni degli ambasciatori veneti*, ser. II., t. IV., p. 283.

disposal, it might still be regarded as an open question whether Gregory XIII. gave his moral approval to the projects for murdering Elizabeth set on foot during his pontificate, and furthered them by his authority.[1] The view that he did so has so far depended, first, on the avowal of the Jesuit Tyrrel (1581). This man travelled to Rome with Ballard in order to hear from the pope's own lips whether the murder of Elizabeth was a good work or not. The pontiff said it was, but enjoined, at the same time, that the attempt should be carried out in such a way as not to bring discredit on his (the pope's) reputation. But this avowal was extorted on the rack, then revoked later on, and once more sworn to.[2] On this account, as well as because of the questionable character of the conspirators (p. 155), Tyrrel's assertion cannot by itself be regarded as proof. The assertion of Gregory's complicity with these murderous plans rests, secondly, on the correspondence between the nuncio at Paris and the cardinal secretary of state. In the spring of 1583, the nuncio Castelli[3] wrote to Cardinal Tolomeo Galli (called from his birthplace, the cardinal of Como) that he had declined to lay before his Holiness for his approval a plan for assassinating Elizabeth which had been submitted to him, "for although I believe everything would be lawful to the pope by which

[1] J. H. POLLEN, S.J., concludes his investigations into this question with the words: "In every case something is certainly wanting to the definiteness of our knowledge. But in some cases very little is wanting, and the concurrence of the three cases proves this conclusion at least, that there was *some sort* of toleration of assassination." *The Politics of the English Catholics during the reign of Q. Eliz.*, The Month, July, 1902, p. 77.

[2] STRYPE'S *Annals*, III., ii., p. 425 ; III. i., p. 698. J. A. FROUDE, *Hist. of Engl.*, XI., pp. 43–45.

April 22/May 2, 1583. See the correspondence in KNOX'S *Card. Allen* (1882), pp. 412 *et seq.* Also in KRETZSCHMAR, *Invasionsprojekte*, pp. 162 *et seq.* ; *cf.* POLLEN, *Politics of Engl. Catholics*, The Month, June, 1902, p. 607. PLATZHOFF, *op. cit.*, p. 80.

God might chastise His enemy (Elizabeth), still it would be unseemly that His earthly representative (the pope) should do it by such means as these." The cardinal communicated the contents of the letter to the pope, and wrote at his orders: " His Holiness can only feel pleased that that kingdom should be set free from oppression by whatsoever means (*in qual si sia modo*) and restored to God and our holy religion." These are very damaging words for Gregory XIII., still they contain no more than a covert approval of assassination, and in no sense convey praise of the deed. In support of this view we can, thirdly, appeal to a remarkable grant of an indulgence. In the winter of 1583-84, Dr. Parry, a real or pretended conspirator against Queen Elizabeth, asked and obtained through the cardinal of Como a plenary indulgence in view of a dangerous (but not clearly defined) undertaking which was to restore England to obedience to the Holy See.[1] According to the idea then prevalent in Rome, this " restoration " could only be effected by putting Elizabeth out of the way. The circumstances under which Parry presented his petition for an indulgence must at least rouse a suspicion that the undertaking in question is to be understood as an attempt on Elizabeth's life. However important this fact may be in our investigation, it, too, is no proof, but merely a fresh ground for suspicion against the cardinal of Como, and, therefore, against the pope.

The decisive answer to this much debated question is contained in a hitherto unknown letter of the cardinal secretary of state (the cardinal of Como) to the nuncio in Madrid, Filippo Sega. In 1580, there appeared at the nunciature in Madrid an Englishman, Humphrey Ely, who not long afterwards became a secular priest and

[1] More fully in POLLEN, The Month, July, 1902, pp. 72-77.

figured as one of the chief opponents of the Jesuits.[1]
On this occasion, Ely came at the bidding of certain
English noblemen and of the English Jesuits to obtain
an explanation from the pope through the nuncio Sega.
The nobles, whose names were not given, had entered
into an agreement to murder Elizabeth, but, as the deed
might cost them their lives, they were willing to attempt
it only on condition that the pope assured them, at least
verbally, that they would not thereby incur sin. The
nuncio at once explained to Ely personally that they
might rest easy on this point since the bull of excommunication of Pius V., of blessed memory, gave leave to
all the queen's subjects to take up arms against her. At
the same time, Sega promised to write to Rome on the
question and obtain the opinion of his Holiness. He
added the assurance that the pope, in case he did not
declare his opinion before the deed was done, would at
all events grant the survivors the necessary absolution
afterwards. In conclusion, he exhorted them to make
haste lest the plans of the conspiracy should get known.
He reported everything fully to Rome and also asked for
an absolution on his own account, in case he might have
gone somewhat too far in the matter.[2]

This letter of the nunico Sega to the cardinal secretary
of state forced the pope openly to take up his position
respecting the question of assassination. The reply of the
cardinal of Como conveying the pope's decision to the

---

[1] Cf. the pamphlet referred to above, p. 105, note 1.

[2] Hitherto the correspondence has only been known in substance
up to this point. The most important part of Sega's letter was first
printed by M. PHILIPPSON, *Ein Ministerium unter Philipp II.
Kardinal Granvella am spanischen Hofe* 1579–86 (Berlin, 1895), p.
204, note 1. CREIGHTON, *Queen Elizabeth* (new impression, 1899),
p. 196. J. H. POLLEN, *The Politics of Catholics*, The Month, June,
1902, p. 605, made use of Philippson's extract. I give the letter in
full in Appendix XVIII., A.

nuncio [1] is the most damaging piece of evidence that so far has come to light in support of the adoption of the doctrine of political murder by Gregory XIII. It makes no material difference that the pope in it does not speak directly with his own lips but through the lips of his prime minister and confidant. "Since that guilty woman of England rules over two such noble kingdoms of Christendom and is the cause of so much injury to the catholic faith, and loss of so many million souls, there is no doubt that whosoever sends her out of the world with the pious intention of doing God service, not only does not sin but gains merit, especially having regard to the sentence pronounced against her by Pius V. of holy memory. And so, if those English nobles decide actually to undertake so glorious a work, your Lordship can assure them that they do not commit any sin. We trust in God also that they will escape danger. As far as concerns your Lordship, in case you have incurred any irregularity,[2] the pope bestows upon you his holy benediction."

These words go far beyond what canon law permits to be done to excommunicate persons. Excommunication in canon law corresponds to outlawry in civil, to kill an excommunicate person is not regarded as murder by canon law, but rather as a deed which calls for penance, "lest the discipline of the church suffer harm," and because impure motives can easily prompt the deed.[3] Inasmuch as Gregory represents the assassination of Elizabeth as "meritorious" and as "a good work," he, who previously was such a stickler for legal exactitude, abandons the standpoint of the canonists and takes his stand among the

---

[1] Hitherto unknown. Appendix XVIII., B.

[2] Participation in a murder entails *ipso facto* "irregularity" for priests. *Cf.* Sega's request for absolution above.

[3] *Decreti Grat.*, pars. ii., causa xxiii., *qu.* V., c. 47.

advocates of the doctrine of political murder. Keener and more determined than his ministers the nuncios, he supports murders with the weight of his authority. He is the same pope who ordered a *Te Deum* to be sung on receiving news of the massacre of St. Bartholomew and ordered a procession to thank God for "the grace bestowed on Christendom." [1] No other pope of the counter-reformation is more completely the child of his age than Gregory XIII.

The conclusion drawn from the evidence hitherto available, *i.e.* that under Gregory XIII. there was "some sort of toleration of assassination," [2] is now shown to fall short of the truth. Assassination is not merely tolerated, it is distinctly encouraged, and that, not in passing, but on principle. The unambiguous statement of 1580 now lends support to the hitherto inconclusive evidence already quoted as to the pope's attitude towards the question of Elizabeth's assassination. There is now no longer any reason for doubting the truth of Tyrrel's avowal of 1581, for it agrees in all essentials with the papal declaration of 1580. The general statement of 1583 quoted above, that the pope would welcome any means of setting England free, forms the third link in the chain, and the indulgence granted to Dr. Parry the fourth. Elizabeth's assassination was not an object which merely entered for the moment into the pope's political programme in the reign of Gregory XIII., it formed one of his constant and cherished aims. It is true the pope himself in no instance hired and dispatched the assassins, but in each case, as it was brought before him, he gave the assassins his moral support.

---

[1] Dispatch of the Card. of Como to the nuncio in Paris, Sept. 8, 1572. PHILIPPSON, *Die Römische Curie u. d. Bartholomäusnacht*, Deutsche Zeitschr. f. Gesch.-Wiss., VII., pp. 134 *et seq.*

[2] See the quotation from Pollen above, p. 268, note 1.

The influence at work during the pontificate of Gregory XIII. was Spanish. In political morality as well as in political aim,[1] Rome sided with Philip II. When the papacy shook itself free from the political influence of Spain, under the great Sixtus V., it also freed itself from Spain's views on bloodshed. Gregory XIII., although so deeply imbued with Spanish influence, had little in common with Philip II. as far as his own personal character was concerned. But still, he did not belong to that small number of men who were in advance of their age. Both in moral force, as well as in mental endowments, he did not rise above the common run of men. His character was free from ignoble traits, but, nevertheless, there are cases in which deficiency in moral greatness amounts to a fault. Only a really great man would have been able in those years, when the counter-reformation was at fever heat, to raise the papacy well above the ordinary level of the period.

Gregory's failure to do this had its tragic effect upon English catholics. As usually happens, the sheep suffered for the faults of the shepherd. The pope and his nuncios had it in their power to nip in the bud nearly every plot formed against Elizabeth, for almost all of them came to their knowledge and were even expressly laid before them for approval. None of these plots were at any time a serious danger to Elizabeth's life, and for this she had to thank the unceasing care taken for her safety by the agents of Burleigh and Walsingham, but each plot added fresh fuel to the agitation against the catholics, and intensified the distrust with which the mission was regarded. Had there been no plots, the unfair judgment passed on

---

[1] HERRE, *Papsttum u. Papstwahl i. Zeitalter Phil. II.* (1907), pp. 245-250. P. O. v. TÖRNE, *Ptolémée Gallio. Card. de Côme* (Helsingfors, 1907).

the catholic mission would have been impossible, and the penal legislation of the last decades of the century,[1] and all the terrible animosity to which it gave rise, would never have been heard of.   It was only after 1580 that the secret societies were formed whose members swore to protect the queen with life and limb, and to pursue her enemies with all their might, even to their complete extermination.[2] This passionate anxiety for the protection of the queen's life was amply justified by the failure of an acknowledged heir to the crown.   Elizabeth's death during the lifetime of Mary Stuart would in all probability have renewed the struggle of the fifteenth century for the succession to the throne.   The value of the queen's life for the preservation of the country's peace could scarcely be overestimated. But the pope and the rest who wished to put an end to her life exaggerated its importance for the maintenance of English protestantism.   Most of the plans of invasion hatched in Rome and elsewhere between 1570 and 1590 started with the supposition that the English state church would lose its chief support with Elizabeth.[3]   Hence the conclusion ; the queen's assassination must precede the restoration of catholicism in England—it must prepare the way for the invasion.

The diplomatic history of these plans of invasion is still far from being complete.[4]   It is neither necessary nor

[1] *Vid. ante*, pp. 147, 150.   *Cf.* T. G. LAW'S remarks to the same effect in *Cambr. Mod. Hist.*, III., p. 290.

[2] " The instrument of association " has been often printed, *e.g.* Harleian Misc. VII., p. 132 ; COLLIER, *The Egerton Papers*, Camden Soc. (1840), pp. 108–110 ; WILLIS-BUND, *State Trials*, I. (1879), pp. 246 *et seq.*

[3] " Quando si levasse il nutrimento et il caldo di colei [Elizabeth], senza dubbio la santa religione si ricuperarebbe in Inghilterra." From an undated memorial of the pope to Philip II. on the invasion of England.   Arch. Vat., Nunz. Inghilterro I., fol. 160–165.

[4] J. KRETZSCHMAR'S book, *Die Invasionsprojekte der kathol. Mächte*

profitable to discuss the matter here, for the changes and chances of diplomacy are of merely secondary importance in dealing with the question of England's relation to the catholic church.   No other sources of information give us so clear an idea of the estimate of England's moral and physical power formed by Spain and the papacy—the two great champions of the counter-reformation—as the judgments expressed by the politicians who were exerting themselves in favour of invasion.

In Rome, between 1570 and 1590, the prevailing opinion was that England was the centre of the evil. At the frontiers of no other country had the counter-reformation to come to a halt so helplessly as at the coasts of England.   And so the conviction arose in men's minds, a conviction fostered by English catholic exiles, that with the return of England to catholicism the divisions of Christendom would practically cease.   The Huguenots in France and the rebels in Flanders would lose their strongest support and return to the church, Germany, being then isolated, would soon follow their example.   "What glory it would be, by winning back England, to rob the nest of heresy, to purge France and Flanders, and give an example to Germany!" [1]   Such is the usual train of thought which

geg. Engl. z. Zt. Elisabeths (Leipzig, 1892), does not go sufficiently deeply into the subject.   Not only is his acquaintance with unpublished sources of information imperfect, but even his knowledge of what is already printed leaves much to be desired.   One of the most important publications on the subject, KNOX's Card. Allen, has been entirely overlooked by him.

[1] Discorso per la ricuperatione del regno d'Inghilterra alla chiesa a Gregorio XIII.   A tract without name or date.   Arch. Vat., Arc. S. Ang. Arm. XI., caps. 6, No. 77.   The original of the quotation runs : " Quanta gloria le fia con il ricuperare il regno d'Inghilterra di haver tolto il nido all' heresia et di averne purgato il regno di Francia et di Fiandra, che potranno essere essempio a Germani!"   Cf. the Discorso sopra l'impresa d'Inghilterra (circ. 1585) in Bibl. Vat., Urb. 854, p. I., for. 242.

recurs at first with wearisome reiteration in the letters and memorials of catholics exiled from England. The same song is set to every key. " The state of Christendome dependethe uppon the stowte assallynge of England." [1] The mischief which sprang from England is depicted in the darkest colours, and the detested island appears not only as the hotbed whence heresy spread to France and rebellion to Flanders, but as the support of the infidel in Africa in their resistance to the Portuguese, and of the Turk in the Mediterranean against Spain and Italy—in fine, as " the source whence all evil and corruption spring." England's overthrow is represented as the duty of universal Christendom wounded in all its members.[2]

The same ideas, translated from the language of passion into that of diplomacy, were repeatedly urged by the papal statesmen who tried to rouse Philip out of his lethargy. About 1580 especially, they attacked the king on all sides with ever-increasing impatience. The nuncio Sega in Madrid, the zealous archbishop Quiroga of Toledo, the cardinal of Como in Rome, the pope's chief adviser—all of them were unwearied in representing to the king that the undertaking against England was the necessary prelude to his conquest of the rebellious Low Countries ; [3]

[1] N. Sanders to Allen, Madrid, Nov. 6, 1577. KNOX'S Card. Allen (1882), p. 38.

[2] Alcuni motivi . . . per rappresentare alla Sua Stà. e gli principi Christiani, per aiutare gli cattolici d'Inghilterra e estirpare gl'heresie [1582], Bibl. Vat., Ottob. 2419, p. I., fol. 3. FROUDE, X., p. 509, says correctly, " So long as England was unconquered, the reformation was felt to be unconquerable."

[3] Cf. two papers by the nuncio Sega—Instruttione data da Mons. Sega, nuntio in Ispagna, a Mons. Taverna, suo successore, July 31, 1581, and Relatione compendiosa della negotiatione della nuntiatura di Spagna di Mons. Sega., Arch. Vat., Borgh. III., 129 D., fol. 23 et seq., 303 et seq.

no remedy was possible until the root of the evil, the queen of England, was torn up ![1]

Hand in hand with the idea of the necessity of the undertaking, went the assurance of its success. No one did more to encourage this belief than the agitators among English catholics on the continent. The exiles in Rome and in the Low Countries, in France and in Spain had, for the most part, left their native land between 1560 and 1570 ; only a fraction of them had come overseas in the twenty years which followed. The England they knew was the England where the two religions were almost equally represented ; they knew neither protestant England nor the land of the " Queen of the Seas " that could mock the world-wide power of Spain with impunity. Their ideas, therefore, both of the moral and physical powers of resistance which England could offer to an invasion from catholics and Spaniards were quite out of date. The one thing they did know, and which was patent to all the world, was the way all enemies of the state church were oppressed by Elizabeth's government. Can anything bind men more closely together than the bitterness of those reduced to slavery ! If only men would strike while the iron is hot ! " The mutual hatred of catholics and heretics is still fresh among those whose brothers, relations, and friends have been tortured and persecuted. Every one longs for revenge. With time and the change of men and things all this will pass away and be forgotten." [2]

[1] " Non pareva che seli potesse apportare rimedio conveniente senza procurare prima di svellere la radice del male, che era la regina d'Inghilterra." *L.c.*, fol. 308.

[2] From the memorial, *Alcuni motivi* (1582), mentioned above, p. 276, note 2. The passage runs : " Hora l' odio di coloro, tanto catholici quanto heretici, li cui fratelli, parenti e amici sono stati tormentati e perseguitati, è fresco e ognuno desideroso di vendetto [*sic*]. Col tempo. tutto quello passarà e si dimenticarà con la morte, con la mutabilità delli costumi, tempi, absenza e governo."

England's powers of moral resistance were also underestimated, because it was thought a country that had
changed its religion three times in the immediate past
must be too deeply shaken within itself to offer resistance
to a serious attack. Moreover, men fancied the queen
must be universally detested on account of her tyranny
and immorality.[1] "Never has a prince in England been
so hated by every one as this queen!" Her own courtiers,
the initiated pretended to know, would forsake her on the
earliest suitable opportunity.[2] In the struggle between
the two religions, the adherents of catholicism were reputed
to have the twofold advantage of larger numbers and
internal unity. Two-thirds of the English people, it was
stated somewhere, were catholic,[3] many reckoned their
numbers much higher. A Welshman, who formed his
opinion of England from his own country, committed himself to the statement that the catholics in England were at
least six times—and in Wales at least a thousand times—
as numerous as the heretics.[4] "The catholics alone," so
people said, "hold close together, with one heart and one
soul, bravely and staunchly, since God gives them force
and courage."[5] The heretics, on the other hand, were
broken up into Calvinists and Lutherans, puritans and

---

[1] *Discorso sopra le potenti cagioni che debbono spingere il re cattolico
più tosto all' impresa d'Inghilterra che a quella di Fiandra, ove si
dimostra, con quanta facilità o non molta difficoltà si potrà conseguire.*
Arch. Vat., Borgh. I., 226–228, fol. 192–223 ; Bibl. Vat., Urb. lat. 857,
fol. 247–287.

[2] Tract by Persons, the Jesuit, 1582. J. KRETZSCHMAR, *Invasionsprojekte*, p. 140. *Cf.* the tract, written after 1570, in K. DE LETTEN-
HOVE, VII., p. 255 ; "Isabella [*i.e.* Elizabeth] es aborrecida."

[3] According to Persons. KRETZSCHMAR, p. 139.

[4] See the quotation above, p. 59, note 3. Of Wales it is said in the
same document : "In Cambria præsertim . . . vix su mille unus aut
ullus hodie invenitur hæreticus."

[5] K. DE LETTENHOVE ; *l.c.*

anabaptists, and, in addition, were thought to be disunited on the question of the succession to the throne, being partly supporters and partly opponents of Mary Stuart. The memory, too, of the affability of Philip of Spain still survived, they believed, from the time of his sojourn in England, and, in conjunction with the weapon of gold, would win him new friends.[1] Some of these statements do contain at least a grain of truth, but no more indeed than a grain ; taken together, they give a completely erroneous picture of the real state of affairs. We can scarcely believe our eyes when we read that Elizabethan England was sunk in hopeless decay, like the Roman empire of old, and needed only a final blow to shatter it to pieces.[2]

England's power of physical resistance was as little appreciated by the advocates of invasion as her moral. For a generation, England had not been engaged in any regular warfare, nor in any great war for a still longer period. Accordingly, in the judgments passed upon the nation's fitness for war, much stress was laid upon its want of experience in military matters. " They know not how to handle a musket, they are without skilled and experienced officers, they have no strongly fortified castles or well-walled towns, and so the war cannot last long." [3] Moreover they have no cavalry, and it is just the country people, upon whom the defence of the island rests, who are

---

[1] *Discorso sopra le potenti cagioni.* It is well known that Philip II. had *not* made a favourable impression upon England.

[2] " Havendo l'Inghilterra per divino giudicio cominciato a declinare, ogni uno sa quanto è facile dare la spinta a chi sta per precipitare, non essendo altro la declinatione che una strada alla corruttione : così l'imperio potentissimo di Romani doppo che cominciò a dare volta si vidde in conseguenza caduto con tutto il peso di una machina smisurata." From the *Discorso sopra le potenti cagioni*, already mentioned, *circ.* 1581.

[3] K. DE LETTENHOVE, VII., p. 258.

good catholics.   Mention was made of the smallness of the invading armies which had conquered England in earlier days, the last time under Henry VII., without its being made clear that one had to deal now with an invasion altogether new in kind and belonging to another period. How little these homeless wanderers were in touch with the new era is best shown by their opinion that the English fleet was of no consequence.[1]   An Italian memorial characteristically employs Cæsar's *Bellum Gallicum* as a source of information in geographical matters in the year of grace 1588![2]

The great review of the English forces held by Queen Elizabeth in the spring of 1580 gave rise to much discussion.   The official report announced that England could put nine thousand cavalry in the field.   In case of a sudden attack twenty-five thousand men could be dispatched within twelve hours to any point within the country.   This statement was with justice severely criticized.   A merchant of Milan, who had passed fifty years of his life in England, remarked upon it that of the ninety thousand infantry and nine thousand cavalry only twenty-two thousand would be found actually in working order, and even these, according to the judgment of English officers, would not be a match for ten thousand Spanish or Italian troops.   In his opinion, between ten and twelve thousand foreign foot soldiers along with one thousand horsemen and one thousand mounted arquebusiers would be quite sufficient for the conquest of England.   "And if any one has a different opinion, I am prepared to satisfy

---

[1] *Discorso sopra le potenti cagioni.   Cf.* K. DE LETTENHOVE, VII., pp. 255, 265.

[2] *Descrittione de porti et fortezze del regno d'Inghilterra, fatta li VI. di Luglio,* 1588.   Arch. Vat., Borgh. I., 132-136, fols. 200-213.

him with well-grounded reasons."[1] This Milanese merchant did not stand alone in his opinion. Castelli, the nuncio at Paris, who was surrounded by numbers of English exiles, thought the same number of troops would be sufficient.[2] Other estimates were lower still, and regarded eight or ten thousand footmen and two thousand horse as large enough for an invading army.[3]

The usually accepted picture of the world-power of Spain was contrasted with this presumably easy undertaking—Spain, with its vast possessions spread over half the world, with its treasures in countless abundance, its mighty and victorious army, its plentiful supply of all the provisions for war, its huge fleet—the amazement of mankind! King Philip is "as it were the umpire and disposer of the world; it seems as if he alone held the reins of power over land and sea."[4] Hopes were at their highest when in 1576 the victor of Lepanto, Don John of Austria, was chosen to be leader of the enterprise against England; "the mere immortal fame of his name and memorable deeds alone will put his enemies to flight."[5] The chief causes of anxiety as to the success of the venture, the dangers of the northern seas and the difficulties of effecting

---

[1] "Informatione per il R^{do.} P. Panigarola circha a le cose del regno d'Inghilterra per la cognitione che Jo. Gio. Sovico, gintilhuomo nato in questa citta di Milano è stato 50 anni in esso regno e traficato in negotii di mercantia per la magior parte delle provincie d'esso regno . . ." etc. The State Archivium, Florence, Sez. Medicea, 4184, fol. 121–125. This letter was addressed to Franc. Panigarola, a famous Milanese preacher of the Friars Minor, afterwards Bishop of Asti. Concerning the muster of the troops, *cf.* Mendoza's report to Philip II., Feb. 20, 1580. *Col. de doc. inéd.*, t. 91, p. 456. SPAN. CAL., 1580–86, p. 9.

[2] Castelli to the Card. of Como, June 10/20, 1583. KRETZSCHMAR, p. 168.

[3] K. DE LETTENHOVE, VII., p. 265.

[4] *Discorso sopra le potenti cagioni.*

[5] K. DE LETTENHOVE, VII., pp. 270 *et seq.*

a landing, were easily disposed of by these prophets of Spain's prowess. Although they did not all scout the idea that the Spanish ships were unfit for these northern waters,[1] yet even military specialists and those well acquainted with the English coast, such as the Italian Filippo Pigafetta, who was both, had so exaggerated an idea of the power of Spain that, notwithstanding their realization of the difficulties of an invasion, they inclined to a hopeful decision.[2] All of them, both the English catholics on the continent and the Italians who remained true to the church, were more or less influenced by the simple creed of the crusaders ; Spain was fighting for the holy faith ; God will be with her ![3]

Gregory XIII. was himself most deeply animated by this belief. Essentially a jurist and theorist, the precepts of canon law often held a more prominent place in his mind than the considerations of statesmanship. " He understands very little about politics," was the judgment of the Venetian ambassador,[4] to whom we owe one of the best sketches of Gregory's character, "and has little liking for it, is unwilling to hear it discussed, and takes no pains to get to the heart of things." He was, on this account, all the more strongly swayed by the ecclesiastical movement of the counter-reformation, which, under his pontificate and partly by his merits, began to reap its firstfruits. Just as Gregory XIII. promoted with all his power the world-wide activity of the Society of Jesus, and, as a forerunner

---

[1] As the author of the *Discorso sopra le potenti cagioni* does.

[2] *Nota delle fortezze principali del' Inghilterra e di porti.* Arch. of the Prussian Historical Institute in Rome ; Minucciana, t. VII., fol. 304-309. Pigafetta is also the author of a *Discorso sopra l ordinanza dell' armata catholica, Roma, Ag.* 27, 1588 (referred to by CORBETT, *Drake and the Tudor Navy,* II. (1898), pp. 211 *et seq.*), and also of a *Discorso sopra liporti della spiaggia Romana.*

[3] *Discorso sopra le potenti cagioni,* and other tracts, *passim.*

[4] Paolo Tiepolo, see his paper in ALBÈRI, II., ser. IV., p. 215.

of Urban VIII., who founded the Propaganda, supported Christian missions in the Near and Far East ; and just as he took up, for a time at least, the cherished idea of the popes—the reunion of the Greek church [1]—so too it was in grim earnest that he laid his plans for winning back England to the catholic church. As early as the second year of his pontificate, 1573, he began to bring pressure to bear on the king of Spain, through his nuncios and legates, that he should liberate Mary Stuart and dethrone Elizabeth. He even proposed to him in all seriousness that he should make one more attempt to convert the excommunicated queen.[2] However often, too, the much occupied and much harassed king might hint at the difficulties of the undertaking and at the need there was for his forces to be employed in other quarters, the pope gave him no peace and never lost hope. When the cardinal of Como, in 1582, described to him a plan of invasion proposed by Henry Duke of Guise, "the pope was filled with as great joy as if it were a question of conquering the Holy Land!"[3] In the language of the curia, the war against England was "the holy enterprise." Many are the references to Gregory's great predecessor, the first of the name, through whom England was won to Christendom. English catholics never tired of encouraging the pope in his intention or of pointing out to him the example of St. Gregory the Great, "in order that, both in heaven and on earth, he may be canonized for delivering us from heresy as St. Gregory has been for delivering us from heathendom."[4]

---

[1] See the paper of Giov. Corraro in ALBÈRI, *l.c.*, p. 274.

[2] F. M. CARNI, *Mons. Niccolò Ormaneto, nunzio alla corte di Filippo II.* (Roma, 1894), pp. 82-93 ; 134-138.

[3] The card. of Como to the nuncio Castelli, May 28, 1582. KRETZSCHMAR, pp. 146 *et seq.*

[4] "Acciochè e in cielo e in terra la S. Stà. sia canonizato liberatore

In the last years of his pontificate, the pope's hopes were perpetually rising and falling. The papal plans for invasion depended at that time chiefly on Scotland and France. So long as the young king, James VI., was governed by the catholic Duke of Lennox, it was possible to entertain the idea of attacking England from Scotland. In spring, 1582, Lennox volunteered to lead the enterprise and carry it through in his king's name.[1] With the fall of the duke in the summer and his death in the following year, the plan was shattered and James VI. fell into the hands of the protestant nobles who were friendly to England. Not long afterwards, however, in the summer of 1583, fresh hopes dawned for the pope, and this time they seemed better founded than ever. The king succeeded in shaking himself free from the power of the lords and called the opposition party, who were hostile to England, to his council-board. "Now or never!" William Allen implored in a letter to the cardinal of Como.[2] In place of Lennox, Henry Duke of Guise was ready to lead the enterprise and set free his relative, Mary Stuart. He counted, of course, on the support of Philip II. A twofold attack, on the north by Spain and Scotland combined, and, on the south, by France, was to be made upon England from both sides.[3] Never, so men thought in Rome, would there be a more favourable opportunity, and so with renewed zeal the pope urged on Spain.[4]

nostro dell' heresie, come Sto. Gregorio del paganismo!" Conclusion of the *Alcuni motivi* (*vid. ante*, p. 276, note 2). *Cf.* BACON, *Notes on the Present State of Christendom*. Works, ed. SPEDDING, VIII., p. 19.

[1] KRETZSCHMAR, pp. 123–126.

[2] Letter from Rheims, Aug. 8, 1583 (n.s.). KNOX'S *Card. Allen*, p. 201.

[3] *Disegno per l'impresa d'Inghilterra* (1583). KNOX, pp. 416 *et seq.*

[4] "Nos urgere Hispanos et alios ad quos ea res pertinet non desinimus, propterea quod tempus magis idoneum magisve aptum ad

Nothing shows more clearly how high hopes had then risen in Rome than the fact that Gregory XIII. decided to renew the excommunication launched by his predecessor. Soon after Elizabeth's excommunication, men recognized in Rome that it was a mistake merely to threaten without striking.   It seems that Pius V. had regretted his action.[1]   The nuncio at the Spanish court wrote in 1574: " The bull ought not to have been published until the army was on its way to conquer England.   Men would then have held the keys of St. Peter (the bull) in one hand, and in the other the sword of St. Paul."[2]   It has been told already how Gregory, when sending forth the Jesuit mission (1580), gave to the bull the fatal interpretation that under existing circumstances it did not bind catholics, but would do so only when its execution might be possible. In this the pontiff acted by the advice of Persons, the leader of the mission.[3]   In two years' time, Persons was already of opinion that the hour for action had come.   He advised the pope to give his moral support to Guise's plan of invasion by renewing the excommunication of Elizabeth.[4] When next year, the Duke of Guise himself also begged for the renewal of the bull, and at the same time, for the grant of an indulgence for all who should take part in the campaign,[5] a fresh bull was then actually drawn up agreeing in the main with the suggestions of Persons and Guise.

---

rem bene gerendam nunquam post hac oblatum iri existimamus." The card. of Como to Allen, Sept. 24, 1583, Arch. Vat., Arm. XLIV., t. 26, p. 101.

[1] POLLEN, *Politics of Engl. Catholics*, The Month, Feb., 1902, p. 141.

[2] Ormaneto to the card. of Como, Oct. 25, 1574.   CARINI, *Mons. Niccolò Ormaneto* (Roma, 1894), p. 135.

[3] *Vid. ante*, p. 138.

[4] KRETZSCHMAR, p. 144.

[5] Instructions for the Roman envoy of the Duke of Guise, Aug. 22, 1583 (n.s.).   ALEXANDRE TEULET, *Relations politiques de la France et de l'Espagne avec l'Ecosse*, V. (1862), p. 310.

The draft bears the date of September 24, 1583 (new style). In spite of the excommunication fulminated by Pius V.—so runs the document [1]—Queen Elizabeth has not repented, but has rather added fresh infamies to the old ones ; she has ordered bishops and priests to be murdered, and has imprisoned the queen of Scotland " out of pure tyranny and hatred towards the catholic faith." Therefore Gregory XIII. makes his predecessor's manifesto his own, and decides to execute the bull forthwith and chastise "that Elizabeth, or rather that Jezabel." He pronounces Mary Stuart to be lawful heir of the kingdom instead of this impure woman (*fœmina impura*). But to all Christians, who repent of their sins and confess them, he grants a crusader's indulgence,[2] on condition they take part in the proposed enterprise against England. No one is to consider himself bound by his oath to the queen.

This second bull was to have been taken by William Allen when he went to England with the invading army to aid in raising the storm against Elizabeth. The bearer of the new bull was appointed bishop of Durham [3] at the same time and accredited as nuncio to Queen Mary Stuart with powers of a legate *a latere*.[4] He was to obtain a solemn oath from the Queen of Scots that she would always be obedient to the Holy See, remain a faithful ally of the king of Spain, restore the catholic religion in England as it was

[1] In what follows I merely give the substance of the draft, for the contents will be published in full by Father Pollen, S.J., who had the kindness to point out the document to me in Arch. Vat., Arm. XLIV., t. 26, pp. 90-95.

[2] "Indulgentiam et remissionem in forma jubilaei, quod procedentibus contra Turcas et ad recuperationem Terræ Sanctæ tribui solet."

[3] Brief of Greg. XIII. to Allen, Sept. 24, 1583, Arch. Vat., Arm. XLIV., t. 26, pp. 104 *et seq*. A northern bishopric was chosen because catholics were more numerous in those parts of England.

[4] Greg. XIII. to Queen Mary, Sept. 24, 1583. *L.c.*, p. 97.

before the apostasy of Henry VIII., and see that her son James VI. was brought up as a catholic.[1] The pope wrote at the same time to the young king of Scotland that, in spite of rumours to the contrary, he was convinced that he professed the catholic faith, and ascribed whatever contradictory measures James may have adopted to pressure put upon him.[2] Whether or not this was meant seriously, it at any rate harmonizes with the apprehensions entertained by the king's presbyterian opponents. The Assembly held in Edinburgh in October, 1583, represented to King James that papists had free access to his court and that his Majesty too openly favoured the enemies of the truth.[3]

In London, too, the new turn of Scottish affairs was taken very seriously. The idea of re-establishing England's impaired influence by force found supporters at the queen's council board but did not succeed in winning over Elizabeth herself, who was always shy of war. The situation, however, seemed sufficiently threatening to Lord Burleigh for him to dispatch to Scotland so trusty and energetic a diplomatist as Walsingham, the secretary of state. In the same days of September in which the pope was renewing the excommunication of Elizabeth and drafting the letters to the king of Scotland and the imprisoned Mary Stuart, the English secretary of state was engaged in a hot though unsuccessful diplomatic conflict with King James and his advisers who were hostile to England.[4] The conflict turned upon Scotland and the union of Great Britain under

---

[1] The pope's instructions to Allen, Sept. 24. *L.c.*, pp. 102 *et seq.*
[2] Greg. XIII. to James VI., Sept. 24. *L.c.*, p. 96.
[3] JOHN SPOTTISWOODE, *Hist. of the Ch. of Scotland*, ed. RUSSELL, II. (Edin., 1851), p. 304.
[4] *Cf.* K. STÄHLIN, *Der Kampf um Schottland u. die Gesandt-schaftsreise Walsinghams i. J.*, 1583 (1902), Leipziger Studien aus d. Gebeit des Gesch., IX., p. 1.

protestant rule: it was a conflict in which religion and national welfare were once more identified as far as England was concerned. England's diplomatic defeat in Edinburgh was a victory for Rome.

Still of what avail were the victories and defeats of diplomatists in the titanic struggle between England and Rome? None whatever, so long as the decision rested not on words but on the sword. And just in these very days of September, when excitement was at its height in Rome, London, and Edinburgh, the decision was taken in Madrid, a decision unfavourable to war. It was not altogether unexpected; still it was bitterly disappointing. Never had Philip II. a stronger navy at his disposal than just at that time. The conquest of the Portuguese mainland (1580) was made more complete and more secure by the naval victory of the Azores, which, in the summer of 1583, the great admiral Santa Cruz gained over Don Antonio, the pretender to the throne of Portugal and protégé of Elizabeth. Henceforth Philip had command over both the colonies and fleets of the two kingdoms. Santa Cruz himself wrote to the king from Terceira in the Azores that now he would be able to turn his victorious army against England.[1] But King Philip repeated, and with good reason, his old answer, "Not yet."[2] The want of the necessities for war, above all of artillery, the difficulty in providing on a large scale for the transport of troops, in short, the realization of the greatness of the undertaking from a *military* point of view, did more in the end than any political consideration to

---

[1] Santa Cruz to Philip II., Aug. 9, 1583 (n.s.). DURO, *La Armada Invencible*, I. (Madrid, 1884), p. 242. Santa Cruz did not advise that steps should be taken immediately, but during the following year.

[2] "Cosas son en que no se puede hablar con seguridad desde agora, pues dependen del tiempo y occasiones que han de dar la regla despues." Philip to Santa Cruz, Sept. 23, 1583. DURO, I., p. 244.

influence Philip once again to resist the pressure put upon him by the pope.[1] In Rome men were very angry. "It is absolutely clear," thought the pope and the cardinal of Como, "that beyond a doubt men were going forth to certain victory."[2] Thanks to the mischievous influence of the misleading accounts given by English exiles who understood little of politics and still less of war, it was impossible for men in Rome correctly to estimate the undertaking against England. Upon one point alone they were clear—that nothing could be done without Spain, and so the second bull of excommunication and deposition, intended to announce to the world the execution of Elizabeth's condemnation, lay an unfinished draft in the dust of the archives and was forgotten.[3]

The difference existing between Rome and Madrid in the judgments they passed on the English enterprise was the difference between the judgments formed by amateurs and professionals. In Rome men found no other explanation for Philip's everlasting procrastination than his luke-warmness and inability to come to a decision.[4] In Madrid, on the other hand, the saying of the Duke of Alva was current—"the king of Spain could make war on any prince in the world provided he was at peace with England."[5] When the Duke of Guise was considering the undertaking,

[1] See the letters of the nuncio at Madrid, Taberna, to the card. of Como, Sept., 1583. KRETZSCHMAR, pp. 117 *et seq.*

[2] *Ib.*, p. 180.

[3] It was in the days of the Armada alone that the curia bethought themselves once more of Gregory's bull of excommunication. The broadside, in which Sixtus V. in 1588 announced the execution of the sentence of excommunication (of which more anon), speaks of the excommunication pronounced by Pius V. *and Gregory XIII.*, and so regards the draft of 1583 as of legal validity.

[4] The card. of Como to the nuncio Taberna in Spain, Sept. 3, 1582. KRETZSCHMAR, p. 152.

[5] Communicated in 1587 by the Venetian ambassador in Madrid. VEN. CAL., VIII., p. 296.

Philip raised his voice in warning: "First make the preparations necessary for carrying it through with honour!"[1] A Spanish seaman, captain Cabreta, declared in 1580, in a memorial presented to the king: "The sea forces which the enemy can collect are very great, and will increase from day to day, unless some strong effort be made to render your majesty's present small number of vessels more than equal to the multitude of the enemy."[2] Here it is frankly admitted that Spain had allowed herself to be outstripped by the English in the equipment of their fleet. Not less important was the report of the enemy's experience in all that pertains to seafaring. "The English," said another warning voice,[3] "set off every year in their ships and sail round the world as merchants or freebooters; such men can in no wise be despised for inexperience." We have already shown (p. 150) how high an opinion of English gunnery and gunners was held in Spain. Until Spain came up to the level of the great revolution wrought in the English fleet between 1570 and 1580, the invasion must have appeared a hopeless undertaking to all well-informed persons.

In Madrid, but not in Rome, there were men who knew the inhabitants of the island from having had personal and commercial dealings with them. "The English," continued the warning voice already quoted,[4] "are naturally brave, and when they find themselves in danger of losing their freedom, they will probably appear on the field in larger

---

[1] The nuncio Taberna to the card. of Como, June 20/30, 1584. KRETZSCHMAR, p. 192.

[2] SPAN. CAL., 1580–86, No. 45.

[3] An anonymous memorial *Sopra l'impresa d Inghilterra*, addressed to Philip II. about 1585. Bibl. Vat., Urb. 854, p. I., fol. 271. The Venetian ambassador in Madrid reports exactly the same judgment as current in Spain. VEN. CAL., VIII., p. 349.

[4] Bibl. Vat., Urb. 854, *l.c.*

numbers and animated by a more warlike spirit than
people think. On this account the English kings have
been of opinion that they can defend the kingdom without
fortresses, and, so far, they have succeeded."

However, in Spain too the opinions of amateurs made
themselves heard alongside those of experts. Along with
officers and seamen, the diplomatists also had their say
on the question of the invasion, and especially *the* diplomatist who brought greater disaster on his country than
any other, owing to his blind confidence in the power of
Spain and equally blind contempt for everything English—
Bernardino de Mendoza, Philip's last ambassador in London.
How completely he deceived himself as to his position
at the English court is shown by a hundred blunders,
but specially by the threat which he addressed to the
queen that, since she refused to listen to words, they
would have to speak to her with cannon—a threat which
did not frighten Elizabeth for a moment and only brought
down upon the ambassador the retort that for the future
he might treat with the members of the queen's council
and think himself fortunate if he were allowed to remain
in the country.[1] Mendoza, who had a record behind him
of many years' honourable service in the Spanish army,[2]
and towards the end of his career aspired to be an historian
of military campaigns,[3] felt himself also called to give his
opinion on naval affairs. He had no hesitation in sending
word to Madrid that the whole English fleet would be no

[1] Mendoza to Philip II., Oct. 30, 1581. *Col. de doc. inéd.*, t. 92,
p. 159. SPAN. CAL., 1580–86, p. 188, where the letter is dated
Oct. 20.

[2] *Cf.* ALFRED MOREL.-FATIO, *D. Bernardino de Mendoza*. Bulletin
Hispanique, VIII. (1906), pp. 20 *et seq.*, 129 *et seq.* In the "Annales
de la Faculté des Lettres de Bordeaux."

[3] He wrote *Comentarios de lo sucedido en las guerras de los Payes
baxos*, 1567–1577 (Madrid, 1592), and *Theorica y practica de guerra*
(Anveres, 1596).

match for a quarter of the Spanish Armada.[1]   His account of England's powers of moral resistance were quite as shallow and superficial as those of many other foreigners. He, too, was under the sway of the fixed idea that the English people were fickle and allowed themselves to be driven like cattle in subservience to every whim of their rulers.   He dwelt upon this point repeatedly, and always in tones of deepest contempt.[2]   But it was just this blustering Mendoza—such is the attraction that widely different characters often exert over one another—who had greater power over Philip's cautious nature than all his other counsellors.[3]   And he, moreover, was not the only Spanish diplomatist whose representation of England was a caricature.   The ambassador in Paris, Vargas, whose reports upon English affairs depended principally on the information given him by English exiles and the agents of Mary Stuart, wrote of England in 1580; "If so much as a cat moved, the whole affair would crumble down in three days beyond repair."[4]   Views similar to those held by Mendoza and Vargas were also repeated in Madrid, and that, too, at a time when people ought to have known better.   This appears from a council of war summoned by King Philip in 1586 to deliberate on the English question.[5] The difficulty of landing was lightly passed over; the

---

[1] Letter of March 23, 1580, *Col. de doc. inéd.*, t. 91, p. 471.   SPAN. CAL., p. 21.

[2] *Col. de doc. inéd.*, t. 91, pp. 215, 489 ; t. 92, p. 35.   SPAN. CAL., 1568–79, p. 574 ; 1580–86, pp. 36, 122.

[3] For the proofs of Philip's deference towards Mendoza, see TEULET, *Relations politiques*, V., p. xi., note 2.

[4] Juan de Vargas to Philip II., Feb. 13, 1580: "Si huviesse un gato que empezasse á moverse, creo darian al traste con todo en tres dias, sin que otra diligencia ni poderse remediar." TEULET, V., p. 207 ; *cf.* p. 212.   SPAN. CAL., 1580--86, p. 5 ; *cf.* pp. 13 *et seq.*

[5] Dispatch of the Venetian ambassador in Madrid, Aug. 6, 1586. VEN. CAL., p. 190.

want of fortified places was dwelt upon as of essential importance; the English themselves, inexperienced in arms, understood nothing beyond the use of the bow!

The judgment of Spain was completely and apparently universally mistaken on the important question of the attitude of English catholics. The great mass of catholics in England were unable to speak for themselves, and instead of them, people gave ear to unauthorized men like Persons and Allen. Persons asserted, with wanton thoughtlessness (1582): "All catholics without a single exception regard the invasion with approval. Nay, they even burn with longing for the undertaking."[1] A memorial written in Spanish had said the same thing at an earlier date: "All the catholics of the country will join your Majesty's troops, will persuade their relations and friends to do likewise, and so will triumph over their lazy and careless enemies."[2] That statements of this kind, showing such obvious signs of exaggeration, were accepted without criticism is chiefly to be explained by the religious excitement of the period. About 1585, it was an axiom among Spanish diplomatists as a body that a general rising of catholics would come to the assistance of the invading army.[3] A Spaniard, Francisco de Valverde, who visited England in 1586, allowed a catholic to expatiate to him while there on the theme that half the entire kingdom was longing to be brought back to the bosom of the church by means of the arms of Spain.[4] Buoyed up with hopes such as these, the Armada eventually put out to sea. The statements of Spanish prisoners of war in 1588 make it quite

[1] KRETZSCHMAR, p. 138.
[2] About 1574. K. DE LETTENHOVE, VII., p. 265.
[3] Juan-Bautista de Tassis, Spanish ambassador in Paris, to Philip II., April 18, 1584. TEULET, *Relations politiques*, V., p. 328.
[4] DURO, *La Armada Invencible*, I. (1884), p. 511; *Noticias de Inglaterra*.

plain that the project of invasion was formed on the supposition that a third or a half of England would make common cause with the Spaniards.[1] Nay, further, we have a draft for the mobilization of troops dating from the year 1586.[2] For every "province" with a high percentage of catholic inhabitants, a list is given (without names) of the influential catholics who are said to be in a position to bring a force of one or two thousand men into the field—over twenty-five thousand all told.[3] In Madrid, a few catholic lords made their appearance in the same year and promised the king that they would engage to order out twelve thousand foot soldiers as soon as the Armada appeared. "But the king is prudent and knows quite well that exiles can never be fully trusted."[4]

Since these engagements were never actually put to the test, the truth or falsehood of the statements can only be proved indirectly. It must also be borne in mind that, as those best acquainted with English catholicism have already admitted,[5] we hardly know anything of English catholics, from the point of view of politics, for the decisive years between 1586 and 1588. Yet we can draw a conclusion from the very absence of information. If a plan of mobilization, such as that just referred to, was something more than an academic essay, it must have had behind it a fully developed organization of English catholics. That

---

[1] LAUGHTON, *State Papers relating to the Armada*, II., pp. 19, 23.

[2] SPAN. CAL., 1580–86, No. 470. TEULET, V., pp. 381–384.

[3] For Yorkshire, instead of giving figures, it is said, "Almost the entire population of the county." The men who were to compose the troops are described as either "catholics" or "schismatics," *i.e.* those who had indeed fallen away from the Roman catholic church, but still remained catholic at heart.

[4] Dispatch of the Venetian ambassador in Madrid, May 1, 1586. VEN. CAL., p. 160.

[5] POLLEN, *Politics of Engl. Catholics*, The Month, April, 1902, p. 409.

this should have left no trace of its existence in the diplomatic correspondence of Spain and Rome cannot be due to the secrecy with which an organization of this kind would be surrounded, for the catholic mission had also to be kept secret, and yet it has left behind it countless traces of its existence. The mission itself would have had to come into touch with this organization in some way or other, had it existed, and would have leant upon it for support. But there is no evidence that the mission had anything to do, either directly or indirectly, with any political organization of catholics.[1] Mendoza, who occasionally tried to employ mission priests for political ends, had to abandon the attempt because the priests proved themselves quite unfitted for the task. " They [the priests], although ardently zealous as regards religion, cannot be trusted with matters of state unless they are taught word for word what they have to say." [2] The most sceptical judge of the mission cannot desire a better witness for the non-political character of the majority of the mission priests than the Spanish ambassador in London. The hope, or dread, of a catholic rising in the event of an invasion may well have been fostered by what transpired in the course of many of the trials of priests between 1580 and 1590. For a considerable number of missionaries declared on trial that in case of war they would side with the invading army.[3] But the existence of a political organization, or of any sort of plan of mobilization, does not become any more probable on this account. The frankness with which the momentous question was answered in court tells rather against the existence of a secret scheme

[1] See ch. ii., *passim.*
[2] Mendoza to Philip II., April 26, 1582. *Col. de doc. inéd.*, t. 92, p. 360. SPAN. CAL., 1580–86, p. 350.
[3] *Vid. ante*, pp. 159–162.

for arming catholics than in its favour. The complete absence of evidence for political or military organization makes it also well-nigh impossible for us to give serious credence to the existence of a scheme by which all English catholics capable of bearing arms [1] were, at a given moment, to join themselves to the Spanish army of invasion.

The doubt thrown on the value of the supposed plan of mobilization is still further increased when we see how it was just those people who weighed the question of invasion with the greatest calmness and common sense who expressed themselves at the same time with the greatest reserve on all plans which pre-supposed a brotherhood in arms between Spaniards and English catholics. Memorials from the pen of Persons or other zealots, who wrote and prophesied with the blindness that springs from hatred—who prophesied the very opposite to what came to pass afterwards—deserve no credit on this question, and can only be used as evidence of the sentiments of the minority, but not of the actual state of affairs. Memorials, on the other hand, of which the verdict on the prospects of the war before the decision was verified by the event, deserve, on this account, to be trusted as well on the further point—what standpoint would the great majority of English catholics assume in the conflict between religion and their duties and sentiments as patriots ? The nameless monitor, already quoted (p. 290), who, about 1585, addressed King Philip, remarks on the catholic question : " Perhaps some one may say that at the news of a victory gained by your Majesty, the catholics would rise and come to your assistance, but I do not think this is to be expected, for although they are also enemies to the heretics, yet, if

---

[1] Granting that the statistics on p. 62 are correct, 25,000 would be one-fifth of the catholic population of England.

matters should come to such a pass, they are still more
enemies to a foreign nation that wishes to deprive them of
their freedom and bring them into subjection." [1]   Another
anonymous memorialist writes to the same effect : " The
English are of such a nature as to be easily won over by
gentleness combined with prudence, but they are not to be
driven by force of arms.   Should a foreign army attempt
to coerce them, catholics and heretics would agree to join
in offering resistance." [2]   In Rome, too, a few warning
voices were raised to the same purpose, though without,
indeed, finding a hearing.[3]

The assumptions, upon which a plan like this for a
general arming of catholics must have rested, had no real
existence except in the heads of excited enthusiasts.   The
alleged plan of mobilization of 1586 deserves to be noticed
merely as a typical instance of the reckless methods by
which a small minority of catholics in England itself, and
the groups of exiles who swarmed round Persons and
Allen in Madrid and Rome, sought to fan the flame.

But even the men who placed their duty to the church
before all else, allowed themselves only by degrees and
much against the grain to be forced into taking up a

[1] " Potrebbe dir alcuno che al rumore della vittoria di V. M. si
levarebbono i cattolici in suo aiuto, nella qual cosa non crederei che si
havesse da sperare, perchè, se bene sono inimici degl'eretici, sono per
aventura più nemici di perder la libertà et cader in soggettione di gente
straniera." Bibl. Vat., Urb. 854, p. I., fol. 283.

[2] " Angli eius sunt naturæ, ut lenitate prudentia coniuncta, facile
persuaderi possint, armis vero aut violentia compelli non patiantur.
Hinc fit ut contra externum militem, qui vim adferre conaretur,
catholicorum cum hereticis ad resistendum in hoc summus foret
consensus.' Arch. Vat., Arm. LXIV., t. 28, fol. 172 : " Capita rerum,
ex quibus modus colligitur, per quem Anglia reduci potest ad pristinum
religionis statum."   Apparently belonging to the period between 1570
and 1588.

[3] A nameless correspondent of the card. protector of England
about 1580. Bibl. Vat., Ottob., 2419, p. I., fols. 15-23.

position of hostility to their own land. Shortly after 1580 this revolution was effected in the minds of the leaders of the English catholics on the continent. As late as 1580, Robert Persons dedicated a pamphlet to Queen Elizabeth in which he complained " that all catholics are regarded as foes and traitors." [1] He concludes his preface with the words : " Jesus Christ, in aboundance of mercye, blesse your Maiestye!" Two years later, he is the most energetic advocate of invasion.[2] Little wonder that he was regarded as a traitor by his protestant fellow-countrymen. But Persons' catholic friends, when summing up their opinion of him, laid special stress just on his love for his native land. When Sir Francis Englefield sought to describe the life-work of this much-abused man, he began with the words : " From the first moment that Father Persons began to work in his order, he devoted himself entirely to the salvation of his native land." [3] Persons himself had no idea that in planning an invasion and the succession of a Spaniard to the English throne he was acting unpatriotically or with the object of subjecting his country to Spanish influence.[4] It may be doubted if the conflict between religion and patriotism ever became clear to his mind or to the minds of many who shared his views. He and his friends fought indeed for the church, not, therefore against their country but *adversus impietatem patriam*.[5] Religion

---

[1] *Vid. ante*, p. 199.

[2] KRETZSCHMAR, pp. 135–146.

[3] " A primo tempore quo Pater Personius in religionis suæ ministeriis se exercere cœpit, totum se impendit in patriæ salutem." Englefield to Clement VIII., Valladolid, Sept. 2, 1596. Arch. Vat., Borgh. II., 448 *ab* fol. 295.

[4] *Cf.* especially his letter of Jan. 4, 1603, to Father Possevin. J.-M. PRAT, S.J., *Recherches . . . sur la compagnie de Jésus en France* (Lyon, 1878), pp. 185 *et seq.*

[5] PAULUS BOMBINUS, *Vita et martyrium Campiani* (Mantuæ, 1620), p. 28.

and patriotism were not distinct sentiments in their mind, but their patriotism was religious in its nature.   Opinions as to what was necessary for the well-being of the country were divided by the reformation ; both sides, however, while engaged in deadly conflict with one another, claimed to be acting from truly patriotic motives.

These men were English patriots in the same sense that Coligny and the Huguenots were French patriots.   Their aim was to be loyal as long as a gleam of hope was left. But when forced to fight against the crown, their forces were fewer and their prospect of success much less than the Huguenots ; they were, therefore, much more dependent on help from abroad than the latter, in fact they were entirely dependent on it.   William Allen, the acknowledged head of the English catholics, as late as 1578, still clung to the idea that England would be converted by peaceful methods and regarded the seminary he had founded as the "sole hope."[1]   Like Persons, even in 1581, he addresses Elizabeth in tones of deepest respect, and besought her in the name of her countless faithful catholic subjects, "that out of banishment, prisons, chains, and dungeons, lift up their hands and hearts to God and your majesty. . . . Incline your heart for Christ's love, gracious lady, to our humble suit, made for your own soul."[2]   The queen was not for him the bastard on the throne, but "the last of all" King Henry's "dearest children."   He passionately rejects the imputation that the bull of excommunication had been published and posted up in the seminary at Douay.[3]

[1] "Agri Anglicani semen et afflictissimi illius gregis dominici spes unica."   Allen to the card. of Como, Rheims, April 4, 1578.   KNOX, p. 40.

[2] ALLEN, *An Apology . . . of two English Colleges*, etc. (1581), fol. 50.   For the full title of this pamphlet, *vid. ante*, p. 145, note 1.

[3] *Op. cit.*, fol. 101.

But Allen, too, whose gentler nature long remained untouched by the harshness and bitterness of his friend the Jesuit Persons, could not maintain this attitude for ever. When the bloody legislation against the mission was inaugurated in the year 1581 (p. 148), and a royal proclamation of 1582 declared all Jesuits and seminary priests to be traitors, he, too, had to change his tactics. In confidential letters to Rome he now spoke of Elizabeth as "our Herodias."[1]   When Gregory XIII. next year resolved to renew the excommunication, Allen was chosen to take part in the projected invasion as the bearer of the bull.   The revolution in his own mind was complete ; in a memorial of 1584, he weighed with perfect calmness the means by which the invasion could best be accomplished, whether by landing the army in Scotland or in England. No word betrays that Allen the patriot reproached himself or had any compunction for the plans which Allen the catholic was propounding.[2]   Outwardly, however, he still followed the course of action which an opposition, loyal at its commencement, has at all times regarded as its last resource ; he still kept up the fiction that Elizabeth herself was innocent, and that it was a few powerful favourites who imposed upon the queen's gentle and confiding nature.   He expressed himself after this fashion in a pamphlet [3] which appeared simultaneously with the memorial on the invasion just alluded to.   No priest, so he says in the publication,[4] questions the queen's

---

[1] Allen to the card. of Como., April 24, 1582. KNOX, p. 131.

[2] THEINER, *Ann. Eccles.*, III., pp. 600 *et seq.* KNOX, pp. 231 *et seq.*

[3] In the preface to his pamphlet against Burleigh (1584). *A true, sincere and modest defence of English Catholiques that suffer for their faith . . . against a false . . . libel intituled " The Execution of Justice in England."* Published also in Latin, *Ad persecutores Anglos pro Catholicis, etc.*

[4] The English edition of the pamphlet, p. 29.

legitimacy either in respect of her birth or her right
to the throne ; no one dares to utter a speech against
the laws that could injure her Majesty or "the state
present." "We are not so perversely affected (God be
praised) as purposely to dishonour our prince and our
country." [1]

This last spasmodic attempt to slur over the opposition
between religion and patriotism must not blind us to the
questionable course of double dealing upon which Allen
now embarked. He kept up an appearance of loyalty
while working for the overthrow of the government. The
impossibility of reconciling duty to the church with duty
to the country must, as things stood, result either in self-
deception or conscious dishonesty. In the years during
which preparations were being made for striking the
decisive blow, it is as if a thick veil covered the features,
once so fair and pure, of the venerable head of the English
catholics. As soon as ever the reasons which drove him
into devious courses were removed, Allen's character stood
out once more in all its greatness and independence. Like
a prophet of the Old Testament, he raised his voice to call
men to battle, and, up to the last moment, remained unshaken in his conviction that victory would be with the
catholics.

III. *The Decision*

These academic and political theories about the war
against England all came to an end when England herself
actually entered upon hostilities.

Spain's last attempt to re-establish diplomatic relations
with England offered, from the first, few hopes of lasting
results, and finally broke down owing to the personal

---

[1] *Op. cit.*, preface.

character of the ambassador.   In his instructions (January 8,
1578), Mendoza had received strict orders only to encourage in general terms those English catholics who
should approach him, and to exhort them to patience, but
he was not to be led into any sort of attack upon the
queen in his dealings with them.[1]   Mendoza deliberately
went beyond his instructions partly from catholic zeal and
partly from diplomatic ambition.   It is sufficient to recall
his endeavours to arrive at an understanding with Mary
Stuart, the Duke of Guise,[2] and the English catholics,
regarding plans for an invasion and the release of the
queen of Scots.[3]   At the same time, he tried—this time
with his king's consent [4]—to get into touch with the
Scottish catholics, and began to prepare the way for the
invasion in that country, and for the young king's conversion to catholicism.[5]   And so Mendoza soon became
an object of suspicion to the English government, his
position at court grew constantly more difficult, and every
step he took was more narrowly watched.   In the course
of 1582, after four years of working behind the scenes, he
practically ceased to be ambassador, although he continued to be so nominally for some time longer.   How
little confidence was then placed in him was shown when
one of the murderous attempts instigated by Philip II.
brought William of Orange to the verge of the grave in
March, 1582.   In the heat of the indignation caused by
the attempt, it was said at once in London that Mendoza
was implicated in the deed.   Two Spaniards were seized

---

[1] *Col. de doc. inéd.*, t. 91, p. 189.   SPAN. CAL., 1568–79, p. 557.   *Cf.*
Philip to Mendoza, Nov. 19, 1581.   SPAN. CAL., p. 219.

[2] Mendoza to Philip, July 16, 1583.   *Col. de doc. inéd.*, t. 92, p. 516.
SPAN. CAL., p. 493.

[3] See Throgmorton's avowal in CAMDEN'S *Annales*, p. 381.

[4] Philip to Mendoza, Dec. 18, 1581.   SPAN. CAL., p. 242.

[5] Mendoza to Philip, Sept. 7, 1581; Feb. 9, 1582.   *Col. de doc. inéd.*,
t. 92, pp. 106, 276.   SPAN. CAL., pp. 169, 288.

as they entered his house and were imprisoned as accomplices.[1] Although the ambassador was innocent of the deed, still the crime laid to his charge was quite in harmony with his own ideas. In joyful words he thanked God for the attempt, and saw the punishment of heaven in the fact that William's sufferings caused by his painful wounds were so prolonged.[2]

The attempt on the Stadtholder's life, however, strengthened the war party in London. The first ill tidings produced a crushing effect. The English sent to William to congratulate him on the preservation of his life, and promised to avenge him.[3] The breach between the court and Mendoza now became more and more manifest. Mendoza was admitted to no more audiences.[4] After the autumn of 1582 he was never once received by the queen's ministers, much as he desired it.[5] Only a man like Philip II. could have accepted all these insults with equanimity; his ambassador suffered acutely under the ignominy of the position.[6] The history of modern diplomacy contains scarcely another example of the representative of a great power being condemned to remain on under such circumstances instead of being recalled. Mendoza stayed on in London in order to work up to the last moment as a spy and informer of the Spanish government. He had to fill a post usually committed to subordinates and not to a nobleman of ancient lineage. Philip II.

[1] Mendoza to Philip, April 1, 1582. *Col. de doc. inéd.*, t. 92, p. 328. SPAN. CAL., p. 325.
[2] *Col. de doc. inéd.*, t. 92, pp. 335, 336. SPAN. CAL., pp. 329, 334. *Col. de doc. inéd.*, t. 92, p. 333. SPAN. CAL., p. 328.
[4] Mendoza to Philip, May 15 and 21, 1582. *Col. de doc. inéd.*, t. 92, pp. 379, 390. SPAN. CAL., pp. 364, 376.
[5] Mendoza to Philip, Nov. 1, 1582. *Col. de doc. inéd.*, t. 92, p. 419. SPAN. CAL., p. 406.
[6] Mendoza to Idiaquez, March 17, 1583. *Col. de doc. inéd.*, t. 92, p. 479. SPAN. CAL., p. 454, *et passim.*

could not prevent the inevitable breach by this means, and it was in vain that he sacrified the dignity of his crown. Only in January, 1584, did Mendoza obtain an interview with Elizabeth's ministers. He was summoned before her council to receive marching orders. The command was based on the ground that the ambassador was seeking to effect the escape of Mary Stuart and disturbing the domestic peace of the country. Once more Mendoza assumed the haughty demeanour of a Spanish grandee, but when, in answer to his scornful words, he received the cool reply that he ought to be very thankful that the queen had not ordered him to be punished for his misdeeds, he lost his temper and flung down a threat of war before the council.[1] With what feelings he turned his back on England may be gathered from his own words : " The insolence of these people has brought me to a state in which my only desire to live is for the purpose of revenging myself upon them, and I pray that God may let it be soon and will give me grace to be His instrument of vengeance, even though I have to walk barefooted to the other side of the world to beg for it." [2]

Mendoza had no authority to declare war, and before Philip II. could give effect to his threat, England herself decided to strike the first blow. The progress of the counter-reformation on the continent in the years 1584 and 1585 removed all obstacles still remaining in the way of the English war party. Orange had succumbed at last to Spain's policy of murder. The last remaining bulwark of

[1] " Pues no le habia dado satisfaccion siendo ministro de paz, me esforzaria de aquí adelante para que la tuviese de mí en la guerra." See Mendoza to Philip, Jan. 26, 1584. *Col. de doc. inéd.*, t. 92, pp. 528–532. SPAN. CAL., pp. 513–515.

[2] Mendoza to Idiaquez, Jan. 30, 1584. *Col. de doc. inéd.*, t. 92, p. 534. SPAN. CAL., p. 517.

freedom in the united provinces of the Netherlands now fell before the victorious Alessandro Farnese ; Bruges, Ghent, Brussels, and Malines opened their gates to the Spaniards, and, in August, 1585, Antwerp at length surrendered. In France the Duke of Alençon had died and the huguenot Henry of Navarre was the next heir to the throne. But the prospect of having a protestant king brought the League to a decision ; the catholic party, headed by Henry of Guise, the strongest in the country, entered into negotiations with Philip of Spain for the purpose of excluding Henry of Navarre. All this was very threatening for England. Lord Burleigh now urged on his unwilling queen to war with greater insistence than ever. In a boldly-conceived plan of attack, he proposed a simultaneous onslaught upon the two extreme flanks of the Spanish empire—the Netherlands and the West Indies.[1] If Elizabeth hesitated any longer, Spain would reap the advantage of being the aggressor. A palpable breach of the peace on the part of Philip II. in May, 1585, opened the eyes even of one who refused to see. A number of English corn-ships, under special offers of protection, put into a Spanish port and were treacherously seized and utilized for the equipment of the Armada.[2] Elizabeth could now no longer resist the pressure put upon her by her people and her ministers, and so gave Sir Francis Drake authority to equip a squadron.[3] At the last moment, indeed, but still in time, England went forth to strike, the first in the field.

The sudden attack in the Netherlands, led by Lord Leicester, came indeed to little, but the young sea-power succeeded beyond all expectations. Drake had once

---

[1] Somers Tracts, I. (2nd ed., 1809), p. 169. Quoted by L. RANKE, *Hist. of England* [Eng. trans.], I. (Oxford), pp. 298-299.
[2] CORBETT, *Drake and the Tudor Navy*, II., p. 11.
[3] In June, 1585. CORBETT, II., p. 12.

X

boasted in his cups that he was the man to cope with Spain, and the Earl of Arundel had upbraided him on the spot for his presumption.[1] Drake now redeemed his word, when, in the last days of September, 1585, he cast anchor before Vigo on the coast of Galicia, and bade defiance to the Spanish governor.[2] The ruin of the Spanish settlements on the Cape Verde islands and of the towns of San Domingo, Santiago, and Porto Praya, were only the beginnings of his triumphal career of combined warfare and robbery on the Spanish main. At the beginning of 1586 he plundered St. Christopher in the Leeward Islands, took by storm San Domingo in Haiti, besieged Cartagena,[3] the capital of Spanish America on the mainland, and destroyed Sant' Agustino on the coast of Florida.[4] Rich in booty and ransoms,[5] Drake's squadron returned home in July, 1586. As early as January, and before news had arrived of these doings in America, Admiral Santa Cruz reckoned that, since the previous August, Spanish subjects had lost over a million and a half owing to England.[6] When the reverses which the colonial empire of Spain had suffered in the West Indies were known in May, one of the first consequences was that the bank of Seville stopped payment. English goods were prohibited in Spain, and a ferment of excitement spread throughout the country. "That will be a cooling to King Philip," says a letter of intelligence at this date, "as never has happened to him since he was king."[7] In the confusion and excitement of the moment, all sorts of impossible projects were in the air ; it was

---

[1] 1582. *Col. de doc inéd.*, t. 92, p. 303. SPAN. CAL., p. 307. *Cf.* CORBETT, I., p. 340.   [2] CORBETT, II., pp. 22–26.

[3] In the existing Columbia.   [4] CORBETT, II., ch. ii.

[5] The ransom for Cartagena alone amounted to 110,000 ducats.

[6] DURO, *La Armada Invencible*, I., pp. 245 *et seq.*

[7] DOM. CAL., 1581–90, p. 327 (May 15, 1586). *Cf.* VEN. CAL., 1581–91, p. 156.

proposed to get ready an Armada of eight hundred ships to go against England ; every man of position was to build one or two vessels ; the entire loss of the West Indies was dreaded ; it was said of King Philip that he was " very melancholy and anxious." [1]

Even in the home waters, Spain could no longer hold her own. As the seas round England were regarded as British waters, so the western basin of the Mediterranean was regarded as the Spanish sea. The lines of commerce between the Iberian peninsula and the kingdom of the two Sicilies ran through these seas, and Spain exacted a salute from foreign ships, just as England did in the Channel. In the summer of 1586, five London merchantmen, with the proud *Merchant Royal*, " a very brave and good ship and of great report," among them, were returning home from the Levant. Philip's Sicilian squadron, comprising two frigates and eleven galleys, under Don Pedro de Leiva, lay in wait for them in the straits between Sicily and Tunis. Close to the island of Pantellaria, the two squadrons came in sight of each other. The Spanish admiral demanded that the English should pay him a visit of courtesy " to acknowledge their duty and obedience to him in the name of the Spanish king, lord of those seas." The English, fearing treachery, declined the invitation and cleared for action. We have a description of the engagement from one of the English combatants.[2] His narrative is pervaded by that love of the sea which characterized the Elizabethan age, and breathes the spirit of the wars of religion. For him the combat " was to the honor of true religion which the insolent enemies

---

[1] VEN. CAL., p. 178 (June, 1586).
[2] PHILIP JONES, *A true Report of a worthy fight . . . at Pantalarea*, printed by RICH. HAKLUYT, *The principal Navigations, Voyages . . . of the English Nation*, VI. (Glasgow, 1904), pp. 46–57.

sought so much to over throwe." The English prayed to God for victory. "Contrarily, the foolish Spaniards cried out according to their manner, not to God, but to our Lady (as they terme the virgin Mary), saying, O Lady helpe, O blessed Lady give us the victory, and the honor thereof shalbe thine." The engagement lasted five hours, and formed a prelude to the decisive conflict fought two years later. As in 1588 in the Channel, so now off Pantellaria, the English guns proved their complete superiority over the Spanish. In spite of their being almost three to one, the Spaniards had to fly because their battered vessels were in danger of sinking. While the Spanish losses were so great that they could scarcely man their guns, the English had only two killed and one wounded. The results were as disproportionate as those of the great battle with the Armada. The Spaniards had to suffer experiences like these just in the years when they fancied their power was at its height both on the sea and in the colonies. The union of the naval forces of Spain and Portugal was celebrated by a medal which bore the inscription, *Immensi Tremor Oceani*.[1] If the bull of Alexander VI. of 1493, which partitioned the globe between Spain and Portugal, still held good, then, since 1580, the entire world beyond the seas belonged to Spain. And even so it seemed as if the limits of Spain's covetousness had not been reached. *Non sufficit Orbis!* met the eyes of the victorious English as they forced their way into the palace of the governor of San Domingo in Haiti. The motto gave the key to a coat of arms representing a horse springing up into the sky from off the terrestrial globe as if the world were not enough for him. The king of Spain, scoffed the lusty victors, would have enough to do only to keep what he had.[2]

[1] DURO, I., p. 163.   [2] CORBETT, II., pp. 43 *et seq.*

The loss of Spain's prestige in the world soon made itself felt. A state like Denmark presumed to offer its friendly services as mediator and to require the religious freedom of the Netherlands as a condition of its doing so.[1] Although Philip declared the condition impossible, he did not altogether reject the offer of mediation.[2] In Rome the time was approaching when the papacy would dissociate itself from the bankrupt kingdom and seek for a sharper "temporal sword" for the church. The new pope, Sixtus V. (1585–90), did not, like his predecessor, regard the world from the point of view of a jurist, but with the eyes of a statesman. The apparent glitter of the power of Spain did not deceive him, but the successes of the English, from the Mediterranean to the West Indies, made a deep impression on him.[3] To representatives of friendly powers he now and then let fall critical and sarcastic remarks about the power of Spain.[4] In the curia the view which had prevailed under Gregory XIII., that the attack on England was an easy matter, now gave place to the opposite idea.[5]

The following year, 1587, brought fresh shocks. It was the year in which Mary Stuart mounted the scaffold as a convicted conspirator against Elizabeth's throne (February). With her a personage disappeared from the conflict, who, although she had herself taken no active part, had still been the centre of all the hopes of catholic England for

[1] VEN. CAL., pp. 175, 179 (July, 1586).
[2] Philip II. to King Frederick II. of Denmark, July 28, 1586, *op. cit.*, pp. 196 *et seq.* Upon the attitude of Denmark to the conflict between England and Spain, and upon the reception which the attempt at mediation received in England, see D. SCHÄFER, *Gesch. v. Dänemark*, V. (1902), pp. 229–232.
[3] HÜBNER, *Sixte-quint*, II. (1870), p. 476; *cf.* pp. 480 *et seq.*
[4] VEN. CAL., pp. 163, 168, 195, 235 (Nos. 349, 359, 395, 451); utterances belonging to the interval between May, 1586, and Jan., 1587.
[5] *Op. cit.*, p. 240 (No. 462).

nearly twenty years.   The eyes of all who longed for a change of government, either peaceful or violent, turned to Mary Stuart.   To set her free and bring her to London as queen had been the ultimate aim of all plots and plans for invasion.   Nothing at this time could have had a more profound effect on the fortunes of the catholic church in England than Mary's death.   English catholics lost their candidate for the throne just at the moment when, owing to the execution of the pope's sentence against Elizabeth, the throne of England was to be made vacant.   Mary left no universally recognized heir belonging to the catholic faith.   Catholics now lost their leader, and consequently their unity amongst themselves was endangered.   The special feature in the programme of the invasion— Mary's elevation to the throne of England—was now obliterated.

This was not the only blow.   While Philip II. was preparing to play the part of heir to Mary Stuart ; Francis Drake, the terror of the Spanish coast, raided the naval base at Cadiz and destroyed, according to the lowest estimate, twenty-four vessels and all the military stores.   This victory was a fresh proof of the superiority of the English men-of-war over the Spanish galleys.   Every engagement in the open sea showed that the English were unassailable, thanks to the longer range of their guns.[1]   Drake's friend, Fenner, wrote triumphantly, "Twelve of her Majesty's ships will make account of all [Philip's] galleys in Spain, Portugal, and all his dominions within the Straits, although they are 150 in number."[2]   To Drake's love of adventure is due the audacious attack upon the fort of Sagres on Cape St. Vincent.   In sight of Lisbon he scoffed at Admiral

---

[1] VEN. CAL., 1581–91, pp. 275, 283.
[2] CORBETT, *Drake and the Tudor Navy*, II., p. 92.   *Cf*. what has been said above, p. 254, upon the reform of English fleet.

Santa Cruz and spread panic within the city.[1] Excitement increased in Spain, and no one knew what to do. Contempt for the enemy gave place more and more to fear. The unfortunate king was severely criticized even among his own people: "The king thinks and plans while the queen of England acts." The cortes roused their lord to avenge the country's disgrace. Desire for revenge on England and for the restoration of their military prestige spread throughout the land.[2]

The year 1587 also came to an end before Spain was fully equipped. The longer the delay, the more the assurance of victory became weakened by anxiety. The approach of the "fatal year" of the astrologers,[3] 1588, combined with the knowledge that decisive action was now at last to be taken, caused "men to believe more than is right in prophecies of calamities which were to fall in the new year, for there are in Spain certain silly women who have much to say about visions of misfortune for this country, which they have seen for the beginning of next year, 1588."[4] Full of anxiety, the nuncio of Madrid observed this spirit of faintheartedness. The counterbalancing force to feelings of this kind was not so much to

---

[1] CORBETT, II., pp. 93, 97. VEN. CAL., pp. 281–283.

[2] According to the reports sent by the Venetian ambassador in Madrid, Girolamo Lippomanno, in May, 1587. VEN. CAL., pp. 272–281.

[3] *Vid. ante*, p. 224, note 5.

[4] Cesare Speciani, bishop of Novara, nuncio in Madrid to Card. Rusticucci, Dec. 14, 1587. "Le cose sono molto accese et ogn'uno vede che si va preparando per un altro anno materie d'incendii molto grandi, et pare che gl'huomini credino più che non conviene alli infortunii che molti vanno dicendo che saranno l'anno che viene, perchè sono in Spagna certe donne semplici che dicono gran cose di visioni che hanno viste in danno di questi paesi per il principio dell'anno seguente 1588—cose sprezzate quando il termine è lontano, ma quando è vicino fanno più impressione nelli animi delli huomini, massime sospesi per altri accidenti, che non doveriano." Arch. Vat., Nunz. Spagna, 34, pp. 117-119.

be found in confidence in the strength of the Armada, now being got ready, as in a marked increase in religious enthusiasm. As early as the summer of 1587, the king had ordered special prayers, daily exposition of the Blessed Sacrament, and the celebration of solemn masses throughout the country.[1]   At Easter, 1588, solemn processions were everywhere to be made. Owing to his shrinking from publicity, the king himself did not take part in these, but in his devotional practices he imposed upon himself an asceticism like that of a monk. "From one who knows," wrote the nuncio,[2] "I hear that every day he spends three hours before the Most Holy Sacrament, commending the Armada and the result of the enterprise to God." When the Armada was on the sea and men were in daily expectation of hearing that the decisive action had taken place, the king wore out his weak, gouty body by attempting the impossible: "Four hours every day his Majesty remains kneeling before the Most Holy without a cushion, with his hands clasped and raised. The prince, his son, performs all the duties of a server at the mass, at which the king his father assists, with such devotion and attention that all are amazed thereat."[3]

[1] VEN. CAL., p. 318.
[2] Speciani to Card. Montalto, April 30, 1588: "Se bene S. M^à non interverrà a queste processioni et messe solenni, nondimeno intendo da chi lo sa certo che ogni dì sta tre hore avanti al s^{mo} sacram^{to}, raccomandando a Dio questa armata et l'esito dell'impresa . . ." Arch. Vat., Nunz. Spagna 34, p. 577. ". . . Domani s'incominciano le processioni generali che si faranno per le cose dell'armata, ancorchè non sia pubblicato il giubileo . . . ogn'uno haveria voluto che ci fosse la persona del re, al quale più volte già io dissi che in simil'attione era bene che S. M^{tà} si trovasse per consolatione delli suoi popoli et per darli animo et essempio ; ma è tanto nemico della vista delle genti che credo che patiria la sua natura estremamente a ritrovarseci " . . . *l.c.* 599 (of the same date).
[3] Speciani to Card. Montalto, July 11, 1588: " S. M^{tà} quattro hore

The austere devotion and loyalty of the Spaniards to the church, and their enthusiasm for orthodoxy now reached a degree the warmth of which can only be faintly realized by a northern imagination, and the like of which no subsequent century has experienced. Just as the papacy of the counter-reformation seized for the last time the ecclesiastical weapons of the middle ages, so, too, the Spain of Philip II. exhibited for the last time in all its greatness the spectacle of that heaven-compelling religious spirit which animated the period of the Crusades. It was declared from the pulpits that no work could be conceived more acceptable to God than the overthrow of the English heretics.[1] By the lips of poets men were summoned to battle against the

> " Ingleses luteranos
> que niegan con gran porfia
> la sancta virginidad
> de la Virgen sacra pia." [2]

The royal standard of the Armada, blessed by the church, called on God by its motto now to judge His own cause—*Essurge, Domine, et judica causam tuam !* [3] The same words of the psalmist with which once Rome, at an important moment in the world's history, had inaugurated the war against the reformation—in the excommunication

---

del giorno sta innanzi al s^{mo} sacram^{to} in ginochione senza coscino con le mani giunte et elevate, et il principe, suo figlio, serve facendo tutti li ufficii di chierico alla messa che sente il re, suo padre, con tanta devotione et accuratezza che ogn'uno se ne stupisce." Arch. Vat., Nunz. Spagna, 34, fol. 706ᵛ.

[1] VEN. CAL., 1581–91, p. 233.

[2] JUAN DE MESA, *Romance de la Armada y Infanteria.* DURO, II., p. 89.

[3] DURO, II., p. 419 (for *indica* read *judica*). *Cf.* also the *Litaniæ et preces pro fælici successu classis regis nostri Philippi adversus Angliæ hereticos, etc.*, in STRYPE'S *Annals*, III., ii. (1824), p. 539.

of Luther [1]—once more became her war cry in the greatest of all trials of strength between reformation and counter-reformation.

A kindred yet different spirit inspired Spain's opponents. The God of Battles of the Old Testament strode through the English lines. Those who cried to Him were the fathers of Cromwell's Ironsides. They felt they were God's children, and wielded the sword of Gideon. "Grant unto them, O Lord, Thy good and honourable success and victory, as Thou didst to Abraham and his company against the four mighty kings; to Joshua against the five kings, and against Amalek; to David against the strong and mighty armed Goliath; and as Thou usest to do to Thy children when they pleased Thee." [2] Theirs was no mystic halo, no ecstasy, no stiff adherence to ecclesiastical forms, but the free play of individual feeling, and, at the same time, that assurance of victory which stands with both feet planted on the ground of reality. The attitude of the English might be summed up in the puritan phrase, "Trust in God, and keep your powder dry!" The piety of the Elizabethan soldiers was no less deep, but was more earthly and practical than that of the Spaniard. "The Lord is on our side," wrote Drake, to the secretary of state, [3] "whereby we may assure ourselves our numbers are greater than theirs." Yet the same letter is full of practical advice—"Powder and shot for our great ordnance. . . . Good my Lords, I beseech you to consider deeply of this; for it importeth but the loss of all." [2]

---

[1] The bull of Leo X. excommunicating Luther (June 15, 1520), opens with the words, *Exurge, Domine!* The quotation is from Ps. lxxiii. 22, in the Vulgate (Ps. lxxiv. 22, A.V.).

[2] STRYPE, *op. cit.*, pp. 16 *et seq.*

[3] Letter of March 30/April 9, 1588. LAUGHTON, *State Papers relating to the Spanish Armada*, I. (1894), pp. 124 *et seq.* Publications of the Navy Record Soc., Vol. I.

Confidence in the fleet is not less than confidence in heaven. " I protest before God, and as my soul shall answer for it," wrote the admiral, Lord Howard, from on board his flagship,[1] " that I think there were never in any place in the world worthier ships than these are." Like master like man—" I assure your Majesty," declared Drake, " I have not in my lifetime known better men, and possessed with gallanter minds, than your Majesty's people are for the most part, which are here gathered together, voluntarily to put their hands and hearts to the finishing of this great piece of work ; wherein we are all persuaded that God, the giver of all victories, will in mercy look upon your most excellent Majesty, and us your poor subjects, who for the defence of your Majesty, our religion, and native country, have resolutely vowed the hazard of our lives."[2]

The consciousness of fighting " against Anti-Christ and all the pillars of his church " was not one whit less passionate than the fanaticism of the orthodox Spaniard. Nowhere does this consciousness find more violent expression than in the " exhortation " of Anthony Marten.[3] The writer had an appointment at court as " sewer of her majesty's most honourable chamber." This makes it all the more surprising that his pamphlet should be inspired by the spirit of thorough-going puritanism. The war with Spain was puritan England's first great opportunity. The Romish anti-Christ has blown the trumpet of rebellion ; *he* is the man of sin who has stirred up rebellion in

---

[1] LAUGHTON, I., p. 85 : Feb. 28/March 10, 1588.
[2] Drake to the Queen, April 13/23, 1588. LAUGHTON, I., p. 148.
[3] ANTH. MARTEN, *An exhortation to stirre up the mindes of all her Maiestie's faithfull subjects, to defend their countrey in this dangerous time from the invasion of enemies* (London 1588). Also in Harleian Miscel., I. (ed. Park, 1808), pp. 161–177.

England, who has insulted the queen and declared her deposed. He it is who has sent forth false hypocrites to steal the hearts of her people from her, who weaves plots against her life, and his herald is the king of Spain! Whenever had England to fight for such a just cause as now ? [1]

In England, as in Spain, religious and patriotic excitement went hand in hand, but in England there was this in addition, that loyalty and patriotism were enhanced by the sentiment of chivalry which surrounded a female sovereign. And Elizabeth's behaviour in the hour of danger kindled this feeling into a flame. Morally she was a coward, and never more so than in the condemnation of Mary Stuart, but physically she was courageous, and never more courageous than now. Her best and her worst years follow close on one another. While her servants, dreading an attack on her life, begged and implored her to take precautions for her safety—" For the love of Jesus Christ, Madam, awake thoroughly and see the villainous treasons round about you ! " [2]—Elizabeth alone showed not the least sign of fear, but did honour to herself and to her people by her unwavering confidence. Philip II. hid himself behind walls—Elizabeth rode through her camp and found words which have never been forgotten. [3]

And so, before the Armada set sail, patriotic and religious excitement in ruler and people, both in England and Spain, exhibited a similar and yet quite different character. The difference lay chiefly in the opposition between catholicism, with its mediæval forms of devotion, and protestantism, with its puritan belief in divine election,

[1] Harl. Miscel., I., pp. 163 *et seq.*, 175.

[2] Howard to the queen, June 23/July 3. LAUGHTON, I., p. 225. Similar warnings, *op. cit.*, pp. 107, 246, 292.

[3] For Elizabeth's celebrated speech in the camp at Tilbury, see Somers Tracts, I. (1809), pp. 429 *et seq.*

though not in this alone. The union between religion and politics in England and in Spain was different in kind. In the former, the union was complete ; religious feeling urged men on in the same direction which a policy of dispassionate self-interest would have taken in any case. The advantages which England reaped from war were not only religious but commercial and political as well. For Spain, the war was a call of duty imposed upon the nation by its position as champion of the counter-reformation. The war between Spain and England was the fruit of the war in the Netherlands, and this, in its turn, was the fruit of Spain's policy in religious matters. How often did Philip declare, " I would rather lose all my kingdoms than consent to liberty of conscience ! " [1] Both these wars, how-ever, were a terrible burden which almost crushed the Spanish nation. England was in the fortunate position that in making war upon catholicism she was fighting against her most dangerous neighbour and for her own greatness at one and the same time. Spain had to carry on the war against protestantism at the cost of her com-merce and so strike a blow at the sources of her own power. Although this distinction may have been clear at the time to only a few Spaniards, and rather revealed itself half-unconsciously in dark warnings, and in the credence given to prophecies of approaching disaster, still, even so, there was an absence of real joyful enthusiasm for the war against England that was being forced upon them. Instead of the positive reasons which urged England onwards—defence of church and state at home, attempts to seize a share of the world beyond the seas, and, in addition, a youthful desire to test her recently increased

---

[1] *E.g.* in 1586, when Denmark offered its services as mediator between Spain and England and the Netherlands. VEN. CAL., 1581–91, p. 197.

power as a nation—the reasons uppermost in Spain were negative—resistance to England's audacity, and passionate longing to destroy English heresy.

To all this another consideration has yet to be added. The very power for which Spain was fighting as if for herself—the papacy—was not wholly one at heart with her. Rome's confidence in Spain was shaken, for Philip had too often disappointed the hopes placed in him. Sixtus V., indeed, at Christmas 1586, renewed Gregory's bull of the crusade (*cruzada*) on the supposition that the proceeds of the indulgence were to be expended on the crusade against the English heresy,[1] but then he shut his fist. This single concession gave him already an opportunity of criticizing the way the money had been spent : " We have granted him church moneys," declared the pope at the end of 1587, after England had dealt some heavy blows at the power of Spain, " and we believe that these moneys, not being spent on their true purpose, are the cause of all his ruin."[2]   During the negotiations concerning the papal subsidy to the war against England, Sixtus V. objected to place sums of money in the hands of the king without receiving a pledge that the undertaking would really be pushed forward.[3] Never yet had a pope so large a sum to dispose of as Sixtus, with his famous 5,000,000 ducats hoarded up in S. Angelo ; still he wished to put it out only at a sure profit.   He promised his co-operation

---

[1] VEN. CAL., p. 130. The *cruzada* bestowed a plenary indulgence on all who, after contrite confession of sin, contributed two Spanish reals to the expenses of a war against unbelievers or heretics.

[2] Communicated by the Venetian ambassador in Rome, Nov. 28, 1587. VEN. CAL., p. 326 (No. 604).

[3] Negotiations of the Spanish ambassador in Rome, Count Olivares, with Card. Caraffa in 1586. KNOX'S *Card. Allen*, p. 258. The letter of Sixtus V. to Philip, printed by GIORGI in the *Archivio della R. Soc. Romana di storia patria*, Vol. XIV. (1891), pp. 172 *et seq.*, is merely the Italian text of a paper already printed by KNOX, pp. 435 *et seq.*

not for the war but for the victory. Sixtus engaged to contribute one million gold scudi, the first half to be paid after the fleet had got to land and the army had disembarked ; the remainder when the war had been in progress for two months.[1] The pope wished to obtain the same security for his subsidy that he was determined to have in the case of a crusade in the Holy Land—the arrival first of all of the army on the enemy's territory.[2]

And even this offer of financial assistance, contingent upon an uncertain stipulation, was only promised on condition that Spain restricted her right of conquest in favour of the pope's feudal suzerainty. Philip's claim to suzerainty over England put forth more than twenty years before, and supported by Paul IV., Pius IV.,[3] and Gregory XIII.,[4] appeared doubly justified after Mary Stuart's death. For had not the Queen of Scots made over her claim upon the English crown to the king of Spain a few weeks before her execution, because her son James—now in alliance with Elizabeth for the repulse of the catholic invasion— was an apostate from the catholic church?[5] Trusting

---

[1] Agreement of July 29, 1587, Appendix XX. According to FROUDE, *Hist. of Engl.*, XII. (1870), p. 361, the financial arrangements of this treaty were settled as early as Dec. 13, 1586, but, unfortunately, he gives no authorities for this statement.

[2] *Cf.* the bull of Sixtus V., *Ad clavum apostolicæ* of April 21, 1586. "Pro recuperatione Terræ Sanctæ. . . tuncque etiam postquam christianus exercitus comparatus erit ac mare ad ipsorum turcarum fines trajecerit." Magnum Bullarium Rom. VIII. (ed. Taur. 1882), p. 695.

[3] *Vid. ante*, p. 228.

[4] According to the definite assurance of the Venetian ambassadors in Madrid (VEN. CAL., 1581–91, p. 171) there was a brief of Greg. XIII. bestowing England upon Philip, but I have myself never set eyes on any brief of this kind.

[5] Letters of Mary Stuart to Sixtus V. and Bernardino Mendoza, Nov. 23, 1586. LABANOFF, *Lettres . . . de Marie Stuart*, VI. (1844), pp. 453, 459. For James's treaty with Elizabeth of July 5, 1586, see DU MONT, *Corps universel diplomatique*, t. V., i. (1728), p. 457.

to this last will of Mary Stuart, and, at the same time, to his own remote descent from the house of Lancaster,[1] Philip repeatedly urged the pope to recognize his claims to the throne of Elizabeth,[2] and protested that he did not desire the investiture of the kingdom, he was about to conquer, for himself but for his daughter Isabella. Yet not even for her could his ambassador in Rome obtain the promise of investiture from Sixtus V. The negotiations which led to the agreement between the pope and Spain as to the subsidies of July 29, 1587, finally settled nothing except that Philip should name as king (*nominet*) a faithful catholic who would be acceptable to the apostolic see and receive investiture from the pope.[3] While the Spanish ambassador and his followers were thinking of the Infanta in this arrangement,[4] the pope, who still had hopes of the conversion of James VI.,[5] kept himself free, by the wording of the agreement, to accept or reject Philip's candidate for the throne. The agreement meant that the apostolic see shared in the cost and in the profit, in case of success, but, if the issue was unsuccessful, the temporal partner was to take all the risk of the enterprise. The distrust, only too well founded, with which Sixtus V. regarded the military efficiency of Spain, gave

[1] For more particulars, see ch. iv., sect. i.

[2] Philip to his ambassador, Olivares, Feb. 11 and March 31, 1587. SPAN. CAL., pp. 16, 58.

[3] See Appendix XX. This agreement, which, as far as I know, has never been studied in its actual wording, demolishes the generally received opinion that Philip "was to hold the crown of England as a fief of the Holy See." RANKE, *Hist. of England* [Eng. trans.], I. (Oxford, 1875), p. 318 ; *cf.* his *Hist. of the Popes* [Eng. trans. 1847], Vol. I., p. 474, note. FROUDE, *Hist. of Engl.*, XII. (1870), p. 394, note 2, knows only the letter of the Spanish ambassador concerning the agreement, but not the agreement itself.

[4] Olivares to Philip II., July 30, 1587. SPA. CALN., p. 128.

[5] Olivares to Philip II., June 19, *l.c.*, p. 107. *Cf.* FROUDE, p. 362.

him the right to move thus cautiously. But Spain, in her political isolation, and with her shattered finances, must have been relieved to obtain the bare promise of assistance.

In addition to his doubtful promise of a contingent subsidy the pope lent his moral and diplomatic support to the attack upon England. Ever since 1580, the English catholics had frequently and urgently petitioned for the appointment of an English cardinal, and Philip II. had seconded their requests.[1] On August 7, 1587, the pope at length yielded and raised William Allen to the cardinalate in order to give a new head to the catholics of England left orphans by Mary Stuart's death.[2] The newly-appointed cardinal received the title of " Cardinal of England,"[3] which he used on all important occasions. On the very day of his creation, the pope wrote to the king of Spain and joined to the welcome news an exhortation to press forward the English undertaking.[4] He wrote that Allen's elevation, which took place at an unusual time, had been understood in Rome as being a signal for war, although he had tried to avoid giving rise to any suspicion of the kind. The announcement seemed to have produced at Madrid much the same effect as at Rome.[5] That the elevation of this influential catholic Englishman had a close bearing on the war is quite clear by the contemporary

[1] Mendoza to Philip II., April 6, 1581 ; Philip to Mendoza, May 28 ; Mendoza to Philip, July 4. *Col. de doc. inéd.*, t. 91, p. 566, t. 92, p. 63. SPAN. CAL., 1580–86, pp. 97, 118 *et seq.*, 139 *et seq.*

[2] Reports of the consistory of Aug. 7, 1578, in HUGO LAEMMER, *Meletematum Romanorum, Mantissa* (Ratisbonæ, 1876), p. 232. BRADY, *The Episcopal Succession in England*, II. (Rome, 1876), pp. 339–341. KNOX'S *Card. Allen*, pp. 297 *et seq.*

[3] VEN. CAL., 1581-91, p. 305.

[4] HÜBNER, *Sixte-quint*, III. (1870), pp. 236 *et seq.*

[5] The nuncio Speciani to Card. Rusticucci, Madrid, Sept. 5, 1587 ; " Qui la promotione del s^r Car^{le} Alano ha consolato ogn'uno, et ha destato nelli animi delli huomini spiriti molto grandi in servitio di Dio et della nostra s^{ta} fede." Arch. Vat., Nunz. di Spagna, 35, p. 493.

action of the papal diplomacy in Paris. The nuncio endeavoured to win over Henry III. and Catherine de' Medici to join in the English enterprise. Catherine declared her son would gladly participate in it, but did not see how he could do so before his own country was at peace. Whereupon the nuncio replied, quite in the warlike spirit of the period, that attractive as the word peace sounded, still, at that time, and in that country, it must be most deeply detested (*odiosissimo*) for the sake of God and the holy religion.[1] The bid for the assistance of France came to nothing,[2] and necessarily so, since a combined undertaking by the forces of Spain and France, acting in concert against England, had no chance of ever being realized.

The pope strove to lend his moral support to the attack upon England in other ways besides the creation of the cardinal and political schemes. When Philip was making ready the Armada he begged the pope to justify his campaign before men, *i.e.* to place it before the world as the carrying into effect of the excommunication.[3] It was the same request which the Duke of Guise had put forward to Gregory XIII. under similar circumstances in 1583 (p. 285). There was all the less reason now for denying the request since the original excommunication of 1570 had only been temporarily suspended in 1580 (*rebus sic stantibus*). English catholics were allowed to be the queen's obedient subjects until they received further instructions.[4] But now,

---

[1] Dispatch of the nuncio at Paris, Aug. 17, 1587. Arch. Vat., Nunz. di Francia, 4, fol. 6.

[2] Concerning the final refusal of the French king, see the nuncio's dispatch of Aug. 30, 1587, *l.c.*, fol. 9.

[3] Philip's instructions to his ambassador at Rome, Aug. 26, 1587. See the ambassador's dispatch of March 2, 1588, in SPAN. CAL., 1587–1603, p. 227.

[4] For further information, *vid. ante*, p. 138.

when their assistance was needed for effecting the invasion, this permission had to be recalled. A renewal of Elizabeth's excommunication would have been the surest way of securing this end, and the most natural thing would have been to promulgate a fresh bull, such as Gregory XIII. had already drafted in 1583 but had not published. Why Sixtus V. did not adopt the same method must be left to conjecture. He perhaps saw that the result was too uncertain and did not wish to subject the solemn act of excommunication a second time to the mockery of the world. The pope who had laid Henry of Navarre under the ban now refrained from publishing a new bull of excommunication against Elizabeth of England.

For the broadside,[1] which older writers styled Elizabeth's excommunication by Sixtus V., contains, indeed, a declaration of the excommunication, but, just on that account, is not an excommunication itself. A papal bull is drawn up in the first person, and must be written in Latin and dated. This manifesto is drawn up in the third person, written in English and undated. These deviations from the style of the papal chancery are so remarkable that the English secular priest, Watson, attacked the authority of the document afterwards (1601) entirely because of its defective form, and sought to characterize it as a trick of Persons, the Jesuit.[2] If the authenticity of the manifesto depended solely upon the *acta* of the papal chancery, it

---

[1] Printed from the original (now lost) by DODD-TIERNEY, *Church Hist. of Engl.*, III. (1840), Appendix, No. XII. Italian translation in GREG. LETI, *Vita di Sisto V.* (Amst., 1686), II., pp. 269–278. *Cf.* Also CAMDEN, *Annal. rer. Angl.* (1625), p. 516; H. SPONDANUS, *Annal. Baronii contin.* (Paris, 1641), ad a. 1588, § 21.

[2] [W. WATSON] *Important Considerations*, etc. (1601), p. 27; "We find Fr. Parson's declaration of Xistus Quintus' sentence of deposition of her Majesty . . . as in the pope's name, to have no warrant at all besides his owne bare affirmation, either of brief or of any other publike instrument, as in such cases had bene most necessarie."

would certainly be undeserving of credence, for this third
excommunication of Elizabeth has not left the least trace
of its existence behind it in the papal archives.[1]   Later
biographers of Sixtus V. mention a speech against Elizabeth
said to have been delivered by the pope in consistory,
and state that orders were sent to all the nuncios enjoining
them to publish the bull throughout Christendom, etc.
These things, however, seem to be merely the offspring of
a fruitful talent of invention.[2]

In spite of its unusual form, and the absence of evidence
in the archives, the genuineness of the manifesto is beyond
doubt.   It appears from the correspondence of the Spanish
ambassador in Rome, Olivares, that this manifesto is
the pope's response to King Philip's request that his
enterprise against England should receive some kind
of justification.   Olivares names Cardinal Allen as its
author, and sent the MS. in April, 1588, to Antwerp for
the approval of the governor, the Duke of Parma, under
whose auspices it was printed as a broadside and published.[3]

The contents of this half-papal, half-Spanish broadside fall into two parts ; (1) the renewal of Elizabeth's
excommunication, and (2) a declaration of the political
aims of the Spanish king.   In solemn phrases, not unlike

[1] I have searched the Consistorial Acta, the registers of bulls and
briefs, and the correspondence of the nunciatures for the years 1587
and 1588 without discovering the least trace of Sixtus V.'s so-called
bull of excommunication.

[2] LETI, *l.c.*, II., pp. 268 *et seq.* 278.   C. TEMPESTI, *Storia della vita e
geste di Sisto Quinto*, II. (Roma, 1754), lib. v., §§ 33–38.   Leti crowns
all by his account of how Elizabeth in St. Paul's solemnly excommunicated the pope and cardinals.   For a criticism on Leti, see
HÜBNER, *Sixte-Quint*, Vol. I. (1870), p. 2.   Leti makes Sixtus "un
héros de roman picaresque."   *Cf.* SARDI, *La politica nella storia*, in
La Rassegna Nazionale, Vol. 163 (1908), pp. 123–135.

[3] SPAN. CAL., 1587–1603, pp. 227, 254, 289.   FROUDE, *Hist. of
Engl.*, XII., p. 453, note.

those of a bull of excommunication, the imminent execution of the sentence formerly pronounced by Pius V., and Gregory XIII.—*i.e.* the deposition of Elizabeth—is announced, and the sentences of excommunication and deposition passed upon her by these pontiffs are renewed. The legal grounds adduced in justification of the excommunication reach far back into the history of the mediæval church, and agree in many points with the contents of a treatise upon the English question, viewed from the standpoint of canon law, which the nuncio Ormaneto had forwarded to Rome from Madrid in 1575, after an exhaustive study of the whole matter.[1]

The second part, the explanation of the aims of Spanish policy, tries to dissipate the idea that the king of Spain or the Duke of Parma wished to conquer England for themselves, and promises a settlement of the succession to the throne by the joint action of the pope, the king of Spain, and the English parliament. Finally, not only is protection from pillage promised to catholics, but the pope's pardon is offered to all repentant heretics.

The origin and aim of this manifesto are now made plain. By the pope's authority English catholics were required to lay aside all hesitation which might restrain them from making common cause with the Spanish invading army. There is now no longer anything strange in the unusual form of the document. English was chosen because the broadside was addressed only to English catholics and because the renewal of the excommunication did not concern the rest of Christendom. Not for them, but for Elizabeth's catholic subjects, had the bull been temporarily suspended. The absence of date, too, is easily explained ; the actual date of the invasion and

[1] .F. M. CARINI, *Mons. Niccolò Ormaneto* (Roma, 1894), pp. 137 *et seq.*

consequent distribution of the broadside could not be given beforehand.

It appears, however, that this manifesto did not fully satisfy those who were responsible for its existence. It was neither a papal bull nor a royal proclamation, but a compromise between the two. For this reason, Cardinal Allen wrote a kind of commentary upon it in the form of a lengthy pamphlet, "An Admonition to the Nobility and People of England."[1]   This, too, was sent by the Spanish ambassador from Rome to Antwerp, and printed there in order to be distributed in England by the Duke of Parma after the successful invasion. Allen's "Admonition" exceeds in freedom of speech all similar writings against Elizabeth, including even the bulls of Pius V. and Gregory XIII.   In its passionate, prophetic, and excited tone, it differs to such a marked degree from everything else written by this hitherto peace-loving man that many contemporaries regarded Robert Persons as its real author.[2]   The evidence of style makes it, indeed, more than probable that the Jesuit's pen played a part in its composition.

As long as it was at all possible, the cardinal of England had preserved at least the outward forms of loyalty,[3]

---

[1] *An admonition to the nobility and people of England and Ireland concerninge the present warres made for the execution of his Holines sentence by the highe and mightie Kinge Catholike of Spaine. By the Cardinal of Englande* [WILLIAM ALLEN], 1588 [Antwerp]. At the end ; *From my lodginge in the palace of S. Peter in Rome this 28th of April,* 1588.   No translation into a foreign tongue appeared either of this admonition or of the broadside, while none of Allen's other writings appeared in English alone.   Solely for the information of the Duke of Parma and the pope a MS. Italian translation was prepared.   SPAN. CAL., p. 289, and Arch. Vat., Pio 170, fols. 84–113 ; the translation was made by Nicholas Fitzherbert.

[2] [W. WATSON] *A decacordon of ten quodlibeticall questions* (1602), p. 240.   *Cf.* DODD-TIERNEY, III., p. 29, note.

[3] *Vid. ante,* pp 299 *et seq.*

but now he declares the queen of England to be "an incestuous bastard, begotten and borne in sinne of an infamous curtesan,"[1] and her kingdom to be "a place of refuge and sanctuarie of all Atheystes, Anabaptistes, heretikes, and rebellious of all nations."[2] Pages are filled with the enumeration of Elizabeth's crimes against God and man; both the public and private life of the queen are recklessly denounced. The catholic king has accepted the sacred and glorious task of driving this woman from the throne for the honour of God, the welfare of Christendom, and for "your deliuerie (my good brethren) from the yoke of heresie and thraldom of your enemies." The catholics of England must now show whether they will endure "an infamous, depriued, accursed, excomunicate heretike; the uery shame of her sexe, and princely name; the cheife spectacle of sinne and abhomination in this our age; And the onely poison calametie and destruction of our noble Churche and Cuntrie."[3]

"Feight not, for Gods loue, feight not, in that quarrel, in which if yow die, you are sure to be damned: feight not against all your auncesters soules, and faith, not against the saluation of all your deerest, wiues, children, and what so euer you wolde wel to, ether now or in the time to cum. Matche not yourselues against the highest: this is the daie no doubte of her fall, this is the hower of Gods wrathe towardes her and all her partakers: Forsake her therefore betime, that you be not inwrapped in her sinnes, punishment, and damnation."[4] An assurance of victory, to which neither the pope nor the king of Spain could attain, animated the cardinal of England. He promised the "valiaunt Champions of Gods Churche" the blessing of

---

[1] ALLEN, *An Admonition to the Nobility*, etc., p. xi.
[2] *Op. cit.*, p. xvi.   [3] *Op. cit.*, p. liv.
[4] *Ib.*

Christ and the intercession of all the saints. With a prophet's assurance he proclaimed that victory will attend the catholic army !

As these prophecies were rendered ridiculous by the result of the undertaking, efforts were made to suppress all the printed copies of the manifesto and Allen's pamphlet as far as possible.[1]   Nevertheless, the existence of at least the "Admonition" came to the knowledge of the English government, and Lord Burleigh suppressed the "vile book" under pain of high treason.[2]

In fact, only men who had entirely lost touch with the majority of their fellow-countrymen, like the cardinal of England and his friends, could have put out a pamphlet such as this "Admonition to the Nobility and People of England."   Loyalty was the ruling passion of Elizabethan England, and no party in the state was unaffected by it. The puritan member of parliament, Peter Wentworth, a victim of Elizabeth's capricious tyranny, wrote from his prison in the tower, "Our nation is of itself more inclined to the subjection of our prince, to obedience to our laws, to reason and to right than any other people which is between the two poles."[3]   Certainly Elizabeth was not beloved by English catholics.   Yet the priest, of whom it is related that on the scaffold he joined in the cry, "God save the queen,"[4] and the puritan, who started the same cry and waved his cap in the air with his left hand after the executioner had hewn off his right,[5] were fuller of the

---

[1]   WATSON, *Decacordon*, *l.c.*

[2]   DOM. CAL., 1581-90, p. 488.

[3]   Written in 1594.   *A treatise containing M. Wentworth's judgment concerning the person of the true and lawfull successor to these Realmes of England and Ireland (Imprinted* 1598), p. 66.   Supplement to *A pithie exhortation to her Majestie for establishing her successor to the crowne.*

[4]   [BRIDGEWATER] *Concertatio* (Aug. Trev., 1583), p. 276.

[5]   J. R. GREEN, *Hist. of the Engl. People*, II. (1878), p. 428.

spirit of Elizabethan England than the cardinal, whom his admirers celebrated as "the Father of his Country."[1] And further, chivalry in the service of woman, that delicate bloom of social culture, flourished in the stormy atmosphere of "Merry Old England," and so invectives, like those cast by Allen at Elizabeth, could not fail to wound both the sentiments of the subject towards his sovereign and of the gentleman towards a woman.

So, too, thanks to Allen's lack of address, the moral support which Spain received from Rome was of still more questionable value than the practical aid. The benefits which Philip II. derived from his alliance with the papacy in the English undertaking were on the whole, so insignificant, that compared with the demands which the war made on his resources, they amounted to little or nothing. But Philip had no other ally than the pope. The rest of Europe remained neutral and stood aside in expectation.[2] The enterprise of 1588 was *not*, as it has indeed been called, "a joint undertaking of the catholic world!"[3] Spain alone had to bear the burden of the gigantic task.

Cardinal Allen was convinced that Spain could bear it. He wrote to King Philip in the same prophetic style as to the English people, that the ever-victorious arms, which had prevailed against Turks and rebels, would also "chastise our heretics and that woman hated by God and man."[4] This assurance of victory was something foreign to Philip's humble submission to the will of God. In the instructions given by him to his admiral, the duke of Medina-Sidonia, on April 1, 1588,[5] we find it stated at the beginning:

---

[1] Letter of the Jesuit Southwell. POLLEN,'*Unpubl. doc.*, Cath. Record Soc., V. (1908), p. 316.

[2] *Cf.* HERRE, *Papsttum und Papstwahl*, p. 391.

[3] E. MARCKS, *Königin Elisabeth v. Engl.*, p. 67.

[4] Allen to Philip II., March 19, 1587. KNOX, p. 275.

[5] DURO, II., p. 6.

"Since victories are the gift of God, who gives them or denies them, according to His will," the admiral is straitly to insist that the soldiers show themselves not unworthy of the divine good-pleasure, and chiefly is to punish severely all blasphemy, in order that the wrath of God may not fall upon them all.

The progress and outcome of the great enterprise do not immediately enter into the scope of this book, and can only be touched upon here in their chief features. A reorganization of the Spanish fleet had been attempted with the means at the nation's disposal, which were still considerable in spite of the burden of war and debt. Gold from America supplied the place of the millions which the pope had refused.[1] Yet although gold was forthcoming, time, equally indispensable, failed for carrying through the naval reform. The idea of a fleet of galleys was abandoned, although it was impossible to man sailing ships, whose gunnery was for the most part of a provisional nature, with sufficiently instructed gunners, while the guns themselves, in spite of the considerable number of pieces, fell far short of the English naval artillery in effectiveness. The Armada numbered 130 vessels, carried nearly 2500 guns,[2] and was thus equipped for fighting at a distance, and yet at the same time, Medina-Sidonia received instructions which seemed drawn up for the admiral of a fleet of galleys. He was to approach close to the enemy's ships and try to board them.[3] In other words, the tactics of Lepanto

[1] According to a dispatch of the Venetian ambassador in Madrid there arrived from America "four millions of gold" in the summer of 1587, just in time to pay for the equipment. VEN. CAL., p. 309.

[2] *Relacion sumaria de los navios que van en la felicisima Armada* DURO, II., pp. 82 *et seq.*

[3] "Que el designio del enemigo será pelear de fuera por la ventaja que tiene de artilleria y los muchos fuegos artificiales de que verná prevenido, y que, al contrario, la mira de los nuestros ha de ser envestir y aferrar, por lo que les tienen en las manos." DURO, II., p. 9.

were pitted against those of the Elizabeth seamen, *i.e.* the tactics of the middle ages against those of the new era. These facts essentially determined the result of the naval engagement. For while the English fleet was almost equal to the Spanish in the number of large vessels, it had the advantage over it in small ships,[1] and the effectiveness of its guns was thrice as great,[2] and so the instructions given to the Spanish admiral could not be carried out, and the 17,000 soldiers[3] on board the Armada counted for nothing. They had no more chance of coming to close quarters with the enemy than the almost equally large forces of the Duke of Parma, which were to have been conveyed by the Armada from the Netherlands to England.

From the diplomatic correspondence of the months preceding the decisive action, it is clear that there was a widespread feeling that the Spanish preparations would lead to nothing. The undertaking was universally regarded as quite impracticable, and men refused to believe that the fleet would ever actually set sail. Even in January, 1588, the nuncio in Madrid contemplated the possibility of a peace at the last moment.[4] The Venetian ambassador wrote from Madrid in April that it was generally believed the king of Spain would not yet run the risk of so vast an undertaking.[5] When the premature news of the Armada's sailing reached Venice in May it was not believed. In

---

[1] *Cf.* CORBETT, II., pp. 189–202.

[2] LAUGHTON, *State Papers*, I., Introd., p. l.

[3] Originally 20,000, but reduced by desertion to 17,000 when the fleet set sail from Coruña. DURO, II., p. 199.

[4] "Non si è fuori di speranza di qualche accordo con Inghilterra et perciò non si lavora così gagliardamente intorno all armata come si potria, et ogni dì si stanno aspettando lettere di Fiandra dal duca di Parma, il che però qui non è creduto dalli più." The nuncio Speciani to Card. Montalto, Madrid, Jan. 18, 1588. Arch. Vat., Nunz. Spagna, 34, p. 214.

[5] VEN. CAL., p. 349.

the city of the lagoons men were well acquainted with the Spanish fleet. "Many maintain," wrote the nuncio from Venice,[1] "that the Armada cannot cope with the English unless it first joins forces with the Duke of Parma,[2] and this is considered to be very difficult."

At length the Armada sailed from Lisbon at the end of May, and discouraging accounts arrived in June that many of the ships were unseaworthy, and that the provisions were not fit to be used and had, for the most part, to be thrown overboard.[3] At the end of June, the admiral, Medina-Sidonia, wrote to the king from Coruña, where he once more touched land, "that the Armada was unequal to the task before it ; it was much inferior to the enemy's fleet in the opinion of all experts.[4] Philip's answer was the command not on any account to relinquish the undertaking but to prosecute the war.[5] In this he was right, for the avowal of failure before action would have inflicted a deeper wound on Spain's political prestige than a defeat afterwards. The admiral resigned himself to the inevitable.

The course of the three engagements in the channel, the appearance at night of the English fire-ships off Calais roads, the panic-stricken terror which drove the Armada once more out to sea, and, finally, the decisive combat next

---

[1] "Molti persistono nell'ostinazione che non possa uscire a far faccia a quella di Inghilterra, quando non s'unisca prima con l'altra del duca di Parma, che reputano difficilissimo, e per se sola assolutamente non la tengono bastante, essendo li legni fiacchi e carichi di pochi soldati inesperti e di poca disciplina, essendone morti molti e non trovandosi in essa nervo di gente forastiera." The nuncio Matteucci to Card. Montalto, Venice, May 11, 1588. Arch. Vat., Nunz. Venezia, 26, fol. 199ᵛ, 200.

[2] Alessandro Farnese, the governor of the Spanish Netherlands.

[3] The nuncio Speciani to Card. Montalto, Madrid, June 16, 1588. Arch. Vat., Nunz. Spagna, 34, fols. 667ᵛ, 671ᵛ.

[4] Medina-Sidonia to Philip II., Coruña, June 24, 1588. DURO, II., pp. 134-137.

[5] *Op. cit.*, pp. 150-154.

morning off Gravelines (July 28/August 8) — all these
are familiar events which need not be repeated here in
detail.[1]   The greater agility of the English ships and the
superior experience of the English seamen, the greater
rapidity and accuracy of the English firing gained the
victory in each encounter and prevented grappling and
boarding which would have given an opportunity for the
Spanish soldiers to show their superiority.   Alongside the
English ships, " the fastest vessels in the Spanish fleet
looked as though they were at anchor." [2]   The spectacle,
here presented for the first time in history, of a great
artillery fight at sea was so amazing that in order to
describe vividly the effect produced by the firing, men
compared the cannonading of the ships to " a skirmish
with small shot on land." [3]   Medina-Sidonia himself was
so unfamiliar with this novel kind of warfare that he noted
down in his diary, how the enemy fired off salvos of cannon
" without attempting to grapple "![4]   Amazement at the
agility of the illusive enemy, horror at the *gran furia de
artilleria*, and impotent rage at his own helplessness give
a special character to the Spanish admiral's narrative
which is written with all the directness of a diary.[5]   In

---

[1] *Cf.* chiefly CORBETT, II., chs. vi.–viii.   The engagements lasted
from July 21/31, to July 29/Aug. 8.

[2] CORBETT, II., p. 261.

[3] Sir George Carey to Sussex, July 25, o.s.   LAUGHTON, I.,
pp. 323 *et seq.*

[4] *Diario de la jornada de Inglaterra* by MEDINA-SIDONIA.   DURO,
II., p. 230.   *Cf.* the words of Speciani ; " Mai si è combattuto con
attaccarsi le navi insieme, come si suole, quando si combatte da
dovere."   Speciani to Card. Montalto, Madrid, Sept. 26, 1588.   Arch.
Vat., Nunz. Spagna, 34, fol. 796.   This view, that only a fight at close
quarters and not firing at a distance counted really as a battle, helped
on the acceptance of the legend that the Armada was destroyed by
the forces of nature and not by human power.

[5] See especially the *Diario*, *l.c.*, pp. 230, 238, 241 *et seq.*, and *cf.* the
other accounts in DURO, II., pp. 249, 258, 261, 275, 280.

the last and hottest encounter of the two fleets off Grave-lines, the fighting power of the Spaniards was already so enfeebled that they replied to the English cannonade with arquebuses and muskets.[1]

Then, when the stricken Armada took to flight, with the enemy close upon its wake, and attempted to gain the North Sea, a strong north-west wind drove it straight towards the sandbanks of Zealand. "God alone could save them." [2] To a Spaniard it seemed "the most terrible day in the world;" [3] all expected death. But, at the last moment, just as the vessels were running into shallow water near the coast,[4] "it pleased God to change the wind to the west-south-west, and the Armada made its way unharmed into the North Sea." So little historical justification is there for the legend about the wind and waves driving the Armada to its doom, that according to the admission of the Spaniards themselves, the wind alone saved it from complete destruction !

There was no danger that the Spaniards would be pursued into the North Sea, for the English, too, were short of ammunition. The idea of an artillery engage-ment at sea, although clearly grasped by the English admiralty, was not yet carried out to its full extent—the annihilation of the enemy by cannonades—and, in the then state of development in gunnery, it was also scarcely practicable. The reproach of niggardliness cast at Eliza-beth,[5] then as well as now, shows a failure to see that in the attack upon the Armada new, and for the most part untried, tactics were employed, and that no previous naval battle in history gave any idea of the amount of

---

[1] DURO, II., pp. 241 et seq.
[2] Medina-Sidonia in his *Diario*.   DURO, *l.c.*, p. 245.
[3] DURO, p. 271.
[4] "A seis brazas y media de agua," *l.c.*, p. 245.
[5] LAUGHTON, Vol. I., Introd., pp. lxiv. et seq., Vol. II., pp. 65, 259.

ammunition that would be required.   If the victory was incomplete from the point of view of modern methods of annihilation, it was yet complete enough to secure England against the danger of invasion.   The enemy's fleet retreated from the contest entirely disabled, and, for the most part, leaky and unseaworthy—with shattered masts and torn tackle, its anchors lost and its provisions spoiled.   The vessels pursued their way manned by crews of wounded and dying men.[1]   It was no longer an Armada, but a fleet of plague-stricken vessels which succumbed to the storms of the North Sea and strewed the coasts of Scotland and Ireland with wreckage.

IV. *After the Armada*

And so at last the decisive battle was fought between England and the catholic church.   The attempt to execute the bull of Pius V. and bring the apostate island back by force to the bosom of the Roman church was a miserable failure.   What effect did it have on the world ?

There are possibilities which fill the imagination with such dread that men are unable to contemplate them seriously.   The destruction of the Spanish fleet was a possibility of this kind for all those whose hopes were placed in the galleons of the " Invincible Armada."   Great as had been the anxiety with which Spain and catholic Europe had witnessed the sailing of the Armada, the thought of its defeat surpassed the power of men's imagination. Hopes of victory rose in men's hearts as soon as the Armada was out of sight of the Spanish coast.   On June 29, the nuncio in Madrid wrote : " The Lords of

---

[1] In addition to Duro *passim*, *cf. Certain advertisements . . . concerning the losses and distresses happened to the Spanish Navy . . .* London, 1588.   Harleian Miscell., I., pp. 132–141.

the council of war and the council of state regard the undertaking as accomplished and victory certain."[1]   Men encouraged one another with the thought of the dread which
the Armada inspired, and how the enemy were losing heart
beforehand.[2]   Then, suddenly, in August, by way of
France, came tidings of victory.   The English fleet had
been defeated and half destroyed—victory and the command of the seas belonged to the Armada.   It appears that
the ambassador Mendoza, who still continued to reside in
Paris, was the credulous source whence the news of this
victory spread.[3]   The strain of weeks and months of anxiety
now changed into exultant jubilation.   From Paris the
papal legate wrote on August 8 (new style), "All good
catholics and all friends of the common good are full of joy
and gladness."[4]   From Madrid the nuncio wrote soon
afterwards :   "The joy of the king and of the whole court
cannot be expressed in words.[5]   "Philip II. himself wrote
to Medina-Sidonia that he hoped the Armada would be
able to follow up its victory.[6]   In Italy the news was
received with mixed feelings.   In Turin, the Duke of Savoy
ordered a *Te Deum* to be sung forthwith, and took part
in a procession of thanksgiving along with his whole

[1] "Questi del conseglio di guerra et di stato tengono l'impresa per
fatta et la vittoria sicura." Speciani to Card. Montalto, Madrid,
June 29, 1588. Arch. Vat., Nunz. Spagna, 34, fol. 690ᵛ.

[2] Speciani to Montalto, Madrid, July 14, 1588, *l.c.*, fol. 710.

[3] FROUDE, *Hist. of Engl.*, XII. (1870), pp. 518 *et seq.   Cf.* the news
from Rouen of Aug. 7, Arch. Vat., Nunz. Francia, 22, p. 29.   A similar
communication in Nunz. Spagna, 34, fol. 760.   Dispatch to the Spanish
Consul in Venice, Nunz. Venez, 26, fol. 319.

[4] Morosini to Montalto, Paris, Aug. 8, Arch. Vat., Nunz. Francia,
22, p. 27.

[5] Speciani to Montalto, Aug. 19 and 26, Arch. Vat., Nunz. Spagna,
34, fols. 756, 768.

[6] On Aug. 18, n.s. DURO, II., p. 224.   For a collection of false
reports of victory by the Spaniards, see *A Pack of Spanish Lies*,
Harleian, Miscell. III., pp. 385 *et seq.* Somers Tracts, I., pp. 453 *et seq.*

court.[1]   In Venice people contended with one another on the squares of the city as to whether they ought to consider the news good or bad!   Catholic sentiment was here at variance with political foresight, which saw a danger to the independence of the Italian states in every increase of the already threatening power of Spain.[2]   In Rome, Cardinal Allen celebrated a grand festival in honour of the victory and invited to it all the English, Irish, and Scotch residing in the city.[3]

Soon afterwards, when, beginning at Paris, dismal tidings of the defeat of the Armada began to circulate, people refused to believe them.   The first authentic report was sent by the cardinal legate Morosini from Paris to Rome on August 17 (new style), with the remark that it was unworthy of credit.[4]   As early as August 28, he wrote with increasing anxiety, " God grant it be not true ! "[5]   Men were kept in doubt as to the fate of the fleet for several weeks.   The following skit was to be read on Pasquino[6] in Rome :—

" 1000 YEARS' INDULGENCE

will be granted by the Pontiff out of his supreme authority to whosoever gives him certain information of the whereabouts of the Spanish Armada.   Whither is it gone? Taken up into heaven or thrust down into hell ?   Suspended in air or floating somewhere on the sea ? "[7]

In Madrid, the first disturbing tidings were not known

[1] The nuncio Ottinelli to Card. Montalto, Turin, Aug. 22 and 25. Arch. Vat., Nunz. di Savoia, 21, pp. 665, 667.

[2] See the lively letter of Giuleo Sarvognano, an old soldier in Venice, to Filippo Pigifetta in Rome, Sept. 3, 1588. Arch. Vat., Misc., Arm. II., 90, fols. 29–31.

[3] STRYPE'S *Annals*, III., ii. (1824), p. 48.

[4] Arch. Vat., Nunz. Francia, 22, pp. 85 *et seq.*

[5] Il che piaccia a Dio che non si verifichi !   *L.c.*, p. 149.

[6] An antique torso near the Palazzo Braschi to which satirical notices were affixed.

[7] STRYPE'S *Annals*, III., ii., p. 22.   A similar notice was to be seen in Paris.   HERRE, *Papsttum u. Papstwahl* (1907), p. 391.

until the beginning of September. "God grant," wrote the nuncio, "that the evil tidings are false and the good ones true!"[1] About the middle of September anxiety increased at the Spanish court. Men began to fear that even the worst news did not yet completely correspond to the actual facts. Their only consolation was the king's demeanour; he alone kept up his spirits and gave no sign of what was passing in his mind.[2] Then, once more, came good news which prolonged the anxiety,[3] to be followed again by uncertain rumours to the contrary; until the end of September, men still remained in uncertainty. Conscious that he had acted rightly, Philip bore up under these trying circumstances. "I would rather have sold everything I have, even to the candlesticks here on the table, than have given up the English enterprise."[4] And so, while the king alone preserved his wonted bearing and good spirits amid the general distress,[5] criticisms were passed at court upon

[1] Speciani to Montalto, Madrid, Sept. 1. Arch. Vat., Nunz. Spagna, 34, fol. 778.

[2] "Tutta questa corte sta molto afflitta, perchè si dubita che le buone nuove già scritte in favore della nostra armata non siano vere, et che le male siano assai peggiori che non si disse, et che perciò non si discoprino li corrieri se bene vengono. . . . Il bene che dà qualche consolatione è che S. M^{tà} se ne sta allegramente, et si pensa che non staria così, se ci fossero male nuove; ma è anche vero che S. M^{tà} è così forte et constante nell'adversità che non si suol movere, nè si può conoscere da atti suoi esteriori alcuna sorte di mala satisfattione interiore." Speciani to Montalto, Madrid, Sept. 13. L.c., fol. 784.

[3] See Speciani to Montalto, Sept. 17. L.c., fol. 790.

[4] "Il medesimo re disse che haveria venduto quanto teneva nominando sino li candelieri che all'hora teneva su la tavola prima ch'abbandonare questa impresa d'Inghilterra, il che è creduto facilmente da quelli che conoscono la natura del re." Speciani to Montalto, Madrid, Sept. 24. Arch. Vat., Nunz. Spagna, 34, fol. 793. Cf. the Venetian dispatch of Nov. 1 in RANKE, History of the Popes [Engl. trans., 1847], Vol. I., p. 477, note.

[5] "Il re se ne sta con la solita misura et allegrezza." Speciani to Montalto, Oct. 2. L.c., fol. 807.

the responsible leaders which increased in vehemence as the certainty of the disaster became clearer.[1] At the beginning of October, the first remnants of the Armada, with thousands of fever-stricken men on board, reached home, and doubt was no longer possible. Then, at last, Philip put a stop to the prayers for the success of the enterprise and ordered others to thank God that the catastrophe had not been greater than it was.[2]

Spanish pride was deeply wounded. " Every one here would have preferred that the soldiers had fallen in battle at sea than return home like this." [3] " One hears nothing here but talk of the new Armada which must be got ready by next year ! " The sense of shame and the longing to repair the disaster dominated for the moment every other feeling.[4] The surviving soldiers of the Armada themselves begged to be sent out once more to retrieve their lost honour.[5] Only a few entertained doubts of the practicability of a fresh undertaking. The cities of Spain vied with one another in offering the king materials for a new fleet.[6] Wealthy private individuals made noble offers of money and gifts.[7] The nuncio was convinced that his

---

[1] Speciani to Montalto, Sept. 26. *L.c.*, fol. 796.

[2] Speciani to Montalto, Oct. 10. *L.c.*, fol. 812. DURO, *Armada Invencible*, II. (1885), p. 314.

[3] " Tutti qui haveriano voluto che più presto fossero morti li soldati combattendo in mare che ritornati a casa nel modo che si è fatto." Speciani to Montalto, Oct. 5. *L.c.*, fol. 810.

[4] Speciani to Montalto, Oct. 10 and 14. *L.c.*, fols. 812, 833.

[5] Speciani to Montalto, Nov. 12. *L.c.*, fol. 877.

[6] DURO, II., pp. 459–464.

[7] " Tuttavia si offriscono da diversi diverse quantità di denari a S.M. per la nova impresa d'Inghilterra, della quale pare che tuttavia si parli gagliardamente, se bene li più stanno nella solita opinione che non si farà per an altro anno, et il conte di Bondia ha donato al re cento trenta mila ducati contanti." Speciani to Montalto, Nov. 24. Arch. Vat., Nunz. di Spagna, 34, fol. 893ᵛ.

Majesty could have as much gold as he wanted.[1] It was only as people waited in vain week after week for the ships that never came, and heard of the disaster on the Irish and Scottish coasts and of the appalling loss of life, that they began at last to see that the preparation of a new Armada was by no means a mere question of money. People saw now that the chief difficulty lay in providing the necessary number of seamen and marines.[2] The new nuncio, who arrived in Spain in November, 1588, met so many people in mourning on his way to Madrid that he inquired the reason. He was told they were the relatives of those who had perished in the Armada.[3] And only then did the magnitude of the disaster dawn upon him.

The tendency to regard the event as a divine chastisement, natural in that age, grew stronger than ever under these circumstances, and operated equally on both conquerors and conquered. The victors saw a manifestation of God's anger chiefly in the storm which beat upon the stricken fleet, "which is the only work of God to chastise their malicious practices, and to make them know that neither the strengths of men nor their idolatrous gods can prevail when the mighty God of Israel stretcheth out his finger against them."[4] Amid the chorus of those who thanked God, the voices of the puritans were louder than all the rest. Their prayers arose to the "God of Israel," the God of the chosen people.

[1] Speciani to Montalto, Oct. 31. *L.c.*, fol. 855.

[2] Speciani to Montalto, Nov. 5. *L.c.*, fol. 860.

[3] Dispatch of the nuncio, Annibale de Grassi, Valencia, Nov. 23, 1588. Arch. Vat., Nunz. Spagna, 35, fol. 9.

[4] Thos. Fenner to Walsingham, Aug. 4/14, 1588. LAUGHTON, *State Papers*, II., pp. 41 *et seq.* *Cf.* Drake's letter, *l.c.*, p. 61, and Thos. Cooper's Thanksgiving in STRYPE'S *Annals*, III., ii., p. 21.

The conquered, however, found themselves face to face with a riddle. "Every one here is stupefied," wrote the nuncio from Madrid at the beginning of November,[1] "for the hand of God seems almost openly to be *against* us." Philip II. had to hear from his ghostly adviser that his prayers and processions were very good things, yet God gave ear to other voices before his, and when the king asked "What voices?" the reverend father replied, "The voices of the poor oppressed who stay about the court in pain without being paid and without having their business attended to."[2] Although Philip kept so brave an exterior, he was, nevertheless, deeply affected by so inconceivable a disaster. He withdrew more than ever from the world, and for a time gave audiences to no one. He made a new will, and passed long hours with his confessor.[3]

Outside Spain there was little sympathy for the vanquished. In Paris, Mendoza scarcely dared to show himself in the streets. Street urchins and porters mocked him with cries of "Victoria, Victoria!"[4] Among the Italian states the ancient hatred of Spanish interference revived and made itself felt in diplomatic affairs. Venice and Tuscany began to break away from Spain.[5] A

[1] "Ognuno sta turbato vedendo quasi manifestamente la mano di Dio contra di noi." Speciani to Montalto, Madrid, Nov. 8, 1588. Arch. Vat., Nunz. Spagna, 34, fol. 869ᵛ.

[2] According to the dispatch of the Venetian ambassador, Lippomano, Oct. 1, 1588. VEN. CAL., 1581–91, p. 396.

[3] Lippomano's dispatches of Sept. 6 and Oct. 1. *L.c.*, p. 386.

[4] "Mendoza at Paris, before the fight at sea crijng out openly before ye victori ' Victoria !' after the disconfeture of the Spanish fleet durst no more come forth of his houss for very shame, because the boyes and porters mokked him, as he rodd through the street upon his mule, crijng to him ' Victoria ! Victoria !'" MS. Marginal note by a contemporary on *The Copie of a letter sent out of England to . . . Mendoza* (London, 1588), p. 14. Brit. Mus., 440, i. 16.

[5] HERRE, *Papsttum u. Papstwahl*, II. (1907), pp. 391 *et seq.*

German broadside bore the following concise moral beneath a picture of the engagement :—

> "Was die Armada, aussgesant
> Vom Spannier wieder Engellandt,
> Verrichtedt hab, weiss jedermann :
> Kein macht ohn Godt gewinnen kan." [1]

On the whole the feeling in the anti-Spanish world was well represented by the design on a Dutch commemorative medal—the terrestrial globe slipping from the hands of the king of Spain.[2] Satire was mercilessly directed against the *Armada Invencible*. Carricatures were circulated with the inscription, " She came, she saw, and fled." [3]

What effect had the collapse of the enterprise on the man who next after the king of Spain had had most to do with it—the pope ? The feelings of Sixtus V. towards Elizabeth were a mixture of hatred and admiration. " He cannot refrain," narrates the Venetian ambassador,[4] " from esteeming her very highly and lauding her masculine courage and bravery to the skies. If she were only a catholic, he says, she would be his favourite daughter." We know that Philip II. was not his favourite son, and that the pope had not thrown himself heartily into the crusade against England (p. 318). To the end of his life the pope, though so clear-sighted a man in other respects, could not bring himself to relinquish all hopes of Elizabeth's conversion.[5] The political quidnuncs of Rome set on foot ridiculous stories of a secret agreement between the pope and the queen—mere fables, which a later history,

---

[1] Bodleian Library, Sutherland Collection, 122.

[2] DURO, *Armada Invencible*, I., p. 217.

[3] *Ib., l.c.* C. TEMPESTI, *Storia . . . di Sisto V.*, Vol. II., lib. vi., § 22.

[4] ALBÈRI, *Relazioni*, ser. II., Vol. IV., p. 344.

[5] See his conversation with the Venetian ambassador, Badoer, in Feb., 1590. HÜBNER, *Sixte-Quint*, Vol. III. (Paris, 1870), p. 359. RANKE, *Hist. of the Popes*, [Eng. trans., 1847], Vol. I., pp. 503 *et seq.*

itself half a romance, took in sober earnest.[1] So much, however, is certain, that the Spanish ambassador in Rome, Olivares, felt himself injured by the manner in which the pontiff received the news of the Armada. "When good news comes he shows no sign of pleasure, but rather the contrary, whilst evil reports do not appear to concern him so much as is fitting. This is the general opinion."[2] To the Venetian ambassador, Sixtus let fall some words about "great princes who needed a counterpoise, lest they should become too powerful."[3]

We cannot tell what the great pope thought in his innermost heart, whether his human admiration for Elizabeth, and, at the same time, the longing to be free from Spanish tutelage were stronger in him than the wish to see the catholic arms victorious. The attitude taken up by Sixtus V. towards Philip II. after the defeat of the Armada was at any rate an additional blow to the king and to Spain's deeply shattered prestige. Sixtus V. held to the letter of his agreement by which he had pledged himself only to pay the subsidy on condition that the troops had actually landed (p. 319), and met the Spanish ambassador's demands for money with a flat refusal. He burst into a rage when Olivares suggested to him that Philip II. had fulfilled the spirit, if not the letter, of the agreement, and deserved compensation under any circumstances for the sacrifices he had made.[4] The church's temporal protector, after fighting for

[1] GREG. LETI, *Vita di Sisto V.*, II. (Amst. 1686), pp. 238 *et seq.* The saying quoted by Leti, "a better Englishman in Rome than a catholic in England," belongs to the time of Urban VIII., not to Sixtus V. More will be said on this point in the second volume of this work.

[2] On Sept. 26, HÜBNER, III., p. 259. SPAN. CAL., 1587–1603, p. 452.

[3] Giov. Gritti to the Doge. Rome, Dec. 7, 1588. HÜBNER, II., p. 514.

[4] See above, note 2, for the references for Olivares' letter.

thirty years to maintain her power and unity, had now to learn the lesson that his life's work and the expenditure of the best energies of his people would be accepted by the church simply as the discharge of an obvious duty for which he was to receive no earthly recompense. Of all the painful experiences which the year 1588 brought to the aging monarch, this was one of the most painful. One consequence of it was that, towards the end of his life, he occupied himself in first setting to rights the temporal affairs of his shattered realm before taking in hand the affairs of the catholic church, although he had believed himself specially called to the latter task.[1]

This alteration in Philip by no means excluded the thought of retaliation on England. It was impossible that it should do so, for Spain, either for better or worse, had to carry on the war when once it had been started. This is not the place to go into all the details of the naval warfare of which neither Philip nor Elizabeth lived to see the end (1604). It is sufficient to remember that on two subsequent occasions (1593 and 1596–97) Philip prepared to invade England, but both attempts proved that the forces of Spain were unequal to the task. But while Philip was far from admitting even to himself that his world-wide empire was to find its master in the small island kingdom, England also found it difficult to grow accustomed to the thought that the danger of a Spanish invasion was past and gone for ever.

Sir Fulke Greville, the friend and biographer of Sir Philip Sidney, and a contemporary of Spain's greatness, paints in vivid colours the impression which the resources

---

[1] The proof of this change in Philip II. is due to HERRE, *Papsttum u. Papstwahl* (1907). *Cf.* however, on the other hand, Erich Marck's criticism on the too great emphasis which Herre lays upon this point, Hist. Zeitschrift., CIV. (1909), p. 157, with which I agree.

of Spain in king Philip's days made upon Englishmen.[1]
" Spain managing the popedome by voices and pensions
among the cardinals and having the sword both by land
and sea in his hand, seemed likewise to have all those
western parts of the world laid as a *tabula rasa* before him
to write where he pleased *Yo el Re*. And that which made
this fatal prospect the more probable was his golden Indian
mines, kept open not only to feed and carry his threatening fleets and armies, where he had will and right to goe,
but to make way and pretense for more where he list, by
corrupting and terrifying the chief counsels both of Christian
and heathen princes." The prestige of a world-wide empire,
such as that of Philip II., survived defeats. While certain
far-seeing spirits might despise the dread of the Spanish
danger as a mere prejudice,[2] the large mass of the people
did not feel safe from invasion even after the victory over
the Armada. In 1588, it was only the fleet, and not the
land forces of England, that had been put to the test, and
confidence in the latter was no greater then than it is to-
day. The idea of a whole nation in arms and of the duty
of universal service, which, since the appearance of Macchiavelli's prophetic *Libro dell' Arte della Guerra* (1521), had
taken such firm root in Germany and Italy,[3] found zealous
upholders in England too, after 1588. It is no mere accident that just in this year Peter Whitehorn's English
translation of Macchiavelli's book was republished[4] and
was supplemented and brought up to date by other
handbooks of Italian and English writers on the art of

---

[1] SIR FULKE GREVILLE'S *Life of Sir Philip Sidney*, ed. NOWELL
SMITH in the Tudor and Stuart Library (Oxford, 1907), pp. 86 *et seq.*

[2] *E.g.* FRANCIS BACON, *Observations on a Libel*, etc. (1592). *Works*,
ed. SPEDDING, VIII. (1862), pp. 163, 169.

[3] H. V. ZWIEDINECK-SÜDENHORST, *Gegenreformation in Deutschland* in PFLUGK-HARTTUNG'S *Weltgeschichte* (1907), pp. 426 *et seq.*

[4] *The Arte of Warre* first appeared in 1560.

war.[1]   In a work on "The Defence of the Realm," Sir
Henry Knyvett[2] advocated only a few years afterwards
(1596) military training for English youths and the introduction of universal service between the ages of 18 and 50.
No less a personage than Lord Bacon adopted the idea as
his own at a later date.[3]   Along with all her pride and
confidence in her victorious fleet, England was still fully
conscious of the weakness of her land forces.[4]

This consciousness of a weak point in her armour, added
to the passion excited by war, would alone sufficiently
explain a fact which might at first strike one as strange,
i.e. that *after* 1588 English catholics were watched and
oppressed with the same severity as before, or even with
greater.   When once the danger was past, the persecuted
ones complained that England turned her arms and her
hatred of Spain against her own sons.[5]   In the days of
peril, catholics had been faithful to the government of the
country, although their fidelity had not been put to the
test. Allen's quickly suppressed "Admonition" found
little response from his co-religionists in England.   Many
catholics had given evidence of undoubted patriotism, and
were prepared to serve their country without any hesitation
(p. 297).   The conduct of the overwhelming majority of
English catholics gave no occasion whatever for the

---

[1] WHITEHORNE, *Certain waies for the ordering of souldiers in
battlery.* G. CATANEO, *Most brief tables to know redily how manie
ranckes of footmen . . . go to the making of a just battile.* Both
books were published in London, 1588.

[2] SIR HENRY KNYVETT, *The Defence of the Realme.* Reprinted
by CH. HUGHES, Tudor and Stuart Lib. (Oxford, 1906), p. 13.

[3] LORD BACON, *Of the True Greatness of the Kingdom of Britain*
(1608).   *Works,* ed. SPEDDING, VIII. (1859), pp. 48 *et seq.*

[4] "The problem was almost the same as at the present time."
HUGHES, introd. to his edition of Knyvett's *Defence,* dedicated to Lord
Roberts, p. xxvii.

[5] R. Southwell to Claudius Acquaviva, Aug. 31, 1588. POLLEN
Unpubl. doc., Cath. Record Soc., V., p. 322.

unusually large number of death sentences and executions which followed upon the victory over the Armada. No other explanation than the intense excitement of those weeks and the increased dread of assassination can be given of the holocausts of August, 1588.[1] On a single day, no less than thirteen men—six priests, and seven laymen who had given asylum to priests—were handed over to the executioner.[2] But the fact that a more humane treatment and a fairer judgment of catholics were not adopted, when the excitement of this critical year had subsided, is to be explained by the combined influence of constant fear of invasion and the growth of the puritanic spirit, a spirit of implacable enmity against Rome.

In 1589 the puritan press fulminated for the first time against the episcopalian church of England.[3] There was, indeed, no immediate causal connection between this and the victory over the Armada or the increased persecution of catholics. Nevertheless, there was more in it than mere coincidence. The puritanical spirit was strong in the English marine, and the puritans had been foremost in urging on the war against Spain and Rome. The victory of 1588 meant, consequently, an increase of moral force for that party. A catholic pamphlet clothes the thought in the following words: "After the destruction of the catholic fleet, being set free from the restraint of fear, they began to carry themselves more insolently, to stir up fresh tragedies, and throw everything into confusion."[4] Robert Persons was well informed when he wrote a few years after the Armada: "The puritan parte at home in

[1] *Vid. ante*, p. 316.
[2] POLLEN, *op. cit.*, p. 323.
[3] *Cf.* WILLIAM MASKELL, *A History of the Martin Marprelate Controversy* (London, 1845).
[4] [J. CRESWELL, S.J.] *Exemplar literarum missarum e Germania ad D. Guil. Cecilium, cons. reg.* (1592), p. 8.

Ingland, is thought to be most vigorouse of any other, that is to say, most ardent, quick, bold, resolute, and to have a great part of the best Captaines and souldiers on their side, which is a pointe of no smal moment."[1]   The spirit of this party, which was to have a preponderating influence on England's future, finds words of powerful incentive in a pamphlet of the year of the Armada already mentioned, written while the impression made by the victory was still fresh.[2]   Wrath against Anti-Christ in Rome and exaltation over the catastrophe inflicted on his fighting power are here mingled with attacks on the pleasure-seeking of the age, on the " gay-coloured silk and bright glittering gold." In the comfortableness, refinement and luxury of his fellow-countrymen, in the good cheer and display in dress, this stern censor sees not only an offence to God but also more especially a danger to the English people's power of resistance.   From this, by a natural transition, he gives expression to exhortations similar, though not completely thought out, to those of the advocates of universal service.[3] And so we find the threefold tendency of hatred to Rome, severity in morals, and care for the national defence already at work in the puritanism of the Elizabethan age, just as we find them later on during the civil war.

Although the queen's council contained more than one member who was a puritan at heart, the English government as a whole cannot yet be reproached with being

---

[1] R. DOLEMAN [*i.e.* R. Persons].   *A Conference about the next succession to the Crowne of Ingland* (1594), p. 244.

[2] ANTHONY MARTEN, *An Exhortation*, etc. *Vid. ante*, p. 315, note 3.

[3] " All yee good men of the Realme and well willing subiects, in whose courage and assistance standeth a great part of our defence, prepare your selves unto all service and loyaltie, be strong and hardie ! . . . Convert your ploughes into speares, and your sithes into swords ! Turn your boules into bowes and al your pastimes into musket shot !" Quoted from the original. *Cf.* Harl. Misc., I. (1808), p. 172.

deeply imbued with the new spirit. But it was one of its marked characteristics not to oppose, without necessity, strong currents of opinion among the people. It therefore placed no restraint upon the eagerness of the puritans for war against Rome, and was all the less inclined to do so as this eagerness coincided with the universal anxiety about the Spanish danger and the protection of the queen's life. The dread of assassination never altogether died down. It was before men's minds, not only in the days when the decisive action was taking place, but, after the collapse of the invasion, it constantly assumed new forms, and about 1590 developed into a nervous panic. Access to the court and to the sovereign's person was then more closely watched than had been usual during the earlier years of Elizabeth's reign. A sharp look-out was kept upon all idle vagabonds and unknown petitioners.[1] The government gave vent to the feeling caused by this combined anxiety and irritation by framing new measures against catholics.

One of these was the royal proclamation of October 18/28, 1591, against Jesuits and seminary priests—a document of unusual length, and falling short of none of the earlier proclamations in harshness of language.[2] Theoretically, the view was still maintained that it was not the

---

[1] Shortly after 1590, many proclamations were issued, such as: "A proclamation to reform the disorder in access of greater number of persons to the court than have just cause so to do," or, "A proclamation to restrain access to the court . . . ," or, "A proclamation for suppressing of the multitude of idle vagabonds and avoiding of . . . dangerous persons from Her Maj. Court." Similar decrees were issued by the Privy Council. HUMPHRY DYSON, *Book of Proclamations* (1618), *passim.*

[2] The original was printed on three folio pages. *A declaration of great troubles pretended against the Realme by . . . seminarie priests and Jesuists . . . under a false pretence of Religion. . . . Published by this her Maiesties Proclamation.* Brit. Mus. G. 6463, fols. 297–299. Also in the Harleian Miscellany, III. (ed. PARK, 1809), pp. 95–99.

catholic faith, but only the disloyalty of the priests to the state, that was to be suppressed and punished. Practically, however, this new police regulation essentially increased the strictness of the inquiry into attendance at the state church, and led to still closer restrictions being placed on the exercise of catholic ministrations in secret. Commissioners for the examination of catholics were instituted by the government in every shire. These county commissions nominated a committee of eight persons for each parish, comprising the minister, the constable, and the church-wardens. Once a week, at least, this committee was to go from house to house in order to examine the inmates as to their belief and attendance at church. Whenever the answers were not satisfactory, the individual was delated to the county commissioners for further examina-tion. It was hoped that by this organized inquisition of the laity disguised priests could be most surely tracked down.[1]

No puritan could have surpassed in bitterness and hatred the terms in which the mission priests were alluded to in this proclamation: "a multitude of dissolute yong men who have partly for lacke of living, partly for crimes committed become fugitives, rebelles, and traitours, and for

---

[1] In addition to the proclamations mentioned in the notes on previous page (cf. also p. 206), see Verstegan's letter to Persons, March 5, 1592. Westminster Cathedral Archives, MSS. IV., pp. 293–296. "By the new Cecillian Inquisition there are certaine comissioners ordayned in every shyre to take the examinations of Catholiques, and thease comissioners do in every parish apoint 8 persons, of which number must be the minister, constable and churchwardens. Thease 8 do once a weeke (or every day in the weeke, yf they please) go from house to house and examine those they fynde, of what religion they are and whether they do go to the Churche; and [such] as they fynd doubtfull in their answeres they do present them to the further examina-tion of the comissioners. The servants of recusants they do eyther perswade by flattery or compel by torture in hanging them up by the hands to betray their masters in discovering what priests he doth relieve, what persons do frequent the house and the lyke."

whome there are in Rome and Spaine and other places certaine receptacles made to live in, and there to bee instructed in schoole points of sedition, and from thence to be secretly and by stealth conveyed into our dominions with ample authoritie from Rome to moove, stirre up, and perswade as many of our subiects as they dare deal withall, to renounce their naturall allegeance due to us and our crowne, and upon hope by a Spanish invasion to bee enriched and endowed with the possessions and dignities of our other good subjectes."

If one asks how unfair generalizations and exaggerations like the above could have made such a misrepresentation of the truth possible, two names must be mentioned at the offset—two names which occur in the proclamation itself—Persons and Allen. The proclamation is drawn up in a style similar to that of the latest publications of these two writers. Because Persons and Allen always made their voices most clearly heard amid the strife, the fact escaped notice that they were the mouthpiece of only a small minority. Now, too, it was Persons who replied—a reply full of bitterness, hatred, and scorn—written with all the effectiveness characteristic of the man, and circulated throughout Europe with great effect and rapidity, thanks to the organization of the Jesuits.[1] His answer to Elizabeth's proclamation was published in Italy and Germany, in

---

[1] *Elizabethæ Angliæ Reginæ hæresim Calvinianam propugnantis sævissimum in catholicos sui regni edictum . . . promulgatum Londini, 29 Nov., 1591. Per D.* ANDREAM PHILOPATRUM, *Presb. a Theol. Rom., ex Anglis olim oriundum.* Philopater is a pseudonym for Persons. The date, Nov. 29, obviously refers to the publication of the proclamation in London, for the proclamation itself is dated Oct. 19. I give the following editions from the Brit. Mus. and Bodleian Library. In Latin : *Augustæ*, 1592 ; *Lugduni*, 1592, 1593 ; *Romæ*, 1593 ; *sine loco* [Rome], 1593. In German : *Ingolstatt*, 1593. In French : *Lyon*, 1593. The English broadside, *A declaration of the true causes*, *etc.*, follows much the same lines as Philopater (Persons).

the Netherlands and France. It spoke in every language, and was at once an indictment and a justification. The pen, indeed, was the only weapon left to the vanquished since the Spanish guns had been silenced off Gravelines. No one can deny the power shown in this desperate defence of a lost position, or the man's unshaken belief in the justice of his own cause.

"'I have not troubled Israel, but thou and thy father's house, who have forsaken the commandments of the Lord.' This is the true cause, from this, believe me, spring all the confusion, all the misfortune of thy country, Elizabeth, forasmuch as thou hast forsaken the Lord and gone astray from the royal road of the Christian and catholic religion, for it is written, 'Who hath resisted him, and hath had peace?'"[1] Persons addresses Elizabeth just as if it was her cause that was lost, and not his. Vanquished as he is, he still utters threats and warnings. "Learn this, Elizabeth, that God is, and that He is the same who has chastised other kings, queens, monarchs, and emperors before thee and far more powerful than thou art."[2] That God decided *against* the Armada does not disconcert him; he compares England to the barren fig-tree in the gospel to which the husbandman grants yet one more year to live, "to see if it will bring forth fruit."[3]

In hardly any other work is the cause of the English mission priests pleaded so brilliantly as in this. "Has history, since the memory of man, anything more wonderful to tell than of youths nobly born and wealthy for the most part, who could live quietly and comfortably at home, and who solely from zeal for the faith have left parents and friends, and all that is dear to them in this life in order to go into voluntary exile, with such greatness of soul and

[1] PHILOPATER (PERSONS), § 50.   [2] *Op. cit.*, § 81.
[3] *Op. cit.*, § 146.

steadfastness that they fear neither spies nor prisons, neither executioner nor instruments of torture for the sake of religion and the salvation of souls." [1]   They could have gained honour and consideration in the anglican church ; in the career they have chosen, none of these things fall to their lot. [2]   " They are not descended from the dregs of mankind like your ministers of the Word, but frequently from noble families and wealthy parents, and I venture to say that in the three English seminaries of Rome, Rheims, and Valladolid, there are more flowers of nobility than among all your clergy at home." [3]

It is plain that Persons was attempting to restore the despised mission priests to honour. But he did the catholic cause little service when he thundered against England's " herodian " legislation and designated Walsingham, the late secretary of state, as " well-nigh crazy," or when he passionately charged Burleigh with being the cause of all the misery in England, and compared the cruelty of Elizabeth to that of Diocletian, Decius, and Domitian. [4]   The consequence of this new outburst of impotent wrath, like that of Allen's in 1588, could only be to increase the amount of already excessive inflammable material. The secular priest Watson passed a severe judgment on Person's pamphlet. " What malice and contempt can devise, that might provoke her Majesty to indignation against us, is there set out very skilfully." [5]   Every new

[1] *Op. cit.*, § 73.

[2] It is absurd to attribute to the seminarist "golden dreams of mitres, titles, and commands," as does M. A. S. HUME (*Treason and Plot*, etc. [London, 1901], p. 87), in his sketch of the students at Valladolid !

[3] PHILOPATER (PERSONS), § 214. For the Latin of this passage *vid. ante*, p. 102, note 2.

[4] *Op. cit.*, §§ 1, 19, 25, 47, 76 *et seq.*

[5] [W. WATSON] *Important Considerations*, etc. (1601), p. 32. Reprinted in *A Collection of Several Treatises*, etc. (London. Printed for Richard Royston, 1675), p. 80.

controversial work issuing from the catholic exiles gave
the puritans, and others too, a fresh weapon against
English catholics at home. "It is strange," wrote Francis
Bacon with reference to the pamphlets put out by catholics,
and especially the most recent attack of the eloquent
Jesuit,[1] "what a number of libellous and defamatory books
and writings, and in what variety, and with what art and
cunning handled, have been allowed to pass through the
world in all languages against her Majesty and her
government."[2]

While Persons was circulating this new war-cry of his
all over catholic Europe in 1593, the English parliament
passed its last and severest law against the confessors of
the Roman faith. Catholics were denied the liberty of
moving about freely in their own country, and catholic
parents the right of educating their own children.[3]   So
boldly did the puritan party now lift up its head that one
of the members declared in parliament that the children
of papists should not be intrusted to the bishops to be
educated, "because their chancellors are so much affected
to the canon law that some are infected with popish
religion"; it was more fitting the children should be sent
to courts of justice for their education![4]

The war of extermination had reached its highest point,
beyond which it could scarcely go. Men only asked

[1] *Observations upon a Libel*, etc. BACON'S *Works*, ed. SPEDDING
VIII. (1862), p. 147. Bacon had not the original form of the book
before him but only the broadside, *A Declaration*, etc., which is closely
related to it. *Vid. ante*, p. 351, note 1 at end.

[2] At the same time as Philopater (Persons') pamphlet appeared
there appeared also the more temperate *Exemplar literarum missarum
e Germania ad D. Guil. Cecilium cons. reg.* (1592), by the Jesuit JOS.
CRESWELL.

[3] *Vid. ante*, pp. 149, 174.

[4] Speech of Nathaniel Bacon in the House of Commons, Feb. 28,
1593. SIMONDS D'EWES, *The Journals of all the Parliaments of
Q. Eliz.* (London, 1682), p. 477.

themselves how long were the majority going to suffer for
the sins of the minority?

The year 1588 marks, too, a division in the internal
development of English catholicism. The defeat of the
Armada was a terrible experience for all those who had
trusted that the invasion would effect a change by violent
means. And what the religious agitation of the moment
could not achieve, the increasing pressure of the following
years accomplished. The existing opposition between the
minority who were in favour of invasion and the majority
who were opposed to it now became open and gave rise to
a cleavage between moderates and extremists.

After 1590, the question of invasion was discussed
among English catholics on its religious, legal, and
patriotic sides. The priest Wryght proposed the question,
"Whether catholics in England might take up arms to
defend their queen and country against the Spaniards?" [1]
It was not easy to establish an affirmative without coming
into collision with canon law and the papal authority.
The bull expressly forbade men to support Elizabeth,
the latest manifesto from Rome had urged them to side
with the invading army, and Spain was acting officially
as executor of the bull. Opposition to a Spanish invasion
could only be justified if it was possible to prove the
invalidity of Spain's claim, and to show that its position
as defender of the faith was a mere pretence. Wryght
now endeavoured to prove this. He maintained that for
many years the Spaniards had done nothing to keep alive
the catholic faith in England, that they had at last drawn
sword not to defend the church but themselves against

---

[1] *An licitum sit catholicis in Anglia arma sumere et aliis modi
reginam et regnum defendere contra Hispanos?* Written after 1590
and translated into English in STRYPE'S *Annals*, III., ii. (1824),
pp. 583–597.

England's attacks and encroachments. "For to defend his money he could presently be ready; but to defend religion he could not be ready." Dare a nation, asks **Wryght**, assume the office of champion of Christendom if, instead of converting them, it exploits poor heathen so cruelly as the Spaniards do the natives of America? And is a king the obedient son of the pope, if he watches so jealously over the rights of his crown in ecclesiastical matters as does the king of Spain?[1] The conclusion—certainly not beyond question—which followed from this subtle dialectic was naturally, Spain's pretended vocation to protect the catholic religion is nothing else than a mask for her political aims. The pope made a mistake when he appointed the Spaniards to be the executors of the bull, and English catholics need not follow him on this point, but ought to defend their country against Spain.

Wryght's out-pourings were meant to be a sort of programme. His advice in brief is—shake yourselves free from Spain and give up all idea of catholicizing England by force. "Wherefore, I think, we must yield to the time; and for a time bear the yoke which Christ hath laid upon us with all humility." These words contain the lesson which the large majority of English catholics drew for themselves from the fate of the Armada. We have seen that they had become estranged from Spain in their own minds long before 1588,[2] and the collapse of the power of Spain put the finishing touch to this development. It

---

[1] It may be observed here that Spain's encroachments upon the rights of the church, and the friction between the royal and papal authority attracted the attention of English catholics. Creswell, in a remarkable letter, warns the pope to put up with these annoyances. England's apostacy from Rome came from small beginnings! J. Creswell to Clement VIII., Madrid, April 26, 1596, Arch. Vat., Borgh. III., 124 g 2, fol. 93.

[2] *Vid. ante*, pp. 244–252.

became a commonplace to attribute Spain's entire policy solely to greed of territory ; Philip II. had merely set his heart on the English crown, and that was all—such was the reproach cast at the Spanish party by patriotic catholics.   Watson, the secular priest, a man given to indulge in paradox, went so far as to maintain that Philip II. would have liked to destroy English catholics as well as English protestants from off the face of the earth.[1]

Spain made no attempt to counteract this tendency. She did not raise a finger to draw the catholics of England nearer to herself, nay, rather, she actually alienated them from her.   The little band of exiles, who, after 1588, still continued in the service of Spain, now suffered more deeply than ever before from the irreconcilable divergencies of character between Englishmen and Spaniards. "Their misery is so extreme that all, or most of them, would at once renounce their obedience to Spain and return to England if the least assurance were given them of being allowed to practise their religion."[2]   Robert Persons himself, the acknowledged head of the "Spanish party," in a fit of depression, once addressed words to the Spanish secretary of state which, coming from him, are full of significance, and reveal the whole tragedy of these homeless exiles.   He who for years had been working on behalf of a Spanish invasion, and who at the time had pointed to its failure as a proof of God's long-suffering towards

---

[1] [W. WATSON] *Important Considerations* (1601).   See *Epistle General.*

[2] ". . . extremæ miseriæ, quam patiuntur omnes Angli, qui serviunt regi Hispaniarum, quæ tanta est, ut data minima securitate religionis omnes vel plurimi catholici statim relicto obsequio Hispanorum in Angliam sint redituri." *Ex relatione* GABRIELIS COLFORDI, *nobilis Angliæ* [1595], Arch. Vat., Borgh. II., 448 ab fol. 335.

reprobate England, writes three years later that God had destroyed the Armada to preserve English catholics, who had already suffered so much from heretics, from suffering still worse things at the hands of the Spaniards.[1]   These words are no mere rhetorical outburst, but must be taken in bitter earnest, and only become intelligible when we picture the scenes which Persons witnessed again and again in the seaport towns of Spain. Englishmen, not only prisoners of war, but catholics of good family too, were employed as a matter of course by the Spanish government as galley-slaves, as if they had been criminals. Between 1590 and 1600, Persons himself, after a hard struggle with the Spanish authorities, liberated one hundred and thirty victims of Christian slavery whom he had found " in the galleys on the rowers' benches in extremest misery." [2]

And so, for the overwhelming majority of English catholics, the significance of the Armada year was— lasting estrangement from Spain, and renunciation once for all of a restoration by forcible means.

This movement in English catholicism corresponded with a similar change in the papal policy.   After 1588, the papacy turned away from vanquished Spain and, unwillingly enough, allowed the thought of conquering England gradually to fall into the background.   The altered attitude of the curia towards England is most clearly shown in the change in the treatment of Englishmen who visited Rome before and after 1588.   Previously to that decisive year, it happened fairly often that English

[1] Persons to Don Ydiaquez, Seville, April 4, 1591. KNOX'S *Card. Allen*, pp. 330 *et seq.*

[2] He obtained the freedom of ninety-three in 1591 at Cadiz, of thirty-four in 1598 in the harbour of Naples.   KNOX, *l.c.*, p. 329, note. T. G. LAW, *The Archpriest Controversy*, I. (Camden Soc., 1896), p. 37.   *Cf.* DOM. CAL., 1598-1601, pp. 101, 325.

protestants coming to Rome fell into the hands of the Inquisition and suffered imprisonment and torture, and, in a few instances, were burnt to death.[1] That they did not suffer loss of life in greater numbers is partly due to the fact that comparatively few English protestants went to Rome, partly, too, because the city of Rome never figured largely as a stage for burning heretics.   In any case, however, Rome was feared and avoided from choice by English travellers of the protestant persuasion in Italy.[2]

Matters, however, changed after England's victory over Spain.   There is very little evidence to show that Englishmen were imprisoned by the Roman Inquisition after 1588.[3]   No less a personage than William Allen, "the cardinal of England," acted as protector to his heretical fellow-countrymen.   After his deplorable exhibition of himself as herald of the Armada, he separated himself from the extremists.   Gentle by nature, and now advanced in years and longing for peace, he submitted without bitterness to a state of things he was powerless to alter. It is just in the last years of his life that he let fall

[1] A. MUNDAY, *The Englishe-Romayne Life* (1582), pp. 72-75; burning of Richard Atkinson for irreverence to the Sacred Host in 1581. Also in the Harleian Miscell., VII., p. 136. For other cases see STRYPE'S *Annals*, I., ii., p. 226; III., i., pp. 54 *et seq.*, 191; III., ii., pp. 187 *et seq.*

[2] Even Parry, the real or suspected conspirator against Elizabeth, avoided Rome in 1583, "spaventato dall' esempio di molti Inglesi mal trattati in Roma." The nuncio Campeggi to the card. of Como. Venice, April 16, 1583. Arch. Vat., Nunz. Venez. 24, pp. 146 *et seq. Cf.* Burleigh's undated instruction to John Arden to discover "by what meanes they [Englishmen in Rome] escape ether troobles or the danger of the Inquisition." Publ. Record Office, State Papers, Foreign, Italian States, 2.

[3] I find only one notice of 1600: "Some of our Englishmen are clapt up in the Inquisition." Letters written by J. Chamberlain, ed. S. WILLIAMS (Camden Soc., 1841), p. 71.

expressions of deep love for his native land.[1]   The gentleness which accompanies old age, combined with political considerations, may have induced him after 1588 to extend his protection to English protestants visiting Rome.   He protected them from the Inquisition and answered for their safety so long as they held their tongue and gave no scandal.   Only, to satisfy his sense of duty, he begged them to receive instruction in the catholic religion during their stay in Rome.   Allen's change of conduct soon became known, and it became the custom for protestants from England, while staying in Rome, to pay their respects to the cardinal.   One of these protestant visitors who enjoyed his protection, Fynes Moryson, saw him shortly before his death (1594), and describes the aged prince of the church as "of goodly stature and countenance, with a grave looke and pleasant speech."[2]

Yet it is by no means to be attributed to the cardinal's personal influence alone that the English were able to venture into Rome after their great victory, for the curia itself had changed its attitude.   Before 1588 English ships in Italian waters were not safe from the Inquisition.   In 1582 an English vessel was detained in Malta by the papal inquisitors, although the crew had given no provocation by any bad behaviour on their part.[3]   English seamen dreaded the "snares" of the Inquisition.[4]   In 1589, on the other hand, we find an English merchantman, *The Farewell*, provided with a papal passport, and, what is especially novel and surprising,

---

[1] *Cf.* especially his letter to Hopkins, Rome, Aug. 14, 1593. STRYPE'S *Annals*, IV., p. 203.   KNOX, p. 349.

[2] FYNES MORYSON, *An itinerary, containing his ten yeeres travell* (1617), p. 121.   New ed., Vol. I. (1907), pp. 259 *et seq.; cf.* III., p. 414.

[3] FOREIGN CAL., 1582, No. 211.

[4] *Ib.*, No. 162.

when, notwithstanding, she was seized along with her cargo in a Spanish port, the papal nuncio in Madrid exerted himself to obtain the release of the ship and her cargo of alum from the Spanish government. King Philip in granting the release represented to the pope that he might exercise more caution in furnishing English ships with passports.[1]

It is easy to understand that Philip II. objected to the encouragement given by his ally the pope to English ships in the Mediterranean. For Spain's war with England dragged on in the form of piracy, and, on the whole, Spain was getting the worst of it. In the three years between 1590 and 1593 eight hundred Spanish vessels were said to have fallen a prey to English privateers.[2] The statement may be exaggerated, but still the coasts of Spain were not safe for a moment from hostile inroads. Even a city like Seville, with the English seminary established within it, lived in constant dread of English freebooters.[3] If Sixtus V., in spite of all this, did not identify himself with the cause of Spain, but rather ceased to regard England as a hostile power after 1588, the explanation is chiefly to be found in the fact that the pope was not only the spiritual head of the church but also the temporal sovereign of the States of the Church—a district with extended coast-lines. Open hostility to England might have been quite as dangerous for the coasts of the Papal States as for the coasts of Spain. About the end

[1] The nuncio Annibale Grassi to Card. Montalto, Madrid, Jan. 6, 1589. " S. M^{ta} mi ha detto in questo proposito che prega S. Sta andar ritenuta in concedere più simili salvocondotti, perchè questi Inglesi sene serveno per venir a far la spia et altri mali." Arch. Vat., Nunz. Spagna, 35, fol. 61, 63.

[2] ALBÉRI, *Relazioni venete*, ser. I., Vol. V., p. 412.

[3] " Li aggravii et molestie che questa città sustiene perpetuamente delli heretici et corsarii inglesi." J. Creswell, S.J., to Clement VIII., Seville, April 19, 1593. Arch. Vat., Borgh. III., 124 g 2, fol. 52.

of the sixteenth century and the beginning of the seventeenth, the Holy House of Loreto was more than once in danger of being sacked by English freebooters.[1] It was not wise to provoke unnecessarily these dangerous visitors by putting vexatious restrictions on English shipping.

And again, Elizabethan England, thanks to its fleet of merchantmen, was reckoned among the powers of the Mediterranean. It was on friendly terms with the states of Northern Italy, especially with Tuscany and Venice. Its merchants went openly in and out of Florence and Venice untouched by the inquisition established in these states.[2]   By its trade with the Levant, England had influence in Constantinople. It throws light on the position held by the young sea-power in the world that the king of Poland, in 1590, should have thanked Elizabeth for her diplomatic support in the question of the adjustment of the boundaries between Poland and Turkey,[3] and that the Sultan, with oriental politeness, should have gone so far as to say that he had put a peaceable end to his quarrel with Poland for her sake alone.[4]   For a long time Sigismund of Poland gave the excommunicated queen

---

[1] Evidence in the Arch. della Sᵗᵃ Casa di Loreto.   I give one account in Appendix XXIII.

[2] F. MORYSON'S *Itinerary*, III. (ed. 1907), p. 413.   *Cf.* the *Relatione di Vinetia dell' anno*, 1591, Arch. Vat., Borgh. I., 8, fol. 337.   "Il libero commercio che quei signori permettono a molti Thedeschi, Inglesi, e d' altre nationi, che publicamente conosconsi per heretici, senza che al Santo Offitio si permetta di poterli inquirere, come sarria il dovere."

[3] Sigismund III. to Elizabeth, Warsaw, Aug., 1590: "Serᵗⁱˢ Vᵣᵃᵉ orator . . . ita se in negocio hoc tractavit, at partim Serᵗⁱˢ Vᵣᵃᵉ auctoritate interponenda, partim dexteritate, studio, opera sua magnum ad constituendam pacem eam momentum attulerit."   Publ. Record Office, State Papers, Foreign, Poland, No. I. (103).

[4] Eder Pasha to Elizabeth, June 26, 1590.   RYMER, *Fœdera*, XVI. (London, 1715), p. 74.   Elizabeth boasted of her success to the emperor, *l.c.*, p. 207.

the title of *Fidei Defensor*. It is true he desisted from this upon express warning from Rome,[1] but he still set a high value on his friendly relations with Elizabeth. And so England's friendship was sought from Portugal to Poland, and its flag respected from Gibraltar to the Bosphorus. By the events of a single year, 1588, the prestige attached to the chief sea-power and the reputation of invincible might passed from Spain to England.[2] Was the sovereign of the States of the Church to close his ports to English ships? Was he to swim against the stream and forbid the produce of the papal alum works to be conveyed to England? When Sixtus V., in 1588, desired peace with the island kingdom of the north, he only showed that he understood the spirit of the new age in which the natural and commercial interests of states once more took precedence over the quarrels between different religions. This change of attitude and ideas, slow at first but increasing, was silently acquiesced in by the papacy—not all at once, but gradually, as it grew accustomed to what it was powerless to alter.

The change of policy inaugurated by Sixtus V. was continued under Clement VIII. (1592-1605). Instead of thinking of a crusade, wiser methods were adopted, and the propaganda was carried on by spiritual weapons. Before long voices were raised in England that the new era of friendly dalliance with Rome was more dangerous

[1] Card. Montalto to the nuncio in Warsaw, Rome, Sept. 9, 1589. Arch. Vat., Nunz. Polonia, 23, fol. 210. The Polish chancery, in answer to the charge, laid the blame on an heretical employé, and stated that the fault had only happened once. THEINER, *Vetera Monum. Polon., etc.*, III. (1863), p. 123. As a matter of fact the title *Fid. Def.* occurs constantly up to 1589, and even after that occurs at least once (Oct. 3/13, 1590). See the letters of the king of Poland to Elizabeth in the Publ. Record Office, S. P., For., Poland, No. I.

[2] *Contarini's Relazione* of 1593. ALBÈRI, *op. cit.*, pp. 412-414.

than the era of excommunications.[1]   For all this, the idea
of invasion was not forgotten in Rome.   It came to the
front more than once, but was no longer able to effect
a return to the papal policy of the days before 1588.
When Philip II. was arming his last Armada (1597),
Clement VIII. discussed the possibility of invasion with
the French ambassador in Rome, Cardinal d'Ossat.   To
the objections of the cardinal, who had doubts as to the
practicability of the attempt, the pope replied that
England had been conquered in earlier times, and, therefore, the same thing could be done now.[2]   Still
Clement VIII. at no time went beyond considering the
question from an academic point of view.

Not even did he do so when, at the close of the century,
catholic Ireland rose against English rule and begged for
help from Rome.   The rebels still lived in the age of the
fighting popes, Pius V. and Gregory XIII., and the excommunication of Elizabeth, still fresh in their memory, served
to fan the flame.[3]   They besought the pope for extensive
moral support,[4] and, where possible, practical assistance.
It was impossible to refuse moral support to the catholic
rising, and so in the year of Jubilee, 1600, the pope bestowed
a crusade indulgence upon the leader of the rebellion, the
earl of Tyrone, " captain-general of the catholic army,"
and all his followers, " in order ye, both leader and soldiers,
may carry on the campaign against the heretics with the

[1] See the criticism on the policy of Clement VIII. by Sir Henry
Wotton in his letter to Salisbury, Aug. 18, 1605.   L. P. SMITH, *Life
and Letters of Sir H. Wotton*, I. (1907), p. 332.

[2] Card. d'Ossat to Villeroy, Feb. 1, 1597.   *Lettres de l'illustre . . .
Card. d'Ossat* (1624), pp. 250 *et seq.*

[3] Sir Thos. Norreys to the Privy Council, Cork, Dec. 9, 1598.
CAL. OF STATE PAPERS, IRELAND, 1598–99, p. 400.

[4] Undated petition of the "Dux generalis fœderatorum, Hugo
princeps Naelius," [*i.e.* Hugh O'Neill, Earl of Tyrone] to Clement
VIII., Arch. Vat., Borgh. III., 124 c, fols. 37 *et seq.*

greater alacrity."[1] It appears, moreover, he threatened the Irish adherents of Elizabeth with his ban,[2] but he did not repeat the mistake of Gregory XIII. by himself providing troops and ships (p. 263), and took care to pay no attention to the inopportune request to excommunicate Elizabeth afresh.[3] Men had given up hopes of bringing about better times for English catholicism by the overthrow of Elizabeth, but set their hopes on her successor, who, in the natural course of events, must take her place before long. The young king of Scotland became a more important personage in the conflict between England and the catholic church than the vanquished king of Spain.

And so 1588 was, in fact, a fateful year. A new era dawned both for English Catholics and the papacy. Nevertheless it would not be correct to regard the battle off Gravelines as in itself the determining factor. The victory of the English fleet merely confirmed a decision made long before. England's supremacy on the sea was, however, only *one* indication among many of the flourishing state of the country in general, and of the wonderfully varied development of the forces latent in the English people. These manifested themselves by a series of political and commercial successes, combined with a powerful outburst of poetic genius, and an awakening of the religious

---

[1] Bull of April 8/18, 1600. Publ. Record Office, State Papers, Ireland, Eliz., Vol. 207, pt. ii., No. 95. " Ut vos, ac dux et milites prædicti, alacrius in expeditionem hanc contra dictos hæreticos opem in posterum etiam præstare studeatis . . . plenariam omnium peccatorum suorum veniam et remissionem ac eandem, quæ proficiscentibus ad bellum contra Turcas, etc. . . . in Domino concedimus." *Cf.* above, p. 286, note 2.

[2] CAL. OF S. P., IRELAND, 1599–1600, p. 494; 1600, pp. 135, 250, 257.

[3] In O'Neill's petition it is said: " Petit, ut sententia excommunicationis a Pio V. lata contra reginam Angliæ et ejus adhærentes a S^{mo} D. N. innovetur in auxilium præsentis belli."

spirit, the like of which the world had scarcely ever seen. The first great protestant power came forward to take its place in history, a match for the greatest nations of the past.

England's development contradicted the catholic conception of the world, which was based upon the assumption that worldly prosperity was bound up with the profession of the true faith.   Spain's possession of so many rich countries was understood, and not alone by Spanish writers, as the divine reward for the catholic policy of her kings.[1] When for a short space England was brought back into communion with Rome by Mary the Catholic (1554), Charles V. thought that with the ancient faith the ancient felicity would return too.[2] Alberto Lollio, the orator and poet, composed a well-turned oration[3] in which he prophesied that now the land would grow in power and the glory of its name would resound from north to south, from the Indian to the Moorish seas, and be beloved by friends and dreaded by enemies. The prophecy came true, but not in the way the orator intended. It was fulfilled not by the catholic England of Mary, but by the protestant England of Elizabeth. A catholic, rather than admit that an heretical country could flourish and prosper, would shut his eyes to plain facts.[4] The protestants, too, were deeply impregnated with belief in the inner bond between religion and worldly well-being. The leading spirits of Elizabethan England never tired of pointing the moral

[1] See G. Riedel, *Draconicidium* (Ingolstadt, 1691), p. 82, quoted by Krebs, *Politische Publizistik der Jesuiten* (Halle, 1890), pp. 85, 204.

[2] Conversations of the emperor with the English ambassador, Nov. and Dec., 1554. P. F. Tytler, *England and Ed. VI. and Mary*, Vol. II. (1839), pp. 455, 458, 464.

[3] *Nel ritorno dell' Inghilterra all' obedienza della Sede Apostolica, etc. Delle orationi di* M. Alberto Lollio, Vol. I. (Ferrara, 1563), p. 173ᵛ. Also in the *Orationi volgarmente scritte da diversi huomini illustri de' tempi nostri*, lib. i. (Vinegia, 1584), p. 117.

[4] *E.g.* Persons, in the work mentioned on p. 351, note 1.

that their country began to prosper just at the time it broke away from Rome. Lord Burleigh seldom found more eloquent words than those in which he described the fulness of blessing bestowed by God on the England of Elizabeth. "By Gods singular Goodnes, her Kingdome hath enioyed more vniuersall Peace, her People increased in more Nombers, in more Strength, and with greater Riches, the Earth of her Kingdoms hath yeelded more Fruits, and generally all Kind of worldly Felicitie hath more abounded since and during the Time of the Popes Thunders, Bulles, Curses, and Maledictions, then in any other long Times before, when the Popes Pardons and Blessings came yerely into the Realme ; so as his Curses and Maledictions haue turned backe to himselfe." [1]   Francis Bacon followed up Burleigh's train of thought when, in 1592, he drew a picture of England in which he contrasted it first of all with its own past, and secondly with the condition of contemporary Europe—both contrasts being of a nature to heighten the picture of the Elizabethan age : "Whoso-ever hath been an architect in the frame therefore . . . needs not to be ashamed of his work." [2]

And Queen Elizabeth herself, in spite of her lack of religious feeling, placed great store on the fact that the catholic world should realize that Heaven was with her and her protestant people. When the historian, Girolamo Pollini, who lived in Florence, wrote a misleading account of schismatic England, Elizabeth addressed a forcible letter to the Grand Duke of Tuscany,[3] and begged him

[1] BURLEIGH, *Execution of Justice* (1583), Somers Tracts, I. (1809), p. 204.   Harleian Miscell., II. (1809), pp. 150 *et seq.*

[2] BACON, *Observations on a Libel*, etc., II. ; *Of the present state of . . . England, whether it may be truly avouched to be prosperous or afflicted. Works*, ed. SPEDDING, VIII., pp. 153–177.   See also BACON'S *In felicem memoriam Elizabethæ, Works*, VI., pp. 291 *et seq.*

[3] Of April 6/16, 1592.   To the best of my knowledge the letter is

to suppress the slanderous work. The assurance bred of success and the self-consciousness of the mistress of an aspiring nation find expression in this letter. Those slanders must be false, "for it is clear as daylight to the world that God's blessing rests upon us, upon our people and realm, with all the plainest signs of prosperity, peace, obedience, riches, power, and increase of our subjects." The letter concludes with the haughty declaration that Elizabeth rules over her country with success and honour "in spite of the hostility of no inconsiderable monarchs." [1]

Thoughts such as those which Burleigh, Bacon, and Elizabeth laid before catholics on the continent, had something of the obviousness of a truism for Englishmen at home. It is inconceivable that English catholics who lived in the midst of their country's progress at home could avoid being affected by the national sentiment of pride in the greatness of their country. Many even of those living abroad did not escape its influence. An exile who had passed twenty-eight years out of England, Anthony Standen, could not restrain himself when an opportunity of returning home was presented to him. "An extraordinary longing burned within me once more to see it before I die, and also my serene queen and gracious lady,

hitherto unknown. State Archiv., Florence, Sez. Medicea, 4183, fols. 30, 31. The original is signed, "Dalla Nostra Reggia di Westmynster, alli 6 d'Aprile, 1592," etc. The particular letter of Pollini which Elizabeth had in view I have been unable to determine. His *Historia ecclesiastica della rivoluzion d'Inghilterra* did not appear until 1594.

[1] ". . . chiarissimamente apparisce al mondo la benedittione di Dio sopra di Noi, del nostro popolo et regno con tutte le più certe marche di prosperità, di quiete, d'ubbidienza, di ricchezze, di forze et d'aumento di sudditi . . . È piaciuto all'Omnipotente Dio di farci heredi di così grande padre et glorioso re, di cui nessun'altro fu nel suo tempo di più alta famma, et di esser noi Sacra Reina di questi christiani regni, gli quali noi per divina gratia con grande prosperità et honore reggiamo contro la nemicitia di non piccioli prencipi . . . "

who rules over it with so much felicity."[1] The sense of joy at the greatness of Elizabethan England could not indeed allay the conflict between church and country, but it had great weight on the side of patriotism, and thereby exercised a pacific influence.

A further modification of the conflict arose from the general reconstruction of the political situation brought about by the conclusion of the French wars of religion. The leader of the huguenots, Henry of Navarre, became the catholic Henry IV., king of France. His relations with Elizabeth were for a time impaired owing to suspicions roused by his conversion to the Roman church, but, owing to the alliance formed between France and England against Spain, the catholic king was as much the ally of England as he had been when leader of the huguenots. In May, 1596, this offensive and defensive alliance between England and France was concluded at Greenwich. With it, England's relation to the catholic church entered upon an entirely new phase ; for the first time since the establishment of the Elizabethan church settlement, England became the ally of a catholic power. Communion of political interests was stronger than even their differences in the matter of religion.

Small as was the political and military importance of this compact, still, in the development of the relations between England and the catholic church, it meant the opening of a new era. To begin with, it was an innovation that Elizabeth should send two ambassadors for the

---

[1] ". . . mi si accese una voglia straordinaria prima che morire di rivederla [*i.e.* mia terra natia] insieme con questa mia Ser^ma Regina et benignissima signora, la quale con tanta felicità la regge et governa." Anthony Standen to the Grand Duke of Tuscany, whose servant he had been for many years, *Di Grassinne* [Gray's Inn] *ne'borghi di Londra alli* 7 *di Luglio* 1593. State Archives, Florence, Sez. Medicea, 4185, fol. 226.

ceremony of swearing to the alliance—one a good protestant, the other a staunch friend to the catholics. To
place in this way the two religions on an equal footing
appeared obviously the best solution of the diplomatic
difficulty.   The cardinal legate resident in Paris did not
know whether he ought more to rejoice over the one
ambassador or take umbrage at the other.[1]   He did his
best to obtain that the investiture of Henry IV. with
the Order of the Garter should not take place with full
solemnity in church, but less solemnly in the audience
chamber, or if in church, then at least " near the door and
at the hour of vespers."[2]   His endeavours to rob the
solemn act of its glory, however, were quite as fruitless as
his later remonstrances over the enormity of a friendship
between His Most Christian Majesty and the heretical
queen.[3] All this opposition was out of date ; just as it was
to no purpose, and bordering on the comic, to protest
against history by refusing to give Elizabeth the title of
queen in the official language of papal diplomacy, and to
speak of her as " she of England " or bluntly as " the bad
woman " (*la mala femina*).

The curia found it difficult to fall in with the new
current of affairs, but the English catholics were very
thankful. The *rapprochement* between the English government and a catholic power tied the hands of the persecutors. What Spain's threats were unable to accomplish

---

[1] In the dispatch of the nuncio in Paris, Oct. 24, 1596, he says of
the catholic ambassador : " Ha visitato in Roano molte chiese, per
modo però di vederle, et ha mostrato in confidenza non piccolo
desiderio di conoscere l'ill^mo legato"; and of the protestant ambassador :
" L'altro è tutto il reverso, ostinato nel suo errore et alienissimo dalla
fede cattolica."   Arch. Vat., Borgh. II., 464, beginning.

[2] " Circa il dare la gerettiera a Sua M^ta Chr^ma il sig. legato fece
qualche officio, acciò almeno non fosse ricevuta in chiesa, parendoli
che fosse manco errore il pigliarla privatamente in camera," etc.   *L.c.*

[3] Dispatches of the nuncio at Paris, Oct. 8 and Nov. 25.   *L.c.*

was brought about by the friendly advances of France.
As soon as the preliminaries of the alliance were set on
foot in the summer of 1595, the persecution diminished,
and the dreaded Topcliffe fell for a while into disgrace.[1]
As ,long as the arms of England and France were united
against Spain (1596, 1597), the number of death sentences
pronounced against catholics fell to half or a quarter of
the average in the preceding and following years, but the
moment France dissolved her alliance with England, the
breathing space for English catholics came to an end.
When Henry IV. concluded the peace of Vervins with
Spain in May, 1598, leaving England to carry on her war
with her ancient enemy single-handed, the number of
executions of catholics at once rose to its old figure.[2]

England's alliance with France had at first scarcely any
other significance for English catholics than that about a
dozen of them escaped the gallows. The real significance
of this period of scarcely three years' improvement in
their lot lies just in this, that it showed catholics a way
in which they might possibly find salvation from their
misery. By alliances, not by war, the catholic nations of
the continent might come to their aid. The union of
England with a catholic power whether by treaty or
by marriage, formed the political programme of English
catholics for the next ninety years. The seventeenth
century saw the realization of this programme to a degree
which they could never have dreamt of in Elizabeth's

[1] "Multum imminuta est persecutio catholicorum in Anglia, licet
non permittatur liberum catholicæ religionis exercitium," etc. As
causes for this, the influence of Henry IV. was set down in the first
place. *Ex relatione Gabrielis Colfordi, nobilis Angli qui* 16° *Junii*
[1595], *appulit Antverpiæ ex Anglia.* Arch. Vat., Borgh., II., 448,
ab fol. 335. *Cf.* Father Holt's report in KNOX, *Douai Diaries*,
p. 379.

[2] Statistics in POLLEN'S *Catalogue of Martyrs*, Cath. Record Soc.
Publ., V. (1908), p. 14.

time.   The marriage policy of the house of Stuart, rich
in consequences for the dynasty, brought with it the
desired alliance with a catholic power, and led to times
of refreshing for English catholics, which fell little short
of actual religious freedom.   But the first glimpse of this
future state of affairs was given by this short period of the
Anglo-French alliance at the end of the sixteenth century.

Only the irreconcilables, with Robert Persons at their
head, regarded the new departure with anxiety.   They
longed to see England under the sway of a catholic
sceptre, neither more nor less!   Every compromise was
distasteful to them.   An alliance between England and
France was to them altogether unendurable ; it destroyed
their dream of a Spanish succession to the English throne,
and doomed to disappointment the hopes still cherished
by a man like Persons.   "The king of France will never
suffer the Spaniards to come nearer to him than they are
already," explained the leading French statesman, Béthune,
in reply to the fruitless representations of the Jesuit.[1]
If Persons had not yet admitted this, he had to admit it
now.   His idea of catholic England's liberation by Spain,
whether by invasion or succession, was a phantom which
faded away in the light of common day.   The lamentable
failure of the last Armada (1597)[2] forced from him, too,
the reluctant avowal that "the forces of the Spaniards do
not correspond to either their wishes or ours."[3]   Towards
the close of the century, a tone of resignation makes itself
occasionally felt in his correspondence.   He scarcely
ventures to hope that there will be at least a clause in

[1] COUZARD, *Une ambassade à Rome sous Henri IV.* (Paris, 1900),
p. 79.

[2] M. A. S. HUME, *Treason and Plot.   Struggles for Catholic
Supremacy in the last years of Eliz.* (London, 1901), pp. 250 *et seq.*

[3] J. H. POLLEN, *The Question of Elizabeth's Successor*, The Month,
May, 1903, p. 531.

favour of the English catholics inserted in the articles of agreement. When this opportunity too was lost, the idea struck him at last that it was now too late, and a great change and discouragement would come upon the English catholics.[1]

In the curia itself, people were tired of him and his schemes. With the death of Philip II. (September, 1598) his sun set, and for a long time Persons was completely laid on the shelf in Rome. When doors were closed to him through which he had for so long passed freely in and out, he found it hard to bear. The papal chamberlain put him off whenever he requested an audience of the pope, and the cardinal nephew, Aldobrandini, was always occupied whenever Persons called.[2] From marginal notes which the cardinal made from time to time on the reports sent in by the nuncios, it is quite clear that they had more than enough of his high-flown plans for securing a catholic succession to the English throne, each one of them as impracticable as the other. Power had always been wanting, and now, since Philip's death, the will was wanting too. When a premature report of Elizabeth's death was current in the summer of 1600, the nuncio wrote from Brussels[3] that the English catholics had proposed to the governor, the archduke Albert, that as soon as Elizabeth was dead he should dispatch three regiments of infantry to England and proclaim the Infanta Isabella queen while the pope should send word to the catholics of England that they were to support the Spanish troops. This last[4] plan of invasion,

[1] R. Persons to Card. Aldobrandini, Naples, Aug. 7, 1598. Arch. Vat., Borgh., III., 124 g 2, fol. 18.

[2] R. Persons to Card. Aldobrandini, Rome, Feb. 13, 1599. Arch. Vat., Borgh., II., 448, ab fol. 244.

[3] Ott. Mirto Frangipani to Card. Aldobrandini, Brussels, June 24, 1600. Appendix XXII.

[4] Or last but one, for the same project reappeared in 1602. POLLEN, *The Accession of King James I.*, The Month, June, 1903, pp. 579 *et seq.*

belonging to Elizabeth's time, merely drew from the cardinal the peevish gloss—" the pope is weary of the general coldness," [1] a reproach aimed at the feeble policy of Spain in general and at the archduke Albert in particular. Another time he remarked upon the proposal that the pope should regulate the succession to the English throne, " Fine words, but what's the good of it ? " [2]   And on yet another occasion, " It is easy to talk.   Who is the man whom the pope could name with any chance of success ? " [3]

In Rome no one was deceived as to the fact that the settlement of the succession to the English throne was beyond the reach of the pope's power.   There was naturally, a wish for a catholic successor, and when the decisive moment seemed approaching, the pope encouraged the English catholics to give their support only to a catholic candidate.[4]   Still no one in Rome was clear who the catholic successor was to be, or was willing to be drawn into political complications for his sake.[5]   People felt the less inclined to interfere in the course of events because they had formed the highest hopes of Elizabeth's presumptive successor, the king of Scotland.   While the pope was yet hesitating whether or not to adopt a policy of strict

[1] The note on the margin is difficult to decipher, but it seems to be : " Questo e quello straccan il papa, il veder la debolezza et la freddezza di tutte le parti."   Appendix XXII.

[2] " Bel discorso ! ma che iuva ? "   Note by Aldobrandini on the margin of a dispatch of the nuncio Frangipani in Brussels, July 15, 1600.   Arch. Vat., Borgh., III., 98 c I., fol. 126.

[3] " È facile il discorrere.   Veggia chi è quello che possa nominare il papa con speranza di riuscita ? "   Note by the cardinal on Frangipani's dispatch of Aug. 19, 1600.   L.c., fol. 165.

[4] Letter of July 12, 1600, to the archpriest and clergy of England ; printed in my article, *Klemens VIII. and Jakob I.* in Quell. u. Forsch. aus ital. Arch. u. Bibl., VII. (1904), p. 278.

[5] More fully in POLLEN, *The Question of Elizabeth's Successor*, The Month, May, June, 1903.

neutrality on the question, James VI. of Scotland finally influenced his decision by his system of clever double-dealing.   The king knew how to rouse and keep alive in Rome the hope that when once he was at the head of affairs, a catholic era would begin.[1]

So far as the papal policy comes into the question, the historian might pass over in silence these phantastic attempts to obtain the succession of a Spaniard or of some one dependent on Spain, but he cannot do so in view of the inner development of English catholicism ; for the long-existing cleavage of catholics into two hostile factions was intensified, and their sad dissensions were painfully embittered by the controversy over the succession to the throne.   Blindness and fanaticism alone could give rise to this controversy, for it was nothing else than a meaningless anachronism after the defeat of the Spanish Armada.

[1] The details are given in my article referred to, p. 374, note 4.

CHAPTER IV

DIVISIONS AMONGST ENGLISH CATHOLICS

IT is the purpose of this book to represent England and the catholic church as hostile powers on the stage of history, and to trace the internal development of English catholicism only in so far as it bears upon the conflict between reformation and counter-reformation. The picture of party strife, which we shall attempt to portray in what follows, may therefore seem at first sight out of place in this work. Still it cannot be omitted without injury to the picture as a whole. For, first, these internal quarrels are closely interwoven with the external disputes, and their result—the prolonged divisions among English catholics—turns upon the question of Rome's authority in England. Then, secondly, the domestic disagreement derives its importance from the fact that it is the repetition in miniature of what had been happening on a large scale in the world ; the great conflict between national ideas and the universal church which fills English history during the sixteenth century is here once more fought out within a confined space. If, consequently, the story of these manifold disagreements cannot be omitted here, it is, nevertheless, more imperative in this connection than in any other question relating to the history of English catholicism to confine our remarks to the chief points in the series of events. For nowhere else do purely personal considerations—and that too in their pettiest and narrowest

forms—obtrude themselves into the struggle so persistently
and so prominently as here.   The fundamental questions
round which the contest waged can only be distinguished
after close examination, and the fact alone that the struggle
lasted for a generation, during which individual actors
came and went, proves conclusively that the conflict arose
out of matters of real moment and was not due to personal animosities.   The large part which this element
of personal bitterness played in the strife of parties has
caused the sources for this unpleasant chapter in the
history of English catholicism to be so numerous that no
investigator has hitherto succeeded in fully mastering them.
And, paradoxical as it may seem, an exhaustive use of
the documents at our disposal might in this case lead to
confusion rather than to clearness.

I. *The Period of Disorganization among the English Clergy*

The disunion among English catholics started with the
priests, and from them spread to the catholic laity.   The
part played by the latter, however, was always secondary,
and they never actively interfered in the conflicts among
the clergy.   The first signs of dissension among the clergy
appear as early as 1577, *i.e.* three years after the beginning
of the catholic mission from Douay.[1]   The imprisoned
Mary Stuart, wary and well-informed as she was, at once
impressed upon Allen, the leader of the mission, the necessity
of exerting himself to preserve unity among the different
parties.[2]   From Allen himself we have a detailed memorandum, written also in 1577, as to the cause of these misunderstandings, which leaves no room for doubt on the

---

[1] The mission began in 1574, *vid. ante*, p. 132.
[2] Mary Stuart to Card. Allen, Aug. 3, 1577.   LABANOFF, *Lettres de Marie Stuart*, IV. (1844), p. 376.   Also in KNOX's *Card. Allen*, p. 30.

question. "The cause wherof this is specially (which many one seeth not that reprehendeth yt) that in this state of things our catholice churche or the religques and seede thereof in England hath no forme of externall common wealth, no one that governeth the rest, no discipline or censures neyther to dryve the preists nor people into order, no man subject to his fellowe, no way to call disorders to accoumpt, no common conference, no soveraignty nor subjection; but every one living severally and secretely by himself, and often farre frome any fellowes, is ruled onley by his owne skill and conscience; which even amonge the apostoles had bredd disturbance, yf by sundry meetyngs, counsels, and conferences yt had not bene looked unto."[1]

The want of organization among the catholic priesthood, due to the destruction of the ancient hierarchy, produced a state of things calculated to foster misunderstandings and factions among them. Seeing then, between 1570 and 1580, it was not mere insignificant matters which were under dispute, but the really important question connected with the cure of souls—whether attendance at protestant worship should be permitted or not [2]—it would have been strange if nothing but perfect peace and concord had prevailed between the old priests surviving from catholic times, who plied their ministry in hiding places and travelled about from place to place, and the young mission priests trained in the strict observances of the seminary. In what form their different ways of looking at things found expression is not recorded. The silence of our sources of information points to the conclusion that an open breach was avoided.

Whether the dissensions between 1570 and 1580 were

[1] Allen to P. Chauncy, Aug. 10, 1577. KNOX, p. 35.
[2] *Vid. ante*, p. 201 ; *cf.* pp. 68 *et seq.*

serious or not, the view which the secular clergy put forth twenty years later, at a time when the quarrel turned chiefly upon the question of organization, is untenable, *i.e.* that the disturbances had been first introduced into the hitherto peaceful mission by the Jesuits and their schemes.[1] That people should subsequently reproach the Jesuit missionaries for their first attempts to create some sort of organization, *i.e.* their modest efforts at synodical action in 1580 (p. 201), and treat it as a sign of their lust for domination, can only be explained by the bitterness which prevailed at a later period.[2] In all this the Jesuits had only done what the father of the secular mission, William Allen, had indicated a short time before as a pressing need ! It is quite possible, and indeed probable, that even in these first attempts at drawing up certain rules for the work of the mission, they had to contend against the suspicions of the other missionaries. When the English college in Rome was placed under Jesuit government in 1579 (p. 111), a warning was given by the secular clergy that the Jesuits did not understand English ways, and that their "trade of syllogizing" did not go down with English people.[3] Yet as, notwithstanding, the sources for the history of the mission between 1580 and 1590 say practically nothing about disputes between seculars and Jesuits, we must conclude that the tact of

---

[1] [JOHN MUSH] *Declaratio motuum ac turbationum, quæ ex controversiis inter Jesuitas . . . et sacerdotes seminariorum, etc.* (Rhotomagi, 1601), p. 82.

[2] See the quotation in T. G. LAW, *A Historical Sketch of the Conflicts between Jesuits and Seculars in the Reign of Q. Eliz.* (London, 1899), p. xxii.

[3] "That the Jesuits have no skill nor experience of our country's state, nor of our men's nature ; and that their trade of syllogizing, there [in Rome], is not fit for the use of our people." Words of the priest Hughes recorded by Allen. *DODD-TIERNEY, Ch. Hist. of Engl.*, II. (1839), p. ccclxx. Also in KNOX'S *Card. Allen*, p. 82.

the first Jesuit superiors had been successful in over-
coming all suspicions. Along with isolated statements
which point to the existence of *occasional* friction,[1] we
find expressions which would have been simply impossible
if the peace of the mission had been seriously disturbed.
When news of the disturbances in the English college
in Rome and the rebellion of a certain number of
the students against Jesuit rule (1585, p. 112) reached
England, the Jesuit missionary Southwell could give expression to his amazement that the demon of discord
should have been able to put asunder in Rome what in
England was so closely united.[2]   And so those complaints
of the secular priests are nothing else than a natural
ante-dating of subsequent feelings and misunderstandings.

We may suppose that *before* the Armada year things
had certainly not come to an open quarrel.   It nevertheless appears that the blow dealt to the catholic cause
by Mary's death made an epoch also in the divisions
among English catholics.[3]   Again, *after* 1588, we see
nothing more than the broad division into a minority
favourable to an invasion and a majority hostile to it
(p. 355).   There is no indication as yet of definite hostility
between Jesuits and seculars such as appears after 1590.

However, the attitude taken up with regard to the

---

[1] As early as 1585 we find complaints of the domineering spirit of
the Jesuits in England among the grievances of those students of the
English college who were under the influence of secular priests.   See
Appendix XIX. [§ 32].   *Cf.* also the contradictory complaints of the
Jesuits.   LAW, *Archpriest Controversy*, II. (Camden Soc., 1898),
p. 80, and the statement made about 1595—"Nunquam defuerunt
æmulationes in Anglia et privatæ discordiæ inter eos et sacerdotes
nostros."   DODD-TIERNEY, III., Appendix, p. lxxvii.

[2] Letter of Dec., 1586.   POLLEN, *Unpubl. doc.*, I. (1908), p. 315.
Cath. Record Soc. Publ., V.

[3] USHER, *The Reconstruction of the English Church*, I. (1910),
p. 143, note 1.

question of invasion was closely connected with that of the succession to the English throne. Elizabeth's feelings as a sovereign were actively opposed to a legal settlement of the succession during her lifetime, and she also threatened with death, as felonies, all private predictions and prophecies concerning her probable successor.[1] This uncertainty about the heir to the throne gave all the greater scope for secret schemes. The catholic exiles on the continent had left their country in the hope that the next change of government would bring back a catholic era, and they manifested the most decided opposition to the idea of a protestant successor. It happened that Philip II., the protector of the English catholics, like many other European princes, could boast of a king of England among his ancestors, for he was descended from Edward III. in the eighth degree.[2] This gave at least the semblance of legal justification for the idea of a Spanish-Hapsburg succession to the throne of England. As soon as the direct heir to the throne was removed out of the way in Mary Stuart (Feb., 1587), the leaders of the exiles, William Allen and Robert Persons, S.J., became immersed in genealogical studies in order to forge legal weapons for their master, in addition to the Armada which he was preparing.[3] But the drawing up of so extensive a genealogical tree was no easy task in the existing state of knowledge, and, with the help they had at their disposal in Rome, remained imperfect.[4] The papal and Spanish

[1] 23 Eliz. c. 2, § 5 (1581).

[2] The table of descent is given most clearly by J. H. POLLEN, *The Question of Q. Elizabeth's Successor*, The Month, 1903, p. 520.

[3] Memorial of March, 1587. KNOX, *Card. Allen*, pp. 281–286. *Cf.* SPAN. CAL., 1587–1603, p. 43.

[4] " Per non haver hauto qui l'historie et croniche Inglese insieme con quella varietà de genealogia che in Parigi et altrove haveriamo havuto non è etato possibile far quella essata calculatione." KNOX, *l.c.*

manifesto of 1588, which endeavoured to justify the invasion,[1] is silent upon Philip's claims as heir, not only from political reasons but probably from genealogical reasons as well. The defeat of the Armada put an end for the time to studies of this kind.

The opposition between those who favoured the invasion and those who opposed it—the Spanish and anti-Spanish factions—was thus unaffected at the time of the Armada by the controversy over the succession to the throne. Even Persons, the leader of the "Spanish party," was in nowise so Spanish as his opponents wished to make out later on. He was ready at any time to recognize any catholic successor who was strong enough to hold his own. His only reason for favouring the Spanish succession more than another was because—even after 1588—Spain was the only power that could interpose on behalf of the catholic pretender in England with any chance of success, small though it might be. Persons never advocated the union of England and Spain under one sceptre, it was not King Philip, but his daughter, who was to inherit Elizabeth's throne. It is worthy of notice that the papal diplomatist in Madrid, under whose eyes Persons worked between 1590 and 1600, the nuncio Caetani, specially praised the Jesuit's skill in steering a middle course[2]—a piece of evidence which the historian may not indeed accept as impartial, though it must be weighed against equally one-sided judgments of a hostile nature. The idea of the Spanish succession, as Persons understood it, was not conceived as an attempt upon England's political independence ; but even so it was an idea which could only have taken shape in the head of a man who was out of

---

[1] See more particularly, pp. 323–328.
[2] See Caetani's dispatch of Nov. 6, 1596.   BELLESHEIM, *Card. Allen* (1885), pp. 290 *et seq.*

touch with his fellow-countrymen.   It is as if Persons had
not lived to see the year 1588.

Three years after the decisive action of the war, in 1591,
the controversy over the succession took a new shape.
The question so thoroughly tabooed by the queen was now
being discussed among the puritans.   Peter Wentworth, a
member of parliament, ventured to write a book on the
succession.   "It was a great sin to tempt God," he said,
"by protracting the establishment [of the succession] . . .
Until a successor is appointed, the papists will never cease
to practise against [the queen's] life ; but they would then
cease in fear of a heavier yoke." [1]   Wentworth, thereupon,
brought the matter before parliament in 1593, and had to
atone for this piece of audacity by going to prison.[2]   It
was certainly advantageous to the well-being of the
commonwealth that there should be no ambiguity on a
question, uncertainty as to which had on former occasions,
and that not so long ago, led to civil war.   Now was the
moment for Persons also to bring to light the plans which
he had matured in silence for seven years.   He might be
quite certain, when in 1594 he came before the public with
his "conference" on the succession, published under a pseudonym,[3] that his book was one which dealt with a burning
question of the moment.   The importance of the book lay

[1] Wentworth to Burleigh, Sept. 27, 1591.   DOM. CAL., 1591–94,
p. 107.   Wentworth's production of 1591 is not forthcoming.   It must
have agreed in substance with *A Pithy Exhortation to her Majesty for
establishing her Successor to the Crown*, by P. WENTWORTH, published
in 1598 along with his answer to Doleman (Persons), *vid. ante*, p. 328,
note 3.

[2] See article on P. Wentworth in the *Dict. of Nat. Biogr.   Cf.*
DOM. CAL., 1591–94, p. 484 ; POLLEN'S *Elizabeth's Successor, l.c.,*
p. 523.

[3] R. DOLEMAN [*i.e.* Persons], *A Conference about the next
Succession of the Crowne of Ingland, Imprinted at N. with licence,*
1594.   A MS. Latin version of 1596 is in the Arch. Vat., Borgh., IV.,
103 ; *De regiæ successionis apud Anglos jure libri duo, etc.*

in its being not a private venture but the programme of a party. "Before yt was printed," the author assures us,[1] "yt passed through the handes and viewe of the wisest and gravest Inglish catholickes lyvinge then in banishment," among them Cardinal Allen and Sir Francis Englefield.[2] This assurance, although given only after the death of the persons named, is thoroughly deserving of credit. Englefield had expressly declared his approval, after the appearance of the book;[3] and in 1587 Allen had already taken part in the genealogical researches on which the book was based.

In this work, Persons starts with the proposition that succession according to the degree of blood-relationship is not of divine but of human law, and can be altered for grave reasons. Religion is a reason of this kind. With the help of a genealogical tree of wide ramifications, Persons indicates, along with James VI. and Arabella Stuart—Elizabeth's nearest blood relations—some ten other princes or nobles who had more or less right of succession. He prudently refrains from coming to a decision as to who was the worthiest. He does not reject unconditionally the king of Scotland, though he distrusted him, and men at that time held very different opinions about him.[4]   But still he makes the object of his " Perfect

[1] "Wherof twoe ar now deade and therefor I may name them ; our late cardinall in Rome and Sir Francis Inglefield in Spayne, others ar yet alyve and yt is not perhaps convenyent to mencion them." Persons to the Earl of Angus, Jan. 24, 160⁹. Pub. Record Office, State Papers, Foreign, Italian States, 2.

[2] Privy councillor and member of parliament under Queen Mary, lived in banishment since 1559 supported by a pension from Spain. *Dict. of Nat. Biogr.*, Vol. XVII., p. 372. *Cf.* Appendix I..

[3] He regards the succession of the Infanta as "el mejor y mas suave [medio]." Englefield to Philip II., Sept. 8, 1596. DODD-TIERNEY, *Ch. Hist. of Engl.*, III. (1840), Appendix, p. l.

[4] "The poyntes that maye invite are his youth, his beinge a kynge, his moderate nature in that he hath shed little blood hetherto,

and Exact Arbor and Genealogy "—the Spanish succession —to appear clearly enough. The daughters of Philip II., the Infanta Isabella, and Catherine married to the Duke of Savoy, figure as the worthiest heirs, and of the two sisters again, Isabella is given the higher place—"a princesse of rare partes both for bewty, wisdome and pietie." [1]

The book was understood by both parties as a defence of the Spanish-Hapsburg succession. Persons passed among his fellows as the "discoverer" of the Spanish claims upon the English throne,[2] and King Philip ordered the welcome book to be at once translated into Spanish.[3] It gave, however, a fresh impetus to the spirit of discord among English catholics, and caused the deepest indignation in anti-Spanish circles. "It is the most pestilential thing ever written." Constitutional feeling at the same time rose up against a purely dynastic conception of the succession to the throne. "In every way Persons will make England into an absolute monarchy, by fair means or foul."[4] It availed not that the followers of the Jesuit

his affection in religion to such as like therof, and the like ; but on the other side, the reasons of state before laid against him, do seeme to be of very great force and to weigh much with Inglishmen, especially those of his allyance with the Danes and dependance of the Scottish nation. And as for his religion, it must needes displease two parties of the three before mentioned [i.e. Protestants, Puritans, Papists], and his manner of government therein perhapps al three." DOLEMAN [PERSONS], II., pp. 248 et seq.

[1] Ib., II., p. 256. Cf. p. 263.

[2] Sir Francis Englefield to Philip II. (1596), DODD-TIERNEY, III., Appendix, p. li.

[3] At least it seems to me that a passage in a dispatch of the nuncio in Spain can only refer to Person's book. "Si stampa per ordine di Sua Mᵗᵃ un libro tradotto [dall'] inglese in castigliano, nel qual si mostra che quel regno di ragione tocca a questa corona." The nuncio Camillo Borghese to Card. Aldobrandini, Madrid [March 26], 1594 (deciphered in Rome on April 27), Arch. Vat., Borgh., III., 94 c, fol. 277ᵛ.

[4] "È cosa la più pestilentiale che si sià mai scritta . . . 83 [i.e. Persons] vuole in ogni maniera l'assoluta monarchia d'Inghilterra

described his book as a mere investigation of facts in which
"the author only weighed the pros and cons without
favouring one party more than another."[1]   It was in vain,
too, that Persons himself defended his work on these lines,
and denied the imputation that it was aimed against the
king of Scotland.   "If he is a catholic, nothing is said
against him, but rather much in his favour."[2]   When
speaking in confidence, Persons left no room for doubt that
when he wrote the book he considered the Scottish king's
conversion out of the question.[3]   King James himself was
intensely annoyed at this book, in which a controversial
aim was veiled beneath the disguise of a scientific inquiry.[4]
With the increase of disunion from other causes among
English catholics between 1594 and 1600, the more bitter
became the judgment passed upon the author and, along
with him, upon the whole Jesuit order.   Owing, at last, to
the underlying connection between the questions of the succession and the invasion, the Jesuits, or their leader, Robert
Persons—for in the controversial literature of the time the
two terms are used indiscriminately—figured as the real
culprits of 1588.   The priest Watson regarded the Armada
as "an everlasting monument of jesuiticall treason and

per fas et nefas."   Dr. W. Gifford to Thos. Throgmorton, undated
[1594 or 5].   Arch. Vat., Borgh., IV., 209 B, fol. 197.   Cf. DOM. CAL.,
1595-97, No. 66, I.

[1] " Per quello che io ho notato nel libro, ch'io ho letto più volte,
mi pare che tutte le pretensioni si dichiarano con tanta indifferentia
allegando le ragioni solamente pro et contra, che non mostra di
favorire più una parte che l'altra l'autore."   From an unsigned memorial
addressed to the pope, which from internal evidence is to be ascribed
to 1595 ; Le differenze che sono tra gl' Inglesi cattolici sopra la
successione, etc.   Arch. Vat., Borgh., IV., 209 B, fol. 198 201.

[2] In the letter to Angus mentioned on p. 384, note 1.

[3] Persons to Creighton, 1596.   KNOX, Card. Allen, p. 382.

[4] "Atrociter regem offendit," Edw. Drummond [James' ambassador]
to the Grand Duke of Tuscany, undated [winter of 1599–1600], State
Archives, Florence, Sez. Medicea, 4183, fols. 74 et seq.

crueltie." [1]   To another secular priest, John Mush, Persons himself seemed to be an incendiary guilty of causing all sorts of external and internal disturbances. By the way he mixed up religion and politics, by the way he promoted the invasion, and, lastly, by this book of his on the succession, Mush considered he had exasperated the English government to the last degree, and had stirred them up to a war of extermination against his innocent co-religionists. Little was wanting to give the penal legislation against the catholic church the appearance of being the consequence of this unscrupulous book—contradictory as such an idea would be to the actual course of events. "We have to do penance at home for his sinning abroad." [2]

In the same year, 1594, in which Persons stirred up the strife over the succession by his book and thereby increased the divisions of the catholic camp, the chief support of unity among English catholics disappeared from the scene. Cardinal Allen closed his weary eyes on October 16. Death saved him from witnessing the quarrels which his highly venerated personality might, at any rate, have lessened, but had not been able to prevent. To those indeed who had been most closely united with him in the controversy, the Jesuits, his death seemed to be a punishment sent by heaven for his inward breach of fellowship with them, the chosen champions of God's church.[3] William Allen had been in a difficult position since 1588. We have told already how, when overwhelmed by the crushing disappointment of a great disaster, he had dissociated himself inwardly from the extremists, and, partly from the need of peace in his old age, and partly from

[1] [W. WATSON] *Important Considerations*, etc. (Newly imprinted 1601), p. 25.

[2] "Quicquid ille foris peccat, nos domi plectimur."   [JOHN MUSH] *Declaratio motuum*, etc. (Rhotomagi, 1601), p. 24.

[3] See Agazzari's words quoted below, p. 389.

considerations of prudence, had met his protestant fellow-countrymen in a friendly spirit (p. 359). As he retired from the arena of politics, he once more resumed with renewed ardour his beloved studies and the performance of the religious duties of his office, in which he had formerly found his greatest delight. It was natural that the man under whose direction and with whose assistance the Rhemish Bible (p. 98) came into existence should be called by the pope to sit on the commission which ever since its institution by the Council of Trent had been occupied in the revision of the text of the Vulgate.[1] The Spanish ambassador in Rome, Count Olivares, speaks of the cardinal in 1591 as being quite engrossed in his work, and the best informed member of the commission, and the strongest opponent to any alteration in the text.[2] In addition, he busied himself with a critical edition of the works of St. Augustine.[3] Under Gregory XIV. he became cardinal librarian of the Holy See. His own study and the Vatican library formed the quiet world in which the life of the English cardinal drew to a close.

This last phase of Allen's earthly career led, as its necessary consequence, to a certain degree of estrangement between him and his former companions. It must have been during these years that John Mush, the secular priest heard Allen repeatedly declare that Persons was "a man of too violent and hard a nature."[4] There was,

---

[1] More fully in A. BELLESHEIM, *Wilhelm Cardinal Allen* (Mainz, 1885), pp. 186 *et seq.*

[2] Olivares to Philip II., Rome, April 28, 1591. KNOX, *Card. Allen*, p. 332.

[3] N. FIZERBERTI, *De . . . Alani Card. vita libellus* (Romæ, 1608), p. 89.

[4] The open letter of John Mush to Persons, London, Nov. 13, 1600: "Well, well, F^a Parsons, I pray God send you a more sincere and quiet spirit. I finde that true daily more and more, which

indeed, no absolute breach between the cardinal and the prominent Jesuit. By his antecedents, Allen was too deeply committed to the cause for which Persons and the other Jesuits were still contending. He owed his cardinal's hat to the king of Spain. His name was attached to the *Admonition* of unhappy memory which was to have prepared the way for the invasion of 1588.[1] And so Allen could not, without being untrue to his own past, have raised a protest when the momentous book on the succession was submitted to him for his opinion. Although a breach was avoided, the estrangement was nevertheless felt, and Allen's death was accepted by the Jesuits with relief. Alfonso Agazzari, S.J., rector of the English college, who was in close touch with Persons, gave vent to this feeling of relief in words which, in their *naïveté*, give an almost startling insight into the inner life of these zealots who regarded themselves as God's chosen instruments. " In fact," wrote Agazzari,[2] " it seems to me a great indication of God's will and a great sign of the love He bears to the Society (of Jesus), to the college, and to the cause of England, that, when human means fail, He, as it were, miraculously puts forth His divine hand. While Allen remained true to the Society, the Blessed God preserved and advanced him, but, as soon as he began to forsake this way, in a moment the thread of his plans and of his life was severed." Since

often I heard good Cardinal Allein, Father Holt and others of your owne coate report of you : that you were a man of too violent and hard a nature." Printed by [WILLIAM BISHOP] in *The Copies of Certaine Discourses which were extorted from divers*, etc. (Roane, Ja. Walker, 1601), p. 178. *Cf.* also on the question of Allen's estrangement from the Jesuits, T. G. LAW, *A Historical Sketch of the Conflict between Jesuits and Seculars* (1889), p. 16, note 1.

[1] *An Admonition*, etc. *Vid. ante*, p. 326, note. 1.

[2] Agazzari to Persons, Sept. 25, 1596. KNOX, *Douay Diaries*, p. 387.

Persons, on another occasion,[1] evinced the same spiritual arrogance, and the same chilly lack of charity, and had the same unshaken belief that only those affairs in which he was interested met with God's approval, we may consequently regard this spirit, not as something singular and personal, but as typical, and we are bound to take it into consideration when forming a judgment in the conflict now beginning between Jesuits and seculars.

Not long after Allen's death the conflict burst into flame almost simultaneously in Rome and England. According to the account of the seculars, the Jesuits' "insolencie burst foorth as a flame that had bin long suppressed."[2]   According to the Jesuits' account, the spirit of unbridled licence had set itself against all rule and authority.[3]   From the bitterness of feeling shown and the length of time this conflict lasted, one thing alone is clear at the start—on both sides there was an accumulation of ancient grievances. Charges such as those of ambition and insubordination throw little light on the subject.   The catholic clergy of England, indeed, were not less lacking in cohesion at this time than they had been ever since the start of the mission ; no all-embracing organization, no hierarchical system, held them together. Who then was the master and who the rebel ?

The answer is easily given with regard to the small battlefield of the English college in Rome. There the

[1] See the short paper of 1589, *An observation of certayne apparent iudgments of Almightye God againste such as have beene seditious in the Englishe Catholique cause.*   Printed by J. H. POLLEN, Cath. Record Soc. Miscell., II. (1906), pp. 202–211.

[2] [CHRISTOPHER BAGSHAW] *A True Relation of the Faction*, etc. (1601), reprinted by T. G. LAW, *Conflict of Jesuits and Seculars*, p. 17.

[3] KNOX, *Douay Diaries* (1878), pp. 368–375 ; Memorial of Dr. Worthington and Dr. Percy to Card. Caetani, the Protector of England (1596).

Jesuits were the masters, and a number of scholars rose in rebellion against them about 1595. This college outbreak attracted attention [1] far beyond its immediate neighbourhood. An Englishman living in Florence wrote to Sir Robert Cecil, Elizabeth's minister, at the beginning of 1595 that in the management of the college "the Jesuites have showed themselfes not such sayntes as the world thinkes ; they rest in such termes as a litle help would dissolve yt [the college]." [2] Although it was the most dangerous storm which had arisen in the seminary, it was not the first. To say nothing of the quarrels which broke out in the year of its foundation,[3] the system of education followed by the Italian Jesuits and the espionage practised by the " guardian angels " had once already (1585) led to a rising against the heads of the establishment.[4] From the severity with which this rebellion was put down at the time, it is not strange that a second disturbance should break out from the same causes. And as a matter of fact, the same causes were at the bottom of the disturbances of 1585 and 1595.[5] But then there were other causes as well, which had nothing whatever to do with the training given in the seminary. The students brought charges against the Jesuits which could only have come to their knowledge through the secular clergy at work in England. They charged the Society of Jesus with aiming at the supremacy over the entire English mission and at a monopoly of the education of

[1] [WATSON] A decacordon (1602), p. 69. " All Europe talking of the iars there, by reason of the Jesuits tyrannicall government."

[2] Ger. Markham to Sir Rob. Cecil, Florence, Feb. 2, 1595. Publ. Record Office, State Papers, For., Ital. States, 2.

[3] I.e. the quarrels between English and Welsh students.

[4] Vid. ante, pp. 105-108, 113 et seq.

[5] Cf. the reports of the two visitations, that of 1585 in Appendix XIX., and that of 1596 in Bibl. Vat., Ottob., 2473, fols. 187-226, given in English in FOLEY'S Records, VI. (1880).

priests.   This charge had been heard indeed in 1585,
but only in general terms,[1] but now, ten years later, it is
insisted upon and supported by an appeal to facts.   The
Jesuits, so it was said, find readier welcome in the houses
of leading catholics than secular priests, because they
have authority to dispense the holders of church property
from censures.   The payments made in compensation
are diverted by the Jesuits to their own uses and not
expended, as they ought to be, upon those suffering
under persecution.[2]   Serious reasons for believing these
charges are not forthcoming ; but the assertion that the
Jesuits possessed the spiritual authority in question is
true,[3] for it seems the Jesuit missionaries had been
furnished with special privileges after the death of
Cardinal Allen.[4]

How is it possible that the students of the seminary in
Rome found cause for complaint in things of this kind,
which did not immediately concern them ?   There is only
one answer to this question—an answer already given
by the Jesuits ; the English secular priests, who fancied

[1] Report of the visitation of 1585, Appendix XIX. [§ 32].

[2] "Patribus [Soc. Jes.] . . . nobilium et magnatum ædes multo
facilius patent, eorum præsertim, qui ecclesiastica bona occupant,
quia nimirum huius rei veniam concedendi ab hac sancta sede patres
facultatem habent ; occupatores vero cum satisfactionis nomine certam
pecuniam dependere teneantur, hanc sollicite colligunt patres atque
in suos usus convertunt, quæ potius in subsidium eorum distribui
deberet, qui varias variis in locis pro Christi fide persecutiones
patiuntur. . . . Jam vero si cui sæculari sacerdoti aliquæ etiam
[facultates] ab hac sancta sede fuerint concessæ, iis tamen præ patrum
metu vix ille audet uti."   From the Report of Sega's visitation of the
English college in Rome, 1596, Bibl. Vat., Ottob., 2473, fol. 200.
In English in FOLEY, loc. cit., p. 20.

[3] See the faculties given to Jesuit missionaries in 1580.   Appendix
XVII., A [§ 6], and B, 3.

[4] Report of Mons. Malvasia to Card. Aldobrandini (1596).
BELLESHEIM, History of the Catholic Church in Scotland [Eng.
trans., 1889], Vol. III., pp. 460 et seq.

themselves thrust into the background, kept up secret communications with the alumni of the English college.[1] Jealous of the Jesuits, who were furnished with more ample faculties than themselves, they attempted to under-mine their position at its very centre, in Rome itself. According to a highly probable statement of Persons, the source of this anti-Jesuit agitation was not in England itself but in the Netherlands.[2]   And indeed a number of those who stirred up these quarrels in Rome had, as a matter of fact, passed from the Douay-Rheims seminary (under the management of secular priests) to the English college.[3]   The English seminaries in Spain, equally under Jesuit management, were not selected by the seculars as objects of attack, for it promised better success to locate their centre of operations in the chief city of the catholic church, where favours, graces, and spiritual faculties were to be bestowed.   While the rebellion of the Roman students was going on, the Jesuit Joseph Creswell [4]

---

[1] *E.g.* the anonymous memorial of Jesuit origin drawn up in 1595, *Le differenze che sono tra gl' Inglesi cattolici*, etc., and presented to the Pope, Arch. Vat., Borgh., IV., 209 B, fols. 198-201.

[2] Persons to [Blackwell(?)], 1598.   T. G. LAW, *The Archpriest Controversy*, I. (Camden Soc., 1896), p. 28.   For the divisions among English catholics in the Netherlands, see LACHAT, *Les réfugiés anglais dans les Pays-Bas* (Louvain, 1914), pp. 160 *et seq.*

[3] Memorial drawn up by Worthington and Percy in 1596. KNOX, *Douay Diaries*, p. 371.   The account which E. L. TAUNTON gives in his *Hist. of the Jesuits in Engl.* (London, 1901), p. 177, as usual, blames everything done by the Jesuits and passes over in silence the underhand dealings of the seculars.

[4] J. Creswell, S.J., to Card. Aldobrandini, Madrid, Sept. 14, 1595 : " Questi [collegii inglesi] di Spagna non sanno che cosa è dissentione per star liberi del tratto di spie et mali huomini che fuggono il pericolo della inquisitione spagnuola et ci lasciano vivere in pace." Arch. Vat., Borgh., III., 124 g 2, fol. 72.   There were disturbances in the Spanish seminaries also, at the beginning of the seventeenth century, between Jesuits and Benedictines.   See the articles by POLLEN and CAMM in The Month, Oct., 1898, Sept., Oct., 1899.

wrote from Madrid : " The seminaries in Spain know nothing of dissension because they are free from spies, and evil men who flee from the danger of the Spanish Inquisition, and let us live in peace." The assertion, made by Creswell and others,[1] that in the stirrers-up of sedition one must recognize spies of the English government, may have been an erroneous, though quite conceivable,[2] generalization, drawn from particular instances. Similar fears must have existed in Rome. In order to calm the uneasiness, it seemed to Cardinal Sega, the visitor of the English college, that the first most pressing need was to place an English priest in charge of the English colony in Rome, and to bring some rather dubious individuals among them under ecclesiastical supervision.[3]

We see, therefore, that the charge brought forward by the Jesuits of unrestrained licence being the cause of all disturbances both in England and Rome is not altogether without foundation. Still it would be an exaggeration simply to attribute, as the Jesuits do, the dissensions in Rome to the underhand machinations of the seculars. These latter could scarcely have found the ground so well prepared in the English college to receive their seed, had not the chief of the Jesuits, Robert Persons—quite apart from the mistakes made by the authorities in the management of the students—stirred up excitement in Rome, too, by his unfortunate book on the succession. This is quite clear from a report which the rector Agazzari sent during the disturbances to the author of the book, who, in spite of his

---

[1] *E.g.* in a letter of *Dottore Thornello*, canon of Vicenza, May 24, 1596 : " Senza ogni dubio la regina d'Inghilterra ha la sua parte in questa fattione." Westminster Cathedral Archives, V., p. 177.

[2] *Vid. ante*, p. 172.

[3] See the conclusion of the report of the visitation of 1596, *l.c.*, fol. 226ᵛ. FOLEY'S *Records*, VI., p. 66.

pseudonym, was well known.[1] " [The rebellious students]
speak frequently and cuttingly against the book on the
succession to the English throne and against its author,
that is to say Father Persons, as they think, and they can
hardly endure to hear his name mentioned. All openly
rejoice over the Spanish reverses, as, for instance, lately at
Cadiz,[2] and grieve over their successes, as recently at
Calais.[3] I know not whether they hate the Society (of
Jesus) more on account of the Spaniards, or the Spaniards
on account of the Society, or both on account of the
Scotchman[4] or the Frenchman,[5] or for some worse
reason still." The alumni, says an English Jesuit, are
so hostile to the Spaniards that they cannot endure the
sight of them and refuse to raise their hat to the Spanish
ambassador.[6]

The causes of the college revolt are thus essentially
laid bare ;[7] they are threefold, (1) the students rebelled
against a discipline which was not frank and open,
(2) they were incited against their Jesuit superiors by the
secular clergy, (3) their national feeling revolted against
the idea of the Spanish succession and especially against
the Spanish policy of the Jesuits.

Cardinal Sega, the papal visitor of the college,
endeavoured to restore the impaired discipline by siding,
with all the weight of his authority, with the heads of
the college. But the result was unsatisfactory. A few

---

[1] Agazzari to Persons, Rome, Aug. 27, 1596. DODD-TIERNEY, III.,
Appendix, p. lxxv.

[2] The descent of the English on Cadiz, June 20/30, 1596.

[3] Calais taken by the Spaniards, April 14/24, 1596.

[4] James VI., next heir to the throne.

[5] Henry IV., the ally of England.

[6] DOM. CAL., 1595-97, p. 356.

[7] To this must also be added that the students wished to have an
Englishman, and not an Italian, as their rector.

months after the visitation, the rector Agazzari complained that the peace of the college was still in a precarious condition.[1] "We have gained nothing here so far beyond a certain outward show of peace and quiet in avoiding scandals." To the rector's distress, the pope and the cardinal protector, Caetani, declared themselves satisfied with the result and refused to interfere further. This dread of scandal on the part of the ecclesiastical superiors played into the hands of those among the alumni who opposed the rector. In the late summer of 1596, six months after the visitation, Agazzari wrote to Robert Persons in Madrid that the agitators could twist the cardinal protector round their little fingers, for both he and the pope were sick of the disturbance and noise, and desired peace at any price, while the opposition party had sworn to withstand the Jesuits to the uttermost. "They have such a hatred against the Society that I fear that they would be ready to join hands with the heretics in order to be delivered from them, as the French have done, in order to withstand the Spaniards."[2]

Persons, who was residing in Spain, realized from Agazzari's cry of alarm how matters stood. Merely to keep in order a body of unruly alumni, he would not have hastened over land and sea and placed himself finally at the head of the English college. It was not the discipline of an ecclesiastical seminary only which was upset, it was the reputation of the English Jesuits in Rome, and their

[1] Agazzari to Creswell in Madrid, Rome, July 28, 1596 : "Nec aliud hactenus lucrati sumus nisi externam quandam significationem pacis et quietis ad vitandum scandalum et offensionem proximorum." West. Cath. Archives, V., p. 207.

[2] Agazzari to Persons, Aug. 27, 1596. "Tantum enim odium in Societatem conceperunt, cui ut aversentur timeo quod etiam cum hereticis se conjungerent, sicut Galli faciunt, ut resistant Hispanis." *L.c.*, fol. 215.

share in the management of the mission in England, which were in danger. Their enemies were certain that Persons was the one man who, at this juncture, thanks to the important recommendation he brought with him from Spain, won over the pope to the side of the English Jesuits and prevented their recall from England.[1] Before leaving Madrid—ostensibly for the purpose of informing the pope of the state of the English seminaries in Spain—Persons took care to prepare the ground for himself in the curia. The nuncio at the Spanish court, in a report [2] to the chief mover in papal politics, Cardinal Aldobrandini, was ready to bear flattering witness to the activity of the leader of the English Jesuits in the mission, in the management of seminaries, and in political affairs, to his behaviour and character, ability, and practical knowledge of everything connected with English catholicism. Owing to these warm recommendations, Persons was able to win over influential personages to his side, and to secure for the Jesuits the direction of the English college, and, for a time at least, their position in Rome and England. His skill in dealing with men was shown more remarkably than ever with respect to both superiors and inferiors. Persons had ranged against him the hatred of the seminary students, the loss of the confidence of the ecclesiastical authorities, and, in addition, the lack of energy of the heads of the Jesuit order themselves.[3] He made concessions to the alumni, yielded to their just demands, listened to what they had to say with so much

[1] CAL. OF STATE PAPERS, DOMESTIC, 1598–1601, p. 61.

[2] Of Nov. 6, 1596. BELLESHEIM'S, *Allen*, pp. 290 *et seq.*

[3] " When I came to Rome, I found the Collegde as a field with two hostile campes, within it, Father Generall, and his assistants wholly aversed and thoroughly resolved to leave the government." Letter of Persons of July 13, 1598. [WATSON] *A decacordon*, etc. (1602), p. 127. LAW, *Archpriest Controversy*, I., p. 29.

patience and good will that in a few days he had won over the youths. One of them, who had inveighed most loudly against Persons, declared afterwards : " He whom we most feared and whom we accounted for our greatest enemy had been our greatest friend." [1] Persons took credit to himself that his appearance on the scene had saved the college.[2] His triumph within the college was enhanced by his equally complete victory in the curia. He had long negotiations with the cardinal protector and the pope, the particulars of which did not transpire. He did not have an easy time of it—" I found [these troubles and disagreements here in Rome] to be greater and more deeply rooted than ever I could imagine, though I had heard much " [3]—but his satisfaction was all the greater in the end. In September, 1597, only a few months after the restoration of peace, some of the students who were ordained priests were sent to England. At the audience which the pope was wont to give the young priests on such an occasion, one of them, who had been a ringleader of "the discontented," delivered the customary address to the pope. Clement VIII., whose custom on former occasions had been to reply with all suavity, this time represented to the priests in emphatic terms that they had enjoyed the benefit of ecclesiastical education in Rome, alluded to the example given by the martyrs of a supernatural strength which sprang from humility, and, in conclusion, inveighed strongly against the unchristian spirit of pride from which no good was to be hoped. Persons, who was himself present at this stormy scene, had every reason to

[1] Edward Bennet to Hugh Griffin, May 16, 1597.   DODD-TIERNEY, III., Appendix, pp. lxxx. *et seq.*

[2] [PERSONS] *A Manifestation of the Great Folly* (1602), fol. 36.

[3] Persons to Father Holt, S.J., Rome, May 5, 1597.   DODD-TIERNEY, III., Appendix, p. lxxviii.

be satisfied with the change in the pope's manner.[1] He
was all the more pleased because Clement VIII. was
essentially cooler in his attitude towards the Jesuits than
his predecessors had been, and was in no wise impressed
with the idea that the order was indispensable to the
world's existence.[2]

Persons attached a significance to the restoration of
peace in the English college which extended far beyond
the walls of the institution and the walls of Rome itself.
He considered his position and that of the Jesuits at the
papal court now so secure that he spoke of peace with the
Society having been established not only in the English
nation, but everywhere else.[3] If Persons really entertained
this belief, we can only wonder whether he fell into the
error of over-estimating his own influence, or into that of
under-estimating the hatred and mistrust which had
sprung up against the Jesuits. Not even in England, let
alone everywhere else, was the conflict at an end. The
pacification of the English college by the enforcement of
Jesuit rule was anything but an earnest of peace. The
students of the college might, indeed, have less to complain of in future as to mistakes in the system of education,
for Persons, who, not-long after his successful intervention,
took over permanently the rectorship of the college, held
sounder views on the education of youths than had
hitherto obtained under the regime of the Italian Jesuits.
Straightforwardness and confidence seemed to him the
best principles to adopt with young people. "And for

---

[1] *Responsum S^{mi} D^{ni} N^{ri} Clem. VIII.*, West. Cath. Arch., VI.,
p. 191. Printed from another source by LAW, *Archpriest Controversy*,
I. (Camden Soc., 1896), p. 4.

[2] See the words of the pope to Dr. Barret (Sept., 1596) : " Putasne
quod totus mundus periret si Societas [Jesu] relinqueret guberna-
tionem ? " KNOX, *Douay Diaries*, p. 386.

[3] Persons to Holt. DODD-TIERNEY, III., Appendix, p. lxxix.

spyeries and sentinels . . . [that] is the waye to mar all." [1]
The watchfulness of the new rector may also have
been successful in suppressing attempts of the seculars
to stir up agitation, and in putting a stop to all
grumbling against the Jesuits' Spanish policy. But in
spite of all this, the stone of stumbling for the secular
priests in England was not yet removed out of the way,
i.e. the unfair competition, as they felt it to be, in the
affairs of the mission and the programme in favour of the
Spanish succession ! The seculars, after the Jesuits' victory
in Rome, had all the more reason for complaint at the
course things were taking at home.

In England, too, the conflict between Jesuits and seculars
broke out first of all within a small area. Wisbeach Castle
in the diocese of Ely,[2] already mentioned, within which
many priests were imprisoned, was the scene of the earliest
"stirs." Some thirty priests, of whom the authorities
did not wish to make martyrs but desired to render
harmless, were detained there at their own charges in
a sort of easy confinement. Owing to the indulgence
of the keeper of the castle, the life of the prisoners
became a standing evasion of the penal laws against
catholics to which no parallel is to be found elsewhere
in Elizabethan England. The priests received visitors,
went to and fro in the town, did pastoral work and,
when able, received converts.[3] And so in Wisbeach
Castle, for the first time since the persecution of catholics
began, an opportunity was given for English priests to live
and work together on English soil, sharing a common

---

[1] Persons to Creswell (1591).   POLLEN, *St. Alban's Seminary
Valladolid 1602-8*, The Month, Oct., 1899, p. 359.

[2] *Vid. ante*, p. 165.

[3] LAW, *Conflicts between Jesuits and Seculars* (1889), pp. xxxviii.
et seq.

dwelling and a common table—in fine to live a common life. Disputes over the domestic arrangements among the prisoners were the cause and prelude to more important disputes about the organization of the English clergy, and from them sprang dissensions among the whole body of English catholics.

Among those imprisoned at Wisbeach, we find the Jesuit William Weston, known as Father Edmund, who, before his imprisonment, had held the office of superior of the English Jesuit mission.[1] He was a man of strictly ascetic life, who felt himself called to be the censor of his fellow-prisoners. Feeling how powerful a high standard of conduct would be for the fame of the catholic mission, Weston persuaded the majority of his companions in misfortune, in February 1595, to join him in binding themselves to follow a strict, but by no means monastic, rule of life, and, at the same time, to elect him as the superior of the community. Weston's successor and superior, the head of the English Jesuit mission, Fr. Henry Garnet, gave his consent and reported what had been done to the general of the Society of Jesus.[2] The out-voted minority resisted the introduction of a special rule of life as meaningless for prisoners, and protested most of all against the setting up of any disciplinary authority on the part of the Jesuits over the secular clergy. The "stirs" among the prisoners in Wisbeach Castle became noised abroad. Priests and catholic laymen throughout the country took sides either for or against the Jesuit superior of Wisbeach. The one side waxed wroth over the ambition of the Society which brought discord into every community, and did not even stop

[1] *Instructions of 24th March*, 1586, Arch. Gen. S.J. Instructiones an. 1577–96.

[2] Letters of Weston's party to Garnet. Wisbeach, Feb. 7, 1595 ; Letter of Garnet to Acquaviva, London, July 12. DODD-TIERNEY, III., Appendix, pp. civ.–cix.

short at prison walls ; they inveighed against the want of moderation of these zealots who alone fancied themselves capable of maintaining law and order, " as if the catholicke faith had neuer beene trulie preached nor any good order rightlie established or practised by us poore secular priests." [1]   The other side gladly welcomed the fact that the order which had deserved so well of the mission should assume the direction of the priests at Wisbeach and considered, moreover, all opposition to the powerful Society useless.[2]

It was disastrous for English catholicism that these domestic broils coincided with the beginning of better times for the persecuted catholics.   The laxer application of the penal laws, introduced in the summer of 1595 (p. 371), only made the spread of these internal divisions possible, for, until then, the pressure of persecution had kept the warring elements together.   The contending parties themselves already clearly recognized the disciplinary value of their time of suffering.[3]   Priests from outside succeeded in establishing peace once more among the prisoners at Wisbeach.   With tears of tenderness the opponents celebrated their reconciliation in November, 1595, and, in a new set of rules signed by all of them, threatened that all future disturbance of the peace should be punished with a fine.[4]   Still the irritation caused by all sorts of insignificant things remained, and,

---

[1] BAGSHAW'S *True Relation* in LAW, *Jesuits and Seculars*, p. 54. *Cf.* pp. 30, 37.

[2] *Ib.*, p. 48.

[3] Wm. Holt, S.J., speaks of the " persecutio quæ instar disciplinæ ecclesiasticæ plurimos in officio continere consuevit."   Memorial of 1596.   KNOX, *Douay Diaries*, p. 379.

[4] *Orders agreed upon to be observed by us whose names are above written*, Wisbeach, Nov. 6, 1595.   West. Cath. Arch., V., pp. 97–104; Report of the mediators Dudley and Mush to Garnet, Nov. 8. DODD-TIERNEY, III., Appendix, No. XX.

towards the end of 1596, scarcely anything survived of the
new regulations.[1]   Worse still, the divisions amongst
catholics throughout the country became more pronounced
also.   The fruitless controversy over the succession to the
English throne, which Persons had evoked, did its work
of breeding discord in England, just as it had done in the
English college in Rome.   Fantastic as the idea of the
Spanish succession was, it was quite clear that its originator had a following behind him.   The initiated thought
that if the pope was minded to support the succession of
the king of Scotland, he would first have to recall all the
Jesuits and their friends from England.[2]

To this grave difference in political views, however, were
now added all those petty vexations arising from jealousy
over the cure of souls—vexations, not indeed confined to
England, but observable more or less universally wherever
the Society of Jesus entered into the practical life of the
church.   The "stirs" among the students of the English
college already described (p. 391), show that the complaints of the English secular priests sprang from a
grievance well known at that time—the exclusion of the
secular clergy from influential positions in the pastorate
of souls by the more businesslike Jesuits who possessed
fuller faculties.   Wherever they were able—so those who
were ousted complained[3]—the Jesuits either insinuated
themselves in person or worked through other clergy
dependent upon them.   "And if happilie there be any

---

[1] BAGSHAW, *Relation* in LAW, *l.c.*, p. 67.

[2] Letter of John Petit, a well-informed agent of the English government in the Low Countries, who kept in touch with the catholic
mission.   Oct., 1597.   DOM. CAL., pp. 520 *et seq.*

[3] What follows is taken from the *Brevis declaratio miserrimi
status catholicorum in Anglia degentium* of 1597.   West. Cath.
Arch., VI., pp. 203-209.   English translation in LAW, *Jesuits and
Seculars*, pp. 97-110, with notes on the authors of the memorial.
Cf. the similar memorial in LAW, *Archpriest Controversy*, I., pp. 7-15.

that do deny the faculties graunted by them, or will not take notice that such assemblies or companies of catholicks depend on them, or will not obediently (as it were at a beck) execute those things that they haue commaunded, such shall be censured either as apostataes, or hereticks, or taynted at least with some infection of heresie. So holie, so godly, so religious would they seeme to be, as nothing is holie that they haue not sanctified, no doctrine catholick and sound that commeth not from them, no dispensation auailable that is not graunted by them, and, which is worse, they haue beaten into the heads of the most, that the masse is not rightly and orderly celebrated of any but a Jesuite!" Furthermore the Jesuits were charged with seeking to divert all alms and offerings to themselves in order to go about "in great gallantry," and travel "from one place to another . . . richly apparelled and attended on by a great train of servants," as if that were the only way of concealing their priesthood.[1] Through their ambitious desire that England should be converted by them or not at all—so said the seculars—they were professedly working for the destruction of the seminary for secular priests at Douay, and were endeavouring by obstacles and threats to prevent students from being sent there from England. In a word, the object of these attempts was spiritual supremacy over all England and over the entire English clergy!

These complaints bear the mark of party feeling and malicious exaggeration, and yet, on the other hand, they

[1] With regard to this complaint, *cf.* the description of English missionaries on p. 205. With regard to the charge of inaccurate book-keeping, see also DOM. CAL., 1598–1601, p. 139. I do not go into the question of the conflict over alms, but merely state that the final decision of the pope on the whole archpriest controversy (the brief of Oct. 5, 1602), decided also the question as to the alms. DODD-TIERNEY, III., Appendix, p. clxxxii.

undoubtedly contain a nucleus of fact. Partisans of the Jesuits praised them—to mention one point alone—just for their readiness to sacrifice themselves and render every assistance in their power, and for their charities, which far exceeded the alms they received and made heavy claims on their own resources.[1] This is not the place to lay down the limits between truth and invention in these conflicting judgments. It is sufficient to show here to what lengths the bitter feeling had already gone before the actual strife broke out. After the heroic period of the mission from 1570 to 1590, a relapse into human frailty quickly followed. A letter of expostulation written by a secular priest (about 1600) concludes all the complaints against the Jesuits with the gloomy general confession: " The spirit which ruled in the seminaries in our fathers' time—unquenchable zeal for souls—is extinct ! " On one occasion indeed,[2] Robert Persons, to encourage the down-cast, made the pertinent remark that quarrels between regulars and seculars reach far back into the early middle ages, and so are no sign of deterioration.[3] This judg-ment shows not only historical insight, but still more clearly the man's unshaken belief in the victory of the catholic cause and in the mission thereby laid upon the Jesuits. Possibly the feeling that they were God's chosen instru-ments was more strongly impressed upon the English Jesuits, who laboured amid such grave difficulties, than upon

---

[1] Blackwell to Card. Caetani, 1597. LAW, *Jesuits and Seculars*, p. 138.

[2] Undated memorial of one *Bascheus* (Bagshaw ?). Incip. *Ad reformanda ea quæ circa regimen ecclesiasticum* . . . Expl. *hyerarchiam ordinariam non observari innotescimus.* A mutilated copy is in Bibl. Vat., Barb. lat. 8618, fols. 48–52 (the quotation is from fol. 50).

[3] PERSONS, *A Storie of Domesticall Difficulties*, ed. POLLEN in Cath. Record Soc. Miscell., II., p. 51. *Cf.* LAW, *Archpriest Controversy*, I., pp. 116 *et seq.*

those working in other countries. When Father Gerard, S.J., held out under the frightful tortures on the rack which were repeated on several successive days, and yet did not reveal the hiding-place of his fellow Jesuit Garnet, he said of himself, with a remarkable mixture of humility and pride: " If there was any strength in my soul, it was the gift of God, and given, I am convinced, because I was a member of the Society, though a most unworthy one." [1]   These men believed and openly declared that no other order was so useful to the church as the Society of Jesus.[2]   The comparison with a second baptism, which had been applied to the vows of renunciation of the world in the early days of Christianity [3]—so hotly attacked by Luther as " monks' baptism "—was applied by these men to reception into the Society.[4]   From the lips of the very men who went to the furthest extremes of self-abasement fell words of self-appreciation bordering on irreverence.   When the Jesuit Southwell—the poet who delighted in visions of the other world—was asked his age by the examining magistrate, his answer was " that he was about the age our Saviour was of when He was brought before Pilate." [5]   The Scotch Jesuit and heroic martyr, John Ogilvy, rejoiced to play the same part.   When the Archbishop of Glasgow boxed his ears, he exclaimed: " I thank my God that in this I am like unto Christ," and in the midst of his tortures on the rack, he groaned, " Lord, forgive them, for they know not what they do ! " [6]

[1] JOHN MORRIS, *Life of Father Gerard* (3rd ed., 1881), p. 247.

[2] FOLEY'S *Records*, Vol. I. (1887), p. 170.

[3] *E.g.* by St. Jerome and St. Bernard.   H. DENIFLE, *Luther u. Luthertum*, I., i. (2nd ed., 1904), pp. 228 *et seq.*

[4] *Cf.* Southwell's words in POLLEN, *Unpub. doc.*, V., p. 297.

[5] POLLEN, *op. cit.*, p. 334.

[6] Report of March, 1615, composed of letters to the rector of the Scots' college in Rome.   Bibl. Vat., Barb., 8618, fols. 117–119.

These and similar touches contribute scarcely anything new to the psychology of the Jesuit order in the first century of its existence,[1] but they must at least be mentioned here in order to explain the bitterness against the Society which grew up among the neglected and slighted seculars. The secular priest Watson thought[2] "the Jesuits would take it in scorne to haue any poore secular or seminarie priest compared with them in prudence and pollicie." Allowing that the Jesuits had many reasons for the high estimation they had of themselves, and granting that they were the most active force in the catholic church at that time, still the want of consideration for others, in which this feeling found vent, coupled with the idea, natural to them, that opponents of the order were opponents of the church, could not fail to arouse indignation.

The "stirs" among the prisoners at Wisbeach over their domestic concerns—a constitutional conflict on a small scale—first set all this long smouldering bitterness ablaze. Still these squabbles were a mere storm in a teacup compared with the conflict, to which they were the prelude, concerning the constitution of the catholic clergy in England as a body. In this conflict, the numerous and varied differences between seculars and Jesuits, centring round individuals and matters of fact, coalesced into one great struggle over the constitution of the church. This constitutional question the seculars wished to solve by the erection of a congregation or brotherhood based on voluntary association.[3] They

---

[1] Cf. the chapter, "Der Glaube, dass kein Jesuit verloren gehe," in DÖLLINGER-REUSCH, Gesch. der Moralstreitigkeiten, I. (1889), pp. 524 et seq.

[2] W. WATSON, A decacordon (1602), p. 109.

[3] DODD-TIERNEY, III., p. 45, note 1. LAW, Jesuits and Seculars, pp. 69 et seq., note 2. LAW, Archpriest Controversy, I., p. 207 et seq.

wished, moreover, in addition to have a bishop of their
own choosing, not because they wanted to set up a
hierarchy, but because they wanted some one with
episcopal powers.[1]   There was no one in England who
could confirm, ordain, etc.!   The Jesuits, on the other
hand, strove, as far as circumstances permitted, to revive
the ancient hierarchy overthrown by Queen Elizabeth.
They also naturally urged the consideration respecting
episcopal powers,[2] but what weighed most with them
was the desire for a stricter exercise of ecclesiastical
discipline and a closer union of the English church with
Rome.[3]   The idea of an independent form of organization floated before the minds of the seculars as being
best suited to local circumstances, while the Jesuits,
whose fixed centre is Rome, dwelt upon the principle
of ecclesiastical centralization.

Reckoning by numbers, the decision rested with the
seculars, for in 1596 three hundred secular priests at least
were working in England and only about a dozen Jesuits,[4]
although, owing to their having been educated in Jesuit
seminaries in Rome and Spain, a portion of the secular

---

[1] That this consideration chiefly moved the seculars to ask for a
bishop is clear from their petition of Aug., 1598. DOM. CAL.,
1598–1601, p. 86.

[2] The need had been already emphasized in 1580 by Persons.
THEINER, *Annals. Eccles.*, III., p. 216.

[3] See Persons' draft of 1597, specially §§ 6–8. DODD-TIERNEY, III.,
Appendix, p. cxviii.

[4] Statement from the memorial of the seculars. *Quomodo seculares
sacerdotes a patribus Societatis in Anglia degentibus opprimuntur.*
West. Cath. Arch., V., p. 427. According to the *Rationes . . .
instituendi canonicam potestatem*, etc. (1597), also emanating from
the seculars, their numbers were five hundred. *L.c.*, VI., p. 281. A
catholic report from the Netherlands estimates the priests resident in
London alone as four hundred. L. WILLAERT, *Négociations politico-
religieuses entre l'Angleterre et les Pays-Bas.* Rev. d'hist. ecclés., VI.
(1905), p. 569. *Cf.* p. 570.

clergy must be numbered among the Jesuits' partisans. But the Jesuits had the advantage in the Roman curia. The cardinal visitor of the unruly college, Filippo Sega, was on their side, and had borne witness that the Jesuits had "diuers other special helpes . . . by the institute of their order, and are more practised therein by the exercise both of their nouiciate and the rest of their lyfe . . . [and] cannot but haue more force, skil, and use in spiritual mannaging of souls than euery other priest."[1] The cardinal protector of England and Scotland, Enrico Caetani, also took the Jesuits' part, while the pope himself, Clement VIII., along with his influential minister, the cardinal nephew, Pietro Aldobrandini, was at least not to be numbered among their opponents, as the result of the recent disturbances in the English college had shown.

Immediately after his victory in the English college, in the summer of 1597, Persons, the most prominent man among the Jesuits, came forward with a scheme for the organization of the English clergy. In a suit to Cardinal Aldobrandini, he petitioned for the appointment of two English bishops each with a staff of six or seven arch-priests, one to reside in England and the other in the Low Countries, the chief centre of the English exiles.[2] At the same time he asked for restrictions to be put upon the taking of the degree of doctor. This request is easily explained by the Jesuits' aversion to titles and dignities, and in fact the students of the English college, much to their disgust, had not been allowed to take part in public disputations upon theses or to take degrees and

[1] [PERSONS] *A Manifestation of the Great Folly*, etc. (1602), fol. 74. *Cf.* FOLEY'S *Records*, VI., pp. 50 *et seq.*

[2] Arch Vat., Borgh., III., 124 g 2, fol. 23.   *Cf.* DODD-TIERNEY, III., Appendix, No. XXI. LAW, *Jesuits and Seculars*, Introd., lix. POLLEN, *Politics of Eng. Cath.*, The Month, Aug., 1902, p. 183.

distinctions.[1] This second and subordinate object of the
suit to the cardinal, alone met with approval, and a papal
brief of September 19, 1597, laid down stipulations concerning the taking of degrees by English catholics which
were highly prejudicial to the academic studies of secular
priests, and were consequently regarded by them as an
unfriendly move on the part of their Jesuit opponents.[2]
The refusal of the other request was due to the same
reasons which had hitherto influenced Rome in refusing to
restore the fallen hierarchy. So long as the Elizabethan
penal laws against catholics were in force, a bishop who
had received ordination in Rome would either be martyred
on setting foot in England or would find himself in a situation that would ill correspond with his episcopal dignity.
The Jesuits' suggestions on this point were accordingly
set aside.

But the need for organization among the clergy in some
shape or other had already become too urgent and too
widespread in England to be resisted any longer in Rome.
The seculars, too, declared that they were in pressing need
of organization.[3] Their means of livelihood, they said, must
be regulated in order that they might not be dependent on
alms. Owing to their being forced to wear lay attire without any outward sign of their priestly office, no restraints
could be placed on their liberty. Priests were unable to

[1] The report of the visitor Sega mentions among the students
grievances : " Impediunt patres, quominus theses publice disputandas
proponant alumni, nec eos patiuntur allis gradibus literariisque titulis
insigniri." Bibl. Vat., Ottob., 2473, fol. 203. English translation in
FOLEY'S *Records*, VI., p. 24, § 6.

[2] The brief is given in DODD-TIERNEY, III., Appendix, No. XVIII.
Cf. LAW, *Jesuits and Seculars*, p. 109, note.

[3] What follows is taken from the memorial of 1597 : *Rationes quibus
breviter ostenditur necessitas extrema instituendi canonicam aliquam
potestatem superiorem in clero Anglicano.* West. Cath. Arch., VI.,
pp. 281–283.

observe a common life in houses of their own, but had to be billeted on private families where they were thrown in the company of women. Now just in these latter years—the account I am following dates from 1597—the number of young priests had increased and the difficulties of their maintenance had become greater owing to the decrease in the liberality of catholics. Their necessities would be relieved if all priests united themselves together into a corporation and formed a common fund out of the pious bequests and alms bestowed upon them. Otherwise beardless youths of twenty-four, who have just left college and have no knowledge of life, are left without income and without superiors to whom they could turn. There is no direction, no order—"so many priests, so many popes!" If the absence of order, the impossibility of being called to account, and the lack of authority able to inflict punishment give rise to ill-feeling and injure the work of the mission, it is nothing to be wondered at! In a word, the disorganized state of the catholic clergy, which William Allen bewailed at the beginning of the mission as long as twenty years ago (p. 378), had become in course of time quite unendurable and was proving in the opinion of all, both Jesuits and seculars, a real danger to the catholic cause.

II. *Disagreement over the Form of Organization. The Archpriest Controversy*

Persons was not the man to rest content with the rejection of his scheme of organization. If *he* did not act, his enemies would. Material as well as personal considerations naturally make both parties anxious to secure the largest amount of co-operation possible in the framing of a constitution. It was not difficult for Persons and the

Jesuits, owing to the recent increase in the strength of their position in the curia, to get the better of the wholly unorganized seculars in distant England. This accounts for the fact that the organization of the English secular clergy took shape under the preponderating influence of the Jesuits instead of at the motion, and with the co-operation, of the seculars themselves. Persons had not been able to set up bishops for the entire catholic clergy of England, yet it is due to him that the secular clergy were organized under an archpriest with a staff of twelve assistants. The details of the transactions which led to the institution of this novel form of organization have hitherto not been made clearly known, and will hardly ever be fully divulged. For since the verbal negotiations between Persons, the cardinal protector of England, and the pope, which preceded the appointment of the arch-priest, have left no traces in the *acta* of the Holy See, we have no alternative but to fall back upon the prejudiced statements by which the anti-Jesuit party sought to explain whatever was unprecedented in the transaction.[1] The unusual features of the arrangement consisted in giving a new scope to an ancient form ; the title of archpriest was coupled with entirely new functions, but, still more unusual was it, that it was not the pope who appeared as the originator of this novel form of ecclesiastical govern-ment, as might have been expected, but merely Cardinal Enrico Caetani, the protector of England. According to the tenor of the brief of institution dated March 7, 1598, the cardinal had only received from the pope authority to take such measures as should seem necessary to him for the preservation of peace among the English clergy. In appointing George Blackwell as archpriest with

[1] E. L. TAUNTON bases his verdict upon them.   *Hist. of the Jesuits in Engl.* (1901), p. 213.

authority over the secular clergy working in England and Scotland, the cardinal, who was favourably inclined to the Jesuits, seems to have acted not without authorization indeed, but still without the full knowledge of the pope, who was less well disposed towards the Society. He himself named six of the assistants at the same time, and placed the nomination of the other six in the hands of the new archpriest.[1]

By the cardinal's letter, the archpriest received authority to preside over the secular clergy, to direct them, and, when necessary, to punish them by restricting or revoking their faculties, also to fix their place of residence as would be most advantageous for the mission. He was to allay strifes and heal schisms, and had the power of summoning each one to appear before him, of convoking assemblies under his own presidency, and of passing censures upon the contumacious. Nevertheless he did not receive episcopal consecration or faculties, and so had no power, for instance, to ordain priests. The twelve assistants were subordinated to him ; they were merely to share in his labours without being able to limit his authority. The maintenance of ecclesiastical discipline, and of concord between seculars and regulars—" especially with the fathers of the Society of Jesus "—was declared to be the aim of the new hierarchy. The services of the Jesuits to the English mission were extolled in glowing words, and all jealous feeling towards these men, who neither had, nor claimed, jurisdiction over seculars, was pronounced to be due to the suggestion of the devil. In the special instructions sent at the same time

---

[1] Draft of the cardinal's decree to Blackwell in Arch. dei Brevi, Diversorum Clem. VIII., lib. ix. (1592 ad 1604), fols. 404 *et seq.* Printed in DODD-TIERNEY, III., Appendix, No. XXII. On the problematical share of the pope in the appointment, see LAW, *Archpriest Controversy*, I., p. 126, note ; *Jesuits and Seculars*, Introd., pp. lxiii. *et seq.*

to the archpriest, the cardinal protector directed him, for the sake of peace and concord, to ask the advice of the superior of the English Jesuits on important matters.[1] Momentous as this suggestion was in its bearings upon the independence of the secular clergy in the future, there is, nevertheless, no reason for thinking that Cardinal Caetani wished by it to make the seculars dependent upon the Jesuits. The contents of the instructions lend no support to this view. The words of the brief of institution, that the Jesuits had no authority over seculars, rather tell against it, and the cardinal would have placed himself in opposition to the prevailing views of the curia had he endeavoured to subject the secular priests to the Jesuits. An impartial interpretation, which must be based on the state of things at the time and not on what happened later, does not attempt to find more in the words than they actually say.[2] Since the English mission was henceforth to have two heads, the archpriest for the seculars and the superior of the Jesuits for that order, it is obvious that the cardinal protector should expect them to work together.

And so the secular clergy of England saw their desires for a constitution realized, but in what a form! They could not feel content with the solution, either in respect to its form nor in respect to the individual chosen as their head. For, as to form, the cardinal's letters meant the disillusionment of those who had set their hearts on a free and independent form of government, while the choice of the person to be archpriest threatened the independence of the secular clergy even more seriously than the institution of the office itself. The future superior of the seculars,

[1] John Gerard, *The Archpriest Controversy*, The Month, Jan., 1897, p. 51.

[2] In this I differ from Law, *Archpriest Controversy*, II., Introd., pp. xvi. *et seq.* For this controversy, *cf.* Gerard, *l.c.* and Pollen in The Month, Aug., 1902, p. 186, note 1.

the archpriest, George Blackwell, was a man whose government seemed neither more nor less than the government of the Jesuits. Although Blackwell was not a pupil of the Jesuits, but had received his ecclesiastical education in the Douay seminary, he was known to be one of the unqualified admirers and panegyrists of the Society of Jesus, who reverenced the fathers as the highest examples of priestly excellence, and was fully persuaded that "they that discommend them know neither themselves nor them."[1] On one occasion he summed up his opinion of the opponents of the Jesuits in the phrase : " There is no greater perversity than to be the enemy of the best ! "[2]

No doubt, indeed, has ever been felt that the hitherto unknown Blackwell had to thank his friendship with the Jesuits alone for his election to the office of archpriest. One point only is open to question, i.e. the object which this momentous appointment, due apparently to Person's inspiration, was intended to serve. The seculars always saw in it an attempt on their independence by the Jesuits, while the latter as persistently denied the imputation whenever it was made. As a matter of fact, for all that, the Jesuits have not succeeded in obtaining a judgment in their favour either from their opponents at the time nor from history since. The most recent historian of "the Jesuits in England" entitles his account of the archpriest controversy, "subjugating the clergy."[3] So pointed an epigram as this sounds like an echo from the controversial writings of the period. Of course, the Jesuits wished to

---

[1] Blackwell to Card. Caetani, London, Jan. 10, 1597. LAW, *Jesuits and Seculars*, p. 138.

[2] " Nulla major potest esse vitiositas quam optimis esse inimicum." Blackwell to Caetani, Dec. 10, 1597. West. Cath. Arch., VI., pp. 253 *et seq.*

[3] E. L. TAUNTON, *Hist. of the Jesuits in Engl.* (1901), ch. ix., " Subjugating the Clergy."

increase their influence in England by working for the nomination of an archpriest for the seculars who would be well disposed to themselves, but any stronger expression than this does violence to facts.   Still, considering the overwhelming majority of secular priests, every increase of Jesuit influence must have been felt as an injustice to the seculars.   And, moreover, this increase of influence was not now due to high appreciation of the services of the Jesuits to the English mission, as had been the case in the years after 1580, nor was it the work of a single individual of great moral superiority, such as Campion, but it was entirely due to the power of the Jesuits with the curia ; it had not been won in fair field, but by strategy.   It was this which led to so much bitterness, and in this consists the blame which attaches to the Jesuits in the history of the English mission.

Regarded as an act of the curia, Blackwell's appointment as archpriest was a piece of red tapism and an administrative blunder, and Cardinal Caetani, who certainly wished for nothing but the internal peace of the mission, thought in this way to bring about a better understanding between regulars and seculars.   But neither he nor Persons were in touch with the mind of the secular clergy in England.   To these priests, whose projects of organization had been passed over in silence, the appointment of a friend of the Jesuits as archpriest seemed, to quote the words of the most moderate of its critics, a violation of " the golden rule "—*regularia regularibus, sæcularia sæcularibus*.[1]

As might be expected, the institution of an unusual office in an unusual manner did not meet with universal

---

[1] " That golden rule, *Regularia Regularibus*, lett religious men deale in matter appertayninge to religion and the cloister, and leave *Secularia Secularibus*" [HUMPHREY ELY].   *Certaine briefe notes*, etc., *imprinted at Paris by Peter Sevestre* [1603], see *General Preface*, fol. 9.   Ely was professor of canon law at Pont-à-Mousson.

acceptance. The resistance, for the reasons already given, was directed partly against the thing itself, but principally against the individual concerned. Not many months after his appointment, the archpriest found that he could only make headway against the stream that set in against him if the legal basis of his office was made plain beyond all doubt. In August, 1598, Blackwell, along with his twelve assistants, petitioned for a papal confirmation of his appointment, which owed its existence to the cardinal protector alone.[1] The appointment of "an archpriest in the place of a bishop" [sic],[2] as is stated in their petition, had met with a joyful approval from all well-disposed persons, both clerical and lay. Nevertheless, the new hierarchy required the pope's protection and confirmation to defend it against a minority composed of ambitious priests, who were moved to envy against the Jesuits. The letter contains a very significant warning against refractory and contentious men—"only few in numbers compåred with the large number of the good "—to whom no hearing or favour ought to be given.[3] And so even now we meet with the determination, which was carried into effect later on, not to allow opponents on any account to gain a hearing.

The opposition party was undoubtedly inferior in numbers, especially at the outbreak of the controversy. For

[1] Blackwell and his twelve assistants to Clement VIII. "Ex Anglia primo Augusti, 1598." Arch. Vat., Borgh. II., 448, *ab* fol. 262.

[2] "Loco episcopi, ad invidiam nominis apud hæreticos vitandam," *l.c.* Blackwell could not draw the conclusion from his faculties (*vid. ante*) that he was set " in the place of a bishop."

[3] ". . . si refractariis ac contentiosis hominibus, si qui erunt (erunt vero respectu totius corporis bonorum paucissimi) aditus aut favor allus (quod absit) contra unionem hanc alicubi daretur, maximarum profecto perturbationum materies inde nasceretur, quod S^tis Vestræ auribus significandum hoc primo quoque tempore communi omnium nomine duximus."

many who were dissatisfied with the solution of the question, submitted when the archpriest let it be known that his authority had received papal confirmation.[1] The idea of a friendly settlement of the archpriest controversy, therefore, did not seem at first hopeless, and would perhaps actually have been realized had there been in Blackwell's place a tactful and diplomatic person. In the days preceding his elevation, Blackwell had passed as a quiet, learned, and virtuous man, even in the estimation of his subsequent opponents.[2] But he was intoxicated by his elevation to the dignity of archpriest. The new superior of the secular clergy, whose character is revealed to us in his style, which abounds in fine quotations and is full of a self-important and pompous kind of edification, embittered his opponents by misplaced severity and harshness of tone. Blackwell's intimate relations with the Jesuits, moreover, gave him the appearance in the eyes of the seculars of being the incarnation of the Society's party-programme. Still, all the blame must not by any means be laid at his door. Side by side with a moderate opposition, which regarded the Jesuits not as enemies but as valuable fellow-labourers in the mission field deficient only in a just estimation of themselves, there was an extremely combative party which declared that the Jesuits and their friends were ambitious hypocrites and likely to bring about the destruction of the catholic religion in England.[3]

Now this ill-will towards the Jesuits is not to be attributed solely to the irritation of rivals who were getting the

[1] Charnock to Bagshaw. LAW, *Archpriest Controversy*, I., p. 71.

[2] [HUMPHREY ELY] *Certaine briefe notes* (Paris, 1603), p. 103.

[3] The difference between these two points of view was well illustrated at the beginning of the archpriest controversy by the moderate John Mush and the violent William Watson. *Cf.* their statements in LAW, *op. cit.*, I., pp. 53–62 and 90–98.

worst of it, but reveals the existence of something behind itself. Blackwell very soon cast the reproach of schism at his gainsayers [1] when onlookers would feel inclined to tax them merely with disobedience and insubordination. His reproach has its origin in the fact that among the opposition party the idea had been current for some time that Rome ought not to impose a spiritual superior over catholic England without the clergy and laity having first expressly given their consent.[2] In other words, the principle of national independence, the principle of the " Gallican liberties," came into conflict with the principle of the centralization of the church's government. The latter was urged by the Jesuits in their character of faithful champions of papal supremacy ; the former by the seculars, to whom the strengthening of the church's central power was of less moment than the creation of tolerable relations with the home government. The greater the dependence on Rome, the less prospect was there of coming to terms with the state, which treated the recognition of Rome's supremacy as high treason. Until now the hostility of the " national " catholic priests and laymen to the Jesuits had rested on the same ground as their hostility to Spain—a protest against the policy of a Spanish invasion and succession. But now the " national " party found itself, moreover, drawn into a certain opposition to Rome by its " Gallicanism," which also caused it to lean upon the University of Paris as an intellectual ally, and, therefore, to rely on France, Spain's ancient enemy. The result of this was that under the protection of France they were able to enter into relations with the English government—and in the end these " national " catholics, who may be described as anglican in policy though Roman

---

[1] Blackwell to Colleton, March, 1599: LAW, I., p. 86.
[2] LAW, I., pp. 78, 99, and further on *passim.*

in belief, were forced to make terms with the anglican state church !

Such was the development that gradually took shape during the five last years of Elizabeth's reign. Behind the archpriest controversy, which at first sight exhibits nothing but a drama of personal animosities and quarrels to gain the upper hand, great differences on matters of principle lay concealed.

How pronounced and deliberate this Gallican tendency was in the minds of some at least of its supporters appears in a small but scholarly treatise, which, although not in any way to be regarded as forming part of the programme of the party, must not be underestimated as an indication of what a certain number of people were thinking. The treatise, which appeared in 1598,[1] was written by an English catholic called John Bishop, who until then had come little before the public. It is not a product of the archpriest controversy, for it rather contemplates the state of English catholicism from a higher standpoint than that of a mere question of the hour. The author places before the seculars six propositions concerning the pope's authority, and seeks to prove their validity from canon law, scripture, and the fathers of the church. The fundamental idea underlying all these propositions is the subordination of the spiritual to the secular power. Christ did not give His disciples earthly dominion, nor did He give the apostle Peter any higher authority than that given to the other apostles. Therefore the pope has no earthly sovereignty, cannot depose princes, nor release subjects from their fealty. The theological proof was strengthened by practical considerations : " These madde bulles haue killed

---

[1] JOHN BISHOP, *A courteous conference with the English Catholickes Romane, about the six articles ministred unto the seminarie priestes* . . . (London, 1598).

many and hurt more of the pope's friendes and fauourers, but not done one halfepennyworth of harme unto them against whome they were sent." [1] To quiet the consciences of those catholics who felt oppressed by the canon of the Lateran council of 1215 on the power of deposing heretical princes, Bishop maintains that the Lateran canons had never been received in England.[2] The idea of national autonomy for the church in England was here expressed with such distinctness that, if carried out logically, it must have led to the establishment of a state church, retaining much that was catholic in doctrine and practice, such as had existed under Henry VIII.

So far-reaching a programme was plainly out of the question for the small body of the archpriest's opponents. The point of law upon which the opposition took its stand was the fact that the letter of March 7, 1598, appointing George Blackwell archpriest emanated from a cardinal, and not from the pope, and, therefore, possessed no final authority. Accordingly, in the late summer of 1598, the opposition dispatched two envoys to Rome, William Bishop and Robert Charnock, to lay their appeal before the pope.[3] The envoys were to request the appointment of a bishop chosen by the secular clergy, and, at the same time, to obtain for the seculars the right to form themselves into a " sodality " of their own. They were further to ask that the government of the English college should be taken out of the hands of the Jesuits, and, finally, to procure an order forbidding the publication of all books written against the queen and the English government, except those with the approbation of the ecclesiastical superiors,[4] since writings of this kind only added fuel to

---

[1] *Op. cit.*, p. 51. [2] *Op. cit.*, pp. 75–82.
[3] DOM. CAL., 1598–1601, p. 86.
[4] Plainly the superiors to be appointed in the future.

the fire and did no good whatsoever.   All these wished-for measures, including the last, were aimed against the Jesuits, especially against Persons, as he was the most prolific author of works of political controversy.   The national idea, which with John Bishop went the length of demanding national autonomy for the church, lies at the root of this programme of the seculars, and shows itself negatively in resistance to the international principle adopted by the Jesuits, and positively in an approximation to the " Gallican liberties," and to some sort of agreement with the home government.   A body of men who believed that ideas of this sort could be carried through in Rome must have lost touch with the spirit animating the papacy of the counter-reformation.

When the two priests reached their journey's end in December, 1598, they naturally asked for hospitality at the English college.   The rector, none other than Persons himself, received them ungraciously enough. Then the two appellants (to give them the name applied afterwards to their party) took steps to gain the support of the French ambassador, Cardinal d'Ossat, who they hoped would be able to smooth the way for them at the papal court.   Even as early as this, the leaning towards France showed itself.   But as the priests brought with them no recommendations from the French court, the ambassador could do little for them.[1]   Meanwhile the superior of the English Jesuits, Father Henry Garnet, made a counter move.   In a letter to the pope, signed not only by members of Garnet's[2] order, but by some

---

[1] Law, *Jesuits and Seculars*, Introd., p. lxxi.

[2] Written from London on Oct. 30, 1598.   Arch. Vat., Borgh. II., 448, *ab* fol. 320.   There are nineteen signatures.   Among the Jesuits the best known names are Thos. Lister, Rich. Holtby, John Gerard, Edw. Oldcorne, Rich. Blount, Edm. Weston, Ralph Emerson. Among the seculars may be noted the later opponent of the archpriest,

secular priests as well, the writers obediently declared their full acceptance of the institution of, and appointment to, the office of archpriest, and laid the blame of the contentions and divisions on "a few priests of restless mind,"[1] who held different opinions. They begged the pope to confirm the appointment of the archpriest, to admonish sharply the two appellants, and to permit them to return to England only on condition that they repented and altered their views.

Persons took care that these petitions should be answered beyond all expectation. Since he had on his side both the cardinal protector of England, Caetani, and the vice-protector, Cardinal Borghese, he was able to cut off the appellants from all access to the pope. Not satisfied with this, he employed the favour he enjoyed with his patrons to procure a warrant for arrest, in virtue of which he placed the two priests under confinement in the English college. In February, 1599, a court was held under the presidency of the two cardinals, the verdict of which must have been a foregone conclusion to the two men who were not even allowed to employ a proctor in their own defence. Their experiences so far on their mission had already opened their eyes to the fact that Persons, the conqueror of the rebellious students, enjoyed the complete confidence of the ecclesiastical authorities, not only as rector of the English college, but in everything connected with the settlement of disputes in England. In fulfilment of his duty, Bishop did indeed make a further attempt to lay before his judges the plan for forming the secular priests into a "sodality," but he did not meet with the least disposition to give it serious consideration, and, later on, himself advised those whom

John Bennet, the author of the pamphlet *The Hope of Peace* (1601). *Cf.* p. 428, note 1.

[1] "Paucos illos inquietioris ingenii sacerdotes."

he represented to give up the idea.[1]   Not until April was judgment delivered on the two men ; they had to leave Rome without having seen the pope, but were not allowed to return directly to England.   Bishop was "banished" to Paris and his companion, Charnock, to Lorraine.   All intercourse with one another was strictly forbidden them, and they must not even travel in company.[2]

Mush, the secular priest, gives vent to his indignation at this ignominious ending of the appeal to Rome in a grim pleasantry—" Our statute of *premunire* may well be repealed now, Father Parsons, a Jesuite, hath laid a plot sufficient enough to hinder appellation or accesse to the See of Rome."[3]   Deep as was their feeling of resentment against Persons, the appellants obediently submitted as soon as Rome had spoken.   A papal brief confirming in unmistakable language both the institution of an archpriest and the appointment of Blackwell to that office, was published on April 6, 1599, almost simultaneously with the judgment of the cardinals on the two envoys.[4]   Any hope that the pope would disavow the cardinal protector of England was thereby finally destroyed.   Those who hitherto had been refractory now abandoned their position as impossible, and almost all submitted with a readiness which at first seemed to promise a lasting peace.

---

[1] " A long tyme I stood in defence of our sodalitie intended," etc. Letter of Bishop from Rome, Feb. 20, 1599.   LAW, *Archpriest Controversy*, I., p. 124.

[2] The judgment is given in DODD-TIERNEY, III., Appendix, No. XXVI.   For the rest, see LAW, *l.c.*, pp. 101 *et seq.; Jesuits and Seculars*, Introd., pp. lxx. *et seq.*

[3] J[ohn] M[ush] to Persons, London, Nov. 13, 1600.   Printed by [WILLIAM BISHOP].   *The Copies of Certaine Discourses*, etc. (*Imprinted at Roane*, 1601), p. 180.

[4] Draft in the Arch. dei Brevi, Diversor. Clem. VIII., lib. ix., fol. 403.   Printed in DODD-TIERNEY, III., Appendix, No. XXVII.

For a time, too, during the summer of 1599, peace prevailed, at least outwardly. The archpriest met those who had submitted in a friendly manner,[1] and Persons wrote a conciliatory letter to William Bishop his former prisoner : "And now God be thanked, by the good order which his Holinesse hath setled, all is well ended and remedied, if men can be contented; and now [secular] priests have their head and subordination and Jesuites also theirs, and both are happilie united together, and all strife is ended in England, to God's great glorie and our common good, I hope."[2]

But the restoration of peace by the exercise of papal authority did not appease the hatred existing between the parties. Among those who found themselves in subjection to the archpriest not all were reconciled to their defeat, and in some the feeling of animosity was so deeply rooted that they sought to curry favour with an ally of a very dangerous character—the English government. The first attempt of English secular priests to enter into an understanding with the protestant state had been made at the very beginning of the archpriest controversy, but without producing any result.[3] Just at the time when Persons had defeated the appeal to the pope, a secular priest, William Watson, and Charles Paget, a layman hostile to the Jesuits and to Spain, acting independently of one another, though almost at the same moment, took the momentous step of denouncing their Jesuit opponents to the English government. Each man acted on his own responsibility, without any authorization from his party. Not until later did the

---

[1] BAGSHAW'S *True Relation*, in LAW, *Jesuits and Seculars*, p. 87.
[2] Persons to Bishop, Rome, Oct. 9, 1599. Printed by [WILLIAM BISHOP] in *The Copies of Certaine Discourses*, p. 63.
[3] See Bagshaw's memorandum of Oct., 1598, etc., in LAW, *Archpriest Controversy*, I., pp. 205 *et seq.*; *cf.* Introd., p. xvii.

party of the seculars follow their lead. In April, 1599, Watson presented to the attorney-general a denunciation of the Jesuits for high treason, grounding his accusation on their attempt to secure the succession of a Spaniard to the English throne.[1] A few weeks later, Paget betook himself to Sir Henry Neville, the English ambassador in Paris, and gave him information about the Jesuits, leaving with him for his approbation the MS. of a controversial pamphlet aimed against them.[2] The knowledge, which, in the course of the ensuing period, the English government obtained from these and other sources, comprised even unimportant details. All the most important documents relating to the archpriest controversy were made known to the government *in extenso*.[3] The government's description of the leading individuals among the Jesuits corresponds with the description given by the secular priests in their denunciations of their foes ; Persons, for example, is set down as " a meere polititian, and a man voyde of all conscience and honestye."[4]

With that wily reserve, so characteristic of its proceedings, Elizabeth's government did not at once mix itself up with the archpriest controversy, but at the beginning confined itself to the rôle of a watchful observer. The tactlessness of the archpriest and the excessive zeal of the Jesuits soon drove the secular clergy in the direction already taken independently by the two informers.

---

[1] *Op. cit.*, I., 210–226, especially, p. 216.

[2] See the dispatches of the ambassador, June 27, Aug. 14, 20 (o.s.), 1599. *Memorials . . . of Sir Ralph Winwood*, ed. SAWYER, I. (1725), pp. 51, 90, 94 ; *cf.* 101.

[3] This is evident from the *Forty-five Articles of Enquiry*. LAW, I., pp. 226–238. The papal brief of April 6, 1599, confirming the appointment of the archpriest was forwarded to the government on Nov. 13/23 by the ambassador in Paris. *Winwood Memorials*, I., p. 128.

[4] LAW, I., p. 237.

By an act which it is difficult to comprehend, Blackwell once again rendered doubtful the victory he had just gained over the appellants. I have mentioned already that he considered the non-recognition of his authority as an act of schism. Instead, then, of being content with the recognition he now received, he required—apparently in the summer or autumn of 1599—that the secular clergy who had sub-mitted to him should acknowledge that, by their past opposition to him, they had incurred the guilt of schism. In support of this pretension he appealed, though in ambiguous terms, to "a resolution from Rome"; not, however, from the curia, as the impartial reader would think, but from English Jesuits living in Rome![1] Where-upon the controversy broke out anew. The secular priests refused to submit to this second and greater humiliation, and when Blackwell persevered in his pretensions, they applied for a decision from the theological faculty of the university of Paris. The decision, given on May 3, 1600, was entirely in their favour. As a reply to this, the archpriest put forth a sharp decree in which he punished clergy and laity with interdict (exceeding in this the limita-tions of his faculties) should they directly or indirectly, in word or in writing, defend the censure of the university of Paris.[2] Blackwell's opponents took no notice of this prohibition—"Can it be iudged by any of reason to be a thing unlawful in itselfe to defend a censure of the most

---

[1] Not, however, Persons. DODD-TIERNEY, III., Appendix, p. cxxxvi. Blackwell in this affords us a typical example of *æquivocatio*, or of a phrase with two meanings, which was *intended* in one sense and *understood* in another. Bagshaw complains of the Jesuits' use of *æquivocatio* in 1598. LAW, *Archp. Contr.*, I., p. 206. More will be said in the second volume on the effect of *æquivocatio* in the history of English catholicism.

[2] Both the decision from Paris and Blackwell's decree are printed by William Bishop, *op. cit.*, pp. 37–39. DODD-TIERNEY, III., Appendix No. XXIX.

famous universitie in the world?"[1]   They were determined to maintain their position to the uttermost.
Blackwell was no less firm on his side, and the archpriest
controversy entered upon its second stage. The opposition's prospect of success was now essentially brighter
than at the beginning of the quarrel two years before. It
was not they, but their adversaries, who cast moderation
to the winds.

The second phase of the archpriest controversy is distinguished from the first chiefly by the greater *esprit de
corps* in each party, the increased sharpness of the weapons
employed, and, above all, by an alteration in the programme of the secular clergy. These now fought less for
the overthrow of the archpriest organization than for the
expulsion of the Jesuits from England. In pursuit of this
object they made use of any weapon that came to hand,
and even allied themselves with the common foe, Elizabeth's
government. Indeed, it may be said with equal justice
that they both sought the aid of the government in
order the better to fight the Jesuits, and exerted themselves to get the Jesuits expelled in order to come to a
better understanding with the government. The tragic
conflict between religion and patriotism, which runs all
through the history of the catholic mission in Elizabethan
England, here appears again, at the close of the period, as
hopeless and irreconcilable as ever. Each party was
regarded by its opponents as traitors because they were
trying to put an end to the conflict by the use of expedients
different from their own. The secular priest looked upon
the Jesuit as a traitor to his country, and the Jesuit looked
upon the secular priest as a traitor to the church.

When the archpriest Blackwell took up the position that

J[OHN] B[ENNET] *The Hope of Peace*, etc. (Franckford, 1601),
p. 38.

his vanquished opponents must acknowledge that they had incurred the guilt of schism, he had the Jesuits on his side and was zealously supported by them when the feud broke out afresh. In October, 1600, he praised them to the pope as his "protection and shield against the disturbers of the church's peace."[1] Among these disturbers of the peace were included, in his opinion, two of the most respected and hitherto moderate members of the secular clergy, Mush and Collington (Colleton), because they had refused to seek absolution for their schism, as he had desired them to do. Both of them, although they were among the oldest and most deserving mission priests, were declared suspended from all ecclesiastical functions by a decree of Blackwell, dated October 17.[2] This autocratic use of his power as archpriest was the signal for the renewal of the strife.

The indignation of the suspended seculars was directed perhaps more against Persons in Rome, who seemed to them the real culprit, than against Blackwell himself. Persons, indeed, was not responsible for this fresh outburst,[3] but ever since he had succeeded in defeating the appeal of 1598 to the Holy See, by an unfair use of his influence, men were accustomed to see in him the originator of every measure directed against the seculars. And it seems that in the course of 1600 he had still further increased their dislike of him by certain imprudent letters, which had come to their knowledge.[4] Even those who were most inclined for peace no longer suppressed their grievances.

---

[1] Blackwell to Clement VIII., London, Oct. 22, 1600 ; " Certe mihi ad hospitium, ad periculum, ad aciem atque præsidium contra perturbatores pacis ecclesiasticæ præsto sunt." Arch. Vat., Borgh. III., 124 g 1, fol. 47.

[2] This order is printed in DODD-TIERNEY, III., Appendix, p. cxxxii.

[3] *Vid. ante*, p. 427, note 1.

[4] DODD-TIERNEY, III., Appendix, p. cxxxviii.

As a protest against the way he had been treated, John Mush, one of the suspended priests, wrote a letter to Persons which represents the views held at that time by the best of the secular priests,[1] for in this letter he maintains throughout a tone of deepest indignation without exceeding the limits of decorum and priestly dignity. " It were high time that you should permit yourself and us to carrie our gray haires in peace to our graues. The trouble and scandall you haue wrought in our church these late yeares by your politicke courses[2] doo quite cancel all your former desert. Was our peace and union made at the comming of his Holines breue (of April 6, 1599), . . . that presently after we had . . . submitted ourselves to it, you and yours might more safely and liberally renew the infamie against us and by the archpriestes authoritie . . . at your pleasures persecute and oppresse us ? " With renewed indignation, he upbraids the leader of the Jesuits for the violence done to the appellants in Rome, and finally flings down the glove with the words : " For defame us before wee come ; imprison us at our arrivall ; keepe us close from being seene or heard—yet shall you not goe so away with your iniquitie. We are resolved verily that with our good names you shal bereve us also of our lives before we sit downe with this undeserved calumnie. Either will wee bee prooved no schismatickes or found no living men ! "

The second appeal to Rome, already announced in these words, followed on November 17, 1600, and was dated from

---

[1] J[OHN] M[USH] to Persons, London, Nov. 13, 1600. [WILLIAM BISHOP] *The Copies of Certaine Discourses* (Roane, 1601), pp. 178–181.

[2] " By your politicke courses." The term must be taken as expressing his estimation of the Jesuits' actions from a moral point of view, and not as referring to their political activity. *Cf.* "the polliticke shifts," *l.c.*, p. 179, and also the use of "policie" in the quotation given above on p. 407.

Wisbeach, the same place where resistance to the Jesuits had first taken shape.[1] The disregard for matters of form, which had marked the somewhat ill-advised first appeal, and had done it no little harm, was avoided on this occasion, and, most important of all, the correct steps to be followed in presenting the appeal were duly observed. The letter, signed by thirty-three secular priests, was presented to the archpriest to be forwarded by him to the authorities in Rome. A long list of complaints against Blackwell's exercise of his office, chiefly bearing on the accusation of schism which he had made against them, was put forth in the document and evidence produced in proof of every instance. The striving after definiteness and accuracy is unmistakable, the language temperate, and the whole document skilfully composed. Taking it all in all, it was a letter so full of weighty matter that it could not fail to make an impression on the authorities before whom it was laid. The best proof that this second appeal to the apostolic see did make an impression in Rome is the fact that the curia allowed seven or eight months to pass before it finally assumed the thankless office of mediator and published a carefully weighed decision.

This long delay in giving an answer was too severe a test of patience for excited passions. "With sharp-pointed pens, venemous tongues, and slanderous books," says Camden, who as a protestant belonged to neither party,[2] "did Jesuits and seculars fight with one another." The archpriest and his followers bitterly reproached the appellants with having brought their controversial writings before public notice, without waiting for the result of their appeal. This charge occupies a prominent place in the denunciation of his adversaries which Blackwell lodged

---

[1] DODD-TIERNEY, III., Appendix, pp. cxxxiii–cxliv.
[2] CAMDEN'S *Annales rec. Anglic.* (1625), p. 842.

with the Inquisition in 1601.[1] Certainly this appeal to
the public led to momentous consequences, but the chief
blame attaches to those who made the first move in
this direction, *i.e.* the Jesuit party.   The small but spiteful
pamphlet of the Jesuit Lister, *Adversus Factiosos in
Ecclesia*,[2] gave the impetus to the increasing flood of
"libels" published between 1601-1603.   Blackwell, in spite
of repeated and urgent prayers that he would suppress
this book, would not consent, but, on the other hand,
supported it with the full weight of his authority, because
in it Lister defended the charge of schism which the archpriest had brought against the appellants.   The grievances
caused by this pamphlet and the archpriest's attitude
towards it are prominent features in the appeal of
November, 1600.[3]   Feeling that they had need of a fuller
and more detailed defence than was possible within the
limits of this document, the seculars had recourse to literary
weapons in the early months of the next year, before the
decision of the curia had been given.   Although they can,
therefore, scarcely be regarded as instigators of the feud,
nevertheless, they left the Jesuits far behind in the number
of writings which they published.

It would take us too far to follow the course of this
paper war in detail.[4]   The pens were more and more
deeply dipped in gall, the facts of the case receded more

---

[1] *Denunciatio ad Sacrum Inquisitionis officium de gravibus quibusdam excessibus, qui in religionis catholicæ præjudicium in Anglia
fiunt, per Georgium Blackwellum, ejusdem regni archipresbyterum
facta aº dⁿⁱ*, 1601.   West. Cath. Arch., VII., pp. 51–76 ; Draft, 39–49.
Copy.

[2] Published in 1598 or 1599.   Printed in [BAGSHAW'S] *Relatio
compendiosa turbarum, quas Jesuitæ Angli concivêre* [1601], pp. 37–49 ;
partly also in LAW'S *Jesuits and Seculars*, pp. 143–145.

[3] DODD-TIERNEY, III., Appendix, pp. cxxxiv. *et seq.*

[4] The best bibliography is given in LAW'S *Jesuits and Seculars*,
Introd., pp. cxxviii–cliii.

and more into the background, and their place was taken
by personalities of the grossest kind. The leaders on both
sides burst all bounds of moderation in the descriptions
which they gave of each other in their pamphlets. Persons
was represented even by John Mush, who had hitherto
maintained a tone of moderation, as a wholly unscrupulous
intriguer,[1] but the much-abused Jesuit, superior in the
use of the pen to all his adversaries, felt, not without pride,
that he was " the only butt against which all their fiery
darts of hellish hatred and serpentine intrigues are
directed."[2] He knew well how to inflict the deepest
wounds upon his foes by treating them with contempt and
scorn. In this way he lost all sense of proportion in
estimating the share which the two parties had in the
work of the mission. On one occasion, he went so far as
to tell the seculars that had it not been for the Jesuits,
most of them would not be even catholics, let alone
priests.[3] It was this sense of personal superiority which
made him so unjust. A man like the worthy but vain
and blundering secular priest, Watson, who loved to
indulge in pathos, and tried to give an impression of
euphuism by adorning his style with flowers of rhetoric,
was no match for the great Jesuit. It would be unfair to
Persons to expect him to regard a writer of this stamp as
a worthy opponent. No wonder, then, if his satirical side
came to the fore or if his portraits were caricatures. Just
because he knew so well how to use his pen, he yielded
more frequently perhaps than his opponents to the
temptation to manipulate facts to please himself. Hence
the reproach brought against him, with varying degrees

---

[1] " Absque . . . minimo conscientiæ scrupulo." [JOHN MUSH]
Declaratio moluum, etc. (Rhotomagi, 1601), p. 25.

[2] [PERSONS] *A Manifestation of the Great Folly*, etc. (1602),
fol. 89.

[3] *Op. cit.*, fol. 25ᵛ.

of indignation, that he had small regard for truth. Of one of his earliest polemical pamphlets (published anonymously in 1601) it had been said by Charles Paget,[1] who was personally attacked therein, that he had "greate cause to suspect [Persons] to be the author of the libell . . . because it is without a name and full of lyes."[2] And yet this book is comparatively free from the venomous bitterness of his later writings. The impression which this exhibition of internecine strife within English catholicism made upon fellow-countrymen and co-religionists abroad may be gathered from the words of Humphrey Ely, who was living as professor of canon law at Pont-à-Mousson. He was indeed an avowed enemy of the Jesuits, whom he had known ever since he had been at the seminary,[3] but he entered the lists on behalf of the secular with greater restraint than others. "What good Christian would not wonder to see men esteemed otherwise neither folish nor dishonest so to forgett themselues in their owne cause that they seeme, duringe the moode and humour, eyther to haue lost their wittes or to haue cast aside all honesty?"[4] The feeling of disgust at length overcame even Persons himself, well-seasoned as he was to literary affrays, and, at the conclusion of his last and bitterest publication he declares, "We are weary and therefore we desire to make an end."[5]

But to put a stop to the strife, which, from being the private

[1] *A brief apologie or defence of the catholic ecclesiastical hierarchie* . . . (1601).

[2] *An answere made by me, Charles Paget, . . . to certayne untruthes and falsityes, tochinge myselfe, contayned in a booke, intitled, A Briefe Apologie*, p. 13. Included in [HUMPHREY ELY'S] *Certaine Briefe Notes . . . Imprinted at Paris* [1603].

[3] *Vid. ante*, pp. 105 *et seq.*

[4] H. ELY, *l.c.* [111]; *An answeare unto the particulars obiected in the apology against Master Dr. Byshope*, fol. 18ᵛ.

[5] [PERSONS] *A Manifestation*, etc., fol. 106.

concern of the English catholics, had become a public
scandal, was no longer in the power of the contending parties.
At first the English government gained its information
secretly and only through informers, but with the outburst
of pamphleteering, indiscretion became almost a principle
of conduct at least among the seculars, and by this means
the government was now kept sufficiently well informed of
all the phases of the quarrel.   The broader the cleavage
became between the hostile parties, the narrower became
the distance between the appellants and the English
government.   The unnatural alliance finally entered into
between them—an alliance between the persecuted and
their persecutors—was due solely to the common motive of
hostility to the Jesuits.   The advantages to be derived from
this alliance were overwhelmingly on the side of the government.   For since by law every priest had forfeited his life,
the alliance was only possible on the assumption that the
penal laws against catholics were at least provisionally
set aside, and thus the appellants depended on the grace
of the power which they had called to aid them against
the Jesuits.

The programme which took shape among the appellants
under these circumstances was made public in various pamphlets during the summer of 1601, and may be described as
an effort to turn the English laws against catholics into
laws against Jesuits.   The struggle was to be carried on,
correct relations with the apostolic see being, at the same
time, duly maintained ; the object was to make peace
in London without breaking it in Rome.   In order to
obtain religious toleration from the government, it was
necessary in the first place to show that the Jesuits
alone, and not the seculars, were dangerous to the
protestant state.   It was necessary, moreover, to prove
to the curia that the church's cause in England could

only be won through the recall of the Jesuits from the English mission. The first proposition necessarily implied the recognition of the right of a protestant state to exist, *i.e.* the recognition of a state of things irreconcilable with the principles prevailing in the catholic church at the period of the counter-reformation. On this account, the appellants did not make any very explicit statement as to their own recognition of the protestant state, but left it as the practical conclusion to be drawn from their writings, as when, for example, the secular priest Watson stated in the earliest of his pamphlets (1601): [1] "We wish with all our harts (and grone euery day at the contrary) that her Maiestie had continued in her obedience to the See Apostolick, as Queen Mary, her sister of famous memorie, had left her a worthy example ; but seeing that God for our sinnes would haue it otherwise, we ought to haue carried ourselves in another manner of course towards her, our true and lawfull queene, and towards our countrie, than hath bene taken, and pursued by many catholickes, but especially by the Jesuits." Watson exhorted his co-religionist to make up for the past, " better late than never ! " It was a surprising revolution in their ideas which he urged upon English catholics. He tried to show that the wrong had been all on the catholic side and the right all on the side of the government. The leading theme throughout this pamphlet, which was of the nature of a manifesto, was that the treatment of English catholics by Queen Elizabeth from the beginning of her reign had been mild and gracious ! He placed obedience to the civil power infinitely above obedience to the pope.

[1] [WILLIAM WATSON] *Important Considerations*, which ought to move all true and sound catholikes who are not wholly jesuited, to acknowledge . . . that the proceedings of her Majesty and of the state with them, since the beginning of her Highnesse raigne, have bene both mild and mercifull. (Newly imprinted, 1601), p. 5.

In case of a conflict, like that which had been caused by the "surreptitious" sentence of excommunication against Elizabeth, *i.e.* in case the pope should in some way or other order the catholics of England to lend their aid in placing an enemy of their country on the throne, there is no civil or natural law which could compel them to obey.   In a conflict of this kind their place would be on the side of the state and of the queen of England.

Watson's views on the relation of church and state are thus closely allied to the more clear-cut views of John Bishop already quoted (p. 420).   But while Bishop's pamphlet, published in 1598, had not spoken in the name of the party, Watson's book of 1601, in which very likely other seculars had a hand, may be regarded more or less as a manifesto of his party.[1]   The idea of making peace with the English state at the expense of the Jesuits, an idea at first put out in secret, and as if with an uneasy conscience, was now boldly paraded in the light of day, and formed part of the avowed programme of the secular priests. This programme is based on national aspirations in general and in particular on the maxims of Gallicanism ; nevertheless it is qualified by what is added at the end of Watson's book : "Whatsoever is written or contained in these books, we submit all to the censure and judgment of our Holy Mother the Catholick Church."

Decisive steps towards giving practical effect to this new programme were taken in the summer of 1601.   The secular priest, Thomas Bluet, a prisoner in Wisbeach castle, was examined by Richard Bancroft, bishop of London, and expressed himself to the effect that the Jesuits were dangerous to the state while the seculars were

[1] See the statement in the title page, " Published by sundry of us, the secular priests."   The *Important Considerations* seem to have been retouched by several hands.   *Cf.* LAW, *Jesuits and Seculars*, Introd., p. cxxxvi.

loyal subjects of the queen suffering from unjust persecution.   In subsequent negotiations with the bishop, with
the privy council, and, finally, with the queen herself, Bluet
succeeded so well in interesting the English government
in the carrying out of the pending appeal to the curia,
that he ventured to ask if it might be permitted to him,
along with some other secular priests, to go to Rome
in furtherance thereof.   Our only knowledge of the
transactions of this adroit priest with Elizabeth's government is gained from the official report which in March,
1602, he himself presented to two Roman cardinals.[1]   It
is easy to understand that in this report he says nothing
that might be detrimental to the cause of the secular
clergy in Rome.   His account sounds credible though
incomplete.   The question remains open ; how did Bluet
succeed in obtaining so unwonted a concession from the
government ?   The earliest law of Queen Elizabeth, and
the one hitherto observed with the utmost rigour, forbade
all appeals to a judge beyond the seas, *i.e.* to the
apostolic see.   The penal, legislation of 1585 made it
high treason to be a priest.   Bluet, already guilty of
death as a priest, asks permission to perform a second
act also punishable with death, and not only obtains the
permission but, in addition, the support of the government !   What had he to offer in return ?

There is only one answer to the question.   From the
course of the negotiations between Bluet and the government, on the one hand, and, on the other, from the
turn taken by the controversy between appellants and
Jesuits, the conclusion is highly probable (and, when
we take Cecil's evidence into account, even absolutely
certain) that Bluet assured the government that in Rome

---

[1] Printed by LAW, *op. cit.*, pp. 153–158.   In English in DOM. CAL.,
1601–03, pp. 167–171.

he would bring about the recall of the Jesuits from England.[1] This assurance might seem to some not beyond the bounds of possibility, for, as people in London knew well, the prevailing estimate of England in Rome after 1588 was very different from what it had been before. It might be assumed from this that the change of attitude in political matters would now be extended to religious questions as well, and so lead to the curb being put on the Jesuits' contentiousness.

The English state had conquered its foreign foe, but was still constantly at war with catholicism, that illusive enemy within her gates, but by this division in the enemy's ranks she saw a prospect at last of gaining a decisive victory over them. It seems that Queen Elizabeth, in order to make full use of this unparalleled opportunity, put forth all her skill and inspired the appellants with hopes she did not intend to realize, and, indeed, could not, on account of the penal laws. Only in this way can the belief of the appellants in the possibility of carrying out their programme, and their hopes of gaining toleration from the government for non-Jesuit confessors of the catholic faith be explained. The queen's subsequent protestation that she was guiltless of starting this idea[2] is certainly no proof that she had not played

---

[1] The Secretary of State reproached the appellants on their return from Rome with not having redeemed their promise, for they had not succeeded in getting the Jesuits recalled from England, or in deposing Blackwell, etc. So a confidential dispatch, *Avvisi di Londra*, of Jan. 29, 1603, in the Arch. Vat., Borgh. III., 124 g 1, fols. 67 *et seq*. To this must be added the evidence of the nuncio in Belgium, Ottavio Mirto Frangipani, bishop of Tricarico, who was mixed up with the quarrels among English catholics. He wrote (Ghent, Aug. 22, 1602) to Card. Aldobrandini, that Queen Elizabeth had given the priests permission to go to Rome, because she hoped by this means to get rid of the Jesuits. Arch. Vat., Borgh. III., 98 d 2.

[2] *Cf.* p. 452. Royal Proclamation of Nov. 5, 1602.

a double game with the priests. With this agrees a statement of hers, evidently intended to reach the pope's ears, recorded by Bluet, which may well be genuine, *i.e.* Elizabeth praised Clement VIII. in contrast to his predecessors, Pius, Gregory, and Sixtus, as a peace-loving pope who had given her no cause for complaint, but rather was, as his name implied, *Clemens !* [1]

And so in the beginning of November, 1601, we find this remarkable state of things full of contradictions; English secular priests and prisoners of state are provided with passports by the English government [2] to go to Rome to prosecute an appeal to the pope. Nearly a year had passed since the appeal had been forwarded, and no word had as yet been received from the curia. It was entirely owing to Rome's long silence that in the first half of 1601 matters in England reached the crisis just described ; but that the envoys of the appellants, when they started for Rome in the late autumn of the year, had not the least suspicion that the decision had already been given, was not the fault of the curia's leisurely way of doing business, but of a piece of unfair dealing on the part of the archpriest.

On August 17, 1601, eight months after the presentation of the appeal, the papal judgment had been delivered. It took the form of a letter to the archpriest,

---

[1] LAW, *op. cit.*, p. 156.

[2] I have found copies of the following passports: (1) for John Mush and Francis Barnaby, Richmond, Aug. 14, 1601—" transituri sunt in partes transmarinas propter negotia quædam nobis cognita, etc." ; (2) for Christopher Bagshaw, Thomas Bluet, Fr. Barnaby and William Finch, alias Bennett, Richmond, Oct. 25 ; (3) Permission for them to take with them over the sea seven or eight horses, Richmond, Oct. 27 ; (4) Pass for their servants, Whitehall, Nov. 1, 1601. Arch. Vat., Borgh. III., 98 d 1, fol. 231 ; *cf.* fol. 235ᵛ. See also J. R. DASENT, *Acts of the Privy Council*, new series, XXXII. (1907), pp. 205, 300, 316. *Cf.* LAW, *Archpriest Controversy*, II., p. 29.

the catholic clergy, and the laity of England, a letter
both diplomatic and pastoral.[1]   The appeal was rejected
in form but granted substantially in all important points.
Blackwell's accusation that the priests who had not
acknowledged his appointment as archpriest before the
papal confirmation were guilty of schism—the accusation
which had kindled the strife anew after it had died
down and reopened wounds that were healing—was dismissed as unfounded, and the mere use of the word
schism was condemned under pain of excommunication.
The controversial publication of the Jesuit Lister (p. 432),
so detested by the seculars, and the entire literature to
to which these quarrels had given rise, were condemned
under the same penalty, and all publications of a similar
nature were forbidden.   The archpriest Blackwell, whose
appointment was confirmed afresh, was soundly lectured
at the same time on the duties of his office, which had
been given him "for the edification and not for the
destruction of souls."   With equal emphasis the christian
duty of humble obedience was urged upon his opponents.

This decision shows in the happiest manner Rome's
twofold effort to be just, and, at the same time, to maintain
ecclesiastical discipline.   Had the letter been made public
immediately after its arrival in England, it would, in spite
of its late arrival, have produced good results.   But, just
at the time of its arrival, the prohibition it contained to
publish anything bearing upon the controversy was most
unwelcome to the archpriest, for there was an immediate
prospect of the appearance of a bulky volume in which
Persons himself attempted to justify the archpriest
against all the pamphlets hitherto aimed at him.   Blackwell, therefore, kept back the brief for some months and

[1] Draft in Arch. dei Brevi, Diversor., Clement VIII., lib. ix., fols.
401 *et seq*.   Printed in DODD-TIERNEY, III., Appendix, No. XXXIII.

only published it in January, 1602, immediately after the looked-for book by the leader of the Jesuit party had made its appearance, bearing upon it all the signs of hasty editing.[1] This clumsy device, which was instantly detected, had the result of making the appellants feel that a papal prohibition, which the Jesuits, with the connivance of the archpriest, had evaded as soon as it was published, did not bind them either. And so the brief of August 17, 1601, by Black-well's fault—or perhaps still more by Persons'—remained a dead letter, and the war of pamphlets continued more vigorously than ever.

The second journey to Rome which the appellants, supported by the English government, had undertaken with the highest expectations of success would therefore have been too late, had its object been nothing more than to obtain an answer to their appeal. It soon became evident that the mere fact of receiving an answer to their appeal failed to satisfy all the desires of the appellant party. The brief, kept back by the arch-priest, had been communicated to the deputies of the appellants by Frangipani, the nuncio in Belgium, as they passed through on their way to Rome, in December, 1601. But neither the knowledge of the papal decision, now communicated to them, nor the exhortation of the nuncio, induced them (with one exception) to give up their journey to Rome.[2] What the conciliatory decree of the pope had conceded to them fell far short of what they hoped to obtain, and, indeed, must obtain, if the expectations which

---

[1] *A Briefe Apologie*, etc. *Cf.* LAW, *Jesuits and Seculars*, Introd., pp. lxxxvii. *et seq.*, cxxxiii. DODD-TIERNEY, III., Appendix, p. clv.

[2] Dispatches of the nuncio Frangipani to Card. Aldobrandini, Nieupoort, Dec. 7, 1601, and Jan. 25, 1602. Arch. Vat., Borgh. III., 98 d 1, fol. 235 ; 98 d 2. *Cf.* LAW, *Archpriest Controversy*, II., pp. 30 *et seq.*

they had raised in the mind of Elizabeth's government were to be realized.

The archpriest and the Jesuits were not idle spectators of their adversaries' activity. In February, 1602, they too sent a deputation to Rome in order to lodge still heavier charges as a counter-blast to the grievances of the appellants. "To such lengths have they (the appellants) gone that they prefer to enter into treaty with the deadly enemies of the faith rather than obey their superiors and keep in charity with their fellow members in Christ."[1] The nuncio Frangipani, who had exerted himself in vain to mediate between the hostile parties, regarded with anxiety this new crisis in the never-ending controversy. He was afraid the catholic religion in England would be destroyed by these quarrels and by the insubordination of the clergy.[2]

The story of the negotiations at Rome, which lasted from February to October, 1602, has been recorded in diaries and reports composed by the appellants.[3] Two letters which Bluet wrote from Rome to Bishop Bancroft have recently come to light,[4] and these complete the material at our disposal, so that hardly any important point still remains in question. We shall here give a

[1] " Immo sunt eousque progressi, ut cum capitalibus fidei hostibus, maluerint inire societatem, quam superioribus obsequi et cum suis in Christi visceribus colere charitatem." Rich. Parker and Aegid. Archer to Clement VIII. *Ex Seminario Anglicano Audomaropoli* [the college of English Jesuits at St. Omer] *prope Caletum, die Feb.* 2, 1602. Arch. Vat., Borgh. II., 448 *ab* fol. 168. This letter preceded the deputation. On April 9, 1602, Parker and Archer announced their arrival in Rome. *L.c.*, fol. 369.

[2] Frangipani to Aldobrandini, Nieupoort, March 8, 1602. Arch. Vat., Borgh. III., 98 d 2.

[3] LAW, *Archpriest Controversy*, Vol. II. *Cf.* LAW, *Jesuits and Seculars*, Introd., § 7.

[4] Printed by R. G. USHER, *Reconstruction of the English Church*, Vol. I. (1910), p. 179.

summary only.   First, there are the political bearings of the case.   As the rivalry between Jesuits and appellants was closely bound up with the rivalry between supporters of the Spanish and non-Spanish (Scottish) succession to the English throne, the appellants received hearty support in Rome from French diplomacy which was then influential in the Eternal City, and for this Elizabeth expressed her thanks to Henry IV.[1]   The Jesuits, on the other hand, enjoyed the patronage of the declining power of Spain, which was of much less account.   And so the great rivalry between these two nations, which had played so important a part in the world's history, had its bearing upon the quarrels among the English priests.   In this connection it is important to note that just then, in the beginning of 1602, the versatile Persons wrote to the Scottish envoy in Paris to excuse himself for having written his book against the king of Scotland,[2] and to offer him his services, "upon the smallest shews that he shall make of his inclination towards the favour of the catholiques."[3]   He who had hitherto been the most devoted adherent of Spain among the English Jesuits was now willing, when too late, to forsake the sinking ship of Spanish power.   Important as these political considerations were in their bearing upon the course of the affair,[4] they did not decide the matter.

[1] Dispatch of the French ambassador in London, Beaumont, Oct. 2, 1602, to Henry IV. AL. TEULET, *Relat. polit. de la France et de l'Espagne avec l'Ecosse*, IV. (Paris, 1862), pp. 264 *et seq.* For the part played by France in the archpriest controversy, see R. COUZARD, *Une ambassade à Rome sous Henri IV.* (Paris, 1900), pp. 82 *et seq.* Couzard is inexact in some details and his view of the controversy is not without bias.

[2] On the succession to the English crown, *vid. ante*, pp. 383 *et seq.*

[3] Communicated to Cecil, secretary of state, by Winwood, the English envoy in Paris, Feb. 27/March 9, 160½. *Winwood Memorials*, I. (London, 1725), p. 388.

[4] *Cf.* the letter of the appellants from Rome, March 31, 1602. DODD-TIERNEY, III., Appendix, p. clvii. LAW, *Archpriest Controversy*, II., *passim.*

The pressure put upon the pope by French diplomacy did not make him approve of the policy of political and ecclesiastical compromise advocated by the appellants. However much they tried to represent their negotiations with the English government as unobjectionable from a catholic standpoint and even beneficial to the church at large,[1] the damaging fact remained that they had been willing to conclude a peace with the heretics and their excommunicated queen on a basis that had never yet been heard of. They wished to purchase freedom of conscience, and the price they were willing to pay was the recognition of the protestant state.

Freedom of conscience! No word was more disliked by the counter-reformation. Seldom did it fall from the lips of the princes of the church, of popes, or of nuncios, without the addition of some such adjective as *detestabilis*, *execrandus*, etc.[2] In most cases, freedom of conscience seemed deserving of anathema because advocated by protestants and not by catholics. But how about it now when, as in England, the parts of oppressor and oppressed were reversed? Clement VIII. answered the appellants sternly, that persecution was more profitable for the church than freedom of conscience. "Do you wish to be among thorns and yet not be pricked?" Bluet showed how much he had been mistaken as to the pope's mind when, in writing to Bishop Bancroft in London, he stated that he was unable to get the better of the Jesuits and Spaniards in the curia for the simple reason that he could produce no definite proposals made by the queen of England!

"Three lynes of Her Majestie's hand had sufficiencie to

---

[1] LAW, *op. cit.*, pp. 62 *et seq.*
[2] See the references given in the author's *Nuntiaturberichte aus Deutschland,* 17 *Jahrhundert. Die Prager Nuntiatur des Ferreri,* etc. (Berlin, 1913), pp. xlix. *et seq.*

drowne all [my opponents in the curia]. The good old man [the pope] did demaunde it of me not once."[1] As far as his Holiness was concerned, there is no reason for doubting that Bluet told the truth. The pope was naturally anxious to have authentic information about Elizabeth's attitude of mind towards her catholic subjects. But all the evidence is against Bluet's inference that Clement would, as it were, have gone halfway to meet the queen in a policy of religious toleration. He blamed the appellants for their negotiations with the heretics and upbraided them for calling the excommunicated and deposed Elizabeth their queen. Although himself no friend to the Jesuits, he regarded with deep distrust the hostility of these priests towards the Society, a hostility concealed beneath "the chimera of freedom of conscience."[2]

The sentence, in which the pope once more and for the last time gave judgment on this second appeal, was in part a reiteration of the brief of August 17, 1601. The previous judgment condemning the charge of schism brought against the appellants by the archpriest had, of course, to be maintained. In April, 1602, quite at the beginning of the negotiations in Rome, the minds of the two deputies had been set at rest on this point.[3] The Inquisition, which had already been charged with the detailed investigation of the controversy, and before which Blackwell had denounced the impugners of his authority (p. 431), could not do otherwise than conform itself to the pope's decision on this point. In a decree of July 20,[4] the Holy Office declared that the archpriest, inasmuch

---

[1] Bluet to Bancroft, June 3, 1602. USHER, *op. cit.*, I., 179.

[2] LAW, *op. cit.*, pp. 6, 48, 112.　　　　　　[3] *Ib.*, p. 194.

[4] *In congr^ne habita die XX.* 1602, *super rebus Anglicis.* West. Cath. Arch., VII., 263-265. Arch. dei Brevi, Diversor. Clem., VIII., lib. ix., fol. 517-27. Extracts printed in DODD-TIERNEY, III., Appendix, p. clxxvii., note.

as he had treated the appellants as schismatics and rebels, had given them just cause for complaint. At the same time, however, they made allowances to the archpriest for extenuating circumstances, and were quite clear that the form of government under an archpriest ought to be maintained now that it had once been set up. Blackwell must be warned a second time not to exceed the limits of his authority. All consultation with Jesuits, either in England, Rome, or anywhere else, about the affairs of his office must be forbidden, and his earlier instructions (p. 413) ought to be declared null and void. In the place of these instructions he must now regard himself as absolutely bound in duty to report to the pope in person, or to the cardinal protector, everything concerning the government of the English clergy.[1]

Certainly these suggestions were sufficiently plain, and, if the pope sanctioned them, they would entail no small humiliation on the Jesuits! Persons thought that the archpriest and his party were so roughly handled in them that they were bound to be made the laughing-stock of the heretics, and so he did his best to get the decree of the Inquisition modified.[2] Still, in the minds of the appellants all the concessions which the Inquisition was prepared to make in their favour were scarcely worth the paper they

---

[1] " Iniungendum preterea eidem archipresbytero, ut omnia negotia ad suum officium spectantia tractet et expediat absque ulla communicatione cum provinciali Soc. Jesu vel aliis patribus eiusdem Societatis in Anglia existentibus, et in hoc abrogandam et tollendam esse instructionem sibi datam a bo. me. Card[ii] Caetano. Ad hoc præcipiendum esse eidem archipresbytero, ne de Eccl. Anglicanæ gubernio seu regimine, vel de rebus ad dictum regimen aliquo modo spectantibus per litteras seu interpositam personam cum patribus eiusdem Societatis in Romana curia vel alibi agat, sed omnia ad S. D. N. vel pro tempore existentem protectorem referat." Westm. Arch., *l.c.*

[2] Persons to Card. Pinelli, Aug. 22, 1602. West. Cath. Arch., VII., p. 273. Pinelli belonged to the *Congregazione del S. Offizio.*

were written on, so long as Blackwell continued in office, and the Jesuits remained in England, and the appellants were prevented from negotiating with the English government concerning the vital question of toleration. It was far removed, however, from the mind of the Inquisition to grant any freedom of this sort. On this point it took up the same position as Persons, who could not find words strong enough to condemn the alliance between the appellants and the government. The recognition of the protestant state was, in his opinion, irreconcilable with a man's duty to the catholic church. When the decree was about to be published, he wrote to the Inquisition : " So long as the appellants depend upon the will of the queen and have dealings with her ministers they cannot really conform themselves to the intention of his Holiness, no matter what they may say or promise." [1] The Inquisition was quite of one mind with Persons, when in its decree it requested the pope to forbid under pain of excommunication " all dealings and communications with heretics to the prejudice of catholics " [2]—a point unmistakably directed against the appellants.

Nearly three more months elapsed before the decree of the Inquisition received the pope's final approbation—the unusual difficulty of the affair fully explaining this additional delay. The idea of making terms with the English government, which the appellants entertained but which

---

[1] *Considerationes quædam præcipui momenti ad causam Anglicanam recte terminandam* by PERSONS, West. Cath. Arch., VII., pp. 255–261. *Cf.* Arch. dei Brevi, *l.c.*, fols. 521 *et seq.* The passage runs : " Sequitur istos Appellantes quamdiu a reginæ voluntate pendunt et cum ejusdem ministris tractant, non se posse vere, quidquid interim dicunt vel promittunt, ad S. S^{tis} intentionem conformare."

[2] " Ac sub eisdem pœnis prohibendam esse quamlibet participationem et communicationem cum hæreticis in præjudicium catholicorum." West. Cath. Arch., VII., p. 265. In English in DODD-TIERNEY, III., Appendix, p. clxxvii.

the Jesuits and the Inquisition regarded as heretical, was by no means looked upon as altogether inadmissible, even in the official circles of the church. The conversations already mentioned which Frangipani, the nuncio in Belgium, had held with the representatives of the appellants on their way to Rome made a great impression upon him. Bluet, the leading spirit of the deputation, may very probably have told him then exactly what he afterwards said in Rome : " If I who am a worm and no man could prevail so much with the queen, what might not your Holiness do, with the aid of the Most Christian King (of France), towards obtaining consolation for the English catholics? " [1] Ever since that time the question of Elizabeth's real intentions towards the catholics had never been out of the nuncio's mind. At length, in August, 1602, during the period of uncertainty before the final decision was given, he came forward with an adventurous plan.[2] How would it be if he himself, without in any way committing the pope, and with the greatest secrecy, were to negotiate in person with the great heretical queen ! Suppose, for the sake of appearances, he allowed himself to be taken prisoner by some English ship in the waters of Nieupoort and carried before Elizabeth in order to treat with her about the peace of her own country and of Europe ? For a long time, as he assures Cardinal Aldobrandini, he had kept this plan to himself lest he should seem frivolous ; he now proposed it in order that the pope might have that certitude which was unattainable through intermediaries, but was, at the same time, so indispensable for the papal policy.

" The idea is charming," wrote the cardinal nephew,

---

[1] Curtailed from Bluet's report in LAW, *Jesuits and Seculars*, p. 158.

[2] See his letter to Card. Aldobrandini in Appendix XXIV.

Aldobrandini, ironically on the margin of the letter containing the proposal. His cautious master, Clement VIII., would never have been won over to take part in so risky a game. He resigned himself to the fact that it was impossible for him to learn Elizabeth's secret thoughts, and at length gave his sanction to the decree of July 20. On October 5, 1602, this judgment was made public in the form of a letter to the archpriest Blackwell.[1] Once again he was warned not to exceed his powers,[2] and these were more plainly defined than heretofore, especially on their negative side. It was made clear to him what he could *not* do. In important points, especially in his powers of inflicting punishment on the clergy, the faculties previously granted him were curtailed. His relation to the Jesuits and the duty of forwarding reports to Rome were regulated in full accordance with the decree of the Inquisition. Furthermore, the humiliated archpriest was ordered to admit three priests from the appellant party among the number of his assistants as soon as there were vacancies. Finally, every publication of a controversial nature emanating from either party, and all dealings with heretics to the prejudice of catholics were threatened with the church's heaviest censures. Both sides were exhorted to unity and Christian love.

This second and final decision of Rome resembled its predecessor in its anxious striving after a fair settlement of the dispute. If impartiality could have established peace, all differences would now have been buried, but the appellants would have no peace that did not entail the banishment of the Jesuits from England. While the

---

[1] Draft in Arch. dei Brevi, Diversor. Clem. VIII., lib. ix., fols. 515 *et seq*, 528 *et seq*. Printed in DODD-TIERNEY, III., Appendix, pp. clxxxi. *et seq*.

[2] As, for example, he had done by threatening an interdict, p. 427.

envoys were urging their charges against the archpriest and his Jesuit friends in Rome, their party was fighting with sharper weapons in England. The Jesuit Rivers wrote to Robert Persons in June, 1602 :[1] "It is already a common received position amongst them that it is not only lawful but meritorious to discover a Jesuit to the state." Seeing that three years before Watson had presented a wholesale denunciation of all the Jesuits in a body to the attorney-general, it followed logically from the alliance between the appellants and the government that individual Jesuits would now be denounced.

The only possible way for the appellants to retrace their steps was to renounce their scarcely formed relations with the Elizabethan state. If they wished to abide by these, and so side with the government in attacking the Jesuits, they must withhold obedience to the papal brief. They stood at the parting of the ways—Rome or England, church or country !

The decision was urgent. Even before the appellants returned to England, Queen Elizabeth placed her ultimatum before them. About six weeks after the publication of the papal letter in Rome, on November 5, 1602 (o.s.), possibly in consequence of receipt of secret information from the Eternal City or, more likely, from impatience at the delay, the queen published a proclamation against the Jesuits and secular priests.[2] The tone of this declaration is one of exhausted patience, while at the same time it shows that Elizabeth was endeavouring to exonerate herself in the eyes of zealous protestants from the reproach of undue leniency towards popery. The queen declares that she had tried in vain to bring the disobedient to a

[1] June 9, 1602. FOLEY'S *Records*, I., p. 38.
[2] A Proclamation against Jesuits and Secular priests. Nov. 5/15, 1602. Brit. Mus. G. 6463 (397). Printed in RYMER, *Fœdera*, XVI. (1715), pp. 473–476, and DODD-TIERNEY, III., Appendix, No. XXXV.

better mind by clemency, still she is willing to make a distinction between the treasonable conduct of the Jesuits and of a section of the secular clergy "combined with them" and the less heinous but still reprehensible disobedience of the rest of the seculars, who were "in some things opposite unto the Jesuits." The former, who stirred up foreign princes to invade England and murder the queen, must forthwith depart out of the country, or else run the risk of having the penal laws set in motion against them with the utmost rigour. The latter, who condemn, indeed, the high treason of the others and are ready to fight for their country, but yet "steal away the hearts" of the queen's people "to unite and knit them to our mortal enemy the pope," receive grace until January 1, or at latest February 1 (o.s.), by which date they must "acknowledge sincerely their duty and allegiance to us" before the authorities, or leave the country like the others. Those who acknowledge their allegiance will be treated "as shall be thought by us to be most meet and convenient."

The system of uncompromising hostility to catholicism, which for some time past had broken down in practice, is here formally waived. This proclamation of Elizabeth, which was her last upon the catholic question, is also the first sign of better times for the outlawed confessors of the Roman faith—a sign, indeed, given with the utmost caution so as not to call forth noisy acclamation. If the appellants had hoped to deserve the boon of freedom of conscience by attacking the Jesuits, they must have been bitterly disappointed. In an outburst of righteous indignation, the royal proclamation scouts the shameless insinuation "that we have some purpose to grant toleration of two religions within our Realme, where God (we thanke Him for it, who seeth into the secret corners of all hearts) doth not onley know our owne innocencie from such imagination, but how fare it hath bene from any about us, once to offer to our eares the perswasion of such a course, as would not only disturbe the peace of the Church but bring this our State into confusion."

The Jesuits, then, had been perfectly right when they declared in Rome, as the archpriest's cause was being tried, that Elizabeth had no idea of granting the freedom of conscience of which the appellants dreamed ; and that even if she wished to grant it she could not, because she dare not change the law of England without the consent of parliament.[1] Now, Elizabeth never entertained any idea of the sort, for we have a witness to prove that this proclamation perfectly represented her personal views, and that Elizabeth held the reins of government up to the very end. The French ambassador in London, Beaumont, records a conversation which he had with the queen early in October, 1602, about the archpriest controversy and the question of religious toleration.[2] The words used by Elizabeth agree perfectly with the tenor of the proclamation issued a month later. While acknowledging the good will of the appellants, the queen emphatically rejected the idea of toleration ; her people were not capable of standing the exercise of two religions ! She would take great care not to disturb the peace of her kingdom ; she must refuse the catholics' demands ; still she was ready to treat them with clemency and not persecute them if they lived agreeably to her laws. Upon these statements Beaumont comments that it is all one could expect from the queen who, in her old age, held very stiffly to her own opinions.

The idea of religious toleration continued to be as

---

[1] LAW, *Archpriest Controversy*, II., p. 78.
[2] Beaumont to Henry IV., Oct. 2, 1602. TEULET, *Relat. polit.* etc., IV. (Paris, 1862), pp. 264 *et seq.*

much tabooed in London as in Rome during the whole of the Elizabethan age—in this respect there was no difference between the catholic church and protestant England. Both were wholly intolerant in theory and both waived points in practice. The clause in the proclamation in favour of the seculars who acknowledged the queen's authority was a compromise of this kind. Whether they should accept or reject it was now the great question which the party had to consider when their envoys returned from Rome. The end of the period of grace was no longer distant when, in the last days of 1602, the secular priest, Thomas Bluet, the organizer of the second appeal to the pope, was once more brought before the bishop of London.[1] This time we have no account of his interview with the bishop from Bluet's own pen, but Bishop Bancroft wrote to Cecil a few days after "his commitment as prisoner" that the result of the transactions in Rome were unacceptable to the appellants.[2] Therefore Bluet must have acknowledged to him that they had gained none of the things there of which they had held out hopes to the English government. The secretary of state, with whom the appellants now entered into communication, upbraided them that they had effected neither the recall of the Jesuits nor the removal of the archpriest Blackwell, as they had promised.[3] It is as if the appellants now sought to make up for the bad impression which the news from Rome had made by an outward show of disobedience to the papal brief of October 5. They were in and out of the bishop's house "as before and perhaps still oftener." Bluet resided and took his meals

---

[1] DOM. CAL., 1601–03, p. 272.

[2] *Ib.;* cf. USHER, *op. cit.*, I., 183.

[3] *Avvisi di Londra*, Jan. 29, 1603.   Arch. Vat., Borgh. III., 124 g I, fols. 67, 68.

for a time with Bancroft, as though he was his guest, and not a prisoner of state. Just as the prohibition to consort with heretics was disregarded, so, too, was the other prohibition, *i.e.* not to continue the paper war. With the bishop of London's consent, the appellants published new pamphlets against the Jesuits.[1] Through a representative in Paris they tried to keep in touch with the French government so as to be able to carry on the war against the Jesuits with diplomatic weapons at the same time. The English ambassador in Paris received constant information concerning the negotiations between the appellants and the ministers of Henry IV.[2]

The Jesuits, who indeed had no cause either to rejoice over the papal pronouncement, were now all respectful obedience. The superior of the English province, Henry Garnet, even before he received official intimation of the brief, directed a circular letter to the members of his order which was a model of correctness, every phrase overflowing with love of peace and unity, and, at the same time, he exhorted them, with a certain show of generosity, to give the appellants the right hand of fellowship.[3] From the catholic standpoint, the conduct of the Jesuits was at once the most dignified and the most skilful. The path of resistance, which the appellants made a show of taking, must inevitably have led them sooner or later out of the catholic church into the anglican. It was probably the instinctive feeling that such would be the result of their

[1] *Ib.; cf.* DOM. CAL., 1601–03, p. 300. For the new controversial writings, see LAW, *Jesuits and Seculars*, Introd., pp. cxlvi. *et seq.*

[2] So says a memorial which the appellants presented to James I. shortly after his accession. *Succincta relatio memorabilium punctorum, quæ Suæ M^tis servitium concernunt negotiatione, sacerdotum appellantium Romæ et Galiæ*, etc., Aug. 10, 1603. Arch. Vat., Borgh. III., 86 a, fols. 55, 56. English text: fols. 59, 60.

[3] Circular letter of Nov. 16, 1602. LAW, *Archpriest Controversy*, II., pp. 227–229.

action that finally restrained the majority of them from coming to terms with the English state by taking the required oath of allegiance. In the last weeks of 1602, the prospect of grace opened up by the proclamation had induced only one priest, so far as we know, to make his submission and beg for release from his legal disabilities.[1] One more priest appealed to the proclamation as an excuse for declining to receive and publish the papal brief, in open disobedience to the archpriest.[2] As the new year approached and the time for making up their mind grew shorter, the priests, once so eager for the fray, still hesitated, and only at the last moment, on the very day on which the time of grace came to a close (January 31, 1603), did they meet, thirteen in all, and sign a conjoint declaration of loyalty—and Bluet was not among them, the man who had been the life and soul of the second appeal! The same feeling of shrinking from a possible breach with the church, which even to the present day is visible whenever a crisis arises in the history of catholicism, restrained the majority of the appellants from openly siding with their country in the conflict between church and state.

"The Protestation of Allegiance," dated January 31 (o.s.), was drawn up by William Bishop, one of the two priests who had acted in the first appeal to the pope in 1598.[3] The chief points in this weighty and dignified document are briefly as follows :—

　　1. The queen has the same sovereign power over us as

---

[1] It is significant that the petitioner does not give his name in writing. LAW, *op. cit.*, pp. 221–223.

[2] Anthony Heborne. LAW, *op. cit.*, pp. 230 *et seq.*

[3] English text in DODD-TIERNEY, III., Appendix, No. XXXVI. Summary in DOM. CAL., 1601–03, pp. 285 *et seq.* Two Latin texts in West. Cath. Arch., VII., pp. 393–410. *Cf.* LAW, *Archpriest Controversy*, II., pp. 246–248.

any of her predecessors had ; nothing in the world can release us from the obedience we owe her in all things temporal.

2. We swear to defend the queen and the state against conspiracies, attempted invasions, and attacks of all kinds whatsoever.

3. If the pope, in fulfilment of his excommunication, commands us to forsake the queen and take part with her enemies, we shall refuse him obedience, even if he threatens us with excommunication.

4. At the same time we acknowledge the pope to be our spiritual chief pastor and the successor of St. Peter who has "as ample and no more authority or jurisdiction over us " as Christ committed to that apostle. For as we are most ready to spend our blood in the defence of her majesty and our country, so we will rather lose our lives than infringe the lawful authority of Christ's catholic church.

The long struggle to bring about a reconciliation between duties to the church and duties to the state—a struggle which fills the history of English catholicism in Elizabeth's days—has perhaps found its most memorable expression in this declaration of allegiance of the thirteen priests. The declaration amounts to a revision of canon law adapted to the needs of the modern state. The supremacy of the pope was set forth as being spiritual in the strictest sense, and every claim on the pope's part to domination in worldly affairs was condemned as an abuse. The "bloody questions " of the catholic persecution, which had been an instrument of torture to hundreds of catholic consciences (p. 159), were all of them answered in a manner entirely favourable to the secular power, while the papacy of the counter-reformation, as it existed from Pius V. down to Sixtus V., was tacitly condemned. The modern papacy indeed has never formally acknowledged this revision of canon law, but in practice accepted it as time went on. The question, "may the pope depose sovereigns?" maintained its central position in the history of the relations between England and the catholic church during the greater part of the seventeenth century, although it had then ceased to have any practical importance for England. The declaration of allegiance signed by these thirteen priests, which answered this question in the negative, is consequently both the close of one period and the starting-point of another; it carried within it the future of English catholicism.

For the moment, indeed, it seemed to have no importance whatever. Whether it was that the government refrained from carrying at once into effect the threats contained in the proclamation of November 5 in the hopes of increasing still more the dissensions among English catholics,[1] or whether it was that the queen's fatal illness, which began about this time, put a stop to any decisive action, the government took no notice of the declaration of allegiance either as regards the loyal priests or the others. We only know that Bishop Bancroft held it to be inadequate.[2] The execution of one priest in February, side by side with the pardon by the queen of four others unnamed,[3] are not events which throw any light on the government's attitude towards the new state of things. Nor did the catholic church take notice, at

---

[1] According to the *Avvisi di Londra* (which as a rule are based upon good information), Jan. 29, 1603 (Arch. Vat., Borgh. III., 124 g 1, fols. 27 *et seq.*), the privy council met on Jan 22, and Cecil and Bishop Bancroft, against the wish of the Lord Chief Justice Popham, succeeded in hindering the proclamation from being put into force for the reason given above.

[2] USHER, *op. cit.*, I., pp. 184 *et seq.*

[3] DOM. CAL., 1601–03, p. 301.

least officially, of the disobedient priests who had made their peace with the protestant state and the excommunicated queen. The reason for this restraint on the part of the authorities of the church can easily be conjectured. For the news of the allegiance of the thirteen priests arrived at the same time as the news of Elizabeth's approaching end, and, therefore, for Rome to take any sharp measures against those English clergy who had given proof of their loyalty to the state, would have been the surest means of forcing the future sovereign to continue Elizabeth's ecclesiastical policy. As Rome entertained great hopes of the probable successor, James of Scotland,[1] a prudent reserve was for the moment the best policy.

And so it fell out that the important declaration of January 31, 1603, remained unnoticed. It was a mere chance if the dying queen ever heard of this last victory of hers. A victory for the crown, nevertheless, this act of allegiance was, although it did not lead to any consequences. Here, too, we are reminded of Bacon's words on Queen Elizabeth : "she reigned over forty-four years without having outlived her good fortune."[2] And in relation to the whole course of the history of the Elizabethan period this last triumph, apparently so small, assumes a symbolical importance. The submission of the thirteen priests is the proclamation of the victory of the modern secular state over the claim of the mediæval universal church to political power. The blow thus dealt at the leadership hitherto exercised by the Jesuits marks, at the same time, the collapse of that system of ecclesiastical

[1] *Cf:* my article *Clemens VIII. und Jakob I.* in the Quellen und Forschungen aus röm Arch. u. Bibl. VII., pp. 268–306.

[2] FRANCIS BACON, *In felicem memoriam Elizabethæ Angliæ Reginæ*, Works, ed. SPEDDING, VI. (1858), p. 291.

politics which had given its strongest manifestations in the excommunication of Elizabeth by Pius V., in the encouragement of political murder by Gregory XIII., and in the attempt of Sixtus V. to give practical effect by means of the Armada to his predecessor's excommunication of the queen of England.

The century which is occupied more than any other with the conflict between the ancient church and the modern state, the century of the reformation and counter-reformation, can tell of no nation or government that carried on the conflict with such far-reaching aims, so consistently and so mercilessly, as the England of Henry VIII. and Elizabeth. The reign of Elizabeth is the greater period of the two, and its work was more lasting in its effect. Not until then did the ecclesiastical creation of Henry VIII. become animated by an inward religious life, and then only did the new-born state church hold its own in grim earnest against the spiritual, and still more against the temporal, power of the Roman church.

Elizabethan England was able to carry on this conflict because throughout the period, and especially after 1570, her ecclesiastical and religious unity was threatened only by feeble minorities. The idea of a strong catholic party, needing but a favourable opportunity, or the advent of a catholic sovereign, or a victory of the Spanish arms in order to carry everything before it—an idea not yet fully exploded—contradicts all the results of the investigation now laid before the reader. This idea was fostered and spread among the irreconcilables who could not endure the idea of a protestant England or believe in its future. They either did not see the truth as to the comparative strength of the two religions, or purposely coloured the picture for their own political ends. Equally untenable is a second idea closely bound up with the first, *i.e.* that the great mass of the English people became anglicans and protestants less from choice than from the pressure put upon them by the civil power. It was not the tyranny of absolute monarchy, but the tendency of the national mind which triumphed in both the state church and in protestantism.

Again, it was in the name of the national sentiment and of the national conception of the state that liberty of doctrine and practice was denied to the small catholic minority. Owing to their foreign connections, catholics seemed the most dangerous of all the parties which kept aloof from the state church. This is a point of view which we can easily understand, in spite of its exaggerations. It is easy to understand it, because the national ideas found their bitterest opponents in the ranks of the catholics ; yet the point of view was exaggerated, because the opposition came only from the band of enthusiasts led by the Jesuits, and these were only a minority even among their co-religionists. The majority of catholics, even before 1588, and certainly after the defeat of the Armada, would have nothing to do with any settlement of the religious question which made England dependent on a foreign power, and in general they would have nothing to do with any forcible solution of the discord between church and country. And so the national idea prevailed, not only among the adherents of the state church, but also among the majority of those whose mother church remained the church of Rome. The ideas which centre round the state and national sentiment prevailed more completely in the English ecclesiastical settlement than in either France or Germany.

The external history of Elizabethan England which comes to a climax in the war with Spain—the political

champion of the catholic church—is the glorious counter-
part of her inner development. By fighting at first with
only light weapons, but keeping well on her guard, by
acting always on the offensive, by instantly returning
every blow—never retreating, but becoming more and
more conscious of her own strength in the ever-widening
circles of the conflict—greatly favoured, indeed, by the
political situation, but, in the decisive moment, relying
on herself alone and having only herself to thank for her
final victory—thus did Elizabeth's England wage her
great fight against the combination of Rome and Spain.
The sons of the English renaissance and fathers of puritan
England carried on the fight not so much for the sake of
religion as for their country and earthly advantage, yet,
at the same time, they were not devoid of religious
enthusiasm and even fanaticism.   More fortunate than
Spain, who squandered the best strength of her people
for the sake of a barren ecclesiastical idealism, England
knew no contradiction between her political and material
needs and her religious sentiment and ecclesiastical
problems.   On the contrary, England's duties as regards
the next world did not hinder, but rather furthered, her
interests in this.   Her religious energy was just strong
enough to produce warmth and action, but not strong
enough to sacrifice exigencies of state to religious enthusiasm.   And so England's war against Spain and Rome
combined had nothing of that strained *doctrinaire* character
which marked the policy of Philip II. in the Netherlands.
The English nation, free from that spasmodic over-exertion
which their Castilian pride forced upon the Spaniards,
attained to its rank as a world-power with the spontaneity
due to a sound national development.

England's victory over Spain brought the career of the
counter-reformation in western Europe to a standstill.

The defeat of the Armada was the salvation of the faith and freedom of the Low Countries. The vanquished power slowly withdrew from the position of champion of the catholic church. The papacy itself formed a new estimate of its foe and abandoned forthwith the use of the mediæval weapons which it had hitherto employed. Pius V., with the holy zeal of a crusader, stands at the opening of the period; he it was who began the war against England—Clement VIII., gentle, cautious, reserved, stands at its close—the forerunner of that subtile, diplomatic man of the world, Urban VIII., who was lavish with his compliments to Charles I. The attempt to win back England to the catholic church continued during the new age; the object remained the same, only the old methods were abandoned. But all the advances and carefully planned manœuvres by which Rome tried to regain puritan England were only the finale to the real decision taken by the England of Elizabeth.

The catholic church, however, in England during the period which we have been considering, was greater in her defeat than in many of her victories; Rome triumphed in England, not by domineering over the world, but by rising superior to it. The persecution by the state aroused great moral strength and a spirit of martyrdom—qualities which were not called forth in countries where the counter-reformation was in league with the civil power. And so, in spite of all conspiracies and schemes for assassination, and in spite of the approbation which these received from a pope who was a true child of his age, nay, even in spite of internal divisions and quarrels, the history of the catholic church in the England of Elizabeth is the most glorious page in the bloody annals of the counter-reformation. Neither in the greatness of the combatants nor in the value of the prize at stake, does this conflict fall below any other of the same period. But its full significance was only to be manifested in the future.   The combatants who then joined battle afterwards became the two greatest forces of the modern world —England and the Catholic Church.

APPENDIX

NOTE

THE appendices have been annotated only so far as the object of this book requires. Several of the pieces have important bearing on other subjects, as, for instance, Nos. XVI. and XIX. on the history of the life in Jesuit seminaries, and the latter, furthermore, throws light on the personal history of English catholicism which has lately been made its own special field of research by the Catholic Record Society. The names of the students in the English College, in several cases given in a corrupt form, have been identified, but I have abstained from adding notes of a biographical character. For the correct form of some names I am indebted to the friendly assistance of the Rev. J. H. Pollen.

I. *Sopra li negotii d'Inghilterra.* [1559 *or beginning of* 1560. *Rome.*]

Proposals for an amicable treatment of the English religious question.

Arch. Vat., Arm. LXIV., t. 28, fols. 299, 300 : undated, without place and signature. Apparently from an English catholic in Rome.

Considerato il presente stato del regno d' Inghilterra, il quale nuovamente è ritornato al scysma et all'heresie per mera volontà della moderna regina et contra il sentimento di molti signori principali di quel regno et della maggior parte delli populi, li quali desiderano la religione catholica et l'unione della chiesa ; considerato ancora che essa regina, non obstante la sua perversa religione, non ha sin qui voluto usare severità alcuna contra la persona di quei signori secolari et ecclesiastici, li quali non hanno voluto fargli il giuramento dell'obedientia nè manco negare la religione catholica, ma quelli solamente ha privati delle dignità et delli beni che possedevano et permette che possino stare nel regno, et ad alcuni che possino stare fuori et godere le loro entrate ; per tutte le sudette ragioni si può sperare che col successo di tempo et con le occasioni che puonno nascere, che sarà forzata la regina

overo sarà inspirata da Dio a dovere restituire l'obedientia di
quel regno alla sede apostolica et ritornare alla religione
catholica. Per questo la Santità di N. S^{re} si dignarà fare consideratione al tutto, et col pio et prudentissimo animo suo si
dignarà conservar questa speranza viva più che si può, senza
lasciarsi tirare dalli principi alle arme contra di essa regina, come
facilmente la potrebbe essere ricercata et pregata di voler fare.
Et se pure Sua Santità giudicarà bene di lasciarsi intendere
per alcun mezzo che, volendo ritornare essa regina all' unione
della chiesa, la sarà più volontieri raccolta più tosto amorevol-
mente che per violentia delle arme, questo pio et paterno officio
si potrà fare per mezzo d' un signor inglese chiamato Inghilfeildt,[1]
il qual era delli più confidenti et amati consiglieri che havesse la
regina passata, et s'è partito dal regno per poter vivere catholica-
mente, et gli è stato concesso di poter godere le sue entrate,
purchè non venghi habitare a Roma, et hora habita a Padova,
dove al presente deve andare un gentilhuomo inglese detto m.
Nevel,[2] chiamato dal decto Inghilfeildt per dover habitare con
esso; et si potrebbe far capace il decto m. Nevel della buona
volontà di Sua Santità, per doverne fare relatione al detto signor
Inghilfeildt, acciocchè habbia da prendere animo da mantenersi
nella buona religione, et che possa nutrire gl'animi degl'altri
catholici che sono rimasti in quel regno, et dirgli similmente
che, volendo lui scrivere o mandare personaggio per informare
Sua Santità delle occorrenze, a chi in tal caso haverà da far capo
in questa corte senza temere di poter essere scoperto et cadere
nell' indignatione della regina sua.

Il decto m. Nevel, il quale al presente ha d'andare trovar il
decto Inghilfeildt, è gentilhuomo da bene et alquanto parente
della bona memoria del cardinal Polo ; et perchè vorrebbe partire
fra dui giorni per suo viaggio, si dignarà Sua Santità fargli sapere
la volontà sua.

Sono similmente fuori del regno alcuni prelati et preti catholici,
li quali sono stati privati delle chiese et benefitii loro per non
voler seguire la nuova religione, et, piacendo a Sua Santità, potrà

---

[1] Sir Francis Englefield, Privy Councillor under Mary the Catholic, abroad
since 1559. *Dict. of Nat. Biogr.*, XVII., 372. *Cf.* R. LECHAT, *Les réfugiés
anglais dans les Pays-Bas espagnols* (Louvain, 1914), p. 45 *et passim.*

[2] Christopher Neville ? See *Dict. of Nat. Biogr.*, XL., 246.

commandare che l'entrate dell' hospitale degl' Inglesi qui in Roma debbino essere conservate et amministrate per li detti prelati et preti, et non da secolari, acciocchè possino nutrire quei gioveni inglesi, li quali vorrano imparare la dottrina christiana et le ceremonie ecclesiastice, atteso che col tempo potranno servire alle chiese in Inghilterra, se a Dio piacerà.

Il signor dottor Karn,[1] Inglese, il quale si trova qui et è stato ambasciatore della regina passata, sarà forzato di doversene ritornar alla sua patria, dove ha lasciato moglie et figlioli et l'entrate sue di qualche importanza, et pare che habbia havuto commandamento di non doversi partire di Roma,[2] la qual cosa potrebbe essere occasione che la regina si sdegnarà contro di lui, et lo privarà delle sue entrate, lui, la moglie et li suoi figlioli. Imperò Sua Santità potrebbe rimediargli con lasciarlo andare dove meglio gli parerà, purchè non ritorni in Inghilterra, et facilmente la regina si contentarà che, stando lui fuori di Roma, possa godere l'entrate sue, sicome ha concesso a molti altri. Et tutto ciò si dice per aviso, rimettendo il tutto nel prudentissimo giuditio di Sua Santità.

II. *Abbot Girolamo Martinengo to Cardinal Morone.* [*Beginning of March*, 1561. *Rome.*]

The abbot asks for instructions for his embassy to England ; the cardinal answers him in the margin.

Arch. Vat., Arm. LXIV., t. 28, fols. 287, 288 : undated with notes on the margin in Card. Morone's handwriting.

Ricordo a Monsignor Illmo et Rev^mo cardinal Morone sopra la instruttione dell'abbate Martinengo.[3]

Poichè per commandamento di V. S. Illma io ho da proporle

---

[1] Sir Edward Carne, the last English ambassador in Rome before the cessation of diplomatic relations. See above, p. 20, note 2.

[2] As a catholic, Carne preferred to remain in Rome. In order to avoid causing injury to his relations and belongings in England, he obtained from the pope a prohibition to leave the city, and so remained outwardly a hostage but really in full possession of his freedom until his death in Rome (1561). *Dict. Nat. Biogr.*, IX., p. 134. *Cf.* the inscription on his memorial slab in the atrium of San Gregorio : *sponte patria carens ob catholicam fidem.*

[3] Endorsed in Morone's handwriting : Dal s.^r abbate Martinengo per l'andata sua in Inghilterra.

alcune cose circa la mia instruttione, io noterò qui appresso
quanto mi occorre per sapere più certamente come portarmi in
servitio di S. Beat^he, rimettendomi poi nel resto a quello che
V. S. Illma con la sua prudenza si degnerà commettermi et
ordinarmi.

Et prima, quanto all' habito, io desidero intendere come io
doverò vestire, cioè da protonotario o pure in altro modo ? [1]

Appresso, se la S. Sta si contenta ch' io habbia alcune facoltà
per usarle, massimamente in Fiandra, dove potranno esser a
proposito o forse necessarie ? [2]

Se io harò da andare per le poste o vero a buone giornate,
ricordando a V. S. Illma che dalla età et dalla complessione mia
non si può aspettare nel viaggio estraordinaria prestezza ? [3]

Se in Fiandra mi converrà communicare la mia commissione
con madama di Parma ? [4]

Da chi harò da aspettare o domandare il salvocondotto per il
mio passaggio ? [5] Et in caso ch' io vedessi di dover esser troppo
intertenuto per ottenerlo, o che non si potesse alla fine ottenere,
se mi bisognerà fare qualche protesto, et in qual modo et con
quali solennità ; et, s' io potrò partirmi senza aspettare sopra
questo altra risposta da Roma ?

Se in Inghilterra io harò a smontare et alloggiare dall'-
oratore di S. M^ta Cath^ca o in altra parte dove più mi verrà
commodo ? [6]

Se con lui et con l'ambasciatore del Re Christianissimo dovrò
communicare il mio negotio in tutto o in parte, et fino a quanto
et con qual più et con qual meno ? [7]

Se la prima mia audienza alla reina doverà essere con introdut-
tione di ambedue e di alcuno de' sopradetti oratori, et se in
presenza loro haverò a fare la mia proposta ? [7]

Se la reina, come lontana della fede catholica, mostrasse di
non ricevermi per nuntio del pastore universale della santa

---

[1] Morone : Si porti l'habito ordinario !
[2] Morone : Et bisognerà fermarsi per aspettar il salvo condutto.
[3] Morone : Si vadi per le poste commode ; questo porta la sanità.
[4] Morone : Si communichi.—Margaret of Parma, Regent of the Netherlands.
[5] Morone : Si dimandi.
[6] Morone : S'alloggi. Obviously add : da sè. *Cf.* the Instructions, No. III.
[7] See the answer in No. III.

chiesa,[1] ma solamente di un principe, o in altro modo nel quale fosse diminutione della dignità apostolica; et se, parlando meco, oltra ciò ella usasse qualche parola irreverentemente verso la persona et potestà di S. B[ne], come [devo] io portarmi?[2] et massimamente in caso ch'ella mostrasse di non accettare il concilio per esservi chiamata o invitata da N. S[re], ma per qualche altro rispetto?

Se dopo la mia proposta ella pigliasse tempo a rispondere col parere del consiglio o parlamento suo, et ch'io vedessi che questo fosse fatto per mandare più in lungo la risolutione del negotio, qual partito dovessi prendere?[3]

Se mi bisognerà far alcuna instanza con la reina per intendere la volontà sua, occorrendo ch'ella pensasse di non rispondermi in voce niuna cosa, et in tutto mi rimettesse alle lettere scritte a S. S[tà] in risposta?[4]

Come s'harà a trattare della liberatione de' vescovi catholici, et se doverò intendere la mente della reina sopra il negotio del concilio prima ch'io le faccia parola di questo, o se pure harò a parlare dell'uno et dell'altro insieme?[5]

Quanto alla mia provisione, sebene i mille scudi non saranno a sufficienza per le spese del viaggio, tuttavolta presupponendo che Dio mi doni gratia di poterlo finir in assai breve tempo, non mi pare di dire altro a V. S. Illma; ben la supplico che, quando occorresse per alcuna difficultà del negotio ch'io fossi sforzato a dimorare in Fiandra o in Inghitterra, ella si degni operare ch'io non sia trattato peggio del signor abbate di S. Saluto[6] nell'assegnamento ordinario che gli fu fatto per questo medesimo viaggio.

Se in questo mentre sopravenesse la morte della reina, o qualche notabile tumulto nel regno, che partito si doverà prendere?

---

[1] MORONE: Non occorre consultar questo, perchè non sarà, et quando fosse, si facci quello che si conviene.

[2] MORONE: Si rispondi accortamente et con quiete.

[3] MORONE: Si scrivi.

[4] MORONE: La farà scrivere.

[5] Answer given in No. III.

[6] Abbot Vincenzo Perpaglia. See above, pp. 39, 40.

III. *Instructions for Abbot Girolamo Martinengo as nuncio in England.*[1] [*March* 9, 1561. *Rome.*]

Queen Elizabeth to be exhorted to send representatives to the council of Trent.

Florence, Bibl. Naz. II., II., 380, fol. 703: Copy.

Farà il camino per Germania et capiterà à Brusselles, dove con Madama d'Austria et con il cardinal d'Arras [*Granvella*] communicherà il negocio suo richiedendogli di consiglio, aiuto et favore. Di Fiandra manderà un huomo suo in anzi a dimandare salvo condotto alla regina, prima che s'imbarchi, et se per sorte non l'ottenesse, avviserà qua et aspetterà risposta.   Ottenendolo et passando nell'isola, non allogierà con l'ambasciatore del Re Catholico nè con altri, ma ben communicherà con lui et con quel di Francia la sua commissione, per intendere il parer loro.[2]   Et all'audienza della regina anderà da sè.

Alla regina presenterà la bolla del concilio[3] insieme col breve,[4] l'eshorterà et pregherà a voler mandare li suoi prelati et ambasciatori al concilio, come fanno gli altri prencipi christiani, dove si termineranno tante dissensioni et varietà di sette che tengano oppressa la povera christianità.   L'esshorterà anchora a liberar quei poveri vescovi carcerati et lasciarli andar liberamente al concilio.   Dirà che, facendo lei tutto questo, può promettersi da N.ᵒ S.ᵉ ogni paterna benevolenza et affettione et ogni gratia et favore per honore et commodo suo.   Et non lo facendo, non potrà se non dolere a S. Sᵗᵃ che una regina si nobile et nel resto si prudente non riconosca il singular beneficio che Dio gli manda di poter sanar sè stessa et il regno suo col mezzo di questo concilio.   Se la regina piglierà tempo a rispondere, lui aviserà qua et aspetterà risposta.

Della liberatione delli vescovi non parlerà se non doppo rissoluto il negotio del concilio.   Nel resto la prudenza del signor

---

[1] PALLAVICINI, *Istoria del concilio di Trento*, lib. xv., c. 7, § 1, gives an abridgment of these instructions from the original, but with additional explanations of his own.

[2] Omitted in PALLAVICINI.

[3] Of Nov. 29, 1560. See above, p. 41.

[4] Brief of March 4, 1561.   Printed by C. G. Bayne, *Anglo-Roman Relations*, 1558–65 (Oxford, 1913), Appendix XXX.

abbate supplirà, al quale S. S.^{tà} rimette il deliberar di quelle cose che nascano alla giornata et che per adesso non vengano in nostra consideratione.

IV. *Cardinal Borromeo to the papal legates in Trent.* [*June 2, 1563. Rome.*]

Refers to the question of Elizabeth's excommunication.

Arch. Vat., Concilio, t. 27/68, No. 41.   Original ; autograph signature.

. . . Sua S.^{tà} dice che, dovendosi per li decreti del concilio condennare la regina d' Inghilterra, li protestanti et gli Ugonotti, sarà bene che VV. Ill^{me} SS. comincino a pensare quel che esse haveranno a fare circa ciò et quel che Sua S^{tà} haverà a far lei, et ne scrivano qua quanto prima il parer loro, massime circa la regina d' Inghilterra. . . .

V. *Cardinal Morone to Cardinal Borromeo.* [*June 21, 1563.   Trent.*]

The committee appointed by the council wishes to know the views of the emperor and the pope regarding Elizabeth's excommunication.

Arch. Vat., Borgh. I., 184, fol. 328 : Copy.

. . . V. S. Illma havrà con questa nostra una scrittura che di Fiandra fu mandata [1] qua a questi giorni pertinente alle cose d'Inghilterra, per cagione delle quali ci riducemmo insieme, essendovi anco il cardinale di Loreno [2] e gl'ambasciatori ecclesiastici dell' imperatore, di Polonia e di Savoia, e, discorsovi sopra, parve a tutti noi cosa di gran momento, e che fosse d'havervi sopra gran consideratione, e concludemmo che se ne dovesse pigliare il parere non solo di N. S^{re}, ma dell' imperatore ancora : onde havendo gl'ambasciatori di S. M^{tà} tolto carico di darlene avviso, lo damo similmente a S. B^{ne} col mezzo di V. S. Illma, pregandola a farci poi sapere quel che parerà alla S^{tà} Sua. . . .

---

[1] The petition of the English catholics in Louvain concerning the excommunication of Elizabeth.   Printed in a report of the imperial envoys at Trent, by F. B. Bucholtz, *Geschichte der Regierung Ferdinand I. Urkundenband* (Vienna, 1838), pp. 700 *et seq.*

[2] Charles de Guise, Cardinal of Lorraine.

VI. *Card. Morone to Card. Borromeo.* [*June* 28, 1563. *Trent.*]

The imperial envoys strongly dissuade from the excommunication.

Arch. Vat., Borgh. I., 184, fol. 334 v. 335 : Copy.

. . . I medesimi ambasciatori [cesarei] ci dissero anco della regina d' Inghilterra conforme quello che a noi et a V. S. Illma similmente n'haveva scritto il nuntio Delfino,[1] mostrandoci che, se qui si tentasse cosa tale, saria la total ruina non solo di quella poca religione che è rimasa in quel regno e la morte certa di quei poveri vescovi, ma ancora di quanti cattolici sono in Germania, perchè gl'avversarii dubitando che a loro non avvenisse il medesimo che alla regina d' Inghilterra, s'accorderiano a scacciare tutti li cattolici, e per la loro potenza saria facile l'essequirlo ; e noi rispondemmo loro come havevamo anco risposto al nuntio predetto, che, ricevuto quell'avviso, non ci era parso di far altro, che di notificarlo a N. S^{re} et alla cesarea M^{tà}, li quali come prudenti e di suprema auttorità nel christianesimo si degnassero e di considerarvi sopra, e di farcene sapere il parer loro. . . .

VII. *Card. Borromeo to the papal legates in Trent.* [*June* 30, 1563. *Rome.*]

The pope expresses himself in favour of Elizabeth's excommunication.

Arch. Vat., Concilio, t. 27/68 (Lettera di S. Carlo), No. 61. Original ; autograph signature.

. . . Quanto a quella scrittura [2] che tocca la regina d' Inghilterra, a S. S^{tà} par bene che si dia questa consolatione a li catholici di quel regno, secondo la forma del memoriale che le SS. VV. Ill^{me} hanno mandato. Et forse nel canone de l' institution de vescovi, o con occasione di quello, saria il luogo d' inserir questa materia. . . .

---

[1] Delfino to the legates at the council, Innsbruck, June 17, 1563. *Nuntiaturberichte aus Deutschland*, II. Abt., 3 Bd., ed. by STEINHERZ (1903), 351.

[2] See Appendix V.

VIII. *Card. Borromeo to the legates in Trent.* [*July* 6, 1563. *Rome.*]

The pope recalls his previous declaration and adopts the emperor's reasons against the excommunication.

Arch. Vat., Concilio, 27/68, No. 69. Original; autograph signature.

... Le cause che moveno l' imperatore [1] a consigliare che non si proceda contra la regina d' Inghilterra paiono a S. S^tà prudenti et ben considerate ; però, non obstante quel ch' io scrissi loro ultimamente, doveranno in questo satisfare a Sua M^tà Ces^ea, facendogli poi intendere, o per mezo del nuntio o come a lor meglio parerà, che hanno voluto tribuir più al giuditio di lei sola, che a infinite altre persone, et Inglesi proprii, a' quali pareva il contrario, et che per questa via si potesse più presto guadagnare qualche cosa con quella donna. . . .

IX. *Card. Morone to Card. Borromeo.* [*July* 7, 1563. *Trent.*]

Since Granvelle in the name of the king of Spain, as well as the emperor, is against the excommunication of Elizabeth, the question may be dropped.

Arch. Vat., Borgh. I., 184, fol. 346 : Copy.

... Quanto alla cosa della regina d' Inghilterra V. S. Illma havrà poi visto quel che li havemo scritto [2] esser di mente dell'imperatore, e vedrà similmente dalla lettera che qui alligata le mandamo, scrittaci da monsignor ill^mo Granvela,[3] come sarebbe per sentirla il Re Cattolico. Onde se da N. S^re non ci sarà, come credemo, comandato altro, lasceremo scorrer la cosa, finchè piacerà a Dio di mostrare e che e come e quando s' havrà da fare. E se pur S. S^tà fosse di parere che hora si facesse intorno a ciò qualche cosa, giudicamo esser bene che ella ne scriva non solo all' imperatore, ma anco al re predetto per quello che ne tocca il cardinale di Granvela, e si faccia di concerto delle MM^tà Loro. . . .

---

[1] See Appendix VI.
[2] On June 28. Appendix VI.
[3] On June 27. Cf. the references given, p. 53, note 2.

X. *Card. Borromeo to the legates in Trent.*
[*July* 10, 1563. *Rome.*]

Out of consideration for the emperor, the pope abandons the idea of excommunicating Elizabeth.

Arch. Vat., Concilio, 27/68, No. 75. Original; autograph signature.

. . . Scrissi a li VII[1] che N. S^{re}, attribuendo al giuditio del' imperatore più che a ogni altra persona, si contentava ch'elle
andassero ritenute et non procedessero per ancora contra la
regina d' Inghilterra. Hora Sua S^{tà} per i medesimi rispetti ha
voluto ch' io replichi loro il medesimo, aggiungendo di più che in
questo et in tutte l'altre attioni, che possono concernere la quiete
di Germania et altri paesi pericolosi d'alterarsi per conto de la
religione, Sua S^{tà} haverà caro che si governino secondo il
consiglio et parere de l' imperatore, del cui giuditio et bontà Sua
B^{ne} ha causa di poter fidarsi, conoscendolo prudentissimo et pieno
di zelo christiano. . . .

XI. *Card. Borromeo to the legates in Trent.*
[*July* 17, 1563. *Rome.*]

The pope abandons the idea of excommunicating Elizabeth, out of regard
for the king of Spain.

Arch. Vat., Concilio, 27/68, No. 78. Original ; autograph signature.

. . . Le SS^{rie} VV. Ill^{me} haveranno visto per altre mie, come
N. S^{re}, rivocando il primo ordine circa il fatto de la regina
d' Inghilterra, si contenta che elle procedano secondo il parere et
consiglio del' imperatore ; onde hora, per risposta di quel che
scrivono con l'occasione de la lettera del signor cardinale
Granvela, Sua S^{tà} replica lor il medesimo ; anzi giudica tanto più
necessario che si habbia questa consideratione, quanto che ci
debbono mover assai li rispetti del Re Catholico, considerati
prudentemente dal prefato cardinale et altre volte ancora allegati
da li ministri qui di Sua Cat^{ca} M^{tà}. . . .

---

[1] Mistake for VI. See Appendix VIII.

XII. *Thomas Harding and Nicholas Sanders to Card. Morone.* [*June* 11, 1567. *Louvain.*]

Request : (1) a clear statement from the pope that only those shall be absolved from heresy who abstain not only from receiving the protestant communion, but from joining in any other religious service with the heretics ; (2) an extension of the Tridentine decrees of marriage, in the sense that any catholic priest may serve as witness to the marriage ; (3) the preparation of a translation of the bible for catholics.

Arch. Vat., Arm. LXIV., t. 28, fols. 60, 61.   Orig. ; autograph signature.

Cum Deus Tuam Celsitudinem genti Anglorum protectorem constituerit, quoties causae maioris momenti occurrunt, molestiam tuis gravissimis occupationibus exhibere cogimur, quod tamen non auderemus facere, nisi quia experti sumus libenter id oneris a Tua Illma D. perferri, quodcunque Dei et religionis causa imponatur. Ita vero se res habet.   Annis ab hinc tribus cum Sua Sanctitas locum generalis inquisitoris Romae obtineret, ad optimorum hominum preces concessit viva voce absque ullo scripto quatuor presbyteris Anglis archiepiscopalem potestatem in foro conscientiae, ut vel ipsi eos Anglos absolverent, qui ad catholicae ecclesiae gremium reversuri essent, vel aliis auctoritatem id faciendi delegare tam coniunctim quam divisim possent.   Eorum autem nomina erant Thomas Hardingus [1] et Nicolaus Sanderus,[2] doctores theologiae, Thomas Wilsonus et Thomas Pecocus,[3] viri graves et docti.   Ex iis quatuor viris duo in Anglia iam degunt, quorum alter Thomas Wilsonus de iis ipsis rebus certiores nos fecit, alter vero Pecocus longius aberat quam ut id facere posset. Nos reliqui duo Thomas Hardingus et Nicolaus Sanderus, qui Lovanii agimus, omnem operam adhibuimus, ut per graves et catholicos viros hoc in Anglia fieret quod in animarum salutem fore putabatur.   Et antea quidem propter dissentientes multorum sententias absolutio iis laicis dabatur, qui se abstinuissent a communione haereticorum in sacramentis, etiam si ad ecclesiasticas preces in schismate celebratas se contulissent.   Nuper autem et

---

[1] THOS. HARDING, prominent controversialist on the catholic side (1517-72).
[2] NICHOLAS SANDERS, author of *De origine ac progressu schismatis Anglicani. libri tres* (Romae, 1586), and other historical and theological writings.
[3] THOS. PEACOCK (1516 ?- 1582 ?).   For him and the others, *cf.* the *Dict. of Nat. Biogr.*

communi consilio doctissimorum hominum et Suae Sanctitatis praecepto iussimus nullum absolvi nisi qui abstineret a schismaticis precibus ac tam facto quam verbo suam fidem profiteretur. Atque hac quidem ex re multo verius profici res ipsa declarat. Quamdiu enim iis indulgebatur qui ex parte aliqua claudicassent, nihil firmum aut stabile reperiebatur. Postquam autem coacti sunt catholici aut in peccatorum vinculis manere, aut omnino ab omni gradu schismatis recedere, tum multo plures a precibus abstinent, tum multo facilius eis gratia divinitus datur, ut fidem intrepide apud quaecunque tribunalia confitentes etiam carceres et vincula cum gaudio perferant, adeo ut multae nobilium familiae statuerint iam deinceps numquam iterum communicare in sacris precibus cum schismaticis. Haec cum ita essent, iamque et ea res literis publice mandata et sermo per totam Angliam perlatus esset, occlusam iis esse ianuam regni coelorum, qui non in totum se a schismate revocarent, ceptum est inquiri a nobilissimis quibusdam cuius auctoritatis esset hic rumor. Cumque aliqui ex iis vocarentur quibus nos potestatem absolvendi commiseramus, responderunt, quod res erat, se hanc potestatem scripto comprehensam a sede apostolica non habere, sed in foro conscientiae eam exercere ex mandato generalis inquisitoris, quo tunc officio Sua Sanctitas fungebatur. Alii autem intulerunt nihil se videre, cur iis hominibus fides haberi debeat, qui mandati sui auctoritatem scriptam exhibere non possint, tunc vero parituros, cum certo sciant eam esse mentem et sententiam sedis apostolicae. Habebant sane illi iustissimas causas, cur de concilii Tridentini sententia hoc nobis opponerent. Itaque iis de causis putavimus faciendum ut scriberemus ad sedem apostolicam, humillime illi significantes videri nobis valde expedire ut haec potestas absolvendi in scriptum aliquod redigatur, in quo et praeterita confirmentur et futura accurate praescribantur. Cuius scripti authenticum et originale exemplar possit Lovanii ab iis custodiri, quibus ea res committetur, ac inde per notarii manum alia exempla describi poterunt, quibus ii sigillatim utantur, quibus ea potestas subdeleganda erit.

In tot vero gravissimis causis, quae in reconciliatione poenitentium accidunt, illa primum occurrit quid de concilii Tridentini publicatione in Anglia censendum sit ; nam si ea matrimonia, quae absque vero parocho celebrantur clandestina et propterea omnino

irrita erunt, cum nullus ibi legitimus parochus propter schismati-
cam pseudepiscoporum iurisdictionem existat, omnia prorsus
matrimonia erunt adulteria. Deinde etiamsi catholici velint
legitimo matrimonio copulari, tamen cum nullum habeant
proprium parochum, ea non erunt matrimonia, etiamsi a presbytero
catholico iungantur, nisi Sua Sanctitas interpretabitur eum
in hoc necessitatis articulo pro parocho habendum esse quicunque
sit catholicus presbyter, qui eos iungit, aut qui auctoritatem a
commissariis sedis apostolicae habeat.

Item cum ex concilii Tridentini decreto libri de rebus sacris
vulgari idiomate perscripti (quales iam multos ab iis catholicis
qui Lovanii exulant summo cum fructu editos constat) absque
licentia episcopi aut alicuius inquisitoris hereticae pravitatis legi
non possint,[1] salvo Suae Sanctitatis iudicio, profuturum arbitramur
ut in Anglia fervente iam haeresi aliter fiat, ne ii qui coguntur
ubique venenum imbibere, pharmacum differre cogantur, donec
medicus accedat, qui aut nullus aut rarus est et longe abest et
semper latet. Illud omnium est maximum, quod, cum haeretici
verbo Dei abutantur ad fallendum rudes et indoctos, id
potissimum efficiunt prava bibliorum interpretatione. Porro
experientia didicimus populum tam aegre a se dimittere haec
ipsa biblia etiam cum catholici iurisdictionem exercebant, ut quo
magis ea legum vinculis prohibebantur, eo vehementius a populo
retinerentur. Cui malo videtur quibusdam remedium afferri posse,
si saltem historici et morales libri veteris testamenti atque
evangelia et epistolae vulgari idiomate a catholicis ederentur. Ita
enim demum persuaderi posset populo, ut veteres libros corrupte
interpretatos abiiceret, si novi accurate ad vulgatae editionis
fidem conversi eis traderentur. Qua in re nos sedis apostolicae
iudicio et praescripto subiicimus.

Aliae sunt causae, quas si enumeraremus nullus finis orationi
poneretur. Nunc autem reliqua omnia tum Tuae Ill^mae Domina-
tionis prudentiae tum Suae Sanctitatis iudicio relinquentes,
alterius pedes alterius vero manus pro eo ac decet animo ac
desyderio nostro osculantes, divinam precamur clementiam, ut
tantam huius pontificis pietatam ecclesiae suae diuturnam esse velit,
Tuamque Ill^mam Dominationem in aeternum tueatur et conservet,

---

[1] *Cf.* Decretum de editione et usu sacrorum librorum (Sessio IV.). See
below, Appendix XVII., A [§ 8].

nostris autem precibus quicquid respondebitur, id quantum in nobis erit re ipsa per Dei gratiam impleri curabimus.   Quicquid autem in hoc genere petitur, non alia mente petitur, quam ut valeat in eum usque diem, quo regnum Angliae ad sedis apostolicae obedientiam reversum per veriores possit legatos administrari. Datum Lovanii tertio idus Junii 1567.

> Tuae Ill^mae Celsitudinis observantissimi servitores
> Thomas Hardingus.
> Nicolaus Sanderus.

XIII. *Giovanni Castagna,*[1] *Bishop of Rossano, nuncio in Madrid, to Card. Michele Bonelli (surnamed Alessandrino).*[2] [*July* 17, 1570. *Madrid.*]

Ill-humour at the Spanish court at Elizabeth's excommunication.
Arch. Vat., Borgh. I., 607, fol. 245 : Copy.

. . . È stato detto qui che Sua Santitá ha fatto un breve [!] contra la regina d'Inghilterra di dichiaratione, privatione et similia, del quale non mostrano[3] molta contentezza, et dicono haverne havuta copia d'Inghilterra et non da Roma, se ben dicono che detto breve[!] è stato mandato al re di Francia da S. Santità, et insomma va qualche bisbiglio sopra questo. Io ho risposto la verità, cioé che non so niente di tal breve, ma che sono ben certo che S. Santità non haverà fatto cosa che non sia bene considerata et tirata tutta a fine del bene della christianità, et per dare animo alli cattolici di quello regno et per eccitare li prencipi cattolici, et similia. . . .

XIV. *The nuncio Giov. Castagna to Card. Bonelli.* [*Aug.* 4, 1570. *Madrid.*]

Philip's explanation of his attitude towards the English Catholic question— we must wait for a favourable opportunity.
Arch. Vat., Borgh. I., 607, fol. 249 v. 251 : Copy.

Per l'indispositione che il re ha havuta, della quale per gratia di Dio è già assai ben sanato, non ho potuto prima dell'altro hieri

---

[1] Afterwards Pope Urban VII.   [2] Nephew of Pope Pius V.
[3] *I.e.* the Spanish court.

haver l'audienza, nella quale, doppo rese le gratie della risolutione
ultima che le galere si unissero etc., entrai nella materia d'Inghiltera e Scotia, rappresentando lo agiuto et favore che S. Santità dà
a quelli che in detti regni seguitavano le parti cattoliche, la speranza et argomenti che si hanno che la regina di Scotia habbia in
animo di tenere, sempre che sia libera et che possi, il suo regno
cattolico et di essere grata de gli agiuti et favori che li veniranno
da S. B^{ne} et da S. M^{tà} Cattolica, la occasione che pare ancora sia
in piedi di agiutare quelli nobili sollevati a favore della religione,
et le essortationi et prieghi di S. Santità che li fa, acciò scriva al
duca Alba che li soccorra essendo richiesto, et di gente et di denari etc., sì come V. S. Illma et R^{ma} mi commanda nelle sue lettere.
S. M^{tà} rispose humanissimamente entrando in un certo modo in un
grave discorso; dice che già io stesso havevo saputo che S. M^{tà}
haveva dato ordine al duca di Star [1] preparato di poter in ogni
buona occasione favorire la detta parte cattolica, et hora mi
diceva di più che ciò era stato ordinato non lievemente et così
quasi per una forma, ma con gran proposito ordinato et scritto
con su' propria real mano, perochè, oltre l'universale institute et
desiderio suo di spendere quanto può et la propria persona
bisognando in servitio di Dio et della sua santa fede, essendo S.
M^{tà} stata causa et ministro, che quello regno d'Inghiltera tornasse
alla fede cattolica, gli è doluto et duole fin al cuore di veder
turbata et guastata quella opera che si può dire quasi creatura
sua, et che ben intende che, se volesse fare una demonstratione
vana per la semplice apparenza, potrebbe farla ; ma, come inimico
di simili prospettive, non giudica che sia bene che si discoprino
li dissegni et agiuti de' cattolici, se non nell'occassione et nel
punto che si possi far colpo, et andare alla sostanza della cosa
desiderata ; et questa tale occasione molto poco si è havuta prima,
et molto manco apparisce al presente, perochè nel principio di
questi moti quelli nobili sollevati per la parte cattolica, forsi per
non haver potuto far altro, furono troppo presti a discoprirsi,
perochè devevano firmar prima meglio il trattato tra di loro, et
communicarlo et trattarlo con quel prencipe il cui soccorso
volevano implorare, acciò fosse preparato in tempo et in forma da
potersene giovare.   Ma essendosi immessi [2] intempestivamente,

---

[1] *Sic.* Either incorrectly written or wrongly deciphered for *Alva*.
[2] Conjectural emendation of the meaningless *in esse* of the text.

non hanno operato altro che danno a sè stessi et sicurezza alli avversarii, onde hora non vede quello che si può fare et che sia come conviene di sostanza, poichè li detti nobili, nelli quali soli poteva essere qualche speranza, già sono o presi o fugati et dispersi, il che duole a S. M.^{tà} infinitamente, et li conosce et nomina a nome, et la maggior parte sono stati suoi creati ; nondimeno, per il desiderio che tiene di sodisfare in tutto quello che si può a S. B^{ne}, ha pensato che, essendo gl'avvisi che arrivano qui da quelle parti ordinariamente tanto tardi et rudi per la lontananza et gl'impedimenti del camino, sarà più comodo che questi negotii siano trattati tra S. Santità et il duca di Alba, il quale haverà ordine che s'intenda con S. B^{ne}, et scriva et dia quella sodisfattione che sarà possibile a S. S^{tà}, del qual duca S. M^{tà} confida che, sapendo la mente sua come sa, se li venirà occasione buona da poter fare effetto utile alle religione, non movendosi però vanamente, non lassarà di abbracciarle et d'impiegarsi in servitù et honore di Dio ; sopra di che di nuovo S. M^{tà} li scriverà et darà il debito ordine. Questo è in somma quello che S. M^{tà} mi rispose sopra questa materia. . . .

XV. *The nuncio Giov. Castagna to Card. Girol. Rusticucci.*[1] [*Sept.* 7, 1570. *Madrid.*]

Philip II. regards a blockade of England as impracticable.

. . . Nelle cose d'Inghilterra ho parlato di nuovo et, ponderando la scrittura che ho ricevuta di avvisi mandati a S. B^{ne} da huomini di là,[2] mostrai a S. M^{tà} che quelli cattolici giudicano che, mentre non si può darli soccorso di gente, potria giovare molto il levare per virtù del breve[3] di S. Santità a quel regno il commertio di Fiandra, Francia et Portugallo, perchè così restarebbono gl'Inglesi molto confusi, onde la nominata regina pigliarebbe odio a li suoi conseglieri che così impiamente la consigliano, et sarebbe in un certo modo sforzata a mutar proposito per non esser così abhorita da tutti li prencipi christiani con tanto pregiuditio del suo regno, il quale non ha altro denaro che dalle mercantie et commercio.

---

[1] Relative of Card. Michele Bonelli.
[2] *I.e.* England.
[3] The bull against Elizabeth (Feb. 26, 1670) is meant. The same mistake as in No. XIII.

A questo S. M^tà replicò il medesimo che is scrissi per le precedenti delli 4 del passato, aggiongendo che quando S. M^tà sola volesse levare detto commercio, nocerebbe molto a sè et non farebbe nulla circa la republica ; ma bisognarebbe che gli altri tutti si contentassero di fare il medesimo, il che malamente si può sperare, perochè nelle parti di Alemagna non occorre parlare, in Francia non sarrebbono mai stati per farlo, tanto meno adesso con questa pace saranno ogni giorno li settarii più potenti, et se l'armiraglio torna nel suo officio, la navigatione d'Inglesi et commercio sarà tanto più favorito, nè lo lassarebbero disturbare in modo nessuno. . . .

XVI. Statutes of the English College in Rome.[1]
[June 12, 1579.]

Arch. Vat., Miscell. Arm. XI., t. 94, between fol. 99 and 100 ; Original. Small 8vo, signed by Card. Morone, the first protector of the college ; with seal affixed.

Quod pertinet ad ingressum.

Cum hoc Anglorum seminarium eo sit consilio institutum, ut ab eius alumnis periclitantis Angliae rebus succurratur, ii duntaxat recipiantur, qui ei se operam ac studium, ubi res ac ratio feret, navaturos promittant, ac propterea sacerdotium consequi cupiant illudque se suo tempore inituros promittant atque confirment, neque quicquam habeant quod ecclesiasticorum ordinum susceptioni obstet, quos etiam ubi erit eis praescriptum et rite suscipient et devote gerent.

Qui recipientur, eos pietati christianae deditos, firmitate corporis, seminarii institutis et legibus parendi studio ingeniique bonitate pollere oportet ac minimum ita latine scire, ut philosophiae dare operam possint; ii vero neque maiores quinque et viginti annis neque minores quatuordecim [2] erunt, nisi in aliquibus doctrina suppleret aetatem ; quod si quem fortasse usus ac dies ineptiorem ostendat, is superiorum arbitrio ad decedendum paratus esto.

Polliceantur item omnes ex formula professionis fidei a Pio IIII

---

[1] Cf. the later Constitutiones Collegii Anglorum, Appendix XIX., §§ 56-86.
[2] Afterwards 18 instead of 14. See Appendix XIX., § 54.

constituta [1] se in fide catholica victuros perpetuamque summo pontifici tanquam Christi vicario et universae ecclesiae capiti obedientiam praestaturos, et suo quisque chirographo antequam admittatur obliget fidem, se nunquam nisi bona venia abiturum.

Qui accipiendi erunt per octo decemve dies separati ab aliis habitabunt, ut, adhibita hac quasi praeparatione, considerate postea et constanter tantum munus suscipiant et recte atque ordine poenitentiae atque eucharistiae sacramenta sumendi, Deum precandi, introspiciendi in mentem suam eamque omni cogitatione pertractando percontandi, ipsi se [sic] rationem ac modum percipiant. Interea vero accurate evolvent ipsas seminarii leges atque omnia anteactae vitae peccata salutari confessione expiabunt.

Quod pertinet ad pietatem.

Missam quotidie audient in eaque ut iussi erunt ministrabunt, quotidie etiam horarias Beatea Virginis preces Deo offerent, semihoram praeterea mane in sanctis precationibus ponent, quo tempore qui voluerint partem Beatea Virginis officii recitare poterunt, exceptis iis quibus dominici officii recitandi onus incumbet, aut quibus alia erit a confessario precationum formula praescripta.

Cum eunt cubitum aut surgunt, cum domo exeunt aut redeunt, brevi se aliqua ad Deum prece muniant.

Singulis diebus vesperi per horae quadrantem quaecunque eo qui praecessit die a se facta, dicta, cogitata sunt diligenter examinent.

Singulis ut minimum mensibus sua quisque peccata confessione patefaciat, atque ad sanctissimum dominici corporis mysterium accedat quanta maxima potest tum religione tum proficiendi etiam voluntate. Sacerdotes vero sacrum saepe faciant, atque omnes eo qui erit assignatus confessario utantur omnesque ei animi morbos aperiant, ut is facilius curationem valetudinis praescribat.

Festis diebus aut ad matutinam aut ad pomeridianam concionem se conferant, intersintque aut missis aut vesperis, quae in Sanctissimae Trinitatis templo decantabuntur, quin ipsi quoque

[1] Professio fidei Tridentinae a Pio IV. per constitutionem "Injunctum nobis," Nov. 18, 1564, ex decreto Trid. praescripta. H. DENZINGER, *Enchiridion symbolorum et definitionum*, ed. 6a (1888), p. 233.

iussi concinant; iisdem etiam diebus se in alicuius libri spiritualis lectione, in catechismi Romani, computi ecclesiastici sacrarumque ecclesiae cerimoniarum cognitione exerceant.

In mensa permagna tum taciturnitate tum etiam attentione quae leguntur audient, ibique tum ante tum etiam post epulas praeeuntis sacerdotis Romano ritu orationem praecibus excipient. Quod etiam in litaniis, si quando erunt recitandae, praecipitur. Porro eorum magna semper in templo modestia ac devotio apparebit. Fundant singuli Deo preces pro summi pontificis, pontificiae auctoritatis conservatione, catholicae fidei propagatione, haeresum ac schismatum extinctione, salute Angliae, benefactoribus seminarii, pro huius xenodochii fundatoribus ac prospera seminarii progressione. Quas etiam ob causas quilibet sacerdotum singulis hebdomadis saltem missam, clericorum vero rosarium sive coronam Deo offerent.

De eo quod pertinet ad studia.

Ibit in gymnasium Societatis Jesu [1] ad eas quisque classes ac domi eos libros leget, praestituto tum tempore tum etiam modo, quos superior singulis expedire arbitrabitur.

Consuetudinem capiant omnes ut superioris admonitu acriter propositas questiones tum oppugnare tum etiam defendere, quae audierint repetere, aliquid etiam scribere ac coetera quae pertinent ad doctrinae studia exequi possint, neve a communibus exercitationibus litterariis absint, illudque contendant, ut ad conciones publice habendas doctrinamque Christianam tradendam exercitatione aptiores fiant.

Sint in disputationibus, apud externos praecipue atque extra seminarium, et refellere sine iracundia et refelli sine pertinacia parati.

Ne, quod est tempus in studiis utiliter consumendum, illud sibi aut turpi otio aut importunis sermonibus perire patiantur, neque a vespertino examine, aut legant aut scribant.

Suorum quisque studiorum rationem praefecto reddat, eique se et magistro in iis, quae ad literas spectant, morigerum atque obsequentem praebeat.

Eos tantum libros emant aut habeant quos superior statuet,

---

[1] *I.e.* the *Collegium Romanum.*

atque in iis, nisi quorum est quisque dominus, nihil adscribant aut notarum imprimant.   Dabit porro studiorum praefectus operam, ut ne libri qui erunt necessarii desiderentur.

Latine loquantur omnes, aut italice, eo inprimis tempore, quo relaxare animos debebunt, praeterquam si cum externis colloquatur.

Canere ii etiam discent qui fuerint a rectore delecti, quibus ipse etiam rector discendi tempus modumque praescribet.

Quod pertinet ad domesticam disciplinam.

Obtemperent rectori omnes in rebus omnibus, in quibus studiorum morumque causa [?] versatur, sive aliquid ipse per se, sive per alium, sive etiam per campanae pulsum fieri iubeat.

Capellanos adeo inter se omnes debito honore prosequantur.

Cum erit domo exeundum, superiorem, a quo certum comitem accipere debebunt, quo exire, quid etiam agere cupiant praemonebunt.   Illud vero intelligent, tum non licere sibi rem ullam agere cum quoquam neque invisere officii causa quenquam, tum etiam extra seminarium neque cibum capere neque pernoctare nisi concessu superioris.   Si exierint, ut longissimum ante solis occasum se recipiant[!]; cum egredientur, una omnes eo ordine quem servandum sibi esse a superiore acceperint ac moderatione incedant.   Domi vero ne eo quisquam accedat ubi ii hebitant qui res domesticas curant, neque ad ianuam nisi accersitu ianitoris, neque ad aliorum omnino cubicula nisi concessu superioris, quin etiam illud caveant, ne in eodem cubiculo ad sodalium loca adeant, praeterquam cum necessitas flagitare videbitur.

Cum tempus non postulat, ne loquantur, in templo praecipue ac triclinio, neque mane item ante preces neque post examen vesperi, nisi pauca quaedam aut necessitas aut humanitas poscet, quod idem in externis colloquiis tenendum erit.   Nullas etiam clam rectore, ad quem deferentur omnes ut inspiciat, litteras neque dabunt ipsi neque accipient.

Seminarii victus communis esto atque ad honestorum civium consuetudinem accommodatus.   Si qua vero indicentur ieiunia praeter ea, quae ab ecclesia instituta sunt, ea voluntaria potius quam necessaria sunto.   Xenodochii tamen institutum in 6^{ae} feriae abstinentia servetur.

In moribus, cubiculis, vestibus et aliis id genus aeque immodica nimiumque exquisita diligentia atque agrestis atque inhumana negligentia fugienda. Utatur igitur cultu vestituque honesto et qui sit homini ecclesiastico congruens neque idem sumptuosus. In vestibus porro et sellis et cubiculis et coeteris rebus adhibenda quaedam mediocris neque odiosa munditia.

Ne pecuniam quisquam apud se habeat, sed eam ad sumptus illos quo utiles superiori videbuntur, apud certum hominem cui hoc superior mandaverit deponat, qui rationes accepti et expensi reddet ac quicquid reliquum erit id totum discedenti restituet. Nemo tamen emat, det, accipiat quicquam nisi superioris assensu.

Nimiae inter se familiaritates diligenter vitandae,[1] multo diligentius omnis animorum alienatio atque obtrectatio, adversus eos praesertim qui alterius erunt nationis et linguae. Illud potius omni ratione studeant, ut rebus quoque ipsis, non verbis tantum, communis eorum erga omnes christiana charitas eluceat.

Quicunque admonentur aut obiurgantur, etiam si quae imponentur amoris plenissimae poenae, eas non patienti modo sed libenti etiam animo suscipiant; prae se quoque spem ac speciem mutatae voluntatis ferant. Si qui tamen ita insanabiles et difficiles erunt, ut non pertinacia modo sibi, verum etiam exemplo aliis noceant, sciant se illi, nisi rescipiscant, e seminario exclusum iri.

Quod pertinet ad valetudinem.

Suam quisque valetudinem curet diligenter. Quod si quis in morbum incidat, mature superiorem admoneat, ut ei occurratur, ac toto eo tempore quo aegrotabit tum medico tum ei etiam qui assidebit plene atque integre obtemperet. Die 12 Junii, 1579. Romae.

(autograph) Joannes card^{lis} Moronus protector.

---

[1] *Cf.* THOMAS À KEMPIS, *De Imitatione Christi*, tract. I., cap. VIII.: De cavenda nimia familiaritate.

XVII. *Faculties.*   [*April* 14, 1580.   *Rome.*]

A. Facultates concessae Patribus Roberto Personio et Emundo [*sic*] Campiano pro Anglia die 14 Aprilis, 1580.

Public Record Office, London, State Papers, Domestic Series, Elizabeth, Vol. CXXXVII., No. 26 : Orig. ; No. 27, 28 : Copies—the illegible passages in the damaged original are supplied from the copies.

[§ 1] Ut missas possint celebrare tribus horis ante diem in hyeme et una hora post meridiem, et ubi valde magna necessitas postulaverit, v. g.[1] ad consecrandum hostiam pro viatico, bis in die modo ieiuni sint; et ubi non poterit haberi copia calicum consecratorum, vel corporalium, vel episcoporum consecrantium aut benedicentium, possint iidem sacerdotes pro usu tam nostrorum quam aliorum in iisdem locis corporalia, pallas, vestes et ea omnia, ubi non intervenit chrisma, benedicere; missas etiam coram haereticis et aliis quibuscumque excommunicatis personis in altari portatili in quocumque loco decente celebrare ac propter necessitates aegrotorum et alia eiusmodi sacramentum eucharistiae clam circumferre et loco decenti servare et sine lumine et sine aliis ceremoniis, quibus utitur ecclesia.

[§ 2] Ut possint uti altaribus portatilibus, qualia in Anglia invenient, neque teneantur inquirere, an contineant reliquias necne.

[§ 3] Sacramenta omnia exceptis confirmatione et sacris ordinibus ministrare quibuscumque personis eorumdem capacibus, omissis pro necessitate ceremoniis solitis, non tamen necessariis.

[§ 4] Dispensare in foro conscientiae super omnibus suspensionibus, inhabilitatibus et irregularitatibus, provenientibus (excepto homicidio et bigamia) ex quocumque delicto, non tamen notorio, ad ministrandum in susceptis ordinibus et eosdem ordines exercendos.

[§ 5] In eodem foro dispensare cum iis, qui, cum paterentur aliquem defectum corporis aut natalium, sacros ordines receperunt, ut possint in susceptis ministrare.

[§ 6] Absolvere omnes Anglos reconciliatos a retentione bonorum ecclesiasticorum, accepta ab eis promissione de stando iudicio ecclesiae, ubi Anglia fuerit revocata, circa eorum restitutionem,

---

[1] v. g. = *verbi gratia.*

illis interim admonitis, ut facient eleemosinas de fructibus ex iudicio confessarii in catholicos pauperes, ut memores sint illa bona esse re vera ecclesiae, ut olim concessit vivae vocis oraculo Pius V.

[§ 7] Possint etiam iis, unde spes aliqua divini cultus promovenda appareat, concedere facultatem retinendi apud se et legendi libros quoscumque sacros vulgari sermone conscriptos, etiam de rebus in religione controversis, quotiescumque ita in Domino videbitur expedire.

[§ 8] Ut liceat libros catholicos imprimere et edere tacito nomine auctoris, loci et typographi, non obstante concilio Tridentino.[1] Ut liceat etiam his facultatibus in aliis vicinis regionibus, nominatim in Scotia, Hibernia et Mona[2] et aliis adiacentibus locis, uti, et etiam in eis, qui ex aliis regionibus in haec loca venerint.

[§ 9] Ut possint dispensare cum religiosis, qui olim ex monasteriis suis exierunt, in verbis obedientiae et paupertatis, ut maneant sine habitu religioso, cum commode reverti ad suas religiones non possint, modo portent secreto aliquem habitum suae religionis sub aliis vestibus.

[§ 10] Ut possint mutare recitationem officii divini tam pro se, quam pro aliis in recitationem psalmorum, hymnorum, aliarumve orationum, aut aliud pium opus commutare, quando sine probabili periculo recitari officium non potest.

[§ 11] Petatur a S^{mo} D^{no} N. explicatio [*sententiae*] declaratoriae per Pium V. contra Elizabetham et ei adhaerentes, quam catholici cupiunt intelligi hoc modo : ut obliget semper illam et haereticos, catholicos vero nullo modo obliget rebus sic stantibus, sed tum demum, quando publica eiusdem bullae executio fieri poterit.[3]

[§ 12] Cum in Anglia quidam, tam sacerdotes quam alii, vitam apostolicam imitantes, statuerint apud se soli animarum saluti incumbere et reductioni haereticorum, et, ut hoc melius faciant, decreverint victu et vestitu aliisque rebus necessariis ad statum

---

[1] The Tridentine *Decretum de editione et usu sacrorum librorum* (*Sessio IV.*) forbade *imprimere vel imprimi facere quosvis libros de rebus sacris sine nomine auctoris*, etc. *Cf.* Appendix XII., p. 477.

[2] The Isle of Man.

[3] This was the paragraph printed by Lord Burleigh in 1583. *Cf.* p. 139, note 1.

suum contenti esse, et quod supererit de bonis suis in commune
subsidium catholicorum conferre, eleemosinasque ad hoc commune subsidium non solum per se, verum etiam per alios procurare, aliisque modis reductionem Angliae promovere, dignetur
V. S^tas horum hominum pium zelum approbare et benedicere et
iis omnibus, qui in hoc exercitio se exerceant, suaque nomina ad
id faciendum pro viribus dederint, sive in carcere sive extra carcerem fuerint, plenariam indulgentiam quater in anno concedere,
si confessi fuerint et sanctissimam eucharistiam sumpserint, videlicet in festis S. Georgii, S. Martini, S. Gregorii papae, S. Augustini
episcopi, apostoli Anglorum, et S. Thomae Cantuariensis, patro-
norum Angliae.

[§ 13] Ut qui reconciliati fuerint ab haeresi aut schismate, in
prima communione sua cum ecclesia catholica per sanctissimae
eucharistiae susceptionem indulgentiam plenariam lucrentur.

[§ 14] Ut omnes catholici, tam in carcere quam extra carcerem,
in prima eorum communione cum nostris, hoc est cum prima vice
sanctissimam eucharistiam de manibus illorum accipient, lucrentur
indulgentiam plenariam.

[§ 15] Has praedictas gratias concessit Summus Pontifex patribus Roberto Personio et Emundo Campiano in Angliam profecturis
die 14 Aprilis, 1580, presente patre Oliverio Martino [?][1] assistente.

[§ 16] Die vero 3°, qui fuit 16, de mandato patris generalis
oblatus est libellus supplex illust^mo cardinali Comensi,[2] ut ipse a
S^mo D^no obtineret facultatem ad Dei gloriam et fidei catholicae
propagationem in Anglia, Hibernia et Scotia, ut praedicti patres,
qui modo mittuntur, possint communicare aliis sacerdotibus in iis
locis laborantibus, quos idoneos compererint, illas facultates et
gratias seu aliquas earum, prout animarum profectus postulaverit,
quae ipsis a S. S^te duobus ante diebus concessae fuerunt: quod
concessit, sed tamen non nisi magno hominum delectu et considerate fieri voluit.

[§ 17] Postea, die 3° Junii, 1581, impetratum est breve, prout
liceat nostris in Anglia dispensare iis matrimoniis contractis super
quibuscumque gradibus iure positivo prohibitis excepto secundo
et super reliquis impedimentis.

Laus Deo Opt. Max.

¹ Or Manarco.   ² Tolomeo Gallio (Galli).

B. Facultates spirituales, quae a Suae Sanctitate petuntur pro regno Scotiae.[1]

Arch. Vat., Borgh. I. 715, fol. 124 : Draft, undated.

1. Facultas absolvendi in foro conscientiae ab omnibus peccatis, censuris et paenis ecclesiasticis, reservatis Sedi Apostolicae etiam in bulla Coenae Domini.

2. Dispensandi cum sacerdotibus super omni irregularitate hac tenus contracta, praeterquam in ea quae contrahitur ex homicidio voluntario.

3. Dispensandi super male perceptis beneficiorum ecclesiasticorum fructibus cum quibuscunque ad ecclesiam redeuntibus et cum catholicis, ut possint etiam fructus beneficiorum in posterum retinere, donec religio catholica restituatur, facta parte aliqua arbitrio patris vel eorum, quibus conceditur facultas, in usus pios.

4. Dispensandi super omnibus impedimentis matrimonii contracti, non autem contrahendi, quae sunt de iure positivo, in foro conscientiae et donec restituatur religio catholica, exceptis primis gradibus.

5. Benedicendi et consecrandi calices et altaria portatilia et omnia paramenta altaris et sacerdotis ad biennium.

6. Communicandi has omnes facultates aliis idoneis sacerdotibus ad biennium.

7. Ut Sua Sanctitas dignetur concedere indulgentiam plenariam omnibus catholicis, qui suscipiunt bellum iustum contra haereticos, et eandem in articulo mortis illis, qui in tali bello moriuntur.

XVIII. *Correspondence between the nuncio in Madrid, Filippo Sega, and the Card. of Como [Tolomeo Gallio].*

Public Record Office, Roman Transcripts 77 and 105. Taken from the Arch. Vat., Nunz. Spagna 25, 27, and 30. When I asked for these volumes in Arch. Vat., I was told they were not forthcoming, so I give the document according to the transcripts in London.

---

[1] This paper does not state that the desired faculties were granted : but since they agreed in all essential points with the faculties granted to England, it may be assumed that this draft was sanctioned for Scotland.

A. *The nuncio Sega to the Card. of Como.*[1]
[*Nov.* 14, 1580.   *Madrid.*]

Had assured English catholics, when asked, that they need not regard the murder of Elizabeth as a sin ; had promised to consult the pope on the point ; had recommended them to keep their plot secret, and does not know what will come of it ; hopes he has not gone too far.

Tra le altre cose che mi dice questo dottore Umfrido Elei,[2] una me ne ha detto con molto secreto in nome di alcuni nobili de la isola [e] de li medesimi padri Gesuiti, et è che li sodetti nobili si risolveriano di tentare di ammazzare la regina di mana propria, ogni volta che si assicurassero, almeno con la parola (a la qual dice che crederiano, quando egli scrivesse o gli rispondesse a la presenza, come si offerisce di fare) che S. Stà gli assicurasse che per questo non caderiano in peccato, per il pericolo che gli instaria de la morte lor propria in tentar cosa tanto grave et pericolosa.   Io gli ho risposto che per le parole de la sentenza[3] di Pio V. di sa. me. pare che questi si potriano assicurare, poichè particolarmente dà licenza a tutti li vassali di poter pigliar le armi contra la regina impune ; con tutto questo che io non lasserò di motivar questa propositione per intendere più in individuo quello che S. Stà commanda, havendogli soggiunto che, quando il papa non venisse in voler dichiarar cosa alcuna inanzi al fatto, almeno li assicurarei che S. Stà a quelli che sopravivessero dopo questo fatto daria tutte quelle absolutioni et dichiarationi che fussero necessarie o ad abundante cautela per le persone di detti sopraviventi, soggiungendoli che 'nocuit quandoque differre paratis' ;[4] però che se questa prattica è passata in più di uno o in più di due, non è prattica da tener sospesa per il pericolo che porta seco di poter scoprirsi, ma a sapersi valere de la opportunità et de la occasione.   Et sono attorno a persuaderlo a ritornarsene in Inghilterra, non si assicurando [lui] anco a scrivere del modo

---

[1] Printed in part by M. PHILIPPSON, *Ein Ministerium unter Philipp II. Kard. Granvella am span. Hofe* (Berlin, 1895), p. 204, note 1.

[2] Humphrey Ely, an English catholic, student at the Douay-Rheims college, jurist and theologian, not yet a priest at this time, afterwards priest and professor of canon law at Pont-à-Mousson. Cf. *Dict. of Nat. Biog.* and the book by Ely quoted above, p. 105, note 1.

[3] The Bull of 1570.

[4] LUCAN, *Pharsalia I.*, 281 : *Tolle moras ; semper nocuit differre paratis.*

che haveva concertato con gli amici suoi, mostrando, che se per sorte fussero state intercette le lettere, non essendo cifra la loro, ma gergo, saria stata occasione et di lunga prigionia et di tormenti a quelli che per sorte fussero caduti in mano de la regina.

Io non so quello che egli risolverà, ma lo scriverò con le prime. Intanto saremo insieme domani lui et io con le paroli de la sentenza in mano, per considerarle un poco più in individuo, et se ben egli conosce il pericolo che gli insta dal ritornare in Inghilterra, si risolve nondimeno di ritornar prima che scrivere, quando habbia qualche determinatione, talche con le prime potrò avvisar quello che sarà seguito; et avverta V. S. Illma che da S. Sta non si desidera nè breve nè bolla da questi cavalieri, sed nudum verbum, il quale significato a me da V. S. Illma per sua cifra bastarà, et andandosi, io concertarò con lui una cifra et il modo, come le potrò far capitar le lettere sicure, se però non ho passato troppo inanzi, sicuro però che, quando fusse necessaria absolutione da S. Sta, supplico V. S. Illma a domandarla per parte mia, che certo in questo caso 'zelus domus Domini comedit me.'[1]

B. *The Card. of Como to the nuncio Sega.* [*Dec.* 12, 1580.   *Rome.*]

To murder Elizabeth, the destroyer of many million souls, is no sin but rather a meritorious work.

Non è da dubitare che tenendo quella rea femina d'Inghilterra occupati a la Christianità dui regni sì nobili, et essendo causa di tanto danno a la fede cattolica et de la perdita di tanti millioni d'anime, ciascuno che la levasse dal mondo col fine debito del servitio di Dio, non solo non peccaria, ma anco meriteria, massime stante la sententia contra di lei di Pio V. s^ta me. Però se quelli cavalieri inglesi si risolvono da dovero di far cosi bell' impresa, V. S. gli può assicurar che essi non incorreranno in nessun peccato, et è da sperar in Dio benedetto che siano anco per scampar ogni pericolo. Quanto poi a V. S. in caso che lei fosse incorsa in alcuna irregularità, N. S. le dà la sua santa benedizione.

[1] Ps. lxviii., 10.

XIX. *Report of Card. Sega's first Visitation of the English College in Rome.*[1] [*Aug.* 1585. *Rome.*]

§ 1. Introduction.   § 2, 3. Chapel, College Buildings.   § 4–6. Hist. of Foundation.   § 7, 8. Admission.   § 9, 10. Course of Studies.   § 11, 12. Mission.   § 13–15. Fate of the Students.   § 16. Persecution of Catholics. § 17. List of Students in Residence.   § 18. The Jesuit Authorities.   § 19. Their Character.   § 20. Scheme of this Report.   § 21. Complaints of the Students in general.   § 22. Reply of the College Authorities.   24–40. Complaints and replies in detail.   § 41–55. The Visitor's Rulings.   § 56–86. Constitution of the College.   § 87. Foundation of the Confraternity of our Lady.   [§ 88–139. Its Constitutions (not printed here).   § 88–110. The pious aim of the Confraternity ; rules for the spiritual life, self-discipline, and mutual edification ; Conferences, Spiritual Exercises, Prayers for the conversion of England, etc.   § 111–122. Rules for Admission, Probation, Secret Voting, Ceremonies, Month's Probation, Second Voting, Petition of those Received. § 123–126. Expulsion ; Imposition of further time of probation.   § 129–139. Organization of the Confraternity.]   § 140–151. Rules for · the Monitors. § 152–164.   Domestic arrangements of the College.   [§ 165. Legal matters (not printed here).]   § 166. Medical Evidence.   [§ 167. Finance (not printed here).]

Bibl. Vat., Ottob., lat. 2473, fols. 60–80.

Sixto quinto pontifici optimo maximo.

[§ 1] Etsi non ignoramus, B^me Pater, Sanctitatem Vestram omnium ecclesiarum, praeter instantia totius orbis quotidiana, solicitam esse, vidimus tamen Anglorum illiusque collegii causam pietati suae praecipue commendatam, quae optime noverit, quantum ex alumnis istis et christianae religioni splendoris et Anglis omnibus propter multorum illius gentis ad Deum conversionem utilitatis accrescat, et propterea V. S^tas more pervigilis solicitique pastoris, ut ex grege suo fructum Domino referat, qui non perit, nobis tanto oneri licet imparibus istorum adolescentium totiusque domus visitationem demandaverit [*sic*], ut si quid fortasse reformatione dignum esset, eidem renunciaremus.   Quod, Pater Sancte, pro viribus prestitimus, inprimis ipsorum ecclesiam visitavimus, sacristiam ac universam ecclesiasticam supellectilem, domum, rectorem, ministros, familiam totam et alumnos ; fundationis

---

[1] The Report of Sega's second visitation (1596) is in Ottob., lat. 2473, fols. 187–226, and is printed in an English translation by H. FOLEY, *Records of the English Province of the Society of Jesus*, Vol. VI. (London, 1880), pp. 1–66. *Cf.* Appendix XVI.—The Statutes of the English College.

collegii principia, redditus, impensas, onera, lites, constitutiones, regulas, spirituales exercitationes, missiones, labores, obitus, plurimorum martiria omnemque denique vivendi rationem novimus, quae in libellum hunc brevius quidem quoad eius fieri potuit redacta ad S^{tem} V. attulimus, ut, cum per otium interdum id sibi aliquo pacto licuerit, modo unum modo aliud perlegere dignetur.   Interim quae ad alumnorum pacem collegiive conservationem nostra sententia visa sunt necessaria, S^{ti} V. poterunt citissime nisi fallimur innotescere, quam Deus incolumem ecclesiae suae diuque conservet.

Relatio status Collegii Anglicani.

[§ 2] De Anglorum ecclesia cultuque divino, Pater B^{me}, nihil est quod S. V. referamus : credimus enim latere neminem templum hoc, etsi perexiguum, illustre tamen aspectuque ex diversorum Dei martirum expressis imaginibus[1] iucundissimum esse. Altaria omnia decora valde, supellex magnifica et pro loci facultate copiosa.   Is ministrantium atque sacerdotum in divinis laudibus aliisque sacris muneribus obeundis ordo eaque pietas, ut videntibus aliquando nobis remque tacite considerantibus non esset ultra spiritus.

[§ 3] Domus certe pro alenda iuventute non incommoda, tota conclave unum, atria, viridarium, porticus, coenaculum, culina, prontuaria, cellae vinariae, aulae, bibliotheca rectoris, patrum, alumnorum, praepositi domui, ianitoris servorumque cubicula, peregrinorum hospitia, valetudinarium et id genus alia distincta quidem ac inter se bene disposita, ut hac ratione adolescentibus istis et universo in praesentiarum collegio deesse nihil arbitremur. Pauca de ipsius initio atque progressu dicemus, et ex iis postea de toto statu rerum omnium cognoscetur.

[§ 4] Igitur Anglicani Collegii ex illius gentis hospitali[2] primum origo cepit, et ut rerum omnium parva sunt principia, anno salutis 1576 scholares aliquot ab Alano[3] ex Gallia Romam missi sunt et in hospitale recepti, ut illius sumptibus alerentur, idque

---

[1] By Niccolò Circignani called *Pomarancio*.   See above, p. 109, note 2.

[2] *Cf.* for this Croke's articles mentioned in p. 99, note 2, and the Memorial on the English hospice in Cath. Record Soc. Publ. IX., 89–97.

[3] William Allen, the founder of the Douay-Rheims seminary, afterwards "the Cardinal of England."

iussu tum bonae memoriae cardinalis Moroni (erat enim eo tempore protector[1]) tum foelicis recordationis Gregorii, S^tis V. praedecessoris. Sequenti vero anno ab eodem Alano alii subinde mittebantur, sed cum hospitalis redditus pro scholarium et capellanorum, qui Anglorum et hospitalis ecclesiae inserviebant, sustentatione, ad peregrinosque recipiendos non sufficerent, mandavit pontifex capellanos omnes ex hospitali discedere et eorum loco scholares recipi, praesertim cum inter eos aliqui essent sacerdotes qui templi etiam necessitatibus inservire poterant; capellanis tamen pro eorum victu provisionem menstruam ex errario [*sic*] suo pontifex assignavit. Sed, cum scholarium ad urbem adventantium numerus in dies augeretur, nec hospitalis sumptibus plus quam duodecim ali possent, voluit summus pontifex ut plures etiam reperirentur, quibus ipse necessaria subministraret. Itaque factum est, ut in initio anni 1578 scholares circiter viginti sub Mauritii Clenocii[2] regimine, qui tunc erat hospitalis custos, in hospitale simul degerent.

[§ 5] Eodem tempore archidiaconus Cameracensis obtinuit a pontifice, ut duo patres e Societate Jesu ad Anglorum hospitale venirent et scholaribus collegialem vivendi formam atque disciplinam tam in re litteraria quam in colenda pietate coeterisque exercitationibus ostenderent; quod cum factum esset, tunc primo ceptum est "Collegium Anglorom" dici hospitalisque nomen in collegii nomen transferri.

[§ 6] Patribus[3] collegii curam pontifex demandavit: ex iis Alphonsus [*Agazzari*] scholarium totiusque domus regimini praeficitur anno 79, quo tempore [*nono*] kalendis Maii et collegium erectum[4] et bona iuraque hospitalis universa collegio ipsi pontificis diplomate fuerunt unita, scolarium numero aucto ad quadraginta, ut non posset amplius accrescere, ita iubente summo pontifice; cum tamen plures ab Alano mitterentur, rogatur

[1] Giovanni Morone, died Dec., 1580. FOLEY (*Records*, VI., p. 123) gives a list of the cardinal protectors of the English college.

[2] Maurice Clenock. See p. 110.

[3] The words *Patres* and *Societas* in this document always mean the Jesuits and the Society of Jesus.

[4] The Bull is dated April 23, 1579, not May 1; hence the insertion of [*nono*]. COCQUELINES, *Bullarium . . . Roman. Pontif.*, t. IV., p. iii. (Romæ, 1746), 359–363. DODD-TIERNEY, *Church History*, II., Appendix, No. LVII.

pontifex a rectore quid agendum ? quotquot idoneos ad collegium Alanus mitteret esse recipiendos S^tas S. respondit, sed initio presentis anni 85 per cardinalem S. Sixti,[1] protectorem collegii, septuaginta scholarium tantum collegium debere esse idem pontifex rectori significavit.

[§ 7] Verumtamen non omnes passim in collegium istud admittuntur, sed probati tantum Alani testimonio ac a protectore ex pontificae legis prescripto, qui postquam in collegio fuerint recepti non statim collegii alumni censentur ; prius enim per quatuor aut sex menses, plus vel minus, prout superioribus et collegii moderatoribus visum fuerit, eorum conversatio probatur.

[§ 8] Deinde si collegio digni videbuntur, se iureiurandi[2] religione obstringunt, vitam ecclesiasticam perducturos seque omni tempore ad superiorum iussu in patriam revertendum, et ad animas, quantum in domino potuerint, adiuvandas paratos fore.

[§ 9] Ex his aliqui diutius et aliqui minus Romae commorantur, ad urbem veniunt vel magis vel minus in litteris instructi. Si logicam adhuc non inceperunt, ordinarie per septennium manent, quorum tres in philosophia et quatuor annos in theologia discenda ponunt ; si vero philosophi veniunt, per triennium tantum vel quadriennium.

[§ 10] Aliqui etiam etsi philosophiae non studuerint, triennium tamen in collegio non excedunt, propterea quod ad theologiam positivam audiendam destinantur, quia vel propter aetatem vel propter ingenii imbecillitatem ad schoolastica studia apti mimime videntur. ◦

[§ 11] Missiones in Angliam fieri bis in anno hactenus consuevit, vere sciticet et autumno, et mittuntur tantum sacerdotes, quive theologica studia vel absolverint vel in eis bene profecerint, in ecclesiasticisque ceremoniis atque concionibus ut plurimum exercitati. Transmittuntur ad Collegium Remense, indeque ab Alano, viro in rebus Anglicis exercitatissimo, in Angliam diriguntur.

[§ 12] Scholarium numerus est, qui a primeva collegii institutione Romae fuerunt, centum septuaginta quinque, ex

---

[1] Filippo Buoncompagni, cardinal of S. Sisto, nephew of Gregory XIII.
[2] Cf. above, p. 101.

quibus in Angliam missi sunt quadraginta duo, Rhemos ad praelegendum philosophiam et theologiam sex.

Ingressi Societatem Jesu ex iuratis sex. Ex non iuratis et convictoribus decem.

[§ 13] Convictores sunt, qui etsi in collegio et collegii regulis vivant, non tamen collegii sumptibus sed propriis eorum pecuniis aluntur. Isti iuramentum non praestant in Angliam revertendi ecclesiasticamque vitam perducendi quemadmodum coeteri ; tamen digni visi sunt admitti, ut saltem nobis catholicorum numerus augeretur.

[§ 14] Ex alumnis octo mortui sunt. Ex convictoribus decem. Dimissi ob adversam valetudinem quatuordecim. Ex his obiit Rhemis Ricardus Eduardus et Andreas Gibbonus in itinere. Octo vero tanquam inepti.

Transierunt in ordinem Dominicanorum duo, quorum unus erat ex convictoribus. In Capuccinorum autem alii duo. Reliqui modo sunt in collegio saxeginta septem.

[§ 15] Ex iis autem sacerdotibus qui in Angliam missi sunt (de alumnis loquimur), Rodulfus Cervinus,[1] Luca Kirbeus,[2] Gullielmus Artus,[3] Georgius Addocus,[4] Thomas Emerfordus,[5] Johannes Shertus,[6] post carceres, postquam multa tormentorum genera Deo favente superata pro cattolica fide summique Romani pontificis primatu defendendo (impiissimae reginae eiusque satellitum detestabili immanique feritate undique per Angliam contra christianae veritatis defensores perbacchante) crudelissime necati, martirii palmam adipisci meruerunt.

[§ 16] Aliqui adhuc pro eadem causa in vinculis detinentur. Reliqui strenue in animabus ad fidem cattolicam convertendis elaborant. " Messis quidem magna, sed operarii pauci," [7] tamen fructus uberrimi ; nam ex huiusmodi martirum constantissima nece, Alano teste, multa ·haereticorum millia conversa sunt, longe autem plura ex vivorum laboribus ad ecclesiae gremium reveruntur. Fertur ex patrum Societatis eiusdemque Alani testimonio, sacerdotum istorum opera, exemplo, diligentia sanguineque animarum supra centum millia,[8] quae in haereseos tenebris in

---

[1] Sherwin.   [2] Kirby.   [3] Hart.   [4] Haydock.
[5] Hemerford.   [6] Shert.   [7] St. Matt. ix. 37.
[8] For this and the following figures *cf.* my attempt to arrive at the actual number of catholics, pp. 60 *et seq.*

Anglia iacuissent, Dei modo et illorum auxilio ad evangelii lumen conversae, in ea publice fidem catolicam profiteri, paratasque ·esse vitam prius, si Deo placeret, ac fortunas omnes relinquere quam a nostra religione discedere. Eorum vero qui corde catholici sunt, sed extrinsecus reginae dominationem et imperium reformidantes reginae (inviti quidem) adhaerent, creditur esse hominum millia circiter quadringenta, ex quibus tamen quotidie aliquos, humano timore deposito, sacerdotes isti privatis colloquiis et exhortationibus ecclesiae reconciliant, qui, si rerum status in Anglia vel minimum mutaretur, armis et omni conatu (ita enim sperandum) publicam orthodoxae fidei causam tutarentur. Romano interim collegio atque etiam Remensi plurimum debemus, ex quibus ecclesiae Dei tam ingentia animarum lucra in hanc usque diem ex perditissimo regno brevi tamen divina disponente bonitate provenerunt, idque postremo hoc sex annorum spatio, quo collegium istud Romanum suos in Anglia alumnos direxit, aliqui factum observarunt (nam ab anno 1580 ceperunt esse martires) perinde ac si Romani alumni veluti immediate a Christi vicario Petrique successore missi pro illius primatus defensione, spiritum laborandi, patiendi atque demum moriendi desiderium, ipsis ducibus, in Angliam importaverint, quod sacerdotibus aliis communicarent. Sed maxime patrum Societatis officium, pietas atque vigilantia sanctum hoc opus adiuvarunt, nam ex eis Edmundus Campianus [1] glorioso in Anglia insignique martirio pro eadem fidei defensione coronatus est. Robertus autem Personius, Gaspar Aiodus,[2] Gulielmus Holtus, Vestonus, Rodulphus Angli et Gulielmus Critonius [3] Scotus cum quodam alio cuius nomen ignoramus, qui omnes Jesuitae sunt, adhuc in vinea domini Anglicanaque messe, quemadmodum audivimus, solicite laborant, ex quibus Critonium dicunt et Rodulphum impie in reorum custodia detineri.

[§ 17] Eorum autem alumnorum, qui modo sunt in collegio, viginti duo scolasticae theologiae vacant, scilicet :

P. Rob. Benettus [4]	P. Dan. Alsvortus [6]	P. Gul. Varfordius [8]
P. Christophorus Sodvortus [5]	P. Thom. Varcopus [7]	P. Phil. Udvardus [9]

---

[1] For Edmund Campion, see pp. 192–195.   [2] Jasper Heywood.
[3] William Creighton, see Appendix XXI.
[4] Bennet.   [6] Ailsworth.   [8] Warford.
[5] Southworth.   [7] Warcop.   [9] Woodward.

P. Robert Xaiirus [1]   Jacobus Vavaxorus [6]   Thomas Evanus [11]
Guglielm. Ciadocus [2]   diaconus   Caesar Clemens [12]
Gulielmus   Ruge-   Robertus Cernoltus [7]   Henricus Ansleus [13]
   rius [3]   Riccardus Lichius [8]   diaconus
Joannes Phiserus [4]   diaconus   Edm. Tornellus [14]
Joannes Petrus [5] sub-   Gulielm. Ardisteus [9]   Thomas Pormortus [15]
   diaconus   Simon Scimbornus [10]   Thomas Vavaxoius [16]

Quindecim vero positive :

P. Eduard. Jacobus [17]   Gul. Eyrtonus [22] diac.   Petrus Flererus [27]
P. Christophorus [18]   Gulielmus Puellus [23]   Thomas Storeus [28]
P. Joann. Zipettus [19]   Jacobus Bolandus [24]   Robertus Graius [29]
P. Thom. Stanneus [20]   Christ. Bugstonus [25]   Richardus Culinus [30]
P. Edm. Carvarleus [21]   Gulielm. Jansonus [26]   Georgius Plosteius [31]

Metaphisici decem :

Eduardus Olcornus [32]   Oliverius   Almun-   Thomas Loflaceus [39]
Joannes Ricardus [33]   dus [36]   Thomas   Parcroph-
Jacobus Fongerus [34]   Ricardus Blontus [37]   tus [40]
Matteus Kelisons [35]   Ricardus Budleus [38]   Joannes Robertus [41]

Novem sunt phisici :

Gulielmus Odoenus [42]   Francisc. Cleitonus [45]   Joannes Nelsonus [48]
Samuel Chenittus [43]   Gulielm. Balduinus [46]   Eduard. Vestonus [49]
Thomas Anxortus [44]   Laurenti. Odoanus [47]   Joann. Stratfordus [50]

[1] Sayers.
[2] Chaddock.
[3] Roger.
[4] Fixer.
[5] Petre.
[6] Vavasor.
[7] Charnock.
[8] Leigh.
[9] Hardesty.
[10] Sherborne (Shirburn).
[11] Evans.
[12] Clement.
[13] Ansley.
[14] Thornell.
[15] Pormort.
[16] Vavasor.
[17] James.
[18] Christopher.
[19] Tibbit.
[20] Stanney.
[21] Calverley.
[22] Heighington. (Heighton).
[23] Powell.
[24] Bowlande.
[25] Buxton.
[26] Johnson.
[27] Fletcher.
[28] Story.
[29] Gray.
[30] Cowling.
[31] Foster (?).
[32] Oldcorne.
[33] Richards.
[34] Yonger.
[35] Kellison.
[36] Almonde.
[37] Blount (Blunt).
[38] Dudley (?).
[39] Lovelace.
[40] Barcroft.
[41] Roberts.
[42] Owen.
[43] Kennet.
[44] Hawksworth.
[45] Clayton.
[46] Baldwin.
[47] Owen.
[48] Nelson.
[49] Weston.
[50] Stratford.

Undecim postremo logici :

Unfredus Usleus [1]	Joannes Ingramus [5]	Polidorus Plasdinus [9]
Antonius Copleus [2]	Georgius Bustardus [6]	Ricardus Valspo-
Antonius Maior [3]	Ricardus Floidus [7]	nus [10]
Edmundus Ducas [4]	Jacobus Bissopus [8]	Ricardus Jornus [11]

Isti omnes habent nomina tum propria tum fictitia, ficta quidem, ne forte ab exploratoribus reginae denuncientur, eorumque patres et consanguinei propterea apud insolentes haereticorum ministros in omnium discrimine fortunarum et vitae sint.

[§ 18] Patres collegii istius moderatores sunt inprimis

Rev^dus Alphonsus Agazarus Senensis, rector.

Camillus Straivanus de Neapoli, minister.

Thomas Martialis Anglus, confessarius.

Robertus Sutvellus [12] Anglus, studiis praefectus.

Gaspar Alonsus Hispanus, repetitor metaphisicae.

Joannes Claivus Polonus, repetitor phisicae.

Jacobus Casamatta ex Romandiola, repetitor logicae.

Vincentius Maria Neapolitanus, praefectus officialibus et famulis pro ministro, ut quisque suo muneri satisfaciat.

Bartolomeus praefectus cellae vestiariae et valetudinario.

Michael Natalis Mantuanus, socius rev^di rectoris et sacristiae praefectus. Sunt omnes numero decem.

[§ 19] Patrum nobis (praesertim rectoris) in universa domo creditaque sibi familia regenda solicitudo atque prudentia probatur. De alumnis audivimus in eos nullum esse crimen, sed pudorem, sed continentiam in omnibus, sed pietatem ut plurimum. Quae vero de collegii dissentionibus circumferuntur, consulto in nostrae huius relationis calce S. V. reservavimus exponenda, ut, iis auditis, ea pro sua prudentia auctoritate constituat quae sibi, rei, personarum et loci qualitate pensata, magis expedire videbuntur.

[§ 20] Centum et unus hoc tempore collegii sumptibus aluntur, alumni scilicet, ut diximus, sexaginta septem, patres decem. Reliquorum autem viginti quatuor nomina et officia, quum mercenarii sunt, infra suo loco, cum de rebus collegii temporalibus

[1] Wolsley.	[5] Ingram.	[9] Plasden.
[2] Copley.	[6] Bustard.	[10] Walpole.
[3] Maior.	[7] Floyd.	[11] Thorney.
[4] Duke.	[8] Bishop.	[12] Southwell.

agetur, describentur. Coeterum alumnorum vivendi rationem, quam ordinem domus appellant, ipsorumque certa onera, sed inprimis quorundam collegii sacerdotum propositiones et gravamina, quibus aliqui se premi sentiunt, scripto S. V. significata cum responsionibus ad singula seorsum ab ista relatione posuimus. Postremo posita coram nobis redituum omnium impensarumque ratione,[1] subducto calculo quod hactenus datum quidve acceptum sit, quae collegii vires quaeve onera, quod aes alienum; si alumnorum numerus ad centum augeretur quid pecuniae deesset; si minuatur quod lucrum; quot denique ex collegii reditu ali sustentarique possent, S. V. planius ex adnotata scriptaque supputatione liquebit.

Multa praetermisimus, Pater Sancte, quae inserere non libuit, nempe reliquiarum inventarium, utensilium domus et librorum indicem, ne libellus iste contra instituti nostri rationem (studemus enim brevitati) in magnum volumen excresceret

[§ 21] Jam ergo ad collegii dissensiones devenimus, et re vera, Pater Sancte, ex alumnis multi multa loquuntur, sed omnia unum sunt. Plerique ipsorum queruntur institutam a patribus in collegio B^mae Virginis Mariae sodalitatem dissidiorum inter eos causam existere; in ea recipi qui rectori videntur addicti quive bene se erga Societatem affectos ostendunt, istos prae coeteris honorari, istos diligi plus aliis, cubiculis praefici, quaestiones philosophiae vel etiam theologicas publice defendere, citius ad ordines promoveri, magis pios existimari, agi cum istis humanius, reliquos hac ratione despici; sodales rectoris partes tueri, coalumnos, quibuscum deambulent, quidve loquantur observàre, rectori omnia, et saepe falsa ac imaginaria quidem, referre; e sodalitate qui rectori non placent pro ipsius imperio eiici, ut propterea pax inter fratres in collegio deturbetur; rem esse ad Societatis et patrum utilitatem compositam, ut ex sodalibus et alumnis aptiores fortasse in ipsorum numerum trahant. Expedire sodalitatem, quamquam in se bona sit, vel dissolvi vel omnibus esse communem. Ante ipsius erectionem tranquillum extitisse collegium; durum quippe videri iuratos in Angliam se ad illius gentis et patriae conversionem adiuvandam reversuros in Jesuitarum Societatem aliamve religionem ingredi, re Anglicana publica miserrime derelicta; quod fieri non debere multis iam argumentis rationibusque

[1] Too long to print here (fol. 80 v–87 v). See § 167.

contendunt; interdum aliquos studiorum cursu non absoluto Rhemos in Galliam ante tempus mitti, qui averso ab rectore animo putantur deterritos discedere. Peregrinorum Angliae curam esse minimam,[1] plerosque vicatim sibi victum querere, qui possent in hospitale recipi, huiusmodi [peregrinos] alloqui Romae alumnis non licere, extra collegium euntibus testis, non autem comes, a rectore datur; divisum esse collegium; occurrendum esse praesenti malo, ne progrediatur ulterius.   Haec alumni, etsi non omnes; istae discordiarum causae.

[§ 22] Rector et alii contra existimant sodalitatem huiusmodi pietatis ac virtutum omnium specimen videri, ab aliquibus rerum novarum cupidis in collegio rumores excitari, infirmiores decipi, regiminis mutationem moliri, non iure conqueri.   Rectorem se omnibus aequalem praebere, omnibus bene velle, scolares ab eorum instituto iuvandi patriam nolle discedere.   Falsum esse sodales tantummodo cubiculos praefici; multos enim extitisse praefectos, non autem ex congregatione, ut patres Philippus, Werfordius,[2] Arturus et alii.   Philosophiam et theologiam defendisse Gilbertum Geffordium,[3] Museum,[4] iique bis, quod nunquam in congregationis sodalibus accidit, patrem Ossonum philosophiam, Warfordium coram summo pontifice orationem habuisse inter missarum solemnia, quod honore non parvo dignum ducitur. Si ex sodalibus plures quam extra congregationem alumni huiusmodi munera subiere, non esse quod patribus imputetur, quandoquidem sodales animo sunt pacato, studiis ac pietati diligentius incumbunt, ideo magis in omnibus proficiunt. Duos extra congregationem hoc anno monitos esse, ut se ad philosophicas defendendas conclusiones parent, fuisse Philippum et Warfordium atque etiam Cecilium, qui tamen de congregatione non erant, citius ad ordines promotos quam ulli unquam alii in isto collegio.   Inquietos observari ex causa, sodales aliquando e congregatione pelli, ut si aliorum commissa revelent, si non obediant, et id genus alia; aliqui siquidem ut humiliores evadant a sodalibus petunt eorum sibi defectus et peccata in os coram fratribus dici, ac per hoc fuit experientia compertum nonnullos sodalium errata detegisse.   Iniustam esse querelam illam de his qui hactenus Societatem ingressi sunt, cum et de summo

---

[1] This complaint was repeated in 1596.   FOLEY, VI., pp. 25 (No. 7), 27.
[2] Warford.   [3] Gifford.   [4] Mush.

pontificis atque protectoris et Alani consensu recepti sunt.
Patres non allicere quenquam, aliquos aliquando non absoluto
septennio in Galliam remitti, quia vel cito se expedierunt, vel ad
Alani postulationem missi sunt. Maxima de causa prohiberi, ne
alumni cum peregrinis Anglis libere colloquantur ; nam aposto-
licus apud regem Gallorum nuntius cardinali Comensi[1] litteris
significavit Angliae reginam summa ope niti, ut collegii Romani
iuvenes corrumpantur, magisque reginam collegia ista reformidare
quam alias mundi potestates. Hinc igitur factum est, ut per
cardinalem protectorem summus pontifex scripto quidem rectori
iusserit magnam habendam esse curam, ne scolares cum externis
versentur, quod mandatum ipsi vidimus. Peregrinos non autem
omnes, sed probatos recipi. Unitum fore collegium, si scandalum
tolleretur. Warfordium, Philippum, Fiscerum[2] et Tornellum[3] et
alios paucos istarum dissensionum causam existere, eos praesertim qui in Oxoniensi academia fuerunt interdum educati, ubi
qui graduati sunt maxima abutuntur vivendi libertate, sibique
propterea collegii nostri institutionem videri servitutem. Aliam
esse causam, scilicet superbiam ; tertiam, parvam istorum pietatem,
idcirco tales contra modestiores obloqui ; quartam extrinsecum
favorem atque etiam auxilium opinantur ; quintam moderatorum
humanitatem disciplinaeque suavitatem existimant. Hactenus
rector et qui pro eo sunt.

[§ 23] Quae autem utrinque iurati deposuerint quaeve
scripserint apud nos conservantur. Vidit S. V. verborum con-
gressum, quae igitur ad scolarium victum, quae ad divinum
ecclesiae cultum, quae denique ad rerum temporalium red-
dituumve collegii administrationem pertinent, hoc nobis referente
calculatore, non potuimus non probare.

Gravamina quibus se premi sentiunt collegii Anglicani sacerdotes et alumni aliquot.

[§ 24] Propositio. In primis quod a fundato collegio triplo
plures obierunt et in religione Jesuinorum [*sic*] abierunt, quam in
messem Anglicanam.

Responsio. Quadraginta duo in messem Anglicanam, sex
etiam Rhemos ad prelegendum philosophiam et theologiam missi

---

[1] Tolomeo Gallio.   [2] Fixer.   [3] Thornell.

sunt.   Ex iis autem, qui iuramento collegii [1] tenebantur, obstricti sex in Jesuitarum societatem abierunt, nempe

Joannes Bartonus [2]	Guglielmus Artus [4]	Osvald. Tesimondus [6]
Thomas Writus [3]	Thomas Listerus [5]	P. Ricc. Engeamus [7]

Octo vero mortui sunt ex iuratis in isto collegio, vel in via discendentes :

Lancell. Procterus [8]	Ed. Trocmortonus [11]	Thomas Benettus [14]
Christoph. Owenus [9]	Humfred. Esaggus [12]	Andreas Wagus [15]
Georgius Witingus [10]	Rodulphus Snirleus.[13]	

[§ 25] P. Quod expensis 60,000 aureorum vix viginti sacerdotes sunt in vineam missi.

R. Quot fuerint missi in superiori declaratione definitur. Aureorum millia quae recensentur et in scholarium totiusque domus alimenta (si subductae rationi credimus) et in ea, quae in ipsius collegii fundatione instrui pararique debuerunt, erogata sunt.

[§ 26] P. Cum reditus collegii sint 8000 aureorum annuatim, alumni autem 60 tantum, illi autem viritim non plus 60 aureos expendant per annum, reliquum pecuniae, quomodo evanescit, non apparet (restat autem 4400), nec audet quis Anglus huius rei rationem querere.

R. Annuus collegii reditus aurearum 4674 et 24 summam non excedit; quanquam igitur non sexaginta viritim aureos expenderent, sed tantum quinquaginta sex, mercedum quae servientibus solvuntur aliorumque collegii onerum habita ratione, aureis duobus millibus et octingentis et amplius impensa equidem necessaria, et supputatione, adhuc reditu maior apparebit [sic].[16]

[§ 27] P. Quod omnes apostatae et exploratores in Anglia ex collegio Anglicano prodierunt, scandalo accepto et indiscreto regimine, ut facile est coniicere.

R. Initio ipsius collegii scholares absque ullo fere delectu hic a

---

[1] The college oath which pledged the student to return to England. *Cf.* p. 101.

[2] Barton.	[7] Engham.	[12] Isaac (?).
[3] Wright.	[8] Proctor.	[13] Snirley (?).
[4] Hart.	[9] Owen.	[14] Bennett.
[5] Lister.	[10] Whiting.	[15] Wage.
[6] Tesimond.	[11] Throgmorton.	[16] Text obscure.

protectore recipiebantur, quorum aliqui exploratores inventi sunt,
ut illorum exitus probavit; nam e collegio tanquam inutiles
eiecti, in Anglia se pessime gessere reginaeque consiliariis nostra
omnia, sacerdotes sodalesque suos prodiderunt; sed, ubi coeptum
fuit ab Alano probatos Romam transmitti, nullus amplius ex
nostri collegii scolaribus alumnisve, eodem Alano teste, per
Dei gratiam apostatarunt, inquit enim datis ad patrem rectorem
litteris.

Illud inprimis est iucundissimum, quod in tanto praesbiterorum
numero nullus hactenus vel adversariorum minis vel tormentis vel
ipsi morti cessit, praeter duos qui, metu victi, aliquid religioni
contrarium fecerunt; sed, mox e manibus hostium liberati, ad
cor redierunt ita plane, ut iudicent sapientes homines nosque
gratissime agnoscamus, non sine summo Dei in nos munere et
miraculo fieri, quod in tanto persecutionis aestu et tanta
hominum fragilitate tam pauci a constanti fidei professione
defecerint.   Addo etiam hoc, quod magis ad Dei laudem pertinet,
presbyterorum utriusque collegii ne unum quidem hactenus quod
audivimus ex vita et moribus scandalum dedisse ullum, licet
ibi nullis visitationibus, nullis praelatorum aut episcoporum
praescriptis, nulla denique ordinaria cleri disciplina, sed solis
conscientiae regulis in officio contineantur.   Hucusque Alanus.

[§ 28] P. Quod in dicta causa sacerdos, vir gravis et magnae
expectationis, cum altero Anglo fuerit expulsus non solum e
collegio sed etiam e civitate, ita ut nisi discederet intra tres dies
metuendus illi fuit carcer.

R. Nescitur quisnam fuerit iste sacerdos, itaque responsum
congruum de eo dari non potest, sed quotquot dimissi sunt,
loquimur enim de ineptis, de protectoris mandato dimissos
affirmamus, ut

Gulielmus Caddeus [1]	Thomas Novellus [5]	Cum hoc ultimo
Gilbertus Giffordius [2]	Hurfred. Maxfildus [6]	discessit etiam pater
Thomas Lovellus [3]	Johannes Bigheus [7]	Baglhaus,[9] ita iu-
Johannes Nicolaus [4]	Georgius Potterus [8]	bente protectore.

[§ 29] P. Quod si quis fuerit, qui religionem Jesuitarum

[1] Caddy.	[5] Nowell.	[9] Bakerhouse (?)
[2] Gifford.	[6] Maxfield.	—Bagshaw (?).
[3] Lovel.	[7] Bigge.	
[4] Nichols.	[8] Potter.	

cogitare induci non poterit, aut non in eorum quasi verba fuerit iuratus, interdicunt ei familiaritatem omnium, omni modo vexant et diffamant, exploratores mittunt, observant, omni libertate privant, et huiusmodi hominibus (sunt autem non pauci) melius sit Angliae in carceribus, quam hic vivere in collegio.

R. In relatione cum de collegii discensionibus agitur quid dicendum ad haec planius ostenditur.

[§ 30] P. Magis religionis suae honorem quam causae nostrae necessitatem cogitant.

R. De occultis non iudicamus, sed ex rerum eventu nobis id parum probatur.

[§ 31] P. Vix inter viginti unus sano corpore in Angliam remittitur, quod partim ex äere, maxime vero ex eo quod in uno cubiculo tot simul habitant et pernoctant, partim vero quod sic exploratoribus vexantur et calumniis onerentur, ut servi potius quam alumni efficiantur, partim quod in exilio patiuntur exilium, nec una exules sine exploratoribus possunt colloqui.

R. Medicum interrogavimus, et, si perito sit credendum, non ita se res habet, ut ex eius testimonio dignoscitur. Alumnorum cubicula sunt inter se pro loci qualitate bene disposita.

[§ 32] P. Quod in rebus Anglicanis nihil fieri patiuntur Jesuitae, nisi se auctoribus fiat, quod multum obest causae publicae.[1]

R. Patres in rebus Anglicanis Alani consilio, uti par est, semper utuntur, idque ex eiusdem Alani ad rectorem litteris plane convincitur.

[§ 33] P. Quod in collegio semper sunt ex 60 ad minus 20 qui sanguinem expuunt, quod necessario est eorum regimini tribuendum, qui Anglorum natura quid requirat nesciunt nec curant; quod inde apparet quod alibi in civitate Angli vivunt satis sani.

R. Nemo sanguinem modo expuit, ita medicus testatur:[2] tres nihilominus aut quatuor existere qui dicunt sanguinem expuisse

---

[1] This complaint was repeated with much greater insistence later on. *Cf.* Sega's Report of 1596. FOLEY, *Records*, VI., pp. 19 *et seq*. The document written in 1596 entitled, "Quomodo seculares sacerdotes a patribus Societatis in Anglia degentibus opprimuntur, deque patrum dominandi desiderio in Anglos et Anglicanum clerum," deals very fully with the efforts of the Jesuits to get the upper hand of the secular clergy both in England itself and in the management of seminaries. Westminster Cathedral Archives, V., 427–470.

[2] *Cf.* the medical evidence in § 166.

iam, non autem in quantitate notabili, quod tamen ipse non vidit, ut hoc valeat affirmare.

[§ 34] P. Quod regimen eorum omnino sit puerorum, nec quis posthac vir gravis aut nobilis cum tanto et vitae et salutis et famae et libertatis periculo velit in collegio vivere.

R. Tot [non] posset alere collegium quot in dies Romam mitterentur, et iam pro mittendis instat Alanus. Regimen autem puerorum sit an contra, ex Germanico licebit asserere, quod nobilibus fere illustribusque adolescentibus plenum iisdem ac durioribus institutis regitur.

[§ 35] P. Quod respectu tantarum impensarum nihil omnino causam iuvat (quid enim prodest ad tantam messem duos vel tres in anno mittere?) collegium istud, nisi quod notam faciat pontifici causam, quae ipsa per se satis est miseranda.

R. Plures in anno mittuntur quam S. V. significetur; missiones autem bis in anno fiunt, vere scilicet et autumno, ut in relatione [1] dicitur. Missionum fructus, ita credimus, et inter omnes constat, maximi sunt.

[§ 36] P. Aequum est itaque ut de redditibus computos faciant annuos, ut ad causae necessitatem convertantur directius, ut saluti provideatur melius, nedum alii infirmi evanescant, alii moriantur, alii in religionem trahantur, causa comunis [2] . . . pulcherrimis ingeniis privetur.

R. De administrationis rerum collegii ratione reddenda iam decrevimus; de praeteritis autem, subducto calculo, in administratione fraudem abesse, nobis qui supputationi praefuit scripto confirmavit.

[§ 37] P. Quam parum causae publicae proficiat iste lautus sumptus, hinc videre licet, quod ex 500 sacerdotibus, qui in Anglia pro salute animarum laborant, vix triginta ex hoc collegio prodierunt, omnes alii Rhemis [3] missi in vineam, et tamen sibi omnia in hac causa arrogare patres non dubitant.

R. Quid causae publicae proficiat collegium Romanum, hinc profecto licet arguere, in Anglia perduellionis lege teneri qui in

---

[1] See above, § 11.

[2] Original imperfect.

[3] This is almost double the actual number. Until 1585 the Douay-Rheims seminary had only sent upwards of 200 priests to England (vid. ante, p. 61, note 1), not 470 as stated here.

Romano educantur collegio. Collegium istud a legislatore timetur, et ex eo 42 in Angliam missi sunt, sex autem Rhemis.[1]

[§ 38] P. Levari possunt miseriae istae, vel Anglum aliquem in regimine cum patribus Jesuitis coniungendo, qui naturas eorum bene norit, et quod saluti prosit bene intelligat.

R. Videat S. V. quid proponatur! unum scimus : in initio collegii, cum alumnis bonae memoriae cardinalis Moronus, tunc protector, Mauritium Cleonociumpraefecisset,[2] iussissetque scolares Mauritio parere vel discedere, aegreferentes hoc alumni inito discedendi consilio, ex eis triginta tres una die e collegio discesserunt ; quod cum audisset summus pontifex, ad se con- quisitos adduci iubet, coram interrogat, auditos ad collegium remittit, patrum Societatis regimen iisdem ad ipsorum peti- tionem spondet. Removetur Mauritius, patribus eius loco suffectis. Res usque modo quievit.

[§ 39] P. Vel si tantum misertus fuerit nostri summus pontifex, ut velit iis, qui hoc äere et regimine se sentiunt gravari, dare alibi in Italia sub patribus alterius religionis seminarium, ubi vivant et Anglice apti efficiantur.

R. Si qui forsan aërem Romanum timent, poterunt Rhemos remitti, ubi et in aëre fortasse puriori et fere patrio ab Anglo collegii sumptibus alantur, absque eo quod nova his inutilibus gravioraque S. V. dispendia proponant.

[§ 40] P. Magna cautio habenda est, ut ista mira charitate tractentur, ne haeretici scandalum inde accipiant, neve [re] infecta durius tractentur alumni, si in his conatibus nihil proficiant.

R. Etsi credamus conscientiam alumnorum aliquem suspiciosum facere, tamen hoc saepe rectorem admonuimus, ut iuvenes istos ea semper qua decet charitate complectatur et foveat.

---

[1] The text has *Rhemos*, which agrees badly with the context.

[2] As if Clenock had been an Englishman ! It throws a good deal of light on the sincerity with which the students' complaints were investigated, that Maurice Clenock should be brought forward as an example of a rector of English nationality, for it was just the undue preference which Clenock showed towards the Welshmen, his own fellow-countrymen, over the English students which caused all the troubles in the college ! "Tam impossibile est naturaliter. . . . Wallum bene tractare Anglum, si illi praesit, atque est Mau- rum amanter tractare Hispanum." DODD-TIERNEY, II., Appendix, p. cccxlvi. For more particulars, see the sources of information quoted on p. 97, note 1.

Decreta.

[§ 41] Igitur per ea quae vidimus et audivimus nihil, Pater Beatissime, remittendum in huius collegii Anglicani regimine de iure patrum arbitramur, et si placet S. V., nobis haec in presentiarum decernenda pro temporum conditione videntur.

[§ 42] Regulae collegii quaecunque ab alumnis omnino serventur.

[§ 43] Non liceat alumnis de lege lata patrumque regimine disceptare; sed si aliquis eisdem expostulandi locus praebeatur, id erit rectori proponendum, ut ipse pro sua prudentia pietateque scholarium saluti atque necessitatibus prospiciat; quod si rector alumnos non audierit, in re tam gravi ill^{mus} protector adeatur, qui pro eius summa in omnes auctoritate providebit.

[§ 44] Illicitae alumnorum conventiculae debita rectoris arbitrio poena puniantur.

[§ 45] Sodalitatem Assumptionis B^{mae} Virginis omnes venerentur uti decet, contraque sodales et eorum statuta obloqui murmurareve nemini liceat.

[§ 46] Alia infra mensem titulo nativitatis eiusdem S^{mae} Virginis iisdem regulis vel etiam diversis arbitrio rectoris erigatur. Qui primo in eam ingredi voluerint, a visitatoribus, rectore praesente, examinentur; coeteri vero pro regulae instituto vel admitti, vel, si minus idonei sint, reici debebunt.

[§ 47] Tempus missionibus praefinitum, nisi protectore consulto et ex causa a collegii praefecto, nolumus alterari.

[§ 48] Alumnorum nemini qui solus fuerit cubiculum absque praefecto concedatur, exceptis parocho aut valetudinariis sive etiam infirmis arbitrio rectoris.

[§ 49] Alumnis egredi volentibus e collegio nominatim sibi socium petere non liceat, sed a rectore, qui melius alumnorum ingenia moresque norit designato comite libenter utantur.

[§ 50] Litteras neque dent scolares, nisi prius a rectore impetrata licentia, neque recipiant, neque eodem inconsulto peregrinos Anglos publice vel privatim alloquantur.

[§ 51] Recreationis tempore (ut aiunt) in collegium praesertim laici, quive ad collegium non pertinent, non admittantur.

[§ 52] Qui sub hisce nostris collegiique constitutionibus vivere

nolle infra octo dierum spatium a praesentium publicatione decla-
rarint, Rhemos ad Alanum honorifice in paceque remittantur.

[§ 53] Musicae statis horis alumni operam superiorum arbitrio
navare non omittant.

[§ 54] Curae sit rectori, ut, qui de coetero rationibus con-
ficiendis in collegio praeerit, codicem habeat, in quo distincte
peregrini omnes ad hospitale Anglorum adventantes, annus,
mensis atque dies ipsorum adventus, patria, commendationis
testimonium, quicquidve in eorum sustentationem erogari con-
tigerit, ordine describantur, in eisque recipiendis hospitalis ipsius
constitutiones omnino serventur; de universa denique rerum
collegii administratione singulis annis coram deputandis ab ill^{mo}
protectore calculatoribus ratio reddatur.

[§ 55] Quae in decretis istis poenae non exprimuntur, rectoris
arbitrio, etiam ad realem dimissionem usque, ill^{mo} tamen protectori communicato consilio, relinquuntur.

MOTUS PROPRIUS ERECTIONIS COLLEGII ANGLICANI.[1]

Constitutiones collegii Anglicani.

[§ 56] Omnis reipublicae status et aliae hominum societates et
collegia, cum demum recte gubernantur, cum pacis et concordiae
vinculis continentur. Quod cum sine lege fieri non posse certum
sit, ut nostrum hoc Anglorum collegium recte dirigi et administrari possit, leges aliquot prescribendas duximus, quibus alumni
instructi velut unius moris in domo mutua charitate coniuncti,
unam eamdemque disciplinam adiscant et ad optatum finem
perveniant.

De admittendis.

[§ 57] Quicumque ergo in hoc collegium admittendi erunt,
Angli sint necessarium est, tantum ex Angliae regno eiusque
provinciis delecti, quorum aetas 18 aut circiter[2] anno non sit
inferior, ut citius ad iuvandam patriam mitti possint et facilius ea
percipiant, quae de ecclesiastici hominis officio et ratione
iuvandarum animarum illis proponantur. Sint igitur et sano

---

[1] Omitted here because already printed in DODD-TIERNEY, *vid. ante*, [§ 6],
note 2.

[2] Originally (1579) fixed at 14 years. See above, p. 481.

corpore, et quod honestatem et bonam indolem referat. Sint quoque necesse est bonae valetudinis, ut studiorum labores tollerare possint; linguam autem habeant expeditam ad munus illud, cui destinantur, recte peragendum, videlicet ad proponendum in lectionibus et concionibus verbum Dei et alios publicis vel privatis colloquiis iuvandos. Sint denique ii, de quibus digna sit expectatio, fore ut christianis moribus, disciplina doctrinaque cattolica commode possit instrui.

[§ 58] Nemo admittatur, qui religionis semel susceptae temere habitum deseruerit; habeant testimonium aliquod honestae anteactae vitae et bonae famae, et quod extimentur utiles fore operarii in vinea domini.

[§ 59] Venturi ad hoc collegium intelligant finem illius esse, ut alantur in eo et instruantur ii tantum, qui spiritualibus Angliae necessitatibus pro talento a Deo accepto possint opitulari.

[§ 60] Statim in ingressu iurare teneantur se sub obedientia summi pontificis ac Romanae ecclesiae victuros, iuxta formam iuramenti professionis fidei felicis recordationis Pii quarti.[1]

[§ 61] Qui tanquam alumni admittentur in collegium post aliquot menses ab ingressu, vel quandocunque superiori videbitur, iureiurando polliceantur se paratos esse vitam ecclesiasticam agere et quotiescunque fuerit iniunctum in Angliam ad iuvandas animas proficisci, et suo quisque chyrographo fidem suam astringet ad promissa servanda.

[§ 62] Admoneatur non debere eos in hoc collegio aliis studiis operam dare nisi tantum philosophicis et theologicis, et propterea admittendi non erunt nisi qui saltem ad cursum philosophiae proxime inchoandum reperti fuerint idonei. Quibus absolutis, in Angliam se profecturos intelligant, ut aquisita in animarum salutem impendant, prout Dominus dare dignabitur.

De instruendis.

[§ 63] Quoniam autem ea demum utilis et salutaris doctrina est, quae pietatis habet fundamentum, sub ipsum ingressum in collegium de rebus spiritualibus ad tuendam animi pietatem et puritatem una cum timore Domini spatio decem dierum aut plurium, prout superioribus videbitur, separatim ab aliis habitent et instruantur ac generalem peccatorum suorum confessionem

---

[1] *Cf.* p. 482, note 1.

faciant, ut, adhibita hac quasi praeparatione, considerate postea et constanter tantum munus suscipiant, et interea collegii regulas evolvant, et an sub tali disciplina vivere possint, attente considerent.

[§ 64] Moneantur etiam hoc tempore, quod quamvis ad studia admittantur, non tamen statim inter alumnos censeri debeant, sed per quatuor menses, plus minus arbitrio superiorum, eorum ingenium et mores explorabuntur; qui apti sint ad ecclesiasticas functiones, et tunc antedictas promissiones faciant de vita ecclesiastica et profectione in Angliam; quod si minus idonei reperti fuerint, arbitrio superiorum dimitti poterunt.

[§ 65] Tempus studiorum illis a superioribus definiendum meminerint pro cuiusquam ingenio et aptitudine, communiter tamen (nisi quid impediat) concedentur tres anni ad philosophiam et quatuor ad theologiam, nisi aliter expedire visum fuerit superioribus. Qui vero mediocris fuerint ingenii aut provectioris aetatis, his concedentur tres anni ad logicae institutiones, ad casus conscientiae et controversias addiscendas.

Observanda ab omnibus circa pietatem.

[§ 66] Postquam surrexerint et agenda peregerint, dimidiatam horam in pia aliqua meditatione impendant, ad quam qui non erunt apti, ex consilio confessarii officium vel rosarium Beatae Virginis recitabunt. Vesperi autem antequam eant cubitum quartam horae partem in examine conscientiae et litaniis insumant, et post examen vel ante matutinam precationem in studio vel colloquio diffiniantur, sed omnes in silentio et eodem tempore orent et cubitum eant.

[§ 67] Singulis diebus missae sacrificio omnes intersint et ea qua decet devotione illud audiant. Divinum officium, vesperas et missam certis diebus festis et solemnibus (ut par est) in choro decantent, ceremonias item, ecclesiasticos ritos atque sacramentorum administrationem accurate perdiscant.

[§ 68] Sit aliquis inter eos sacerdos, vir pius et eruditus et prudens bonique exempli, qui, ex superiorum mandato, curam habeat animarum tam alumnorum quam famulorum in collegio degentium. Sit unus confessarius a superioribus constitutus, qui omnium audiat confessiones et in rebus spiritualibus omnes

instruat. Teneantur omnes saltem singulis mensibus et celebrio-
ribus diebus festis ad sacramentum confessionis bene preparati et
praescripta hora accedere et sacram eucharistiam reverenter
sumere, nisi confessarius differendum consuluerit.

[§ 69] Habeant pios libellos, quibus certis horis, sacris
praesertim diebus, utantur et res gestas sanctorum perlegant, et ad
omne genus virtutum et ecclesiastici hominis excellentem pietatem
se ipsos excitent.

[§ 70] Certis anni temporibus, praesertim in vacationibus au-
tumni, ac preterea cum ad sacros ordines accedere debent, dies
aliquot in divinarum rerum meditatione vel in aliquibus spiritualibus exercitiis ad iudicium superioris insumant.

Circa studia.

[§ 71] Quoad studiorum rationem et litterarias exercitationes
pertinet, nemo suum sensum et voluntatem sequatur, sed potius
superioris iudicio se gubernari promittant.   Illi enim erit curae et
studia cuiquam prescribere et auctores seligere, quibus potissimum
operam dari convenit, ut maiorem fructum percipiant, et ideo
nemo libros habeat, qui a superiore non probentur prius et non
censeantur utiles studiis vel pietate comparanda.

[§ 72] Omnes dent operam, ut ex litterariis exercitationibus
fructum illum consequantur, quo et sibi ipsis et aliis prodesse
possint.   Caveant autem ne sint in disputationibus iracundi,
mordaces aut pertinaces, sed mansueti ac mites, et non solum
magistris, verum etiam privatis praefectis obedientes se praebeant
paratique sint studiorum suorum rationem reddere.

[§ 73] Ubique autem latine communiter loquantur, recreationis
vero tempore italice loqui poterunt.

[§ 74] Nemo e scolis repetitionibus et disputationibus etiam
domesticis aberit sine necessitate et superioris obtenta facultate,
ac semper e scolis modeste et simul domum redeant et ad scholas
pariter eodem tempore et simul cum sociis sibi assignatis
accedant.

[§ 75] In libris quos acceperint nec scribant nec ullas ducant
lineas neque mutuo illos praesertim extra collegium ulli concedant
et eorum catalogum habeant, ut cum ab eis repetentur omnium
rationem reddere possint, nec fractos reddant.

[§ 76] Certas diei horas, prout superioribus videbitur, studiis vacabunt ac horarum omnium distributionem secundum collegii consuetudinem diligenter observabunt.

[§ 77] Theses aut publicas aut privatas ex superiorum iudicio et consilio, dum in collegio versantur vel cum discessuri sunt, ex academiae consuetudine deffendant.

Circa domesticam disciplinam.

[§ 78] Communem cum coeteris vitae rationem omnes sequantur seque ad collegii institutionem et consuetudinem accommodent neque quicquam peculiare in lectulo, vestibus, libris, mensa aut alia in re usurpent. Nulli eorum liceat apud se pecunias ullas habere, sed quascunque vel ipsi attulerint vel amici vel cognati ad eos miserint, eas collegii procuratori ad ipsorum necessarios usus tradent, et ex iis absque rectoris facultate nemo quicquam emere poterit.

[§ 79] In domesticis officiis et actionibus, in colloquiis inter se vel cum externis, in iis denique omnibus, quae ad scholasticorum in doctrina et pietate institutionem spectant, omnes obedientiam rectori exhibeant; litteras autem mittere aut accipere nemo debet sine licentia superioris, cui etiam ostendendae erunt, ut si velit legere possit.

[§ 80] Si quis in crimen aliquod inciderit, qui pacem, bonos mores et disciplinam collegii perturbet, et emendationis nulla sit spes, is e collegio dimittetur. Si quis autem levius aliquid comiserit, paratus esse debet pro superioris arbitrio eam poenam subire, quae illi pro disciplina retinenda et communi bono fuerit iniuncta.

[§ 81] Tempore studiorum per collegium ne vagentur neque uspiam colloquantur, nisi quid breve necessitas postularet, sed ad studia se conferant, loca etiam ministrorum domesticorum aut opificum ne adeant, neque cum iis tractent vel quicquam ab iis aut a quovis alio accipiant, nisi a superiore prius impetrata venia.

[§ 82] Nemo e collegio sine facultate et comite a superiore declarato egrediatur et cum eodem praescripta sibi hora redeat: neque ullus extra collegium pernoctet prandiumve sumat nisi impetrata a rectore facultate, quam tamen raro graves ob causas concedere oportebit. Qui deambulandi gratia egredientur, simul cum sociis sibi assignatis atque cum suis praefectis exeant, quos nulla ratione aut occasione deserant, et domum saltem ad 24 horam revertantur.

[§ 83] Superiores suos et praefectos observent et eos modeste alloquantur, inter se vero ne sint litigiosi aut acerbi, sed paternam pacem e animorum unionem conservent.

[§ 84] Eo tempore, quod animorum et corporum relaxationi conceditur, nihil agant immodeste, neque locum recreationi attributum egrediantur, nisi particularem vel generalem a superiore habeant facultatem.

[§ 85] Nobilium aut amicorum visitationibus non occupentur, ad quos tamen si ob gravem causam accedere debeant, non nisi honesto aliquo loco cum iis colloquantur; et quandocunque aliquod negotium expediendum acciderit, mature rectorem admoneant et ab eo facultatem obtineant.

[§ 86] Omnes denique sciant tanto se aptiores futuros huic esse collegio et ad finem praescriptum consequendum capaciores, quanto ad pietatem comparandam alacriores et ad studia capescenda diligentiores et denique ad optemperandum promptiores se exhibuerint.

Institutio sodalitatis B^{mae} Virginis in collegio Anglicano.

[§ 87] Sodalitas sacratissimae Virginis Dei matris Mariae in collegio Anglicano post diligentem ac lungam consultationem, rem multis et praecipuis ex ipsius collegii alumnis iam a multo tempore vehementer exoptantibus et flagitantibus, instituta est anno salutis nostrae 1581, ipso B^{mae} Virginis in coelum gloriosissimae assumptionis die,[1] erecti a Gregorio XIII. pontifice maximo huius collegii anno tertio, persecutionumque in catholicos tempestatibus vel maxime in Anglia saevientibus, rectore r^{do} patre Alphonso Agazario Societatis Jesu.   Fuerunt autem duodecim qui primi huic se divae Virginis tutelae tradiderunt et consecrarunt:

Ricardus Barrettus[2]	Andreas Gibbonus[6]	Alexander Righeus[9]
Ricard. Engehamus[3]	Oliver. Holowellus[7]	Joannes Boltonus[10]
Guglielm. Bissopus[4]	Joannes Cornelius.	Christ. Soutwartus[11]
Rodulphus Bicleus[5]	Guglielm. Coulinus[8]	Joannes Zippettus[12]

[1] August 15.
[2] Barrett.
[3] Engham.
[4] Bishop.
[5] Bickley.
[6] Gibbons.
[7] Holliwell.
[8] Cowling.
[9] Rigbie.
[10] Bolton.
[11] Southworth.
[12] Tibbit.

[§§ 88-139] Sodalitatis B^{mae} Virginis
in collegio Anglicano leges et instituta.

. . . . .¹

Regulae pro praefectis cubiculorum.

[§ 140] Praecipua praefecti cura ea esse debet, ut ipse inprimis
ac sui omnes in regulis tam collegii quam cubiculi accurate ser-
vandis atque in omni pietatis genere proficiant, ad cuius direc-
tionem haec pauca praescribere visum est.

[§ 141] Quamprimum mane surgendi signum datur, id curet ab
omnibus fieri sane diligentur, quod ipse ita prestet, ut aliis exemplo
ea in re esse possit.

[§ 142] Vesperi post orationem curabit, ut, quamprimum commode fieri poterit, scholares cubitum sese recipiant nec in studiis
aut rebus aliis occupentur.

[§ 143] Quibus autem diebus confiteri peccata solent, ut omnes
simul confessarium adeant curabit; quod si aliqui non iverint vel
negligentes hac in parte fuerint, superiori significet.

[§ 144] Cum domo egrediuntur, faciat ut ordinatim ac modeste
incedant, praesertim per vias publicas, ubi parce ac moderate
loquendum esse meminerint.

[§ 145] In cubiculo munditiem curet diligenter, ac ut quisque
suum locum statuto tempore verrat, ac omnes habeant lucernas
mundas; denique ut in lecto, vestibus, mensis aliisque rebus
omnibus nihil non mundum, compositum ac decens appareat.

[§ 146] Novorum alumnorum, cum in cubiculum primum veniunt, peculiarem curam habeat eisque legem cubiculi ostendat et
commendet atque ad domesticam disciplinam vivendique rationem
instruat, eosque inprimis ad obedientiam hortetur.

[§ 147] Habeat aliquem subpraefectum ex fidelioribus sui cubiculi secundum superioris iudicium, qui ipso absente observet, quae
contra regularum observationem fiant, sibique redeunti referat.

[§ 148] Valetudinem suorum sedulo curet, ac si quomodo
laborare quenquam animadvertat, superiorem vel praefectum
infirmariae certiorem faciat.

[§ 149] Si aliquid peccetur a suis circa regulas collegii vel

---

¹ Omitted because of its length and practical unimportance. *Cf.* the brief
summary at the heading of this piece.

cubiculi, patri ministro quamprimum significabit. Patrem vero rectorem saltem semel in hebdomada statuto die certiorem faciet de iis omnibus, quae maioris momenti fuerint.

[§ 150] Audito signo, ut in cubiculum se recipiant, praefecti omnibus aliis negotiis ad tempus relictis sint hac in re coeteris exemplo, ut negligentes observare possint et patri ministro significare.

[§ 151] Ut melius praedicta servet, ea singulis mensibus legat. Tempore studiorum nisi magna urgente necessitate nunquam cubiculo absit; quod si etiam [*sic*] de superiorum facultate vel etiam mandato alio se conferat, patrem ministrum moneat, ut cubiculo provideatur, id quod etiam faciet, cum propter aliquod negotium diu a cubiculo abesse cogetur.

Ordo domus.

[§ 152] Primo datur signum ad surgendum, quo audito omnes surgunt, lectos componunt et se ad orationem parant. Post mediam horam datur ad orationem signum, quo audito omnes, in suis cubiculis genua flectunt, et quibusdam praescriptis orationibus a praefecto cubiculi voce intelligibili recitatis, omnes in silentio per integram mediam horam meditantur vel orant pro cuiusquam captu et confessarii iudicio et instructione.

[§ 153] Oratione completa, itur ad sacrum audiendum in templo; quo absoluto, ad studia se conferunt, quousque pulsetur ad scolas. Hora consueta datur signum ad scholas, quo audito omnes theologi ad ianuam se conferunt et simul cum sociis sibi assignatis ad collegium patrum proficiscuntur; hora deinde elapsa pulsatur pro philosophis, qui pariter et eodem ordine ad scholas vadunt, comitante illos omnes semper aliquo patre.

[§ 154] Absolutis lectionibus et repetitionibus, omnes simul et cum iisdem sociis domum redeunt, ubi per dimidium horae qui reperiuntur idonei a magistro capellae in cantu exercentur. Finito cantu pulsatur ad prandium, et omnes conveniunt in refectorium, ubi data ab uno ex sacerdotibus benedictione, omnes discumbunt quibus aliqui ex scholaribus in mensa ministrant, et unus ex suggesto vel legit vel concionatur usque ad finem prandii.

[§ 155] Peractis de more gratiarum actionibus, omnes simul eunt in templum, ubi paulisper orant, deinde se in hortum vel in

aulam conferant seseque per integram horam piis et utilibus colloquiis recreant. Post recreationem ad propria cubicula redeunt et
se ad repetitiones ac disputationes parant.

[§ 156] Post mediam horam pulsatur ad repetitiones, quae in
diversis locis pro classium diversitate habentur, et singulis singuli
patres praesunt, qui omnes difficultates dilucidant et dubia dis-
solvunt, necnon et modum disputandi et argumentandi docent.
Post repetitiones demum ad studia redeunt, donec iterum ad
scolas pulsetur et tunc eodem plane ordine et modo quo supra
diximus eunt et revertuntur a scholis.

[§ 157] Ubi domum venerint, datur signum ad cubicula ver-
renda, et tunc omnes simul propria cubicula mundant lectosque
et mensas accommodant. Post quartam deinde horae partem
datur signum ad coenam, ubi omnia fiunt sicut in prandio.

[§ 158] Finita recreatione recitantur litaniae in templo ab uno
sacerdote, praesentibus omnibus, quibus absolutis, omnes in silentio
proprias examinant conscientias, et post quartam horae partem
omnes cum silentio discedunt et cubitum eunt, et post septem
horas cum dimidia omnes excitantur, ut initio diximus.

[§ 159] Dominicis aliisque praecipuis diebus festis omnes com-
municant, facta die praecedenti suorum peccatorum confessione.
Cantatur deinde sacrum solemne, praemissis de more litaniis.
Post prandium absoluta recreatione omnes in aulam conveniunt,
ubi in modo concionandi instruuntur, et paulo post suo tempore
in templo vesperae cantantur, quibus finitis eunt ut plurimum ad
aliquas ecclesias vel pia loca visitanda. Die sabbathi litaniae B.
Virginis solenniter in templo cantantur.

[§ 160] Sciendum est etiam novem esse scholarium omnium
cubicula, singulis autem eorum alumnus rectori probatus praeficitur, sed cubicula sanctorum nominibus nuncupantur, scilicet
primum S^{mae} Trinitatis, secundum B^{mae} Virginis, tertium S.
Michaelis arcangeli, quartum S^{torum} apostolorum, quintum S.
Francisci, sextum S. Thomae, septimum S. Georgii, octavum
S. Edmundi, nonum S. Albani.

[§ 161] Demum ex onere collegii per alumnos et patres quotidie
celebratur in altare S. Joannis pro anima bonae memoriae cardinalis Poli. In altare S^{mi} Crucifixi pro anima benefactoris Angli
ter in hebdomada. In capella S. Edmundi ter in hebdomada.
Pro benefactore, qui domum collegio legavit, semel in hebdomada.

Pro benefactoribus vivis semel in hebdomada cum recitatione
rosarii sive coronae, ut aiunt.   Idem servatur pro benefactoribus
defunctis.   Pro summo pontifice quilibet sacerdos in hebdomada
missae sacrum facit, reliqui vero singuli coronam dicunt.   Quot
autem patres et alumni pro benefactoribus vivis atque defunctis
et pro summo pontifice praestant, id sua sponte faciunt; piam
tamen hanc institutionem perpetuo servaturos promittunt.

[§ 162] Diebus autem dominicis aliisque solemnibus festis, qui
ex ecclesiae praecepto sanctificantur, missa decantatur sacerdoti
adhibitis ministris, diacono scilicet et subdiacono, magistro cere-
moniarum, canonicis sex vel octo (ita enim appellantur [qui]
superpelliceis induti in ecclesia deserviunt), duobus accolytis et
thuriferario, ultra cantores et musicos in choro, qui etiam solemni
vesperarum decantationi semper intersunt.   Diebus festis alumni
sex cum eorum superpelliceis praesto sunt in sacristia, ut celebrare
volentibus statis vicibus ministrare valeant, estque illis curae et
altaria praeparare et alia peragere ad divinum cultum pertinentia,
idque per hebdomadam totam sedulo praestant, sed non sunt
semper iidem ; ordine enim mutantur, et ex alumnis duo sunt
praefecti ecclesiae, quorum officium est cartulam conficere, in qua
eorum nomina notantur, qui hebdomada sequenti servituri sunt,
quam in refectionis loco legere non omittunt, lectamque ponunt
in sacristia, ut omnibus quid cuique demandetur innotescat.

[§ 163] Idem collegium ad Anglos peregrinos recipiendos
tenetur, quos alere per octo dies ac etiam, si opus fuerit, cathe-
chizare debebit.   Non omnes tamen passim admittuntur, sed
commendati tantum aliquorum testimonio ; omnibus nihilominus,
quicunque ii sunt, etsi minime recipiantur, elemosinam rector
impartitur, ut illos consoletur, ne amaro discedant animo.

De alumno parocho.

[§ 164] Quoniam patres ex eorum instituto animarum curam
exercere aliisque extra Societatem, sacramento poenitentiae excepto, ministrare non solent, semper aliquis alumnus ex probati-
oribus et examinatus in urbe tanquam aliorum parochus deputatur,
qui praeter eum, qui ex patribus a confessionibus est, scholarium
confessiones audit illisque ecclesiae sacramenta ministrat, et uno
vel decedente vel dimisso alius eodem ordine sufficitur.

[§ 165] Index causarum et litium collegii Anglicani.

. . . . .¹

Attestatio medici.²

[§ 166] Iste Marsilius medicus interrogatus de infirmis qui sunt in collegio, quae infirmitas, quae causa infirmitatis, an aliqui sanguinem expuant, et si qui remittuntur in Galliam ex alumnis ob adversam valetudinem ipsius consilio remittuntur, in hunc modum respondit :

Io Marsilio Cognati medico del collegio de gli Inglesi, dimandato dalli signori visitatori che sorte d'infermi sono al presente nel detto collegio, rispondo che non vi è alcuno che stia nel letto, ma vi sono bene dui quartanarii et uno che di fresco è stato amalato di disenteria et febre, ma hora è convalescente et non sta più nel letto.   Dimandato di più se vi è alcuno che sputi sangue, dico non vi essere hora alcuno il quale evidentemente lo sputi, ma essere bene tre o quattro li quali dicono haverne sputato, ma non quantità notabile, et non si è veduta che se ne possa fare testimonio.   Dimandato della causa dello sputo di sangue in questi gioveni, dico concorrere più cose : le fatiche de gli studii et massime dello scrivere, l'affetto dell'animo et molta sollecitudine, et anco come si sospira, la qualità dell'aere, ·perchè questo medesimo milita anco in altri collegii, come il Germanico, S. Andrea, il Romano ; et si sono di mio parere et d'altri medici meco aggionti, fattone partire alcuni dal detto collegio de gli Inglesi di Roma, li quali si sono trovati bene, benchè non tutti. In fede delle cose dette di sopra io Marsilio sopradetto ho scritto la presente di mia mano questo di 2 di settembre 1585.

[§ 167] Rendite annali del collegio inglese di Roma.

. . . . .³

---

¹ Concerns the house-expenses and lawsuits of the English college, followed by an enumeration of its legal advisers, and a list of offices (sacristan, doorkeeper, cook, barber, etc.).

² *Cf.* above, § 33.

³ Summary of the income and expenditure of the English college from 1579 to 1585.

XX. *Terms of agreement between the pope and Spain for the invasion of England.* [*July* 29, 1587. *Rome.*]

The pope is willing to aid the king of Spain in his pious undertaking against England. If this is carried out in 1587 the pope will give one million gold ducats. The money will at once be placed in readiness. Payment of 500,000 ducats to be made as soon as the Spaniards have landed in England; the remainder in payments every two months. If England is conquered, the Spaniards to set up a good catholic sovereign, of whom the Holy See may approve, and who shall receive investiture from the pope. The church's property and rights, alienated since the apostasy of Henry VIII., to be restored to her. The king of Spain must agree to these conditions on his royal word, must ratify the terms of agreement, and on his part see that they are also ratified by the future king of England.

Two texts are extant : *A*, Arch. Vat., Borgh. III., 124 c, fols. 140, 141 ; *B*, Phillipps' MSS. 2753, privately printed under the title *De Conquestu Angliae per Hispanos tempore Elizabethae reginae* 1588. Ex MSS. Phillipps. Impensis et cura Dni. Thomae Phillipps, Bart. Typis Medio-Montanis Jacobus Rogers impressit 1869." (*Medio-Montanis* is Middlehill in Worcestershire ; the MSS. are now in Cheltenham, Gloucestershire.)

Both texts are copies, the original of the treaty is not forthcoming. I here follow the better text *A*, giving the alternative readings of *B* in notes.

The documents mentioned in the footnotes are also only copies.

Sixtus papa quintus.

Quod intimis affectibus florentissimam olim, nunc plane perditam Angliae et Hiberniae conditionem miserantes assiduis a Deo lachrimis votisque precati sumus, ut qui nostris illorumque populorum peccatis offensus ea regna iuste a[1] se abiecit, placatus piorum precibus et sanguine servorum suorum in eis effuso, ad se misericorditer revocaret, nunc tandem veluti signo ad bene sperandum de illorum salute divinitus elato haud dubie nostro hoc tempore confidimus eventurum. Siquidem[2] charissimus in Christo filius noster, Philippus Hispaniarum rex, christianae pietatis zelo accensus et catholicae religionis[3] studio inflammatus, iam accingitur ad prelianda bella domini, nempe adversus impiam foeminam, iampridem ob impurissimas eius hereses notoriumque schisma anathematis mucroni[4] percussam,

---

[1] ab B.
[2] si quidem B.
[3] religionis vindicand^{ae} studio B.
[4] mucione B.

quae cum se caput Anglicanae ecclesiae mandet appellari,[1]
cumque catholicae religionis edictis et poenis atrocissimis pro-
hibuerit, execrandum vero impietatum atque heresum publice
introduxerit exercitium, nobilissimas insulas ab unitate catholicae
ecclesiae seiunctas, oppressas[2] violenta tirannidi detinet[3]
secumque illas in exitium miserrime pertrahit, crudelius saeviens
in animas eorum, quos impietati suae obsequentes dimittit
incolumes, quam in illos, quos pro veritate catholicae fidei
reluctantes inaudita immanitate novis cruciatuum generibus iubet
excarnificari. Quem sane gloriosum motum, divino spiritu
afflante, in catholici regis pia mente excitatum sicut nos nostris
consiliis et adhortationibus saepius urgere hactenus non destitimus,
ita nostris et Sedis Apostolicae collatis opibus temporalibusque
auxiliis ad Dei omnipontentis gloriam et catholicae fidei exalta-
tionem, pro ea quae[4] nos angit omnium gentium regnorumque
sollicitudine, omni conatu promovere paratos nos esse profitemur.

Quapropter si hoc anno 1587 fiet expeditio, nos ex nostro Apo-
stolicaeque Sedis aerario decies centena millia aureorum nummûm
conferemus. Utque Cath^{ca} M^{tas} ob assignatam hanc pecuniae
summam ex credito commoditatem praemature possit accipere,
iam nunc tradimus singrafas mercatorum,[5] qui M^{ti} Suae cavent
hanc summam solutum[6] iri terminis et modis infrascriptis :
nempe quingenta millia statim ac classis regia in Angliam
appulerit et exercitus in terram fuerit expositus,[7] et deinceps

---

[1] The mistaken idea continued to be held in Rome—just as in 1570, when
the bull of excommunication was first drawn up—that Elizabeth had adopted
the same title as her father and brother, (*supremum*) *caput ecclesiae!* See
above, pp. 82, and 83, note 1 ; *cf.* p. 24.

[2] oppressasque detinet B.

[3] et secum B.

[4] quae violenta tirannide nos B.

[5] These *mercatores* were Castellino and Giovanni Agostino Pinelli, and
Geronimo Gentili in Rome. The bond drawn up by them on July 29, 1587,
contains the above-mentioned conditions concerning the payment of the million
ducates. Arch. Vat., Borgh. III., 124 c, fol. 154, 155. The papal instructions
for the payment of Pinelli and Gentili, dated July 30, are to be found *l.c.*, fols.
156, 157.

[6] solutam in terminis B.

[7] Philip II. had made a vain resistance to this clause—an indirect witness to
the fact that he was by no means sure of victory ! In place of the stipulation that
the troops must have landed, he wished *poner palabras que obligasen al Papa
aunque no hubiese armada en el affecto*. Letter of the king to Olivares, his

hoc eodem bello in eadem insula durante,[1] vel dicto Angliae regno Dei miseratione capto, alia quingenta millia[2] in uno quoque bimestri usque ad integram predictorum decies centenûm millium solutionem.

Ob id nos in verbo Romani Pontificis, tum nostro tum huius Sanctae Sedis nomine,[3] ita praestare atque[4] adimplere promittimus, et statum, dominium omniaque Sanctae Romanae Ecclesiae bona obligamus, nec non ad maiorem M^{tis} S. cautelam iisdem de rebus publicam scripturam, decretum aut instrumentum de consensu venerabilium fratrum nostrorum S. R. E. cardinalium conficiemus.

Preterea, ubi S. M^{tas} proposuerit gratias,[5] quas ad hanc expeditionem promovendam desiderat, eas considerabimus, et quantopere ad satisfaciendum[6] eius M^{ti} prompti simus re ipsa ostendemus, cum persuasum nobis sit postulationes non nisi rationabiles atque honestas neque admodum onerosas fore.

Quam sane oblationem et promissionem non aliter quam cum conditionibus, conventionibus et pactis infrascriptis fieri intelligimus.

Ut si predicta Angliae et Hiberniae regna, quemadmodum speramus in Domino, recuperentur, eum S. M^{tas} eorumdem regnorum nominet regem, de quo sperari tuto possit, ut catholicam in eis religionem stabiliturus et conservaturus sit, quique huic Sanctae Apostolicae Sedi gratus existat et ab ea eorumdem regnorum investituram accipiat.[7]

Ut Apostolica Sedes restituatur redintegreturque ad census, iurisdictiones, iura et actiones, quas habebat in iisdem regnis,

ambassador in Rome, Nov. 18, 1586. FROUDE, *Hist. of England*, Vol. XII. (1870), p. 361, note.

[1] vel de Angliae Regno Dei B.

[2] alia 50,000, intra quinque terminos Romae persolventur, *scilicet*, 100,000 in unoquoque bimestri usque ad integram B.

[3] *I.e.* the pledge was to bind the successors of Sixtus V., a condition to which Philip attached especial importance. *Ib.*, p. 361.

[4] et B.

[5] Chief among these was the elevation of William Allen to the cardinalate on Aug. 7, 1587. T. F. KNOX, *The Letters and Memorials of W. Card. Allen* (1882), Intro., civ. *et seq.*

[6] satisfaciendum Maiestati ejus promptissimus re ipsa B.

[7] This shows that Philip II. himself was not to be invested with England. *Cf.* p. 320.

antequam Henricus octavus a Romani Pontificis et huius[1] Sanctae Sedis obedientia se subtraheret.

Utque detur opera quam diligentissime, ut ecclesiastica bona ecclesiis, monasteriis, collegiis, hospitalibus et locis piis re ipsa plenarieque restituantur, ea ratione temperamentoque adhibito, quod huic Sanctae Sedi eiusque M^{ti} pro tempore, ad Dei obsequium illorumque regnorum utilitatem, magis visum fuerit expedire.

Insuper eius M^{tas} recipiat et promittat praedictas conditiones, conventiones et pacta se observaturam sub verbo regio per publicam scripturam seu publicum et autenticum instrumentum ac propterea constituat suum legitimum procuratorem dilectum nobis filium Don Henricum de Guzman comitem de Olivares, S. M^{tis} apud nos oratorem ordinarium,[2] vel quempiam alium eiusdem M^{tis} ministrum, cum ampla facultate obligandi M^{tem} S. etiam sub verbo regio ad effectum conficiendi publicum instrumentum super praemissis.   Quod ubi stipulatum confectumque fuerit, eadem M^{tas} S. ratificabit,[3] et[4] ut suo quoque tempore a primo futuro Angliae Hiberniaeque rege[5] a M^{te} S. ut supra nominando, ratificetur,[6] efficiet.

In quorum omnium fidem praesentes fieri[7] mandavimus, easque[8] nostra manu subscripsimus.   Romae in Esquilio[9] die 29[10] Julii, 1587.

Ita promittimus F

---

[1] ejus B.

[2] Olivares promised at the conclusion of the articles of agreement, on July 29, 1587, that the king would ratify everything.   Arch. Vat., *l.c.*, fol. 142. His subsequent authority for ratifying the terms of the alliance is dated Sept. 12, 1587.   *L.c.*, fol. 148.   There is a declaration by Philip II. of the same date, concerning his ratification of the alliance.   *L.c.*, fol. 150.

[3] The king's ratification of the treaty is dated Feb. 22, 1588.   *L.c.*, fols. 152, 153 ; *cf.* 145, 146.

[4] ac B.

[5] regni B.

[6] ratificentur B.

[7] scribi B.

[8] quas B.

[9] Esquilitio B.

[10] Die 24 Julii anno MDLXXXVII. B.

XXI. *William Creighton to Card. Enrico Caetani, Protector of England and Scotland.* [*Sept.* 7, 1595. *Louvain.*]

Concerning the Scottish catholic nobles. The foundation of the Scotch seminary in Louvain.

Archiv. Caetani (Rome), No. 92, 124. Orig. holograph MS. Seal—monogram of Christ with a cross above, and a heart beneath.

Delle cose publice della Scotia non c'è cosa particolar de scrivere fuora delle fattioni particolari de segnori, lequali tengono gli heretici occupati tra sè, che non pensano tanto contra gli catholici, se non in prediche et escomuniche di predicanti heretici contra i catholici. Gli duoi conti de Huntley et Errol,[1] conestablio, chi stanno in queste bande, stanno bene per la gratia di Cristo et de buonissimo animo de far bene. Il terzo chi sta in Scotia, ch'è il conte d'Angus,[2] sta bene, ma in estrema povertà, perchè questi duoi conti, chi stanno qui, godono delli lor beni, ma lui non può ottener pace nè compositione nessuna, ma sta privo de tutti gli suoi beni et in continuo pericolo della sua vita per haver havuto communicatione col conte de Bothvel, tanto odiato dal re, de sorte che questo conte non tiene con che puoter uscire dal regno, nè per mantenersi di dentro, se non volesse consentire alli heretici contra sua conscientia, quel ch'e risoluto de non fare, et però faria la S^{ria} V. Illma grandissima opera di misericordia et grande adgiuto alla causa catholica, d'ottener da S. S^{tà} qualche mezzo et adgiuto per puoter conservar questo signor alla causa catholica; altrimente è pericolo che non perisca, essendo pur il primo et principal segnor de tutto il regno in titolo et dignità. Abandonato de tutti quasi gli suoi parenti et sudditi per la sua constantia nella regligione catholica, per amor de Cristo et l'amor che V. S. Illma porta a quel regno, del quale è protettore, ch'adgiuti la conservatione de questo segnore. Perchè nel regno, benchè il numero de catholici sia grande, pur non ci sono comparsi,[3] nè in particolare perseguitati,

---

[1] George Gordon, 6th Earl of Huntly, and Francis Hay, 9th Earl of Errol, 1589, leaders of a catholic rising in Scotland, advocates of the Spanish invasion.

[2] William Douglas, 10th Earl of Angus, in league with the two former.

[3] *I.e.* had not appeared before the justices of the peace to justify their absence from protestant worship.

se non questi duoi, chi stanno qui, et il conte d'Angus, del quale scrivo.

Il detto conte d'Angus alcuni mesi fa mandò qui a me il suo fratello, molto garbato giovane, ma ostenato heretico et pur adesso per la gratia de Cristo molto fervente catholico, il quale è di buonissimo ingegno et studia alla philosophia. Qui anche teneamo un fratello del segnor conte de Huntley, et fra dieci giorni espettiamo il fratello del segnor conte de Crauford,[1] chi saranno tre fratelli delli tre primi conti de Scotia, et per tali saria facile de retirare gli beneficii ecclesiastici dalle mani della nobiltà, gli quali altrimente saria molto difficile de ricuperare; anzi il più grande impedimento della restitutione della religione catholica è la paura, ch'ha la nobiltà, d'esser privata dell'intrata, che tiene della chiesa, ch'è molto grande in Scotia. Poi quando saria restituta la religione, non ci trovarà ecclesiastici per fare o prelati o parochi, perchè tutti gli vecchi ecclesiastici sono morti, non c'è vescovo anticho in vita se non l'archivescovo de Glasgo [2] et il vescovo de Rossa,[3] chi sta qui tutto asmatico. Non habbiamo havuto seminarii come gli Inglesi per far gente. Et al presente habiamo comminciato una casa [4] qui et comprato il fondo, ch'è molto bello, sotto la speranza che S. Stà et Mtà Catholica ci adgiutaria, quel che non dubito che S. Stà farà, se piacesse a V. Sria Illma impiegharsi; et anche ci adgiutariano quei altri segnori Illmi, come ha ben comminciato l'Illmo Cardinale de Stà Severina,[5] et se così fosse, mandaressimo un huomo espresso in Scotia et subito n'haveressimo huomini maturi già graduati in philosophia et atti per sentire theologia, et così fra duoi o tre anni n'haveressimo buona provisione, perchè dalle tre università, c'habbiamo in Scotia, ne caveressimo buon numero, benchè heretici, perchè subito li facciamo catholici. Habbiamo

---

[1] David Lindsay, 11th Earl of Crawford. The brother alluded to here is probably Sir James Lindsay, who later on acted as go-between between James VI. and Clement VIII. *Cf.* my article, "Klem. VIII. u. Jak. I. v. Engl.," Quell. u. Forsch. aus ital. Arch. u. Bibl., VII., pp. 282, 294, 304–306.

[2] James Beaton, died 1603.

[3] John Leslie, Bishop of Ross, died 1596.

[4] For the Scotch seminary, see above, pp. 115 *et seq.*

[5] It is not certain who is meant by the cardinal de Stà Severina. There was no cardinal of this name. Alfonso Pisani, archbishop of Stà Severina was not a cardinal. Perhaps *Severina* is a mistake for *Sabina* or some other cardinalitial title.

qui duoi, chi vennero duoi mesi fa tutti heretici; ma nel principio li trattiamo col maggior carità che possiamo, quel che non trovorono tra lor heretici, poi poco a poco et con patientia et dolcezza li facciamo solamente capaci della verità, et presto da lor stessi si convertono et dicono, che la più grand mortificatione che hanno è la vergogna d'haver stati tanto tempo in tali heresie si grosse et lontane da ragione et dalla verità. Speriamo che S. S^(tà) ci adgiutarà, come ci dà anche buona speranza mons. ill^(mo) Malvasia, nuntio qui. Piaccia a V. S. Ill^(ma) avisarci de quel che possiamo haver o sperar, perchè secondo quello vorrei mandar un espresso in Scotia per menarci gente et comprar per tempo mobili et preparar luogho per ricevirli, et spero de puoter haver gentilhuomini de buona qualità.

Verrà presto verso V. S. Ill^(ma) un particolar con bastante instruttione, come si possia adgiutar la Sua Scotia, che non può esser bene se no per il re stesso e sua nobiltà, perchè altri non hanno il puotere. La S^(ria) V. Ill^(ma), credo, haverà materia grata per proporre a S. S^(ta). Si dice che sono discesi in Irlanda 4000 Spagnogli, et che le cose nostre de Scotia andaranno bene, come intendiamo de Spagna, et dirà a V. S. Ill^(ma) et R^(ma) il padre Tyrio, con che humilmente bascio le mani, etc. Da Lovanio adì 7 di settenbre 1595.

Della S^(ria) V. Ill^(ma) et R^(ma)
Humiliss.° servitore
Guglielmo Creytton.[1]

XXII. *Ottavio Mirto Frangipani, nuncio in the Netherlands, to Card. Pietro Aldobrandini.* [*June* 24, 1600. *Brussels.*]

Negotiations for peace between England and Spain. Elizabeth's approaching death. Attitude of the catholics towards James VI. Proposal for installing the Infanta Isabella as Elizabeth's successor by force.

Arch. Vat., Borgh. III., 98 c 1, fol. 93. Original; autograph signature.

Quel ch'io posso scrivere adesso per aviso, non dandomi materia di risposta l'essere passata questa settimana senza lettere di V. S. Ill^(ma) et R^(ma), sarà primieramente il negotio d'Inghilterra, qual,

---

[1] In the original the name seems to be rather *Creylton* than *Creytton*. He usually wrote his name *Creitton*.

caminando come camina lentamente, è quasi nel termine già scritto nelle precedenti ; [1] et ciò se vede nell'alligate copie di lettere [2] dell'huomo di questi paesi intelligente et fedele, ch'in Bologna [3] tengo occulto, et le mando a V. S. Illma et R^{ma} in vece di quel ch'io saria obligato scrivergli, essendo le lettere nel tempo della data et nella sustanza conformi all'altre publiche et private che di là se scrivono.

Et benchè in dette lettere non se faccia mentione dello stato della vita della regina, tuttavolta il tempo ci posta ferma credenza che sia per finir presto ; onde s'intende ch'il re di Scotia s'habbia fatto rinovar il giuramento da tutto il suo regno per prepararse all'entrata d'Inghilterra subito udito il caso della morte.

Et già s'intende anchora che, per farsela facile, promette alli cattolici inglesi la libertà di conscienza et ch'i cattolici se risolveranno d'accettarlo con questa conditione, s'altro non potranno ottenere, poichè vedeno ch'a lor non se nomina alcun prencipe cattolico per re, et se sminuisse ogni giorno la speranza ch'han posta su le forze di Spagna.

Per questo li cattolici inglesi che sono qui esuli ricordano spesso a questa Ser^{ma} A. [4] che non trascurass'il negotio di tal successione, proponendosegli mezo facile di far cadere il regno nella persona della ser^{ma} infanta, [5] con destinare tre reggimenti di fantaria a quell'effetto, traiettandoli subito dopo la morte delle regina in Inghilterra, perchè bastariano con li cattolici del regno a impedir i dissegni di qualsivoglia principe di religion contraria ch'aspirass'alla corona, purchè alli cattolici fusse da N. S^{re} proposta et nominata. Ma non rispondendo altro S. A. fuorchè : "Vi si pensarà," [6] fa giudicare a questi zelosi della religione et delle salute della lor patria ch'il negotio di questa successione o

---

[1] The preceding dispatches of the nuncio describe the beginning of the negotiations between England and Spain in Boulogne, and his last letter, June 17, speaks of the difficulties about the choice of a building in which the proceeding could take place, and the quarrels over precedence among the representatives on both sides, who had not yet paid visits to each other.

[2] Not forthcoming.

[3] Boulogne-sur-mer ; *cf*. note 1.

[4] The governor, the Archduke Albert.

[5] Isabella, wife of Albert.

[6] Marginal note by Card. Aldobrandini : "Questo e quello stracan il papa, il veder la debolezza e la fredezza di tutte le parti."

se governa con qualche mezo non manifesto al mondo, et ciò
non credeno vedendose mal governati questi stati, ch'è il suo ben
proprio, o che se trascura a fatto, et di ciò se maravegliano con
lor scandalo. . . .

XXIII. *Threatened Attack upon Loreto by English Pirates.* [*January*, 1602.]

Arch. della Santa Casa di Loreto, Registro di lettere apostoliche 1581–1645, fol. 31.

A. Copia d'un aviso ricevuto mons. governatore da certi mercanti. . . .

Merchants give warning of English freebooters to the governor.

Ne pare nostro debito avertirvi che da un pirato inglese con
bel modo si è inteso che in Ancona, luoco di questo regno, si
apprestino quatro bone nave da guerra et commissione d'un
signore inglese, e par disegni far colpo alla Madonna di Loreto,
che intende essere molto richa, dovendo levare più di 500 homini,
pensando potere effettuare simil sua mala intentione in una notte
e imbarcarsi inanzi comparischi il giorno, che pur stentiamo a
vederlo, pur vedendoci che questi pirati metono le sue azioni [a]
cose molto dificultose, et che molte volte li riescono, non può che
servire l'avertimo.

B. Card. [Ant. Maria] Galli, Protector of Loreto, to Card. Aldobrandini. [Jan. 21, 1602. Osimo.]

Measures of defence.

Il governatore di Loreto per via de mercanti ha havuto questo
aviso che io mando a V. S. Illma, et se bene lo sbarco è difficile
assai et l'impresa non è loro riussibile, comme sperano, nondimeno, perchè i corsali sogliono essere arrisicati, et acciochè dal
canto nostro il tenersi sicuri non cagioni qualche pericolo, ho
fatto, per abondare in cautela, voltar alcuni falconetti[1] verso la
marina.   Ho similmente dato fuori alcune poche arme che vi
sono a i serventi della S. Casa, et ordinato agl'habitanti che stiano

[1] Culverins.

provisti ciascuno d'armi a bastanza, che si facciano guardie dentro e fuori alla spiaggia, e quali sorprendo vascelli armati diano segno. Ne mancherebbe se non che V. S. Illma se degnasse di comandare che ci si dia della polvere dalla Rocca d'Ancona, et che venga ad habitare un bombardiero in Loreto, poichè non v'è alcuno. Se paresse poi alla somma prudenza di V. S. Ill^{mà} d'ordinare a mons^r governatore d'Ancona che capitando bertoni[1] inglesi in quel porto faccia diligenza, se portano moltitudine d'homini et d'arme insolita, io mi rimetto a Lei, a i soli cenni della quale ubbidirò sempre, etc.

Poi l'Illmo Sig^r Card. Gallo, protettore, si trasferì a Loreto, dove ordinò doi capitani, uno d'infanteria et l'altro d'archibugieri a cavallo, fece revedere l'artellarie, arme, resarcire muraglie, far fare guardie, levar terraci et altre imunditie intorno alla città, et fatte altre provisioni scrisse al Illmo Sig. Card^l Aldobrandino l'infrascritta littera e poi sene tornò in Osimo. Il tenore della quale è l'infrascritto :

C. Card. Galli to Card. Aldobrandini.
[Jan. 24, 1602. Loreto.]

Further news.   Reassurance.

Scrissi a V. S. Illma da Osimo l'aviso che s'haveva havuto del disegno d'alcuni bertoni inglesi di sacheggiare questo santo luogo et gli diedi conto delle provisioni da me fatte. Hora trasferitomi qua havendo voluto penetrare più a dentro la qualità dell'aviso, trovo che viene da Londra per via de mercanti conosciuti, li quali per interesse del negotio non vogliono essere publicati. Il tutto si è assicurato di maniera che posso liberar affatto l'animo a V. S. Illma da ogni sospetto, poichè qui non manca modo di resistere ad ogni maggiore incontro et in ogni caso di provisioni presenti se non per questo almeno gioveranno per altri bisogni. Però domani mene ritorno alla mia chiesa[2] dove aspetterò con summo dessiderio i comandamenti di V. S. Illma.

---

[1] *Bertone* was a threemaster, such as was used especially by the Bretons and English, with square sails, a broad hull slightly curving inwards towards the deck, and a high poop, having a displacement of 500 to 1000 tons, and so for that age a ship of considerable size. A. GUGLIELMOTTI, *Vocabolario marino e militare* (Roma, 1889).

[2] Card. Galli was bishop of his native city of Osimo near Loreto.

XXIV. *Ottavio Mirto Frangipani, nuncio in the Netherlands, to Card. Pietro Aldobrandini.* [*Aug.* 9, 1602. *Ghent.*]

The nuncio is desirous of being taken secretly to Queen Elizabeth in order to learn her real views.

Arch. Vat., Borgh. III., 98 d 2.   Original ; autograph signature.

L'ordinario d'Italia mi ha portata questa settimana la di V. S. Illma et R^{ma} delli 20 di luglio, intorna la quale occore solamente il particolare d'Inghilterra, sopra di che assicuro N. S. che, dopo ch'io intesi quei preti inglesi,[1] pensai molte volte come senza offenderse l'honore di Sua B^{ne} et il decoro di quella santa sede potesse da per me solo, senza mezo d'altri, accertarmi dell'animo della regina, poichè conoscevo et conosco anchora ch'il negotio della salute di quel regno potria condurse a qualche segno di qualche poco acquisto, quando ciò segretamente si tentasse in nome di N. S. con tal donna, et mi entrò nell'animo un pensiero[2] di farmi fare con participation della regina preggione un giorno in quel mare di Neoporto[3] dalla sua gente per condurmi inanzi a lei, el con opinione di cattivo trattare seco, non già della conversion sua, ma della stabilità della pace nel suo regno et nell' Europa, attesochè, al mio parere, se fa più difficile la materia per il rispetto dell'interessi d'altri che per natura propria ; onde sempre sarà dubia et pericolosa la fede che se ne presta a persone quali spontaneamente ne raggionano sotto titolo di zelo ; ma lo tacqui per non farmi giudicar leggiero et vano, et lo comunico adesso, perchè vedo col tempo darse poca luce alla Sta S. del modo come possa esseguir i suoi santi pensieri su la salute particolare di quel regno et pace universale nel cristianesmo, humilissimamente dimandandogli perdono et a V. S. Illma et R^{m} insieme del mio fallo, se fusse questo pensiero giudicato temerario et imprudente, poichè l'era solamente fondato

---

[1] Bluet, Mush, and Champney, the representatives of the appellants, who on their way to Rome had had interviews with Frangipani in Dec., 1601, and in Jan., 1602.   See above, p. 442, note 2.   *Cf.* pp. 446 *et seq.*

[2] Marginal note by Card. Ald. : "Il concetto è bellissimo."

[3] Nieupoort.

nella necessita di conoscersi l'animo della regina per sicurezza di N. S., et nelli mezzi ch'io non vedevo nè vedo facili et certi ad investigarlo ; con tutto ciô vi uso diligenza per via di corrispondenti amici, quali trovo varii per non tutti tirare al nostro fine : ch'è quanto posso dire in risposta della sudetta lettera di V. S. Illma et R^{ma} . . .

CHRONOLOGICAL LIST

OF

UNPUBLISHED DOCUMENTS

THIS list is intended first of all to facilitate the student in obtaining a general view of the new sources of information utilized in the foregoing pages, over and above those documents which are printed in the Appendix. At the same time it may also be of use to the future investigator by directing the course of his researches. The references to the volume, etc., in the various archives are not given in full, as they can easily be found in the body of the book by means of the reference in the last column. After 1582, the dates are given in accordance with the new style (wherever double references are not given) ; in a few cases only an asterisk indicates that the style adopted for the date is uncertain.

A. B.   = Archivio dei Brevi (now forming part of the Secret Archives of the Vatican).
A. C. A. = Archivium Collegii Anglorum de Urbe.
A. P.   = Archivio della Propaganda.
A. S. J. = Archivium Societatis Jesu.
A. V.   = Archivio Vaticano (Arch. Segreto della Sta Sede).
B. M.   = British Museum.
B. V.   = Bibliotheca Vaticana.
Fl.   = State Archives of Florence.
P. H. I. = Prussian Historical Institute in Rome.
P. R. O. = Public Record Office in London.
Ven.   = State Archives of Venice.
W. C. A. = Westminster Cathedral Archives.

No.	Date	Description	Place	Reference (page, note)
1	1560 June 20	The Emperor Ferdinand to Queen Elizabeth	A. V.	40, 4.
2	[1561]	Anonymous paper without date .	A. V.	38, 2.
3	1561 Apr. 24	Philip II. to Cardinal Morone . .	A. V.	35, 2.
4	[1561 May]	Anonymous report of the sitting of the Privy Council, May 1, 1561. No date. Headed *Pro rebus Angliae*	A. V.	44, 2.
5	1562 Dec. 6	Maurice Clenock to Cardinal Morone	A. V.	241, 1.
6	1566 March 8	200 exiled English catholics to Pius V.	A. V.	229, 1.
7	1567	Engl. broadside, *A Bull*, etc. .	A. V.	126, 1.
8	1570	*Copia d'un discorso, venuto d'Inghilterra del* 1570 *in Venetia* .	A. V.	67, 3 ; 242 3.
9	[after 1570 ?]	Instructions of Lord Burleigh to John Arden in Rome . . .	P. R. O.	359, 2.
10	1570 May 26	Sir Francis Englefield to Cardinal Morone	A. V.	126, 5.
11	1571 May 5	Giov. Castagna, nuncio in Madrid, to Card. Michele Bonelli (Alessandrino)	A. V.	232, 2.
12	1571 July 3	The same to Card. Rusticucci . .	A. V.	232, 2.
13	[after 1572]	*Attioni e costumi di Pio V.* . . .	A. V.	73, 4.
14	1575	*De ratione et progressu seminarii cleri Anglicani in universitate Duacena*	A. V.	211, 5.
15	[between 1572 and 1580]	*Ad consolationem et instructionem quorundam catholicorum in angustiis constitutorum quaestiones aliquot*	A. V.	136, 1 ; 140
16	1578	*Alcune cose di consolatione, cavate parte dalle lettere annali del seminario inglese di S. Sta in Fiandra per l'anno* 1578, *parte da lettere private di là . . . intorno il progresso della religione catholica in quelle bande* . . .	A. V.	132, 2 ; 134 1 ; 184 1 ; 239, 4

No.	Date	Description	Place	Reference (page, note)
17	1578 July 5	The Cardinal of Como to the nuncio Bolognetti in Venice	A. V.	265, 3.
18	1578 Nov. 8	The same to the same	A. V.	265, 3.
19	[about 1580]	Memorial of an unnamed Welshman on the invasion of England addressed to Gregory XIII. Incip.: *Cum primum Elisabeta inauguraretur*	A. V.	59, 3.
20	1580 March 26	The Cardinal of Como to the nuncio Bolognetti in Venice	A. V.	266, 1 ; 266, 2.
21	1580 April	Instructions of the general of the Jesuits for Rob. Persons and Edm. Campion	A. S. J.	142, 1; 143; 143, 2; 202, 3-5.
22	[after 1580]	Appeal [undated] to Philip II. in the name of Gregory XIII. concerning the invasion of England	A. V.	274, 3.
23	,,	*Discorso pee la ricuperatione del regno d'Inghilterra alla chiesa, a Gregorio XIII.*	A. V.	275, 1.
24	[about 1581]	*Discorso sopra le potenti cagioni che debbono spingere il re cattolico più tosto all'impresa d'Inghilterra che a quella di Fiandra*	A. V., B. V.	278, 1; 279 1, 2; 280, 1; 281, 4 282, 3.
25	1581	*Informatione per il R^{do} P. Panigarola circha . . . Inghilterra per la cognitione che Jo. Gio. Sovico*	Fl.	281, 1.
26	1581	*Relatione compendiosa della negotiatione della nuntiatura di Spagna di Mons. Sega*	A. V.	276, 3; 277, 1.
27	1581 July 31	*Instruttione data da Mons. Sega, nuntio in Ispagna, a Mons. Taverna*	A. V.	276, 3.
28	[1582]	*Alcuni motivi . . . per rappresentare alla Sua Sta e gli principi christiani, per aiutare gli cattolici d'Inghilterra*	B. V.	276, 2; 276, 3; 283, 4.

No.	Date	Description	Place	Reference (page, note)
29	[1582]	*Brevis narratio de origine ac pro-gressu Collegii Anglorum in civitate Romana ab a. d. 1578 usque 1582 . . . . . .*	B. V.	100, 1.
30	1582	*Annuae litterae Collegii Anglorum de Urbe . . . . . .*	A. C. A.	109, 4 ; 20; 2.
31	[1583?]	*Capita rerum, ex quibus modus col-ligitur, per quem Anglia reduci potest ad pristinum religionis statum . . . . . .*	A. V.	297, 2.
32	[1583?]	Anonymous memorial against making war on England, ad-dressed to the Card. Protector of England	B. V.	11, 1 ; 29 3.
33	1583	*Annuae litterae Collegii Anglorum de Urbe . . . . .*	A. C. A.	187, 1 ; 21(4.
34	1583 Apr. 16	The nuncio Campeggi in Venice to the Card. of Como . . .	A. V.	359, 2.
35	1583 Sept. 24	Draft of a second bull of excom-munication against Elizabeth .	A. V.	286.
36	,,	Gregory XIII. to James VI. of Scotland	A. V.	287, 2.
37	,,	Gregory XIII. to Mary Stuart .	A. V.	286, 4.
38	,,	,, ,, to William Allen	A. V.	286, 3.
39	,,	Instructions of Gregory XIII. for Allen	A. V.	287, 1.
40	,,	The Cardinal of Como to Allen .	A. V.	284, 4.
41	[about 1585]	*Discorso sopra l'impresa d'In-ghilterra . . . . . .*	A. V.	275, 1 ; 29(3, 4 ; 29; 1.
42	1585	*Annuae litterae Collegii Anglorum de Urbe . . . . .*	A. C. A.	107, 4 ; 10(1.
43	1586 March 24	Instructions of the General of the Jesuits for Henry Garnet, S.J., and Rob. Southwell, S.J. . .	A. S. J.	401, 1.
44	1587 July 29	Bond of the merchants Castellino, Giov. Ag. Pinelli, and Geron. Gentili	A. V.	

No.	Date	Description	Place	Reference (page, note)
45	1587 July 30	The pope's order for the payment of the million ducats	A. V.	
46	1587 Aug. 17	Dispatch of the nuncio in Paris .	A. V.	322, 1.
47	1587 Aug. 30	,, ,, ,, .	A. V.	322, 2.
48	1587 Sept. 5	Cesare Speciani, nuncio in Madrid, to Card. Rusticucci	A. V.	321, 5.
49	1587 Sept. 12	Authorization to the ambassador Olivares to conclude a treaty with the pope	A. V.	
50	1587 Sept. 12	Declaration of Philip II. as to his consent to the treaty	A. V.	
51	1587 Dec. 14	Speciani, nuncio in Madrid, to Card. Rusticucci	A. V.	311, 4.
52	[1588?]	Filippo Pigafetta, *Nota delle fortezze principali dell' Inghilterra e di porti*	P. H. I.	282, 2.
53	1588 Jan. 18	Speciani to Card. Rusticucci . .	A. V.	331, 4.
54	1588 Feb. 22	Philip's ratification of the treaty with the pope	A. V.	
55	1588 Apr. 30	Speciani to Card. Montalto . .	A. V.	312, 2.
56	1588 May 11	Matteucci, nuncio in Venice, to Card. Montalto	A. V.	332, 1.
57	1588 June 16	Speciani to Card. Montalto . .	A. V.	332, 3.
58	1588 June 29	,, ,,	A. V.	336, 1.
59	1588 July 6	*Descrittione de porti et fortezze del regno d' Inghilterra*	A. V.	280, 2.
60	1588 July 11	Speciani to Card. Montalto . .	A. V.	312, 3.
61	1588 July 14	,, ,, . .	A. V.	336, 2.
62	1588 Aug. 7	News from Rouen, etc., about the Armada	A. V.	336, 3.
63	1588 Aug. 8	Gio. Fr. Morosini, Cardinal-legate in Paris, to Card. Montalto	A. V.	336, 4.
64	1588 Aug. 17	,, ,,	A. V.	337, 4.

No.	Date	Description	Place	Reference (page, note)
65	1588 Aug. 19	Speciani, nuncio in Madrid, to Card. Montalta	A. V.	336, 5.
66	1588 Aug. 22	Ottinelli, nuncio in Turin, to Card. Montalto	A. V.	337, 1.
67	1588 Aug. 25	,, ,,	A. V.	337, 1.
68	1588 Aug. 26	Speciani to Card. Montalto . .	A. V.	336, 5.
69	1588 Aug. 28	Morosini to Card. Montalto . .	A. V.	337, 5.
70	1588 Sept. 1	Speciani to Card. Montalto . .	A. V.	338, 1.
71	1588 Sept. 3	Sarvognano (Venice) to Pigifetta (Rome)	A. V.	337, 2.
72	1588 Sept. 13	Speciani to Montalto	A. V.	338, 2.
73	1588 Sept. 17	,, ,, ...	A. V.	338, 3.
74	1588 Sept. 24	,, ,, ...	A. V.	338, 4.
75	1588 Sept. 26	,, ,, ...	A. V.	333, 4; 33 1.
76	1588 about the end of Sept.	Marginal note on an English pamphlet	B. M.	341, 4.
77	1588 Oct. 2	Speciani to Montalto	A. V.	338, 5.
78	1588 Oct. 5	,, ,, ...	A. V.	339, 3.
79	1588 Oct. 10	,, ,, ...	A. V.	339, 4.
80	1588 Oct. 14	,, ,, ...	A. V.	339, 4.
81	1588 Oct. 31	,, ,, ...	A. V.	340, 1.
82	1588 Nov. 5	,, ,, ...	A. V.	340, 2.
83	1588 Nov. 8	,, ,, ...	A. V.	341, 1.
84	1588 Nov. 12	,, ,, ...	A. V.	339, 5.
85	1588 Nov. 23	A. de Grassi, nuncio in Spain, to Card. Montalto	A. V.	340, 3.
86	1588 Nov. 24	Speciani to Montalto	A. V.	339, 7
87	1589 Jan. 6	Grassi to Montalto	A. V.	361, 1.
88	1588 Sept. 9	Card. Montalto to Annibale de Capua, nuncio in Warsaw . .	A. V.	363, 1.

No.	Date	Description	Place	Reference (page, note)
89	1589 Oct.	Minuccio Minucci, *Informatione della lega di Hansa et del commercio che ha con Inghilterra*	B. V., P. H. I.	88, 2.
90	1590 Aug.	Sigismund III. of Poland to Queen Elizabeth	P. R. O.	362, 3.
91	1590 Oct. $\frac{3}{13}$	,, ...	P. R. O.	363, 1.
92	1591	*Relatione di Vinetia*	A. V.	362, 2.
93	1592 March 5	Richard Verstegan to Robert Persons, S.J.	W. C. A.	350, 1.
94	1592 Apr. $\frac{6}{16}$	Queen Elizabeth to the Grand-Duke Ferdinand I. of Tuscany	Fl.	367, 3.
95	1592 Nov. 3	Letter of Clement VIII., sanctioning the foundation of the seminary at Valladolid	A. B.	118, 2.
96	1592 Dec. 1	Jos. Creswell, S.J., to Clement VIII.	A. V.	119, 1.
97	1593	Recusant Rolls of the English treasury	P. R. O.	168, 5.
98	1593 Apr. 19	Jos. Creswell to Clement VIII. .	A. V.	119, 2; 361, 3.
99	1593 July 7	Anthony Standen to the Grand-Duke Ferdinand I.	Fl.	369, 1.
100	1594 Feb. 9	Letter of Clement VIII., confirming the foundation of the seminary at Seville	A. B.	118, 2.
101	1594 [March 26]	Camillo Borghese, nuncio in Madrid, to Cardinal Pietro Aldobrandini	A. V.	385, 3.
102	[1594 or 95]	*Cavato d'una lettera scritta da Guiglielmo Gifordo . . . a Tomaso Throcmorton . . . residente in Roma in casa del vescovo di Casano, laqual lettera fu intercetta dagli heretici et mandata a quelli del conseglio della regina d'Inghilterra, et da questi al re di Scotia* .	A. V.	385, 4.
103	[about 1595]	Jos. Creswell, S.J., to ? . . .	A. V.	175, 2.

No.	Date	Description	Place	Reference (date, note)
104	[1595]	*Le differenze che sono tra gli Inglesi catholici sopra la successione et modo della riduttione di quel regno. Per Sua Santità* . . .	A. V.	386, 1; 393, 1.
105	[1595]	*Ex relatione Gabrielis Colfordi, nobilis Angli, qui 16 Junii appulit Antverpiae ex Anglia* .	A. V.	357, 2; 37, 1.
106	1595 Feb. 2	G. Markham to Sir Robert Cecil	P. R. O.	391, 2.
107	1595 Sept. 14	Jos. Creswell, S.J., to Card. P. Aldobrandini	A. V.	393, 4.
108	1595 Nov. 6	*Orders agreed upon to be observed by us whose names are above written (Chr. Southworth, Alex. Gerarde . . .)—Wisbeach Castle*	W. C. A.	402, 4.
109	[1596]	*Quomodo seculares sacerdotes a patribus Societatis in Anglia degentibus opprimuntur, deque patrum dominandi desiderio in Anglos et Anglicanum clerum* . . .	W. C. A.	408, 4.
110	1596	*De regiae successionis apud Anglos iure libri duo. Ex dominorum iurisconsultorum disputatione excepti et per R. Dolmanum anglice primum* [1594] *editi, nunc vero latine redditi sunt* . . . A.D. 1596	A. V.	383, 3.
111	1596 March 4	Report of Card. Filippo Sega upon his visitation of the English college in Rome	B. V.	106, 1; 11, 1, 4; 17, 4; 17, 2; 39, 5; 39, 1, 2; 39, 3; 410,
112	1596 Apr. 26	Jos. Creswell, S.J., to Clement VIII.	A. V.	5, 1; 356,
113	1596 May 24	*Cavati d'una lettera del sig. dott. Thornello, canonico da Vicenza*	W. C. A.	394, 1.
114	1596 July 28	Alfonso Agazzari to Jos. Creswell .	W. C. A.	396, 1.
115	1596 Aug. 27	Agazzari to Rob. Persons . . .	W. C. A.	396, 2.

No.	Date	Description	Place	Reference (page, note)
16	1566 Sept. 2	Sir Francis Englefield to Clement VIII.	A. V.	298, 3.
17	1596 Oct. 24	Dispatches of the nuncio in Paris and the Card. Legate Alessandro de Medici to Card. Aldobrandini		
18	1596 Oct. 28			
19	1596 Nov. 25		A. V.	370, 1, 2, 3.
20	1597	*Brevis declaratio miserrimi status catholicorum in Anglia iam degentium*	W. C. A.	403, 3.
21	1597	*Rationes, quibus breviter ostenditur necessitas extrema instituendi canonicam aliquam potestatem superiorem in clero Anglicano* .	W. C. A.	408, 4; 410, 3.
22	[1597]	Robert Persons to Card. Aldobrandini	A. V.	409, 2.
23	1597 Dec. 10	George Blackwell to Card. Enrico Caetani	W. C. A.	415, 2.
24	1598 Aug. 1	Blackwell to Clement VIII. . .	A. V.	417, 1, 3.
25	1598 Aug. 7	R. Persons to Card. Aldobrandini	A. V.	373, 1.
26	1598 Oct. 30	19 English Jesuits and secular priests to Clement VIII. . .	A. V.	422, 2; 423, 1.
27	Between 1598 and 1600	Memorial of *Bascheus* (Bagshaw ?) concerning the quarrels between Jesuits and secular priests	B. V.	405, 2.
28	[About 1599]	Hugh O'Neill, Earl of Tyrone, to Clement VIII.	A. V.	364, 4; 365, 3.
29	1599 Feb. 13	Rob. Persons to Card. Aldobrandini	A. V.	373, 2.
30	Winter of 1599/1600	Edw. Drummond to the Grand-Duke of Tuscany	Fl.	386, 4.
31	[About 1600]	*Discourse of the Providence* . .	P. R. O.	228, 6.
32	1600	Statutes of the Scots' College in Rome	B. V.	116, 4.
33	1600 April $\frac{8}{18}$	Indulgence granted by Clement VIII. to the Earl of Tyrone and his adherents	P. R. O.	365, 1.

No.	Date	Description	Place	Reference (page, note)
134	1600 July 15	Ott. Mirto Frangipani, nuncio in Brussels to Card. Aldobrandini	A. V.	374, 2.
135	1600 Aug. 19	,, ,, ...	A. V.	374, 3.
136	1600 Oct. 4 *	*Da Londra.* Anonymous Reports.	A. V.	169, 2.
137	1600 Oct. 22 *	George Blackwell to Clement VIII.	A. V.	429, 1.
138	After 1600	Various *acta* and documents relating to the history of the Scots' colleges in Rome and Paris . .	B. V.	116, 3, 117, 2.
139	1601	Blackwell's denunciation of the appellants to the Inquisition .	W. C. A.	432, 1.
140	1601 Jan. 24	Rob. Persons to the Earl of Angus	P. R. O.	384, 1; 38
141	1601 Aug. $\frac{14}{24}$	English passports for the priests Mush and Barnaby		
142	1601 $\frac{\text{Oct. 25}}{\text{Nov. 4}}$	Do. for the priests Bagshaw, Bluet, Barnaby, and Finch (= Bennet)	A. V.	440, 2.
143	1601 $\frac{\text{Oct. 27}}{\text{Nov. 6}}$	Supplement to the above . . .		
144	1601 Nov. $\frac{1}{11}$	Passport for the servants of the above named		
145	1601 Dec. 7	Frangipani, nuncio in Brussels, to Card. Aldobrandini . . .	A. V.	442, 2.
146	1602	Persons' petition to the Inquisition: *Considerationes quaedam praecipui momenti ad causam Anglicanam recte terminandam* . .	W. C. A.	448, 1.
147	1602 Jan. 25	Frangipani to Aldobrandini . .	A. V.	442, 2.
148	1602 Feb. 2	Parker and Archer (St. Omer) to Clement VIII.	A. V.	443, 1.
149	1602 March 8	Frangipani to Aldobrandini . .	A. V.	443, 2.
150	1602 Apr. 9	Parker and Archer to Clement VIII.	A. V.	443, 1.
151	1602 July 20	Decree of the Inquisition concerning the archpriest controversy .	W. C. A., A. B.	446, 4; 44 1.

No.	Date	Description	Place	Reference (page, note)
52	1602 Aug. 22	Frangipani to Aldobrandini . .	A. V.	439, 1.
53	1602 Aug. 22	Persons to Card. Domenico Pinelli	W. C. A.	447, 2.
54	1603 Jan. 29 *	*Avvisi di Londra*	A. V.	439, 1 ; 454, 3 ; 458, 1.
55	1603 Aug. 10	Petition of the appellants to James I. : *Succincta relatio memorabilium punctorum, quae Suae M^{tis} servitium concernunt negotiatione sacerdotum appellantium Romae et Galiae, quorum pregnantes et evidentes probationes pro praesenti sunt in manibus episcopi Londinensis*	A. V.	455, 2.
56	1615 March	Account of the martyrdom of two Jesuits in Scotland based on letters to the rector of the Scots' College in Rome	B. V.	406, 6.
57	1635 May 9	Card. Franc. Barberini to Gregorio Panzani, papal agent at the English Court	B. V.	5, 1.
58	1636	Greg. Panzani, *Relatione dello stato della religione cattolica in Inghilterra*	A. P., B. V., B. M.	64, 1 ; 120.
59	1637 May $\frac{5}{15}$	George Con, papal agent in London to Card. Fr. Barberini	B. V.	245, 3.
60	1670 Jan. 10	Piero Mocenigo, Venetian ambassador in London to the Senate	Ven.	64, 2.
61	1679 Feb. 10	Paolo Sarotti, Venetian ambassador in London to the Senate .	Ven.	188, 1.

INDEX

Catholics, English—*continued*—
supervision of, 90, 125, 169 f., 175, 205, 349 f.
arrested, 40, 89, 124, 126, 166, 184
relations with Spain, 33 f., 123, 235, 239-241, 244-253, 357-359
loyalty, 243 f., 296 f., 299, 328, 346 f., 456
divisions of, 355 f., 376-380, 385 f., 389 f., 400 ff. *passim ; see also* Persons
See also Emigrants, Invasion, and Catholics, persecution of
Catholics, persecution of—
political and religious character, 123 f., 129, 162, 164 f., 172–176, 349
fanaticism, 129, 176–178, 185 f., 188
manner of persecution, 165
the power of punishing, 22, 147, 166–169
legislation, 149–162
judicial murder, 152 f., 162
executions, 165, 186, 213 f., 347, 371, 458 f.
number of victims, 163, 184 [6]
women and children, 175 f., 354
mitigation, 370, 402
at its height, 146 f., 263 f., 346
See also Penal Laws and Religious Persecution
Cecil, alumnus, 501
Cecil, Sir Robert, 391, 438, 454, 458 [1]
Cecil, William, Lord Burleigh, 179 f., 273, 328, 353, 367
in Elizabeth's confidence, 16, 89
attitude towards the Catholic Church, 42 f., 55 f., 89, 92 f., 125,[1] 139, 144, 164,[2] 175,[2] 214
attitude towards Spain, 48 f., 75, 232 f., 259, 260, 305
attitude towards Scotland, 287
as publicist, *vide* Printed Matter
Celt, hatred for the Anglo-Saxon, 241, 507 [2]
Chaddock, William, alumnus, 498
Champney, Anthony, archpriest, 530 [1]
Charles I. of England, 190, 245, 463
Charles V., Emperor, 17, 366
Charles, Archduke, 58
Charnock, Robert, alumnus, late archpriest, 421, 424, 498
Cheshire, 167
Chester Castle, 166
Christopher, alumnus, 498
Church lands, dispensation of unlawful possession of, 203, 392

Circignani, *vide* Pomarancio
Civita Vecchia, 263
Clayton, Francis, alumnus, 498
Clement VIII., 116, 364, 372 f., 398 f., 409, 440, 445, 450, 463
Clement, Cæsar, alumnus, 498
Clenock, Maurice, rector of the English college, 110, 241,[1] 494, 507 f.
Clergy, English, organization of the, 377 f., 401, 407-414, 421, 423
Cobham, Henry, English ambassador, 232,[2] 237 [1]
Cognati, Marsilio, Roman physician, 453 f.
Collegium Anglorum de Urbe, *vide* Seminary, English, in Rome
Collegium, Germanicum, 506, 519
Collegium, Romanum, 103, 197, 483, 519
Collington (Colleton), archpriest, 429
Commercial Treaty, Spanish-English, 242 f.
Common Prayer-book, 22, 68
Como, Cardinal of, 269-271, 276, 283, 284, 289, 489-492, 502
Conscience, liberty of, 128, 180, 188, 445, 451-454
Conspiracies against Elizabeth, 90, 154, 268-273, 490-492
Conspiracies detected, 127 f., 157
Constantinople, 362
Continental boycott, 87 f., 480 [2]
Convertb, 60-62, 103, 196, 214
Convocation of Bishops (1559), 25
Copley, Anthony, alumnus, 499
Cornelius, John, alumnus, 514
Cowling, Richard, alumnus, 498
Cowling, William, alumnus, 514
Crawford, Earl of, 525
Creighton, Mandell, 139 f.
Creighton, William, S.J., 114, 203,[2] 497, 524-526
Creswell, Joseph, S.J., 5,[1] 175,[3] 361 [3]
Cromwell, Oliver, 15, 38, 135, 256
Crusaders' indulgence, 286, 318, 365
Cruzada, 318

D

Darnley, Lord, 74
Defensor Fidei, 43, 363
Delfino, nuncio, 472
Denmark, 309
Dennum, E., spy, 30,[2] 172 [1]
Devotion, objects of, 90, 202 f.
Dobson, *vide* Wright

---

* In the following only those references are given in which the title of the pamphlet is quoted in full.